D1006268

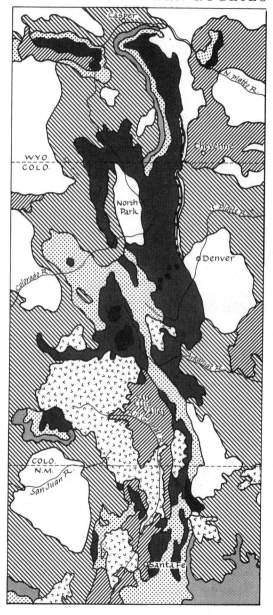

Casper

N. Platte R.

Cheyenne

WYO
COLO.

North
Park

Platte R.

Denver

Colorado R.

Kansas R.

S.L.s
Valley

COLO.
N.M.

San Juan R.

Santa Fe

THE SIERRA CLUB NATURALIST'S GUIDES

A Sierra Club Naturalist's Guide to

THE SOUTHERN ROCKIES

The Rocky Mountain Regions of Southern Wyoming,
Colorado, and Northern New Mexico

by Audrey DeLella Benedict

**WITH ILLUSTRATIONS BY
BARBARA BASH**

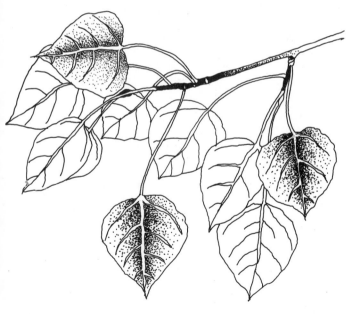

SIERRA CLUB BOOKS   *San Francisco*

The Sierra Club, founded in 1892 by John Muir, has devoted itself to the study and protection of the earth's scenic and ecological resources—mountains, wetlands, woodlands, wild shores and rivers, deserts and plains. The publishing program of the Sierra Club offers books to the public as a nonprofit educational service in the hope that they may enlarge the public's understanding of the Club's basic concerns. The point of view expressed in each book, however, does not necessarily represent that of the Club. The Sierra Club has some sixty chapters coast to coast, in Canada, Hawaii, and Alaska. For information about how you may participate in its programs to preserve wilderness and the quality of life, please address inquiries to Sierra Club, 730 Polk Street, San Francisco, CA 94109.

Library of Congress Cataloging-in-Publication Data

Benedict, Audrey D.
   A Sierra Club naturalist's guide : the Southern Rockies : the Rocky Mountain regions of southern Wyoming, Colorado, and northern New Mexico / by Audrey D. Benedict.
      p.   cm.
   Bibliography: p.
   Includes index.
   ISBN 0-87156-741-5
   1. Natural history—Rocky Mountains.   2. Rocky Mountains—Description and travel.   I. Sierra Club.   II. Title.
QH104.5.R6B46   1990
508.78—dc20   91-10569
                                                 CIP

Production by Janet Vail

Book design by Ronna Nelson
   based on a series design by Klaus Gemming

Illustrations by Barbara Bash

Printed in the United States of America on recycled paper

10   9   8   7   6   5   4   3   2   1

TABLE OF CONTENTS

ACKNOWLEDGMENTS

THIS BOOK would not have been possible without the help and encouragement of many people. I extend my sincere thanks to Constance Brown, who first involved me in the project and who was an enthusiastic companion during the nearly 8,000 miles traveled in conjunction with the initial fieldwork. I have relied on the research and descriptions published in the professional literature by a great many geologists, climatologists, and biologists, far too numerous for me to list individually but without whom no book such as this could be attempted. Several individuals have been influential in shaping my thinking about the natural history of the Southern Rockies: Dr. David M. Armstrong, Dr. James B. Benedict, Dr. William C. Bradley, Dr. David J. Cooper, Dr. Emmett Evanoff, Susan Quimby Foster, Dr. John W. Marr, Dr. Robert Michael Pyle, Dr. Richard T. Reynolds, Dr. William A. Weber, and Dr. Olwen Williams. I owe a tremendous debt of gratitude to Dr. James B. Benedict and Dr. David M. Armstrong for their critical review of the entire manuscript, a monumental task. Several individuals critically read one or more chapters: Dr. Peter W. Birkeland (geology), Dr. Emmett Evanoff (geology), Dr. Brainerd Mears, Jr. (geology), Dr. William C. Rense (geography, climate, and weather), Dr. Freeman Hall (climate and weather), Dr. Arthur Mears (snow and avalanches), Deborah Tewell, and Frances Enright. Their criticisms, comments, and ideas significantly strengthened the scientific content of the book. In addition, Judith Schaefer, Liz Caile, and Abigail Bridges read the manuscript in its entirety, making invaluable stylistic and editorial suggestions. Dr. William A. Weber, curator of the Herbarium at the University of Colorado, reviewed the plant species list for accuracy. Dr. Robert M. Pyle provided lists of the most common butterflies for each ecosystem. If any errors slipped through the review process, they are mine alone. The wonderful illustrations that grace the pages of this book are the work of Barbara Bash; the times that we spent in the field together were rich with shared discoveries. My thanks to Emmett Evanoff for suggesting and drafting several of the illustrations in the chapters on geology. I am grateful to James B. Benedict and the photographic team of Robert Rozinski and Wendy Shattil for allowing me to use several of their photographs. I thank my editor at Sierra Club Books, James Cohee, for his faith in the Naturalist's Guide Series and his patience through the many years this book was in preparation, and my copyeditor, Barbara Fuller.

No project of this sort can be undertaken without the support of one's family. I extend special thanks to my parents, George and Louise DeLella, my mother-in-law, Katharine T. Benedict, and my stepsons, Robert and William Benedict, for their belief in me and for their patience as the book absorbed more and more of my time. My greatest debt of gratitude is to my husband, James B. Benedict, whose moral support was a constant source of encouragement. Jim's many years of research in the Colorado Front Range are a continuing inspiration to me—this book is as much his as it is mine.

INTRODUCTION

A MAP OF THE Southern Rocky Mountains is musical with the names of ranges: Sangre de Cristo, La Garita, Jemez, Never Summer, Medicine Bow, La Plata, Sawatch, Culebra, San Juan, Grenadier, and many more. To those who have had the pleasure of exploring this most complex of North American mountain regions, these names bring to mind memories of summers gladdened, meadows rich with the colors of flowers, snowmelt cascades, and peaks lit with alpenglow. But the scenery does not stop at mountains. Deep canyons and broad, sweeping valleys cleave the ranges and create a landscape of extraordinary beauty and diversity.

To the geologist or biologist, the urge to unravel the histories of landscapes or the complex relationships governing natural communities is irresistible. "To understand the fashion of any life," Mary Austin said in *The Land of Little Rain*, "one must know the land it is lived in and the procession of the year." Our exploration of the ecosystems of the Southern Rockies begins with a geographical introduction to its mountain ranges, plateaus, and basins. To appreciate the scenic diversity that is the region's hallmark, one must walk through the geologic archives—from nearly 3 billion years ago to the tectonically restless present. The tumultuous geologic story of the Southern Rockies occupies several chapters of this book and is crucial to understanding the landforms we see today. The effects of climate and weather, the subject of chapter 8, are clearly imprinted on the land and its people, setting the stage upon which all physical, chemical, and biological processes operate. Snow, the subject of chapter 9, is a critical component of the mountain environment, influencing landscape processes, controlling the distribution and composition of plant communities, and shaping many of the adaptations that plants and animals must have for survival.

The second half of this book is a field guide to the major ecosystems—beginning with the shortgrass prairie and ending with the alpine tundra. Each is described in terms of its environmental setting, principal plant and animal species, and community characteristics. The emphasis throughout is on the adaptations of the organisms associated with these ecosystems—their form, physiology, and behavior—

1

and the ways in which these adaptations are shaped by the environments in which the organisms live. To maintain the usefulness of this guide over such a broad region, ecosystem descriptions and species lists have been somewhat generalized. Readers primarily interested in identification should refer to the comprehensive field guides listed in the Bibliography. Plant and animal species lists, once again limited by space constraints, are provided to give an idea of the representative species associated with each ecosystem.

This book follows the current format of the Sierra Club Naturalist's Guide series by listing the scientific names for plants and animals in the species lists rather than including them in the body of the text. This is intended to improve readability of the text without sacrificing the greater precision of scientific names or the usefulness of the guide. In some cases, subspecies and varieties are indicated where their use has become essential in identifying a particular organism occurring in the Southern Rockies. Nomenclatural differences are also noted where appropriate. Editorial policy has also dictated that all measurements be given in English units without metric equivalents.

Human-wrought changes threaten nearly every corner of the Southern Rockies—we trample, build roads, clearcut, overgraze, bulldoze, drain, fill, flood, and poison with reckless abandon. Even in the once-remote, pristine watersheds of our highest mountains we are beginning to see the effects of acid rain. Sadly, we need to be as wary of the impacts of recreation and all its accouterments as we are of the effects of unregulated logging or mining. Every habitat altered or destroyed, whether through unwitting overuse or through careless disregard, makes every remaining habitat exponentially more important—and with it the crucial web of life strung through all its parts.

We are only beginning to understand the intricate relationships that characterize natural communities. My intent with this book is to provide an introduction to the varied ecosystems of the Southern Rockies and to share some of the marvelous adaptations that bind organisms to their environments. In so doing, my ultimate wish is to underscore the fragility of such systems and the importance of stewardship.

CHAPTER ONE .

Mountains in the Clouds: The Southern Rocky Mountains

TO THE TRAVELER journeying west across the Great Plains, the first sighting of the cloud-capped ramparts of the Rocky Mountains makes a lasting impression. Appearing on the western horizon like a line of storm clouds, the Rockies form the eastern front of an immense cordon of mountain ranges, the Western Cordillera, that extends from Alaska to the southern tip of South America. Within the United States, the Rocky Mountains are divided physiographically into four provinces: the Northern, Central, and Southern Rocky Mountains, and the Wyoming Basin. The Wyoming Basin, separating the Central and Southern Rocky Mountains, is connected by narrow passages to the Great Plains Province to the east and the Colorado Plateau Province to the south.

A Geographic Orientation

The Southern Rocky Mountains lie mostly in Colorado, with extensions north into Wyoming and south into New Mexico. These mountains dominate the landscape from the northern edge of the Laramie Mountains to north-central New Mexico. The region covered by this book extends beyond the eastern mountain front to include the High Plains, Colorado Piedmont, and Raton sections of the Great Plains Province, all lying within the rain shadow of the Southern Rockies. The western boundary borders the mesa and canyon country of the Colorado Plateau, along a line roughly drawn through the towns of Jemez Springs, New Mexico;

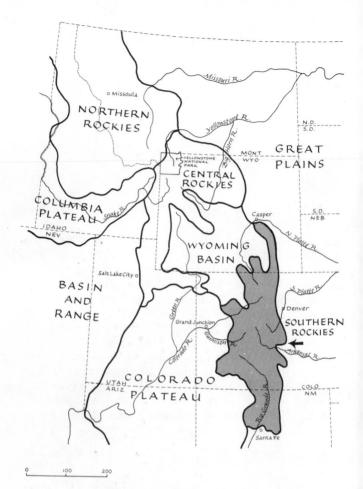

Physiographic provinces of the Rocky Mountain region.

Durango, Grand Junction, Rifle, and Craig, Colorado; and Saratoga, Wyoming.

With the exception of the San Juan Mountains in southwestern Colorado, the principal mountain ranges of the Southern Rockies fall into two north-south belts. The eastern ranges include the Laramie Mountains, the Colorado Front Range, the Wet Mountains, and the Sangre de Cristo Range. The principal ranges of the western belt are the Sierra Madre, Park, Gore, and Sawatch ranges, and the Elk, San Juan, and

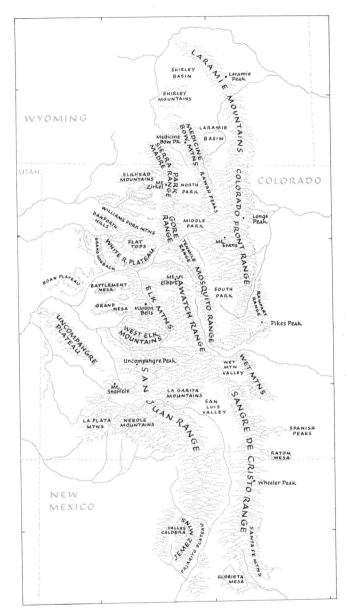

Index map of the Southern Rocky Mountains.

Mountains in the Clouds

Jemez mountains. Separating the two mountain belts is a chain of large, intermontane basins: Laramie Basin, North Park, Middle Park, South Park, the San Luis Valley, and the Rio Grande Valley.

High Peaks

Alpine scenery—high country—distinguishes the Southern Rockies. During the opening of the American West, the scenery that now attracts millions of visitors each year proved to be a major barrier to transmountain travel. The most heavily used emigrant trails followed routes around the northern and southern ends of the Southern Rockies—never through their heart. Colorado contains the loftiest summits in the entire Rocky Mountain system, including all of the chain's fifty-four "Fourteeners" (mountains that exceed 14,000 feet). In fact, excluding Alaska, Colorado contains more high mountains than any other state; more than one thousand Colorado summits rise above 10,000 feet, and three hundred exceed 13,000 feet. Looking west from Denver, the difference in elevation between the peaks and the nearby lowlands is particularly striking; the square-topped silhouette of Longs Peak, northernmost Fourteener, towers 9,000 feet above the adjacent plain. North and south of Colorado, the ranges of the Southern Rockies decline only slightly in elevation.

The Continental Divide

The Continental Divide charts a sinuous course as it travels along the jagged backbone of the Southern Rockies. Not surprisingly, the Divide attains its highest elevations in Colorado. It enters the Southern Rockies from the north along the crest of the Sierra Madre and Park ranges. At the southern end of North Park the Continental Divide swings east around the headwaters of the Colorado River in Rocky Mountain National Park and then south along the highest peaks of the Indian Peaks Wilderness Area; Sawtooth Peak, a conspicuous landmark at the northern end of the wilderness area, marks the extreme eastern point reached by the Continental Divide in the United States. Near the southern end of the Colorado Front Range, the Divide swings sharply west around the head of the Arkansas River to ride the crest of the Sawatch Range. In a great looping switchback that roughly defines the headwaters of the Rio Grande, the Divide then traverses the San Juan Mountains before angling south into the San Juan Basin, between the San Juan and Chama rivers.

The Continental Divide marks the geographical boundary between the Eastern Slope and the Western Slope of the Southern Rockies. Along the Eastern Slope of the Continental Divide, rivers such as the Platte and the Arkansas roll down from the mountains and out across the plains, eventually mingling their waters with those of the Gulf of Mexico. Nearly two-thirds of the Southern Rocky Mountains drains eastward, toward the Atlantic Ocean. Along the Western Slope of the Divide, the Colorado River and its many tributaries wind their way down spectacular canyons to the Gulf of California.

The Continental Divide's influence on regional climate — and politics — cannot be denied. More than three-quarters of the Southern Rockies' precipitation falls on the west side of the Divide, 60 percent in the Colorado River Basin alone. This natural imbalance, paired with the concentration of the population and much of the political power in the Eastern Slope's urban corridor, has placed Western Slope rivers at the center of a controversy that has no easy resolution. In response to the unquenchable thirst of Front Range cities, transmountain diversion projects proliferate. In Colorado, a massive network of ditches and tunnels diverts nearly 700,000 acre-feet of water a year — water once bound for the Pacific via the Colorado River and its tributaries — over, under, and around the Continental Divide to meet the burgeoning needs of Eastern Slope urban and agricultural users. A single acre-foot of water is equivalent to 325,851 gallons of water — enough to supply the needs of four families for an entire year or to fill twenty-five Olympic-sized swimming pools! Without serious efforts at water conservation, the future of the Western Slope's rivers — as well as of the species that depend on them — remains in jeopardy.

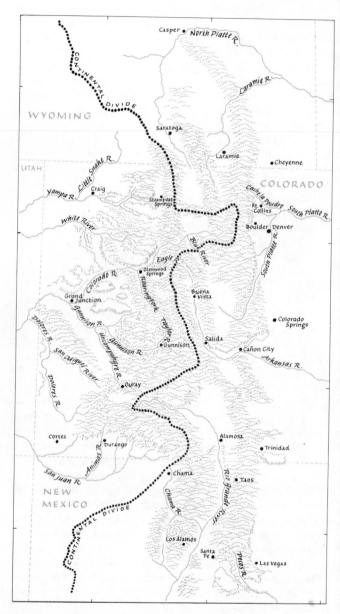

Continental Divide and major rivers.

THE SOUTHERN ROCKIES

Eastern Ranges of the Southern Rockies

Laramie Mountains

The low, weather-beaten Laramie Mountains mark the western edge of the High Plains in southern Wyoming. These rolling, unglaciated mountains contrast sharply with the rugged, ice-sculpted scenery of the Medicine Bow Mountains to the west. Rounded bedrock knobs and unusual rock formations characterize much of the range crest, particularly in the Vedauwoo Rocks and Sherman Mountains section. Laramie Peak, the highest peak in the range at 10,272 feet, was a famous landmark along the Oregon Trail, which passed just to the north of the mountains. Early exploration accounts referred to the Laramie Mountains as the "Black Hills" because of their dark profile when viewed from the east, near old Fort Laramie. Along their eastern front, the Laramie Mountains merge with the plains along a ramplike slope called the Gangplank. This unusual landform, located about 16 miles west of Cheyenne and visible from U.S. I-80, marks the only place between Mexico and Canada where the thousands of feet of sediments that once buried the Rockies remain largely undisturbed — the only place where you can step from the High Plains surface directly onto the ancient Precambrian rocks that distinguish the crest of the range.

Medicine Bow Mountains

In the Medicine Bow Mountains, two groups of glaciated, snow-capped peaks rise above the otherwise flat, benchlike surface of the range: the Snowy Range in Wyoming and the Rawah Peaks in Colorado. The white quartzitic peaks of the Snowy Range rise nearly 2,000 feet above the thickly forested Medicine Bow upland, appearing like whitecaps on a storm-tossed sea. Medicine Bow Peak (12,006 feet) marks their highest point. A seasonal road over Snowy Range Pass (10,847 feet) provides easy access to the willow-rimmed lakes and trout streams that characterize the rolling upland.

Flanking the eastern edge of North Park and extending from Cameron Pass to the Wyoming border, the Rawah Peaks mark the southern end of the Medicine Bow Mountains. The 76,000-acre Rawah Peaks Wilderness Area was one of the first areas to enter the National Wilderness Preservation System. The East Sand Hills and North Sand Hills, east of Cowdrey, nestle against the Rawah foothills and form a northern analog to sand formations found at Great Sand Dunes National Monument, on the western slope of the Sangre de Cristos.

Colorado Front Range

Looking west from Denver, the mountains appear to rise from the plains in two giant steps, from an average elevation of 5,600 feet to alpine summits above 14,000 feet. Beginning at the north fork of the Cache la Poudre River, near the Colorado-Wyoming border, the Colorado Front Range stretches south to the Arkansas River near Cañon City. Along much of its length, the eastern slope of the Front Range is edged by a conspicuous ridge of buff-colored sedimentary rocks known as the Dakota Hogback — the frayed, upturned edge of a vast sheet of sedimentary rock that spreads out for thousands of square miles beneath the surface of the eastern plains.

Several mountain ranges are collectively referred to as the "Colorado Front Range." These include the Never Summer Mountains and the Mummy Range (both in Rocky Mountain National Park); the Indian Peaks (west of Boulder); and a lower, more timbered series of ranges south of the Indian Peaks that define the Williams Fork Mountains, Vasquez Mountains, Platte River Mountains, Tarryall Mountains, Kenosha Mountains, and Rampart Range. The Lost Creek Wilderness Area, located on the northeastern slopes of the Tarryall Mountains, preserves a region of uniquely weathered granite formations.

The Colorado Front Range contains some of the most accessible alpine scenery to be found in the Southern Rockies. Rocky Mountain National Park preserves thousands of acres of mountain meadows, glacier-fed streams, deep U-shaped valleys, rolling alpine uplands, and glacially carved peaks. Trail Ridge Road in Rocky Mountain National Park traverses a 50-mile sky-scraping sampler of the Colorado Front Range between the resort communities of Estes Park and Grand Lake. As you travel the 11-mile section of the road that lies above treeline, you parallel the Continental Divide, surrounded on all sides by a seemingly endless expanse of alpine tundra and snow-capped peaks. More than 300 miles of hiking trails provide access to remote areas of the park.

The highest peaks in Rocky Mountain National Park, such as Longs Peak (14,255 feet) and Ypsilon (13,514 feet), challenge rock climbers from all over the world. Longs Peak was first officially climbed in 1868 by a small party that included the one-armed explorer and geologist John Wesley Powell. The infamous Diamond of Longs Peak, which ranks as the largest, highest, and steepest wall in the Southern Rockies, remains as alluring to rock climbers as El Capitan in Yosemite. Several early attempts to climb the Diamond failed and the wall remained unconquered until 1960, when two California climbers made the first ascent. Enos Mills, the self-taught naturalist who led the fight to establish Rocky Mountain National Park in the early 1900s, was to Longs Peak what Thoreau was to Walden Pond; his books on regional natural history, written "in the evening shadow" of this legendary peak, remain classics in their field.

The North Fork of the Colorado River comes to life each spring in a snowy amphitheater beneath Thunder Mountain, in the northwestern corner of Rocky Mountain National Park. From there and from tributary streams along the western side of the National Park and the Indian Peaks, the Colorado River gathers force and begins its 1,450-mile odyssey to the Gulf of California. At Shadow Mountain Reservoir, between the towns of Grand Lake and Granby, the river encounters the first of man's many attempts to tame it; from here to its mouth it bears only an occasional resemblance to the snow-nourished streams of its youth.

South of Rocky Mountain National Park, the Indian Peaks and a long string of alpine summits extend south along the Continental Divide to reach their greatest elevation at Grays Peak (14,270 feet). The 70,000-acre Indian Peaks Wilderness Area sits astride the Divide, providing a network of hiking trails that forms a scenic complement to that in Rocky Mountain National Park. Mountains in the Indian Peaks area are named for the Indian tribes that frequented the Southern

Isabelle Glacier from the north flank of Niwot Ridge, Indian Peaks Wilderness Area. *Audrey D. Benedict.*

Rockies and the eastern prairies: Ogallala, Kiowa, Pawnee, Shoshoni, Arikaree, Arapaho, and others. Two influential Arapaho chiefs, Niwot and Neva, are commemorated in the naming of Niwot Ridge and Mount Neva; Niwot Ridge is the site of the University of Colorado's Mountain Research Station and is one of the most thoroughly studied alpine environments in the world.

The Front Range skyline, south of the Indian Peaks, is dominated by three Fourteeners: Mount Evans and the twin peaks of Grays and Torreys. Mount Evans boasts the highest automobile road in the United States, providing seasonal road access to the 14,264-foot summit and a panoramic view of the Colorado Front Range from Longs Peak, 50 miles due north, to Pikes Peak, 58 miles to the southeast. In 1863, Albert Bierstadt, one of the world's great landscape artists, was among the first white men to climb Mount Evans. Grays and Torreys peaks are named for two nineteenth-century American botanists, Asa Gray and John Torrey, whose extensive collections and classification of western plants paved the way for the modern botany manuals used in the Southern Rockies today.

South of Mount Evans, the benchlike crest of the Rampart Range is broken only by the pyramidal outline of Pikes

Peak, near the southern end of the range. Pikes Peak, the "small blue cloud" that Zebulon Pike first sighted as he made his way across the High Plains in 1806, has become one of the world's most famous mountains. Major Stephen Long's expedition in 1820, sent to chart the boundaries of the Louisiana Purchase, made short work of Pike's claim that the mountain would never be climbed. The expedition's surgeon and botanist, Dr. Edwin James, scaled the peak in three days, making the first collections of the Colorado Columbine, now Colorado's state flower, as well as a wide assortment of previously unknown alpine plants. During the gold rush years, the slogan "Pikes Peak or Bust" became synonymous with events that heralded the opening of the American West.

With the discovery of gold in 1858, the high-mountain valleys of the Colorado Front Range were inundated by prospectors and settlers. Countless mining claims were filed, roads built, towns established, and enormous quantities of gold sluiced from gravels along the channels of most of the major streams. With few passes lower than 11,000 feet, engineering bravado was necessary to breach the formidable crest of the Front Range. John Rollins pioneered the first wagon road across the Continental Divide west of Denver in 1873. The Rollins Pass Road (or Corona Pass Road, as it was also called) was soon joined by many others — Berthoud Pass, Loveland Pass, Argentine Pass, Guanella Pass, and Kenosha Pass, to name just a few.

Wet Mountains

The green, somewhat flat-crested range known as the Wet Mountains extends from the Arkansas River southeast to Badito Cone. No doubt the name "Wet" was coined by some weary prairie traveler in response to the respite these mountains offered after the long, dusty march across the Great Plains. This narrow, 45-mile-long range is separated from the rugged ramparts of the northern Sangre de Cristo Range by the Wet Mountain Valley. Rounded granite knobs are typical of the higher portions of the Wet Mountains, with discontinuous patches of volcanic rock particularly prominent along its western margin. Elevations along the north-northwest–trending crest of the Wet Mountains vary from around 9,200 feet at Tanner Peak to more than 12,000 feet at Greenhorn Mountain. Aspen and Douglas-fir forests, interspersed with streams and lush meadows, are characteristic of the range's eastern flanks and provide a striking contrast to the arid grasslands and open stands of bristlecone pine that typify the western slope.

Spanish explorers preceded the American and French frontiersmen by nearly a hundred years in their familiarity with the mountains that lay between their Santa Fe and Taos outposts and the Arkansas River country. In 1779, while American colonists were fighting for independence from England, Juan Bautista de Anza, then governor of Spanish-controlled New Mexico, was pursuing the defiant, elusive Comanches through the verdant valleys of the Wet Mountains. Greenhorn Mountain was named by de Anza in grudging admiration for the Comanche chief Cuerno Verde (meaning "greenhorn"), who died in a fierce battle with the Spanish along its flanks.

Spanish Peaks

The twin cones of the Spanish Peaks rise abruptly out of the arid plains southwest of Walsenburg and the Cucharas River. Indians named the Spanish Peaks *Huajatolla,* meaning "breasts of the Earth." Isolated from the main Sangre de Cristo Range, the Spanish Peaks are the much-eroded remnants of ancient volcanoes. Vertical walls of solid rock—called dikes—radiate from the flanks of the two peaks and run for miles up and down the foothills, bearing a striking resemblance to the man-made Great Wall of China. These dikes are all that remain of the lava-filled fissures that developed as the volcanoes grew. The Apishapa Pass and Cuchara Pass roads skirt the flanks of East and West Spanish Peaks (13,626 feet and 12,683 feet, respectively), offering travelers an unparalleled look at the underground plumbing system of an ancient volcano.

Some tribes, like the Utes, traditionally believed the Spanish Peaks to be the home of evil spirits and avoided them. Spanish explorers, disregarding Indian superstitions, were drawn to the peaks. Legend has it that one of the priests left behind by the Coronado Expedition in 1541 traveled north to Huajatolla after hearing tales of rich Indian gold mines there. As the story goes, the priest found the gold and,

THE SOUTHERN ROCKIES

after loading his mules with as much as they could carry, started south for New Mexico — never to be heard from again. Hundreds of years later, stories of lost Spanish gold entertained travelers at such places as nearby Bent's Fort.

Sangre de Cristo Range

The crest of the Sangre de Cristo Range stretches south, almost unbroken, for more than 200 miles, from the Arkansas River near Salida to Glorieta Pass southeast of Santa Fe. As late as 1827, an American map of the Santa Fe Trail showed no routes through this seemingly impenetrable range. In the autumn of 1540, however, Francisco Coronado and his men made their way east from Pecos Pueblo through present-day Glorieta Pass, becoming the first Europeans to cross the Continental Divide north of Mexico. The Spanish named this range Sangre de Cristo, meaning "the blood of Christ," inspired by the rich red glow of these mountains at sunset.

For 250 years, the fortunes of the Spanish waxed and waned in missions established along the foothills of the Sangre de Cristos. As Spanish dreams of empire faded, French and American traders, followed by U.S. Army explorers and surveyors, poured into the Sangre de Cristos in ever-increasing numbers. The Santa Fe Trail became a bustling trade route, and mountain men such as Ceran St. Vrain, Antoine Robidoux, and Kit Carson explored the Sangre de Cristo high country and trapped beaver along the streams that danced down its side canyons.

In the winter of 1807, Zebulon Pike and his men crossed the Sangre de Cristos from the east, most likely along Mosca Pass. Upon descending from the pass, the Pike expedition viewed a startling geologic phenomenon — vast dunes of sand trapped in a cul-de-sac at the foot of the mountains. Today, Pike's "sandy hills" are preserved within Great Sand Dunes National Monument and rank among the world's tallest inland dunes.

The northern portion of the Sangre de Cristos, extending from the Arkansas River south to La Veta Pass, is geographically and structurally considered to be part of the western belt of mountain ranges. Seven Fourteeners — Kit Carson Peak, Humboldt Peak, Crestone Peak, Crestone Needle, Mount Lindsey, Little Bear Peak, and Blanca Peak —

Great Sand Dunes National Monument. *Wendy Shattil and Robert Rozinski.*

grace the northern crest of the range. South of Blanca Peak and La Veta Pass, the range is offset to the east by a fault, rejoining the ranges that form the eastern mountain belt. From La Veta Pass south to the Colorado–New Mexico border, the Sangres are known locally as the Culebra Range (*culebra* means "snake" in Spanish). Culebra Peak (14,047 feet), the southernmost Fourteener in the Southern Rockies, and Purgatory Peak (13,676 feet) mark the high points along this section of the range.

Between the Colorado–New Mexico border and Taos, the Sangre de Cristo Range folds into two north-south–trending groups of mountains, the Taos Mountains on the west and the Cimarron Range on the east, separated along their length by the Costilla and Moreno valleys. Wheeler Peak (13,160 feet), northeast of Taos, is the highest peak in New Mexico and is encompassed by the 6,000-acre Wheeler Peak Wilderness Area. The Cimarron Range is located on private land and special permission from the current landowners (Philmont Scout Ranch and Vermejo Park) is required prior to entering this area.

From Taos south, the Sangre de Cristos form two north-south ridges: the Truchas Peaks and the Santa Fe Range on the west and the Mora and Las Vegas ranges on the east.

Near the Truchas Peaks, an east-west ridge connects the Santa Fe Range with the Las Vegas Range, enclosing the upper Pecos Valley. First climbed by the Wheeler survey party in 1874, South Truchas Peak, at 13,103 feet, is the second highest point in New Mexico. The Sky Line Trail, beginning near Aspen Basin and extending in a 48-mile arc around the entire upper Pecos River drainage basin, offers an unparalleled sampling of the 167,000-acre Pecos Wilderness Area.

Western Mountain Ranges

Jemez Mountains

The Jemez Mountains mark the southern end of the western ranges of the Southern Rockies. Rising along the rim of an enormous volcanic depression, the Valles Caldera, the Jemez Mountains were created by volcanoes active as recently as 10 million years ago. Lava and volcanic ash associated with the Jemez volcanoes spread over an area of nearly 2,000 square miles, producing a range that extends from Cerro Pedernal, west of Abiquiu, to Borrego Mesa, near Jemez Pueblo. The highest summits in the range, Santa Clara Peak (11,561 feet) and Polvadera Peak (11,232 feet), distinguish the caldera's rim.

Hot springs, reminders of the region's turbulent geologic past, are common in the Jemez Mountains. Spanish explorers visited the Jemez Sulphur Springs as early as 1542. Today, these mountains are the site of the only known high-grade, subsurface geothermal reservoir in New Mexico; in the main geothermal area, a localized "hot spot" raises subsurface water temperatures to more than 500°F, providing a possible geothermal resource for electric power generation.

Pajarito Plateau

Massive eruptions of volcanic ash spewed from Valles Caldera around 1 million years ago to form the Pajarito Plateau, a gently sloping bench skirting the eastern flank of the Jemez Mountains. The striking canyons and mesas of the Pajarito, with their stacks of vertical colonnades and cone-shaped "tent rocks," were carved from the volcanic tableland by the erosive forces of water and wind.

The Pajarito Plateau contains a wealth of archeological ruins, which provides evidence of almost five hundred years of Indian occupation. Bandelier National Monument, south of Los Alamos, occupies the southernmost section of the Pajarito Plateau and preserves the finest examples of these ruins. At Bandelier, early peoples used stone scrapers to enlarge the natural caves and depressions found in the ashflow tuff, creating chambers that were used for dwellings, storage, or ceremonial purposes. The most impressive and beautiful ruins are located within easy walking distance of the Visitor Center in Frijoles Canyon.

Nacimiento Mountains

The Nacimiento Mountains form a low, north-south ridge that parallels the Jemez Mountains for nearly 50 miles from San Ysidro to beyond Cuba. Unlike the volcanic Jemez Mountains, the Nacimiento Mountains are cored with crystalline rock and flanked along their eastern side, near Jemez Springs, by spectacular red cliffs of sedimentary rock. Deposits of travertine and calcium carbonate are common around once-active hot springs along the southern portion of the range, most notably in the Arroyo Penasco area and at Ojo del Spiritu Santo. The Nacimiento Mountains are largely forested, with ponderosa pine and aspen typical of higher elevations and Gambel oak and New Mexican locust common along valley walls at lower elevations.

San Juan Mountains

Rugged and colorful, the San Juan Mountains encompass more than 10,000 square miles, space enough to enclose the entire state of Vermont and a sliver of New Hampshire. Unrivaled as the largest single range in the U.S. Rockies, the San Juans include at least seven mountain groups: the Sneffels Range, the Grenadier Range, the Needles and West Needles, the La Plata Mountains, the Rico Mountains, and a north-western offshoot called the San Miguel Range. A south-eastern arm of the San Juans — the La Garita Mountains and the Cochetopa Hills — forms the hill country along the western boundary of the San Luis Valley. South of the Colorado border, the Brazos Mountains rise between Tres Piedras and Tierra Amarilla and include the prominent landmarks of the Brazos Cliffs along the Rio Brazos and the great volcanic dome of San Antonio Mountain (10,935 feet).

No other range in the United States contains as much land above 10,000 feet as the San Juans, with almost a dozen peaks exceeding 14,000 feet. The San Juans include three National Forests: the Rio Grande, San Juan, and Uncompahgre. Within these public forestlands are currently six wilderness areas — Weminuche, South San Juan, Big Blue, La Garita, Mount Sneffels, and Lizard Head — protecting more than 800,000 acres.

The San Juans are split nearly in half by the Rio Grande, the third longest river in the United States. The Rio Grande arises deep within the heart of the San Juans near Stoney Pass, bearing little resemblance in its headwaters to the muddy, powerful river that sweeps 1,885 miles to the Gulf of Mexico. The Conejos River and the Rio Chama, both originating in the San Juans, are among the Rio Grande's main tributaries. In addition to the Rio Grande, the Dolores, the San Juan, and at least ten other rivers have headwaters in the high San Juans; some of these rivers, such as the Piedra and the Los Pinos, are candidates for inclusion in the Wild and Scenic Rivers System.

Much of the beauty of the San Juan Mountains can be attributed to their geologic history — a unique mixture of fire and ice. The western portion of the range is constructed of vividly colored layers of sedimentary rock. The central and eastern portions reflect thousands of years of violent volcanic activity. Between 40 and 25 million years ago incredible out-pourings of lava and ash covered most of the central and eastern San Juans and extended north to merge with volcanic rocks in the West Elk Mountains. Ice cap and valley glaciers reworked the volcanic landscape, scouring the spectacular U-shaped valleys and multicolored peaks we enjoy today. Wheeler Geologic Area, near Creede, preserves some of the most interesting rock formations to be found in the Southern Rockies.

Sunshine Peak, San Juan Mountains. *Colorado Tourist Bureau.*

Once the homeland of the far-ranging Ute Indians, the San Juans were among the last regions in the Southern Rockies to be overrun by settlers and gold seekers. Discoveries of rich lodes of gold and silver in the early 1870s increased public pressure to displace the Utes. In 1873, the Brunot Treaty removed a large rectangular area of the San Juans from Ute control and paved the way for white settlement. As the trickle of prospectors and miners became a raging torrent, towns sprang up in the richest parts of the range: Silverton, Ouray, Telluride, Lake City, and Creede. The new prosperity attracted the interest of some of the West's most legendary outlaws. Butch Cassidy began his bank-robbing career in 1889 with a stickup of Telluride's silver-rich San Miguel County Bank. To combat the growing lawlessness and to tame their more colorful citizens, Silverton's town fathers imported the infamous Bat Masterson from Dodge City.

As the mining boom continued, the need for year-round access into the heart of the San Juans intensified. The Denver and Rio Grande Railroad, a slim ribbon of track climbing up from Durango along the Animas River, ended Silverton's isolation in 1882. A journey on the narrow-gauge Silverton-Durango train remains a popular way for travelers to sample the historic and scenic flavor of the San Juans. Several spectacular roads — Engineer Mountain, Cinnamon Pass, Ophir Pass, Imogene Pass, Black Bear Pass, and Stony Pass — penetrate the San Juan backcountry but are passable today only by four-wheel-drive vehicles. Avalanches still pose a serious threat to winter travel on even the paved, more civilized routes over Red Mountain and Wolf Creek passes; avalanche sheds protect the highway in several areas along these routes.

Uncompahgre Plateau

A forested tableland, the Uncompahgre Plateau stretches northwest from the San Juan Range for nearly 100 miles. *Uncompahgre,* a Ute Indian word meaning "red-water canyon," was first applied to the area by the Spanish friars Domínguez and Escalante, who traveled through the region in 1776. Linked geologically to both the Colorado Plateau and the Southern Rockies, the Uncompahgre Plateau forms a scenic and ecological unit with nearby ranges in the Southern Rockies. Crystalline rocks, similar to those that form the cores of other ranges in the Southern Rockies, lie at the heart of the Uncompahgre Plateau. Unlike most of those other ranges, however, the plateau remains draped with a thick overlay of the same colorful sedimentary rocks so characteristic of the canyon country to the west. Unaweep Canyon, one of the major scenic attractions of the Uncompahgre, slices through these rocks to expose the plateau's crystalline core. Geologists believe this canyon was carved by a large river, probably the ancestral Colorado or the west Gunnison, and then abandoned as a result of stream piracy. At the northeast edge of the plateau, high above the Grand Valley of the Colorado River, the geologic story of the Uncompahgre is spectacularly revealed at Colorado National Monument.

Grand Mesa and Battlement Mesa

Grand Mesa and Battlement Mesa rise abruptly from the flat, fertile sweep of irrigated green that defines the Grand Valley of the Colorado. Both mesas are erosional remnants of a lava-capped plain that once spread across much of west-central Colorado. Grand Mesa, the larger of the two, begins near the confluence of the Colorado and Gunnison rivers and extends eastward to the Elk Mountains, encompassing nearly 800 square miles; Battlement Mesa is situated about 15 miles to the northeast of Grand Mesa.

Climate and vegetation vary enormously from bottom to top of each mesa, encompassing four distinct biological zones within a remarkably short vertical distance. The summit of Grand Mesa, averaging about 10,000 feet in elevation, lies almost a mile above a valley floor dotted with desert scrub. The Lands End Road, one of the most dramatic roads in the Southern Rockies, spirals downward over the lip of the mesa and offers spectacular views of the confluence of the Gunnison and the Colorado. During glacial times, Grand Mesa was host to a succession of thick ice caps that covered most of the mesa top and, in places, cascaded down the flanks along old stream courses. Later, landslides created a broad bench of rotated lava blocks along the mesa's flanks and dammed numerous small lakes. In all, there are some three hundred lakes on the bench and the glaciated upland of Grand Mesa. Many of these lakes have been developed as reservoirs to augment the water-intensive agriculture of the Grand Valley.

West Elk Mountains

Like the San Juans, the West Elk Mountains are somewhat detached from the two north-south–trending mountain belts that comprise the Southern Rockies. This northwest-trending range lies north of the San Juans and is bounded on its southern and eastern flanks by the Gunnison River. Essentially circular in outline, the West Elks cover an area no more than 30 miles in diameter. Two spur ranges, the Anthracite Range and the Ruby Range, angle off from the main mass of the West Elks toward Crested Butte. High and relatively inaccessible, the West Elks contain a number of peaks that exceed 12,000 feet; West Elk Peak (13,035 feet), located in the West Elk Wilderness Area, is the highest peak in the range.

The West Elk Mountains were formed during the same interval of intense volcanic activity that produced the San Juans. Castlelike outcrops of a distinctive volcanic rock, called the West Elk Breccia, edge the mountain front with colorful spires and form the Palisades along the Gunnison River. The peaks and ridges in the southern half of the range, which contains West Elk Peak, are carved from layers of lava and consolidated ash that were once continuous with those of the San Juan region. Summits in the northern West Elks, on the other hand, are carved from the once deeply buried roots of enormous volcanoes.

Lava flows originating in the West Elk Mountains played havoc with the course of the ancestral Gunnison River. Once volcanic activity came to an end, about 18.5 million years ago, the river was able to cut its way through the layers of lava and ash, through the underlying sedimentary rocks, and into the ancient crystalline rocks beneath the West Elk Mountains—a process that took nearly 2 million years. Black Canyon of the Gunnison National Monument protects a 13-mile, nearly 2,000-foot-deep section of the canyon. No other North American canyon combines the depth, narrowness, sheerness, and forbidding countenance of the Black Canyon.

Elk Mountains

For many people, the sunset-hued peaks of the Elk Mountains rank among the most beautiful in the entire Rocky Mountain chain. This northwest-trending range extends for nearly 50 miles, from the central Sawatch Range to the Huntsman Hills near Glenwood Springs. Unlike most mountain ranges in the Southern Rockies, a number of the highest peaks in the range are capped with enormous thicknesses

Maroon Bells and Maroon Lake, Elk Mountains. *Robert Rozinski.*

of steeply slanting red sedimentary rocks. In the central portion, richly colored peaks such as the Maroon Bells and Castle Peak contrast sharply with the gray, crystalline summits of Capitol and Snowmass peaks. Of the six Fourteeners that grace the crest of the Elk Mountains — Castle Peak, Pyramid Peak, North and South Maroon peaks, Capitol Peak, and Snowmass Mountain — only one has a walk-up route to the summit. Today, these peaks are included within the 175,000-acre Maroon Bells–Snowmass Wilderness Area.

Situated high on the western slope of the Continental Divide, the Elk Mountains are drained on the north by the Roaring Fork and Crystal rivers, and on the south by the East and Taylor rivers, tributaries of the Gunnison. Stream valleys within the Elk Mountains are generally steep-sided and narrow, their walls dramatized by cliffs of red rock; waterfalls cascade from hanging valleys left behind by long-vanished glaciers. Passes between drainages are high and treacherous, the primitive roads that cross them — Schofield, Pearl, Conundrum, and Taylor — legendary for their difficulty.

Following the Leadville silver boom in the late 1870s, prospectors swarmed across the Sawatch Range, along Independence Pass, searching for similar lodes in the Elk Mountains. They were not disappointed. In 1879, silver was discovered along Castle Creek, near the historic town of Ashcroft, and on Aspen Mountain. During the early days of the boom, before a wagon road was built over Independence Pass, miners using Taylor Pass were forced to dismantle their wagons and lower them piece by piece, along with their cargo, over drops of about 40 feet. By 1890, Aspen—then known as Ute City—surpassed Ashcroft as a mining center, its population of nearly ten thousand served by two railroads, three newspapers, and a municipal electric lighting system. Elsewhere in the Elk Mountains, mining activity concentrated on extensive deposits of coal and marble, leading to the establishment of the towns of Redstone, Marble, Crystal, and Crested Butte. The town of Marble became nationally famous for its high-grade marble, known as Yule Marble; one enormous, 56-ton block of this frost white marble was quarried for the Tomb of the Unknown Soldier.

During World War II, the Tenth Mountain Division ski troops trained for mountain duty near the former boomtown of Aspen. Some of these men returned to Colorado after the war and were influential in the development of a downhill ski area at Aspen Mountain, which today ranks as one of the finest winter-sports centers in North America.

White River Plateau and the Flattops

The White River Plateau towers above the valley of the Colorado River north of Glenwood Springs. This steep-sided, forested upland extends northwest for some 40 miles, its southwestern flank bordered by a sinuous ridge of steeply upturned sedimentary rock known as the Grand Hogback. Along its northern edge, the plateau is defined by the low Yampa Williams Fork Mountains (not to be confused with the string of peaks paralleling the Blue River). Much of the White River Plateau is parklike in character, the large open meadows interspersed with aspen or coniferous forests and dotted with small lakes.

The White River Plateau ranges in elevation from 6,000 feet along its southern margin to 12,493 feet at Flattop Mountain, near the northern end, where the plateau is capped with thick layers of dark volcanic rock. Almost 660 feet of layered volcanic rocks, representing at least three periods of volcanic activity, are exposed at Trappers Peak (11,990 feet). Elsewhere on the White River Plateau, in striking contrast to the volcanic terrain, the upland surface is blanketed with multiple layers of light-colored sedimentary rocks. Deep Creek Canyon, slicing 2,300 feet into the White River Plateau, winds its way between Deep Lake and the Colorado River, exposing almost 300 million years of sedimentary deposits. Just below the canyon's rim, an exposed layer of limestone forms near-vertical walls up to 250 feet tall. Because of its high solubility, the limestone provides an ideal environment for the formation of solution caves. The greatest concentration of caves in the Southern Rockies is found within this limestone layer; Groaning Cave, with an estimated 12 miles of passageways, is believed to be the largest.

Trappers Lake, situated at the headwaters of the White River, lies just within the boundaries of the 174,000-acre Flat Tops Wilderness Area. A visit to this timber-rimmed lake inspired Arthur Carhart, a young Forest Service engineer, and Aldo Leopold to promote the idea that certain federal lands could best serve the needs of the public if left in their wild state. The year was 1918. Though the idea of protecting wilderness was slow to gain support, Congress finally created the National Wilderness Preservation System in 1964, and the Flat Tops Wilderness Area became one of the first to join the system.

Sawatch Range

Sailing into the distance like a row of battleships, the Sawatch Range dominates the high country south and east of the Elk Mountains. Beginning at the Eagle River, near Wolcott, the range stretches south for almost 100 miles. Peak after peak line up to form a towering wall that ranks as the highest range in the U.S. Rocky Mountains. Fifteen Fourteeners mark the crest of the Sawatch Range, including the three highest peaks in the Southern Rockies: Mount Elbert (14,433 feet), Mount Massive (14,421 feet), and Mount Harvard (14,420 feet). Unlike the mountain ranges to the east and west, all traces of the sedimentary rocks that once draped the range crest have been stripped away by erosion.

Isolated within the heart of the northern Sawatch, Mount of the Holy Cross (14,005 feet) stands guard over the 126,000-acre Holy Cross Wilderness Area. The peak is named for the snowy, cross-shaped couloir on its northeast face. The first photograph of the peak, made in 1873 by Hayden Survey photographer William Henry Jackson, brought the mountain and its photographer international fame. Inspired by Jackson's photograph, Thomas Moran, the noted English landscape artist, traveled to the Sawatch Range to paint the peak. Moran's painting of this famous peak, with its cross wreathed in clouds, ranks among the finest examples of nineteenth-century landscape painting.

South of Leadville, a group of Fourteeners known as the Collegiate Peaks—Mounts Harvard, Yale, Columbia, Oxford, and Princeton—graces the central section of the Sawatch Range. The three symmetrical summits of Mount Princeton, at the southern end of the Collegiates, are flanked to the southeast by a 2,000-foot escarpment known as the Chalk Cliffs. These striking white cliffs are formed of kaolinite, a soft, chalklike rock produced by hot springs percolating through the fault-riddled crystalline rocks at the core of Mount Princeton. Hot springs persist along the eastern mouth of the Chalk Creek Valley, and at Mount Princeton Hot Springs there is a public health spa and swimming pool. South of Mount Princeton, across Chalk Creek, several summits—Mounts Antero, Shavano, and Tabeguache—break above 14,000 feet before the Sawatch Range merges with the northernmost foothills of the Sangre de Cristos and the San Juans.

Bounding the Sawatch Range are some of the most scenic rivers in the Southern Rockies: the Arkansas on the east, the Eagle on the north, the Roaring Fork on the northwest, and the Taylor and Gunnison drainages on the west. In its first 125 miles, the Arkansas River tumbles 5,000 feet in a series of deep green chutes—a spectacular beginning for the second-longest tributary of the Mississippi. From its headwaters to Royal Gorge, the Arkansas ranks as one of the finest whitewater rivers in the country; more than seventy-five thousand people a year ride rafts and kayaks through rapids such as the Zoom Flume and the Giant Steps in Browns Canyon.

By the 1880s, mining camps had sprung up in almost every valley of the Sawatch; nearly every outcrop bears the mark of some hardrock miner's can't-miss claim. Roads built of bravado and greed were pushed over Monarch, Tincup, Cottonwood, Independence, and Marshall passes, connecting the Sawatch communities with mining centers west of the Continental Divide. During the winter, horse-drawn sleighs replaced the wagons and stagecoaches that rumbled along these tortuous routes. An army of men with shovels was required to keep the freight traffic moving. The windswept summit of Independence Pass must have presented an eerie spectacle to the winter traveler in 1880 — a solid double line of traffic moving in opposite directions through 20-foot-deep trenches shoveled through the snowdrifts. During the summer, specially trained dogs raced ahead of the stagecoaches to warn uphill traffic to get out of the way. Independence Pass, at 12,095 feet, remains the nation's highest passenger-car crossing of the Continental Divide.

Mosquito and Tenmile Ranges

The Mosquito Range rises from a low gap in the mountains near Hoosier Pass and angles due south to Trout Creek Pass, paralleling the Sawatch Range and separating the windswept grasslands of South Park from the upper Arkansas Valley. At its southern end, near the dark summits of the Buffalo Peaks, the Mosquito Range loses elevation rapidly and merges with the low volcanic country of the Arkansas Hills. A cluster of Fourteeners — Lincoln, Democrat, and Bross — marks its northern end.

With scarcely a break, the comparatively small Tenmile Range curves north from Hoosier Pass to Tenmile Canyon, near Frisco. Bordered on the east by the Blue River and on the west by Tenmile Creek, the Tenmile Range forms a lofty and somewhat linear ridge as it angles northward to the Gore Range. One Fourteener, Quandary Peak (14,264 feet), marks the southern end of the range; north from Quandary, several peaks — Pacific, Fletcher, and Crystal — approach 14,000 feet as the narrow crest winds toward Tenmile Peak at the northern end of the range.

Layers of sedimentary rock still drape much of the Mosquito Range, giving the upland surface a broad, rolling appearance. These sedimentary layers are best displayed west of Fairplay, where glacial erosion has created the spectacular bowl of Horseshoe Cirque. In contrast, the rugged peaks of the Tenmile Range and the cluster of high peaks that graces the northern end of the Mosquito Range are capped with crystalline rocks. Buffalo Peaks, the double-summited mountain southwest of Fairplay, is an erosional remnant of the many layers of volcanic rock that once spread over this portion of the range.

In 1859, gold-rich gravels were discovered near Fairplay and Breckenridge, and at California Gulch, north of Leadville. The gentle pull up Kenosha Pass and the flat expanse of South Park proved to be a veritable speedway for prospectors heading to these new gold fields. From the summit cairns to the valleys below, nearly every inch of the Mosquito and Tenmile ranges has felt the impact of miners' picks. By 1873, however, the first placer boom was on the wane, leaving the valley bottoms littered with gravel piles. Prospect fever began once again when miners at Leadville discovered cerussite — a silver ore — along with the gold in their gravels. This second boom period produced nearly $100 million worth of silver and made Horace Tabor the bonanza king of Colorado.

The numerous roads in these ranges are a legacy of the frenzied mining activity more than a century ago. During the winter of 1863–64, Methodist preacher John Dyer pioneered a route across Mosquito Pass in order to make regular mail deliveries between the communities of Fairplay and Leadville. Dyer made his trips across the pass alone and at night, when the hard-frozen snow allowed him to make good time on his homemade skis. Eventually, a road was built over the pass, and by the summer of 1879, some 150 wagons and stagecoaches were traveling the route daily. Life insurance policies issued to miners during the boom period stipulated that no payoffs would be made if the insured met his end on Mosquito Pass. Once the railroads arrived in Fairplay and Leadville, however, the treacherous pass route fell into disuse.

Gore Range

The Gore Range rises steeply from the glaciated valley of Tenmile Canyon and angles northwest along the Blue River Valley. Except along its western flank, few traces remain of the sedimentary rocks that once draped the crest of the range. A line of serrated peaks distinguishes the southern end of the range, with several peaks breaking above 13,000 feet — Eagles Nest, Mount Powell, Keller Mountain, and several unnamed summits. North of the Gore Range—

Eagles Nest Wilderness Area, at Gore Canyon, the Colorado River has carved a 4-mile-long, 2,000-foot-deep gorge, exposing pastel-hued sedimentary rocks as well as the crystalline core of the range. North of Gore Canyon, the range loses elevation gradually as it winds north to Rabbit Ears Pass. Unlike so many other ranges in the Southern Rockies, the Gore Range has offered very little to the prospector, and few roads penetrate its high country.

The Gore Range is named for the Irish baronet Lord George Gore. Colorful to a fault, Gore seems an unlikely candidate for immortality. Arriving at Fort Laramie in the summer of 1854, Gore was intent on trophy hunting his way up the North Platte. Jim Bridger, legendary mountain man and scout, signed on as hunting guide for the expedition — inflating his guiding fee to thirty dollars a day to compensate for Gore's nasty disposition. No luxury was spared: Gore's entourage included 40 attendants, 112 horses, 12 yoke of oxen, 14 dogs, 6 wagons, and 21 carts full of wine and champagne. Lord Gore had few qualms about the wholesale slaughter of wildlife in the name of sport. During three summers spent hunting in the Rockies, Gore's party is believed to have killed more than two thousand buffalo, sixteen hundred elk and deer, and a hundred bear.

Rabbit Ears Range

The jumble of ancient volcanoes and lava flows that forms the Rabbit Ears Range carries the Continental Divide eastward from the southern tip of the Park Range to the Never Summer Mountains. North of the Rabbit Ears Range lie the broad basin of North Park and the headwaters of the North Platte River; to the south lie the rolling hills of Middle Park and the headwaters of the Colorado River. The range is named for the prominent stone "ears" of Rabbit Ears Peak, the eroded remnant of a volcanic plug marking the west end of the range; Rabbit Ears Peak can be seen from the middle of North Park all the way south to near Kremmling, Colorado.

Parkview Mountain (12,296 feet) dominates the crest of the range, and several mountains — Radial, Elk, Gravel, and Little Gravel — exceed 11,000 feet in elevation. Muddy Pass (8,772 feet), at the western end of the range, is the lowest crossing of the Continental Divide in Colorado. John Charles

THE SOUTHERN ROCKIES

Fremont, during his 1844 expedition, was the first explorer to use this well-trodden buffalo trail — now the route of U.S. 40 — linking North and Middle parks. Fremont was deeply impressed by Muddy Pass, noting in his journal that it was one of the most beautiful passes he had ever seen.

Park Range and the Sierra Madre

The Park Range rises sharply from the gray-green sagebrush flats along the western edge of North Park. From its southern tip, near Rabbit Ears Pass, the rugged alpine ridge stretches northward for nearly 35 miles to the Colorado-Wyoming border. There the range becomes known as the Sierra Madre as it continues on into Wyoming, where it resembles the Medicine Bow Mountains to the east but lacks the latter's broad upland surface. Except for a cluster of 12,000-foot peaks at the southern end of the Park Range, in the Mount Zirkel Wilderness Area, the landscape seems gentler and more welcoming than ranges to the south. The broad alpine uplands that characterize the crest of the Park Range are speckled with lakes — Luna, Bighorn, and Lake of the Crags. Along the western slope of the range, streams such as the South Fork and the Wolverine cascade through forests to join the Elk River and, ultimately, the Yampa.

The crystalline core of the Park Range has been exposed only along the crest of the range, and in places sedimentary rocks extend to or across the crest. Valleys along both sides of the range head in steep-walled cirques and end in a rippled series of glacially deposited bouldery ridges. In a number of areas along the eastern slope of the mountains, ridges of glacial rubble have dammed small ponds and lakes that offer excellent fishing. Along the western slope, the flat-floored Yampa River Valley is littered with enormous boulders flushed from glacial deposits upvalley by periodic flash floods. More than 150 hot springs issue from faults along the west side of the range. One of these springs — for which the town of Steamboat Springs is named — used to make a rhythmic noise like the chugging of a steamboat.

Economically valuable mineral deposits are uncommon in the Park Range except in the Hahns Peak area. John Hahn discovered placer gold in the 1860s near the peak that bears his name. By 1874, area gold ore yields approached $5 million a year. North of the Colorado-Wyoming border, one of the earliest large-scale mining operations in Wyoming—the Ferris-Haggerty Copper Mine—led to the founding of the town of Encampment.

Due to the absence of widespread mining activity, the Park Range and Sierra Madre lack the extensive backcountry road network found in so many areas of the Southern Rockies. The road over Buffalo Pass is the only crossing of the range between the Wyoming border and Rabbit Ears Pass. With the development of a major downhill skiing facility at Steamboat Springs' Mount Werner, skiers and other winter-sports enthusiasts are now taking full advantage of the ample snowfall and beautiful terrain.

Elkhead Range

This rolling, 18-mile-long range rises just to the north of the Yampa River, west of the Park Range. Geologically, the Elkhead Range is a by-product of the violent volcanic eruptions that shaped the White River Plateau and the Flattops to the south. With the exceptions of Welba Peak (10,801 feet), Bears Ears Peak (10,577 feet), and Mount Oliphant (10,670 feet), most summits in the Elkheads barely exceed 10,000 feet. Although considerably lower and drier than the nearby Park Range, the Elkheads receive sufficient moisture from winter storm systems to nourish the Elk, Little Snake, and Yampa rivers.

During the 1870s, the Elkheads provided one of the last refuges and principal hunting grounds for the northern Utes. Nathan Meeker, a fanatical reformer and the imperious Indian agent living at White River, had dreams of building an agricultural utopia at the base of the Elkheads—to be populated by Utes civilized by his personal efforts. In 1879, finally goaded to violence by Meeker's attempts to force them to the plow, the Utes made a defiant stand against a unit of two hundred soldiers at the mouth of Elkhead Creek. In the fierce battle that followed, which came to be known as the Meeker Massacre, the Utes killed several soldiers and more than 250 packhorses. A war party, sent to the Indian Agency, killed Meeker and several associates, and took his wife, daughter, and two small children hostage. Sadly, public outrage over the incident led to the 1880 Ute Removal Act, which transferred Colorado's remaining Utes to a reservation in Utah.

THE SOUTHERN ROCKIES

The Mountain Parks

Broad, treeless basins are a distinguishing feature of the mountain landscape of the Southern Rockies. Although small intermontane basins are scattered throughout the mountains, the largest — North, Middle, and South parks and the San Luis Valley — form a chain between the main north-south ranges. Explorer and geologist John Wesley Powell was so impressed by the parklike character of these large basins that he identified the Southern Rockies as the Park Mountains on his regional map of the United States. The term "park" continues to be used to refer to any extensive basin or lowland that is essentially treeless and enclosed on all sides by well-defined groups of mountains — hence, Estes Park, Taylor Park, Saguache Park.

North Park

The rolling sagebrush country of North Park and its enclosing circle of snow-capped peaks epitomizes the dramatic beauty of the mountain parks. Spreading south from a series of low hills near the Colorado-Wyoming border, North Park extends for nearly 60 miles to the Rabbit Ears Range. It is bounded on the east by the Rawah Peaks and along the west by the Park Range. High and windswept, the mean elevation of the basin floor exceeds 8,000 feet; areas of higher relief include the prominent landmarks of Owl Ridge, Peterson Ridge, Delaney Butte, Independence Mountain, and Pole Mountain. Tributaries of the North Platte River — the Canadian, Michigan, Illinois, Grizzly, Little Grizzly, and North Fork — form a meandering network before joining the North Platte near North Gate Canyon. Arapaho National Wildlife Refuge is situated in the heart of North Park, serving as an important link in the chain of refuges available to birds migrating along the Central Flyway.

When trappers and mountain men first arrived in North Park in the early 1800s, they shared the sage-dotted basin with Ute and Arapaho hunting parties. Herds of buffalo, deer, elk, and antelope were abundant. By the beginning of the twentieth century, however, professional hunters and North Park settlers had decimated wildlife populations to satisfy the booming meat trade in communities outside the park.

Abandoned cabin, North Park. *Audrey D. Benedict.*

During the 1870s, Wyoming-bred English and Scottish cattle dominated cattle herds throughout North Park. A string of severe winters in the late 1880s caused the downfall of the English cattle empire throughout the Rocky Mountains. The lessons of those first winters were never forgotten. North Park ranchers replaced English cattle breeds with hardier white-faced Herefords and began harvesting wild hay and clearing large expanses of sage and willow to cultivate more hay. Now, each autumn, breadloaf-shaped haystacks dot the meadows—insurance against the coming winter. North Park old-timers still like to joke that the snow there never melts—it just blows around until it wears out.

Middle Park

Middle Park, the smallest of the major mountain parks, lacks the expansive quality of its northern and southern counterparts. It lies within an irregular, eastward bend of the Continental Divide, enclosed by mountains—on the east by the Front Range, on the north by the Rabbit Ears Range, on the west by the Gore Range, and on the southwest by the Williams Fork Mountains. This is rough, rolling country—a patchwork of sage, aspen, and pine. Lateral spurs from the surrounding mountains and the ragged remains of ancient lava flows disrupt the basin floor, compressing its stream valleys and partitioning its meadows. A dense thicket of cottonwoods, bright gold in autumn, follows the course of the Colorado River as it snakes its way west through Middle Park to exit at Gore Canyon.

By the late 1870s, Middle Park seems to have attracted the attention of every sort of adventurer — trapper, explorer, prospector, botanist, and surveyor. Its relative seclusion ended with the construction of direct wagon roads over Rollins and Berthoud passes, linking Middle Park with Denver and other Eastern Slope communities. The summer of 1874 witnessed the beginning of real settlement in the area. The severe, seemingly endless winters, however, dashed the hopes and fortunes of all but the hardiest. Surviving ranches joined forces each autumn to stage a cattle drive, chiefly over the alpine tundra of Rollins Pass, delivering their herds to the Eastern Slope markets.

Today, water is Middle Park's most sought-after commodity. The first plans for the diversion of irrigation water from the North Fork of the Colorado to the semiarid Eastern Slope were proposed in 1889. By 1906 a major canal had been slashed across the slopes of the Never Summer Mountains, diverting a portion of the Colorado's water to the east-flowing Cache la Poudre River. Another Middle Park diversion project, the ambitious Colorado–Big Thompson Project, gathers water from the Colorado and from Willow Creek and channels it through a tunnel 3,780 feet below the Continental Divide, supplying water for more than 700,000 acres and 400,000 people in the South Platte River Basin. A complicated network of power plants along the system generates sufficient hydroelectric power to meet the project's needs as well as those of customers in northern Colorado, eastern Wyoming, and western Nebraska.

South Park

South Park, the beloved "Bayou Salado" of the mountain men, is the best known of the mountain parks. Viewed from a distance, this enormous grassy expanse appears strikingly flat. To the west lies the snow-rimmed wall of the Mosquito Range; to the north, the smooth balds of the Kenosha Mountains and Tarryall Mountains; to the east, Pikes Peak and the forested ridges of the Rampart Range; and to the south, a confusion of rough volcanic hills. In most places the basin floor lies well above 9,000 feet. The South Platte and its upper tributaries curve through South Park on their way east to an exit at Eleven Mile Canyon.

South Park gained prominence when significant deposits of gold were found in gravels along the South Platte River. Fairplay, established in 1859, was by all accounts an unruly gold camp in the western tradition. The stream of newcomers arriving on the newly built Denver, South Park, and Pacific Railway included enterprising businessmen who quickly set about supplying the prosperous mine owners with whatever luxuries they desired — everything from Steinway pianos to pressed-brick privies and vintage champagne. Fairplay was slow to give up its love affair with gold, maintaining operations until 1952; the last gold dredge still floats on its self-made pond a few miles south of Fairplay. Beyond it lie the giant heaps of dredge tailings — a reminder of the days when gold fever held the Southern Rockies in its grasp.

Today, South Park is ranching country. Water has become a pivotal commodity, as it has for Middle Park. The mountain parks of the Southern Rockies are dry, lying within the rain shadows created by the mountains along their western margins, and South Park is drier than most. Faced with the grim economics of ranching, most landowners have been unable to resist the inflated prices that their water rights are bringing in the urban marketplace. Consequently, the once-irrigated hay lands are drying up as water rights are sold to the Denver Water Board, the city of Aurora, and other municipal users. With irrigation water siphoned away to the cities, the prospects for South Park ranches remain troubled; a traditional way of life hangs in the balance.

San Luis Valley

The saltbush and greasewood flats of the San Luis Valley stretch for 50 miles between the San Juan Mountains and the Sangre de Cristo Range. Uncompromisingly flat and nearly three times the size of Delaware, the San Luis Valley sweeps south from Poncha Pass for more than 100 miles to straddle the Colorado–New Mexico border north of the

Taos Plateau. Situated in the long rain shadow cast by the San Juans, the region receives less than 10 inches of precipitation a year. With the exception of the Rio Grande, streams flowing into the valley along its margins sink into the sand and gravel of the valley floor. Along the eastern edge of the valley, at Great Sand Dunes National Monument, sands blown across the arid valley floor have built some of the highest inland dunes on Earth.

Until 1848, Spanish territory stretched north into the Southern Rockies as far as the Arkansas River, encompassing all of the San Luis country. During the early 1800s, Spanish patrols crisscrossed the lands south of the Arkansas at every rumored U.S. presence. In 1807, tracking Zebulon Pike to his winter quarters in the San Luis Valley, the Spaniards took him to Santa Fe as a political prisoner. In the years that followed, however, the Missouri–New Mexico fur trade began in earnest, and the Spanish could do little to keep the American and French trappers from ranging north from Santa Fe into the San Luis Valley and beyond.

The first permanent Spanish settlement in the valley was established at San Luis in 1851. The influx of Spanish settlers continued unabated during the next two decades, with more than two thousand making their homes in the valley by 1860. San Luis and other early communities—Costilla, San Pablo, Guadalupe, Conejos—were patterned after New Mexican territorial settlements. Individual farmsteads, most of adobe, were strung out like beads along the rivers at the valley's edge. At least forty irrigation ditches constructed during this period brought water to the arid bottomlands of the valley and thus expanded the agricultural base. Today, artesian wells supplement the network of irrigation ditches, and the San Luis Valley continues to be an important agricultural area for potatoes, malting barley, and lettuce.

Wildlife refuges at Monte Vista and Alamosa, encompassing thousands of acres of marshland and desert scrub, provide critical migratory and nesting habitat for waterfowl and shorebirds. Monte Vista National Wildlife Refuge is the main stopover for migrating sandhill cranes enroute between their wintering ground at Bosque del Apache Refuge in New Mexico and their nesting area at Grays Lake, Idaho.

CHAPTER TWO

Landscape Evolution: A Geologic Introduction

DRIVING WEST ACROSS the Great Plains, one barely notices as the road begins to climb — 1,000, 2,000, 5,000 feet — on debris shed from the Rockies and spread across the floors of long-departed oceans. Rising like a wall out of these outfanning sediments, the Southern Rocky Mountains form a succession of north-south–trending, folded and faulted uplifts, cored with ancient crystalline rocks and interspersed with volcanics. The sedimentary rocks that once spread across this entire region have largely been eroded, their broken ends forming a hogback escarpment along the flanks of the mountains that displaced them. Broad basins between the ranges form a distinctive chain of high mountain valleys — the parks described by John Wesley Powell in his geologic survey of the region.

Compared to mountain ranges such as the Appalachians, the Southern Rockies are geologic newcomers. They began their rise from the bed of an ancient sea only 70 million years ago, during the last 2 percent of the Earth's history. The entire story of the Southern Rockies, however, spans nearly 3 billion years and encompasses a complex series of changing environments. Here, mountain ranges have risen time and again, only to be buried in their own debris. Shallow seas swept across the land, lapping at beaches edged by lush subtropical forests. Volcanoes erupted, searing the land with lava and filling the air with white-hot ash. While volcanic fires were still smoldering, rivers of glacial ice plucked at summits and scoured valleys.

Landscape evolution is generally measured in thousands or even millions of years. The expansion of geologic knowledge resulting from the advent of radiometric dating has provided a measure of the vastness of geologic time and has allowed geologists to develop a reasonably well-dated chro-

Era	Per.	Epoch	Years (before present)	Geologic Events in the Southern Rockies
C E N O Z O I C	Q U A T E R N A R Y	Holocene		End of conditions favoring full-scale glaciation; growth and decay of "Little Ice Age" glaciers. Active mass-wasting; development of periglacial features; stream erosion. Evidence from the Colorado Front Range suggests that Paleo-Indian hunters were making seasonal use of high altitude valleys by at least 8500 years ago.
			10,000	
		Pleistocene		Climatic fluctuations result in the growth and decay of "Ice Age" ice sheets and valley glaciers; the glacial record is represented by three major glaciations (pre-Bull Lake, Bull Lake, Pinedale); glacial erosion and deposition processes create the U-shaped valleys and other landscape features typical of glaciated mountains. Dune fields develop in several areas at the close of the Pleistocene. Widespread mammalian extinctions.
			2 million	
	T E R T I A R Y	Pliocene		Regional uplift continues. Widespread erosion and canyon-cutting; development of modern drainage patterns. Late Cenozoic (Pliocene and Pleistocene) volcanism results in the massive, flow-on-flow basaltic rocks that cap mesas and plateaus in north-central Colorado and many other areas.
			5 million	
		Miocene		Broad regional uplift (as much as 5,000 ft. in some areas) and local block-faulting exhumes the Laramide uplifts and redefines the structural basins along their flanks. The Rio Grande Rift develops along the crest of the uplift dome and is accompanied by intense volcanic activity in the Jemez volcanic field and elsewhere.
			25 million	
		Oligocene		Catastrophic volcanic eruptions occur repeatedly and are believed to correspond to the emplacement of a massive, near-surface batholith beneath the San Juan Mountains and the region that extends northeast from the Elk Mountains and the Sawatch Range to the Rocky Mountain front; explosive volcanism produces enormous calderas, massive floods of lava, and extensive ash falls.
			40 million	
		Eocene		Post-Laramide erosion and basin development prevail throughout much of the region. Fossil plants and animals indicate a warm temperate to subtropical climate.
			60 million	
		Paleocene		The continuation of Laramide Orogeny is associated with the emplacement of igneous plutons and mineralization along the trend of the Colorado Mineral Belt. Many economically important ore bodies are emplaced as crack and fissure fillings in Precambrian-age rocks during this time.

Era	Per.	Epoch	Years (before present)	Geologic Events in the Southern Rockies
M E S O Z O I C		Cretaceous	65 million	The subtropical climate sets the stage for the explosive development of the flowering plants. Geologic events reflect the interplay of global changes in sea level and tectonic forces; shifting shorelines of the Western Interior Seaway result in sequences of rocks (Pierre Shale, Dakota Formation, Mancos Formation, Mesaverde Formation, and many others) representative of both deep and shallow-water marine environments as well as nonmarine settings; economically important coal-bearing rocks develop in many areas. The long history of subsidence and deposition comes to an end about 70 million years ago with the onset of beginning of the Laramide Orogeny.
		Jurassic	135 million	The earliest Jurassic rocks (Wingate, Navajo, and Entrada Formations) represent coastal dune deposits of enormous proportions that developed along the leading edge of the Sundance Sea as it spread south along the north-south trending Western Interior Basin. The geologic record corresponds to the cyclic transgression and regression of this sea; the sea's final withdrawal during the late Jurassic is represented by the fossil-rich interbedded shales and sandstones of the Morrison Formation. Morrison sediments yield one of the richest dinosaur faunas in the world.
		Triassic	195 million	Geologic events reflect the beginning of the breakup of the supercontinent Pangaea. The fine-textured sandstones and shales that characterize the distinctive "redbeds" of the Triassic were deposited under semiarid to arid conditions in mudflats, on alluvial plains, and in dune fields adjacent to the eroding highlands of the Ancestral Rockies. Conifers flourish in moister sites, joined by tree ferns, cycads, and scouring rushes. Dinosaurs dominate the land toward the close of the Triassic.
P A L E O Z O I C		Permian	230 million	Fossil-poor, coarse textured redbeds record the continued erosion of the Ancestral Rockies, largely completed by the Middle Permian, when shallow seas invade the region from the west and east. Dune fields form along the western margin of Uncompahgria (represented by the Weber Formation) and along the northern flanks of Frontrangia (represented by the Lyons Sandstone). By the close of the Permian, the continents have coalesced to form the supercontinent Pangaea, giving rise to semiarid and arid conditions worldwide.
		Pennsylvanian	290 million	Tectonic quiescence ends with the progressive collision-suturing of continental plates and the

Era	Per. Epoch	Years (before present)	Geologic Events in the Southern Rockies
P A L E O Z O I C	Pennsylvanian (cont.)		rise of the Ancestral Rockies. Mountain-building activity is concentrated along two main belts: Front-rangia and Uncompahgria. Shallow seas invade the region along the Central Colorado Trough during the early stages of uplift; thick sequences of evaporites (gypsum, anhydrite, and halite) form in the trough's center as the seaway evaporates. Thick sequences of sediments eroded from the uplifts consolidate to form colorful redbeds in many areas (Fountain, Maroon, Sangre de Cristo, and Cutler Formations).
	Mississippian	325 million	Widespread submergence characterizes the Southern Rockies during this period. Shallow-water carbonate sedimentation results in the formation of massive, gray limestones such as the Leadville Formation. Towards the end of the Mississippian, tectonic activity begins along the Transcontinental Arch and in the wake of the retreating seas the surface of the limestone undergoes extensive solution weathering.
	Devonian	355 million	At the start of the Devonian, the region lies only slightly above sea level and is situated close to the equatorial zone. By late Devonian time, embayments of a western seaway spread across the central Southern Rockies and the rock record is dominated by soft shales, fossiliferous limestones, and quartz-rich sandstones.
	Silurian	410 million	The most widespread submergence of North America occurred during the Silurian. Silurian-age rocks are exceedingly rare in the Southern Rockies as a result of erosion; the only evidence of the region's submergence comes from blocks of fossiliferous limestone preserved in later volcanic tubes.
	Ordovician	440 million	Seas deepen locally throughout the region, continuing a pattern of cyclic transgression and regression. A scattering of islands persist along the trend of the Transcontinental Arch. Ordovician limestones and sandstones (Harding Sandstone, Fremont Limestone, etc.) contain a diversity of marine organisms.
	Cambrian	500 million	At the beginning of the Cambrian, the largely eroded Precambrian ranges are part of the emergent North American continental platform. Ocean basin displacements resulting from plate tectonics cause seas to spread from west to east across the region. By the late Cambrian, highlands along the northeast-trending upwarp known as the Transcontinental Arch persist only as islands.
		570 million	

Era	Per.	Epoch	Years (before present)	Geologic Events in the Southern Rockies
P R E C A M B R I A N		Late	1,600 million	Late Precambrian history is highlighted by two intervals of igneous intrusion resulting in the emplacement of batholiths such as the Pikes Peak Granite, the Laramie Anorthosite, the Sherman Granite, the Silver Plume Granite, and others. During the final years of the Precambrian (the Lipalian Interval) much of the region was eroded to a nearly featureless plain.
		Middle (Proterozoic)	2,500 million	Evidence suggests that the region encompassing the present-day Southern Rockies was joined to the southwestern edge of the ancestral North American craton during the period 1,800–1,600 m.y. as a result of tectonic accretion. A lull in tectonic activity at this time resulted in the deposition of sediments in oceanic troughs along the edge of the Wyoming Province. The onset of intense regional metamorphism, intermittent erosion and sedimentation, and two intervals of massive igneous intrusion punctuate the remainder of the Middle Precambrian.
		Early (Archean)	4,500 + million	The oldest Precambrian rocks in the Southern Rockies, dated at more than 2,500 m.y., are found along the southern margin of the Wyoming Province (part of the Archean nucleus of North America); these rocks are separated from the younger Proterozoic rocks that comprise the remainder of the present-day Southern Rockies by a northeast-trending zone of faults and fractures known as the Cheyenne Belt.

nology of the Earth's history. To understand the modern geologic landscape of the Southern Rockies, we must view these landscapes within the framework of geologic time, deciphering clues left behind by forces that create mountains as well as those that wear them down. The five chapters that follow this brief introduction to rocks and landscape processes describe the changing geologic environments that have shaped the face of the Southern Rockies during nearly 3 billion years.

Raw Materials of the Southern Rockies

The geologic history of the Southern Rockies is written in its rocks and landforms. In many ways, it is far more useful to be able to recognize differences in the origins of certain rocks than to be able to identify rocks by their specific names. Geologists recognize three basic types of rocks: igneous, sedimentary, and metamorphic, each type characterized by the process that formed it.

IGNEOUS ROCKS

Igneous rocks are formed by the crystallization of molten material called *magma*. Geologists define two broad classes of igneous rocks based on the environment of their formation: *plutonic* (intrusive) and *volcanic* (extrusive). Plutonic rocks form when magma cools and crystallizes beneath the Earth's surface. Volcanic rocks form whenever magma erupts at the surface as lava or as airborne ejecta. Rocks in each group are given specific names (for example, granite) that precisely describe their mineralogy and texture.

Plutonic and volcanic rocks are chemically similar, but they differ markedly in texture and general appearance. The proportion of light and dark minerals in an igneous rock determines its color. *Felsic* (light-colored) igneous rocks are composed largely of late-crystallizing minerals, such as quartz and light-colored feldspars. *Mafic* (dark-colored) igneous rocks contain high proportions of early-crystallizing minerals, such as hornblende, pyroxenes, and dark-colored feldspars. The texture of an igneous rock reflects the rate at which the magma cooled. The slower the rate of cooling, the larger the resultant crystals. Plutonic rocks, insulated during their formation by the rock into which the magma is intruded, tend to cool slowly, resulting in a medium- to coarse-grained texture, with the individual minerals visible to the naked eye. Volcanic rocks tend to be fine-grained or glassy because eruption at the Earth's surface brings about more rapid cooling. *Porphyries* are rocks characterized by crystals of two markedly different sizes and are typically formed when magma undergoes two cycles of cooling, the first at depth, permitting the growth of the large crystals (*phenocrysts*), and the second when the magma moves to shallower depth, increasing the cooling rate and resulting in smaller crystals.

Volcanic eruptions generally produce variable quantities of liquid lava. In addition, magmas that are heavily charged with gas may explode from a surface vent or fissure, producing a shower of porous rock fragments and ash. The term *pyroclastic* refers to volcanic rocks that form as a result of an explosive ejection. Pyroclastic agglomerates and ash-fall tuffs, common on the Pajarito Plateau and in the San Juan Mountains, are formed from the consolidation of nonsorted ejecta—volcanic bombs, cinders, and ash. Welded tuff, a common pyroclastic rock encountered at Lava Cliffs in Rocky Mountain National Park and other volcanic areas of the Southern Rockies, is formed from ash believed to have been so hot that it fused immediately upon deposition.

The silica content of magma plays an important role in landform development. Silica-rich (*rhyolitic*) lavas are generally so viscous that they flow with difficulty, increasing in size by mounding. In contrast, basaltic lavas typically flow freely across the landscape, producing plateaulike topographic features. When basaltic lavas cool, they tend to crystallize from the outside inward, causing the lava to contract and to develop a columnar joint pattern. Excellent examples of columnar jointing can be seen in the basalt flows exposed along the Rio Grande in northern New Mexico, at Wagon Wheel Gap (near Creede), on Grand Mesa (near Land's End), and east of Cochetopa Pass (Colorado Highway 114).

Igneous intrusive bodies, or *plutons*, come in many shapes and sizes and are formed as magma pushes forcibly into preexisting host rocks or moves along zones of weakness in the host rock. The largest pluton is the *batholith*, which melts its way upward, assimilating whatever rock it intrudes. Batholiths typically exceed 40 square miles in size; Pikes Peak is formed by a batholith that marks the southern end of the Colorado Front Range. *Stocks* are somewhat smaller, cylindrical plutons that cut across or are discordant with the structural trend of the preexisting host rocks. *Laccoliths* are essentially large, blisterlike bodies that create domes in the overlying rocks but generally conform to or are concordant with the preexisting structural trend of the host rocks; laccoliths are common features in the West Elks. *Dikes*, such as the wall-like features that radiate from the flanks of the Spanish Peaks, are distinctly smaller, sheetlike bodies that typically cut across the structural grain of the host rock. *Sills* are sheetlike bodies that, like laccoliths, are concordant with the structural trends of the host rock.

SEDIMENTARY ROCKS

Sedimentary rocks are formed when sediments—rock fragments, chemical precipitates, or organic matter—consolidate on land or in the water under temperature and pressure regimes typical of the Earth's surface. Geologists separate sedimentary rocks into three general groups: *clastic, non-clastic,* and *organic.* Many sedimentary rocks are gradational between these simplified groups, while others may have a composite origin.

Clastic sedimentary rocks consist of fragments, or grains, of preexisting rocks that have undergone compaction and cementation to form new rocks. They are classified according to grain size into the following general categories: conglomerate (gravel-sized), sandstone, siltstone, and shale (laminated clay and silt-sized particles). For example, sandstone is formed by the cementation of sand-sized grains, usually quartz. Close examination of a clastic sedimentary rock reveals the environmental factors that played a role in its formation. Sediments are transported to a depositional site by processes that involve the flow of air, water, or ice, or by gravity-driven processes, which may or may not involve water as a support mechanism or lubricant. The size and sorting of particles in a clastic sedimentary rock reflect the size of grains weathered from the source area, the character of the transporting medium, the energy characteristics of the environment in which the sediments are deposited, and any postdepositional changes that have occurred in this environment. Silt- and sand-sized particles can be transported by both water and wind. The presence of cobbles, gravel, or sand generally implies a high-energy depositional environment, such as might be found in a stream channel or along a marine beach; clastic materials associated with beach, stream, and sand-dune environments are often distinctly rounded. Fine particles, such as silt and clay, typically settle out in quiet water or from air, and are associated most commonly with lake, deep-ocean, estuarine, or swamp environments.

Many clastic sedimentary rocks are conspicuously layered, each layer representing an episode of deposition. Layers may be several feet thick or paper-thin, depending on the character and duration of each depositional interval. Boundaries between successive layers may be observed as subtle changes in grain size or color, or as distinct changes in rock type. Sedimentary structures, such as ripple marks, cross-bedding, mud cracks, and the tracks or other signs of animals, may pattern the surfaces of certain layers. Wherever wind or water currents have swept sediment into bars, dunes, or ripples, we are able to determine the direction of current flow or, in the case of cross-bedding relationships, changes in the current direction within the depositional environment.

Nonclastic sedimentary rocks (such as dolomite, rock gypsum, and rock salt) are derived from sediments that either precipitate out of water or are produced through the evaporation of water containing dissolved solids. Cherts are nonclastic rocks that consist largely of silica and have been formed either from chemical precipitation or by silica replacement of plant or animal material; agates, jasper, and some petrified wood are examples. Secondary segregations, such as nodules, concretions, and geodes, are often found in sedimentary rocks, and all result from the orderly precipitation, or segregation, of mineral matter in the sediment after deposition. *Organic* sedimentary rocks are derived from the accumulation and consolidation of plant or invertebrate remains; most limestones (formed from coral reefs or shell fragments) and coal are examples.

The color of a sedimentary rock provides information on the mineralogy of the parent material as well as indications of the oxygen levels present in the original depositional environments or of the chemistry of waters flowing through the rock after burial. In most cases, however, the mineral pigments we see are released by chemical weathering and later alteration of the sedimentary grains in place. Light colors prevail in sedimentary rocks in which the mineral grains or rock fragments and the cementing material are dominated by quartz or calcite. Bright colors are generally produced by the chemical alteration of dark, iron-bearing minerals in the sediments. Buff, brown, and red hues result from the presence of ferric oxide (hematite) and are often associated with oxygenated depositional environments or groundwaters. The green, gray, and blackish hues common in many shales reflect a poorly oxygenated, or reducing, environment in which organic decay was limited. Certain dark-colored rocks, such as coal, owe their color largely to the amount of organic carbon present. Glauconite (potassium iron silicate) grains in sufficient quantity are responsible for the greenish hues prevalent in certain sandstones, such as the Sawatch Sandstone of central Colorado.

Geologists recognize relatively consistent, thick, and extensive sedimentary rock units as formations, to which they assign two-part names (for example, Leadville Limestone) that provide both a geographic and geologic identity. Because sedimentary rocks often contain fossils, they provide not only a record of past life forms, but they allow geologists to correlate specific intervals of geologic time from one area to another. Based on their knowledge of modern plant and animal habitat requirements and distributional patterns, paleontologists have been able to reconstruct many of the ancient environments of the Southern Rockies.

METAMORPHIC ROCKS

Metamorphic rocks result from the recrystallization of igneous, sedimentary, or preexisting metamorphic rocks beneath the Earth's surface. The primary factors involved in the formation of the various kinds of metamorphic rocks are: (1) heat, resulting either from contact with rising magma, radioactive decay, or deep burial; (2) intense pressure; or (3) hot, chemically active solutions. The high heat and intense directed pressure of the metamorphic environment can cause the constituent minerals in the parent rock to form parallel layers, or *folia*. Geologists separate metamorphic rocks into two groups: *foliated* and *nonfoliated*. The bands in foliated rocks commonly consist of dark-colored concentrations of biotite mica and hornblende. In metamorphic rocks associated with the intense deformational pressures of mountain building, such as schists or gneisses, the folia may be spectacularly bent and folded. Nonfoliated metamorphic rocks, such as hornfels and marble, develop from rocks that lack mineralogic diversity and have been subjected only to the heat of an intruding magma and not to any directional pressures.

Two types of metamorphism are important in the Southern Rockies: *contact* and *regional*. Contact metamorphism, which produces nonfoliated rocks, occurs along the margins of small igneous intrusions, such as dikes and sills, and is initiated by the heat of the intruding magma. Because small igneous intrusions cool more rapidly than large ones, the contact metamorphic zones adjacent to them form relatively thin, nonfoliated sheaths, seldom exceeding a few feet in width. Yule Marble, quarried in central Colorado for use in the Lincoln Memorial, is an example of a rock type produced by contact metamorphism of a thick bed of Leadville Limestone.

Massive intrusions, such as those that formed the cores of many of the mountain ranges of the Southern Rockies, were slow to cool and therefore gave rise to large-scale regional metamorphism. Rocks such as schist and gneiss are produced by regional metamorphism and are associated with the axes of the large mountain ranges where deformational pressure has been particularly intense.

Internal Processes

Seismic studies show that the Earth is made up of three major zones, arranged in concentric layers of differing densities: an extremely dense molten *core*, a moderately dense, iron-rich, mobile *mantle*, and an outermost layer of relatively low-density materials called the *crust*. This differentiation by density is the most fundamental structural feature of the Earth and is crucial to our understanding of the geologic events that have shaped the face of the Southern Rockies.

Geologists use the term *tectonics* to refer to all deformation of the Earth's crust. These crustal movements may range from minor disruptions that affect small bodies of rock to the folding and faulting that produce mountain ranges and, on a global scale, to the forces that cause continents to move and sea floors to split. The causes of crustal deformation are complex. Many geologists believe that large-scale tectonic activity is generated by the development of huge convection cells in the mobile zone that underlies the crust and includes the upper region of the mantle. Since these processes cannot be observed, we can only speculate about the triggering mechanisms necessary to generate global-scale movements.

PLATE TECTONICS AND THE SOUTHERN ROCKIES

The theory of plate tectonics provides us with a broad outline of the forces that create mountains and initiate volcanic eruptions — but with few details to explain the events that have occurred in the Southern Rockies. The general model for plate tectonics embodies the idea that the Earth's crust is broken into several rigid plates, which move at varying speeds over the underlying mantle. Plate boundaries do not correspond to standard geographic units but extend

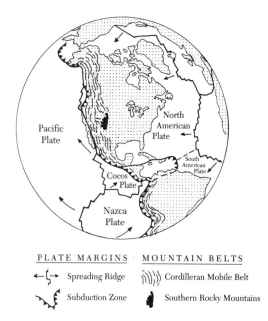

Generalized map of the major lithospheric plates of the Western Hemisphere. Arrows indicate direction of plate movement. *Emmett Evanoff.*

through continents, along the edges of continents, and down the middle of oceans. The Earth's plates include two types of crust: continental crust and oceanic crust. Continental crust consists largely of lightweight, silica-rich (felsic) rocks; oceanic crust consists primarily of dense, iron-rich (mafic) rocks.

The North American continent includes two major tectonic features. A large, tectonically stable platform, or *craton*, encompasses much of the present-day continental interior and is underlain by Precambrian-age granitic and metamorphic rocks. The craton is characterized by subdued topography and low elevations. Tectonic disturbance of this stable platform occurs by broad, gentle upwarping—only the craton's edges participate in the violent creation of mountains. The long, narrow, and generally arc-shaped zones of structural instability that form along the leading edges of a moving craton are called *mobile belts*. These belts are the loci of volcanoes, granitic batholiths, regional metamorphism, and earthquakes, and are characterized by thick sequences of sedimentary and volcanic rocks that have been folded, metamorphosed, and intruded by plutons. The Southern Rockies are unique in that they overlap the southwestern portion of the craton as well as the Cordilleran mobile belt that extends along the west coast of North, Central, and South America.

Mountain building, or *orogeny*, occurs as a result of mobile-belt disturbances along the zone where two plates converge. When an oceanic and a continental plate collide, the leading edge of the oceanic plate, being denser and less buoyant, plunges beneath the margin of the continental plate — by a process called *subduction* — where it undergoes progressive melting; the zone of intrusive and volcanic activity along the continental plate margin is believed to correspond to the trajectory of this descending plate. The surface expression of a subduction zone is delineated by an oceanic trench on one side, and by a curvilinear line of volcanoes, called a *magmatic arc* (including both island arcs and intracontinental volcanic arcs), on the other side.

The axis of the oceanic trench marks the zone in which sediments from both the oceanic plate and the continental plate are accumulating. Deep-ocean sediments — fine clay and ooze — that have settled to the ocean floor are carried along on the moving oceanic plate. From the continent, terrestrial sediments — sand and mud — are carried to the shore by streams and then swept into deep ocean waters by currents. In the bottom of the trench, sediments from both sources are mixed and then deformed as they are dragged downward by the subducting oceanic plate. In this way, the continental margin is built outward and new continental crust is created by the addition (*accretion*) of these metamorphosed sediments.

Most of the world's great mountain belts lie along the margins of continents and fit neatly into the framework of the plate-tectonic model. But the Southern Rockies are located in the interior of the continent, far from the current boundaries between colliding plates. The actual mechanism behind their final rise during the Cenozoic era remains enigmatic, only partially explained by the modern plate-tectonic paradigm. Some scientists suggest that the episodes of mountain building that produced the Southern Rockies were an intraplate response to the collision of the North American and East Pacific plates. Whatever the answer, it seems probable that episodes of intense regional orogeny in the Southern Rockies were initiated at times when the geographic positions of convergent plate boundaries were different from those we see today.

CHAPTER THREE

Opening Scenes:
Precambrian Landscapes

WE TEND, IN discussing the events of the Precambrian era, to compress the uncompressible. Spanning roughly three-fourths of geologic time, the Precambrian began with the Earth's formation some 4.6 billion years ago and ended with the appearance of the first shell-bearing animals about 600 million years ago. Precambrian mountain ranges of vast dimensions appeared repeatedly across the region of the present-day Southern Rockies—only to be worn away and engulfed by the advancing seas of the Paleozoic era. Today, the uncovered, uplifted roots of these Precambrian ranges form some of the most spectacular scenery in the Southern Rockies.

Precambrian Rock Provinces

Precambrian rocks form the foundations—the so-called basement rocks—of the continents. In many areas, the Precambrian basement rocks are blanketed by later strata; outcrops of these ancient rocks are visible only in a few deep canyons, such as the Grand Canyon of the Colorado and the Black Canyon of the Gunnison, or in the cores of deeply eroded mountain ranges, such as the Colorado Front Range and the Park Range.

The Precambrian basement rocks that make up the continents can be subdivided into distinct regions, or provinces, based on rock ages. Radiometric dating has shown that the North American craton can be divided into seven provinces, each distinguished by characteristic rock assemblages of differing rock ages and by generally similar deformational

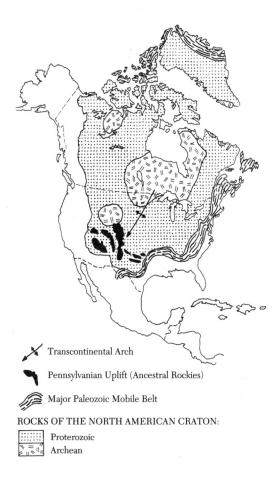

Precambrian and Paleozoic features of North America.
Emmett Evanoff.

trends that have been preserved in the rocks; adjacent
provinces have different deformational trends and appear
to be separated by abrupt metamorphic boundaries known
as *orogenic fronts.* Radiometric dates of rock samples taken
from deep wells and scattered exposures of Precambrian
rocks in western Canada, the United States, Mexico, and
Greenland have enabled geologists to develop models that
explain the growth of the continents during the Precambrian.

Archean History: The Early Precambrian
(2.5 Billion Years Ago)

Details of the Precambrian history of the Southern Rockies are slowly unfolding after nearly a century of study. The oldest rocks in the Southern Rockies are found in the Medicine Bow Mountains and the Sierra Madre Range of southern Wyoming and consist of early Precambrian or Archean-age gneisses, granites, and quartzites, dated at more than 2.5 billion years. These crystalline basement rocks form the southern margin of the Wyoming Province, part of the Archean nucleus of North America, and provide the most complete and best-exposed record of Archean and early Proterozoic events in the western United States. Correlated in age with rocks of the southern Superior Province of Canada, the rocks of the Wyoming Province reflect widespread deformation, granitic plutonism, and volcanic activity, culminating about 2.5 billion years ago.

Rocks of the Wyoming Province are separated from a distinctly younger, Proterozoic basement complex to the south by a broad, northeast-trending zone of faults and fractures known as the Cheyenne Belt. This well-defined shear zone extends through the Sierra Madre, Medicine Bow, and Laramie mountains just north of the Colorado-Wyoming border. South of the Cheyenne Belt, in the Proterozoic province that encompasses the remainder of the Southern Rockies and much of the Southwest, the oldest basement rocks are dated at about 1.8 billion years. Some geologists have suggested that the Cheyenne Belt defines the southern margin of the Archean continental nucleus — a zone they believe has been characterized by plate convergence, the development of offshore island arcs, and crustal accretion. According to this model, the juxtaposition of these two contrasting age provinces can be explained by the tectonic accretion (addition) of a 720-mile-wide band of Proterozoic crust to the Wyoming Province during the period 1.8 to 1.6 billion years ago.

Proterozoic History: The Middle Precambrian
(2.5–1.6 Billion Years Ago)

Geologists believe that by earliest Proterozoic time the region encompassing most of the present-day Southern

Rockies was joined—some use the term welded—to the southwestern edge of the ancestral North American craton. The beginning of the Proterozoic is marked by a lull in tectonic activity and by the deposition of thousands of feet of sediments in deep oceanic troughs along the southern margin of the Wyoming Province. The remainder of the middle Precambrian was characterized by the onset of intense regional metamorphism and deformation, intermittent erosion and sedimentation, and two intervals of massive igneous intrusion. Much of the metamorphic activity, including the alteration of the trough-deposited sedimentary and volcanic rocks, was concentrated along the trend of the Colorado Lineament, a 100-mile-wide belt of Precambrian faults that can be traced from the Grand Canyon northeast to the Rocky Mountain front, and possibly on beneath the northern midcontinent region to Lake Superior. Clearly, Precambrian tectonic activity occurred repeatedly, on a scale far greater than in any subsequent time. This early deformation set the course of the Colorado River and, more important, initiated the fragmentation of the Precambrian basement of the Southern Rockies into a mosaic of fault blocks, which, when reactivated during the Cretaceous period of the Mesozoic era, played a critical role in the final rise of the Southern

Medicine Peak Quartzite exposed in a sheer cliff near Snowy Range Pass. *Audrey D. Benedict.*

White pegmatite dikes decorate the sheer face of the Painted Wall in Black Canyon, Gunnison National Monument. *Audrey D. Benedict.*

Rockies. Metamorphic rocks that formed during the middle Precambrian were repeatedly folded and faulted into huge corrugated ridges. Metamorphic activity peaked in the region approximately 1.8 to 1.7 billion years ago, coinciding with diminished movement along the Colorado Lineament.

The earliest Proterozoic rocks are the metasedimentary (partially metamorphosed) rocks of the Snowy Pass Supergroup in the Medicine Bow Mountains and the Sierra Madre of Wyoming. These metasedimentary rocks are unique in the Southern Rockies because they represent cratonic margin, shallow-marine sedimentation. One of the best examples, a sparkling white quartzite called the Medicine Peak Quartzite, forms an impressive cliff in the Snowy Range of southern Wyoming; this quartzite is about 5,600 feet thick and is derived from the metamorphism of sediments deposited on a shallow marine shelf. Younger rocks in the same region, dated at about 1.7 billion years, contain stromatolites, the mound-like accumulations of calcium carbonate produced by reef-forming marine algae. Stromatolites are the only common

THE SOUTHERN ROCKIES

fossil in Precambrian rocks, and, with other ancient stromatolites found in Australia and Africa, are thought to represent
the oldest known evidence of life on Earth.

South of the Cheyenne Belt shear zone, continent-island-
arc collision produced the high-grade metamorphic rocks
typical of Colorado and northern New Mexico. Large outcrops of early Proterozoic gneisses and schists dated at about
1.8 billion years are especially prominent in the walls of
numerous mountain canyons and glacial cirques along the
Colorado Front Range. These distinctive rocks, the first
Precambrian rocks you see as you travel Interstate 70 west
from Denver, are easily observed along Trail Ridge Road
in Rocky Mountain National Park and in Big Thompson
Canyon (west of Loveland). Metamorphic rocks of this age
group form the famous Keyboard of the Winds, a jagged
ridge between Longs Peak and Pagoda Mountain in the park.
At the southern end of the Colorado Front Range, metamorphic rocks are conspicuous in the Royal Gorge of the
Arkansas (west of Cañon City). In Black Canyon of the Gunnison National Monument, the 2,300-foot-high "Painted
Wall" exposes a spectacular cliff of early Proterozoic gneiss
interlaced with a series of younger, light-colored dikes.

In addition to the gneisses and schists typical of middle
Precambrian metamorphism, several other rock types are
common in the Southern Rockies. Outcrops of amphibolite,
a dark greenish black metamorphic rock, form striking cliffs
along the Pecos River in the Sangre de Cristo Range in New
Mexico. Exposures of phyllite (metamorphosed shale), also
common in the Sangre de Cristo Range, are the product of
regional metamorphism and are easy to spot because of their
silky sheen and crinkly foliation. Middle Precambrian quartzites (metamorphosed sandstones) form Pecos Baldy, Chimayosos, and Truchas peaks in the southern Sangre de Cristos.

IGNEOUS INTRUSIONS BEGIN

During the late stages of middle Precambrian metamorphism, dated at around 1.7 billion years, massive igneous
intrusions began to occur throughout the region. These intrusions ranged in composition from granite to gabbro. Later
episodes of intrusive activity occurred around 1.4 and 1 billion years ago, during the late Precambrian. With each episode of intrusion, mountains were built and subsequently
eroded to near sea level. The great variety of shapes and sizes

of these intrusions was determined by the structural characteristics of the host rocks into which they were intruded, the viscosity of the intruding magma, and the rate of its injection. Renewed metamorphism of the host rocks, resulting from the thermal effects of the intruding magma, accompanied each episode of intrusion.

THE FIRST PHASE:
1.7-BILLION-YEAR-OLD GRANITES

Granitic igneous rocks of this first intrusive episode are exposed as batholiths, stocks, dikes, and smaller lenticular bodies. The most typical and well-known granite of this period is the Boulder Creek Granite, a dark blue-gray, faintly banded granodiorite. Outcrops of this small batholith are exposed west of Boulder in the central Front Range. A granite batholith of similar age makes up Mount Evans, one of the Fourteeners dominating the skyline west of Denver. In central Colorado, granite dated at 1.75 billion years can also be seen in the exposed core of the northern Sawatch Range.

A period of major erosion is believed to have followed this first intrusive episode. Evidence of this erosive interval, however, is limited to the Needles Mountains in the San Juans, where an 8,000-foot-thick sequence of metamorphosed sedimentary rocks (quartzites, slates, and phyllites of the Uncompahgre Formation) overlies middle Precambrian granites and is, in turn, intruded by the Eolus Granite, a late Precambrian granite.

The Late Precambrian
(1.6 Billion–570 Million Years Ago)

Late Precambrian history in the Southern Rockies is highlighted by two intervals of igneous intrusion and concludes with a long period of erosion, known as the Lipalian Interval.

SECOND PHASE INTRUSIONS:
1.4-BILLION-YEAR-OLD GRANITES

The first of the two intrusive periods began about 1.4 billion years ago and continued for almost 100 million years. The Silver Plume Granite, locally exposed in the central Colorado Front Range, and the Sherman Granite, conspicuous

Sherman Granite exposed at the Vedauwoo Rocks Scenic Area, Laramie Range. *Audrey D. Benedict.*

along the crest of the Laramie Range and in the Vedauwoo Rocks area of southern Wyoming, are the most representative granites of this second intrusive group. Most rock climbers are familiar with the Silver Plume Granite because it forms the sheer wall of the Diamond on Longs Peak. Related in age to the Sherman Granite is a batholith of anorthosite, an unusual igneous rock composed almost exclusively of the calcium-plagioclase feldspar known as labradorite. This batholith is situated on the Cheyenne Belt where it crosses the Laramie Range and is cut by the northern margin of the Sherman Granite Batholith. Anorthosite plutons are rare on Earth but are very common on the moon, where they form light-colored lunar highlands.

Here and there, 1.4-billion-year-old granites have been intruded by dikes of darker igneous rocks, such as gabbro and andesite. Dikes of this type are especially common in the northern Front Range and in the Sawatch Range. The 40-mile-long Iron Dike, which extends from just south of Boulder northwest across the Front Range, is believed to have been emplaced at this time. Road-cut and surface exposures of this dike are a conspicuous dark brown, due to the dike's high iron (magnetite) content; the Iron Dike can be easily seen in a road-cut about a mile west of Many Parks Curve in Rocky Mountain National Park.

FINAL INTRUSIVE PHASE: 1-BILLION-YEAR-OLD GRANITES

The final episode of granitic intrusion was marked by the emplacement of the Pikes Peak Batholith. Very little infor-

The Diamond on Longs Peak, Colorado Front Range. *Wendy Shattil and Robert Rozinski.*

mation exists on intrusive activity elsewhere in the Southern Rockies during this time. The composition of the Pikes Peak Batholith is highly variable, the most extensive element of which is a coarse-grained pinkish granite called the Pikes Peak Granite. Part of this batholith also forms the core of the Rampart Range, which extends north from Pikes Peak. Aeromagnetic surveys of the Pikes Peak area suggest that the batholith may have fed a volcanic caldera. Decomposition of the Pikes Peak Granite into a coarse sand containing feldspar and quartz grains is widespread throughout the region. Colorado's state mineral, bright green feldspar crystals known as amazonstone, are found in the Pikes Peak Granite and are especially prevalent at Crystal Mountain, north of Florissant.

The End of the Precambrian

The final years of the Precambrian era are characterized by tectonic quiescence and widespread erosion. For an immense span of time, ranging between 600 and 400 million years ago, no rock record exists of mountain-building activity in the Southern Rockies. During this time, known as the Lipalian Interval, much of the region was eroded to a nearly featureless plain, at or just above sea level. In most places, the erosion surface, or unconformity, separating the Precambrian basement from younger strata is smooth and somewhat beveled. Below the unconformity, tremendous thicknesses of granite or metamorphic rocks can be seen; above it are bedded sequences of younger sedimentary rocks. In certain situations, a thick fossil soil may also be seen, such as in a road-cut on Flagstaff Mountain, just west of Boulder. Good exposures of the Upper Precambrian erosion surface can be seen in Glenwood Canyon near Glenwood Springs, at Box Canyon Falls near Ouray, and in the Williams Canyon–Cave of the Winds area west of Colorado Springs.

CHAPTER FOUR

The Paleozoic: Mountain Islands and Desert Seas

VISUALIZE THE FACE of the Southern Rockies half a billion years ago, at the dawn of the Paleozoic. The landscape is barren. There are no plants to soften the contours, no animals except sea-dwelling invertebrates. At times, the land is emergent and marine waters spill only onto the continental margins. At other times, shallow seas sweep across the land, the few remaining highlands forming a chain of islands in the warm, tropical seas.

Geologists divide the Paleozoic era into seven periods, each of which has a characteristic suite of fossils that reflect the environmental conditions at the time of their burial. In the Southern Rockies, the early and middle Paleozoic are characterized by the widespread deposition of predominately marine sediments and by a rapidly evolving marine fauna. The late Paleozoic witnessed the expansion of terrestrial life, both plant and animal; the rise of a major group of mountains, the Ancestral Rockies, in the region of the present-day Southern Rocky Mountains, and the formation of the supercontinent Pangaea. Differences in the Paleozoic sedimentary record from one area to another in the Southern Rockies are the result of variations in the extent of the encroaching seas, changing depositional environments, and the effects of postdepositional erosion.

Cambrian Period
(570–500 Million Years Ago)

At the beginning of the Cambrian period, the Southern Rockies were part of the emergent North American continental platform. The paleocontinents were dispersed around the globe in low tropica latitudes; there were no emergent land masses above latit des 60° north or south. In the Southern Rockies, the set spread from west to east across the eroded, planed-down Precambrian mountains, beginning a series of advances, or *transgressions,* with each advance punctuated by a retreat, or *regression,* of these seas from land areas. This pattern continued intermittently throughout the Paleozoic and Mesozoic eras and is believed to have been the result of ocean-basin displacements associated with plate tectonics. Although similar marine transgressions and regressions occurred during Precambrian time, Cambrian rocks provide the first clear record of these events.

Throughout early and middle Cambrian time in the Southern Rockies, emergent highlands persisted along a broad, northeast-trending upwarp known as the Transcontinental Arch, which extended from New Mexico to Wisconsin. By the middle Cambrian, shallow seas had advanced to the crest of the Arch from both the east and the west in a series of transgressive and regressive events. Most of the sediments laid down in the advancing seas were derived from the erosion of various highlands along the trend of the Transcontinental Arch. The western and eastern seas merged during the late Cambrian along an east-west–trending trough in the Arch called the Colorado Sag; several portions of the highland landscape may have persisted as islands during this time.

In the Southern Rockies, Cambrian sedimentary rocks and fossils are restricted to certain portions of central Colorado, the San Juan region, and the northwestern edge of the Medicine Bow Mountains; no early Paleozoic sedimentary record exists for northern New Mexico. The Sawatch Sandstone (or Quartzite) of central Colorado is the most widespread Cambrian sedimentary formation in the region. Exposures of this ancient beach deposit overlie Precambrian rocks and can easily be identified by the presence of the minerals glauconite (green) and hematite (red), which give the formation a variegated appearance. Sawatch Sandstone can be seen along the flanks of the Sawatch Range (near Red Cliff and Minturn) and the Mosquito Range, on the White River Plateau, in Williams Canyon (west of Colorado Springs), and in Glenwood Canyon (near Shoshone Dam). In the San Juans, the Cambrian Ignacio Formation (quartzite, conglomerate, and sandstone) can be seen along U.S. 550 south of Silverton and a few miles south of Coal Bank Pass (north of Durango). Cambrian igneous dikes, some as many as 98 feet thick and several miles long, occur along a west-northwest–trending tectonic zone believed to be related to a Paleozoic rift structure, or the zone of strike-slip faulting, that extended from southeastern Oklahoma through New Mexico and Colorado into Utah. Outcrops of these largely mafic dikes can be seen in the Sangre de Cristo Range in northeastern New Mexico, in the Wet Mountains, at Black Canyon of the Gunnison, and in Unaweep Canyon.

The Cambrian Explosion

The encroaching seas of the Cambrian witnessed the rapid evolution and adaptive radiation of most of the major phyla of invertebrate animals. Paleontologists refer to the extraordinary increase in species diversity and complexity that occurred during the first 10 to 20 million years of the Cambrian as the Cambrian Explosion. This burst of evolutionary activity was unprecedented, and nothing approaching it has occurred since. In the Southern Rockies, as in most areas where Cambrian fossils are found, the poor preservation of soft-bodied animals (such as jellyfish and worms) has biased the fossil record in favor of animals with hard parts; as a result, records of only a fraction of the total fauna have been preserved. Though not common, fossil trilobites, brachiopods, mollusks, and graptolites can occasionally be found in Cambrian rocks in Williams Canyon and in the Sawatch and Mosquito ranges. Of these, the well-armored trilobites were the most abundant and perhaps the most interesting. These pillbug-like bottom feeders, extinct since the late Paleozoic, are the first animals known to have possessed a compound eye. Fossil evidence indicates that the most complex trilobite eye may have contained fifteen thousand elements, each with its own lens of crystalline calcite oriented to transmit light most efficiently.

Ordovician Period
(500–440 Million Years Ago)

During the Ordovician period, the seas deepened locally in the Southern Rockies, continuing their cyclic invasion of the North American continent. Along the trend of the Trans-continental Arch, a scattering of islands protruded above the tropical seas; the occurrence of warm-water fossil faunas in the Ordovician deposits of the Southern Rockies supports other types of data that place this portion of the North American continent in an equatorial position during the early Paleozoic. By mid-Ordovician time, marine waters were receding throughout much of the region, and fossil-rich sediments were deposited either on top of Cambrian rocks or, in the absence of Cambrian sediments, directly on top of the Precambrian basement rock. Ordovician rocks are preserved primarily in the region of the Colorado Sag in central Colorado; they are conspicuously absent from the San Juan Mountains, southern Wyoming, and the northern half of New Mexico.

In Colorado, the Ordovician is characterized by the deposition of thick sequences of limestone, dolomite, and sandstone. The Ordovician system of central and northern Colorado is composed of three main formations: the Manitou Dolomite, the Harding Sandstone, and the Fremont Limestone. The Manitou Dolomite (or Limestone), named for its type locality near the town of Manitou Springs, is believed to have been deposited in vast subtidal mudflats that surrounded the emergent highlands of the Transcontinental Arch; the carbonate-rich sediments that made up these mudflats were produced largely by the bottom-dwelling organisms (benthos) that proliferated in the warm, shallow waters. Extensive exposures of this red to light gray limestone form the lowermost portions of Cave of the Winds (near Manitou) and can be seen on the fault-riddled slopes above Aspen, at the mouth of Trout Creek Canyon, and in canyons near the towns of Glenwood Springs, Wellsville, and Leadville.

The Harding Sandstone, composed primarily of gray to reddish sandstone and layers of greenish brown shale, formed during at least 35 million years of receding seas and widespread erosion, probably in an estuarine environment. This formation is extremely fossil rich and has produced an astonishing diversity of animals. In 1887, the paleontologist Charles Walcott recovered the bony armor plates of a bottom-feeding fish called *Astraspis* in the Harding Quarry near Cañon City. The Agnathid (jawless) fishes, of which *Astraspis* is a member, are of particular importance because they represent the remains of the Earth's first vertebrates. Tiny fossils called conodonts are also present in great quantities in the Harding

Sandstone. These brown, toothlike fossils are from an unknown marine animal and are used by geologists as index fossils for stratigraphic correlation and as a tool for oil exploration. The best exposures of the Harding Formation can be seen at Phantom Canyon near Florence and at Crestone.

Following deposition of the Harding Sandstone, the sea deepened locally, and the massive Fremont Limestone was deposited. This gray, crystalline limestone formed during the most widespread submergence to which North America has ever been subjected. In contrast to the limited fossil assemblage present in the Cambrian rocks of the Southern Rockies, Ordovician limestones, such as the Fremont, contain an amazing assortment of coral, snail, sponge, brachiopod, cephalopod, crinoid, and many other fossils. The straight-shelled, or hornlike, cephalopods, giant ancestors of the modern chambered nautilus, reached an all-time peak in numbers during this time.

Silurian Period
(440–410 Million Years Ago)

Most geologists believe that carbonate-rich Silurian sediments once covered much of the North American continent but were extensively eroded shortly after deposition. Though the most widespread submergence of North America culminated in the Silurian, rocks of this period are almost completely absent in the Southern Rockies as a result of erosion. The only rocks from this period, as well as the only evidence that the Southern Rockies were covered by seas during this time, are blocks of fossiliferous limestone preserved within volcanic tubes, called diatremes, that penetrated these sediments during some subsequent period of volcanism.

Devonian Period
(410–355 Million Years Ago)

By the early Devonian, the ancestral North American and European continental plates had collided to form a larger continent, called Laurasia. To the east and west of North America's stable interior craton, mountain ranges developed along the continental margins as a result of tectonic activity associated with plate movement. For the first time since the Paleozoic had begun, sediments eroded from these uplifts were swept toward the center of the continent, rather than away from it. During much of the Devonian, the Southern Rockies were situated just a little above sea level. By late Devonian time, however, embayments of a western seaway covered large portions of the central Southern Rockies. The changing climates and landscapes of the Devonian provided the impetus for the colonization of land by the vertebrates.

Devonian rocks in the Southern Rockies are dominated by interlayered beds of soft shales, fossiliferous limestones, and quartz-rich sandstones. Marine fossil assemblages in these rocks continue to reflect the region's proximity to the equatorial zone. In northern and central Colorado, the Devonian is represented by the Chaffee Group, which is subdivided into two well-defined units: the Parting Sandstone and the Dyer Dolomite. The Parting Sandstone is recognized by its quartzitic character and by the inclusion of thin layers, or partings, of shale. The distinctive Dyer Dolomite beds of the White River Plateau are highly fossiliferous and can be identified by their wavy laminations of dolomite and quartz sand. The thin-bedded limestone and shale of the Chaffee Formation can be seen at Deep Creek Canyon on the White River Plateau and near the eastern entrance of Glenwood Canyon, where the rock forms greenish gray slopes and ledges below the massive Mississippian-age Leadville Limestone.

In southwestern Colorado, Devonian strata are represented by the Elbert Formation and the younger Ouray Limestone. The Elbert Formation, made up of sandstones, dolomites, and shales deposited in vast intertidal mudflats, can be seen along Elbert Creek between Coal Bank Pass and Rockwood (on U.S. 550); the shaley beds of the formation contain abundant evidence of stomatolites (algal mats) and salt casts. Exposures of fossiliferous, burrow-riddled Ouray Limestone can be seen at the mouth of Canyon Creek on the outskirts of Ouray.

Mississippian Period
(355–325 Million Years Ago)

The Mississippian period was a time of widespread submergence throughout the Southern Rockies. For the first time since the start of the Paleozoic, tropical seas covered much of northern New Mexico, leaving the Precambrian quartzite highlands comprising Pecos Baldy and Truchas and Chimayosos peaks in the southern Sangre de Cristo Range as islands in the advancing sea. A great diversity of marine animals—mollusks, corals, brachiopods, and crinoids—flourished in the clear warm seas. The period has been called the Age of Crinoids because of the fossilized concentrations of these flowerlike animals in Mississippian limestone beds.

Throughout most of the Rocky Mountains, as well as from Canada southwestward into Arizona, shallow-water carbonate sedimentation resulted in the formation of massive, cliff-forming beds of gray limestone. In Colorado, the most important and widespread of these Mississippian limestones are collectively referred to as the Leadville Formation; this formation can be traced into the subsurface of the Paradox Basin (in southwestern Colorado and southeastern Utah) and the Four Corners region (where Colorado, Utah, Arizona, and New Mexico meet) and on into the Grand Canyon, where it is known as the Redwall Limestone. In the Southern Rockies, good exposures of the Leadville Limestone can be seen at the Rockwood Quarry north of Durango (along U.S. 550), at the eastern entrance to Glenwood Canyon (on Interstate 70), on the slopes of West Aspen Mountain at Aspen, in the Eagle Park area north of Tennessee Pass (along U.S. 24), near Trout Creek Pass (on U.S. 285), east of Monarch Pass (U.S. 50), along the South Fork of the White River, in Arkansas Canyon (near Wellsville), and in Rifle Box Canyon (near Rifle on Colorado 325). The greatest concentration of caves in Colorado is found in the Leadville Limestone layer of the White River Plateau; Groaning Cave, believed to be the most extensive cave in the state, with an estimated 12 miles of passageways, is located near Deep Creek Canyon on the plateau.

Elsewhere in the Southern Rockies, Mississippian limestones include the Madison Limestone in northern Colorado and southern Wyoming, the Williams Canyon Limestone near Colorado Springs, the Hardscrabble Limestone and the Beulah Limestone along the eastern flank of the Wet Mountains and the southern Front Range, the Tererro Formation in the Sangre de Cristo Range near Santa Fe, and the Arroyo Penasco Formation in the Nacimiento Mountains. The Tererro Limestone can be seen in the bluffs along the Pecos

River near Tererro; a cave in the limestone cliff opposite the Tererro post office figures prominately in Pecos Pueblo Indian legends and may also be the cave referred to by Willa Cather in her novel *Death Comes for the Archbishop*.

There is evidence that the Transcontinental Arch was tectonically active during the late Mississippian and that highlands were emerging throughout the Southern Rockies. Erosion intensified with the recession of the seas, and much of the rock record for the late Mississippian was eroded prior to Pennsylvanian deposition (325–290 million years ago). During this time, the climate was humid and the surface of the Leadville Limestone underwent extensive solution weathering, resulting in a cavernously pitted and channeled erosion surface; geologists use the term *karst* to refer to this type of surface. Karst topography can be seen on the upper surface of the Leadville Limestone in Glenwood Canyon, in Rifle Box Canyon, and at a number of localities in central Colorado and northern New Mexico. It has been suggested that Molas Lake and several nearby ponds fill hollows in the karst surface. Weathering of the limestone terrain has caused a rich, red soil to develop, accumulating to depths of up to 75 feet on the karst surface in certain areas. Remnants of this fossil soil, called the Molas Formation, are best preserved in southwestern Colorado and are conspicuous in road cuts near Molas Lake in the San Juan Mountains where U.S. 550 crosses the karst surface; the formation can also be seen along the rim of Rockwood Quarry north of Durango (along U.S. 550).

Pennsylvanian Period
(325–290 Million Years Ago)

The long interval of tectonic quiescence that characterized the Southern Rockies during the early Paleozoic came to a dramatic halt during the Pennsylvanian period. The Pennsylvanian marks the beginning of a series of continental collisions that resulted in widespread deformation and uplift and that concluded, ultimately, in the formation of the Permian supercontinent Pangaea. In the region of the Southern Rockies, tectonic activity intensified during middle Pennsylvanian time, culminating in the uplift of the Ancestral Rocky Mountains some 300 million years ago.

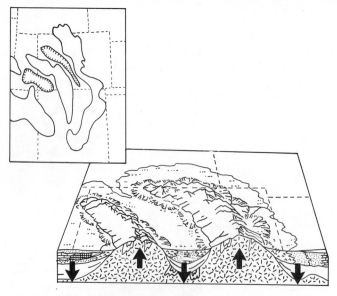

Positions of Pennsylvanian uplifts and basins. Deep basins formed between the uplifts and were filled with thick sequences of Pennsylvanian and Permian strata.

THE RISE OF THE ANCESTRAL ROCKIES

The Ancestral Rockies, like the present-day Southern Rockies, are enigmatic in terms of plate-tectonic theory because they were located in an intracratonic setting as far as 900 miles from any plate margin. One interpretation associates the development of the Ancestral Rockies with collision-related tectonism along the Pacific plate margin at the western edge of North America. This interpretation seems unlikely, however, because the mountain-building activity triggered by these events, the Antler Orogeny of the Great Basin area (late Devonian–early Mississippian), ended well before development of the Ancestral Rockies began. More recently, geologists have proposed that the rise of the Ancestral Rockies was related to the collision of North America with South America–Africa along the southern margin of North America. The progressive collision-suturing of these continental plates is believed to have initiated the Ouachita-Marathon Orogeny encompassing modern-day southern Texas, Oklahoma, and Arkansas and to have sent waves of tectonic activity northwestward to encompass a southwestern peninsular projection of the North American craton; this region, which includes much of northwestern Texas, New Mexico, northeastern Arizona, Colorado, and southeastern Wyoming, was subsequently wrenched, pushed northwestward, and intensely deformed as the collision progressed.

Pennsylvanian tectonism is characterized by block-fault mountain building and the development of actively subsiding basins, or down-dropped blocks, between rising mountain blocks. In certain areas, mountain-building activity resulted in as much as 10,000 feet of relief. The uplifts that formed the Ancestral Rockies were concentrated along two main belts. The eastern belt of uplift, called Frontrangia, essentially parallels the present-day Front Range, but was offset to the west of the modern mountain front by some 30 to 50 miles. The northern prong of Frontrangia extended into Wyoming, where it is known as the Pathfinder Uplift; the southern end of the uplift extended into New Mexico, where it is known as the Sierra Grande Uplift. The western belt of uplift, called Uncompahgria, extended from the present-day Nacimiento Mountains northwest along the western edge of the San Luis Valley to Colorado National Monument, including the area of the Black Canyon of the Gunnison and the Uncompahgre Plateau. The ranges of the Ancestral Rockies are roughly coincident with the modern or Cenozoic features of the Front, Gore, Park, Sawatch, southern Mosquito, and northern Sangre de Cristo ranges, the Wet Mountains, Las Animas Arch, and Uncompahgre, Apishapa, and Sierra Grande uplifts.

During the early stages of tectonic activity, shallow seas invaded the region from the southeast and northwest, depositing marine sediments in the basins that adjoined the mountain uplifts. The most important of these basins, a deep and narrow trough known as the Central Colorado Trough, extended from northwestern Colorado to south-central Colorado between the major mountain belts. Between 10,000 and 20,000 feet of Pennsylvanian and Permian strata of both marine and nonmarine origins accumulated within the trough, recording a long history of marine transgression from the northwest. Pennsylvanian basinal features are roughly coincident with the following present-day basins: Paradox, Denver, Piceance, Sand Wash, South Park, Antero, Currant Creek, Wet Mountain Valley, Raton, and the San Luis–Rio Grande Valley.

The earliest basin-deposited sediments of the Pennsylvanian are the marine-transitional black shales and sandstones of the Glen Eyrie Formation (outcropping near Colorado Springs) and the Belden Formation of the Central Colorado Trough. Exposures of the Belden Formation can be seen in Arkansas Canyon (near Wellsville), near Trout Creek Pass, in Glenwood Canyon (along Interstate 70), between Tennessee Pass and Minturn (on U.S. 24), and in road cuts south of Antero Junction (on U.S. 285). The variegated gray, green, and brown strata of the Minturn Formation overlie the Belden Formation and represent a complex sequence of marine, transitional, and nonmarine sediments deposited in the trough and along the western edge of Frontrangia; excellent exposures of the Minturn Formation (such as the 200-foot banded cliffs near Minturn) can be seen between Tennessee Pass and Minturn and in Arkansas Canyon (near Wellsville). A Pennsylvanian algal "reef" forms the Lionshead above Minturn. The Madera Formation, extending from south-central Colorado into northern New Mexico and correlative with the Minturn Formation, consists largely of gray-green sandstones and interbedded black shales, reflecting the cyclic deposition of marine and nonmarine sediments in a coastal mudflat or delta; exposures of this formation are prominent in the northern Sangre de Cristo Range near Orient and at Crestone.

Within the center of the Central Colorado Trough, between the towns of Avon and Gypsum, thick sequences of interbedded gypsum, anhydrite, halite, black shale, and siltstone are well exposed in bluffs along the Eagle River. These evaporite rocks formed in a warm, arid climate and are derived from thousands of feet of gypsum, salt, and potash precipitated from the brackish waters left behind by the evaporation of a narrow seaway. The most extensive concentration of gypsum and other evaporites is a deposit totaling 7,500 feet near the town of Gypsum. The evaporite rocks of the Central Colorado Trough have undergone extensive deformation, as can be seen along the Eagle River west of Gypsum; landforms developed in these areas are characterized by bedding that has been highly contorted and folded, largely because of gypsum's ability to flow in a solid state. Soils derived from the weathering of gypsum-rich shales provide an environment in which few plants can grow.

Along the flanks of the Ancestral Rockies, sediments eroded from the granitic mountain blocks accumulated as valley fill, braided alluvial (water-deposited) plains, and cone-

THE SOUTHERN ROCKIES

shaped alluvial fans (called bajadas). Thick sequences (from 7,000 to 12,000 feet) of these nonmarine sediments, consisting mostly of arkosic (feldspar-rich) gravels and sand, consolidated to form colorful redbeds in many areas of the Southern Rockies. Because of the association of these redbeds with extensive dune sands and evaporite rocks, geologists suggest that these strata developed in a warm and probably arid climate.

The Pennsylvanian redbeds of the Southern Rockies include the famous Fountain, Maroon, Sangre de Cristo, and Cutler formations. The red arkosic sandstones and conglomerates of the Fountain Formation, deposited by high-energy rivers flowing off the east slope of Frontrangia, are well exposed in several scenic landmarks, including Boulder's Flatirons, Red Rocks Park (near Denver), and the Garden of the Gods (near Colorado Springs). The bright red shales and sandstones of the Maroon Formation, derived from sediments washed from Uncompahgria during Pennsylvanian and Permian time, are prominent along Maroon Creek and form the Maroon Bells (in the Elk Mountains); these sediments are believed to have been deposited in a vast mudflat subject to alternating wet and dry periods. In south-central Colorado and northern New Mexico, the dark red and grayish green sandstones, conglomerates, and shales of the Sangre de Cristo Formation were deposited on sunbaked mudflats crisscrossed by braided, sand-choked stream channels. A conglomeratic unit of the formation, the Crestone Conglomerate, forms the Crestone Needles and extends to Eureka Mountain; other units of the formation can be seen at La Veta Pass (U.S. 160), Huerfano Park, and along the serrated ridge east of Blanca Peak. In southwestern Colorado, the Pennsylvanian-Permian Cutler Formation of the Hermosa Group was deposited along the western flank of Uncompahgria; outcrops form the cliffs along the Animas River Canyon and the striking redbeds just beneath the rhyolite cap of Engineer Mountain (along U.S. 550 at Coal Bank Pass).

Permian Period
(290–230 Million Years Ago)

Early Permian sedimentary rocks record the continued erosion of the Ancestral Rockies and their subsequent burial in their own debris. The fossil-poor, arkosic redbeds laid down during this time are similar to those of the Pennsylvanian, making determination of the stratigraphic boundary between the Pennsylvanian and Permian difficult. Moving away from the uplifts, finer-textured units of the Fountain, Sangre de Cristo, Cutler, and Maroon formations continued to accumulate in stream channels, ephemeral lakes, and intertidal environments. Basin sediments are predominately carbonate and evaporite rocks, reflecting a continued trend toward aridity and stagnating seas.

By middle Permian times, terrestrial sedimentation had slowed, and shallow seas once again invaded the region from the west and the east. The Ancestral Rockies had been extensively eroded and nearly buried by their own debris. Coastal dune fields, built of sand swept south from the Wyoming Arch (central Wyoming), spread along the flanks of the eroding uplifts, stabilizing in front of the advancing Permian sea. One of these ancient dune fields formed along the northwestern margin of Uncompahgria and is preserved as the Weber Formation; outcrops are especially prominent in Dinosaur National Monument, the White River Plateau, and near the towns of McCoy and Wolcott. Several large dune fields developed along the northern flanks of Frontrangia and are represented by the Lyons Sandstone, named for its type locality near Lyons. This buff to reddish quartz-rich sandstone outcrops in a number of localities along the northern Front Range and has been widely used as paving stone for the buildings of the University of Colorado at Boulder.

By the end of the Permian period, all the continents had coalesced to form the supercontinent Pangaea. Lasting for nearly 150 million years, this grouping of continental blocks stretched from pole to pole and was surrounded by an enormous, interconnected ocean. Arid and semiarid conditions prevailed, decimating the tropical jungles that had prospered in certain localities since Mississippian time. These radical changes exerted adaptive pressures on inhabitants of both land and sea. Amphibians were forced to give way to reptiles, whose dryland adaptations foreshadowed their coming days of grandeur during the Mesozoic. Large, carnivorous pelycosaur reptiles, such as *Sphenacodon* or the sail-back "lizard" *Dimetrodon,* represent the most common genera collected from Permian deposits of New Mexico. The appearance of these therapsid reptiles during the Permian is important because it is from this stock that mammals eventually evolved.

PERMIAN EXTINCTIONS

The sharp rise in species numbers at the start of the Paleozoic contrasts sharply with the late Permian extinctions. The Permian extinctions are regarded by many paleontologists as the most profound of several mass extinctions that punctuated the last 600 million years. At least half the known families died out within the span of a few million years. The victims of this mass extinction were primarily marine, including the trilobites, all ancient corals, all but one lineage of ammonites, all fusulinid foraminifera and most bryozoans and crinoids. By the close of the Permian period, 75 percent of the amphibian families and more than 80 percent of the reptile families had disappeared. Few paleontological questions have attracted more attention than the search for an explanation for these extinctions. Paleontologists now believe that widespread habitat destruction, resulting from the coalescing of the continents, and the associated withdrawal of shallow seas greatly reduced ecological space and that those organisms unable to adapt to these changing conditions were doomed to extinction.

CHAPTER FIVE

The Mesozoic:
Rising from the Sea

WHEN THE MESOZOIC began, the seas had withdrawn from large areas of the continents, and a desert climate prevailed over much of the Earth. Spanning some 165 million years, the Mesozoic era embraces three distinctly different periods: the Triassic, Jurassic, and Cretaceous. Popularly known as the Age of Dinosaurs, the era witnessed the triumph of the ruling reptiles (Archosauria), the class of advanced vertebrates that evolved from Permian reptilian stock and includes the birds, dinosaurs, and crocodilians, and their adaptive radiation into every ecological niche available to vertebrates. The Mesozoic fossil record of the Southern Rockies is world famous and startling in its diversity. Of the fourteen reptilian orders present during the Mesozoic, only four survive today, and only two of these, the order Testudines (turtles) and the order Squamata (snakes and lizards), are found in the region's modern ecosystems.

Triassic Period
(230–195 Million Years Ago)

Triassic geologic history reflects the beginning of the breakup of the supercontinent Pangaea. Throughout much of the period, Pangaea lay above sea level, resulting in persistent warm, dry climatic conditions and terrestrial rather than marine sedimentation. By the middle of the Triassic period, continental drift had resulted in a more equal distribution of the Earth's continents between the Northern and Southern hemispheres. In fact, many of the climatic shifts that have occurred since Triassic time can be explained by plate motions and the changing configuration of lands and seas.

In the Southern Rockies, the soft, fine-textured sandstones and shales that characterize the Triassic redbeds were deposited in mudflats, on alluvial plains, and in dune fields adjacent to the eroding highlands. Formation names differ from one area to another in the Southern Rockies — Chugwater, Lykins, Moenkopi, Dolores, Chinle — but the sediments deposited throughout much of the Triassic are remarkably similar in composition and general character.

In southern Wyoming, the redbeds of the Triassic Chugwater and Jelm formations can be seen west of Laramie along the eastern flank of Centennial Valley (along Wyoming 130). Triassic redbeds are well exposed at several localities along the western edge of the Southern Rockies. In the San Juan Mountains, the stream-deposited reddish brown shales and interbedded sandstones of the Dolores Formation are prominent just north of Durango (along U.S. 550), between Dolores and Rico (along Colorado 145), west of Telluride (along Colorado 145), and approximately 5 miles north of Ouray (along U.S. 550). In north-central New Mexico, west of the Sangre de Cristos, the stream- and lake-deposited sandstones and shales that constitute the Chinle Formation are overlain by the dune-deposited, cliff-forming Wingate Sandstone (of early Jurassic age); exposures of these formations can be seen at several localities north of Abiquiu (along U.S. 64/84). To the northwest, rocks of the Chinle Formation contribute to the spectacular scenery of Colorado National Monument, Unaweep Canyon, and the canyon of the Dolores River.

By the end of the Triassic, the archosaurs had given rise to the two great orders of dinosaurs: the Saurischia (having lizardlike pelvic structures) and the Ornithischia (having birdlike pelvic structures). Skeletons of one of the earliest of the Triassic dinosaurs, a small erect predator called *Coelophysis,* were first discovered in the red shales of the Chinle Formation at Ghost Ranch near Abiquiu, in northern New Mexico; the deposit is unique in that the dense concentration of skeletons at the site represents every stage of growth, from juvenile to adult. Weighing less than 50 pounds, and with its upright stance, hollow, birdlike bones, and long, slender tail, *Coelophysis* filled somewhat the same niche as the modern roadrunner of the Southwest deserts. The dryland environment in which *Coelophysis* lived supported nearly four hundred species of plants. Conifers flourished in the moister sites, joined by tree ferns, cycads, true ferns, and scouring rushes. Crocodilian reptiles prowled along the waterways, and amphibians and mammal-like reptiles sought cover in the weedy understory and floodplain ponds.

At the close of the Triassic, the suture zones connecting the massed continents weakened and then failed, allowing several of the continents to pull apart; Africa and South America remained joined until Cretaceous time, but South America separated from North America during the Jurassic. North America–Europe moved in a northwesterly direction, the western margin of North America becoming the leading edge of the westward-drifting plate. From the late Triassic onward, the physical evolution of the continents and ocean basins has been influenced by tectonic events associated with plate collisions and rifting initiated by the progressive breakup of Pangaea.

Jurassic Period
(195–135 Million Years Ago)

The Jurassic rocks of western North America record the geologic events initiated by the separation of the North American and European plates, and by a major change in the direction of plate motions. The divergence of these two plates occurred along a rift that eventually evolved to form the Atlantic Ocean. Sea floor spreading along the trend of this ancient rift zone, now part of an oceanic ridge-rise system called the Mid-Atlantic Ridge, intensified the westward movement and clockwise rotation of the North American Plate. Similar sea floor spreading occurred in the Pacific, along the East Pacific Rise, sending the eastern Pacific, or Farallon, Plate eastward—on a collision course with the westward-moving North American Plate. The western margin of North America underwent massive deformation and volcanism as the two plates collided, the subducting oceanic plate diving obliquely beneath the overriding continental plate. Wave after wave of tectonic activity swept eastward from the western continental margin. The mountain building that resulted from these compressional tectonic movements, known collectively as the Cordilleran Orogeny, occurred almost continuously from late Jurassic to Eocene (Cenozoic) time.

East of the present-day Sierra Nevada Range, the basic framework of the north-south, asymmetrical Western Interior Basin had developed by earliest Jurassic time. In the Southern Rockies, the first of four transgressions by the Ancestral Arctic Ocean entered the region from the north, along the trend of the basin. This Jurassic seaway, known as the Sundance Sea, was limited in its southern and eastern extent by persistent highlands that paralleled the former Transcontinental Arch and the Uncompahgria region of the Ancestral Rockies. The pattern of these uplifts influenced the overall distribution of Jurassic sediments throughout the region. Full marine conditions were never uniformly widespread in the Southern Rockies during the Jurassic, and the sedimentary record for this period reflects the cyclic transgression and regression of the Sundance Sea. A gradual change to a maritime climate accompanied the advances of the Arctic Ocean.

The earliest Jurassic rocks of the Southern Rockies, the Wingate, Navajo, and later Entrada formations, represent dune deposits of enormous proportions. Exposures of these cross-stratified, sometimes salmon-colored sandstones form smooth cliff faces — the slickrock scenery for which the Colorado Plateau is well known. In the Southern Rockies, these formations are typically paler in color than those of the Colorado Plateau and interfinger with marine or saline-lake sediments such as the Todilto Limestone of southwestern Colorado and northwestern New Mexico. Conspicuous bands of the Entrada Formation can be seen at Colorado National Monument, in Unaweep Canyon, south of Ridgway (along U.S. 550), between Lizard Head Pass and Rico (along Colorado 145), and north of Durango (along U.S. 550). Striking exposures of the Todilto Limestone can be seen north of Abiquiu and Ghost Ranch (New Mexico 84/64), where it forms a gray cap above the buff-colored Entrada Sandstone and the reddish sandstones and shales of the Triassic Chinle Formation.

The final withdrawal of the Sundance Sea from the Western Interior Basin occurred in late Jurassic time and is best represented by the widespread, fossil-rich Morrison Formation of Wyoming, Utah, Colorado, and New Mexico. The thick sequences of mudstones, shales, and sandstones that make up this fine-textured formation were laid down on broad floodplains and in shallow lakes that developed following

Triassic through Jurassic stratigraphic sequence north of
Abiquiu, New Mexico. The uppermost gray layer is Todilto
Limestone; the paler layer directly below is Entrada Sandstone;
the lower interbedded sandstones and shales are Triassic-age
Chinle Formation. *Audrey D. Benedict.*

the sea's retreat. The distinctive variegated gray, green, and
maroon colors of the Morrison are the result of both reduction and oxidation of iron under conditions of poor drainage
in some areas, as well as postdepositional alteration of the

sediments by groundwater on better-drained sites. The climate during this time is believed to have been warm and seasonally dry. Plant fossils are abundant in the Morrison Formation and include the conifer *Araucaria* (related to the monkey puzzle tree of South America), ginkgos, cycads, tree ferns, club mosses, and some flowering plants. Exposures of the Morrison Formation can be seen at the interpretive geologic site at the Interstate 70 road cut just west of Denver, near Morrison between Red Rocks Park and the Dakota Hogback, in Colorado National Monument, west of Glenwood Springs along Interstate 70, at Como Bluff in Wyoming, and in the quarry exhibit area at Dinosaur National Monument.

Morrison sediments have yielded one of the richest dinosaur faunas in the world. The first discoveries of dinosaurs in the Morrison were made in 1877 near the towns of Morrison and Cañon City, attracting the attention of paleontologists the world over. Dinosaurs representing fifteen genera were subsequently collected and described from Morrison strata. The most common of these were *Stegosaurus, Diplodocus, Apatosaurus* (formerly called *Brontosaurus*), *Camptosaurus,* and *Camarasaurus;* the top of the Morrison pecking order was dominated by *Ceratosaurus* and *Allosaurus.* At Como Bluff, in southeastern Wyoming, Yale paleontologist O. C. Marsh made a second major discovery of Jurassic dinosaurs in the Morrison in 1878. Today, the most accessible of the Morrison dinosaur localities are those at Dinosaur National Monument. There, in the Quarry Visitor Center, the ongoing excavation of a dinosaur-bone–rich cliff attracts thousands of visitors each year. Southeast of Cañon City, at a site along the Purgatoire River, the world's largest assemblage of dinosaur trackways (more than thirteen hundred tracks and a hundred trackways) has been found in an exposed limestone layer of the Morrison Formation.

Cretaceous Period
(135–65 Million Years Ago)

The Cretaceous geologic history of the Southern Rockies reflects the interplay of tectonic forces and global changes in sea level. The uplift and igneous activity that characterized much of western North America at the close of the Jurassic intensified during the Cretaceous, progressing eastward in a more or less continuous wave of deformation through time. Geologists recognize three distinct belts of Cordilleran tectonism based on differences in timing and in the type of mountain building that occurred in each area: the Nevadan Orogeny (Jurassic) in California and western Nevada; the Sevier Orogeny (late Jurassic–Cretaceous) in western Utah and adjacent regions, migrating eastward to encompass the present-day Basin and Range Province; and the Laramide Orogeny (Cretaceous-Tertiary) in the mountain areas of Montana, Wyoming, Colorado, and New Mexico.

Mountains rose in the Sevier orogenic belt to the west of the Southern Rockies, and sediments derived from these uplifts were carried eastward, accumulating in the Western Interior Basin. As the basin subsided, a vast cratonic seaway spread southward from the Arctic Ocean to merge with the warm waters of the Gulf of Mexico. By late Cretaceous

location of the
modern Southern Rockies

epicontinental seaway

Paleogeography of the Western Cretaceous Seaway.
Emmett Evanoff, after Kauffman, 1977.

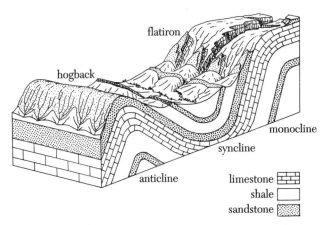

Folds and associated landforms in the Southern Rockies. Limestones are resistant to weathering in the dry climate, and form steep canyon cliffs. *Emmett Evanoff.*

time, the Western Interior Seaway essentially divided North America into two large land masses; at its maximum extent, the seaway was more than 600 miles wide. The shorelines of this seaway were oriented in a general north-south direction, shifting widely from east to west with changes in sea level or in sediment influx. Cretaceous rocks were deposited in constantly changing marine and nonmarine settings, the dominance of one of these over the other alternating through time.

Throughout the region, subtropical climatic conditions nourished forests that included conifer, fig, eucalyptus, ebony, palm, cycad, magnolia, and cypresslike trees. Better-drained highlands supported hardwood forests of oak, walnut, ash, sassafras, and birch, with lush understories of grape, bayberry, and ivy. The explosive development of the flowering plants is well documented during this time; although flowering plants are rare in lower Cretaceous strata, they make up at least 90 percent of the late Cretaceous plant fossils. Not surprisingly, these plants provided food for many groups of animals, including, in their first appearances, the bees, wasps, and butterflies.

The oldest Cretaceous rocks in the Southern Rockies belong to the widespread and economically important Dakota Group. Rocks of this group are found in Utah, Montana, Wyoming, Colorado, New Mexico, North and South Dakota, Nebraska, Kansas, and the Prairie provinces of Canada. The

Dakota Group includes a complex series of clastic sediments derived under a warm-temperate to subtropical temperature regime, first from riverine, delta, and sand-beach environments and then from shallow-marine environments. Today, sandstones of the Dakota Formation form a spectacular hogback ridge that can be traced along the eastern flank of the Southern Rockies for some 200 miles. Good viewpoints of these hogbacks are abundant along the Eastern Slope of the Colorado Front Range. One of the most interesting is Skyline Drive, which traverses a section of the Dakota Hogback west of Cañon City.

Sandstones of the Dakota Formation are often quite porous and permeable, serving as excellent reservoirs for oil and gas. Dakota rocks in the San Juan Basin of northeastern New Mexico and in the Four Corners area of Colorado continue to produce economically important quantities of petroleum. The basal layers of the Dakota Formation include a distinctive chert-pebble conglomerate. Silica, derived from the alteration of the chert, has firmly cemented the sand grains together in some parts of this unit, forming a fine-grained, gray to buff quartzite highly prized by prehistoric peoples because it could be flaked into high-quality stone implements. The famous Spanish Diggings stone quarries near Glendo, Wyoming, are located in a probable Dakota equivalent.

With the deepening of the seaway during the late Cretaceous, fine-textured limestones and shales were deposited in a wide variety of marine environments. Maximum inundation of the Western Interior Basin is marked by the deposition of the Greenhorn Limestone, which reaches its greatest thickness in north-central Colorado; the depth of the water along the eastern margin of the seaway during the deposition of the Greenhorn has been estimated at approximately 1,000 feet. Between Pueblo and Walsenburg, gently tipped mesas, called cuestas, are capped by this resistant limestone and interbedded with darker layers of shale. Along the eastern portion of the seaway, the chalky shales and limestones of the Niobrara Formation were deposited in a shallow-water environment characterized by warm, tropical currents from the Gulf of Mexico. Typical Niobrara fossils include large, corrugated-shelled clams, ammonites (related to modern octopi and chambered nautili), and small oysters in dense colonies.

Localized deepening of the seaway followed, resulting in

the deposition of great thicknesses of dark, marine muds on top of limestones. Gray marine shales of the Pierre Formation are several thousand feet thick in a number of localities along the eastern lowlands of the present-day Southern Rockies. The Pierre Shale is easy to recognize because of its gray-brown color and extremely fine texture. Good exposures are relatively rare because the shale tends to weather quickly. In some areas, the lower units of the Pierre Shale are considerably darker, and fossils of marine invertebrates are uncommon, suggesting that deep-water, barren zones occurred periodically in response to sea-level changes. In most other units of the Pierre Shale, fossil clams and ammonites, as well as the bones of fossil fish (sharks) and swimming reptiles are abundant. Just north of Kremmling, bluffs of Pierre Shale are capped by a resistant sandstone unit. The fossils of straight-shelled ammonites (baculites) may be found at the base of these bluffs. East of Interstate 25, between Colorado Springs and Pueblo, hundreds of conical hills of resistant limestone, known as the Tepee Buttes, rise above the broad expanse of the Pierre Shale. These low hills are rich in marine fossils and appear to have formed as reeflike mounds on the muddy floor of the Cretaceous sea.

Along the western margin of the Southern Rockies, the shales and sandstones of the Mancos Formation form gray and yellow, poorly vegetated badlands. Deposited during roughly the same time interval and under the same circumstances as the Pierre Shale, the widespread Mancos Formation is a variable sequence of interbedded silty to sandy shales and thinly bedded sandstones dotted with occasional nodules of limestone. Some of the best exposures of this formation can be seen near Grand Junction (along Interstate 70) and in and surrounding the towns of Cortez, Mancos, and Durango, Colorado, and Cuba, New Mexico. Swelling clays in the Mancos Formation cause it to expand when wet, making it an unsuitable substrate for roads or buildings.

With the onset of tectonic activity during the late Cretaceous, marine waters receded to the north and east. Along the western margin of the Southern Rockies, sediments of the nonmarine Mesaverde Group were deposited in sand beach, river delta, and swamp environments. Mesaverde rocks often intertongue with the marine, fossil-bearing Mancos Formation. Mesaverde Group sandstones are fairly easy to recognize because of their tan color and tendency to develop honeycomb-like weathering cavities. A spectacular ridge of Mesaverde Sandstone, called the Grand Hogback, extends along the southern margin of the White River Plateau; like the Dakota Hogback to the east, the Grand Hogback delineates the edge of the Southern Rockies, separating it at its western edge from the arid country of the Colorado Plateau.

Extensive deposits of low-sulphur bituminous coal are widespread in the Mesaverde Group and result from the accumulation of organic matter in the marshes and lagoons that formed behind the sand-barrier islands paralleling the shores of marine embayments. Good exposures of coal-bearing Mesaverde strata can be seen along the trend of the Grand Hogback, along the Colorado River near De Beque, near Oak Creek, south of Hayden, and near Redstone. Along the eastern margin of the retreating sea, sand beach and bar deposits formed the distinctive Fox Hills Sandstone and the overlying, interbedded sands and coal units of the Laramie Formation. This pattern of clastic deposits and interbedded coal units characterizes late Cretaceous rocks throughout the Rocky Mountains. Coal fields in the San Juan, Raton, Piceance, Uinta, North Park, and Green River basins rank among the most economically important in the West.

Laramide Orogeny and the Southern Rockies

Beginning approximately 70 million years ago, the long history of subsidence and deposition that had characterized the Western Interior Basin came to an end with the Laramide Orogeny and the rise of the Southern Rockies. To the west, the Sevier Orogeny was drawing to a close. What, then, triggered this final phase of Cordilleran orogeny so far inland from plate margins? Theories abound, but the facts remain elusive. Some geologists propose a plate tectonic origin, suggesting that the Laramide orogenic phase was coincident with, and probably caused by, a long interval of high-speed convergence of the Pacific sea floor and the North American plates. Their argument is supported by a well-documented increase in the rate of spreading along the Mid-Atlantic Ridge during this time, which would have greatly accelerated the westerly movement of the North American Plate and increased the velocity of its impact with the northeast-moving

Pacific Plate. This acceleration is postulated to have caused a flattening of the angle by which the sea floor plate subducted beneath the continent. As a result, the tectonic effects of the impact were redirected along a more horizontal trajectory, ultimately triggering the eastward-moving wave of deformation that would envelop the Rocky Mountain region. In response to this new wave of tectonism, the Colorado Plateau, acting as a discrete unit of the continent and largely undeformed by Cordilleran orogeny, is believed to have rotated slightly in a clockwise direction and moved northward — exerting additional compression and shearing stress along its eastern boundary with the Southern Rockies.

Late Cretaceous

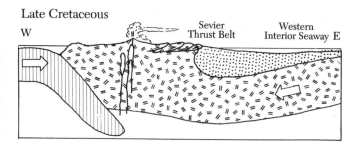

Early Tertiary—Laramide Orogeny

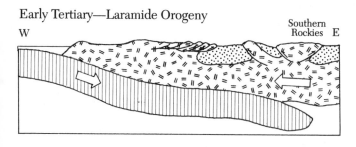

Cretaceous—Early Tertiary Basin Fill

North American Plate

east Pacific Plate

direction of plate movement

Plate tectonic model for Laramide Orogeny. *Emmett Evanoff.*

The Mesozoic: Rising from the Sea

The intense structural deformation that characterized the Laramide Orogeny produced mountain uplifts and deep, bordering basins from Montana to northern Mexico, along the entire Rocky Mountain chain. In the Southern Rockies, the Laramide uplifts rose vertically as narrow, mostly north-south–trending *anticlines* (upfolds), transfigured by block faulting and elevating the once flat-lying layers of sedimentary rock like rippled blankets across the Precambrian basement. Down-dropped blocks and *synclines* (downfolds) developed concurrently between the mountain uplifts and were rapidly filled with sediments eroded from the rising folds. Igneous intrusions and volcanic activity occurred in conjunction with the uplifts, along a northeast-trending zone that essentially defines the Colorado Mineral Belt. Once begun, uplift and igneous activity, accompanied by intense periods of erosion, continued well into the Cenozoic era.

Laramide tectonism was not synchronous throughout the Southern Rockies. The earliest uplift activity began in the Sawatch–San Luis highland and the Wet Mountains and spread outward as an irregular orogenic "front." Rejuvenation of the late Paleozoic Front Range highland followed, producing the Front, Park, and Gore ranges and the Medicine Bow Mountains. North, Middle, and South parks formed as structural sags in the former Front Range highland. The locations and orientations of the Laramide uplifts reflect preexisting Precambrian and Paleozoic tectonic features, and in many cases correspond to the trend of the major Precambrian fault systems. The only major uplifts in the Southern Rockies that lack a pre-Laramide expression are the Sangre de Cristo Range, the White River Plateau, and the Needle Mountains, all of which lie along the trend of the Paleozoic Central Colorado Trough.

Erosion kept pace with the Laramide uplifts, and sediments deposited in basins such as the Denver, Raton, San Juan, and Piceance provide geologists with a detailed record of the sequence of Laramide events. Older and older sedimentary layers were successively stripped from the crests of the anticlines until their Precambrian cores were exposed. The Gore Range is unusual in that fragments of some of the sedimentary rocks that once arched across the Precambrian core of this uplift can still be seen along the crest of the range. The Dakota and Grand hogbacks are representative of the steeply upturned sedimentary rocks that form the sides of the Laramide anticlines. At the close of the Cretaceous, the major uplifts and basins of the Southern Rockies were largely in place—awaiting their exhumation and finishing touches during the Cenozoic.

CHAPTER SIX

The Tertiary Period: Landscapes in Upheaval

BY THE BEGINNING of the Cenozoic era, 65 million years ago, the last vestiges of the inland seas had disappeared from the Rocky Mountain region. Laramide Orogeny still rumbled across the land. The stage was set for high geologic drama—an action epic with a complex script, unusual special effects, and numerous scene changes. The Cenozoic era is divided into two very unequal periods, the Tertiary and the Quaternary; the Tertiary period embraces all but the last 2 million years of the Cenozoic. Much of the topography of our modern world—continental outlines, mountain ranges, and most of the major drainage patterns—reflect Tertiary events.

In the Southern Rockies, Tertiary geologic history can be conveniently divided into three stages: (1) early Tertiary–Laramide events—continuing uplift, pluton emplacement along the Colorado Mineral Belt, erosion, and basin development (Paleocene and Eocene epochs); (2) middle Tertiary events—post-Laramide tectonic quiescence and volcanism (late Eocene, Oligocene, and Miocene epochs); and (3) late Tertiary events—epeirogenic uplift, erosion and canyon cutting, development of the Rio Grande Rift, and late Cenozoic volcanism (Miocene and Pliocene epochs, extending into the Holocene—or Recent—epoch of the Quaternary period).

Laramide Events

UPLIFTS AND MOUNTAIN BUILDING

Evidence of the intensity and influence of Laramide tectonism is written in dramatic detail in the modern landscape. In the Southern Rockies, folding and faulting have acted

Tertiary
Intrusive Rocks

Tertiary
Volcanic Rocks

Upper Tertiary
Sedimentary
Rocks

Lower Tertiary
Sedimentary
Rocks

Cretaceous
Sedimentary
Rocks

Triassic-Jurassic
Sedimentary
Rocks

Paleozoic
Sedimentary
Rocks

Precambrian
Basement Rocks

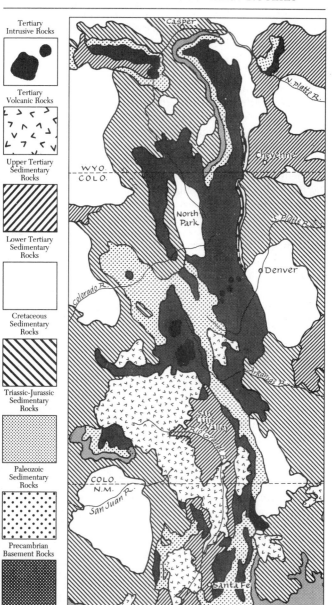

The Tertiary Period: Landscapes in Upheaval 91

singly and in concert to create the landforms we see today. For example, the majority of the region's north-south–trending ranges are faulted anticlines — linear uplifts whose structural characters exhibit folding as well as faulting. In contrast, uplifts such as the White River Plateau, San Juan Mountains, and West Elks are comparatively simple domal uplifts, cored with Laramide-age intrusive rocks and covered with a veneer of Oligocene and Miocene volcanics.

In the Southern Rockies, the amount of movement that has occurred along faults varies from a few inches to as much as several miles. In ranges such as the Colorado Front Range, displacement along fault zones is commonly measured in thousands of feet; a massive overthrust fault delimits the southeastern margin of the Colorado Front Range, extending from Cheyenne Mountain to just north of Monument. Along this zone, Pikes Peak Granite and other Precambrian rocks have been thrust eastward, in some places for nearly a mile, over the Cretaceous sedimentary rocks of the Colorado Piedmont.

Fault zones — clusters of more or less parallel faults — have played a crucial role in landscape evolution and, in many areas, have controlled the development of valleys and determined the courses of certain rivers, such as the Colorado, Laramie, Rio Grande, and Arkansas. Most of the hot springs found in the Southern Rockies, such as those at Manitou Springs, Glenwood Springs, Steamboat Springs, and Jemez Springs, emanate along major fault systems. Additionally, many of our mountain passes, such as Berthoud and Loveland, lie along fault zones that traverse the mountain crest. Recent fault-zone activity can be seen along the eastern margin of the San Luis Valley, where fault movement during the last few thousand years has produced a prominent fault scarp in the alluvial fans that flank the Sangre de Cristo Range between Villa Grove and Great Sand Dunes National Monument; erosion has caused this fault scarp to be segmented into a series of triangular facets, each with its base aligned parallel to the fault trace.

IGNEOUS INTRUSION AND THE COLORADO MINERAL BELT

Igneous intrusion and volcanism were closely associated with Laramide tectonism in the Southern Rockies. The joints and fractures that developed as a result of mountain building permitted mineral-rich solutions to move upward from magma sources deep within the Earth. During the early Tertiary, a series of pipelike intrusions, called stocks, were emplaced along a northeast-trending zone that cut diagonally across the mountain uplifts, extending from Durango to the eastern flank of the Colorado Front Range north of Boulder. These Laramide stocks are believed to be an expression of an underlying batholith or string of batholiths. Mineralization associated with these stocks and their related dikes and sills was concentrated along the 50-mile-wide belt known as the Colorado Mineral Belt.

Nearly all of the economically important gold, silver, lead, and zinc ore deposits in the Southern Rockies are located within the Colorado Mineral Belt. The only significant ore deposits located outside this mineralized zone are those of the Cripple Creek, Westcliffe–Silver Cliff, and Creede gold districts and the western Colorado vanadium and uranium districts. The majority of ore deposits of the Colorado Mineral Belt can be placed into one of five basic categories: (1) Laramide-age and younger crack and fissure fillings in Precambrian rocks (like those in the Central City Mining District); (2) Tertiary vein, karst-fill, and replacement deposits in Paleozoic and younger sedimentary rocks (such as those in the Leadville Mining District); (3) molybdenum mineralization associated with mid-Tertiary porphyritic stocks (as found at Climax Mine); (4) vein deposits in Tertiary volcanic rocks (such as those of mines in the San Juan Mountains); and (5) placer-type deposits in Quaternary glacial and stream gravels (as found at Fairplay and Breckenridge).

LARAMIDE EROSION
AND BASIN DEVELOPMENT

During Eocene time, coalescing alluvial fans, or bajadas, formed along the margins of basins bordering the larger ranges of the Southern Rockies. Remnants of these debris aprons are preserved today as coarse-textured sedimentary rocks. Along the eastern slope of the Front Range, vast quantities of erosional debris were deposited by rivers and streams leaving the mountains and flowing across the eastern plains. These lowland river and alluvial-fan deposits make up the Denver and Dawson formations and are as thick as 2,000 feet in some areas.

The Dawson Arkose formed from weathering products

of the Pikes Peak batholith and, like other arkosic rocks, reflects the character of its granitic parent material. Good exposures of Dawson Arkose can be seen near the U.S. Air Force Academy in Colorado Springs (south of Denver) and in the nearby Black Forest area. In the Black Forest, the formation is of ecological interest because it supports an unusual eastern outlier of ponderosa pine that grows preferentially in the gravelly, feldspar-rich soils developed on the arkose. North of this area, a locally prominent Oligocene rock, the Castle Rock Conglomerate, forms the castle-shaped hill that gives the town of Castle Rock its name. This unusual conglomerate is a remnant of the broad valley fill cut into the Dawson Arkose and deposited by the ancestral South Platte River where it emerged from the Rampart Range.

In south-central Wyoming, Eocene sediments derived from the Medicine Bow, Shirley, and Laramie mountains form a series of variegated maroon claystone beds in the Laramie and Shirley Basin areas. Along the western flank of the Laramie Mountains, the claystone contains deeply weathered cobbles and boulders of Sherman Granite, the 1.4-million-year-old granite that makes up the core of the range. Near the Medicine Bow Mountains, the cobbles that make up an Eocene-age conglomeratic rock are mostly Medicine Bow Quartzite. This distinctive conglomerate forms massive outcrops near Kennaday Peak, on the north flank of the Medicine Bows, and in a series of well-defined hogbacks along the eastern flank of the range.

Along the western edge of the Southern Rockies, the lake-deposited shales that make up the Eocene Green River Formation formed in an immense basin that covered much of northeastern Utah, southwestern Wyoming, and northwestern Colorado. The Green River system consisted of a series of shallow lakes that accumulated plant and animal detritus to such a degree that the resultant shales constitute one of the world's largest oil shale reserves. In the Piceance Basin of Colorado, shales of the Green River Formation are estimated to contain a total of 1.8 trillion barrels of oil.

Fossil animals and plants associated with the Green River Formation indicate warm-temperate to subtropical conditions, contrasting sharply with the desertlike climate of the area today. During the height of Eocene basin filling, the fauna of the Green River lowlands included crocodiles, alligators, boa constrictors, soft-shelled turtles, and a great variety of subtropical fish; the Green River fossil flora suggests that lowland forests were dominated by deciduous trees and subtropical species such as bald cypress, palm, and hibiscus, while the higher elevations were covered by pine forests.

The main mammal-bearing deposits of the early Tertiary are located in the structural basins of the Rocky Mountains. A diverse assemblage of primitive mammals has been recovered by paleontologists working in the Denver, Huerfano, Middle Park, and northern San Juan basins. A single locality in the Denver Basin has produced more than four hundred specimens of the earliest Tertiary mammals known. Along the San Juan Basin, the variegated clays of the San Jose Formation have yielded an early Tertiary bestiary that includes a hippolike animal *(Coryphodon)*, a rhinoceros-like herbivore *(Uintatherium)*, a flightless bird *(Diatryma)*, five species of primates, and the first true carnivorous mammals. East of this area, in the Huerfano Basin, Eocene deposits contain some of the earliest known horse remains, skeletons of a collie-sized animal known as the dawn horse (*Hyracotherium*, formerly *Eohippus*). During the Oligocene and Miocene we see a dramatic shift toward a more modern fauna, with increasing numbers of grazers and the appearance of saber-toothed cats. The first appearance of many of the modern mammalian families occurred in the Southern Rockies during this time.

Middle Tertiary Events: Tectonic Quiescence and Volcanism

AWASH IN DEBRIS: POST-LARAMIDE EROSION

The end of Laramide mountain building was marked by a renewal of widespread erosion, reducing the rugged uplifts of the Southern Rockies to a series of rounded hills and ridges. The magnitude of post-Laramide erosion is documented by the cutting of a relatively flat, high-level erosion surface across the region's uplifts, and by the accumulation of thick sequences of Tertiary sediments in the basins between the ranges. Although large portions of the post-Laramide erosion surface have been disrupted by Miocene-Pliocene uplift and faulting and dissected by modern streams, examples of this surface can still be seen in a number of localities. Remnants of the surface are well preserved only on the broader ranges, such as the Rampart Range and the northern Colorado Front Range; narrow ranges, such as the Sangre de Cristos, have lost nearly all traces of the erosion surface.

FIRE IN THE SKY:
OLIGOCENE VOLCANISM

Catastrophic volcanic eruptions occurred repeatedly in the Southern Rockies between 40 and 25 million years ago. Oligocene volcanic activity is believed to reflect the emplacement of large, near-surface batholiths beneath the San Juan Mountains and the region that extends northeast from the Elk Mountains and Sawatch Range to the Rocky Mountain front. Widely scattered volcanoes spewed lava and ash over hundreds of miles, with volcanic centers eventually coalescing to form a giant volcanic field that covered large portions of the southern and central Southern Rockies; individually named volcanic fields, such as the San Juan or West Elk fields, are merely the much-eroded remnants of this larger composite field. The southern segment of the Oligocene volcanic field covered all of south-central Colorado and adjacent New Mexico, and the northern segment extended from central Colorado to the eastern mountain front; the two segments were linked along the trend of the Colorado Mineral Belt. Local volcanic centers existed north of the Colorado Mineral Belt, in the Never Summer Mountains, and in the Park Range.

The Oligocene volcanoes of the Southern Rockies produced lavas largely of intermediate and felsic composition — andesite, rhyolite, and quartz latite — reflecting the presence of shallow batholiths beneath the volcanic piles. Rocks of basaltic (mafic) composition are rare in Oligocene volcanic assemblages and are more commonly associated with late Cenozoic volcanism related to the development of the Rio Grande Rift, a major intracontinental rift extending from central Colorado to northern Mexico. Because andesitic and rhyolitic magmas are less fluid than basalt, they tend to trap gases within the volcanic vent, resulting in more explosive eruptions — much like when the cork on a bottle of champagne is popped. This phenomenon resulted in the development of large craters, called calderas, and in the accumulation of tremendous thicknesses of pyroclastic rocks.

The largest ash-flow deposits and most of the calderas

formed in the San Juan Mountains. Recent estimates suggest that as much as 5,400 cubic miles of ash and other ejecta were erupted during the height of volcanic activity in the San Juans. In comparison, the fateful May 18, 1980, eruption of Mount St. Helens, in Washington, is estimated to have produced only one-quarter cubic mile of ash — a minor volcanic event by San Juan standards.

The successive lava flows of the first phase of volcanic activity in the San Juans, between 35 and 30 million years ago, formed a shieldlike volcanic field that was approximately 100 miles in diameter. Many of the high peaks of the San Juan Mountains are carved from the welded ash-flow tuffs and fine breccias produced by these eruptions. The distinctive San Juan Tuff, conspicuous in several exposures between Ouray and Silverton, is easily eroded and has slumped and flowed in many areas. The most famous and recent of these slumps is the Holocene-age Slumgullion Earthflow that dams San Cristobal Lake, near Lake City.

A second eruptive phase began in the San Juan Mountains around 29 million years ago and is represented by at least eight layers of lava, ash-flow tuff, and welded tuff, and by an interval of widespread caldera formation. One of the second-phase volcanic domes, reaching a height of more than

Spires of eroded volcanic tuff at Wheeler Geologic Area, San Juan Mountains. *Audrey D. Benedict.*

2,000 feet, was centered near the modern town of Creede. Following an intense series of pyroclastic eruptions, the dome collapsed into the magma chamber, creating a caldera nearly 10 miles in diameter. The fine, ashy sediment that accumulated in the crescent-shaped lake that formed in the caldera preserved a diversity of middle Tertiary plants and insects. Wheeler Geologic Area, near Creede, is a fairyland of lavender-and-white spires eroded in the volcanic tuff associated with these eruptions.

A final phase of eruptions, which began about 26 million years ago, bore little resemblance to the eruptive activity that preceded it. Volcanic fissures erupted massive floods of black basalt all along the central and eastern portions of the San Juan volcanic field, coincident with the development of the Rio Grande Rift. Basaltic lavas are common along the western edge of the San Luis Valley, and are particularly well exposed at Wagon Wheel Gap, where the columnar jointing of the basalt gives the appearance of a log stockade.

Along its northern periphery, the San Juan volcanic field merged with another volcanic center in the West Elk Mountains. The thickening volcanic cover in this region consisted primarily of streams of molten rock and fragmental debris known as the West Elk Breccia. Remnants of this breccia, its original volume believed to have been more than 150 cubic miles, are common along the southern half of the West Elks and make up the Dillon Pinnacles near Blue Mesa Reservoir, and Castle and Cathedral peaks southeast of Crawford. In certain areas, thin layers of heat-welded tuff cap the less resistant breccia pinnacles, creating a variety of fanciful shapes. Elsewhere, deposits of loosely consolidated pumice and ash-flow tuff produced by a later sequence of eruptions form light-colored, easily eroded foothills.

Along the eastern margin of the San Juan volcanic field, a nearly continuous sheet of mid-Tertiary volcanic rocks once linked the San Juan Mountains with the Wet Mountains and the Spanish Peaks, whose twin domes are believed to represent the much-eroded roots of former volcanoes. Today, at places like Cuchara Pass, we can see the resistant, wall-like dikes that formed as the magma forced its way into the vertical cracks that developed in the surrounding sedimentary rocks as these volcanoes grew.

In the southern Front Range, Oligocene volcanic activity was concentrated around the cluster of volcanoes that make up the Thirty-nine Mile volcanic field. The southwestern perimeter of the field closes off the basin of South Park and merges westward with the volcanic Arkansas Hills and the San Juan volcanic field. The most interesting event associated with the Thirty-nine Mile volcanic field is the formation of ancient Lake Florissant — today the site of Florissant Fossil Beds National Monument. Nearly 35 million years ago, lava and mudflows dammed an ancient valley near the present-day community of Florissant and created a sickle-shaped lake that was nearly 12 miles long and 2 miles wide. Towering sequoia, white cedar, and numerous deciduous species lined the ancient lakeshore. Intermittent volcanic activity showered the lake with ash and pumice, and on shore, mudflows and volcanic ash buried the trees and low-growing vegetation. Plants and animals washed into the lake were buried by successive layers of ashy mud. The Oligocene shales at Florissant form the most extensive fossil record of their kind in the world. Since their discovery in 1874, the lakebeds have provided scientists with the exquisitely detailed fossils of more than 1,100 species of insects, more than 140 species of plants, and several kinds of fish, birds, and small mammals.

To the west of Florissant, beyond the low volcanic hills of the Thirty-nine Mile volcanic field, the dark mass of the Buffalo Peaks rises from the floor of South Park. The Buffalo Peaks and the flows capping several small buttes nearby are all that remain of the many thick layers of andesitic lava and volcanic ash that accumulated in this basin from sources in the southern Sawatch Range. Volcanic activity in the southern Sawatch Range was probably triggered by the mid-Tertiary emplacement of the Mount Princeton batholith, which fed a major volcano or cluster of volcanoes along the crest of the Collegiate Range.

North of the Colorado Mineral Belt, volcanic activity was concentrated in the Never Summer Mountains and in the Rabbit Ears Range. In the Never Summer Mountains, multiple layers of silica-rich lava and ash-flow material were erupted from volcanic centers near Mount Richtofen, and from Lulu, Lead, and Specimen mountains. Light-colored layers of volcanic ash and pumice can be seen in numerous road cuts along the western half of Trail Ridge Road in Rocky Mountain National Park. The ash-flow deposits from these and from other volcanic centers filled deep canyons along the west side of the park. Welded ash-flow tuff, possibly the same as that at Specimen, can be seen in the 500-foot-high cliff above Iceberg Lake, along Trail Ridge Road.

The Rabbit Ears Range, an east-west–trending ridge of mid-Tertiary volcanic rocks, connects the Park Range with the Front Range, separating North Park from Middle Park. Rabbit Ears Peak, formed of the same reddish volcanic breccia that makes up most of the range, is the much-eroded plug of an Oligocene volcano. Just to the south, a prominent pointed mountain called Whitley Peak is capped with basalt that shows well-developed columnar jointing.

By early Miocene time, deposits of windblown volcanic ash, originating from volcanoes in the Southern Rockies as well as from those in Wyoming and Montana, blanketed large portions of the eastern plains. The widespread Oligocene White River Formation, extending from north-central Colorado to South Dakota, is characteristic of the alternating layers of volcanic ash and coarse erosional debris that accumulated during this time. Outcrops of the White River Formation can be seen in North Park, at Pawnee Buttes in northeastern Colorado, and near Bates Hole along the western flank of the Laramie Range.

The White River Formation has yielded a rich assemblage of Tertiary mammals — including the rhinolike brontotheres, ancestral horses, and a gazellelike camel — that is suggestive of an open woodland environment. The Miocene Creede fossil flora is allied to genera living within a radius of 100 miles of the Creede area today. When compared with the Florissant fossil flora of Oligocene age, it shows evidence of a sharp decline in the number of warm-temperate deciduous species. Regional uplift and changes in climate caused by the tremendous volumes of ash produced by Oligocene volcanoes may have been responsible for the changes in vegetation.

Late Tertiary Events

RAISING THE ROOF:
MIOCENE-PLIOCENE UPLIFT

The last major episode of tectonic and volcanic activity in the Southern Rockies began at the close of the Oligocene and continued to the end of the Tertiary. Unlike the Laramide Orogeny that preceded it, Miocene-Pliocene uplift was characterized by the domal upwarping of the entire Rocky Mountain and Great Plains region. This broad regional uplift was accompanied by local block faulting and by extensive basalt volcanism associated with the development of the Rio Grande Rift along the crest of the uplift dome. Local block faulting rejuvenated and exhumed the Laramide uplifts and redefined the structural basins along their flanks. By the end of the Tertiary, the Southern Rockies had risen at least 5,000 feet; summits over 9,000 feet became Fourteeners, and the western plains were lifted to an elevation of 6,000 feet.

DEVELOPMENT OF THE RIO GRANDE RIFT

The Rio Grande Rift can be traced for nearly 500 miles, from near Leadville to northern Mexico; the upper Arkansas River Valley and the San Luis and Rio Grande valleys of southern Colorado and north-central New Mexico follow its course. Structurally, the Rio Grande Rift consists of a series of interconnected *grabens* (down-dropped blocks) bounded on one or both sides by fault-block mountains. The geometry of faulting along the rift indicates a pattern of crustal extension or spreading, a style characteristic of much of the western United States during late Cenozoic time. Basaltic volcanism has occurred repeatedly along the trend of the rift since its inception about 26 million years ago. The rift, which continues to be geologically active, is characterized by abnormally high heat flow, the presence of shallow magma bodies, crustal thinness, and high seismicity.

The Rio Grande Rift is deepest and broadest in the San Luis Valley, where subsidence of the rift's northern segment occurred simultaneously with the beginning of basalt volcanism in the San Juan Mountains. Basalt flows form an impressive plateau north of Taos, and are as thick as 650 feet in exposures in Rio Grande Gorge. Just to the north of this area, a cluster of twelve volcanic cones and the larger domed volcanoes of San Antonio Peak and Los Mogotes dominate the otherwise flat valley floor. Turquoise, produced by hydrothermal alteration of copper minerals in the volcanic rock, is mined in the basalt-capped hills near Manassa.

The turbulent geologic history of the central portion of the Rio Grande Rift is reflected in the development of the Jemez Mountains of northern New Mexico. This diverse assemblage of volcanic domes, craters, and interbedded ash and lava flows occurs where the Rio Grande Rift is offset eastward from the Albuquerque Basin to the Espanola Basin. The Jemez Mountains are part of the Jemez volcanic field, which covers an area of 2,000 square miles centered around Valles Caldera, one of the largest calderas in the world. Eruptions within the Jemez volcanic field spanned a time period from 10 million to 400,000 years ago.

The earliest eruptions, beginning about 10 million years ago, produced distinctly banded domes and composite volcanoes, such as St. Peter's Dome and Boundary Peak. These volcanoes, now much eroded, were high enough to stand well above the ash flows that later swirled around their flanks. During the period from 7 to 3.5 million years ago, silica-rich lava flows formed the massive rounded peaks that mark the skyline of the Jemez Mountains as seen from Santa Fe and Espanola. By about 3 million years ago, volcanism had shifted to the central portion of the Jemez volcanic field, culminating in the violent ash-flow eruptions that have shaped the present-day Pajarito Plateau.

The catastrophic ash-flow eruptions of 1.4 and 1.1 million years ago were the most important events in the history of the Jemez volcanic field. The volume of silica-rich pumice and ash erupted during these two episodes is estimated to have been some one hundred times greater than that produced by the 1980 eruption of Washington's Mount St. Helens. The collapsed craters of Valles Caldera and the remnants of the earlier Toledo Caldera provide ample testimony to the violence of these eruptions. Pyroclastic flows filled preexisting valleys and canyons along the flanks of the volcanic field and eventually formed the gently sloping surface of the Pajarito Plateau. The orange-brown to light tan pyroclastic deposits associated with these eruptions are collectively called the Bandelier Tuff. Thick layers of Bandelier Tuff dominate the Pajarito Plateau and are prominent in Bandelier National Monument.

LATE CENOZOIC VOLCANISM

A southwest-trending belt of Pliocene and Pleistocene volcanism cuts across the Rio Grande Rift from the High Plains of northeastern New Mexico, through the Cimarron Range and the Jemez Mountains, to the southeast margin of the Colorado Plateau. Within this region, basalt flows cap a number of prominent mesas, such as Oak Canyon, Johnson, Barella, Raton, and Black mesas, and Mesa de Maya. At

Capulin Mountain National Monument, just east of Raton, the well-preserved cone of a volcano that was active as recently as 10,000 years ago rises more than 1,000 feet from base to rim.

Another area of important late Cenozoic volcanism was centered in north-central Colorado. Repeated eruptions, beginning about 25 million years ago, created a basalt plain that covered the White River Plateau, parts of the Gore, Park, and Sawatch ranges, the Elk Mountains, and Grand Mesa. Remnants of this basalt plain still cap mesas in the region. In the Flattops, more than 1,300 feet of flow-on-flow basaltic rocks have been carved by erosion to form such landmarks as Trappers Peak. Basalt flows on Grand and Battlement mesas are 650 feet to nearly 3,000 feet thick in some exposures.

THE EXHUMATION OF THE ROCKIES: PLIOCENE EROSION AND CANYON CUTTING

By the end of the Pliocene, the northern ranges of the Southern Rockies were almost buried in erosional debris. Streams flowing eastward from the Park–Sierra Madre Range spread across the nearly submerged summits of the Medicine Bow and Laramie mountains, depositing a vast apron of debris across the High Plains. A narrow, ramplike portion of this debris apron is still preserved along the eastern flank of the Laramie Range, west of Cheyenne. This geologic landmark, known as the Gangplank, forms a natural bridge between the High Plains and the top of the steeply dipping rocks flanking the Laramie Range. In 1869, the gentle approach of the Gangplank was chosen as the route of the nation's first transcontinental railroad across the Rockies. Elsewhere along the eastern front of the Southern Rockies, features analogous to the Gangplank are nonexistent. Along the Colorado Front Range, a broad valley called the Colorado Piedmont separates the High Plains from the eastern mountain front. Most geologists believe that the South Platte and the Arkansas rivers and their tributaries have removed or greatly modified the debris apron that once lapped against the mountain front.

West of the mountain front, intermontane basins were inundated with erosional debris washed from the rising mountains. In the San Luis Valley, interbedded layers of Tertiary erosional debris and volcanic deposits are as thick as 10,000 feet in certain areas. Groundwater resources in the arid San Luis Valley are uniquely tied to these alternating layers of gravel, clay, and lava. Water, entering the trough-shaped valley from the mountains to the north, east, and west, flows underground along the permeable gravel layers, confined between the impermeable layers of lava or clay. By the time the water reaches the center of the valley, it has developed considerable artesian pressure and can rise to the surface without the aid of mechanical pumps.

With the acceleration of regional uplift during the Pliocene, moist air masses moving eastward from the Pacific were forced upward and robbed of their moisture by the newly risen mountains. Rain shadows developed along the leeward side of the rising ranges, encouraging the development of a more drought-resistant shrub-and-grassland vegetation in these areas. In the mountains themselves, altitudinal differences in temperature and precipitation resulted in a more zonal distribution of forest vegetation, similar to what we see today. Precipitation in the mountains became sufficient to sustain large, perennial rivers and streams. As local gradients increased, streams that once wandered aimlessly across the crests of buried ranges began to straighten, rush, and cut their way through the mountain uplifts.

Ever since John Wesley Powell's epic journey down the Colorado River more than a hundred years ago, geologists have debated the origins of the rivers that flow across the structural grain of the mountains. Some geologists have proposed that the major river systems in the Rocky Mountain region became established in their present positions prior to Miocene-Pliocene uplift and simply continued downcutting as uplift accelerated around them. Others have suggested that the modern drainage systems of the Southern Rockies are relatively young—the product of increased precipitation resulting from Miocene-Pliocene uplift. They propose that the major drainage systems, or at least sections of these drainage systems, have been *superimposed* onto a pre-Miocene landscape, downcutting through the debris mantle as the region was uplifted. In support of this view, geologists studying the upper Colorado River and its tributaries have found that this drainage system had its beginnings near the end of the Miocene, about 10 million years ago; downcutting was rapid until about 8 million years ago, when rates of uplift decreased. Whatever the ultimate conclusion to this debate, water — in both its liquid and crystalline state — would assume a dominant role in landscape evolution during the Quaternary period.

CHAPTER SEVEN

Finishing Touches: The Quaternary Period

THE FINISHING TOUCHES that distinguish the modern landscape of the Southern Rockies — the jagged peaks, ice-carved basins, and U-shaped valleys — reflect the dramatic climatic changes of the Quaternary period. Encompassing only the last 2 million years, the Quaternary period includes the comparatively short Pleistocene epoch, popularly known as the Ice Age, and the Holocene epoch, beginning roughly 10,000 years ago and continuing to the present day. In the Southern Rockies, Pleistocene climatic fluctuations resulted in the growth and decay of enormous ice sheets and valley glaciers, producing distinctive changes in the mountain landscape and controlling the distribution and survival of many plants and animals.

Pleistocene glaciers once covered as much as 32 percent of the Earth's land surface. Continental ice sheets extended more than 2,500 miles across the northern conterminous United States and stretched as far south as the Missouri and Ohio rivers. In the Rocky Mountain region, alpine ice caps and valley glaciers formed as far south as south-central New Mexico (latitude 33° north). In the Southern Rockies, alpine glaciers formed in all major ranges; most were valley glaciers, but ice caps developed in areas of higher precipitation, such as the San Juan Mountains, Grand Mesa, and the White River Plateau. Today, though perennial snowfields persist in many alpine areas of the Southern Rockies, true glaciers are found only in the Colorado Front Range.

We know a great deal about the geologic, climatic, and biological changes that shaped the Southern Rockies during Quaternary time. The story is far from complete, however, and researchers representing a variety of disciplines — geology, paleontology, paleobotany, physics, and climatology —

Late summer photograph of the Arapaho Glacier, Colorado Front Range. Note bergschrund at top of glacier, crevasses, the exposed gray ice of the ablation zone, and the Little Ice Age moraines at the foot of the glacier. *James B. Benedict.*

are continually adding to our knowledge of Quaternary environments. To develop a paleoclimatic history for the Quaternary, the geologist must work backward by examining deposits left behind by Pleistocene and Holocene glaciers, dating these deposits wherever possible, and then reconstructing the climatic scenario that might have produced them. Chronologies of Quaternary events, as well as correlations within and beyond the Southern Rockies, have been established by using an array of absolute and relative dating methods that include carbon 14, or radiocarbon (for dating charcoal, wood, and sediments containing organic carbon), lichenometry (using lichen diameters for dating), pollen stratigraphy (using pollen preserved in sediment samples to infer former climates), rock weathering, and soil development.

Reading the Evidence: Glacial Erosion

The advance and retreat of Quaternary glaciers led to a distinctive pattern of landform development that can be readily observed in every major mountain range in the Southern Rockies. Pyramidal peaks, amphitheater-like basins, hanging valleys, and U-shaped valleys are all trademarks of mountain glaciation. Glaciers modify the landscape primarily through the erosive processes of abrasion and plucking. Abrasive action is achieved by the presence of rock and rock fragments embedded in the base and sides of the moving glacier. Study of the striations (grooves) produced by glacial abrasion can provide information about glacier movement. Good examples of glacially striated bedrock can be seen in Rocky Mountain National Park along the old Fall River Road (west of Chasm Falls) and in the Glacier Gorge area, east of Independence Pass in the Sawatch Range, and near Molas Pass in the San Juans.

Plucking, in contrast to glacial abrasion, involves the lifting and incorporation of loose rock material as part of the bedload of the glacier as it moves downslope. Frost-aided weakening and quarrying of the bedrock in contact with the glacier greatly enhances the subaerial removal of rock from the headwall and sidewalls of the glacier basin. The combined effects of abrasion and plucking can be seen in the streamlined bedrock landforms commonly observed on the floors of glaciated valleys; these features, known as whalebacks or *roches moutonnées,* are abrasion-smoothed and often striated on their upvalley sides, and roughened in response to glacial plucking on their downvalley sides. Good examples of roches moutonnées can be seen in the Glacier Gorge and Moraine Park areas of Rocky Mountain National Park and are common in the Indian Peaks Wilderness Area south of the park.

The most conspicuous landforms associated with glacial erosion are found in the glacier's source area and result largely from the headward quarrying of rock by the glacier. The names of these features—*cirque, tarn, arête, col,* and *horn*—are in the lexicon of every mountaineer. The term cirque refers to the semicircular basin the glacier creates at its head; in longitudinal profile, a typical cirque exhibits a steep, quarried headwall, a circular or elongated basin below the headwall, and an abraded bedrock lip, or threshold. In many cases, the threshold serves to enclose the basin, allowing water to collect to form a cirque lake, or tarn, such as Chasm Lake at the base of Longs Peak and Frozen Lake at the head of Glacier Gorge (both in Rocky Mountain National Park). There are thousands of cirques in the Southern Rockies, and many are visible from the major mountain highways; good examples can be found in Rocky Mountain National Park, in the Indian Peaks Wilderness Area (Colorado Front Range), at Horseshoe Mountain in the Mosquito Range, along the eastern slope of the Sangre de Cristo Range, and in the Elk Mountains.

The artistry of ice is apparent when two cirques develop on opposite sides of a bedrock ridge, eroding the ridge between them to create a high saddle, or col. A narrow, sawtoothed ridge consisting of a series of cols and intervening ridge segments forms an arête. Where two or more cirques intersect, a pyramidal peak, or horn, may persist above the general level of the saw-toothed divide. Good examples of horns are abundant in the Southern Rockies and include peaks such as Wetterhorn and the Matterhorn in the San Juans, Lone Cone in the San Miguel Range of the San Juans, and Lone Eagle on the western edge of the Indian Peaks in the Colorado Front Range.

Valleys that have been heavily glaciated usually have a characteristic U shape when viewed in cross section, in contrast to the V shape typical of unglaciated drainages. Good examples of U-shaped valleys are common throughout the Southern Rockies and include the Animas Valley in the San Juans, the Roaring Fork Valley near Aspen, and both Horseshoe and Moraine parks in Rocky Mountain National Park. The upper end of a glaciated valley sometimes appears stepped in long profile, each step fronted by a cross-valley ledge of more resistant rock and often dotted by a chain of small lakes (as can be seen at Gorge Lakes, viewed from Forest Canyon Overlook in Rocky Mountain National Park). Hanging valleys, small glaciated valleys perched high above the main valley floor, mark the junctions where tributary glaciers joined the main trunk of a valley glacier; streams draining these tributary valleys often form waterfalls as they cascade to the main valley floor. Hanging valleys are common features in the Colorado Front Range and are especially prominent in the San Juan Mountains.

DEPOSITIONAL LANDFORMS

Glaciers transport enormous quantities of erosional debris beneath, within, and on the surface of the ice. Geologists use the term glacial drift to refer to all erosional debris — boulders, cobbles, pebbles, sand, silt, and clay — transported and deposited by glaciers or their associated meltwater streams. The term *till* refers to the unsorted, nonstratified debris that is picked up, transported, and deposited directly by the glacier without being reworked by meltwater streams. Glacial drift that has been transported by meltwater streams is called *outwash;* unlike till, outwash may be stratified or layered as a result of size-sorting of the sediment by the transporting stream.

Landforms constructed of glacial drift, though less spectacular than those sculpted by glacial erosion, are distinctive and often of impressive size. Most glacial deposition takes place as the ice melts and retreats, providing the geologist with a detailed record of the movement of glaciers that have long since disappeared. Like a giant conveyor belt, the glacier delivers much of its load of rock debris to its terminus, or snout, with lesser amounts deposited along the sides and bottom of the glacier. These deposits of till are called *moraines,* consisting typically of a jumble of rock debris and finer sediments; moraines may be ridgelike or somewhat amorphous and hummocky in form. Moraines that form around the glacier's snout are called *terminal moraines.* The smaller, cross-valley ridges that may form as the glacier recedes are known as *recessional moraines.* The long ridges of till that parallel valley walls along the sides of the glacier are called *lateral moraines.* The term *ground moraine* refers to the low, relatively rolling accumulations of till that form a veneer on the floors of many glaciated valleys. Terminal and lateral moraines, such as those that enclose Moraine Park in Rocky Mountain National Park, can be enormous, reaching heights of 1,000 feet or more.

Pleistocene Glaciers in the Southern Rockies

Major glaciation events in the Southern Rockies correspond in a general way to worldwide patterns of Quaternary climatic change. It is important to remember, however, that specific intervals of climatic change were neither synchronous nor of similar intensity in all areas. In contrast to the midcontinent region of North America, which was mantled with continental ice sheets throughout much of the Pleistocene, all evidence for glaciation in the Southern Rockies appears to be restricted to the middle to late Pleistocene and the Holocene. The onset of glaciation in the Southern Rockies is believed to correspond to a sharp drop in temperature coupled with an increase in precipitation, resulting in the development of large perennial snowfields throughout the higher ranges.

During the maximum extent of Pleistocene glaciation, the highest elevations of the Southern Rockies were nearly covered by glacial ice, and massive rivers of ice flowed down most of the major valleys to around 8,000 feet. One icefield in the San Juan Mountains was 60 miles wide and reached a thickness of more than 3,000 feet. In other areas, valley glaciers were as thick as 2,000 feet, creating the classic U-shaped valleys we see today as well as the lofty moraines that delineate former ice margins.

The Pleistocene glacial sequence for the Southern Rockies is represented by at least three major glaciations: (1) pre–Bull Lake, (2) Bull Lake, and (3) Pinedale. The names for these glaciations are derived from localities in the Wind River Range of central Wyoming, where Pleistocene glacial deposits of similar ages were first identified and studied. Evidence of multiple intervals of glacial advance, called stades, are reported for both the Bull Lake and Pinedale glaciations; each of the major glaciations was separated from its successor by an interglacial period in which the glaciers withdrew substantially or melted altogether.

PRE–BULL LAKE GLACIATION

The Pre–Bull Lake Glaciation, essentially middle Pleistocene in age, is the earliest recognized glaciation known for the Southern Rockies. Unfortunately, precise dating of the Pre–Bull Lake Glaciation has been difficult due to the paucity of deposits and because it lies beyond the time range of radiocarbon dating. Limited chronological control provided by potassium-argon–dated volcanic ash units in association with these ancient tills and outwash gravels suggests that multiple advances of the pre–Bull Lake glaciers occurred between 302,000 years ago and 738,000 years ago. Deposits of these sheetlike and deeply weathered tills have been reported in the Colorado Front Range, from Grand Mesa, in the San Juan Mountains, and in the Sawatch and Sangre de Cristo ranges. In the Colorado Front Range, examples of possible pre–Bull Lake till can be seen just east of the Fall River entrance to Rocky Mountain National Park and in road cuts along Colorado 7 in the Tahosa Valley, just east of Longs Peak.

BULL LAKE GLACIATION

In the Southern Rockies, the Bull Lake Glaciation consisted of at least two distinct advances of glacial ice separated by a major withdrawal of ice. Dating of Bull Lake deposits has been problematic in the Southern Rockies, relying largely on relative dating methods. Bull Lake moraines cannot be radiocarbon dated, and opportunities for applying other types of numerical dating techniques are limited. A uranium-trend date of approximately 130,000 years has been obtained for a Bull Lake lateral moraine in the Colorado Front Range. North of the Southern Rockies, in Yellowstone National Park, combined obsidian-hydration and potassium-argon dates ranging between 140,000 and 150,000 years have been obtained.

Evidence of Bull Lake ice caps and valley glaciers is found in nearly every glaciated range in the Southern Rockies. Bull Lake valley glaciers were generally more extensive than later Pinedale glaciers and in many areas were as thick as 2,000 feet in their upper portions. At Grand Mesa, for example, a Bull Lake ice cap covered the entire surface of the mesa, and tongues of ice extended into the surrounding drainages to an elevation of 5,800 feet. Bull Lake moraines can be distinguished from those of Pinedale age by their broad crests and gently sloping sides. Moraine surfaces are less bouldery than Pinedale and Holocene moraines, have well developed soils, do not exhibit the pronounced hummockiness or the undrained depressions characteristic of Pinedale moraines, and typically support a mature forest or sagebrush cover. Where Bull Lake moraines cross major valleys, most have been breached by later stream erosion. Examples of Bull Lake moraines can be seen along Glacier Creek in Rocky Mountain National Park and west of the Beaver Meadows entrance to the park, at the Home Moraine Geologic Site

THE SOUTHERN ROCKIES

in upper Cache la Poudre Canyon, on Grand Mesa near Land's End, along the upper Laramie River Valley, and on the east slope of the Sawatch Range near Lake Creek and Twin Lakes.

PINEDALE GLACIATION

The Pinedale Glaciation was the last major Pleistocene glaciation event in the Southern Rockies. Radiocarbon dating and relative-age criteria suggest that the Pinedale Glaciation began between 40,000 and 30,000 years ago, and that Pinedale glaciers were near their maximum lengths at least once, and perhaps twice, prior to 20,000 years ago. At Devlin Park in the Colorado Front Range, a radiocarbon date of 23,000 years relates to the last advance of a Pinedale glacier close to its terminal limit.

In the northern and central Southern Rockies, Pinedale glaciers occasionally exceeded 20 miles in length and were as thick as 1,500 feet in their source areas. To the south of this area, Pinedale glaciers were considerably shorter, stopping well above the maximum of Bull Lake ice. In southern Wyoming, Pinedale ice sheets accumulated around the flanks of the Snowy Range and spread across the post-Laramide erosion surface, enveloping the major stream valleys of Libby Creek, French Creek, Rock Creek, Brush Creek, and the Medicine Bow River. In the Colorado Front Range, glaciers flowed both east and west from well-developed cirques along the crest of the range. Along the western slope of the range, glaciers grew to such enormous thicknesses that several overflowed their valleys to form a complex network of ice streams. Glaciers flowing eastward from cirques in the Never Summer Mountains merged with glaciers flowing westward from the Continental Divide to form the longest Pinedale glacier in Rocky Mountain National Park: the 20-mile-long Colorado River Glacier.

To the south and west of the Colorado Front Range, Pinedale glaciers formed along the crests of most of the major ranges. In the San Juans, Pinedale ice cap and valley glaciers formed some of the largest ice bodies in the Southern Rockies. An enormous ice cap overflowed the divide between the Animas and the Uncompahgre rivers to form two spectacular rivers of ice: the Animas Glacier, flowing south for nearly 40 miles down Animas Canyon, and the Uncompahgre Glacier, flowing north for more than 20 miles along the Uncompahgre Valley. From the rolling, glaciated terrain around Molas Lake, just south of Red Mountain Pass, it is easy to envision a virtual sea of ice, with only the summits of Mount Sneffels and Engineer Mountain and a number of other peaks protruding above the level of the slow-moving ice.

Large, forested Pinedale moraines are conspicuous features of most glaciated valleys in the Southern Rockies. Pinedale moraines can be distinguished from Bull Lake moraines by their steep sides and sharp crests, which tend to be somewhat hummocky and may contain small ponds. On the whole, Pinedale moraines are more bouldery and less weathered than deposits of Bull Lake age. Good examples of Pinedale moraines include those flanking the eastern edge of the Park Range, those near Animas City and Bakers Bridge in the San Juans, and the extremely large moraines bordering the basins of Horseshoe Park, Moraine Park, and Glacier Basin in Rocky Mountain National Park. In cases where Pinedale terminal moraines formed temporary barriers to glacial meltwater streams, lakes were created, such as Grand Lake (west of Rocky Mountain National Park), Twin Lakes (near Leadville), Lake Marie (in the Snowy Range), and Lake Katharine (in the southern Sangre de Cristo Range).

In most areas of the Southern Rockies, Pinedale glaciers began receding from their outermost positions between 15,000 and 13,000 years ago, with glaciers in the southern portion of the Southern Rockies probably receding first. At Lake Emma and Molas Lake, in the San Juan Mountains, a series of radiocarbon ages obtained for the lowermost lake sediments suggests that Pinedale glaciers had all but disappeared from this region by 15,000 years ago. North of the San Juans, radiocarbon dates obtained for Pinedale deglaciation in the Colorado Front Range and the Park Range suggest that the last of the valley glaciers were in full-scale retreat by 14,000 to 13,500 years ago, and that most were confined to their cirques by at least 12,000 years ago.

The effects of Pinedale glaciation extend well beyond the limits of glacial ice. Meltwater torrents deepened and scoured canyons along both the eastern and western slopes of the mountains — Royal Gorge, Clear Creek, Big Thompson, Cache la Poudre, and the Black Canyon of the Gunnison, to name just a few. In the higher valleys and intermontane basins, downcutting by meltwater-enriched streams removed a large percentage of glacial outwash deposits, leaving the remnants as terraces above the new stream levels. In some valleys, several Pleistocene terrace levels can be seen along the sides of streams and rivers. The upper Arkansas River Valley, near Buena Vista, is noted for the steplike terraces that flank both sides of the river.

Late Pleistocene Dune Fields

Dune fields developed in several areas of the Southern Rockies at the close of the Pleistocene. Those at Great Sand Dunes National Monument and along the eastern edge of North Park remain active and attract thousands of visitors each year. At the national monument, the dune field towers 700 feet above the valley floor and covers 150 square miles. During the last 15,000 years, southwesterly winds have carried trillions of tons of sand across the arid expanse of the San Luis Valley, funneling it into a trap formed by three low passes in the Sangre de Cristos: Music, Medano, and Mosca. The sand, a mixture of volcanic rock fragments and bits of quartz weathered from the San Juan Mountains, has been scoured from the ancient floodplain of the Rio Grande River. As the winds slam into the towering wall of the mountains, the alcove created by the three passes produces additional turbulence, forcing the winds to lose energy and to drop their load of sand. Reverse storm winds, roaring down from the northeast, periodically blow dune crests back to the west, contributing to their great height and keeping them away from the mountain front.

Along the eastern edge of the Southern Rockies and extending into the High Plains, Pleistocene dune fields have largely stabilized and become obscured by their vegetation cover. Deflation hollows, or blowouts, are common features of these dune fields, resulting from renewed wind scour in areas where the vegetation has been disturbed by fire or grazing. Big Hollow, an inactive blowout near Laramie, ranks as one of the largest in North America, measuring 3 miles wide, 9 miles long, and almost 150 feet deep.

Pleistocene Extinctions

For nearly a century, paleontologists have debated the causes of the great wave of mammalian extinctions that occurred at the end of the Pleistocene. With few exceptions, all of the mammals that became extinct were large-bodied species—mammoths, camels, ground sloths, saber-toothed cats, and giant bison. Numerous theories have been proposed to explain their demise, including climatic change, disease, poor synchronization of breeding habits with climate, and overkill by Paleo-Indian hunters. It seems probable that the answer to the Pleistocene extinction puzzle lies in some combination of causal factors rather than in the effect of a single predator, such as man.

Holocene Glacial History

In the Southern Rockies, the beginning of the Holocene epoch marks the end of climatic conditions favoring full-scale glaciation. In fact, there is growing paleoclimatic evidence that summer solar radiation had increased markedly in the Northern Hemisphere by 10,000 years ago. Several hypotheses have been proposed to explain the glacial-interglacial transition between 14,000 and 10,000 years ago, each relying on a different causal agent—changes in the Earth's orbit, sunspot cycles, volcanic activity, solar-lunar tidal forces, differences in atmospheric circulation patterns, and changing carbon dioxide levels in the atmosphere. Indeed, some combination of these factors may ultimately provide a framework for understanding Holocene climates.

In the absence of full glacial conditions, the development and survival of Holocene glaciers in the Southern Rockies depended to a large degree on wind-redistributed snow and favorable cirque orientation. Even the largest of the Holocene glaciers, measuring around a mile in length, were minuscule compared to the Pleistocene valley glaciers and ice caps that preceded them. At least four, and possibly more, Holocene ice advances have been reported from the Colorado Front Range, the Medicine Bow Mountains, and the Park Range. Ice advances in these northern ranges were confined to high-elevation cirques and to north-facing valley walls above present treeline. In the San Juan Mountains, where glaciers flourished under Pleistocene conditions, there is no evidence of Holocene glaciation younger than about 9,000 years.

Holocene Glaciation in the
Colorado Front Range

Much of what we know about Holocene glacial history and climatic change in the Southern Rockies is the result of extensive research in the Indian Peaks region of the Colorado Front Range. Data derived from mapping of the glacial deposits, numerical and relative dating, archeological excavations, and pollen and vegetation studies provide us with a continually evolving record of climatic change. In most cirques, the sequence of terminal moraines suggests multiple glacial advances separated by intervals of near-total disappearance of glaciers. The extent to which this sequence can be extrapolated to other ranges in the northern and central portions of the Southern Rockies remains to be determined.

The oldest of the post-Pinedale cirque-glacier advances occurred around 12,000 to 10,000 years ago; this advance just precedes the formal Pleistocene-Holocene boundary. Terminal moraines deposited by these glaciers are generally found within a mile of cirque headwalls, near present timberline; they are typically well vegetated, supporting trees and a shrub understory in certain situations.

Archeological evidence from several high-altitude sites in the Indian Peaks Wilderness Area indicates that Paleo-Indian hunters were making seasonal use of the high valleys and alpine uplands by 8,500 years ago, enjoying the warmer conditions that followed this early Holocene glaciation.

During the middle Holocene, a prolonged interval of warmth and aridity known as the Altithermal affected large areas of western North America. Glaciers and perennial snowbanks disappeared from the high mountains, and lowland areas underwent severe drought stress. Archeological evidence indicates an extraordinary increase in human occupation of the cool, moist mountain environments during the Altithermal, in sharp contrast to the apparent decline in human populations in drought-susceptible areas of the Great Basin, Colorado Plateau, and Great Plains. Clearly, the mountains offered refuge to early peoples as well as to the large game animals on which they depended for food. More than forty prehistoric game-drive systems, consisting of low stone walls and rock-rimmed blinds, have been located in the Colorado Front Range; these game-drive systems are similar to those used in the Arctic by both prehistoric and modern peoples to hunt caribou and musk-oxen. Archeological evidence indicates that game-drive hunting became important above timberline in the Colorado Front Range by at least 5,800 years ago and continued until hunting by horseback supplanted traditional techniques.

The rebirth of glaciers following the Altithermal assumed the same pattern of intermittent advance and retreat that had characterized the preceding 6,000 years—but on a much smaller scale. Moraines deposited by post-Altithermal ice advances do not extend far from the cirque headwalls; they appear fresh and unweathered, and are only sparsely vegetated. The last of these ice advances, those of the Little Ice Age, began in the Colorado Front Range around 300 years ago, and ended in the middle of the nineteenth century with the start of a global warming trend. Most cirques that still contain glaciers or large perennial snowbanks, such as the Andrews and Tyndall cirques in Rocky Mountain National Park, also contain small ice-cored moraines representing this last advance.

Present-day glaciers in the Southern Rockies are restricted to north- and east-facing cirques in the Colorado Front Range. Glaciers persist in these areas only because they are sheltered from the direct rays of the sun and receive large accumulations of windblown snow. The future of these glaciers is uncertain. Despite short-term climatic fluctuations, such as the warming trend that has characterized much of the twentieth century, a return to glacial conditions appears to be overdue, according to some interpretations of the data. Alternately, other researchers speculate that we are entering a warming phase, or "super-interglacial" period, resulting from human-induced impacts on world climate.

Beyond Glacier Margins: Periglacial Landscapes

In mountain environments, frost action and gravity are the critical variables in the algebra of erosion. Geologists use

THE SOUTHERN ROCKIES

the term *periglacial* to refer to any past or present near-glacial environment in which frost processes (freezing and thawing of water in rock or soil) have dominated weathering and landform development. The results of these processes—rock glaciers, talus cones, blockfields, and various types of large- and small-scale patterned ground features—are common above timberline throughout the Southern Rockies. During the Pleistocene, permafrost (perennially frozen ground) was widespread in the frigid, windswept uplands of the Southern Rockies. Permafrost probably formed during the first major glaciation, and may have formed and disintegrated several times during subsequent glacial and interglacial intervals. Present-day climatic conditions in the Southern Rockies continue to be severe enough to maintain isolated patches of permafrost at elevations above 11,500 feet.

The general tendency of frost action is to cause change and instability through the processes of frost wedging, frost heave and thrust, frost cracking, and the development of needle ice. For example, the coarse, angular rock that mantles alpine summits and slopes in the Southern Rockies is thought to result primarily from the action of frost wedging, which occurs when joints and cracks in bedrock are penetrated by surface water that freezes, generating sufficient pressure to shatter the rock into angular blocks. Frost wedging in nearly flat terrain can result in the development of extensive blockfields; the German word *felsenmeer,* meaning "sea of rocks," is often used to refer to these features.

Frost heave is the major cause of disruption and upheaval of soil and rock in mountain environments and is a critical factor in the development of patterned-ground features. Heaving is favored by silty soils, saturated conditions, and slow, deep freezing. As ice nuclei form in the soil during the fall freeze, free water migrates toward these nuclei, dewatering adjacent sediments and encouraging the development of layers or lenses of clear ice, generally oriented parallel to the soil surface. As these ice bodies grow, the ground expands vertically and may be accompanied by the ejection of rocks from depth. Differential frost heaving, the result of local variations in soil texture, moisture availability, or insulation of the freezing surface by snow or vegetation, creates a blistered or bubbled effect. Earth hummocks, common features in alpine and subalpine wetlands, are thought to result from differential frost heaving. The trouble spots that develop along paved mountain roads at the end of winter can also be partly explained by the process of differential heaving.

Needle ice consists of delicate filaments of ice an inch or less in length that develop at or near the soil surface in response to daily freeze-thaw cycles. The needles may be as densely packed as the bristles in a brush, or scattered loosely through the soil. Soil surfaces affected by needle-ice development often appear somewhat frothy. In alpine areas where the vegetation cover has been disturbed and bare soil exposed, needle-ice development can uproot plant seedlings and discourage natural revegetation.

PATTERNED GROUND

The patterning of rocks, soil, and vegetation into various geometric shapes as a result of frost action occurs widely in alpine areas of the Southern Rockies. Actively forming patterned ground features are restricted to areas with permafrost or to sites where environmental conditions encourage intense frost action, such as the floors of ephemeral ponds or areas that receive meltwater from persistent snowbanks. Patterned ground features are classified according to their shape and the amount of sorting of fine and coarse materials that has occurred. Shape is ultimately controlled by the slope of the surface on which the pattern forms. The basic types of patterned ground are earth hummocks, sorted and nonsorted circles, polygons, nets, steps, and stripes.

Earth hummocks are most common in subalpine and alpine wetlands, where winter snow is deep enough to provide protection from wind erosion but shallow enough to permit deep frost penetration. Nonsorted circles (such as frost boils) tend to form primarily in snow-free zones. Relict or inactive polygons, up to 30 feet in diameter, are common on windswept knolls and in dry saddles, reflecting times when climatic conditions were moister and colder than at present. Arctic-type fossil ice-wedge polygons, ranging from 30 to 80 feet in diameter, have been reported at a single locality at the base of Sawtooth Peak in the Colorado Front Range and in a number of localities in the Laramie Basin of Wyoming. One of the best places to see both active and inactive patterned ground features is along Trail Ridge Road in Rocky Mountain National Park.

Sorted nets with active centers, Albion-Kiowa saddle, Colorado Front Range. *James B. Benedict*

Landforms Produced by Mass-Wasting

Mass-wasting refers to the downslope movement of soil and rock on slopes in response to gravity. Many types of mass-wasting processes are at work in the mountain environment, each exerting a profound influence on landscape development. The processes can be imperceptibly slow, as in frost creep, producing effects visible only when accumulated over a long span of time; moderate, as in solifluction; or catastrophic, as in rockfalls and mudflows.

FROST CREEP

Frost creep, an important process in alpine environments, involves the downslope movement of frost-heaved soils, often in large quantities. Over time, the effects of frost creep can be seen in the development of small steps or terracettes. These miniature terraces, typically aligned approximately parallel to the contour of the slope, are influenced by wind and by the restraining effect of the vegetation cover.

SOLIFLUCTION

Solifluction (soil flow) occurs in areas where bedrock, permafrost, or seasonal ground ice prevents the downward percolation of water. As the upper soil layer becomes increasingly saturated due to seasonal thawing, it tends to lose its cohesive strength and deform downslope as a viscous mass. Solifluction lobes and terraces frequently resemble large tongues of soil, banked along their fronts by piles of rock or vegetation; they may coalesce to form scalloped, lobate terrace complexes extending for considerable distances across a slope. Solifluction features frequently have meltwater pools on their surfaces in summer, and patterned ground may develop on inactive lobes where vegetation cover is limited. Downslope movement rates vary depending on local conditions; rates of nearly 2 inches per year have been reported for the Colorado Front Range.

During the Pleistocene, solifluction was the most important soil movement process on all but the driest of alpine slopes. Under present climatic conditions, frost creep is the most important process, and active solifluction is restricted to areas where the water table remains high enough during the fall freeze to permit development of thick ice-lenses. Both inactive and active solifluction features can be seen in most alpine areas of the Southern Rockies; good examples are easily observed from Trail Ridge Road in Rocky Mountain National Park.

EARTHFLOWS AND MUDFLOWS

The terms earthflow and mudflow are applied to types of mass-wasting that are similar to solifluction but involve more rapid movement. An earthflow characteristically exhibits a spoon-shaped sliding surface, a crescent-shaped cliff at its upper end, and a tongue-shaped bulge at its lower end. The Slumgullion Earthflow, near Lake City in the San Juans, is the most famous example of this type of mass movement in the Southern Rockies. This spectacular earthflow began in supersaturated, strongly weathered volcanic rocks at an altitude of about 11,400 feet and flowed downvalley to an altitude of 8,200 feet, where the flow dammed the valley above the present community of Lake City and formed San Cristobal Lake. Where Colorado 149 crosses the Slumgullian Earthflow, the bumpy pavement provides some indication of continuing movement. Mudflows are more liquid than earthflows and tend to create steep-walled channels flanked by ridges of debris in the form of levees and terminating in debris fans. Evidence of both young and old mudflow activity is common throughout the Southern Rockies.

TALUS AND SCREE

Along the bases of steep slopes, accumulations of frost-wedged rocks commonly form apronlike deposits called *talus,* if they are composed chiefly of large blocks, or *scree,* if they are made up of smaller-sized rocks. In certain volcanic ranges, most notably the San Juan Mountains, rapid scree development in closely jointed volcanic rocks has produced spectacular rock streams and debris mantles.

ROCK GLACIERS

Rock glaciers are lobate or tongue-shaped accumulations of unsorted rock debris that resemble ice glaciers in many ways. Active rock glaciers are ice cored or ice cemented, which accounts for their glacierlike movement. Most rock glaciers head in cirques or are located at the bases of steep-walled cliffs, where they receive a continual supply of frost-wedged rock. They vary in length from a few hundred yards to more than a mile. Depending on local conditions, rock glaciers may be active or inactive. The fronts of active rock glaciers tend to be steep, fresh-appearing, and unstable; evidence of past or present movement is apparent in the arcuate flow ridges that pattern their surfaces. Movement rates for active rock glaciers in the Southern Rockies are quite variable, ranging from less than 8 inches per year in the Colorado Front Range and the Sawatch Range to as many as 24 inches per year in the Elk Mountains.

Rock glaciers can form in several ways. Some are simply ice glaciers that have been buried by rock debris, whereas others originate from the accumulation of massive quantities of frost-wedged rock and the development of an internal ice core. Active and inactive rock glaciers are common in many areas of the Southern Rockies that have long been

Rock glacier at the head of the Columbine Creek, Indian Peaks Wilderness Area. Note arcuate ridges and furrows. *James B. Benedict.*

abandoned by glacial ice. On Mount Sopris, in the Elk Mountains, both types, some more than a mile long, fill all major valleys. Some of the most spectacular rock glaciers in the world are located in the San Juan Mountains; the best examples can be seen in the Imogene, Pierson, Silver, American, and Hurricane basins. Rock glaciers are also common in the Colorado Front, Sawatch, and Sangre de Cristo ranges.

CHAPTER EIGHT

Climate and Weather in the Southern Rockies

THE CLIMATE OF the Southern Rockies is a mosaic, with the differences from one area to another clearly imprinted on the shape and texture of the mountain landscape. Every mountain range, basin, and canyon exhibits a climatic pattern as unique as a signature, one influenced by the interplay of topographic differences and regional climatic controls such as latitude, continentality, altitude, orientation of the main ranges, prevailing wind direction, and storm tracks. These regional climatic controls ultimately determine the distribution of solar radiation, temperature, precipitation, and local winds—the dependent meteorological variables that interact to produce daily weather phenomena.

To a hiker caught above timberline in a sudden thunderstorm or snow squall, the behavior of the atmosphere may appear random, capricious, and even malevolent. In mountain environments, sharp contrasts often occur within short vertical and horizontal distances, as well as within short time spans. Although the interactions that determine day-to-day weather phenomena may seem complex, they conform to predictable patterns and characteristics common to all mountainous areas.

Regional Climate Controls

The term *climate* integrates all of the long-term, variable characteristics of the atmosphere in a particular region: temperature, precipitation, wind speed and direction, radiation, sunshine, cloudiness, and evaporation. Climate, to a large degree, determines the natural environment. It sets the stage upon which all physical, chemical, and biological processes operate. *Weather,* in contrast to climate, reflects short-term fluctuations in atmospheric conditions and describes, in both quantitative and qualitative terms, the state of the atmosphere at a given time and place.

Latitude and Continentality

The Southern Rockies are located in the middle latitudes, where seasonal differences in the angle of the sun above the horizon and in day length account for substantial variations in temperature from summer to winter. Middle-latitude mountains receive a greater proportion of incoming solar radiation than do lowland areas, both because the atmosphere is thinner at higher elevations and because the sun's rays strike slopes oriented toward the sun at a higher angle than they do level surfaces. In the Southern Rockies, latitudinally controlled differences in incoming solar radiation result in a decline in temperature from south to north; the effects of this gradient can be seen in the changing composition of forest communities and in the decreasing elevation of timberline northward along the Rockies.

One of the major climatic controls affecting the Southern Rockies is their midcontinent location, far from the moderating influences of moist, maritime air masses. The region is dominated by a highland continental climate and consequently experiences larger diurnal and seasonal differences in temperature, lower humidity, more sunshine, less cloudiness, and less precipitation than coastal mountain ranges. Eastward-moving storms originating in the Pacific Ocean lose a substantial quantity of their moisture as they pass over mountain ranges to the west of the Southern Rockies, further intensifying the effects of continentality.

Air Mass Source Areas

Day-to-day weather depends primarily on the temperature, stability, and moisture content of the air masses that continually pass overhead. Air masses are classified accord-

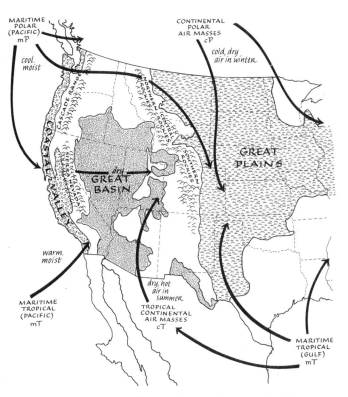

Air mass source areas affecting the Southern Rocky Mountains.

ing to area of origin and moisture content. Two basic types are identified: maritime and continental. Maritime air masses develop over an ocean and are characterized by high water-vapor content and high condensation potential. Continental air masses evolve over the dry interior of a continent and are characterized by low water-vapor content and low condensation potential. Three maritime source areas and two continental source areas influence the climate of the Southern Rockies: (1) maritime polar (cool Pacific, from the Pacific Northwest); (2) maritime tropical (warm Pacific, from the Baja area of southern California); (3) maritime tropical (from the Gulf of Mexico); (4) continental tropical (from Mexico); and (5) polar continental (from north-central Canada).

The Altitude Factor

TEMPERATURE AND ALTITUDE

When temperatures in Denver soar into the 90s on a summer day, those atop nearby Mount Evans (14,264 feet) may only register in the 60s. This altitudinal variation in air temperature, called the *lapse rate,* is the result of a never-ending balancing act going on in the mountain atmosphere. The majority of incoming solar radiant energy is first absorbed by the Earth—by vegetation, soil, rocks, and water—then a portion is radiated back into the atmosphere in the form of atmospheric kinetic energy (as heat). As the air in contact with the surface is warmed it expands and becomes less dense, which causes it to rise; this process is called *convection.* Heat is lost as a result of the kinetic energy of expansion, leading to a decrease in air temperature at the average rate of about 3.5°F for every 1,000-foot gain in elevation. It is important to remember that the lapse rate is influenced by the amount of incoming solar radiation, the slope aspect, winds, and, most important, the amount of moisture in the air.

AIR DENSITY AND ALTITUDE

The heat-holding capacity of air is determined by its density and composition. At sea level, the weight, or density, of the air (the standard atmospheric pressure) is expressed as 29.92 inches of mercury. As elevation increases, atmospheric pressure decreases at the rate of about 1 inch per 1,000 feet. At higher altitudes, the molecules in a given parcel of air are spaced farther apart, so there are fewer molecules to receive and hold heat. Water vapor and suspended particulate matter are important heat-absorbing and radiating constituents in the atmosphere. More than half of the water vapor in the atmosphere occurs below an altitude of 8,000 feet; above this elevation the amount of water vapor diminishes rapidly and is barely detectable at altitudes above 12,000 feet. In the mountains, temperatures tend to drop off sharply after sunset because of the limited ability of the high-altitude atmosphere to hold heat. The orientation of a given slope with respect to the sun exaggerates these effects, and great differences may occur between sunny and shaded slopes, wet and dry slopes, and windward and leeward slopes.

What most visitors to the mountains notice first is the lower oxygen content of the air. As the density of the air decreases, there are fewer molecules of oxygen per unit volume, and consequently, above 8,000 feet, most people begin to experience some shortness of breath. At 10,000 feet, a hiker must take in approximately a third more air to receive the same amount of oxygen as at sea level. Visitors to high elevations are encouraged to allow sufficient time for acclimatization (two to three days are recommended) before undertaking vigorous physical activity. Failure to do so may result in the unpleasant symptoms of *mountain sickness:* difficulty in sleeping, fatigue, persistent headache, and nausea.

Atmospheric Circulation: Westerlies, Jet Streams, and Air Masses

Air Pressure and Winds

Atmospheric convection is the driving force behind the movement of air. When air is heated, it increases in volume and rises because of its greater buoyancy. These vertical air currents rob the surface of some of its air, thus creating regions of slightly lower pressure at the bottom of the rising air column. As air is forced to move from areas of higher pressure toward the newly created low-pressure area, a horizontal pressure gradient develops. These air movements vary in size and in their significance for climate, from local winds, such as dust devils and valley winds, to large-scale air currents in the upper levels of the atmosphere.

The largest-scale wind patterns — the winds aloft — are initiated by pressure systems set up by latitudinal variations in incoming solar radiation. In the Northern Hemisphere, the winds aloft do not flow in the direction the gradient of pressure would suggest but are deflected to the right by the Earth's rotation, spiraling counterclockwise around the lows and clockwise around the highs. In meteorological terminology, centers of low pressure are called *cyclones,* and centers of high pressure are called *anticyclones.* As a result of the Coriolis force, large-scale air motions move perpendicular to the pressure gradient—that is, around regions of low and high pressure—but not directly to or from them. These large-scale pressure patterns, and the upper-air winds they generate, play a critical role in shaping the climate of the Southern Rockies.

Winds Aloft: The Westerlies and the Jet Stream

If we could look down on the atmosphere from above, we would see a broad current of air—the *upper-air wester-lies*—moving generally from west to east around the globe in the midlatitudes. Frequently, atmospheric disturbances in the circumpolar flow of the westerlies produce large, wavelike undulations known as *Rossby waves* in this upper-air current. Rossby waves develop along a narrow zone, called the *polar front,* that marks the contact between cold polar air (the polar easterlies) to the north and warm tropical air to the south. A *trough* (characterized by low pressure and cyclonic flow) and an adjacent *ridge* (characterized by high pressure and anticyclonic flow) constitute a wave. Although Rossby waves vary in number and position, usually five such waves link to encircle the Earth.

Associated with the Rossby waves, and coinciding with the polar front, is a zone of high-speed flow called the *polar front jet stream.* The position of the polar front jet stream is affected by major topographic features, such as the Rocky Mountains, and by such variables as changes in land and sea surface temperatures. The Rocky Mountains, which are oriented almost perpendicular to the prevailing west-to-east airflow pattern, impose disturbances of all scales on upper-air circulation, ranging from the initiation of meanders in jet stream systems to the large-amplitude vertical waves that generate windstorms along the Eastern Slope of the Rockies. Large meanders or displacements of the polar front jet are responsible for some of the recent weather anomalies in the United States. Although the polar front jet stream is the most important jet affecting weather in the Southern Rockies, the *subtropical jet stream,* which forms in the subtropical latitude zone and is the more fixed in position of the two, is also influential in circulation patterns in the mid-latitudes.

The sharp north-to-south temperature gradient that exists in the Northern Hemisphere during the winter months causes the upper-air westerlies to intensify seasonally and with increasing altitude. Consequently, winds in the Southern Rockies are nearly twice as strong in winter as in summer. Another important characteristic of the upper-air westerlies is that their location shifts latitudinally with the seasons in response to seasonal differences in the global pressure regimes. During the summer, when westerly air flow is comparatively weak, the main air current and its associated polar front jet stream stay far to the north over Canada. By winter, however, the westerlies and the main axis of the polar front jet are frequently positioned over the Southern Rockies, guiding Pacific storm systems through the region at fairly regular intervals. As the main belt of westerlies migrates northward in the spring, the windy storms of winter give way to the calmer weather of summer. During those occasional winters when a large ridge in the upper atmosphere keeps the polar front jet along or to the north of the Canadian border, the Southern Rockies may experience a lack of snow, severe drought, and unseasonably warm weather.

Air Masses, Fronts, and Wave Cyclones

The storms that buffet the Southern Rockies are actually small wave disturbances, called *wave cyclones*, embedded in and traveling through the Rossby waves. Sharp contrasts, such as those encountered along the polar front, give rise to a procession of wave cyclones (cyclonic storms), each wave delineated by a vortex that forms, intensifies, and then dissolves as it travels east along the polar front. What we experience at the surface is a migration of cyclones and anticyclones, each disturbance initiated and steered by the winds aloft and then dragged along beneath the core of the polar front jet stream. Traveling cyclones may be mild in intensity, their passage marked by little more than a period of cloud cover and minimal precipitation, or, when pressure gradients are great, they may develop into powerful storm systems.

Understanding Mountain Climates

Solar Radiation

Mountains experience the most extreme and variable radiation climate on Earth. We know that incoming solar radiation, predominately in the form of ultraviolet (short-wave) energy, increases in intensity with height above sea level. Research in the Colorado Front Range shows a 26-percent increase in ultraviolet radiation between the elevations of 5,500 feet and 14,000 feet on a cloudless summer day. There is little doubt that the greater intensity of ultraviolet radiation in mountainous areas has special significance for life and for biological processes. Skin sunburns rapidly at high elevations because of the intensity of ultraviolet radiation. In recent years, the high incidence of skin cancer in individuals working outdoors at high altitudes has received widespread attention. Many plants growing at high altitudes exhibit a wide range of adaptations, such as protective pigments and surface hairs, that serve to reduce the damaging effects of high ultraviolet transmission.

Most people have noticed how much bluer the clear sky looks in the mountains than at lower elevations. This intensity of color results from a decrease in molecular scattering — which primarily affects wavelengths in the short-wave, or blue, end of the spectrum — and the greater availability of short wavelengths at higher elevations because of this decreased scattering.

Slope Differences

Differences in the duration and intensity of incoming solar radiation as a function of both slope angle and orientation of the slope with respect to the sun are the key determinants of *microclimate* — the highly localized climate at or near the ground surface. Topographically controlled differences in energy income are reflected in soil and air temperatures, snow-cover duration, and soil moisture. In the Southern Rockies, south-facing slopes are measurably warmer and drier than north-facing slopes, a pattern that is sharply defined by

THE SOUTHERN ROCKIES

differences in the duration of winter snow cover, evapotranspiration rates, the distribution of vegetation, and the types of habitats available to wildlife. Geologic processes such as frost shattering, soil creep, and rock exfoliation — each an important agent in landscape development — are controlled by variations in the solar income and the associated moisture conditions they determine.

Temperature

Mountains tend to heat up rapidly as a result of the high levels of incoming solar radiation but are quick to lose their heat by radiative cooling, producing a steep temperature gradient in the surrounding air. The Southern Rockies are characterized by strong diurnal and seasonal temperature gradients. At most elevations in the Southern Rockies, the diurnal temperature range is broad, generally between 30° and 40°F. Nocturnal cooling begins shortly before nightfall, reaching maximum rates just before midnight and continuing at a diminishing rate until shortly after sunrise. Summer nights with little or no cloud cover tend to be cool or cold, because the clear night skies permit rapid radiative heat loss. Overcast conditions flatten the diurnal temperature curve by blocking incoming solar radiation in the daytime and retarding radiative heat loss at night.

TEMPERATURE INVERSIONS

Temperature inversions are a common phenomenon in mountainous areas. During a temperature inversion, temperatures are lowest in the valley and increase upward along the mountain slope — a situation clearly at odds with the normal lapse rate rule. Temperature inversions develop best when skies are clear, permitting rapid heat loss to the atmosphere, and when there is no wind to mix and equalize temperatures. As the ground surface becomes colder than the overlying air, the air immediately above the surface begins to lose heat to the surface (by conduction and turbulence) as a result of downward heat flux. Eventually the cool air flows downslope, sliding beneath the warm air along the valley floor and displacing it.

If the valley is open, with no topographic impediment to the free flow of air, there may be continuous downvalley movement, or *cold air drainage*. The magnitude of cold air drainage can range from a cool breeze in a narrow stream valley to a substantial flow, such as that experienced along the Rio Grande Valley in north-central New Mexico. If the valley is encircled by mountains, as is true of the Gunnison Valley, pooling of cold air will occur. Similar conditions are responsible for the low temperatures associated with mountain basins such as the San Luis Valley and North and Middle parks, where diurnal temperature ranges of 50°F are common. The lowest recorded winter temperature in the Southern Rockies, a reading of −63°F at Maybell in northwestern Colorado, was produced by a closed-basin temperature inversion. During recent winters, temperature inversions developing over the Denver metropolitan area, in the natural bowl formed by the South Platte River Valley and the Colorado Front Range, have compounded air pollution problems by trapping dangerous levels of carbon monoxide.

GROWING SEASON

The growing season is determined by the length of the *frost-free period*, defined as the length of time between the last occurrence in spring and the first in fall of a temperature of 32°F or below. In alpine areas of the Southern Rockies, the growing season is no more than forty days, about half that of Alaska's Yukon Valley. Above 9,000 feet, freezing temperatures are possible any night during the year. At Leadville (10,158 feet), the highest city in the Southern Rockies, the growing season averages between sixty and eighty days. Lower elevations fare little better. Red River (8,676 feet), in the southern Sangre de Cristos, averages eighty-three days; Estes Park (7,522 feet), in the Colorado Front Range, averages less than one hundred days. Along the eastern edge of the mountains, Denver's growing season is about 170 days, and nearby Colorado Springs averages 148 days. Grand Junction (4,586 feet), famous for its peach and apple orchards, has perhaps the longest growing season in the Southern Rockies, with a range of 160 to 190 days.

Precipitation: Orographic Effects, Cyclonic Storms, and Convection

Condensation of water vapor into cloud droplets occurs when large quantities of air—individual parcels, entire layers, or air masses—are forced upward and cooled to the saturation point. Three types of lifting mechanisms cause air to rise: frontal wedging associated with cyclonic storms, convective air currents generated by differential heating of the ground surface, and mechanical lifting resulting from *orographic* (topographic) impediments to horizontal wind flow. The highly variable precipitation pattern that characterizes the Southern Rockies results from differences in elevation, slope orientation, seasonal storm tracks, and the trajectories of air masses delivering precipitation.

OROGRAPHIC PRECIPITATION

Orographic effects dominate any discussion of precipitation in mountainous areas. The steeper and more exposed the slope, the more rapidly air will be forced to rise. During its forced ascent, the air is cooled by expansion. As the air cools, it loses its capacity to hold water vapor; clouds form as the excess moisture condenses, and if moisture and temperature conditions are suitable, precipitation will occur. Orographic lifting is most effective when the mountains are oriented—as the Southern Rockies are—perpendicular to the prevailing winds. In the Southern Rockies, as in all mountainous areas, *orographic lifting* serves to intensify cyclonic and convectional precipitation.

Orographic precipitation accounts for a significant percentage of the winter snowfall in the Southern Rockies. How much snow falls is determined largely by how moist the air is and how fast it is moving. The stronger the winds, the more rapidly the air will be forced to rise, producing greater amounts of precipitation in areas west of the Continental Divide. During periods of strong westerly airflow, a massive, wall-like cloud called a crest cloud is commonly observed over the Divide, while leeward slopes and other locations where the air is descending (such as into mountain basins) generally remain clear and receive little precipitation. In contrast, when moisture-laden Gulf of Mexico air is pumped northward along the Eastern Slope of the Southern Rockies

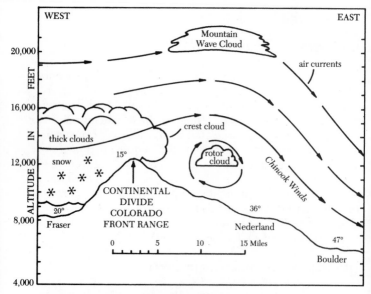

WEST   EAST

20,000 — FEET

Mountain Wave Cloud

air currents

16,000

IN

thick clouds

crest cloud

12,000 — ALTITUDE

snow

15°

rotor cloud

Chinook Winds

CONTINENTAL DIVIDE COLORADO FRONT RANGE

20°

36°

8,000 — Fraser

Nederland

0   5   10   15 Miles

47°

Boulder

4,000 —

Schematic diagram illustrating the characteristic weather phenomena associated with a chinook. The transect extends from Fraser, on the Western Slope of the Colorado Front Range, eastward across the mountains to Boulder. Note the differences in temperature along the transect, especially at Fraser and at Nederland. *(After Hansen, Wallace R., John Chronic, and John Matelock. "Climatology of the Front Range Urban Corridor and Vicinity, Colorado." U.S. Geological Survey Professional Paper no. 1019. Washington, D.C.; U.S. Government Printing Office, 1978.)*

under *upslope* conditions, the eastern foothills and plains may receive significant precipitation or, if no storm system is present, may be blanketed by a stratiform cloud layer, which leaves the higher elevations basking in sunlight. Upslope fog is a frequent phenomenon in the mountains and occurs when moist air near the saturation point is forced upward along a sloping plain or steep mountain slope.

CYCLONIC PRECIPITATION

During a cyclonic storm, the upward spiral of air from the center of the low-pressure system produces clouds and rain as the air cools and ultimately reaches saturation. A typical cyclonic storm, intensified by orographic lifting along the

136

Western Slope of the Southern Rockies, delivers the greatest amount of precipitation to the windward slope of the mountains, while a marked decrease in precipitation occurs on the leeward side. Where the ranges tend to be in echelon, the first mountain range usually receives the largest amount of precipitation, and succeeding ranges downwind receive progressively less. As the air descends the leeward side of the mountains, it is compressed and warmed, making further precipitation unlikely and producing a distinctly dry area, or *rain shadow*, immediately to the lee of the higher ranges.

CONVECTIONAL PRECIPITATION

During the summer months, convection storms dominate the precipitation picture in the Southern Rockies. Daytime solar heating of the ground warms the adjacent air, producing an unstable air layer that may extend upward to a height of 3,000 feet or more. As the air is warmed it begins to rise, setting up organized *thermals,* columns of upward-moving air that are sought by hang-glider pilots and soaring birds alike. If the moisture content of the air is sufficient and if the air rises high enough, the cooling caused by expansion of the rising air will lead to condensation and to formation of small cumulus clouds. Continued heating of the ground will intensify the rising air currents, causing the clouds to increase in size. As the day proceeds and heat input from the sun decreases, the driving force for convection diminishes, resulting in clearing skies by late afternoon or early evening.

During the summer months, cumulus clouds typically develop over the mountains by late morning and, if sufficient moisture is present, produce widely scattered rain showers and thunderstorms by midafternoon. Although the frequency of afternoon showers in the mountains is relatively high, most are of brief duration, producing highly localized precipitation, lightning, and small hail in the higher elevations before drifting with the prevailing winds eastward over the High Plains. With enough heat and moisture, cumulus clouds can mushroom into colossal, anvil-topped thunderheads. At their worst, the subsequent cloudbursts can spawn locally violent winds combined with rain, lightning, thunder, and hail in the mountains; a second peaking of thunderstorm activity over the plains may follow in the early evening.

Mountain Winds: Mountain Waves, Chinooks, and Local Winds

Mountain ranges are windier than nearby lowlands, partly because they intercept the fast-traveling winds aloft and partly because they generate their own localized wind systems. The Rocky Mountains are the longest north-south mountain barrier in the world. When the upper-air westerlies produce a strong, deep flow of air across the Rockies, the peaks along the Continental Divide create ripples in the air currents—in much the same way that a rock in a streambed produces ripples in the surface of the water. Once initiated, these wavelike undulations, known as *mountain waves*, develop over and to the lee of the mountains before settling back into a relatively horizontal flow pattern over the Great Plains. This orographically induced flow pattern is superimposed on the upper-air Rossby wave patterns and smaller wave disturbances that are already in place. Mountain waves with vertical air movement reaching 50 miles per hour can result in the kind of clear-air turbulence feared by pilots.

The lenticular clouds often seen above the mountain ridges of the Southern Rockies during the winter months—sometimes forming caps above individual peaks—provide the best evidence that mountain-wave conditions are present in the upper air. These lens-shaped clouds, known as *mountain wave clouds*, form near the crest of the range because the air there, expanding and cooling as it is forced upward by the peaks, chills sufficiently to condense some of its water vapor; *lee wave clouds* form downwind from the crest and may occur as far as 200 miles downwind from the mountains. The smoothly contoured bases of mountain and lee wave clouds are determined by the altitude at which condensation occurs, and the rounded top corresponds to the undulating shape of the airstream.

CHINOOK WINDS

When a low-pressure system is situated to the lee of the mountains, the westerly airflow, after passing over the mountain barrier, is forced to accelerate downward along the mountains' leeward slopes. The downslope wind that results is known as a *chinook*—an Indian word that means "snow eater." Chinooks are characterized by several distinctive weather phenomena: persistent and often gusty winds, high temperatures, low humidity, and the development of a relatively stationary, cumuliform cloud known as a *crest cloud* along the windward slope of the mountains.

When viewed from the leeward side of the mountains, the shape of a crest cloud may be distinctly wall-like, its top planed horizontally by high winds, or it may be somewhat billowy, with a wind-tattered top. Crest clouds form when moist Pacific air is forced up the windward side of the mountains, where it undergoes cooling and condensation; as the air descends the leeward slopes it warms up and the clouds evaporate. With persistent strong winds, crest clouds may last for several days, and total precipitation may be significant. The amount of moisture contained in a crest cloud is variable. Gray, ominous-appearing crest clouds are associated with moisture-laden Pacific air masses; these wet crest clouds deposit a great deal of snow along the higher elevations and windward slopes of the Colorado Front Range, spilling over as downslope storms along leeward slopes to elevations of 9,500 to 9,000 feet. White crest clouds, on the other hand, generally contain minimal moisture and produce little or no precipitation on either windward or leeward slopes of the mountains. During a chinook, considerable precipitation may occur along the windward slopes of the Southern Rockies, where the air is forced to rise; the leeward or eastern slopes of the mountains, however, will receive little or no precipitation.

The rapid rise in temperature associated with the onset of a typical chinook is due to heating of the air by condensation processes on the windward side and by compression, or *adiabatic heating,* on the leeward side of the mountains. Although periodic chinooks may reduce the snowpack along the Eastern Slope of the mountains, keeping large areas of winter range open for grazing by elk, mule deer, and cattle, the low relative humidity of these winds, often below 10 percent, can also wick away valuable moisture from vegetation and exposed soil.

DESTRUCTIVE WINDSTORMS

Chinook winds attain hurricane force several times each year, with gusts exceeding 100 miles per hour. These destructive windstorms develop when unstable conditions over

Crest cloud on the Continental Divide west of Boulder. Note the smooth-topped surface of the cloud as it appears above Sawtooth Peak. *Audrey D. Benedict.*

the crest of the range are such that they initiate extreme amplification of the mountain wave patterns. Where the wave dips sharply downward along the Eastern Slope of the Southern Rockies, especially between Colorado Springs and Fort Collins, the resulting lee windstorms routinely damage roofs, shatter glass, and litter the streets with branches. Wind velocities during these windstorms are usually highest close to the eastern mountain front and near the mouths of major canyons. Boulder, at the mouth of Boulder Canyon, has recorded wind velocities in excess of 143 miles per hour—nearly twice the strength of minimum hurricane-velocity winds. Lee windstorms are most common during the winter months, particularly during January.

Local Winds: Slope Winds and Mountain and Valley Winds

Local winds are small-scale, short-lived phenomena generated by topographic differences in surface heating. They are best developed under clear skies and in the presence of a weak high-pressure system. When such conditions prevail, the air above a mountain slope warms and begins to rise, producing vertical convection currents. Because the warm air is less dense, it moves upward along the slope. Cooler air from nearby areas flows in to replace the heated air, and a small-scale circulation pattern develops. Meteorologists recognize two types of local winds: slope winds and mountain and valley winds.

Slope winds are thin layers of air that flow up the slope during the day and down at night. Upslope flow begins shortly after sunrise, as the mountain slopes begin to warm, reaching maximum intensity around noontime. By late afternoon the upslope wind has abated, and within half an hour after sunset, it is replaced by a downslope wind that develops as the slopes and the adjacent air layer begin to cool; because of its increased density, the cool air flows rapidly downslope, displacing warm air in the valley bottom.

Mountain and valley winds blow upvalley during the day and downvalley at night, traveling essentially at right angles to the slope winds. Although controlled by similar thermal responses, mountain and valley winds involve greater thermal contrast and a larger air mass than slope winds. During stormy or windy weather, however, the daily pattern of slope winds and mountain-valley circulation may be highly modified or even nonexistent. Valley winds, blowing from the valley toward the mountain, begin shortly after sunrise, reaching a maximum around mid-day and diminishing by sunset. After sunset, as the pool of cold air in the valley bottom begins to build, valley winds are replaced by a mountain or downvalley wind. The cold-air drainage typically associated with mountain winds may significantly delay the budding and flowering of trees and herbaceous plants in the path of the cold air.

Seasonal Weather Patterns

Winter

Winter climate in the Southern Rockies is influenced by storm systems originating over the Pacific Ocean and by high pressure centering over the Great Basin. In most areas, the seasonal snowpack above 10,000 feet begins to accumulate in late October and reaches its maximum depth in mid-April. During most winters, frequent storms produce moderate amounts of dry, powdery snow. Consequently, the mountain resort developments of the Southern Rockies rank among the top destinations in North America for downhill and cross-country skiers. More important, however, the mountain snowpack—specifically because of its depth and water content—is the lifeblood of the watersheds of the Rio Grande, the Colorado, the Canadian, the Pecos, the North and South Platte, and the Arkansas rivers.

Variations in the winter storm patterns affecting the Southern Rockies correspond largely to differences in the orientation of the jet stream and in the air mass source areas and trajectories. Meteorologists recognize four main winter storm patterns, designated here by source area and route of passage: (1) cool Pacific, tracking from the northwest; (2) cool and warm Pacific, tracking from the west; (3) warm Pacific, tracking from the southwest; and (4) Gulf of Mexico, the air mass but not the storm system tracking from the south.

STORM SYSTEMS TRACKING
FROM THE PACIFIC NORTHWEST

A high percentage of early and midwinter snowfall is generated by migrating cyclonic storms that originate over the cool Pacific Ocean (in the Pacific Northwest) and follow a southeasterly route that parallels the Columbia River Valley on the border between Oregon and Washington and the Snake River area of southern Idaho and then sweeps south across the Wyoming Basin. This route coincides with the zone of maximum westerlies and the main axis of the polar jet stream—at a latitude of about 40° north. Precipitation associated with this flow tends to come in relatively frequent storms that drop light to moderate amounts of snow. In general, the amount of precipitation delivered by these storms increases with elevation on the windward slopes of the mountains, usually reaching a maximum slightly windward of the mountain crests; the leeward slopes, especially those east of the Continental Divide, receive relatively little precipitation from these storms. Storm systems tracking southeast from the cool Pacific deliver their heaviest snows to the Park Range. Average annual snowfall at Steamboat Springs, at the western edge of the Park Range, is 166 inches; at Buffalo Pass (10,180 feet), just short of the crest of the Park Range, average annual snowfall is nearly twice that reported for Steamboat.

STORM SYSTEMS TRACKING FROM THE WEST

When the main axis of the winter jet stream crosses the Southern Rockies from the west or southwest, Pacific air is channeled across California, often pumping large quantities of moist, unstable air into the region. With strong westerly flow, air masses originating over both the warm and cool Pacific source areas penetrate the continent with sufficient moisture to produce substantial snowfalls in the Southern Rockies before continuing east. Some of the most intense winter storms occur when the jet stream plunges southward west of the mountains and loops northward once again just east of the mountain front. Under these conditions, a low-pressure center often forms in western Colorado or northwestern New Mexico, moving slowly eastward and producing substantial snowfall on the Eastern Slope as well as in the central and southern mountains.

STORM SYSTEMS TRACKING FROM THE SOUTHWEST

Air masses originating over the warm Pacific generally enter the Southern Rockies from the southwest and are capable of transporting larger quantities of moisture than those originating over the cool Pacific. Considerably fewer of these systems, however, reach the Southern Rockies. For these storms to successfully penetrate the region, their trajectory must angle northwest across Arizona and New Mexico, lingering long enough to draw up large quantities of tropical Pacific air. Maximum winter precipitation from these storms occurs in the San Juan Range, the first major barrier to storm systems tracking from the west and southwest. Snowfall along the windward side of the San Juans often exceeds 30 feet; during the winter of 1978–79, Wolf Creek Pass received nearly 70 feet of snow, establishing a Southern Rocky Mountain record for the greatest snowfall in one season.

STORMS NOURISHED BY MOISTURE
FROM THE GULF OF MEXICO

Major snowstorms can occur along the Eastern Slope of the Southern Rockies as the result of upslope winds laden with moisture carried northward from the Gulf of Mexico. This influx of Gulf air masses is generated by the counterclockwise flow of air around low-pressure areas moving across New Mexico and southern Colorado; the presence of a stalled, cut-off low known as an *Albuquerque low* can produce heavy snowfalls as the Gulf air is forced to rise up the Eastern Slopes of the Southern Rockies. If the low-pressure system is slow to migrate eastward, upslope conditions can persist for several days. Generally, however, upslope conditions are surprisingly shallow; the moisture-laden air being swept toward the Rockies may be only 2,000 to 3,000 feet thick. People looking down on an upslope storm from higher elevations in the mountains often view a sea of clouds swirling in slow motion as they break against the mountain front like waves on a beach. At times, even a low ridge like the Palmer Divide, located at 7,500 feet between Colorado Springs and Denver, can arrest a north-moving upslope — leaving Denver basking in sunshine while Colorado Springs remains overcast.

Occasionally, cold, polar air masses are able to spread south over the High Plains, east of the Rockies, causing a sudden drop in temperature along the eastern mountain front and effectively blocking the passage of cyclonic storms tracking from the Pacific. This situation can produce severe and dangerous blizzard conditions wherever the southern edge of the cold, dry air mass meets warm, moist air moving north from the Gulf of Mexico. These storms ordinarily move in a northeasterly direction, blanketing the High Plains with several inches of snow, but are typically too shallow to push westward over the mountains. Consequently, the High Plains and Eastern Slope experience severe winter storms while areas west of the Continental Divide remain clear and settled.

Spring

Spring in the Southern Rockies tends to be wet and windy. The months of March, April, and May have a distinct character that sets them apart from the winter months. From about the time of the vernal equinox (toward the end of March) through the first two weeks in June, large quantities of moisture periodically stream into the region, especially along the Eastern Slope. The diminished strength of the westerlies allows Gulf air masses to push their way northward into the Great Plains with increased frequency, resulting in heavy spring precipitation both west and east of the Continental Divide. In 1921, a spectacular April upslope storm produced 76 inches of snow in a single twenty-four–hour period at Silver Lake in the Colorado Front Range — the largest twenty-four–hour snowfall ever recorded in North America. At nearby Berthoud Pass, the total snowfall received during the first two weeks of April that same year was nearly 10 feet. Throughout the higher elevations of the Southern Rockies, the snowpack generally reaches its maximum in April, then declines steadily, disappearing almost entirely from lower and mid-elevation areas by mid-June. Temperatures climb rapidly, with about a 10° increase in the mean occurring between April and May. In the mountains, skiers in shirt sleeves revel in the sunshine, carving graceful arcs through fine beds of spring, or *corn*, snow.

Summer

Toward the end of June, the zone of strong midlatitude westerlies shifts northward to Canada, and with them go the cyclonic storms and strong winds of autumn and winter. Consequently, the Bermuda High (situated over the western Atlantic) is able to produce a strong low of moist air from the Gulf of Mexico and north from the tropical Pacific (off the west coast of Mexico) toward the mountains. Climatologists refer to this phenomenon as the *Arizona summer monsoon* because of its impact on the climate of Arizona and surrounding regions. During the months of July and August, and in early September, surges of moist air spread across the southern, southwestern, and eastern portions of the Southern Rockies under the influence of the Bermuda High. Consequently, greater summer precipitation occurs in southern ranges such as the San Juans, Sangre de Cristos, and Wet Mountains than in more northerly ranges such as the Elk Mountains and the Park, Sierra Madre, and Colorado

Front ranges. These northern ranges typically remain under the influence of comparatively dry air masses that must flow east across the arid western interior (Nevada and Utah).

Throughout the summer months, influxes of Gulf moisture fuel the afternoon convective showers and thunderstorms that rumble through the mountains. Occasionally, rainy spells lasting two or three days occur when a persistent tongue of moist air positions itself over the region. When the moist air masses withdraw from the region, cloud buildup may occur, but afternoon convection showers become rare and are quite light. Because orographic lifting of warm, moist air amplifies the processes of convection, severe thunderstorms and flash flooding can occur under certain conditions. Thunderstorms can pose a distinct hazard to the above-timberline hiker and climber; lightning-caused deaths are not uncommon in the Southern Rockies. Hikers should abandon ridges and summit areas when thunderstorms threaten.

Autumn

By mid-September, the Bermuda High has begun its annual migration toward the equator, reducing the amount of Gulf moisture being channeled toward the Southern Rockies. Because the westerlies are not yet ensconced over the Southern Rockies, they guide only occasional storms across the mountains. Thus begins what many residents feel is the Southern Rockies' most beautiful time of the year — Indian summer. The blue of the sky intensifies and the rich hues of autumn paint the landscape in a brilliant wash of color.

In September and October, more than 50 percent of the days are bright and sunny. In most areas, temperatures are often 40 degrees higher in the afternoon than at dawn. Nighttime temperatures above 9,000 feet average below freezing on about half the nights in September, on most of the nights in October, and on every night in November. Passing storms begin to dust the higher mountains with snow in September. By the end of October, winter has gained a firmer foothold at higher elevations. At lower elevations and in the southern portion of the Southern Rockies, precipitation may continue through October as rain rather than as snow. During most years, the westerlies are firmly positioned over the Southern Rockies by December, tracking Pacific storm sys-

CLIMATIC DATA FOR SELECTED STATIONS IN THE SOUTHERN ROCKIES

Station	Elev. (Ft.)	Av. Temp. (°F) Jan.	July	Yearly Precip.
High Plains and Piedmont (Eastern Slope)				
Casper (WY)	5,322 ft.	22	62	16"
Cheyenne (WY)	6,139 ft.	27	68	15"
Denver (CO)	5,292 ft.	29	73	15"
Boulder (CO)	5,420 ft.	34	74	18"
Walsenburg (CO)	6,221 ft.	34	72	15"
Cimarron (NM)	6,427 ft.	34	74	15"
Las Vegas (NV)	6,470 ft.	29	68	17"
High Mountain Basins and Valleys				
Centennial (WY)	8,074 ft.	26	68	16"
Fraser (CO)	8,574 ft.	13	55	17"
Gunnison (CO)	7,664 ft.	10	62	11"
Eagle (CO)	6,497 ft.	18	66	10"
Alamosa (CO)	7,536 ft.	17	64	6"
Lower Western Valleys				
Saratoga (WY)	6,786 ft.	21	71	11"
Craig (CO)	6,285 ft.	18	67	13"
Grand Junction (CO)	4,843 ft.	26	79	8"
Cedaredge (CO)	6,180 ft.	27	72	12"
Durango (CO)	6,550 ft.	26	68	18"
Mesa Verde NP	7,070 ft.	30	73	17"
Espanola (NM)	5,595 ft.	30	70	10"
Mountain Regions				
Colorado Front Range				
Estes Park (CO)	7,522 ft.	26	62	16"
Berthoud Pass	11,314 ft.	10	51	36"
Grand Lake (CO)	8,680 ft.	15	55	20"
Rampart Range				
Ruxton Park (CO)	9,050 ft.	19	56	23"
Sangre de Cristo Range and Jemez Mountains				
North Lake (CO)	8,800 ft.	25	60	41"
Red River (NM)	8,676 ft.	19	58	18"
Jemez Springs (NM)	6,100 ft.	30	66	17"
San Juan Mountains				
Wolf Creek Pass	10,642 ft.	17	52	46"
Rico (CO)	8,700 ft.	21	58	26"
Silverton (CO)	9,322 ft.	17	56	22"
Elk Mountains and Sawatch Range				
Leadville (CO)	10,188 ft.	18	57	19"
Aspen (CO)	7,928 ft.	21	62	19"
Crested Butte (CO)	8,800 ft.	13	58	25"
Park Range				
Steamboat Springs (CO)	6,770 ft.	15	62	23"

tems through the region at regular intervals until the following June.

Regional Climatic Patterns

Distinct patterns begin to emerge as we look at the varied climates of the Southern Rockies. The region can be broken into four geographic divisions: the High Plains and Piedmont areas east of the mountains; (2) the high mountain basins and valleys; (3) the lower western valleys and plateaus; and (4) the mountain ranges. The climates of each of these areas reflect differences in latitude, elevation, prevailing and seasonal storm tracks, and slope position (windward or leeward). Climatic characteristics for each regional division are summarized below, with specific data provided for representative stations within each division. Differences between individual mountain ranges are significant enough to warrant their division into eight subregions. Precipitation amounts provided in the summaries refer to the liquid equivalent of rainfall, snow, sleet, or hail collected in precipitation storage gauges; average annual precipitation amounts for a given site are based on data collected over a twenty-five–year period (1961–85).

CHAPTER NINE

The Winter Landscape

SNOW IS A critical component of mountain ecosystems. In the Southern Rockies, topographic and climatic diversity combine to produce a complex regional snowfall pattern. Above 9,000 feet, snow may cover the ground more or less continuously for as long as nine months; above timberline, in certain alpine basins, it may persist from one year to the next. Variations in the depth, duration, and other physical characteristics of the mountain snowpack influence landscape processes, control the distribution and composition of plant communities, and determine the adaptations that plants and animals must have for survival.

Snow Crystals

All precipitation starts as water vapor in the atmosphere. For snow crystals to form, the air at upper levels in the atmosphere must be at or below freezing and must contain minute particles, called freezing nuclei, around which ice crystallization can occur. Bacteria, as well as clay minerals, dust, minute crystals of sea salt, and even splinters of ice from a shattered, previously formed snow crystal, can serve as nuclei for ice-crystal growth. The embryonic ice crystal is a hexagonal prism, its shape determined by the orderly arrangement of water molecules within the crystal; the lattice of a single snow crystal may contain as many as 100 million water molecules.

The ultimate shape and size of a snow crystal depends on the temperature and the amount of moisture in the cloud in which it forms. In general, large, intricate crystals form at relatively warm cloud temperatures when ample water vapor is present; small, less intricate crystals form at low temperatures when the air holds less moisture. Most snow

149

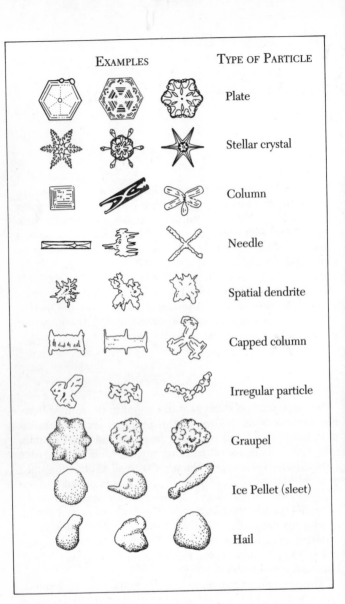

EXAMPLES	TYPE OF PARTICLE
	Plate
	Stellar crystal
	Column
	Needle
	Spatial dendrite
	Capped column
	Irregular particle
	Graupel
	Ice Pellet (sleet)
	Hail

The ten basic forms of solid precipitation as summarized in the International Snow Classification system. *(After La Chapelle, Edward R., Field Guide to Snow Crystals. 1969. University of Washington Press: Seattle.)*

THE SOUTHERN ROCKIES

crystals follow a hexagonal pattern; the most common is the stellar crystal—a flat, star-shaped crystal with delicate, branching arms. Less common are columnar crystals, which form in very cold clouds with limited moisture supplies; these hollow crystals are responsible for producing the colored halos you sometimes see around the sun or the moon. Needle crystals are produced when the air temperature during a snowstorm is near the freezing point. When a snow crystal evolves in or travels through a cloud composed of super-cooled water droplets, it collects a coating of rime. Riming tends to obscure the hexagonal form of the parent crystal, giving it a distinctly whiter and more opaque appearance. When riming continues to such an extent that the original crystal is unrecognizable or nearly so, the result is a grain-like crystal called *graupel,* or soft hail; much rain is melted graupel.

Most of the snow crystals we see have been modified to some degree during their journey to Earth. Turbulent winds or violent updrafts may break off the branches of stellar crystals, or crystals may strike others as they fall and become attached to them. The term *snowflake,* often used errone-ously to refer to a single snow crystal, refers to an assem-blage of individual snow crystals, typically stellar crystals, that have collided and remained hooked together during their fall through the atmosphere. A fresh deposit of snow dominated by stellar crystals tends to be fluffy and relatively cohesive because of the way the branches of the crystals in-terlock with one another. This cohesion produces spectacu-lar snow canopies on tree branches, fence posts, and other exposed objects.

Snowpack Structure

A snowpack consists of many individual layers of snow, each representing a distinct storm or depositional interval. The accumulation of snow on the ground is in many ways analogous to the formation of a sedimentary rock, with each layer reflecting the nature of its origin. Differences between layers may be well defined or almost indistinguishable. Typi-cally, thick layers are deposited by prolonged snowfalls or by wind transport. Thin layers may reflect events that oc-curred at the snow surface between storms, such as a brief interval of wind redistribution or the development of an ice crust resulting from melting and refreezing.

During most of the winter, a temperature gradient exists within the snowpack as a result of differences in the heat energy budget at the snow surface and in the amount of heat flowing into the pack from the ground. The average temperature gradient through a snowpack is determined by the thickness of the pack and the mean snow surface temperature. Under spring conditions, when the snowpack warms to the melting point throughout, temperature gradients vanish and the snowpack becomes *isothermal* (the same temperature throughout).

Snow Metamorphism

Unlike most natural substances, snow exists quite close to its melting point. Newly fallen snow is especially unstable. A few days after deposition it is virtually impossible to identify the original crystalline components of a new storm layer. In contrast to glacier ice, the natural snow deposit is both porous and permeable — an emulsion of ice, air, water vapor, and, sometimes, liquid water. These important characteristics allow air and water vapor to circulate freely through the ice skeleton of the snowpack, transferring water molecules from one area to another. As a result, the changes that begin when the snow crystal forms continue within the snowpack after deposition. The term *metamorphism* is used by the snow scientist to refer to changes in snow texture caused by pressure and temperature conditions. Two types of metamorphism — *equi-temperature* (ET) and *temperature-gradient* (TG) — occur in a dry, seasonal snowpack; a third type, called *melt-freeze*, takes place when snowpack temperatures reach 32°F throughout.

EQUI-TEMPERATURE (ET) METAMORPHISM

Equi-temperature metamorphism occurs only in snow layers that are essentially the same temperature throughout. Common in a newly fallen snow layer, the beginning stages of ET metamorphism require anywhere from a few hours at warm temperatures to a few days at cold temperatures; it proceeds most rapidly at temperatures close to the freezing point. New-fallen snow crystals, especially the finely

THE SOUTHERN ROCKIES

branched stellar crystals, are thermodynamically unstable. The most stable shape for a snow crystal to assume in its new environment on Earth is that of a sphere. To achieve this, water vapor molecules must be transferred from crystal corners and dendritic branches toward the center of the crystal. The result of this transfer of water vapor is a progressive rounding of the original snow crystal, which reduces the ratio of surface area to volume and nearly obliterates the original crystal shape.

The predominate grain size of ET crystals is about .04 inches. The reduction in the space occupied by each crystal, as well as the pressure exerted by subsequent snow layers, cause the snowpack to compact or settle. As the density of the snow increases, individual ice grains tend to become bonded together along their points of contact. This process, known as *sintering*, greatly enhances the mechanical strength of the snow layer. During the final stages of ET metamorphism in a seasonal snowpack, the snow assumes the fine-grained texture typical of *old snow*; the *powder snow* favored by skiers is a transitional stage between new and old snow. In alpine areas, where portions of the snowpack may persist from one year to the next, periodic melting and refreezing of old snow results in *firn*, or *névé* — dense snow at least one year old.

TEMPERATURE-GRADIENT (TG) METAMORPHISM

In contrast to ET metamorphism, temperature-gradient metamorphism occurs in response to a strong temperature gradient in the snowpack. In a moderate climate, snow layers near the ground are usually warmer than those near the surface of the snowpack because of the heat given off by the Earth. As snow accumulates, the temperature gradient generated by the upward flow of stored heat causes water vapor to flow from warmer snow layers to colder snow layers. Water vapor transfers from warm crystal to colder crystal throughout the snowpack until the entire mass of snow has passed through the water-vapor stage and been redeposited in the form of completely new crystals. The new crystals bear no resemblance to the original precipitated snow or to the rounded ice grains produced by ET metamorphism. The large, fragile TG crystals are characterized by a distinctly layered or steplike structure, by alignment in vertical growth

Angular crystals, layering has not begun	Small and poorly layered crystals	Well-developed depth hoar with prominent layering

Progressive stages in the development of depth hoar. (*After La Chapelle, Edward R.*, Field Guide to Snow Crystals. *1969. University of Washington Press: Seattle.*)

columns that reflect the direction of vapor diffusion in the snowpack, and by the virtual absence of sintering.

The net result of TG metamorphism is a general weakening of the snowpack. Snow layers in which TG metamorphism is well advanced tend to collapse into a cohesionless mass of crystals at the slightest disturbance. Because TG metamorphism proceeds most rapidly in warmer snow layers, the process generally begins along the base of the snowpack. Climatic conditions in the Southern Rockies provide an ideal setting for the formation of TG layers, or *depth hoar,* because the snow cover is relatively thin and because ambient air temperatures are cold — resulting in steep snow-temperature gradients. Optimum conditions for TG metamorphism are found on north-facing slopes and in deep, shaded gullies; the probability of forming a TG layer is highest early in the winter when the snowpack is relatively thin and unconsolidated. TG layers more than 3 feet thick have been observed in Colorado.

MELT-FREEZE METAMORPHISM

The third type of metamorphism is controlled by the presence of free water in the snowpack. Melt-freeze metamorphism dominates during occasional midwinter warm periods and during the spring thaw, when the snowpack is essentially isothermal. With the presence of free water in the snowpack, either from melting snow or from rainfall, temperature gradients and their effects all but vanish. Solar heating of the snow surface is the primary cause of melting; newly fallen snow may reflect 80 to 90 percent of the incoming solar radiation, while old granular snow may reflect as little as 40 percent.

The largest amounts of free water will be found adjacent to exposed rocks or trees—terrain features that act as efficient absorbers of radiation and therefore increase the rate of melt. When temperatures are low, ice grains freeze together along their points of contact to form large, multigranular units. Occasionally, meltwater freezes at the surface of the snowpack to form thin sheets of clear ice. These thin ice sheets act like glass in a greenhouse to trap heat underneath and promote further snowmelt.

In melt-freeze metamorphism, the mechanical strength of the snowpack increases during the freeze portion of the cycle and decreases rapidly with the onset of warmer temperatures. This cyclic increase and decrease of snowpack strength is a familiar phenomenon to the spring skier or early summer hiker who has traversed the ice-crusted snow of morning only to sink knee deep in mid-day slush. Under some conditions, melt-freeze metamorphism can also trigger avalanches. Wet-snow instability should be expected after late spring snowstorms when buried ice layers can serve as gliding surfaces for the overlying snow.

Snow in Motion

Of the external forces affecting snow in the Southern Rockies, few are as important as wind. Snow crystals falling to Earth under calm conditions construct a delicate, fluffy mass. Light winds deflect snow in a horizontal direction, driving it against the windward sides of trees or other obstacles. Subjecting a fragile stellar crystal to strong winds is like putting it in a rock polisher. Wind processing shatters the delicate crystals, sorting the fragments by size before depositing them in firm, slablike layers.

The amount of snow transported by the wind depends upon the character of the snow, the nature of the snow surface, and the speed of the wind. The largest amounts are transported during or immediately after storm periods, since newly fallen snow is especially susceptible to wind erosion. Wet snow, on the other hand, resists movement by wind. The density of wind-deposited snow averages two to four times that of snow that falls in a wind-protected site. As a result, wind-drifted snow exhibits amazing strength; well-developed wind slab can fully support the weight of a person on skis or a small over-snow vehicle. The strength of wind-deposited snow is also a factor in the stability and longevity of the drifts that form to the lee of terrain obstacles.

The distribution of snow in the mountain landscape is largely controlled by wind. Mountain terrain is highly irregular, disrupting the free flow of air and exerting a variable frictional force on the wind, which causes it to scour snow from one area and redeposit it in another. Snow is generally eroded from areas where wind speed is increasing and redeposited in areas where the wind is forced to decelerate because of surface obstructions. Wind-transported snow tends to accumulate in localized zones instead of spreading out evenly across the landscape. Accumulation areas are usually depressions bounded by rock outcroppings or groups of trees. The deepest accumulations typically occur in gullies and bowls and along gully walls. Small-scale surface features such as rocks, bushes, and fallen trees can also force the wind to decelerate, producing a variety of beautiful drift forms to the lee of the obstacle.

Wind Sculpture

SASTRUGI

In many alpine areas of the Southern Rockies, beautiful beveled drifts form wherever windblown snow accumulates. These are called *sastrugi,* a word first applied by the Russians to similar wavelike drifts in the Arctic tundra. Sastrugi form ridges parallel to the prevailing winds, with an abrupt, scoured edge pointing into the wind; they are often shaped like the curl of a wave. Because of the durability of wind-packed snow, sastrugi often continue to develop throughout the winter months as wind scour and sublimation rework the original drift patterns.

CORNICES

Where snow accumulates along ridge crests and other sharp breaks in slope, *cornices* develop as the prevailing winds pull snow over the top of a ridge and pack it on the leeward slope in a concave curl to match the eddying air current. The cornice shapes that result resemble waves of frozen surf. Successive snow layers are added to the cornice during each period of snow transport, each layer extending

Sastrugi on Niwot Ridge, Colorado Front Range.
James B. Benedict.

out over the cornice face as a cantilevered sheet; a cornice
may extend as far as 50 feet upward and outward from the
point where it forms. Throughout its life, the cornice de-
forms steadily outward and downward over the slope, its cantilevered projections in an increasingly precarious balance
with the forces of gravity. Collapsing cornices or even falling cornice blocks occasionally trigger avalanches; avalanche
patrols at ski areas routinely destroy potentially dangerous
cornices that develop at the tops of ski runs. Hikers and
skiers should exercise extreme caution around cornices and
remember that these formations can break a considerable
distance back from their edges.

Snow Avalanches

Few natural hazards in the Southern Rockies are more frightening — or more common — than the avalanche. A large avalanche in the Southern Rockies can transport as much as 100,000 tons of snow and can produce a horizontal thrust that ranges between 5 and 50 tons per square meter; thrusts between 3 and 10 tons per square meter can destroy wood-frame structures and uproot mature Engelmann spruce. Fast and deadly, fractures in the snow may propagate as rapidly as 350 feet per second. Once in motion, an avalanche of loose, dry snow may reach a velocity of nearly 140 miles per hour.

Areas such as Red Mountain and Wolf Creek passes (in the San Juan Mountains) and Loveland and Berthoud passes (in the Colorado Front Range) are notorious for their avalanche danger. The narrow, winding road over Red Mountain Pass is threatened by more than twenty named, active avalanche chutes. One of the most compelling reasons for the construction of the Eisenhower Memorial Tunnel under the Continental Divide was to provide a safe detour for Interstate 70 around Loveland Pass, particularly because of the heavy traffic between the Eastern Slope metropolitan areas and the mountain ski resorts. Avalanche sheds, similar to those used in the Cascades of Washington and in Europe, now shelter the most dangerous stretches of all-season highway in the San Juans.

Avalanches occur when the gravitational or external forces acting on a snow slope overcome the forces that tend to keep the snow in place. In the Southern Rockies, avalanches start most frequently on slopes with average gradients of 30 to 45 degrees; the average gradient for the entire avalanche path, however, is much less — as little as 15 degrees in some cases. The slope in the runout zone is often very gentle and sometimes completely flat. Avalanche paths in forested areas are conspicuous, appearing as vertical or curving swaths cut through the forest; many begin above timberline, tracking downward through spruce and fir, and have runout zones in grassy or brushy areas at the base of the slope. Frequent avalanche activity along the same path will prevent the regrowth of conifers along the slide route but may allow other types of vegetation, particularly pioneer species such

THE SOUTHERN ROCKIES

as aspen and willow, which can regenerate from their roots, to colonize the avalanche chute. Those plants that thrive must be able to absorb the impact of small slides and to adapt to the environmental changes characteristic of the open, sunny track.

Avalanches fall into two categories — *loose-snow avalanches* and *slab avalanches* — based on differences in the conditions that produce them and in their behavior. A loose-snow avalanche is a cohesionless failure of dry or wet snow. Slab avalanches, on the other hand, represent failure of a cohesive mass of snow. Of the two types, loose-snow avalanches are more common, but slab avalanches usually involve much more snow.

LOOSE-SNOW AVALANCHES

Fluffy, new-fallen snow on steep slopes is highly unstable. With little internal cohesion to hold the snow in place, a slight disturbance in equilibrium is all that is necessary to get small masses of snow moving downslope. The exact angle of repose for a new snow layer depends on the temperature, wetness, and shape of the snow crystals. Wet snow, for example, has very little strength for its weight and can avalanche off slopes as gentle as 15 degrees. New-fallen, dry snow generally has enough cohesion to cling to a 30-degree slope but exhibits increasing instability on steeper slopes.

Most loose-snow avalanches take the form of small, shallow slides called *sluffs*. They occur with regularity throughout the winter, and many small slides may take place during a single snowstorm. Most begin from a single starting point, spreading out to form a fan-shaped snow deposit. In some cases, loose-snow avalanches can have a stabilizing influence on the mountain snowpack, since frequent small sluffs on the steepest slopes force a continual adjustment in the snow and may prevent major slides from developing.

SLAB AVALANCHES

During a slab avalanche, the snow breaks away as a unit, with enough internal cohesion to release a large, slablike region of the snow slope at the same moment. Slab avalanches can originate in any type of snow, from old to newly fallen and from dry to wet. The starting zone of the avalanche is marked by a smooth, wall-like fracture line — called a *crown* — that may extend across a slope for many yards. Once released, the slab breaks into smaller blocks that tumble and collide with one another as they roar down the avalanche track. The size of the blocks depends on the cohesiveness of the original slab and the roughness of the terrain over which the avalanche travels. When a slab avalanche finally comes to rest, the fine particles and the larger chunks sinter rapidly to form a cementlike mass.

Slab failure is initiated when shear stress exceeds shear strength at the bed surface — the main sliding surface of the slab. Slab failures are most likely to start on slopes in the 30- to 45-degree range. In the San Juan Mountains, for example, 72 percent of the slab avalanches occurring during a four-year period had starting zones located between 30 and 45 degrees; the range of the total sample was 25 to 48 degrees. The mechanics of slab failure are complex. Several situations may set the stage for slab failure: the loading of an avalanche-prone slope by wind redistribution of older snow, a high-intensity snowfall, rapid impact (cornice collapse, explosive blast, etc.), the added load of one or more skiers traversing the slab, weakening of the bed surface by temperature-gradient metamorphism, or weakening of the bed surface due to melting.

Hard slabs, prevalent on the Eastern Slope, are composed of snow that has undergone extensive aging and compaction or has been deposited by strong winds; slides composed of these massive blocks are capable of causing tremendous damage. Soft slabs, on the other hand, tend to break into smaller chunks and may lose their initial character entirely as they tumble about on their journey downhill. Many of the massive avalanches west of the Continental Divide are of the soft-slab type. Wet slabs, initiated by intense spring melting or by rainfall, flow downhill as a fluid mass of chunks and smaller particles.

AVALANCHE SAFETY

Avalanches pose a serious threat to backcountry travel. Deaths from avalanches occur with increasing frequency as winter use of the mountains intensifies. In areas where avalanches are a possibility, each member of a group should continually evaluate the terrain for high-risk areas and should carry a basketless ski pole or a sectional avalanche probe to help in locating victims in the event of a slide; brightly colored avalanche cords or electronic transceivers are also highly recommended for each member of the party. Because changes in weather often provide the best clues to when and where avalanches are likely to occur, backcountry travelers should consult regional weather services for up-to-date information. Roughly 80 percent of all avalanches occur during a storm interval or within twenty-four hours after its passage. Snow is a complex material — there is no substitute for exercising caution in winter backcountry travel. Snow recreationists are encouraged to refer to the excellent references on snow and avalanches listed in the bibliography.

Snow and Life

Snow and winter climatic conditions pose a variety of stresses for plants and animals. Plants, being relatively immobile, respond to environmental extremes through morphological and physiological adaptations. Most cold-blooded animals — insects, reptiles, amphibians, and fish — deal with environmental extremes by escaping them through hibernation or dormancy. Many warm-blooded animals choose to avoid the rigors of winter through migration. Those that overwinter acclimatize to seasonal environmental change by a combination of behavioral and physiological mechanisms. Behavioral mechanisms include the use of advantageous microclimates, adjustments in daily activity patterns, nest building, and communal nesting; physiological mechanisms include periodic torpidity, body-weight reduction, increased insulation, adjustments in the basal metabolic rate, and a variety of forms of thermogenesis, or metabolic heat production. Certain animals, such as the snowshoe hare and the white-tailed ptarmigan, also exhibit morphological adaptations that allow them to cope with, and to some degree even exploit, the winter snowpack.

With regard to life, the most important property of snow is its ability to insulate the ground — not only against low minimum temperatures but also against drastic fluctuations in temperature. It is this property that protects plants, cold-blooded animals, and small mammals from the harsh environment above the snow surface. With the approach of winter, the ground surface cools and then begins to freeze. If there is little or no snow cover, air temperatures at ground level fluctuate diurnally, and the ground will continue freezing to considerable depths. Small mammals — shrews, mice, voles, and pocket gophers — have little physiological capability to withstand environmental extremes for long periods of time. Once the snow accumulates to a depth of about 6 inches, however, small mammals are able to construct tunnels and runways along the base of the snowpack, where they are protected by the moderating influence of the snow.

For those mammals small enough to utilize the subnivean (under-snow) environment, life follows an easy rhythm of sleeping, feeding from a supply of cached food, and foraging along snow tunnels for new sources of food (roots, buds, bark, fungi, etc.). The fear of predation is somewhat lessened, although coyotes and weasels still zigzag over the snow surface listening for faint squeals and scratchings, sounds they can hear through 10 to 12 inches of snow. Communal nesting — a behavioral thermoregulation mechanism — is common for many small mammals. In areas where the snow cover lingers into early summer, some mice and voles may even breed beneath the snow. The southern red-backed vole, an animal characteristic of the subalpine forest in the Southern Rockies, begins breeding in late March, beneath a continuous snow cover up to 100 inches thick.

Throughout much of the winter, the subnivean environment is dark and virtually silent. A 12-inch snow cover transmits only 8 percent of the sunlight reaching the snow surface; midwinter snow depths of 20 inches transmit no light at all. The air beneath the snow is also surprisingly moist. Gaseous by-products produced by continuing bacterial decay at the soil surface are transported upward through the snowpack with the rising water vapor. Carbon dioxide, being relatively heavy, tends to settle into depressions along the base of the snowpack. To avoid concentrations of this gas, voles frequently construct ventilation shafts to the snow surface. These distinctive little holes are common during early winter but become less common after January. It is possible that the development of extensive zones of depth hoar may increase air space along the base of the pack and thus improve subnivean air quality as the winter progresses. As spring approaches, melt-freeze metamorphism destroys the insulative capacity of the snow and increases the amount of light transmitted to the ground surface. This increase in light transmission is believed to play a role in triggering subnivean

THE SOUTHERN ROCKIES

reproductive behavior in many small mammals, so that breeding can take place during or immediately after snowmelt.

Mammals and birds unable to utilize the subnivean environment must cope continually with changes in the distribution, depth, and character of the snowpack if they are to survive. For mule deer, the costs of moving and foraging in deep snow are high. Severe winters can cause massive die-offs. Studies in Middle Park have shown that mule deer abandon all areas where snow depths exceed 18 inches. In some areas, snow may limit usable winter range for deer to less than 1 percent of their normal summer range. Deep snow can also cause critical changes in dietary composition by forcing deer to eat a higher percentage of less-digestible browse—resulting in a decrease in the digestive bacteria necessary to process food effectively. Deer faced with such a diet may starve, their stomachs full of undigestible plant fiber. With their longer legs, elk can tolerate deeper snows but will generally migrate to lower elevations to avoid it. Similarly, when snow blankets the high valleys and alpine basins of the Southern Rockies, bighorn sheep confine their midwinter wanderings to areas sometimes no more than half a mile across; wind-scoured uplands, south-facing slopes, and steep, broken cliffs become preferred habitat at such times.

The snowshoe hare is the undisputed master of deep snow, with its camouflage-white coat and its broad, snowshoe-shaped feet. The white-tailed ptarmigan, like the snowshoe hare, changes to a white winter plumage in late fall and grows stiff mats of feathers on each toe. Lack of sufficient snow when ptarmigan are changing from brown to white, however, can subject them to higher levels of predation than at other seasons. Molting of the white winter plumage, although largely controlled by day length, is apparently also affected by the amount of snow cover present in tundra breeding areas.

Most jumping mammals, such as rabbits and hares, support themselves on all four feet at once and have a distinct advantage in deep snow over predators such as coyotes and foxes, which use the walk-jog-trot-run mode of travel. A coyote can walk easily in 6 inches of new snow, but when the snow is much deeper, the animal must expend more energy to move and is less effective in catching its prey. Smaller predators, such as weasels and martens, bound easily across the snow, initially supported on the two front feet,

White-tailed ptarmigan. *James B. Benedict.*

followed by a quick and efficient transfer of the hind feet into the prints of the front feet. For flying predators, such as owls and hawks, the snow is a fresh, white canvas; the unwary rabbit scampering across the snow surface provides an effortless target.

How readily an animal is able to cope with metamorphic changes in the snowpack depends on the weight of the animal and the structure of its legs and feet. Small and medium-sized mammals continue to maintain their advantage. Recognizing the usefulness of compacted snow, rabbits, hares, tree squirrels, and mice will often reuse trails between feeding areas. White-tailed ptarmigan, on the other hand, move away from areas where the snow has been compacted by wind or glazed by ice crusts, in order to find soft snow in which to construct their roosting burrows. Under some conditions, the snow surface may be so firm that a hunting coyote is unable to dig through it to catch small mammals. Wind slab and ice crusts can prove deadly for elk, deer, and pronghorn, which are heavy in relation to the bearing surface of their hooves; they sink readily into soft snow and break through most crusts—which is extremely costly in terms of expended energy. Deep snow can also immobilize a fleeing deer and make it easy prey for a coyote or mountain lion.

CHAPTER TEN

Landscape Patterns

APPROACHING THE SOUTHERN Rockies from the east, across the grasslands of the Great Plains, the most striking pattern that can be seen is the altitudinal zonation of the vegetation. Changes in the distribution of plant and animal species, as well as in the structure of the vegetation—from grassland and scrub through woodland and forest to alpine meadow—are readily apparent. Mountains are unique in that they extend vertically into different environmental regimes within short horizontal distances. The "elevation gradient" includes decreasing mean temperatures, decreasing lengths of growing seasons, increasing rainfall, increasing wind speeds, and so on. All these factors influence the distribution of plants and animals. For example, one of the most conspicuous features associated with the zonation of vegetation with increasing altitude is the presence of an upper and a lower treeline. Trees are largely excluded from the lowest elevations by drought, and from the highest elevations by cold and strong winds.

Each species of plant or animal has a genetic program that specifies a range of environmental conditions necessary for its survival. This species-specific range of tolerances defines the organism's *ecological amplitude,* which in turn is characterized by a minimum, a maximum, and an optimum. For most species, survival and reproduction (the ultimate test of a species' fitness in a particular environment) are most favorable within a relatively narrow set of conditions ranging around the optimum. At either extreme of its range of tolerance, a given species may be forced to yield the competitive advantage to another species with a different optimal range. Some species, the so-called *generalists,* have exceedingly broad ecological amplitudes and can be found in a great variety of habitats.

The term *community* refers to all the plants and animals found in a particular place dominated by one or more prominent species or by a physical characteristic. For example, we speak of a sagebrush community or a pond community. Used in this way, "community" is spatially defined and includes all the populations within its boundaries. When we examine the structure of natural communities, we find them to be mixtures of plants and animals with different ways of life. Within a given community, species evolve toward difference in habitat and in *niche* (the functional role of the organism) as a means of reducing competition. Habitat and niche are closely related aspects of the species' total adaptation to the environment. A given ecological niche is occupied by a single species. Where broad overlap occurs, such as might exist if two species were to utilize the same resources at the same time and space, one species will eventually displace the other or force changes in behavioral patterns that allow co-existence without direct competition. The number of species, expressed as *species diversity,* appears to increase with the productivity and structural heterogeneity of the vegetation.

The term *ecosystem* refers to the physical environment and all the organisms in a given area. Because plants are the most conspicuous ecosystem components, ecosystems are generally named for their dominant plant species. Ecosystems may be of any size, from the bacteria that populate the gut of a porcupine to a spruce-fir forest covering several thousand acres. In some cases, certain associations of plants and animals are so closely tied to a specific community-type that they are considered *indicator species* for that ecosystem. In recent years, the presence or absence of certain key indicator species have been used as a way of evaluating the environmental health or degree of disturbance occuring within a given ecosystem.

During the latter part of the nineteenth century, biologist C. Hart Merriam introduced the "life-zone" concept to describe the elevational zonation of vegetation he observed on the San Francisco Peaks of Arizona. In Merriam's classification, elevational zones determined on the basis of a given temperature range were correlated with an apparently analogous series of latitudinal zones of climate recognized for North America. Though Merriam's pioneering descriptions of vegetational zonation marked a great stride forward for plant ecology, the theoretical basis for his system was widely criticized because it failed to recognize that vegetation responds not to a single physical factor but to a synergistic array of environmental variables.

Biologists attempting to apply Merriam's life-zone system in the Southern Rockies during the first half of the twentieth century soon noted that the limits of elevation given for each life zone varied considerably from north to south along the mountains and that life zones were seldom stacked in neat horizontal sections. We know from our discussion of microclimate in chapter 8 that north-facing slopes receive considerably less direct sunlight than south-facing slopes and are consequently cooler, lose less water by evaporation, hold snow longer, and have a shorter frost-free season. These differences are significant enough to cause north-facing slopes to support ecosystems more typical of higher elevations than those on nearby south-facing slopes. In addition, boundaries between adjacent life zones or the ecosystems that comprise them are rarely sharply defined. These areas of transition, called *ecotones*, are characterized by a mixture of plant and animal species from the two adjacent zones or ecosystems. Though it is useful to recognize life zones, as Merriam did, it is important to remember that these zones are essentially continuous with one another and that the distributions of the major plant species by which we recognize these zones overlap broadly.

In the 1960s, University of Colorado plant ecologist John Marr developed an eminently workable vegetation classification for the Colorado Front Range that corresponds to the altitudinal zonation of mountain vegetation but is based on regional ecosystems and employs the ecological concepts of *climax* and *succession*. A brief discussion of these concepts is warranted because of their importance in understanding many of the vegetation patterns that we see in the Southern Rockies.

The term *succession* refers to the sequence of changes in the species composition of a newly exposed or a disturbed site over time. The final association of species achieved as a result of these changes is called a *climax*. For example, a plant community that is partially destroyed by fire and eventually replaces itself through a succession of intermediate vegetation types is considered to be the climax for that region. Succession tends to be one-directional; good colonizers with rapid growth and high tolerance of conditions on disturbed or newly exposed sites are replaced by slowly growing species with great competitive ability. Successional species alter the environment by their structure and activities, often to their own detriment and to the benefit of other species. In the traditional sense, succession is viewed as leading inexorably toward an ultimate expression of plant development, the *climax community*. A climax community is defined as one in which the species composition of the community (or ecosystem) remains relatively stable over time (at least for centuries) and the species populations are in a steady state, with a balance between the income of new individuals by reproduction and the outgo of individuals as a result of death. Many ecologists, however, dispute the idea that a region has only one true climax, recognizing that communities are essentially dynamic, open systems whose composition varies at any one locality depending on the particular environmental conditions at that point. Many factors determine the climax community for a given area, including climate, soil, topography, fire, and the activities of animals. Mosaic patterns of vegetation types are common to any climax community where the death or removal of certain individuals alters the environment, creating openings that are then invaded by seral (successional) species within an otherwise stable community.

The vegetation classification that best describes the zonation observed in the Southern Rockies is modified from that of Marr and includes five distinctive zones: Grassland/Semidesert, Foothills, Montane, Subalpine, and Alpine. Each zone within this system designates a region of more or less uniform climate in which distinctive types of climax vegetation occur. Various successional communities occur in each zone, and in some places may be even more common than climax vegetation.

The *grassland/semidesert zone* is characterized by short and mixed-grass prairie at elevations below 6,000 feet along the eastern edge of the Southern Rockies and by semidesert shrub ecosystems dominated by saltbush, greasewood, or sagebrush between 6,000 and 7,000 feet in the arid valleys west of the Continental Divide. On some sites, such as in the San Luis Valley, semidesert shrublands may even reach 8,000 feet under certain conditions. Watercourses occurring within this zone are characterized by lowland riparian ecosystems consisting of broad-leaved cottonwoods, willows, or box elder.

The *foothills zone* (or submontane) marks the transition between the grassland/semidesert ecosystems and the mountain forests and is characterized by mountain shrublands (Gambel oak or mountain mahogany) and by woodlands consisting of piñon pine and various species of juniper. The elevation of this zone is quite variable and ranges between 6,000 and 8,000 feet. Ponderosa pine and Douglas-fir forests often occur in this zone, as they do along the Eastern Slope of the Colorado Front Range, but are at their lower limits of distribution.

The *montane zone* occurs between 8,000 and 9,500 feet and is characterized by ponderosa pine ecosystems on drier, warmer sites and by Douglas Fir forests on moister, cooler slopes. Open stands of limber pine are typical of exposed ridges. Aspen and lodgepole pine ecosystems are common where fires or other types of disturbances have occurred. Mountain meadow and grassland communities are found in locations with suitable moisture and soils. Watercourses are numerous and delineated by distinctive assemblages of mountain riparian forest and shrub communities.

The *subalpine zone* is found between 9,500 and 11,400 feet and is dominated by dense forests of Engelmann spruce and subalpine fir. Limber pine or bristlecone pine form open forests on exposed ridge tops within this zone. Aspen and lodgepole pine may be present in certain areas that have undergone disturbance. Throughout these dense forests, lush meadows, ponds, and various types of wetlands are common. The upper margin of the subalpine forest marks the *forest-tundra ecotone,* which occurs at higher and higher elevations from north to south along the mountains; at the southern end of the mountains, the forest-tundra ecotone may extend to more than 12,000 feet. Trees growing in the forest-tundra ecotone are small and stunted, often forming shrubby patches that extend into the alpine meadows above.

The *alpine zone* begins at treelimit, which ranges from 12,200 feet in northern New Mexico and southern Colorado to 11,400 feet in northern Colorado and southern Wyoming, and extends to above 14,000 feet. This highest life zone is characterized by dwarf willows and a distinctive assemblage of herbaceous plants adapted to cold temperatures and a short growing season.

　　　　　THE SOUTHERN ROCKIES

The chapters that follow describe the most common ecosystems of the Southern Rockies—beginning with the shortgrass prairie and ending with the alpine tundra. Each ecosystem is portrayed in terms of its environmental setting, principal plant and animal species, and community characteristics.

CHAPTER ELEVEN

Land Within the Rain Shadow: The Shortgrass Prairie

WITHIN THE LONG shadow cast by the Rockies, drought and wind have fashioned a beautiful but uncompromising landscape. Plains Indians called this vast ocean of grass the *waho*—the great circle of the horizon. The grasslands of the Great Plains consist of three main types arranged in irregular, north-south belts that succeed one another along a west-to-east gradient of increasing moisture: shortgrasses in the west, mixed short- and tallgrasses in the middle, and tallgrasses in the east. The mixed prairie essentially marks a broad transition between tallgrass and shortgrass prairie types, defining a zone within which the rain shadow effect of the Rockies diminishes. West of this zone, precipitation declines dramatically as one approaches the Rockies, and sod-forming shortgrasses dominate the landscape. Too easily obscured by the dramatic scenery of the mountains, the shortgrass prairie offers visitors a wilderness world of subtle diversity.

Physical Environment

The climate of the shortgrass prairie, like that of the alpine tundra, is one of extremes. Hail, blizzards, tornadoes, parching winds, and dust storms are not unusual. The most significant feature of this semiarid grassland, and what shapes its character, is low precipitation; the shortgrass prairie averages between 10 and 16 inches a year. Most precipitation comes during the growing season—May through July—with a conspicuous increase in storm activity during June. Spectacular to watch, prairie thunderstorms are visible from miles away, black clouds churning, thunder rumbling, lightning flashing, and rain falling in a slanting torrent.

Temperatures in the shortgrass prairie fluctuate enormously, not only from season to season but also from day to day. Winter minimums typically hover in the low teens, but may drop to a bone-chilling −20°F when cold polar air spreads across the plains. The highest temperatures in the region also occur here; summer daily maximums hover in the 90s and each year several locations report temperatures in excess of 100°F.

Wind is a constant presence in the shortgrass prairie. Winter blizzards transform the prairie into a stark, white moonscape. Chinook winds from the mountains quickly melt the snow, but these warm winds also carry moisture away, robbing plants and soil of critical moisture reserves. Where the prairie sod has been plowed or overgrazed, high winds fuel the dust storms so characteristic of the area from Limon, Colorado, south to Las Vegas, New Mexico. The "black blizzards" of the 1930s were of spectacular proportions, sweeping their fury across thousands of acres of shortgrass prairie.

Community Characteristics

Countless acres of shortgrass prairie have been overgrazed; others have been lost to center-pivot irrigation and urban sprawl. Despite these losses, however, much of what remains is uncultivated and supports an assortment of native and introduced perennial grasses. On suitable sites, two native shortgrass species share dominance — buffalo grass and blue grama. In years with average precipitation, a mixture of these two grasses forms a dense, gray-green turf over hundreds of square miles, often making up nearly 80 percent of the native-grass cover.

Various mid-height grasses — such as little bluestem, needle-and-thread, western wheatgrass, side-oats grama, and galleta grass — are also present to varying degrees, depending on topographic differences, grazing pressures, and soil moisture conditions. There can be considerable variation

From left to right: buffalo grass (male plant), buffalo grass (female plant), blue grama.

in the dominance of certain species from year to year and from place to place in response to changing environmental conditions. During wet years, for example, shimmering fields of needle-and-thread tend to obscure the ever-present understory of shortgrass species. Wherever the range has been grazed conservatively, mid-height grasses become increasingly abundant.

The shortgrass prairie is made up of a mosaic of plant communities. The boundaries between communities may be quite sharp. On dry uplands, communities of buffalo grass and blue grama may form a patchy turf interspersed with bare ground and cacti. Bunch grasses such as little bluestem and Junegrass thrive in areas that have not been overgrazed and where deep soils ensure an adequate moisture supply. Moist swales and watercourses, protected from desiccating winds, favor taller grasses such as big bluestem and switchgrass. Concentric bands of desert saltgrass and foxtail barley encircle intermittent ponds and alkaline depressions. Sandhill areas tend to be dominated by sand-tolerant grasses such as sand reed, red three-awn, and sand bluestem. Throughout the prairie, in disturbed sites—such as around prairie-dog burrows and harvester-ant mounds—clumps of sand dropseed, squirreltail, and Indian ricegrass are abundant. Cheatgrass, an exotic from Eurasia, is an aggressive colonizer of overgrazed or disturbed sites and forms large, monotonous stands in many areas.

During years with above-average precipitation, a bewildering variety of showy wildflowers lend their colors to the grassland. Local moisture conditions, grazing pressure, com-

Common wildflowers of the shortgrass prairie, clockwise from upper left: copper mallow, stemless white evening-primrose, prickly poppy.

petition with grasses, and seed availability clearly influence patterns of species abundance and dominance. Drought years may cause an overlapping or telescoping of seasonal aspects, mixing the typical forbs of spring, summer, and autumn in rapid succession. The earliest wildflowers—lavender townsendias, pink locoweeds, sand-lilies, wild onions, and birdfoot violets—make their appearances in late April or May. In years with heavy spring rainfall, drifts of white evening primrose may cover the prairie like new-fallen snow. By late spring, the prairie is patterned with the variegated colors of blue penstemon, prairie larkspur, copper mallow, silky sophora, and many others. Wherever the land has been overgrazed, the yellow and apricot pink flowers of prickly pears and the elegant, cream-colored spikes of yucca dot the landscape. On the windswept tops of isolated buttes, cushion-forming plants like the sandwort and mat vetch are common, their compact growth identical to that of species found on alpine summits.

By mid-July, the yellow composites—common sunflowers, butterweed, gumweed, snakeweed, and prairie coneflower—become conspicuous. Sky-blue lupine and purple prairie clover mix with the silvery green foliage of sand sage. Along roadsides and in disturbed sites, the showy flowers of prickly poppy intermingle with lavender-flowered thistles. In sandy areas, clumps of white sand-verbena, purple-flowered morning-glories, and the carmine-colored, fleshy flowers of sand begonia are widespread. With the coming of autumn, the magenta flowers of blazing star give way to the vibrant yellow of rabbitbrush and to white, woolly clumps of winterfat.

North and west of the Laramie Mountains, shortgrass prairie merges with the sagebrush steppe and forms a distinctive understory. From Cheyenne south to Colorado Springs, blue grama, needle-and-thread, and western wheatgrass intermingle with ponderosa pine along the mountain front to form a savanna-like transition zone. In southern Colorado and New Mexico, shortgrass borders piñon-juniper and oak woodland, which extends far to the east along the Colorado–New Mexico border. South of the Platte-Arkansas Divide, the shrubby cane cactus becomes conspicuous, and as temperature and aridity intensify, blue grama is joined by dryland species such as galleta grass and sideoats grama.

Plant Adaptation:
Designs for Survival

In the shortgrass prairie, water conservation is the key to survival, and the dominant plants have evolved a variety of adaptations that absorb and conserve water efficiently. Grasses are characterized by small, inconspicuous flowers; narrow, parallel-veined leaves; hollow, jointed stems; and fibrous root systems. The narrower leaves typical of most shortgrasses minimize water loss through evaporation. In addition, ranks of special hinge cells parallel the central vein of the leaf, allowing it to fold or roll to reduce surface area further. In some species, a protective, waxy coating called *cutin* covers the leaves; in others, fine hairs entrap a layer of moist air along the leaf surface, insulating the leaf from excessive heat or desiccating winds.

The ability to absorb moisture from several soil layers is especially important in a semiarid environment. Long, vertical roots may reach a depth of 6 feet or more, tapping moisture reserves in the deeper soil layers. Nearer the surface, a multibranched network of fine rootlets spreads laterally to make use of the ephemeral moisture produced by brief showers. With its extensive root system, blue grama is one of the most drought resistant of all prairie grasses, exceeding even buffalo grass in durability. During times of severe drought, both species are able to remain physiologically dormant and to recover quickly after long periods without water.

Many perennial shortgrasses have evolved elaborate methods of vegetative reproduction that allow them to propagate when conditions are unfavorable for sexual reproduction. The continuous mat of stems and roots so characteristic of buffalo grass is formed by modified stems known as *stolons;* these creeping "runners" spread over the ground surface and produce new plants by developing roots and shoots along the prostrate stem joints. Many other prairie grasses, such as galleta and western wheatgrass, produce horizontal underground stems, called *rhizomes,* that bear scalelike leaves and send up new plants from underground nodes. Under the right conditions, a single plant can produce enough rhizomes to carpet the area around it with new plants. Some species, like galleta grass, produce large, woody rhizomes that may spread laterally for up to 6½ feet.

Bison have long been considered agents of natural selection in the shortgrass prairie, encouraging the evolution of plant features that have enabled grasses to withstand the grazer's activities. Whereas most plants grow from their tips, each grass leaf grows from its base. Thus, when the tip of the blade is eaten or broken by trampling, growth continues from the base, and the leaf is able to regenerate. Intermittent grazing also tends to encourage the production of side shoots, called *tillers*, which arise from nodes near the root crown; these ensure that a grassland grazed frequently but not excessively will produce thick, bushy growth. Bison once moved freely from place to place and were able to digest a wide variety of vegetation — leaving the land with ample time to recover after the animals moved on. More recently, domestic cattle and the fences that control their movements have dramatically changed the character of the shortgrass prairie in areas where grazing has been allowed to outstrip vegetative regeneration.

Descriptions of Common Plants

Buffalo Grass, *Buchloë dactyloides.* This native, warm-season shortgrass is easily distinguished by its sod-forming, stoloniferous growth habit. Wiry, gray-green leaves are produced in clusters at the nodes of the stolons and measure 1 to 6 inches in length. Male and female flowers are generally borne on separate plants, the flaglike male flowers on short, upright stems and the burlike female flowers enclosed in the leaves near the base of the plant.

Blue Grama, *Bouteloua gracilis.* This native bunchgrass is taller than buffalo grass and can be identified by its arched, comblike flowering spike and its wiry, blue-green leaves. The flowering stem, arising from a dense cluster of basal leaves, ranges in height from 6 to 24 inches. Blue grama is a warm-season grass, beginning growth in May or June.

Galleta Grass, *Hilaria jamesii.* This native midgrass grows in scattered stands and is distinguished by the cluster of three spikelets that arises from each node along its spike; the spikelets are conspicuously hairy at their bases. The flowering stem, 12 to 20 inches in height, has a ring of soft hairs present

Common grasses of the shortgrass prairie, clockwise from upper left: side-oats grama, needle-and-thread, western wheatgrass, galleta grass, big bluestem.

at each joint. Though resembling a bunchgrass, the species has scaly rhizomes that sometimes extend 6 feet just beneath the soil surface. Galleta grass is a warm-season grass, beginning growth in summer after sufficient rain.

Land Within the Rain Shadow: The Shortgrass Prairie

Side-oats Grama, *Bouteloua curtipendula.* This native midgrass is readily identified by its inflorescence — a one-sided raceme bearing ten to fifty spikelets. The length of the flowering stem is variable, depending on growth conditions, but heights of 18 inches are not uncommon. Leaf blades may be up to 12 inches long, with scattered long hairs along the margins. A warm-season bunchgrass, side-oats grama begins growth in early spring and flowers from July to September; it reproduces by seed, tillers, and rhizomes.

Needle-and-thread Grass, *Stipa comata.* The flowering stems of this elegant midgrass average about 2 feet in height and are tipped with multiple spikelets, each spikelet having a pointed, needlelike base and a long, threadlike awn. When a seed lands on the ground, the ability of the awn to twist and untwist in response to changing moisture conditions may help to position the seed for optimal germination. Needle-and-thread grass is a cool-season species, beginning growth in early spring or when moisture is available.

Western Wheatgrass, *Agropyron smithii.* This native, sod-forming midgrass is identified by its symmetrically arranged, imbricated spikelets. Western wheatgrass reproduces by seed or rhizome, its flowering stems ranging between 1 and 2½ feet in height. A cool-season species, growth begins when daytime temperatures are above 50°F; a period of dormancy is common in summer.

Common Plants of the Shortgrass Prairie

Shrubs

Greasewood, *Sarcobatus vermiculatus*
Rabbitbrush, golden, *Chrysothamnus nauseosus*
Sage, prairie, *Artemisia ludoviciana*
  sand, *Artemisa filifolia*
Sagebrush, big, *Seriphidium tridentatum* (formerly
     Artemisia tridentata)
  silver (or fringed), *Artemisia frigida*

Saltbush, four-wing, *Artemisia canescens*
   silverscale, *Artemisia argentea*
Skunkbrush, *Rhus aromatica* ssp. *trilobata*
Snakeweed, broom, *Gutierrezia sarothrae*
Winterfat, *Krascheninnikovia lanata* (formerly
   Ceratoides)
Yucca, or Spanish bayonet, *Yucca glauca*

Grasses

Barley, foxtail, *Critesion jubatum* (formerly *Hordeum*)
Bluestem, big, *Andropogon gerardii*
   little, *Andropogon scoparius*
   sand, *Andropogon hallii*
Buffalo grass, *Buchloë dactyloides*
Cheatgrass, *Anisantha tectorum* (formerly *Bromus*)
Cordgrass, *Spartina pectinata*
Galleta grass, *Hilaria jamesii*
Grama, blue, *Bouteloua gracilis*
   side-oats, *Bouteloua curtipendula*
   hairy, *Bouteloua hirsuta*
Indiangrass, *Sorghastrum avenaceum*
Junegrass, *Koeleria macrantha*
Muhly, ring, *Muhlenbergia torreyi*
   alkali, *Muhlenbergia asperifolia*
Needle-and-thread, *Stipa comata*
Needlegrass, green, *Stipa viridula*
Ricegrass, Indian, *Stipa hymenoides* (formerly *Oryzopsis*)
Sacaton, alkali, *Sporobolus airoides*
Saltgrass, *Distichlis stricta*
Sand reed, *Calamovilfa longifolia*
Squirreltail, *Elymus elymoides* (formerly *Sitanion hystrix*)
Switchgrass, *Panicum virgatum*
Three-awn, red, *Aristida purpurea*
Wheatgrass, western, *Agropyron smithii*

Wildflowers

Aster, white prairie, *Virgulus falcatus* (formerly *Aster*)
Bindweed, field, *Convolvulus arvensis*

Birdfoot violet, *Viola pedatifida*
Blazingstar, or gayfeather, *Liatris punctata*
Broomrape, *Orobanche* spp.
Butterweed, *Senecio spartioides*
Cactus, candelabra, *Cylindropuntia imbricata*
   green-flowered, *Echinocereus viridiflorus*
   pincushion (or ball), *Coryphantha vivipara*
   prickly-pear, *Opuntia polyacantha*
Chicory, common, *Cichorum intybus*
Coneflower, prairie, *Ratibidia columnifera*
Evening-primrose, prairie, *Oenothera albicaulis*
   white stemless, *Oenothera caespitosa*
   yellow stemless, *Oenothera howardii*
Evening-star, plains, *Nuttallia nuda* (formerly *Mentzelia*)
Fleabane, *Erigeron bellidiastrum*
Gaura, scarlet, *Gaura coccinea*
Gumweed, *Grindelia squarrosa*
Larkspur, prairie, *Delphinium carolinianum*
Loco, Colorado, *Oxytropis lambertii*
   Rocky Mountain, *Oxytropis sericea*
Lupine, Nebraska, *Lupinus plattensis*
Mallow, copper (or cowboy's delight), *Sphaeralcea*
   coccinea
Milkvetch, ground-plum, *Astragalus crassicarpus*
   Missouri, *Astragalus missouriensis*
Milkweed, green, *Asclepias viridiflora*
   showy, *Asclepias speciosa*
Morning-glory, bush, *Ipomea leptophylla*
Onion, wild, *Allium textile*
Penstemon, narrow beardtongue, *Penstemon*
   angustifolius
   white, *Penstemon albidus*
Pepper-grass, *Lepidium densiflorum*
Phlox, moss, *Phlox hoodii*
Plantain, woolly, *Plantago patagonica*
Poppy, prickly, *Argemone polyanthemos*
Poppy-mallow, purple, *Callirhoë involucrata*
Prairie clover, *Dalea enneandra*
Puccoon, narrow-leaved, *Lithospermum incisum*
Ragweed, western, *Ambrosia psilostachya*
Sand begonia, *Rumex venosus*
Sand-lily, *Leucocrinum montanum*

Sand-verbena, *Abronia fragrans*
Sophora, silky, *Sophora nuttalliana*
Spiderwort, *Tradescantia occidentalis*
Sunflower, common, *Helianthus annuus*
Thistle, Russian, *Salsola australis*
   plains, *Cirsium canescens*
Townsendia (or Easter daisy), *Townsendia exscapa*

Environment and Adaptation: Animals of the Shortgrass Prairie

Hunting, agriculture, and urbanization, have taken their toll on the prairie's animals. Despite these impacts, however, a remarkable diversity and abundance of wildlife remains. Pronghorn still number in the thousands. With the wolf gone from the open prairies, the adaptable coyote has proliferated, occasionally at the expense of the more vulnerable swift fox. The reappearance of prairie dog colonies in areas where they were once eradicated by poisons or decimated by plague attracts large wintering populations of ferruginous and rough-legged hawks and an ever-growing number of bald eagles. Burrowing owls stake their claims to the abandoned burrows of prairie dogs and badgers. With the coming of spring, the prairie belongs largely to its nesting birds; the courtship rituals of long-billed curlews, mountain plovers, lark buntings, horned larks, and vesper sparrows fill the air with music and grace.

A Diet of Grass

A magnificent variety of large grazing animals—camels, horses, mammoths, bison, and pronghorn—roamed the grasslands during the Pleistocene. Many ecologists believe that the spread of grasslands and the evolution of grazing animals proceeded together. Unlike most other herbaceous plants, grasses secrete minute grains of silica between their cells; this plant sand abrades the teeth of animals that depend on a grass diet. The first grazers evolved with high-crowned (*hypsodont*) cheek teeth equipped with crescent-shaped ridges of hard enamel on the grinding surface of each tooth. Hypsodont teeth are not only resistant to abrasion, but they are able to compensate for wear by rising within the gum and exposing successive increments of the crown.

A grass diet is especially rich in cellulose, a structural carbohydrate found in plant cell walls. Cellulose is impervious to all vertebrate digestive enzymes and acids and is a source of food energy only for animals with very specialized digestive systems. In some large grazing animals, a digestive system evolved in which the true stomach is preceded by several large-capacity storage and fermentation chambers. The first and largest of these, the rumen, serves as the principal fermentation site, where the swallowed plant food and saliva mixture is exposed to a variety of microorganisms (bacteria and protozoans). These organisms are able to break down the cellulose, reducing it to nutritionally useful metabolites and allowing access to the vital substances housed within the plant cells. Any undigested fibrous materials are partially regurgitated and remasticated, and then swallowed once again to undergo a second round of fermentation. This process, known as rumination, allows the animal to graze quickly through an area and move on, digesting the food at leisure in a more protected spot, minimizing the length of time the animal is exposed to predators. Pronghorns, for example, alternately feed and bed down through the day and night, with ruminating dominating almost 80 percent of bedding time.

Hares and rabbits cope with the problems of cellulose digestion by processing their food twice. During the first round of cellulose digestion, food passes rather rapidly through the digestive system, and a group of soft, greenish pellets forms in a pouchlike organ, called the *caecum*, which is attached to the intestine. These pellets are high in protein, water-soluble vitamins, and other nutrients but require further processing before they can provide any nutritional benefit. The pellets are then voided and reingested for a second round of digestion. This process, known as *coprophagy*, is of critical importance because it allows maximization of the diet's nutritional content. The round droppings typically associated with hares and rabbits represent the final waste product of the digestive process.

Built to Run

For many prairie animals, survival depends on the ability to run fast and far without tiring. Hares are built for the quick getaway, their powerful hind legs allowing them to virtually explode from absolute immobility, bounding across the prairie at speeds up to 45 miles per hour. A jackrabbit on the move is a marvelous sight, taking 15-foot bounds, skillfully shifting directions in midair, and executing a series of "spy-hops" to scan the terrain ahead. The pronghorn is the quintessential running machine. Its legs are unusually long and slender, and the heaviest muscles are bunched close to the body; combined, these modifications serve to reduce and redistribute the weight of the limbs, thus favoring rapid limb movement with a minimum expenditure of energy. While running, the body moves almost in a straight line; little energy is wasted in the up-and-down movements typical of most galloping animals. Enlarged lungs and heart, combined with a large-diameter trachea, enable the pronghorn to maintain high speeds for long periods of time; the pronghorn may cruise at 30 miles per hour for as far as 7 miles, and individuals have been clocked at 50 to 60 miles per hour for short distances, often running with their mouths open and tongues hanging out to increase the supply of air to the lungs.

Burrowers Large and Small

In the shortgrass prairie, the diversity of habitats available for feeding and reproductive activities is severely limited. Not surprisingly, the shortgrass fauna is characterized by a preponderance of burrowing animals that are specially adapted to exploit both the herbaceous layer and the sheltering subterranean environment. Burrows are used to escape predators, avoid environmental extremes, sleep, breed, rear young, and store food. The larger rodents, such as the black-tailed prairie dog, plains pocket gopher, and thirteen-lined ground squirrel, are skillful burrowers, constructing complex underground chambers. Grassland predators such as the coyote, badger, and swift fox dig their own dens or reconstruct burrows abandoned by other animals. The small, nocturnal mammals of the shortgrass prairie — the Ord's kangaroo rat and an assortment of pocket mice—create networks of underground tunnels, complete with predator-fooling dead ends and alternate entrances, and often plug the entrances to their nesting chambers when using them.

Many reptiles and amphibians seek shelter in abandoned burrow systems or have variously modified appendages that allow them to excavate their own burrows or dig out their prey. The western box turtle and the spadefoot toad have appendages modified for digging; the spadefoot toad is named for the hard, spadelike tubercles on the hind feet that it uses to dig resting and hibernation burrows. The western hognose snake, a voracious toad-eater, detects its buried prey by smell and then uses its cornified, upturned snout to dig the toad from its burrow.

Grassland Birds

Grassland birds exhibit adaptations in appearance, physiology, and behavior that differ strikingly from those of forest species. Cryptic (camouflage) coloration is common; in many species—burrowing owls, long-billed curlews, vesper sparrows, and others—the feathers are variously striped or streaked with shades of brown, regardless of sex, so that when the bird is motionless it tends to disappear against its

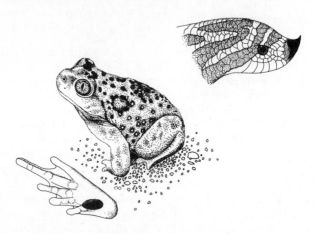

Plains spadefoot toad, with detail of spadelike tubercle on hind foot; western hognose snake, showing spadelike snout.

background. During the nesting season, the long-billed curlew makes concealment a fine art, stretching its neck out along the ground while sitting on its nest to avoid attracting predators. The bold, black bands on the white breast of the killdeer — known as disruptive coloration — serve roughly the same purpose as cryptic coloration by visually breaking up the outline of the bird into unidentifiable pieces. White outer tail feathers, a distinguishing feature of many grassland species — vesper sparrows, lark sparrows, horned larks, and longspurs — are particularly conspicuous when flashed in flight, serving as a group warning mechanism. The white rump patch of the pronghorn serves a similar function.

Male territorial and courtship displays can be spectacular. With few exceptions, grassland birds sing on the wing, often rising several hundred feet in the air to deliver their territorial messages before fluttering or dropping quickly back to Earth. The mountain plover and the longspurs are well known for their song flights. The male chestnut-collared longspur begins its beautiful aerial displays over its nesting grounds by mid-April. Song flights begin with a gradual rise into the air accompanied by singing, wings beating rapidly to the peak altitude of the flight; then, circling briefly, the bird flutters to the ground like a leaf floating down through the air. Other species, like the western meadowlark and the lark bunting, select some suitably conspicuous perch — a fence post, small shrub, tall weed stalk, or boulder — from which to deliver their advertisements or territorial songs.

Life Histories of Selected Animals

Mammals

White-tailed Jackrabbit, *Lepus townsendii.* This large, heavy-bodied hare is easily distinguished from the black-tailed jackrabbit (*L. californicus*) by its pale, buffy gray pelage and pure white tail; winter pelage is mostly white. Distribution is largely restricted to open country, and alpine tundra may be occupied in some areas. White-tailed jackrabbits are herbivorous, foraging primarily in the early morning and from late afternoon well into the night. During the day the

Thirteen-lined ground squirrel.

jackrabbit rests in a "form" (a shallow depression) dug into
the ground. During winter, a snow burrow is often used for
concealment. The breeding period extends from late February to mid-July. During courtship, male jackrabbits fight fu-
riously, kicking out with their hind feet. Ovulation is induced
by copulation, with females producing multiple litters of one
to nine precocial young (fully furred, eyes open). Juvenile
hares can survive on their own at only two weeks of age.

Thirteen-lined Ground Squirrel, *Spermophilus tridecem-*
lineatus. This small, diurnal ground squirrel is easily identified by its dot-and-dash color pattern. Thirteen-lined ground
squirrels seldom occur in defined concentrations and are not
colonial. The winding, shallow burrow systems are constructed in sandy soils on gentle slopes and have separate
nesting and food storage chambers; the earth from tunnel
excavation is scattered away from the burrow entrance.
Thirteen-lined ground squirrels are active above ground
from April through October; hibernation begins in October,
in a chamber sealed off from the rest of the burrow system
by a plug of soil. Insects and the seeds of various grasses
and forbs are preferred as food, but these ground squirrels
will also eat fleshy roots, carrion, and the eggs and nestlings
of ground-nesting birds when available. Females mate soon
after emerging from hibernation; gestation requires about
twenty-eight days, and the young are altricial (naked, eyes
closed).

Black-tailed Prairie Dog, *Cynomys ludovicianus.* This
ground squirrel is identified by its robust size, buffy brown

pelage, and black-tipped tail. Diurnal, herbivorous, and active year-round, prairie dogs are opportunistic feeders, mixing their grass diet with a wide variety of succulent forbs, cacti, carrion, and insects. Black-tailed prairie dogs have a highly organized social system; prairie dog towns are composed of a series of subunits called wards. Each ward houses several coteries; the coterie typically consists of one or two males, several females, and half a dozen young. The dominant male controls the patriarchal society of the coterie, and the mating system is polygnous (one male mates with several females). The communication system of the prairie dog is highly evolved and based on tactile, olfactory, visual, and vocal cues. The most common call is the nasal alarm or warning bark, usually accompanied by a flick of the tail. Mutual grooming reinforces the strong social bonds within the coterie. During the breeding season, from March until April, a litter of four to six altricial young is born after a gestation period of twenty-eight to thirty-three days. Juvenile prairie dogs remain with the coterie until their second year.

Pronghorn, *Antilocapra americana.* The pronghorn is identified by its tan or reddish upper body; white rump patch, belly, and inner legs; and alternating bands of white and tan across the throat. Males have a black band from eye to snout and on the neck. Horns are present in both sexes, surrounding laterally flattened horn-cores that are unbranched and permanent; the larger, branching horn sheaths of the males are shed shortly after breeding. Pronghorn have keen eyesight; the eyes are set in protruding sockets that allow for an extraordinary degree of wide-angle vision. At the first hint of danger, the pronghorn erects the white hairs of its rump patch in a heliograph-like warning display that alerts other members of the herd. Pronghorn are gregarious, especially during winter; in spring and summer, bachelor herds and female-kid groups are common. The rut begins in September, continuing into the first week in October; pronghorn defend their territories with ritualized displays and occasional fights. Twin, precocial young are born in late May or early June, after a gestation period of 230 to 250 days. During the first few days of its life, the pronghorn kid is virtually odorless and will flatten itself against the grass, attracting as little attention as possible, rising only when its mother visits it for nursing. Within as few as four days after birth, pronghorn fawns can outrun a man and are able to keep pace with adults in the herd.

Birds

Burrowing Owl, *Athene cunicularia.* This small, diurnal owl is identified by its short tail, long legs, brown barring on the breast, rounded head (no ear tufts), and ground-dwelling habits. The species is migratory in the shortgrass prairie, arriving in mid-April either singly or paired and returning south in mid- to late October. The diet consists of insects, small rodents, and occasionally small birds, reptiles, and amphibians. Burrow entrances may be littered with regurgitation pellets containing fur, bone, and insect parts. Males return to the same burrow year after year; unpaired males display from their burrow locations by "bowing" and giving their double-noted "coo-coo" song through the night. When approached or flushed, both sexes give a sharp "chatter" call. These owls are often observed standing at the entrance to their burrows or perching on fence posts. Females are fed by males during pair formation, incubation, and brooding. Incubation takes about twenty-eight days, and the young are able to fly after forty-four to forty-eight days.

Swainson's Hawk, *Buteo swainsoni.* This large, dark buteo is distinguished by its chestnut bib, somewhat pointed wings, finely banded tail, and preference for open country. Swainson's hawks hunt primarily from perches such as fence posts

Burrowing owl.

THE SOUTHERN ROCKIES

and low trees, or from prominent knolls. Pairs are monogamous and arrive on their breeding ground in late March or in April, about a month before egg laying begins. These hawks migrate in enormous flocks, making use of thermals during the annual migratory journey to South America. The diet consists of small mammals and insects; migrating flocks sometimes hunt crickets and grasshoppers on the ground. Swainson's hawks build large, bulky stick nests in isolated trees or tall shrubs. Both sexes incubate and feed the young; fledging occurs after about thirty days.

Mountain Plover, *Charadrius montanus.* Despite its name, the mountain plover is largely restricted to shortgrass prairie and is identified by its shorebird-like appearance, sandy brown upperparts, creamy breast, and whitish wing stripe visible in flight. This species frequently crouches low to the ground, well camouflaged by its protective coloring. Mountain plovers are migratory, arriving in late March and often returning to their old territories. Males advertise their territory with calls and an aerial "falling leaf" display; they also practice "scraping," preparing several potential nest bowls in a given territory. Despite pair bonds formed early in the breeding season, some females will mate with new mates within two weeks of completing their first clutch, leaving their original mates to rear the first clutch. While nesting, the adult will defend the nest, using a "crippled-bird act" to lure away potential predators. Nesting occurs in May.

Western Meadowlark, *Sturnella neglecta.* This robin-sized songster is identified by the black V on the upper breast and the bright yellow throat, breast, and abdomen; the outer tail feathers flash white in flight. Meadowlarks typically walk on the ground while feeding, often in pairs, or perch on fence posts, tall weeds, and shrubs while delivering their flutelike song. This species is largely insectivorous but may occasionally be seen scavenging road-kills. Meadowlarks nest on the ground, their nests well hidden in grass clumps. The nest may have a canopy woven into the surrounding vegetation and a lateral entrance. The female incubates the eggs, but both sexes feed the young.

Lark Bunting, *Calamospiza melanocorys.* Male lark buntings are identified by their jet-black plumage, large white wing patches, and white-tipped tails; females and males in winter plumage are brownish with dusky streaking and buff or whitish wing patches. Lark buntings are migratory, moving

From left to right: horned lark, lark bunting.

in large, gregarious flocks north along the Southern Rockies in March from their wintering grounds in Mexico and on the southern plains. Birds at the rear of the flock continuously leapfrog to the front, the flock appearing like some enormous wheel rolling over the prairie. Males tolerate each other during the nesting season, and pairs will often nest only 100 feet apart. Strong fliers, males sing from perches or will often shoot up into the air to deliver their rich, warbling advertisement song. The lark bunting builds its cup-shaped nest of grasses on the ground, usually in a shallow depression.

Vesper Sparrow, *Pooecetes gramineus.* The vesper sparrow is named for its preference for evening singing. This small, inconspicuous brown sparrow is identified by its white outer tail feathers, evident only in flight, and by the absence of strong facial markings and breast spots. Vesper sparrows arrive in small flocks on the nesting ground in March or April. Males sing only from elevated perches, and the song is a mixture of paired opening notes and a descending series of rapid trills. Vesper sparrows forage along the ground and fly only when closely approached. This species is fond of dust baths; several may be observed dusting together in bare patches on dirt roads. Vesper sparrows generally build their nests in depressions in the ground under tall vegetation.

Amphibians and Reptiles

Plains Spadefoot Toad, *Scaphiopus bombifrons.* This small toad is largely restricted to grasslands and sandhills and is identified by its vertical pupils, the wedge-shaped black "spade" on each hind foot, and the hard lump between the eyes. Spadefoots are active from May to September but spend much of their time underground in rodent burrows or in burrows excavated with the cornified "spades" on their hind feet. Rains of an inch or more and temperatures of at least 50°F are necessary to initiate breeding. Males emerge in response to these conditions and give their loud, snore-like calls while floating in the water. During mating, the male clasps the female with his forelegs while the two swim from place to place. Egg masses are laid by the female on submerged vegetation or other objects and are fertilized by the male. Eggs hatch in two to three days. Tadpoles develop rapidly, and metamorphosis requires less than forty days.

Great Plains Toad, *Bufo cognatus.* The Great Plains toad is a large species, with horizontal pupils, warty skin, and a somewhat symmetrical pattern of light-edged dark spots on the back; cranial crests and oval paratoid glands are prominent. This species is common in lowland habitats where soils are relatively soft. Largely nocturnal and active from May to September, this toad spends much of its time in self-dug burrows, but it may be conspicuous after heavy rains. Heavy rainfall and flooding initiate breeding activity, and the male's jackhammer-like trill can be heard anytime from May to July. Each female may lay up to twenty thousand eggs encased in slender tubes of jelly; eggs hatch in two to three days, and tadpoles normally metamorphose within forty days of hatching.

Western Box Turtle, *Terrapene ornata.* This small terrestrial turtle is identified by its domed top shell, patterned with yellowish radiating lines and spots; males have reddish iris and foreleg spots and females have yellowish iris and foreleg spots. Preferred habitat consists of dry, open grassland with sandy soils; the average home range is about 5 acres, and favorable habitat may support three to six turtles per acre. Box turtles are diurnal and active from April to October; most activity occurs in early morning and late afternoon in midsummer. Males reach breeding age after eight to nine years; females become sexually active at ten to eleven years. During mating the male climbs up on the shell of the female and grips her shell with his hind feet. Female box turtles deposit four to six eggs in an underground burrow in May, June, or July; eggs hatch after two months, but young are rarely observed above ground.

Lesser Earless Lizard, *Holbrookia maculata.* This common small lizard is typical of sandhills and in open, sparsely vegetated grasslands. It is distinguished by its smooth, granular scales, the black marks on each side of its belly, and the light-colored stripe down the center of its back; there are no external ear openings. Lesser earless lizards are diurnal and active from March or April to October if temperatures are mild. This species seeks shade during midsummer and may hide in small rodent burrows or bury itself by plunging headfirst into the soil and wriggling frantically until covered. The species breeds in May, the eggs developing underground in June or July; hatchlings appear from late July through August.

Western Hognose Snake, *Heterodon nasicus.* The western hognose is a small snake, identified by the stocky body that narrows abruptly at the tail, the upturned, spadelike snout, and the black belly. This diurnal species is largely restricted to grassland and sandhill areas. Most activity occurs in the morning and late afternoon from April to October. Hognose snakes dig their food, mainly toads and lizards, out of the soil with their snouts. When frightened or disturbed, this snake seldom bites, but it is a magnificent bluffer—flattening its head and neck, hissing vigorously, and pretending to strike. If this tactic fails, it may resort to its famous "death-feigning" act, in which it rolls over on its back and may regurgitate, defecate, and hang its tongue out of its open mouth. If the snake is righted, it will usually flip over again and expose its black belly. This behavior presumably repulses some potential predators. If left alone, the snake will turn over after a few minutes and crawl away. Females breed their second year and then alternate years thereafter; eggs are laid underground in July and hatch after about two months.

Common Animals of the Shortgrass Prairie

Mammals

Merriam's Shrew, *Sorex merriami*
Big Brown Bat, *Eptesicus fuscus*
Desert Cottontail, *Sylvilagus audubonii*
White-tailed Jackrabbit, *Lepus townsendii*
Black-tailed Jackrabbit, *Lepus californicus*
Thirteen-lined Ground Squirrel, *Spermophilus tridecemlineatus*
Black-tailed Prairie Dog, *Cynomys ludovicianus*
Plains Pocket Gopher, *Geomys bursarius*
Plains Pocket Mouse, *Perognathus flavescens*
Silky Pocket Mouse, *Perognathus flavus*
Ord's Kangaroo Rat, *Dipodomys ordii*
Plains Harvest Mouse, *Reithrodontomys montanus*
Deer Mouse, *Peromyscus maniculatus*
Northern Grasshopper Mouse, *Onychomys leucogaster*
Prairie Vole, *Microtus ochrogaster*
Coyote, *Canis latrans*
Swift Fox, *Vulpes velox*
Long-tailed Weasel, *Mustela frenata*
Badger, *Taxidea taxus*
Striped Skunk, *Mephitis mephitis*
Pronghorn, *Antilocapra americana*

Birds

Turkey Vulture, *Cathartes aura*
Red-tailed Hawk, *Buteo jamaicensis*
Ferruginous Hawk, *Buteo regalis*
Rough-legged Hawk, *Buteo lagopus*
Swainson's Hawk, *Buteo swainsoni*
Golden Eagle, *Aquila chrysaetos*
Northern Harrier (or Marsh Hawk), *Circus cyaneus*
American Kestrel (or Sparrow Hawk), *Falco sparverius*

Prairie Falcon, *Falco mexicanus*
Mountain Plover, *Charadrius montanus*
Killdeer, *Charadrius vociferus*
Long-billed Curlew, *Numenius americanus*
Mourning Dove, *Zenaida macroura*
Burrowing Owl, *Athene cunicularia*
Common Nighthawk, *Chordeiles minor*
Eastern Kingbird, *Tyrannus tyrannus*
Western Kingbird, *Tyrannus verticalis*
Say's Phoebe, *Sayornis saya*
Horned Lark, *Eremophila alpestris*
Barn Swallow, *Hirundo rustica*
Black-billed Magpie, *Pica pica*
American Crow, *Corvus brachyrhynchos*
Western Meadowlark, *Sturnella neglecta*
Loggerhead Shrike, *Lanius ludovicianus*
Brewer's Blackbird, *Euphagus cyanocephalus*
American Goldfinch, *Carduelis tristis*
Brewer's Sparrow, *Spizella breweri*
Grasshopper Sparrow, *Ammodramus savannarum*
Lark Bunting, *Calamospiza melanocorys*
Vesper Sparrow, *Pooecetes gramineus,*
Lark Sparrow, *Chondestes grammacus*
Chestnut-collared Longspur, *Calcarius ornatus*
McCown's Longspur, *Calcarius mccownii*
Lapland Longspur, *Calcarius lapponicus*

Amphibians

Tiger Salamander, *Ambystoma tigrinum*
Plains Spadefoot, *Scaphiopus bombifrons*
New Mexico Spadefoot, *Scaphiopus multiplicatus*
Great Plains Toad, *Bufo cognatus*
Woodhouse's Toad, *Bufo woodhousii*

Reptiles

Western Box Turtle, *Terrapene ornatus*
Lesser Earless Lizard, *Holbrookia maculata*
Eastern Fence Lizard, *Sceloporus undulatus*

Many-lined Skink, *Eumeces multivirgatus*
Six-lined Racerunner, *Cnemidophorus sexlineatus*
Racer, *Coluber constrictor*
Western Hognose Snake, *Heterodon nasicus*
Coachwhip, *Masticophis flagellum*
Bullsnake, *Pituophis melanoleucus*
Plains Garter Snake, *Thamnophis radix*
Western Rattlesnake, *Crotalus viridis*

Butterflies

Plains Gray Skipper, *Yvretta rhesus*
Riding's Satyr, *Neominois ridingsii*
Olympia Marblewing, *Amblyscirtes simius*

CHAPTER TWELVE

Shrublands

SHRUB COMMUNITIES FORM a distinctive and important component of the mountain landscape. In many parts of the Southern Rockies, shrublands occupy large areas, often extending for tens of miles across intermontane basins. More commonly, shrublands occur as small patches or as a discontinuous, somewhat narrow transition zone between grassland or meadow ecosystems and the mountain forests. The shrublands described in this chapter are of three types: semidesert scrub (dominated by greasewood or saltbush), sagebrush shrublands (dominated by big sagebrush), and mountain shrublands (dominated by Gambel oak or mountain mahogany). Other shrub-dominated communities are important in wetland, forest-tundra ecotone, and alpine tundra ecosystems; these are described in later chapters.

Sagebrush shrubland west of Laramie, Wyoming.
Audrey D. Benedict.

Physical Environment

Shrublands are generally characterized by hot summers, cool to cold winters, and low precipitation. In the semidesert shrublands of the San Luis Valley and along the Colorado River near Grand Junction, summer temperatures often soar above 100°F. Winter minimum temperatures, on the other hand, may drop below 0°F because of cold-air drainage from surrounding mountain slopes. The coldest temperatures in the Southern Rockies are regularly reported from the sagebrush-covered basins of Middle Park, the Gunnison and Taylor Park area, and northwest Colorado. In the mountain shrublands, summer temperatures in the 80s and 90s are common. The climate in general, especially with regard to winter temperatures, is more moderate than in most other ecosystems because of the predilection of these communities for south-facing slopes and other upland situations that enable them to avoid the extremes of temperature and wind associated with most basins.

In the semidesert scrub, annual precipitation averages less than 10 inches, most coming in the critical spring-and-summer period. During the summer, however, high daytime temperatures and low humidity conspire to produce high rates of evaporation. In sagebrush shrublands, annual precipitation is highly variable and can range from 10 inches in lowland sites to more than 20 inches at higher elevations. Soil moisture recharge in sagebrush ecosystems occurs primarily in the spring, when the snow melts, and is followed by a warm growing season with little precipitation. In mountain shrublands, annual precipitation is normally less than 15 inches.

The balance between the amount and seasonal distribution of precipitation and potential evaporation governs moisture conditions and vegetation patterns in most environments. Plant ecologists use the p/e ratio, in which p is the annual precipitation and e is the potential evaporation, to provide an index of moisture conditions for a given site. The shrublands described in this chapter are most common on sites where the p/e ratio is transitional between that of drought-adapted woodlands such as piñon-juniper, and that of grasslands and semidesert herbaceous communities. The individual character and species composition of shrublands vary considerably depending on local environmental conditions. Shrub stands typical of the driest sites may consist of only one or two shrub species and a sparse understory of herbaceous plants. Sites with deeper soils and more moisture may include several species of shrubs and a rank understory of herbaceous plants.

Plant Adaptation: Designs for Survival

Water stress is the most critical factor influencing the adaptations of plants growing in arid and semiarid environments. The morphological and physiological adaptations that enable a plant to maximize its ability to absorb groundwater efficiently and to moderate the rate at which water loss occurs are of paramount importance. Below ground, most aridland shrubs increase water uptake by developing more extensive root systems. Rapid and deep penetration by a plant's taproot is a common characteristic of many species. The root system of big sagebrush, for example, consists of an extensive lateral network of shallow roots, which take

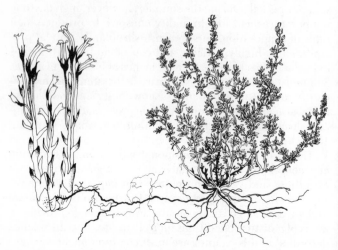

Below-ground detail of root connection between tufted broomrape, shown on the left, and fringed sage, the parasitized host.

advantage of short-term moisture supplies in the upper soil layers, and a cluster of coarse, penetrating roots, which are able to tap groundwater reserves at great depth.

Root Parasites

Many herbaceous species have solved the problem of water and nutrient stress by parasitizing the roots of other species. The most interesting of these parasitic species is broomrape. Broomrape lacks chlorophyll and is unable to manufacture its own food by normal photosynthetic processes—making it totally dependent on other sources for nutrients and water. When first established, broomrape seedlings quickly attach their roots to those of suitable hosts, typically species of sage or buckwheat. Paintbrush, in contrast to the fully parasitic broomrape, is capable of photosynthesis, but is also known to parasitize the roots of other plants. In the case of the paintbrush, root parasitism enables the plant to better withstand periods of drought and to expand its ecological range into areas with nutrient-deficient soils.

Root Nodules and Symbiotic Bacteria

In addition to being dry, shrubland soils are often deficient in nitrogen and other nutrients. Several shrub and herbaceous plants have evolved special structures on their roots that house nitrogen-fixing bacteria. The roots of mountain mahogany have nodules populated by filamentous bacteria known as *Actinomycetes*. These single-celled organisms counteract the relative sterility of the soil by converting atmospheric nitrogen into water-soluble nitrate compounds, which can then be utilized by the plant. In return, the mountain mahogany furnishes the bacterium with nutrients and water. Nodules on the roots of lupine, a common wildflower in sagebrush shrublands, harbor *Rhizobium* bacteria and serve a similar function. During the early stages of this symbiotic relationship, the bacteria gain entrance to the root hairs and are entirely parasitic until nodule formation has been completed.

Leaf Design

Adaptations to water stress are most conspicuous in the anatomical modifications of the leaves, where water loss, as a function of transpiration, occurs through minute openings, called *stomates*, in the leaf surfaces. Stomates are critical to terrestrial plants because they permit the exchange of gases between the living protoplasm of the plant's cells and the atmosphere. Each species has solved its water-balance problem by its own unique combination of adaptive characters. The leaves of most dryland shrubs are smaller than those of species growing in areas where water is abundant. In addition, the leaf blades are somewhat thickened, and in certain species, such as mountain mahogany and big sagebrush, the leaf blades may change their orientation or even inroll during times of severe water stress so as to moderate the amount of leaf surface exposed to direct sun.

Control over water loss is also achieved by the degree of protection that can be afforded to the leaf surface and to the stomates. The leaf surfaces of several species, such as Gambel oak and chokecherry, are covered with a fatty substance, called cutin, that gives the leaves a shiny, waterproof appearance and also reflects a certain amount of incoming solar radiation. Leaf surfaces that are heavily cutinized are very effective in retarding water loss and in protecting the underlying plant cells from desiccation. In some species, such as big sagebrush and golden rabbitbrush, leaves may be covered with fine hairs, which keep moisture-robbing air currents elevated well above the stomata and insulate the leaf surface from excessive heat or cold.

A deciduous growth habit, either seasonal or initiated by prolonged drought, is another efficient means of reducing transpiration. In contrast to the primarily nondeciduous shrub species that dominate the true chaparral of California and Arizona, the principal shrubland species of the Southern Rockies are winter-deciduous. The corky or waxy materials that cover the leafless branches further reduce transpiration.

The Water Balance: Coping With High Salt Concentrations

Water-soluble salts and a variety of other materials are produced from most rocks as a result of normal chemical weathering. In a high-rainfall environment, leaching flushes these salts from the soil, lowering the pH and increasing the acidity. In arid or semiarid environments, however, saline and alkaline soils (pH greater than 7) are common because excessive amounts of soluble salts and carbonate compounds accumulate in the soil due to evaporative concentration. Excess solute accumulations—often appearing as a white crust on the soil surface—are conspicuous in areas where evaporative concentration is enhanced by a high water table. In other areas, periods of above-average precipitation may cause surface salt accumulations to be washed from uplands and to accumulate in depressions.

High soil concentrations of soluble salts interfere with the osmotic balance necessary for normal water uptake by roots. Plants that are adapted to grow in salty or alkaline soils are called *halophytes*. Shrubs such as greasewood and saltbush are highly specialized halophytes, solving the problem of excess salt by absorbing it, so that the concentration of salt in their cell sap exceeds that of their soil-moisture supply. Under conditions of severe soil-moisture stress, the capacity for continual adjustment of internal salt concentration helps these plants cope with increasing salinity in the soil. In addition, salt concentrations in plant tissues may function as an antifreeze during winter, protecting the plant from injury by limiting the development of ice crystals within the plant cells.

Most halophytes, despite their high salt tolerance, must prevent the buildup of toxic levels of salt in their tissues. Salt dilution and salt extrusion are the two most common ways in which they achieve this reduction. The succulent leaves of greasewood have the capacity to store large amounts of water, which provides a means of diluting the amount of salt present in the leaf cells as needed. Saltbush, on the other hand, reduces its salt load by transporting the excess to specialized salt glands or to storage hairs on the leaf surface. The storage hairs, each consisting of a small stalk cell and a large, bladderlike cell, function as reservoirs, filling with salt water until the bladder cell ruptures and releases its contents to the exterior of the leaf.

Reproduction and Growth

Dryland shrubs exhibit several adaptations that help to ensure their reproductive success. The small, inconspicuous flowers of mountain mahogany produce seeds that effectively plant themselves and can respond immediately to microclimatic conditions conducive to germination. Each small, hairy seed is tipped with a long, feathery plume, which functions in much the same way as a parachute, allowing the sharply pointed seed tip to reach the ground first. Changes in relative humidity cause the featherlike tails to coil or twist hygroscopically, drilling the seed directly into the soil so that it can germinate the following spring.

Reproductive versatility—the ability to reproduce by either sexual or vegetative means—is an important advantage for many dryland shrubs. For Gambel oak, such versatility is critical, for the plant must contend, at least in the northern portions of its range, with environmental conditions (such as cold temperatures and insufficient moisture during germination) that often inhibit successful completion of the sexual cycle. At the base of the trunk, specialized anatomical structures called *lignotubers* enclose hundreds of dormant buds, each capable of sprouting and growing out into a leafy shoot. In addition, numerous stems, called rhizomes, lie just beneath the ground surface. Each rhizome has its own supply of dormant buds, which remain dormant until some environmental stress, such as damage to the tree's crown by fire or heavy browsing, ends the hormonal suppression that keeps them dormant. Consequently, a stand of oak typically consists of several spreading *clones* (genetically related plants originating from a single mother plant), which may persist for thousands of years through stress-related suckering.

Plant Defenses

Chemical interactions play an important role in the ecology of shrub ecosystems and are especially important in communities where basic resources are limited and each plant must compete with its neighbors in order to survive. The term *allelochemic* describes a large class of chemical interactions in which one species affects the well-being and growth of another by releasing chemical compounds into the environment. Allelochemic interactions may occur between different species of plants or between plants and animals.

The majority of chemicals involved in allelochemic interactions are produced as by-products of plant metabolism and belong to one of three major groups—phenolics, terpenoids, and alkaloids—or to one of a number of minor groups that include mustard oils and organic cyanides. All are toxic or inhibitory to varying degrees and may be released to the environment either as volatile (airborne) or as water-soluble agents. For the most part, these compounds remain at low levels or are degraded by microbial action in the soil without producing effects detrimental to other organisms. In some cases, however, the concentrations of these secondary compounds in plants are such that substantial quantities are released into the environment, either from the living plant or by decomposition of plant litter. For example, the pungent odor of big sagebrush, especially aromatic after a rain, is produced by the emanation of volatile terpenes (camphor and cineole) from its leaves.

The term *allelopathy* refers to the situation in which compounds produced by one plant species influence the germination and growth of another. In communities dominated by a single species, such as big sagebrush, the chemistry of the soil may reflect the influx of secondary compounds to such a degree that only those species that are tolerant of this chemistry can maintain populations in the community. Terpenes in the litter and fresh leaves of big sagebrush have been shown to inhibit the growth of blue grama and golden aster, and many other would-be competitors. The concentration of toxic compounds in the soil is greatest directly beneath the sagebrush canopy, frequently resulting in areas of bare, vegetation-free soil.

Plants rely on secondary compounds as well as on an impressive arsenal of defensive structures (such as spines, thorns, and trichomes) to deter would-be herbivores. Some secondary compounds exhibit inhibitory effects on animal metabolism and digestion, while others may interfere with reproduction, produce cancerous growths in vital organs, or destroy the central nervous system. Coevolution on the part of many herbivores, however, has included numerous mechanisms that circumvent or counteract these detrimental effects. For example, the foliage of some succulent plants, such as greasewood and prickly-pear, contain large amounts of oxalic acid, a compound toxic to most animals. Animals that routinely utilize these plants for food and as a source of water—jackrabbits, pocket gophers, and pronghorn—have evolved a means of metabolizing oxalic acid and excreting the by-products without harmful side effects.

Though domestic livestock eat big sagebrush sparingly, this terpene-rich shrub is the staple food resource for animals such as the sage grouse, and an important supplementary food for pronghorn, mule deer, and elk. The twigs and foliage of sagebrush are rich in plant fiber, or cellulose, but require prolonged bacterial fermentation in order to break down the cellulose for further digestion. Research shows that a high intake of terpene-rich foods can seriously reduce the microbial population of the herbivore digestive tract—rendering it largely ineffective in terms of cellulose digestion. Birds that subsist on a cellulose-rich diet, such as the sage grouse, possess a pair of sacs—the caeca—located toward the posterior end of the intestine. The caecum functions as a temporary storage chamber in which microbial fermentation can occur. It is especially large in sage grouse, the combined length of the two sacs roughly equal to that of the intestine. Sage grouse are able to concentrate and detoxify terpenoid compounds in the caeca, eliminating all indigestible and potentially harmful residue in the form of a caecal dropping. Caecal droppings are entirely unlike normal feces and are easy to identify because of their tarlike appearance and strong sage smell.

In mule deer and pronghorn, the initial bacterial processing, or fermentation, of cellulose-rich foods takes place in the *rumen,* the first and largest compartment of the multichambered stomach. Studies of mule deer suggest that these animals can tolerate up to 30 percent sagebrush in their diet without incurring significant inhibition of rumen bacterial activity. There is no evidence that ruminants are able to isolate and detoxify harmful substances in the same way that sage grouse do. Feeding experiments have shown that mule deer, and probably other native ruminants as well, are selective in their browsing of sagebrush, choosing plants that have comparatively lower levels of toxic compounds and varying their total daily consumption of sagebrush in relation to other plant foods. These foraging behaviors appear to play a critical role in maintaining an adequate population of rumen bacteria for proper fermentation. The association of heavy deer mortality with excessive feeding on sagebrush, however, suggests that selective browsing may be inadequate when mule deer are forced to subsist primarily on sagebrush.

Environment and Adaptation: Shrubland Animals

Shrublands provide critical habitat for a diversity of animal species. In fact, more mammalian species can be found in rocky shrubland habitats than in any other mountain ecosystem. For small and medium-sized animals, cover from predators is readily available. Many shrubland communities offer a rich harvest of seasonal foods—acorns, seeds, berries, foliage, insects and other invertebrates, small vertebrates, and eggs. Living space, though somewhat limited in terms of vertical differentiation, is less condensed than in herbaceous communities. The majority of animal species make use of shrubland ecosystems on a seasonal or occasional basis. Year-round residents are primarily small mammals, reptiles, some birds, and an enormous variety of invertebrates.

Adaptations to Water Stress

For all animals, the maintenance of water balance is essential for survival. Adaptations for water conservation can be seen in the timing of activity cycles, the kinds of food eaten, and a variety of behavioral, morphological, and physiological features. In environments where the availability of free water is largely limited to the rare instance of rain or snow, carnivorous and insectivorous animals extract water from the body fluids of their prey. Many herbivorous animals obtain sufficient water from the tissues of plants they eat. Ord's kangaroo rat, the undisputed master of water conservation, can live indefinitely on a diet of dry seeds, without any water intake. Though low in moisture content, the seeds that comprise this species' diet are typically high in fats and carbohydrates, which yield a large amount of *metabolic water* as a result of the oxidation of hydrogen that occurs during digestion.

Evaporation is the most important cause of water loss in dry environments, especially when temperatures are high. Moist-skinned animals, such as frogs and toads, are particularly vulnerable to evaporative water loss through the skin and, as a result, are present in shrublands only in microhabitats with consistent water supplies. Birds and mammals must rely on their fur or feathers to reduce evaporative losses and to insulate their bodies from excessive heat. Lung-breathing animals regularly lose moisture to the atmosphere when they exhale. Ord's kangaroo rat has achieved a remarkable reduction in respiratory evaporation. It can exhale air at a lower temperature than that of its body core because the convolutions of its nasal passages function as a *countercurrent heat exchanger*. When the kangaroo rat inhales, the walls of the nasal passages give off heat to the air flowing over them, causing the temperature of the nasal passages to fall below that of the air being inhaled. The inhaled air undergoes further warming and subsequent saturation in the lungs. On exhalation, this warm air passes over the nasal membranes cooled during inhalation and is forced to leave some of its moisture behind as condensation on the membranes. The effectiveness of this system is enhanced by the kangaroo rat's highly efficient kidneys, nocturnal habits, and prolonged periods spent resting and feeding in the relatively humid environment of the burrow.

In arid environments, the ability of the kidneys to concentrate urine is an important adaptation for reducing water loss. The more concentrated the urine, the more economical the use of water for urine formation and the elimination of toxic wastes produced by metabolic processes. Kangaroo rat urine is roughly twice as dense as seawater and five times more concentrated than human urine. Consequently, in excreting comparable amounts of toxic metabolic wastes, the kangaroo rat uses one-fifth as much water as humans do.

Avoiding Heat Stress

All animals must avoid extremely high temperatures. A variety of physiological, anatomical, and behavioral adaptations allow animals to maintain a degree of constancy, or *homeostasis*, in their body temperatures. Cold-blooded animals, such as the rattlesnake or the eastern fence lizard, maintain optimal body temperature behaviorally, by shuttling between a warm, sunlit area and a cooler, shaded refuge. Mammals and birds that remain active above ground during the heat of the day must be able to withstand hours of exposure to an unrelenting sun. Many have pale-colored, reflective pelage or feathers, thus reducing the rate at which heat is absorbed from the environment. Others have evolved morphological features such as large ears that dissipate heat in much the same way that a radiator does. The large ears of the desert cottontail and the black-tailed jackrabbit are crisscrossed with a network of tiny, pulsating blood vessels that give off heat to the air blowing over them.

Under conditions of high heat stress, warm-blooded animals may be forced to resort to evaporative cooling, a function of the respiratory organs or the sweat glands, to prevent overheating. Humans dissipate heat effectively through sweating. Coyotes, in contrast, have few sweat glands, and must pant to produce evaporative cooling. Birds, lacking sweat glands altogether, increase evaporative cooling by panting or by the rapid oscillation of the throat, known as *gular fluttering*.

Semidesert Scrub

Greenish gray shrubs, sparsely interspersed with herbaceous plants, lend their muted colors to the semidesert scrub. Considered an eastern outlier of the Great Basin Desert, semidesert scrub consists of two community types, one dominated by greasewood and the other by various species of saltbush. Species diversity tends to be low, and in many communities, a single species constitutes 90 percent or more of the plant cover. Some communities have greater than 50 percent bare soil. Because of the thin vegetation cover and deflation of the soil by wind, a "pavement" of wind-burnished stones is present in many areas.

Common shrubs of the semidesert scrub, clockwise from upper left: four-wing saltbrush, winterfat, Russian-thistle, greasewood with detail of fruit.

Ecological Distribution

Semidesert scrub is prevalent below 7,500 feet in the upper Rio Grande Basin, from the San Luis Valley south into

New Mexico, on broad valley floors in western Colorado, in the Shirley Basin in Wyoming, and as isolated stands near Pueblo, Cañon City, and Walsenburg. The most extensive scrub communities are developed on a massive Cretaceous marine deposit known as the Mancos Shale. The Mancos Shale, where not protected by more resistant sandstones, erodes into undulating gray and yellow badlands, characterized by swelling clays and by soils rich in gypsum and other salts.

Community Characteristics

Soil factors, in combination with climate, are the primary agents of plant selection in the semidesert scrub. Greasewood predominates in areas with either saline or alkaline soils and a consistently high water table. In the most alkaline bottomlands, greasewood may form single-species stands or may occur in association with saltgrass, alkali sacaton, desert wild-rye, kochia, whiteweed, and marsh-elder. In less alkaline situations, species of saltbush, big sagebrush, rabbitbrush, Russian-thistle, and winterfat may also be common.

Saltbush is most common in areas where the soils are generally drier and less saline or alkaline than those where greasewood grows. Typical associates of saltbush in these communities include copper mallow, galleta grass, Indian ricegrass, blue grama, and ring muhly. Cacti are far less common in these communities than in the warm-temperate deserts of the Southwest.

Descriptions of Common Plants

Shrubs

Four-wing Saltbush, *Atriplex canescens.* Four-wing saltbush is a densely branched shrub, rarely exceeding 4 feet in height, and distinguished from other species by its narrowly oblong leaves, silvery leaf scales, and clusters of four-wing fruits; male and female flowers appear on separate bushes.

The leaves and young shoots of four-wing saltbush are extremely palatable to browsing animals, and many small mammals and birds relish its fruits.

Shadscale Saltbush, *Atriplex confertifolia.* Shadscale, the dominant shrub of the Great Basin salt-scrub, is most common in this region in the Grand Valley and in other arid basins along the western margin of the Southern Rockies. It is a compact, moderately sized shrub, ranging in height from 1 to 3 feet, armored with an array of rigid, spine-tipped branches. The leaves of this species are broader and more oval in shape than those of four-wing saltbush, and its flat fruits have two parallel wings instead of four. At maturity, the fruit turns from pale green to a lovely deep pink.

Mat Saltbush, *Atriplex corrugata.* This distinctive saltbush is identified by its matlike growth form and succulent, oblong-to-ovate–shaped leaves. Mat saltbush often forms single-species communities in extremely water-stressed environments, such as the Mancos Shale badlands in the Grand Valley.

Greasewood, *Sarcobatus vermiculatus.* Greasewood is readily identified by its scraggly, much-branched growth form, spine-tipped branches, and dark green, linear leaves. The inconspicuous flowers of greasewood are unisexual, but both male and female flowers are typically present on the same shrub. Female flowers are pale green, borne in pairs or singularly within the axil of the leaf; the cone-shaped male flowers average about 1 inch in length and are clustered at the tips of leafy branchlets. The fruits develop in the axil of the leaf and are somewhat funnel shaped, consisting of an erect nutlet rimmed by a membranous wing that is characteristically tinged with red.

Winterfat, *Krascheninnikovia lanata.* Winterfat is a low shrub, ranging in height from 1 to 3 feet, and is common throughout the arid West. Its leaves are slender and almost needlelike, with a dense covering of hairs and rolled-under leaf margins. The male and female flowers occur separately but are borne in terminal spikes on the same plant. Winterfat is most conspicuous in seed, when the fruits open and cloak the branches with woolly hairs.

Grasses and Herbaceous Plants

Russian-thistle, *Salsola australis.* This abundant tumble-weed, introduced from Eurasia, is distinguished by its stiffly spreading, prickly branches and by its alternate, threadlike leaves. Though distinctly woody and often tinged with red when mature, this species is an annual. The flowers occur in the leaf axils and are subtended by two bracts; the fruits have five membranous white or pink persistent sepals.

Indian Ricegrass, *Stipa hymenoides.* This tall, graceful bunchgrass is identified by its multiple-branching inflorescence and solitary spikelets appearing at the ends of curved pedicels. The seeds of this native species are high in protein and were ground to make flour by various Indian tribes.

Ring Muhly, *Muhlenbergia torreyi.* Ring muhly derives its name from the large, ring-shaped cushions that it forms on dry, sandy soils and blowout areas; the growth form is maintained because as the clump grows, the inner portion dies, leaving a ring of living grass. *M. pungens,* a common species on the Western Slope, assumes the same growth form. The leaves of ring muhly are greatly curved and sharply pointed, contributing to the compact appearance of the cushion; the inflorescence is much branched, and the spikelets are solitary.

Common Plants of the Semidesert Scrub

Shrubs

Greasewood, *Sarcobatus vermiculatus*
Horsebrush, spiny, *Tetradymia spinosa*
Rabbitbrush, golden, *Chrysothamnus nauseosus*
   small, *Chrysothamnus depressus*
   sticky-flowered, *Chrysothamnus viscidiflorus*
Sagebrush, big, *Seriphidium tridentatum* (formerly *Artemisia*)
Saltbush, four-wing, *Atriplex canescens*
   gardner, *Atriplex gardneri*
   mat, *Atriplex corrugata*
   shadscale, *Atriplex confertifolia*

Snakeweed, broom, *Gutierrezia sarothrae*
Spiny Hopsage, *Atriplex grayi*
Winterfat, *Krascheninnikovia lanata* (formerly *Ceratoides*)

Grasses

Cheatgrass, *Anisantha tectorum* (formerly *Bromus*)
Galleta grass, *Hilaria jamesii*
Grama, blue, *Bouteloua gracilis*
   hairy, *Bouteloua hirsuta*
Muhly, alkali, *Muhlenbergia asperifolia*
   ring, *Muhlenbergia pungens* and *M. torreyi*
Ricegrass, Indian, *Stipa hymenoides* (formerly *Oryzopsis*)
Ryegrass, desert, *Leymus salina*
Sacaton, alkali, *Sporobolus airoides*
Saltgrass, *Distichlis stricta*

Wildflowers

Buckwheat, desert, *Eriogonum ovalifolium*
Cactus, prickly-pear, *Opuntia* spp.
Fleabane, desert, *Erigeron pulcherrimus*
Hyacinth, wild, *Androstephium breviflorum*
Mallow, copper, *Sphaeralcea coccinea*
Mariposa lily, desert, *Calochortus nuttallii*
Marsh-elder, *Iva axillaris*
Milk Vetch, milkweed-flowered, *Astragalus asclepiadoides*
Oreocarya, desert, *Oreocarya longiflora*
Scorpionweed, desert, *Phacelia splendens*
Skeleton-weed, *Lygodesmia grandiflora*
Thistle, Russian, *Salsola australis*

Animals of the Semidesert Scrub

Semidesert scrub provides food and cover for a great variety
of desert species. Where the soil is easily dug, the burrow
mounds and foraging trails of Ord's kangaroo rat crisscross
the landscape. Avoiding mid-day heat, desert cottontails and
black-tailed jackrabbits rest in shallow scrapes beneath the

shrubs. Coyotes prowl the brushy swales in search of prey, and a shrike perches atop a tall shrub as it scans the ground for the unwary mouse. Swainson's and other open-country hawks ride the thermals that rise above the broad, intermontane basins. Flocks of Brewer's sparrows forage for protein-rich seeds among silvery tussocks of ricegrass. In the sparse shade beneath a saltbush, a short-horned lizard ambushes a harvester ant with a quick flick of its tongue. Nearby, in the soft sand of a small dune, a gently curving trail reveals the passage of a bullsnake.

Life Histories of Selected Animals

Mammals

Desert Cottontail, *Sylvilagus audubonii.* This medium-sized, buff gray rabbit is distinguished by its whitish underparts highlighted with rust, and by its large, sparsely furred ears. Water is obtained primarily from succulent vegetation or from the oxidation of food; the ability of the kidneys to concentrate urine surpasses that of other cottontails. The species is largely solitary. Males occupy home ranges of up to 15 acres and maintain strict territories against other males, while home ranges of females average about 1 acre and several females may coexist in a given area. Breeding begins by late April, with two or more litters of altricial young born yearly. Ovulation is normally induced by copulation, and gestation takes about one month. Young rabbits reach full maturity at about six to nine months; few individuals live longer than three years.

Black-tailed Jackrabbit, *Lepus californicus.* This somewhat dark-colored hare is distinguished from the white-tailed jackrabbit *(L. townsendii)* by its large, black-tipped ears, lack of whitish fur on the sides of the body, and black tail patch; there is no winter color change. Semiarid brushlands and grasslands below 7,000 feet are preferred habitat. Usually solitary except during the breeding season, the black-tailed jackrabbit normally has a home range of less than 2,000 acres. Mating behavior is complex, involving long chases, jumping, and frequent fighting between males and females.

Ovulation is induced by copulation, with one to four litters of precocial young born annually. Young hares are capable of moving about at birth and hop well within two or three days; adult size is attained in about ten weeks.

Ord's Kangaroo Rat, *Dipodomys ordii.* Huge hind feet, short forelegs, and a long, bushy-tipped tail make this small mammal unmistakable. Upper body pelage is generally cinnamon buff, shading to white below; white stripes run along each flank to the tip of the tail. Rapid locomotion is bipedal, with the hind feet providing power and the small forelegs carried close to the body; the tail is used for balance. The kangaroo rat is chiefly nocturnal and solitary. Burrow systems are dug in sandy soils, with an opening typically situated at the base of shrubs or bunchgrasses; the animal retreats by day to its burrow, plugging the entrance with soil to protect itself from predators and to maintain optimal humidity. Diet consists mainly of seeds, which are gathered with the forepaws, often by sifting the sand, and then carried to the burrow in capacious cheek pouches. Seed stores are kept in the burrow, occasionally in species-specific piles, and the pilfering of seed caches of harvester ants is fairly common. Courtship is active and reciprocal; males engage in fighting, aerial kicks, hind-foot drumming, teeth chattering, and vocalizations. The female delivers her altricial young with her forepaws and incisors. Adult size is attained by five or six weeks of age.

Birds

Ferruginous Hawk, *Buteo regalis.* The ferruginous hawk is distinguished by its rufous brown upperparts, whitish breast, and white, unbanded tail; seen from below, the dark, barred legs form a conspicuous V against the white body, and dark crescents mark the wrist of each wing. In flight, the wings are held in a V. Hunting is done from a perch, on the ground, while soaring, or in low, rapid flight; the bird often soars in great circles. This species utilizes a variety of nest sites—trees, rock ledges, hillsides, and rocky pinnacles; nests may be used repeatedly by the same pair, and aggressive protection of the nest against predators—red-tailed hawks, great horned owls, and coyotes—is common. Breeding occurs from March to July; incubation is by both sexes and

Open country birds of prey, from left to right, by row: (top row) rough-legged hawk, Swainson's hawk; (row 2) ferruginous hawk, northern harrier with detail showing white rump patch; (row 3) red-tailed hawk, prairie falcon, American kestrel; (row 4) golden eagle, with detail of white wing patch visible on immatures; (row 5) turkey vulture. Silhouettes show wing position while soaring.

averages twenty-eight days. Young fledge forty-four to forty-eight days after hatching. Ages of seventeen to twenty years have been reported for this species.

Loggerhead Shrike, *Lanius ludovicianus.* Often confused with the mockingbird, this robin-sized bird is identified by its black wings, dark gray upperparts, falconlike bill, and conspicuous black mask extending through the eyes and over the bill; white patches flash prominently in flight. Solitary, except during the breeding season, this small predator hunts from a conspicuous perch—the top of a shrub, a small tree, or a fence post. Mice, small birds, insects (especially grasshoppers and crickets), and small reptiles provide the bulk of the diet; undigestible parts (fur, feathers, etc.) are regurgitated as pellets. Excess food items may be impaled on the tips of twigs or on barbed wire for later retrieval. The call of the shrike is short and abrupt, while the song consists of a fluid series of notes. Breeding occurs from April to July; both sexes incubate, and the young fledge within thirty-six days of hatching.

Brewer's Sparrow, *Spizella breweri.* This small, rather nondescript sparrow is distinguished from other clear-breasted sparrows by its slender shape, long, notched tail, whitish wing bars, and lack of rufous cap or strong head markings. In the Southern Rockies, the species is considered the dominant dryland sparrow in many areas. Brewer's are insectivorous in summer and granivorous in winter. On winter range, this species forages in mixed flocks with other sparrows. On nesting grounds, the male sings an elaborate, canary-like song from the end of a branch near the nest; many males may sing in chorus at dawn and at twilight.

Reptiles

Short-horned Lizard, *Phrynosoma douglassii.* This small lizard is distinguished by its rounded and somewhat flattened midsection, spiny head and upper back, and enlarged row of pointed scales on each side of its body. Remarkably well-camouflaged, this species often resembles the soil coloring of its habitat. Dry grasslands and shrublands characterized by sparse vegetation at ground level are preferred habitat. Short-horned lizards are diurnal and insectivorous; ants and beetles are dietary staples. At night or on cool days, this species seeks shelter in small rodent burrows or by burying itself in the soil; activity extends from April to October. Short-horned lizards are relatively easy to catch and handle if treated gently; disturbed individuals may spurt blood from the corner of the eye. Females give birth to live young in underground burrows in July or August; average litter size is seventeen.

Western Rattlesnake, *Crotalus viridis.* This venomous snake is identified by its triangular-shaped head, the presence of a rattle consisting of horny segments on the end of its tail, and a body pattern consisting of splotches of brown on a tan background. Though not generally considered aggressive, rattlesnakes will coil defensively when approached and may strike if harassed; vibration or buzzing of the rattle does not always occur prior to striking. Rattlesnakes are potentially dangerous to humans; any bite victim should be kept quiet and transported to medical facilities as quickly as possible. In this region, the western rattlesnake is found in dry terrain below 8,200 feet. Rattlesnakes do not actively search out their prey (small mammals, nestling birds, toads, and lizards) but rely instead on their ability to ambush warm-blooded animals through the use of special heat-sensing organs that produce an image of the prey in the brain and serve to determine strike range — even in total darkness. Rattlesnakes are largely nocturnal in midsummer, becoming active at dusk and retreating to an abandoned burrow, a rocky crevice, or the shade of a small shrub during periods of inactivity. Group hibernation chambers are common; emergence typically occurs in late April, with a return to den sites in mid-September through early November. Females give birth from late August to early October, producing an average of twelve precocial young.

Common Animals of the Semidesert Scrub

Mammals

Desert Cottontail, *Sylvilagus audubonii*
Black-tailed Jackrabbit, *Lepus californicus*
White-tailed Jackrabbit, *Lepus townsendii*
Least Chipmunk, *Tamias minimus*
White-tailed Prairie Dog, *Cynomys leucurus*
Valley Pocket Gopher, *Thomomys bottae*
Northern Pocket Gopher, *Thomomys talpoides*
Silky Pocket Mouse, *Perognathus flavus*

Ord's Kangaroo Rat, *Dipodomys ordii*
Deer Mouse, *Peromyscus maniculatus*
Northern Grasshopper Mouse, *Onychomys leucogaster*
Coyote, *Canis latrans*
Gray Fox, *Urocyon cinereoargenteus*
Badger, *Taxidea taxus*
Striped Skunk, *Mephitis mephitis*
Mule Deer, *Odocoileus hemionus*
Pronghorn, *Antilocapra americana*

Birds

Turkey Vulture, *Cathartes aura*
Rough-legged Hawk, *Buteo lagopus*
Ferruginous Hawk, *Buteo regalis*
Red-tailed Hawk, *Buteo jamaicensis*
Swainson's Hawk, *Buteo swainsoni*
Golden Eagle, *Aquila chrysaetos*
Common Raven, *Corvus corax*
Loggerhead Shrike, *Lanius ludovicianus*
Horned Lark, *Eremophila alpestris*
Brown Towhee, *Pipilo fuscus*
Vesper Sparrow, *Pooecetes gramineus*
Lark Sparrow, *Chondestes grammacus*
Brewer's Sparrow, *Spizella breweri*

Reptiles

Collared Lizard, *Crotaphytus collaris*
Short-horned Lizard, *Phrynosoma douglassii*
Sagebrush Lizard, *Sceloporus graciosus*
Eastern Fence Lizard, *Sceloporus undulatus*
Many-lined Skink, *Eumeces multivirgatus*
Western Rattlesnake, *Crotalus viridis*
Bullsnake, *Pituophis melanoleucus*

Butterflies

Saltbush Sooty-wing, *Pholisora alpheus*
Great Basin Wood Nymph, *Cercyonis sthenele*

Sagebrush Shrublands

Sagebrush—the word conjures up images of wide open spaces, a silvery green landscape rimmed by billowing clouds and azure skies. By day, the air is redolent of sage and sun-baked earth. Hawks, and sometimes a golden eagle, pass high overhead, soaring on the thermals. Pronghorn, disturbed from their grazing, race into the distance, white rumps flashing in the sunlight. To some, a landscape dotted with sagebrush is a lonesome wasteland, but to most westerners these durable shrublands fill a special niche—a magical place where the eerie howl of a coyote can still be heard at dusk.

Ecological Distribution

Sagebrush covers vast areas of the American West. Two major types of sagebrush shrubland occur in the Southern Rockies. The *sagebrush-steppe association,* dominated by mountain sagebrush, is most common in basins and broad valleys in the northern half of the Southern Rockies at elevations ranging from 7,000 to 10,000 feet and above. Sagebrush-steppe communities are best developed on the Western Slope and occur sporadically on the Eastern Slope, covering large expanses in the Shirley Basin and Laramie River Valley of Wyoming, the Yampa River Valley, the Little Snake River Valley, the Western Slope of the Park Range, North Park, Middle Park, the upper Gunnison Basin, and the Beaver Meadows area on the eastern side of Rocky Mountain National Park. The *Great Basin sagebrush association,* dominated by big sagebrush, is adapted to slightly warmer, semidesert environments and is typical of lower elevation plateaus and river valleys to nearly 8,000 feet. Great Basin big sagebrush communities reach their greatest development in north-central New Mexico, and in the Animas, Colorado, and lower Gunnison river-drainages of Colorado.

Community Characteristics

Sagebrush shrublands are best developed on sites with soils that are moderately deep, well drained, and only mildly alka-

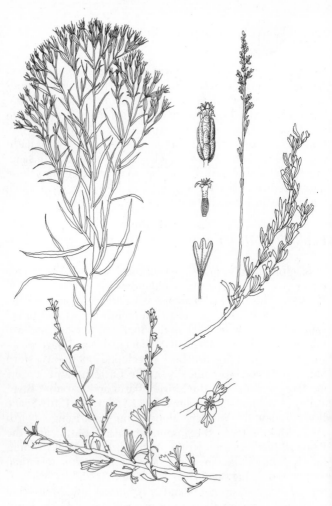

Common shrubs of the sagebrush shrublands, clockwise
from upper left: golden rabbitbrush, big sagebrush (with
enlargements of flowerhead, floret, and leaf), bitterbrush,
with flower detail.

line. In order for sagebrush to dominate a plant community,
the soils must be friable and unrestrictive, allowing root
penetration to substantial depths and easy circulation of air
and water. In contrast to the soils associated with semidesert

scrub, those of sagebrush shrublands tend to be better leached, with lower salt concentrations and a deeper calcium carbonate, or *caliche,* layer.

In most cases, sagebrush-steppe and Great Basin sagebrush communities can be distinguished on the basis of species-specific differences in growth form and preferred habitat. Big sagebrush, the taller of the two sagebrush species, is a shrub of deep soils and is especially common on floodplains and in arroyos. Mountain sagebrush, on the other hand, seldom exceeds 3 feet in height and is associated with shallower soils and cooler and more moist habitats. Wyoming sagebrush, a subspecies of mountain sagebrush, occurs in northern Colorado and southern Wyoming and is typical of sites that are more arid than those occupied by mountain sagebrush. Black sagebrush, a more darkly colored species, is a common component of the sagebrush-steppe at lower elevations and in areas with relatively shallow, calcareous soils. Hoary sagebrush is typical of moist meadow situations in the northern half of the Southern Rockies. Where communities dominated by different species of sagebrush occur in close proximity, community boundaries tend to be sharply defined.

Understory vegetation in Great Basin sagebrush communities tends to be sparse as a result of the competition for available moisture. On the most arid sites, big sagebrush may grow in association with greasewood, various species of saltbush, black sagebrush, and winterfat. Dry, relatively sandy soils may support nearly pure stands of rabbitbrush. Where growth conditions are optimal, and where livestock grazing has been controlled, stands of big sagebrush may include golden and sticky-flowered rabbitbrush, broom snakeweed, spiny hopsage, and cottonthorn. Aridland bunchgrasses and wildflowers such as orange paintbrush, phlox, desert buckwheat, and desert sandwort may be especially common.

Sagebrush-steppe communities often exhibit a greater diversity of herbaceous plants than is found in adjacent coniferous forests. Shrubs such as horsebrush, serviceberry, bitterbrush, wild rose, and snowberry are common in many stands. During years with above-average precipitation, a surprising abundance of wildflowers lends color to these shrublands. The most conspicuous species include larkspur, lupine, balsamroot, mule's ears, penstemon, scarlet gilia, paintbrush, fleabane daisies, and buckwheat. Among the wildflowers, grasses such as blue grama, wheatgrass, Junegrass, needle-and-thread, and various species of fescue may be common. With extreme grazing pressure, the herbaceous understory is quickly removed and the living crust of mosses and soil lichens trampled beyond recovery; many such areas have been invaded by exotic plants, such as cheatgrass and Russian-thistle.

Successional Patterns

On certain sites, sagebrush ecosystems represent a long-lived successional stage. In relatively moist environments, these successional stands are replaced by grasses and moisture-loving trees and shrubs, such as aspen and willow. The existence of small and largely isolated stands of mountain sagebrush, such as those found in the Front Range, are difficult to explain. Some biologists believe that these stands are relicts of larger populations that flourished during a time when climatic conditions favored their development.

Grazing and fire can dramatically alter normal successional patterns in sagebrush communities. Under heavy grazing, big sagebrush and other woody species increase in size and number at the expense of more palatable, herbaceous species. In contrast, fire selectively destroys sagebrush and favors the spread of grasses—a fact range managers have exploited to increase forage yields for livestock. Following a range fire, the niche of the fire-intolerant sagebrush is often assumed by the proliferation of fire-adapted plants, such as rabbitbrush and snakeweed, which sprout from their stumps when burnt.

Descriptions of Common Plants

Shrubs

Big Sagebrush, *Seriphidium tridentatum.* Sagebrush is generally identified by its silvery green, wedge-shaped, three-

lobed leaves; the crushed leaves give off a strong scent somewhat similar to that of the culinary sages (*Salvia* spp.). Its
clusters of small, yellowish green flower heads bear little
resemblance to those of more showy members of the
sunflower family. Each flower head consists of numerous
tubular florets; flowers are produced during late summer or
early fall and are wind pollinated. Big sagebrush, in contrast
to mountain sagebrush *(S. vaseyanum),* tends to be tall and
robust, with its flower heads arranged in numerous open
panicles.

Golden Rabbitbrush, *Chrysothamnus nauseosus.* Golden
rabbitbrush, or *chamisa,* as it is known in New Mexico, is
easily distinguished from big sagebrush by its narrow, non-
lobed leaves and the absence of a sagelike odor. The branches
are slender and flexible, and young twigs are covered with
feltlike matted hairs. The pungent odor and unpalatable
qualities of rabbitbrush are caused by the presence of latex,
a viscous fluid composed of terpenoid particles suspended
in water; the latex has been investigated as a commercial
source of rubber. Masses of narrow flower heads, with about
five tubular, chrome yellow disk flowers per head, begin to
appear in August and build to a spectacular, golden climax
in September.

Antelope Bitterbrush, *Purshia tridentata.* Antelope bitterbrush is readily identified by its much-branched growth
habit and small, three-lobed leaves, which resemble those
of big sagebrush but lack the conspicuous covering of fine
hairs and the distinctive sagelike odor. Like most members
of the rose family, the fragrant, pale yellow flowers have five
sepals, five petals, and multiple stamens. The single carpel
ripens to a tapered, yellow-orange capsule, containing numerous small black seeds; despite their bitter, quininelike
taste, the seeds are a favorite with small mammals. In areas
where browsing is severe, heavily pruned shrubs of antelope bitterbrush are generally no more than 2 feet tall.

Wildflowers

Lupine, *Lupinus* spp. Lupines are among the most common wildflower associates of sagebrush and are distinguished
by their palmately compound leaves and pealike, blue flow-

Common wildflowers of the sagebrush shrublands, clockwise
from upper left: Indian paintbrush with detail of flower,
lupine, larkspur, mule's ear.

ers borne in elongated clusters or racemes. Each flower consists of five different petals: an upright or nearly upright petal
known as the *banner* or *standard,* two lower petals joined

along one edge to form the *keel,* and two lateral petals, the so-called *wings,* one to each side of the keel. The stamens, generally ten in number, are enclosed within the keel and form a sheath around the carpel. Following fertilization, the carpel elongates to form a podlike fruit enclosing a single row of seeds and splitting open into two halves at maturity. Lupine pods contain poisonous alkaloids that can be extremely toxic to livestock, particularly sheep.

Mule's Ears, *Wyethia amplexicaulis.* Few species can match the spectacular floral display of this golden, sunflower-like wildflower. Mule's ears is distinguished from a similar species, balsamroot *(Balsamorhiza sagittata),* by its leathery-textured, hairless leaves, its leafy flowering stems, and the presence of two or more flower heads per stem; some hybrid populations in western Colorado may have pubescent leaves.

Indian Paintbrush, *Castilleja* spp. The striking colors associated with the paintbrushes—shades of palest cream, yellow, pink, magenta, orange, and crimson—are due not to the flowers themselves, which are small and greenish, but to the brilliantly colored bractlike leaves and sepals that surround the flowers. The flower consists of a two-lipped corolla, with the upper lip (or galea) elongated like a beak and enclosing the four stamens. Paintbrush flowers are a favorite with nectar-seeking pollinators, especially hummingbirds.

Larkspur, *Delphinium nuttallianum.* This common wildflower is identified by its largely basal, linearly palmate leaflets and its blue-purple flowers; the flowers are bilaterally symmetrical, with the uppermost sepal elongated to form a conspicuous spur. The Latin name for this species is derived from the word *delphinus,* meaning dolphin, and refers to the flower's unusual shape.

Tufted Broomrape, *Orobanche fasciculata.* Broomrape is a small, easily overlooked plant identified by its clustered, coral-colored flowering stalks, each bearing a single penstemon-like flower, and its coral-colored, scalelike leaves. The petals of the flower are fused into a slightly arched tube with five lobes. Stems, leaves, and flowers are typically covered with sticky, glandular hairs. Broomrapes are root parasites; a single broomrape flower produces enormous numbers of small seeds, as many as fifty thousand in some species, which can remain dormant in the soil for ten to fifteen years, or until suitable germination conditions are met.

Common Plants of the Sagebrush Shrublands

Shrubs

Bitterbrush, *Purshia tridentata*
Chokecherry, *Padus virginiana* (formerly *Prunus*)
Greasewood, *Sarcobatus vermiculatus*
Hopsage, spiny, *Grayia spinosa*
Horsebrush, *Tetradymia canescens*
Rabbitbrush, golden, *Chrysothamnus nauseosus*
   sticky-flowered, *Chrysothamnus viscidiflorus*
Rose, wild, *Rosa woodsii*
Sagebrush, big (or Great Basin), *Seriphidium*
      tridentatum (formerly *Artemisia tridentata*)
   black, *Seriphidium novum*
   hoary, *Seriphidium canum*
   mountain, *Seriphidium vaseyanum*
   Wyoming, *Seriphidium vaseyanum* ssp. *wyomingensis*
Saltbush, *Atriplex* spp.
Serviceberry, Utah, *Amelanchier utahensis*
   western, *Amelanchier alnifolia*
Snakeweed, broom, *Gutierrezia sarothrae*
Snowberry, *Symphoricarpos rotundifolius*

Grasses and Sedges

Cheatgrass, *Anisantha tectorum* (formerly *Bromus*)
Fescue, Arizona, *Festuca arizonica*
   Idaho, *Festuca idahoensis*
Galleta Grass, *Hilaria jamesii*
Grama, blue, *Bouteloua gracilis*
   side-oats, *Bouteloua curtipendula*
Junegrass, *Koeleria macrantha*
Mutton-grass, *Poa fendleriana*
Needle-and-thread, *Stipa comata*
Ricegrass, Indian, *Stipa hymenoides* (formerly *Oryzopsis*)
Sedge, valley, *Carex vallicola*
Squirreltail, *Elymus hystrix* (formerly *Sitanion*)

Wheatgrass, *Agropyron* spp.
Wild-rye, giant, *Elymus cinereus*

Wildflowers

Aster, *Aster occidentalis*
Aster, golden, *Heterotheca villosa*
Balsamroot, *Balsamorhiza sagittata*
Bitterroot, *Lewisia rediviva*
Broomrape, tufted, *Orobanche fasciculata*
Buckwheat, desert, *Eriogonum ovalifolium*
   sulphur flower, *Eriogonum umbellatum*
   wild, *Eriogonum racemosum*
Flax, blue, *Adenolinum lewisii* (formerly *Linum*)
Fleabane, Eaton's, *Erigeron eatoni*
   little, *Erigeron pumilus*
Geranium, common wild, *Geranium caespitosum*
Gilia, scarlet, *Ipomopsis aggregata*
Larkspur, *Delphinium nuttallianum*
Lily, mariposa or sego, *Calochortus gunnisonii*
Loco, Rocky Mountain, *Oxytropis sericea*
Lupine, Baker's, *Lupinus bakeri*
   lodgepole, *Lupinus parviflorus*
   silky, *Lupinus sericeus*
   silvery, *Lupinus argenteus*
   spurred, *Lupinus caudatus*
Milkvetch, silver-leaved, *Astragalus argophyllus* var.
      martinii
Mule's Ears, *Wyethia amplexicaulis*
Paintbrush, Indian, *Castilleja chromosa, C. integra, C.
      linariifolia, C. miniata*
Penstemon, Colorado, *Penstemon linarioides*
   grayleaf creeping, *Penstemon teucrioides*
   mat, *Penstemon caespitosus*
   showy, *Penstemon secundiflorus*
   Watson's, *Penstemon watsonii*
Phlox, *Phlox hoodii, P. longifolia,* and *P. austromontana*
Pussy-toes, *Antennaria rosea, A. dimorpha,* and *A. rosulata*
Salsify, *Tragopogon dubius*
Sandwort, desert (or Hooker's), *Eremogone hookeri*
      (formerly *Arenaria*)
Yarrow, *Achillea lanulosa*

Animals of the Sagebrush Shrublands

Sagebrush shrublands provide food and cover for a diversity of wildlife species. Though domestic livestock find it unpalatable, sagebrush is an important food for elk, pronghorn, and mule deer, especially during the winter months when other forage is scarce. Sage grouse are almost totally dependent on sagebrush for food and cover, often moving long distances during the winter to find snowfree stands. Sagebrush and other shrubs provide perching areas, escape cover, and nesting sites for birds such as the sage thrasher, lark sparrow, and green-tailed towhee. Black-tailed jackrabbits and cottontails escape the heat of summer days in the shade beneath the shrubs, emerging only at dusk to forage. The lush understory of some stands offers concealment for the runways and foraging activities of small mammals such as the northern grasshopper mouse and the sagebrush vole. The deep, friable soils are ideal for burrowing mammals — prairie dogs, northern pocket gophers, badgers, and several species of ground squirrels. Unfortunately, the widespread use of herbicides, chaining, and fire to open up sagebrush habitat for cropland and grazing will continue to chart the futures of the animals that rely on the sagebrush shrublands.

Rites of Spring

Elaborate courtship and territorial displays are characteristic of many birds that breed in open country. Few are more impressive than those of the male sage grouse — the classic lek-forming species of North American grouse. From late March until May, males and females begin congregating at traditional strutting grounds, called *leks*. Most leks consist of a small, windswept clearing in the sage, often on a knoll or other prominent area. During the peak of the breeding season, fifty or more males may be present at a single lek. With their tails fanned and their yellow air sacs inflated, the cocks strut and swoop, ending each display with an abrupt deflation of the air sacs; a single display sequence

Territorial and courtship display of the male sage grouse.

lasts a few seconds and is repeated frequently. Each male maintains a distinct territory within the lek. Dominant cocks defend territories closest to the lek center, while the younger males remain on the periphery. Females appear somewhat passive during the display, gathering in the center of the lek to await copulation with a dominant male. Once copulation has been completed, the females leave the lek and proceed to the nesting grounds.

Life Histories of Selected Animals

Mammals

Sagebrush Vole, *Lagurus curtatus.* This pale, ash-gray vole is identified by its whitish underparts and extremely short tail; color and sagebrush habitat distinguish it from other voles (or "meadow mice"). Sagebrush voles feed on the leaves of sagebrush, greasewood, and other shrubs. A lackluster climber, the vole depends on deer mice to scale the shrubs and clip off the foliage, whereupon the vole steals the fallen harvest. The sagebrush vole lives in small, social colonies; the burrow and runway systems of the colony form an interconnected cluster. Colonies are mobile, changing location seasonally and in response to changes in the distribution of the snow cover.

White-tailed Prairie Dog, *Cynomys leucurus.* This robust, buff-colored ground squirrel is identified by its white-tipped tail. (Gunnison's prairie dog, *C. gunnisoni,* also has a white- or grayish-tipped tail but is considerably smaller in size.) White-tailed prairie dogs are common in the drainage of the Laramie River, North Park, and the valleys of the Colorado River and its northern tributaries. Gunnison's prairie dog is common in mountain parks from central Colorado south into the upper Chama Valley and upper Rio Grande Valley of New Mexico. The white-tailed prairie dog is gregarious, and its vocal communication, consisting of shrill whistles and barks, is well developed. Daily activity in summer revolves around foraging, basking in the sun, and territorial behavior. Animals enter hibernation in early fall and emerge in spring, when body fat stores have been depleted.

Badger, *Taxidea taxus.* Grizzled gray coloring, prominent black-and-white facial pattern, and waddling gait distinguish this large member of the weasel family. The badger is a fast and powerful digger, literally sinking out of sight under a geyser of flying dirt; the neck and legs of this species are short and muscular; the front claws are extremely long. Conspicuous excavations, with entrance holes about 8 to 12 inches in diameter, are the most common indication of badger activity. Badgers are carnivorous, their diet consisting mostly of small mammals and ground-nesting birds. Though largely nocturnal and active year-round, badgers may be seen at any time of the day. Badgers are solitary except during the breeding season, which occurs in late summer and fall.

Birds

Golden Eagle, *Aquila chrysaetos.* The large size (average adult wingspan is 6.5 feet), uniform brown coloring, and broad wings distinguish the golden eagle from smaller avian predators; golden neck feathers are inconspicuous except at close range. Juveniles, seen in flight from below, show white wing patches and a broad white tail band. Rabbits, hares, and small rodents comprise nearly 90 percent of the diet; carrion is utilized when available, and may comprise as much as 60 percent of the winter diet. Golden eagles hunt while soaring, with wings held horizontally rather than in the position typical of vultures, or from perches; they will soar for hours over mountain ridges, sometimes diving with tremendous speed to capture prey or in presumed play. Courtship involves soaring and undulating flight displays. Pairs may remain mated for life; some — as well as successive generations of eagles — may use the same nest site. Nesting success is usually limited to one eaglet; human disturbance can cause nest abandonment. The female incubates, but the male may help; incubation time is about forty-five days, and eaglets fledge at around seventy days.

Sage Grouse, *Centrocercus urophasianus.* The largest North American grouse species, the sage grouse is identified by its mottled gray-brown plumage, black belly, and stiff, pointed tail feathers; the male is distinguished by its greater size, yellow eye combs, black throat patch, and white breast. Sage grouse are relatively common in sagebrush habitat in the northern half of the Southern Rockies and are considered uncommon south of this area. Sagebrush foliage comprises the bulk of their diet; juveniles eat insects and forbs during their first few weeks. Seasonal movements between sheltered wintering areas in dense sagebrush, traditional springtime strutting grounds, and nesting and brooding habitats in more open sagebrush are common.

Sage Thrasher, *Oreoscoptes montanus.* This small, slender thrasher is distinguished by its gray-brown upperparts, strongly streaked breast, bright yellow eyes, and white-cornered, narrow tail. This migratory species is largely restricted to sagebrush shrubland and semidesert scrub. The sage thrasher forages for insects by running over the ground like a robin. Shy and difficult to approach closely, the male perches atop sagebrush to deliver its rich, mockingbird-song; males may also sing in flight. The nest of coarse twigs and finer plant fibers is normally built in a low shrub.

Green-tailed Towhee, *Pipilo chlorurus.* The smallest of the towhees is identified by its rufous crown, white throat patch with vertical dark stripes, gray sides, white belly, and olive green upperparts. This denizen of dense underbrush is often observed scratching and scuffing as it searches for seeds, berries, and insects on the ground. When disturbed, the towhee runs swiftly over the ground as it heads for cover. During the breeding season, males deliver their trilling song from a conspicuous shrub-top perch; the call is a catlike "puee."

Reptiles

Sagebrush Lizard, *Sceloporus graciosus*. This small, spiny lizard is identified by the pale stripe along each side of its back; males have a blue-mottled throat and blue patches on each side of the body. Sagebrush lizards occasionally climb trees or bushes in search of insect prey. They emerge from winter chambers in large numbers in April; males typically emerge first. Adults are diurnal and active throughout the summer and into mid-September, juveniles until early October. Females generally lay two clutches of eggs, the first in early June and the second in early July; first clutch eggs hatch in August, second clutch eggs in mid-September.

Common Animals of the Sagebrush Shrubland

Mammals

Black-tailed Jackrabbit, *Lepus californicus*
White-tailed Jackrabbit, *Lepus townsendii*
Nuttall's Cottontail, *Sylvilagus nuttallii*
Desert Cottontail, *Sylvilagus audubonii*
Least Chipmunk, *Tamias minimus*
Wyoming Ground Squirrel, *Spermophilus elegans*
White-tailed Prairie Dog, *Cynomys leucurus*
Gunnison's Prairie Dog, *Cynomys gunnisoni*
Northern Pocket Gopher, *Thomomys talpoides*
Ord's Kangaroo Rat, *Dipodomys ordii*
Deer Mouse, *Peromyscus maniculatus*

Northern Grasshopper Mouse, *Onychomys leucogaster*
Bushy-tailed Woodrat, *Neotoma cinerea*
Sagebrush Vole, *Lagurus curtatus*
Coyote, *Canis latrans*
Long-tailed Weasel, *Mustela frenata*
Badger, *Taxidea taxus*
Mule Deer, *Odocoileus hemionus*
Pronghorn, *Antilocapra americana*

Birds

Rough-legged Hawk, *Buteo lagopus*
Ferruginous Hawk, *Buteo regalis*
Red-tailed Hawk, *Buteo jamaicensis*
Golden Eagle, *Aquila chrysaetos*
Sage Grouse, *Centrocercus urophasianus*
Common Raven, *Corvus corax*
Loggerhead Shrike, *Lanius ludovicianus*
Horned Lark, *Eremophila alpestris*
Sage Thrasher, *Oreoscoptes montanus*
Mountain Bluebird, *Sialia currucoides*
Green-tailed Towhee, *Pipilo chlorurus*
Sage Sparrow, *Amphispiza belli*
Vesper Sparrow, *Pooecetes gramineus*
Lark Sparrow, *Chondestes grammacus*
Brewer's Sparrow, *Spizella breweri*

Reptiles

Eastern Fence Lizard, *Sceloporus undulatus*
Sagebrush Lizard, *Sceloporus graciosus*
Western Rattlesnake, *Crotalus viridis*
Bullsnake, *Pituophis melanoleucus*

Invertebrates

Sagebrush White Butterfly, *Pontia beckerii*
Blue Copper Butterfly, *Chalceria heteronea*
Mormon Cricket, *Anabrus simplex*

Mountain Shrublands

Mountain shrublands occur throughout the foothills of the Southern Rockies. Impenetrable thickets of Gambel oak give a chaparral-like feeling to hillsides in the western and southern foothills. In the northern and eastern foothills, a rough tangle of mountain mahogany dominates dry, rocky slopes between the grasslands below and the coniferous woodlands above.

Ecological Distribution

In the southern foothills of the Southern Rockies, stands of Gambel oak form small, islandlike groves on gentle slopes and dense thickets on steeper slopes in a zone roughly transitional between that of the piñon-juniper woodlands and the ponderosa pine forests. To the north, along the Eastern Slope, stands of mountain mahogany begin to replace Gambel oak in the foothills north of Denver and the Palmer Divide area. Gambel oak reaches its northern limit along the Colorado Front Range near Morrison. Its conspicuous absence in the foothills north of this area suggests a major climatic boundary affecting oak seedling survival, possibly related to the increasing frequency of frost damage or to the probability of summer drought stress associated with the diminished influence of the Arizona monsoon in this region.

Gambel oak.

THE SOUTHERN ROCKIES

On dry, south-facing slopes of the hogbacks north of Lyons, mountain mahogany frequently forms homogeneous stands.

On the Western Slope, thousands of acres of Gambel oak dominate the foothill shrub belt, reaching their greatest development between 7,000 and 8,500 feet. At their lower limit, oak brushlands adjoin piñon-juniper woodlands or sagebrush ecosystems; at their upper limit they merge with aspen and lodgepole pine or other types of coniferous forest. Within this region, oak shrublands are conspicuously absent from South, Middle, and North parks, perhaps as a result of cold-air drainage in these basins. In the northwestern ranges of the Southern Rockies, dense thickets of Gambel oak and stickly-laurel are common on steep slopes, while in other areas the shrubland consists almost entirely of serviceberry.

Community Characteristics

Stands of Gambel oak or mountain mahogany probably represent climax (stable) communities wherever microclimatic and soil conditions preclude the invasion of these habitats by trees. Communities developed on the most xeric sites, such as those dominated by mountain mahogany, generally consist of only one or two shrub species and a sparse understory of herbaceous plants. On less xeric, topographically more diverse sites, mountain mahogany may occur in association with skunkbrush, chokecherry, wild plum, and bitterbrush.

On sites with deeper soils and more moisture, communities generally consist of several species of shrubs and a lush understory of herbaceous vegetation. Oak-dominated brushlands are typical of such sites, and the more common shrub associates include snowberry, serviceberry, chokecherry, big sagebrush, and wild rose. In the southern foothills, Gambel oak forms dense stands in association with mountain mahogany, mountain spray, Apache plume, and New Mexican locust. The earliest written observations of oak brushlands were made by Fra Silvestre Velez de Escalante, when the 1776 Domínguez-Escalante Expedition traveled through the region. Unimpressed with the impenetrable, gnarled woodlands, Escalante might have formed a more favorable view had he seen their brilliant red-and-orange autumn foliage.

Many shrub species typical of the mountain shrublands tend to be aggressive invaders following fire or other disturbances. In the case of Gambel oak, fire stimulates vegetative reproduction by suckering, resulting in a thickening of open stands and a merging of scattered stands to form continuous thickets. In north-central New Mexico, Gambel oak has spread into large areas of the lower montane region in places where ponderosa pine has been burned or logged.

Descriptions of Common Plants

Shrubs

Gambel Oak, *Quercus gambelii.* This deciduous, thicket-forming scrub oak is easily recognized by its leathery, deeply lobed leaves; newly emergent leaves are yellowish green, turning dark green in summer and deep reddish in fall prior to shedding. Flowers appear in spring, shortly before or in conjunction with the growth of new leaves; male and female flowers are produced on the same tree. The fruits, or acorns, are borne singly or in clusters and mature in the fall.

Mountain Mahogany, *Cercocarpus montanus.* Mountain mahogany has small, somewhat oval-shaped leaves arranged alternately on short, spurlike lateral twigs; leaf margins are toothed and the lower leaf surface is densely covered with fine hairs. Large numbers of small, inconspicuous flowers are produced in early spring; the flowers lack petals, but the sepals form a greenish tube with flared, pinkish to reddish petal-like lobes rimming the mouth. The name *Cercocarpus,* from the Greek words for "tail" and "fruit," refers to the feathery, corkscrewlike fruits that grace this shrub in late summer and fall. This is an important browse species.

Western Serviceberry, *Amelanchier alnifolia.* Common names for serviceberry abound — Saskatoon, Juneberry, sarvisberry, shadbush, shadblow. Western serviceberry is a deciduous, thicket-forming shrub or small tree with an erect, rounded crown and usually with several trunks. The leaves of this variable species are simple, alternate, oval to round

Common shrubs of the mountain shrublands, clockwise from upper left: snowberry, with detail of flowers, skunkbrush, chokecherry (center), western serviceberry, mountain mahogany.

in shape, and coarsely toothed, changing from hairy to smooth with age. Clusters of white, star-shaped flowers appear near the tips of the branchlets in early June; each flower has five strap-shaped, white petals, and multiple stamens. In mid- to late summer, dark bluish purple fruits appear in small bunches. The foliage and twigs are heavily browsed during all seasons, and the fruit is a favorite with birds and small mammals.

Chokecherry, *Padus virginiana* (formerly *Prunus*) ssp. *melanocarpa.* This large shrub forms loose thickets in canyons and hillsides and is readily distinguished by its broadly lanceolate leaves and cylindrical racemes of white, roselike flowers. The small, five-petaled flowers appear in June and are followed in late summer by astringent purple-black fruits. The large-pitted fruits are a favorite food of birds, small mammals, black bears, coyotes, and foxes, and make excellent jelly and wine.

Snowberry, *Symphoricarpos rotundifolius.* This small- to medium-sized shrub, also known as buckbrush, is a member of the honeysuckle family and is common in oak scrub and aspen forests from the foothills to the subalpine zone. Snowberry is distinguished by its small, oval leaves, paired tubular flowers (white to pinkish), and clusters of porcelain white berries. This shrub reproduces largely by vegetative means, sending out a network of underground runners.

Skunkbrush, *Rhus trilobata.* This much-branched, rounded shrub is identified by its compound leaves (each leaf divided into three, scallop-margined leaflets) and by its clusters of reddish orange berries. The scent given off by the crushed foliage is produced by resinous oils housed in ducts in the leaves and branchlets. Flowering occurs in spring, with clusters of small, inconspicuous yellow flowers appearing before the leaves. The berrylike fruits, despite their covering of sticky glandular hairs, are sought after by birds and small mammals. The leaves of skunkbrush turn a rich red-orange before they are shed in autumn.

Common Plants of the Mountain Shrublands

Trees and Shrubs

Apache Plume, *Fallugia paradoxia*
Bitterbrush, *Purshia tridentata*
Buckbrush, *Ceanothus fendleri*
Buffalo Berry, Silver, *Shepherdia argentea*
Chokecherry, *Padus* (formerly *Prunus*) *virginiana* ssp. *melanocarpa*
Cliffrose, Mexican, *Purshia stansburiana* (formerly *Cowania mexicana*)
Fendlerbush, *Fendlera rupicola*
Hawthorn, *Crataegus erythropoda* and *C. rivularis*
Locust, New Mexican, *Robinia neomexicana*

Mahogany, curl-leaf, *Cercocarpus ledifolius*
  Mountain, *Cercocarpus montanus*
Mountain Spray, *Holodiscus dumosus*
Oak, Gambel, *Quercus gambelii*
  wavyleaf, *Quercus undulata*
Olive, New Mexican, *Forestiera neomexicana*
Plum, wild, *Prunus americana*
Rabbitbrush, *Chrysothamnus* spp.
Rose, wild, *Rosa woodsii*
Sagebrush, big, *Seriphidium tridentatum*
  mountain, *Seriphidium vaseyanum*
Serviceberry, Utah, *Amelanchier utahensis*
  western, *Amelanchier alnifolia*
Snowberry, *Symphoriocarpos rotundifolius*
Squaw-apple, *Peraphyllum ramosissimum*
Sumac, skunkbrush (or three-leaf), *Rhus aromatica* ssp.
    trilobata
  smooth, *Rhus glabra*
Yucca (or Spanish bayonet), *Yucca glauca*

Herbaceous Plants

Aster, golden, *Heterotheca villosa*
Balsamroot, arrowleaf, *Balsamorhiza sagittata*
Barley, foxtail, *Critesion jubatum* (formerly *Hordeum*)
Blanketflower, *Gaillardia aristata*
Brickellia, *Brickellia grandiflora*
Buckwheat, *Eriogonum subalpinum*
Fescue, Thurber, *Festuca thurberi*
Fleabane, *Erigeron* spp.
Gaura, scarlet, *Gaura coccinea*
Gilia, scarlet, *Ipomopsis aggregata*
Grama, blue, *Bouteloua gracilis*
  side-oats, *Bouteloua curtipendula*
Lily, mariposa, *Calochortus gunnisonii*
Loco, Rocky Mountain, *Oxytropis sericea*
Lupine, *Lupinus* spp.
Muhly, mountain, *Muhlenbergia montana*
Paintbrush, Indian, *Castilleja linariifolia*
Ricegrass, Indian, *Stipa hymenoides* (formerly *Oryzopsis*)
Sedge, Geyer's or elk, *Carex geyeri*

Spring Beauty, *Claytonia lanceolata*
Vetch, *Vicia americana*
Wheatgrass, slender, *Agropyron Elymus trachycaulus*
   western, *Agropyron smithii*
Yarrow, *Achillea lanulosa*

Animals of the Mountain Shrublands

The fauna of the mountain shrublands is remarkably rich, an ecotonal assemblage of species transitional between lowland communities and mountain forests. Where brushy vegetation adjoins cliffs or other rocky areas, denning and nesting sites abound, providing habitat for wildlife species as diverse as hawks, bats, marmots, woodrats, bobcats, mountain lions, and rattlesnakes.

The attractiveness of shrubland habitats for wildlife changes with the seasons. In most areas, mountain shrublands bustle with activity by the middle of May, when th. first leaves appear. The roster of bird species swells to its highest number as resident species, such as the rufous-sided towhee and the scrub jay, are joined by an influx of summer breeders: lazuli bunting, Virginia's warbler, green-tailed towhee, blue-gray gnatcatcher, and many others. Animals that have spent the winter underground, such as the rock squirrel, Colorado chipmunk, and eastern fence lizard, emerge to bask on sun-warmed boulders. Mule deer browse on the succulent new growth before beginning the journey to summer ranges at higher elevations.

By hot midsummer the intense activity of spring has diminished, leaving the shrublands subdued, even silent, the air redolent of resinous foliage. With the exception of the resident species, many of the birds that nested in the shrublands have moved higher into the mountains or begun migrating south to their wintering areas. Small mammals and reptiles remain active but now restrict their activities to the cooler times of the day.

A bountiful supply of seeds and fruit in late summer coincides with the onset of fall bird migration, when high-energy foods must be eaten in large quantities to build up the re-

Common birds of the mountain shrublands, from top to bottom: scrub jay, rufous-sided towhee.

serves of subcutaneous fat that will fuel the long flights to southern wintering grounds. The mountain shrublands fill with noisy flocks of birds—residents and migrants alike feed on the fruits of serviceberry, chokecherry, and skunkbrush. Ripening acorns attract large numbers of scrub jays as well as desert cottontails, woodrats, rock squirrels, and chipmunks. Ground feeders, such as the rufous-sided towhee and the scaled quail, search for fallen fruits and seeds under the protective cover of the shrubs.

In winter, mountain shrublands serve as a refuge for many species that have spent the summer at higher elevations. Escaping the deep snows of their summer ranges, mule deer return to favorite wintering areas. The tracks of the gray fox and the long-tailed weasel are frequently seen in the snow. Mice continue to forage over the ground for seeds and fruit, and the well-packed trails of hares and rabbits zigzag from shrub to shrub. Ground-dwelling squirrels retreat to underground nests and become torpid during long periods of severe weather. Overwintering birds, often in large flocks, forage on the ground for seeds or harvest the dry fruits that remain on the shrubs. Scrub jays search the branches and dead leaves of Gambel oak for nymph-filled galls. Twig gleaners, such as the mountain and black-capped chickadees, scour the branches for dormant insects and eggs attached to the surface or under loose bark.

Of the forty-nine species of mammals reported to occur in the mountain shrublands, sixteen belong to the Chihuahuan Faunal Element, a fauna whose origins can be traced to the semiarid highlands and grasslands of Chihuahua, in north-central Mexico. Mammalogists suggest that this warmth-loving fauna was able to spread north into the Southern Rockies during the early Holocene, when the climate is believed to have been warmer and perhaps drier than at present. These Chihuahuan species, with their affinities for the desert Southwest, include many of our most interesting foothill mammals — Townsend's big-eared bat, desert cottontail, black-tailed jackrabbit, rock squirrel, rock mouse, Mexican woodrat, gray fox, and ringtail. In the Southern Rockies, the Chihuahuan fauna is narrowly restricted to the foothill zone. Along the Eastern Slope, species such as the Mexican woodrat, rock mouse, and rock squirrel reach the northern limits of their distribution just short of the Colorado-Wyoming border. With increasing elevation, Chihuahuan species are replaced by mammals with affinities for the boreal forests of northern Canada.

Life Histories of Selected Animals

Mammals

Colorado Chipmunk, *Tamias quadrivittatus.* The Colorado chipmunk is distinguished from the least chipmunk *(T. minimus),* the common chipmunk of higher elevations, by its larger size, less animated behavior, and preference for rocky sites instead of wooded habitat. The bright cinnamon coloring of this species is similar to that of the least chipmunk, but the black-and-white stripes along the head and sides do not continue to the base of the tail. Common at elevations below 8,000 feet, the species occurs at higher elevations (to 10,000 feet) in the southern portion of its range. Colorado chipmunks are solitary and live in burrows dug beneath rocks, shrubs, or the exposed roots of trees. Winter torpor alternates with consumption of food stores. Mating occurs in late April or early May, and females give birth to one litter of altricial young per year; the young are weaned at six to seven weeks of age.

Rock Squirrel, *Spermophilus variegatus.* The rock squirrel is identified by its ground-dwelling habit, bushy tail, and salt-and-pepper fur. The species is locally abundant in broken, rocky terrain to 8,200 feet; the northern limit of distribution occurs in Colorado near Meeker on the Western Slope and near Livermore on the Eastern Slope. Rock squirrels construct burrows beneath boulders and shrubs, occasionally in steep-sided arroyos. The diet of this semiarboreal squirrel includes acorns, seeds, and other fruits. Rock squirrels are noncolonial, and communication is poorly developed; their call is an abrupt, moderately loud whistle. The annual cycle of activity consists of successive periods of fattening, cold-season torpor, warm-season foraging, and two breeding periods. The altricial young are born in a well-constructed nest and do not appear above ground until they are nearly two months of age.

Mexican Woodrat, *Neotoma mexicana.* This woodrat is distinguished from other species by the presence of a dark ring around the mouth, the absence of pure white fur on the breast, and a short-furred rather than bushy tail. Locally abundant in rocky areas of the foothills to 8,500 feet, the species prefers horizontal crevices in broken, sedimentary rock for denning; man-made structures may also be used. The diet consists mostly of foliage, which is clipped and stored during all seasons, but particularly in late summer and fall. Nocturnal and active throughout the year, the Mexican woodrat has a less developed collecting instinct than other species—dens contain only moderate amounts of sticks and collected debris. The food refuse pile, or midden, serves as a urination perch where plant fragments and fecal pellets are gradually cemented into hard masses that may be preserved for thousands of years. Females breed in March and bear altricial young in April.

Western Spotted Skunk, *Spilogale gracili.* This small skunk has no dorsal stripes, but rather a distinctive "checkerboard" pattern of white spots on an otherwise black body. Spotted skunks are common in broken, shrub-covered terrain along the Western Slope and are uncommon on the Eastern Slope. Den sites are in rock piles, abandoned burrows, brush piles, hollow logs, and man-made structures. Home range is extremely limited, with as many as twelve spotted skunks per square mile in good habitat. Spotted skunks are nocturnal and omnivorous, taking a wide variety of animal and plant foods. They are solitary animals, except during the breeding season and during severe winter weather, when a communal den may hold six or more individuals. Breeding occurs in September, and females are spontaneous ovulators. Implantation of the fertilized egg in the uterus is delayed (six to seven months) until April; the altricial young are born in May. Young are furred at three weeks, and eyes open between four and six weeks; full size is attained at about three months.

Mule Deer, *Odocoileus hemionus.* Mule deer are identified by their large, mulelike ears and somewhat narrow, black-tipped tails. Adults stand about 3 feet high at the shoulder and are about half the size of an elk; bucks average 250 pounds. Seasonal migrations between summer and winter range are common; mule deer tend to avoid dense forests, and snow depths in excess of 18 inches are believed to preclude use of range by mule deer. Active primarily at dawn and dusk, mule deer are moderately gregarious but seldom form large herds. They are most dispersed during the spring fawning period, when does seek isolation and yearlings are driven off. Does give birth to precocial, spotted, and odorless young from June to early July; fawns are kept hidden and does approach only to nurse. Does, fawns, and yearlings form small herds again in midsummer, remaining together through the winter. Socialization breaks down among bucks during the rut (November to December), when food intake declines and aggressive behaviors — involving urine marking, thrashing and rubbing of the antlers in shrubs and trees, and sparring — increase. Antlers are shed in February or March; new antler growth is completed by late summer.

Birds

Scrub Jay, *Aphelocoma coerulescens.* This slim-bodied, crestless jay is identified by its whitish throat, long tail, smoke gray back, and undulating flight; head, wings, and tail are a rich blue, and a narrow white eye stripe is sometimes present. The scrub jay's diet consists of acorns, piñon nuts, wild and cultivated fruits, insects, eggs, nestlings, small mammals, reptiles, and amphibians; acorns may be buried for later retrieval. This conspicuous, noisy jay is often seen perched atop a prominent shrub or hopping about on the ground or in shrubbery. Calls are typically harsh and raucous, but musical "whisper" songs by both sexes are not uncommon. Scrub jays are communal nesters; young jays leave the nest about eighteen days after hatching, remaining in loose family groups.

Rock Wren, *Salpinctes obsoletus.* This small, gray-brown wren is identified by its conspicuously cocked tail and its habit of bobbing as it walks or when alarmed. Rock wrens are found from the foothills to the alpine tundra in suitably rocky habitat. The bird is extremely active, foraging among the rocks for insects. The call is a variety of trills on a single pitch, often given from a perch on top of a rock, and is distinctly different from the beautiful, descending "whistle-song" of the canyon wren *(Catherpes mexicanus).* Rock wrens nest in a rock crevice or in an abandoned burrow on a rocky slope; the entrance to the nesting cavity is often paved with small stones.

Virginia's Warbler, *Vermivora virginiae.* This small, gray-and-olive-yellow warbler has a bold white eye ring, whitish underparts, and a yellow breast patch; males have a seldom-exposed reddish patch on the head. Virginia's warbler is a summer resident in the foothills to 9,000 feet. This somewhat shy warbler can be observed foraging for insects on the ground, in dense shrubbery, or catching insects on the wing. Males sing while foraging or from a conspicuous perch. Females construct a cup-shaped nest on the ground, slightly sunken in dead leaves or loose soil, at the base of a shrub or clump of grass.

Lazuli Bunting, *Passerina amoena.* This small bird is superficially similar to the western bluebird. Males have a turquoise blue head, throat, back, and rump; upper breast and sides are a rich cinnamon, the lower belly is white, and the wings show two white wing bars. Females and immatures are grayish brown but have a hint of blue on the rump and tail. Lazuli buntings are resident here only during the breeding season, with males arriving on nesting areas first, singing from prominent perches and courting females with spreadwing displays. Females build a cup-shaped nest in low shrubs, often near water. Lazuli buntings are insectivorous, foraging on or near the ground or in shrubbery.

Rufous-sided Towhee, *Pipilo erythrophthalmus.* The rufous-sided towhee is identified by its red eyes, black hood and back, cinnamon-colored sides, white breast, and white-cornered black tail; female plumage is more washed out. Nonmigratory and locally common in brushy habitats, towhees are often first detected by their noisy scratching as they forage for insects in the leaf litter. During courtship, males sing from prominent perches in the shrubbery and fan their tails. The song is a buzzy trill; the call resembles a monosyllabic "tweee" or "chweee." This species typically nests on the ground, occasionally in shrubs or small trees.

Reptiles

Eastern Fence Lizard, *Sceloporus undulatus.* This small, variable lizard is identified by the presence of spiny scales on the back and keeled scales on the rear of the thigh. These insectivorous lizards follow a spot-and-pursuit style of hunting, sometimes leaping into the air to catch prey. Fence lizards emerge from underground chambers in late March and April, remaining active until September or October. Most activity occurs in mid-to-late morning and late afternoon, with the animal retreating underground during the warmest times of the day. Males are polygamous, conducting "bobbing" courtship displays from May through early July. The female lays a clutch of eight to twelve eggs that will hatch from mid-July through early September. Longevity seldom exceeds four years.

Smooth Green Snake, *Opheodrys vernalis.* This beautiful snake is easily identified by its grass green coloring, slender body, and smooth scales. Smooth green snakes are found in lush undergrowth and in dry mountain shrublands, especially oak brushland, at elevations to 9,000 feet. This diurnal, shy, and quick snake is active from May to September, seeking shelter underground when not active. Smooth green snakes will climb into low herbaceous plants or shrubs in search of insect prey, and may also enter shallow water. Little is known of breeding; females lay six to seven eggs, which may hatch after as little as four days.

Common Animals of the Mountain Shrublands

Mammals

(C indicates Chihuahuan Faunal Element)
Dwarf Shrew, *Sorex nanus*

Merriam's Shrew, *Sorex merriami*
Townsend's Big-eared Bat, *Plecotus townsendii* C
Small-footed Myotis, *Myotis leibii*
Mountain (or Nuttall's) Cottontail, *Sylvilagus nuttallii*
Desert Cottontail, *Sylvilagus audubonii* C
White-tailed Jackrabbit, *Lepus townsendii*
Black-tailed Jackrabbit, *Lepus californicus* C
Least Chipmunk, *Tamias minimus*
Colorado Chipmunk, *Tamias quadrivittatus*
Yellow-bellied Marmot, *Marmota flaviventris*
Rock Squirrel, *Spermophilus variegatus* C
Prairie Dog, *Cynomys leucurus* and *C. ludovicianus*
Silky Pocket Mouse, *Perognathus flavus* C
Ord's Kangaroo Rat, *Dipodomys ordii* C
Deer Mouse, *Peromyscus maniculatus*
Brush Mouse, *Peromyscus boylii* C
Rock Mouse, *Peromyscus difficilis* C
Mexican Woodrat, *Neotoma mexicana* C
Bushy-tailed Woodrat, *Neotoma cinerea*
Porcupine, *Erethizon dorsatum*
Coyote, *Canis latrans*
Gray Fox, *Urocyon cinereoargenteus* C
Ringtail, *Bassariscus astutus* C
Long-tailed Weasel, *Mustela frenata*
Badger, *Taxidea taxus*
Western Spotted Skunk, *Spilogale gracilis*
Striped Skunk, *Mephitis mephitis*
Mountain Lion, *Felis concolor*
Bobcat, *Felis rufus*
Mule Deer, *Odocoileus hemionus*
Elk, *Cervus elaphus*

Birds

Red-tailed Hawk, *Buteo jamaicensis*
Scaled Quail, *Callipepla squamata*
Wild Turkey, *Meleagris gallopavo*
Northern Flicker, *Colaptes auratus*
Gray Flycatcher, *Empidonax wrightii*
Dusky Flycatcher, *Empidonax oberholseri*
Scrub Jay, *Aphelocoma coerulescens*
Piñon Jay, *Gymnorhinus cyanocephalus*

Black-capped Chickadee, *Parus atricapillus*
Mountain Chickadee, *Parus gambeli*
Plain Titmouse, *Parus inornatus*
Bushtit, *Psaltriparus minimus*
House Wren, *Troglodytes aedon*
Rock Wren, *Salpinctes obsoletus*
Blue-gray Gnatcatcher, *Polioptila caerulea*
Orange-crowned Warbler, *Vermivora celata*
Virginia's Warbler, *Vermivora virginiae*
Black-throated Gray Warbler, *Dendroica nigrescens*
MacGillivray's Warbler, *Oporornis tolmiei*
Green-tailed Towhee, *Pipilo chlorurus*
Rufous-sided Towhee, *Pipilo erythrophthalmus*
Canyon Towhee, *Pipilo fuscus*
Brewer's Sparrow, *Spizella breweri*

Amphibians and Reptiles

Short-horned Lizard, *Phrynosoma douglassii*
Sagebrush Lizard, *Sceloporus graciosus*
Eastern Fence Lizard, *Sceloporus undulatus*
Plateau Striped Whiptail, *Cnemidophorus velox*
Smooth Green Snake, *Opheodrys vernalis*
Bullsnake, *Pituophis melanoleucus*
Western Rattlesnake, *Crotalus viridis*

Butterflies

Aphrodite Fritillary, *Speyeria idalia*
Arrowhead Blue, *Glaucopsyche piasus*
Two-tailed Tiger Swallow Tail, *Pterourus multicaudatus*
Colorado Hairstreak, *Hypaurotis crysalus*
Large Wood Nymph, *Cercyonis pegala*
Tailed Copper, *Tharsalea arota*

CHAPTER THIRTEEN

Piñon-Juniper Woodlands

WOODLANDS OF PIÑON pine and juniper have little in common with the verdure of the high mountain forests. These open woodlands, with their low, round-crowned trees, evoke a feeling of the desert Southwest. Piñon-juniper woodlands cover more than 75,000 square miles in the West, their distribution extending from trans–Pecos, Texas, to the Santa Ynez Mountains of southern California, and from southern Idaho deep into Mexico. Though species composition varies from place to place, the overall character of these woodlands remains much the same. In the Southern Rockies, piñon-juniper woodlands are dominated by piñon pine or, more commonly, by one of several species of juniper: Rocky Mountain juniper, Utah juniper, or one-seed juniper.

Ecological Distribution

In the Southern Rockies, piñon-juniper woodlands occur along both sides of the Continental Divide. They are best developed in a zone between 5,000 and 7,000 feet, but they can be found at elevations as high as 9,000 feet on west- or south-facing slopes. Along their lower margins, piñon-juniper woodlands merge with semiarid grasslands or shrub communities. Near their upper limits, they interfinger with forests of ponderosa pine and Douglas-fir, or with Gambel oak.

On the Eastern Slope, piñon-juniper woodlands are most common from Colorado Springs south along the foothills. Extensive woodlands can be seen along the Western Slope of the Sangre de Cristo Range and in the vicinity of Great Sand Dunes National Monument. At relatively low eleva-

Rocky Mountain juniper (upper left) and Utah juniper (right);
Piñon pine (below) shows mature cone with bracts spread to
expose the seeds.

tions, piñon pine and one-seed juniper dominate Eastern
Slope woodlands; Rocky Mountain juniper is seldom found
below 6,500 feet, except in moist canyon environments. Scattered woodlands occur on canyon and mesa sides well out
into the shortgrass prairie, from Walsenburg to the southern
terminus of the Southern Rockies. North of Colorado Springs,

Rocky Mountain juniper replaces one-seed juniper, and piñon pine becomes increasingly uncommon. At Owl Canyon, north of Fort Collins, an isolated stand of piñon pine marks the northern limit of piñon along the Eastern Slope. North of this area, Rocky Mountain juniper grows alone or in combination with ponderosa pine, Douglas-fir, or limber pine.

On the Western Slope, woodlands consisting of piñon pine and Utah juniper cover hillsides and mesa tops from the Colorado-Wyoming border south into New Mexico. Along the western edge of the Southern Rockies, Utah juniper may form pure stands in areas unfavorable for piñon. Rocky Mountain juniper typically replaces Utah juniper along the upper margin of Western Slope woodlands. Alligator juniper, so named because of the distinctive pattern of its bark, reaches the northern limit of its range in the woodlands of north-central New Mexico, where it grows alone or in small stands in the Jemez Mountains.

Physical Environment

Piñon-juniper woodlands occupy sites characterized by intense sunlight, hot summers, relatively low precipitation, high evapotranspiration, and strong winds. Though daily and seasonal temperatures vary greatly, the frost-free period generally exceeds ninety days—the longest for any forest type in the Southern Rockies. Annual precipitation ranges between 12 and 18 inches. Soil moisture recharge takes place primarily in the spring, when the snow melts. Summer precipitation occurs in cloudbursts, which result in a high percentage of runoff. Drought is common, and potential evaporation exceeds precipitation.

Community Characteristics

Many people refer to these dry, somewhat sprawling woodlands as "pygmy forests." Along the lower margin of the piñon-juniper zone, the trees tend to be widely spaced and rarely exceed 20 feet in height. With increasing elevation and moisture availability, piñon-juniper woodlands become dense and the tree canopy more forestlike. Even under optimal conditions, however, tree height rarely exceeds 40 feet.

Variations in resistance to drought and tolerance of cold temperatures determine the species composition of a given woodland. Piñon pine is better adapted to cold temperatures and dominates higher-elevation woodlands, whereas the more drought-tolerant junipers are prevalent at lower elevations. Piñon pine is commonly associated with one-seed juniper or Utah juniper in areas receiving at least one-third of their precipitation during the summer months, and with Rocky Mountain juniper in areas where a spring precipitation maximum prevails. Soil factors are especially important in the distribution and character of individual stands. The best-developed woodlands tend to occur on rocky substrates characterized by coarse-textured, calcareous soils.

Shrubs dominate the understory vegetation in most piñon-juniper communities. Semidesert shrubs such as greasewood and saltbush are common in low-elevation woodlands with strongly alkaline soils. Elsewhere, shrubs such as skunk-brush, rabbitbrush, bitterbrush, and mountain mahogany may assume local dominance. In the southern woodlands, wavyleaf oak, Apache plume, and candelabra cactus are important shrub associates. Big sagebrush is a common species in areas with relatively deep soils.

The total cover provided by herbaceous species is extremely low, and in many communities may be less than 1 percent. Herbaceous vegetation is most abundant where the overstory is open—for example, in the upper and lower fringes of the woodlands. Where livestock grazing has been extensive, the herbaceous understory is largely depleted. In this region, grasses such as blue grama, Indian ricegrass, and galleta grass tend to dominate the herbaceous layer. Broad-leaved herbaceous plants include such species as golden aster, gumweed, fleabane, bladderpod, copper mallow, and showy four-o'clock. Various species of cactus, such as prickly-pear, claret cup, and the magenta-flowered hedgehog may be common on rocky slopes.

Plant Adaptation: Designs for Survival

Water Stress

The needlelike, wax-coated leaves of conifers are perfectly designed for water economy—whether the tree must cope with a hot, arid environment or a cold one in which ground-water supplies are largely unavailable during the winter. Junipers have carried this adaptation one step further than other conifers, producing leaves that are almost scalelike—an advantage that partially explains their ability to out-compete piñon along the drought-prone lower margin of the woodlands.

The root systems of piñon pine and juniper include long taproots that enable them to exploit rocky substrates and to plumb deep-seated moisture sources below the rooting zone of herbaceous plants. The taproots are capable of rapid elongation and are thus able to adjust to changing moisture conditions—an important adaptation during periods of prolonged drought. In addition to the taproot, a group of branching, lateral roots fans out into the upper horizons of the soil, competing with herbaceous plants for ephemeral moisture supplies produced by rain or snow.

Chemical Defenses

Plant chemical defenses play an important role in reducing herbivory and resource competition in piñon-juniper woodlands. Both juniper and piñon produce an arsenal of secondary compounds that, when released into the environment in sufficient quantities, may affect the growth and well-being of plants or animals that come into contact with them. Some defensive compounds simply taste bad; others inhibit digestion, alter reproduction, or interfere with development in various ways. Many of these compounds are volatile resins and are readily detected by their odor. Volatile terpenes present in both the berrylike cones and the foliage of juniper give gin its distinctive taste and also lend their pungent aroma to the woodlands. The fragrance of woodlands dominated by piñon pine is produced by the volatization of ethyl caprylate, a chemical compound also found in Zinfandel grapes. This same compound is responsible for the spicy-sweet woodsmoke that perfumes the air in towns like San Luis and Santa Fe — wherever fireplaces and woodstoves are fueled with piñon.

The concentration of chemical defenses in a given tree varies from season to season and also with age, and is often greatest in young foliage and developing reproductive structures. This strategy has obvious advantages in reducing predation on new growth. Though some resinous foliage is eaten by animals, most defensive compounds are released to the environment through the roots or through the decomposition of plant litter. Recent studies have shown that, in addition to having anti-herbivore action, many of these defensive compounds function as natural herbicides, inhibiting the growth of would-be competitors such as blue grama and golden aster. The concentration of toxic compounds tends to be greatest directly under the tree canopy, frequently resulting in areas of bare, vegetation-free soil. Furthermore, some of these compounds inhibit the growth of fungi, making the heartwood of piñon and juniper highly durable and resistant to decay.

Descriptions of Common Plants

Trees

Piñon, *Pinus edulis.* First described by Cabeza de Vaca in the early 1500s, this is one of eleven species of piñon native to North America, and it is the only species found in the Southern Rockies. It is distinguished from other pines by its low, rounded growth form and by its needles, which are arranged in bundles of two and are normally less than 2 inches long. The male and female cones occur on the same tree, appearing in early summer from buds formed the previous summer. The male, pollen-producing cones are small and crowded into reddish yellow clusters near the tips of the branches. The newly emerged female cones are pin-cushion-like and purplish, consisting of numerous, spirally arranged, overlapping scales, each scale bearing on its upper surface two tiny ovules. At the end of the third growing season, the egg-shaped cone dries to a yellowish brown. Ripening completed, the cone scales open to reveal plump, paired seeds on the upper surface of each scale; these wingless seeds, numbering about ten to twenty per cone, fall to the ground within a few weeks after the cones open. A good seed crop occurs about every fifth year. Cone production begins at about 25 years of age. Mature piñon pines vary from 75 to 200 years in age, with a maximum age of approximately 400 years.

Rocky Mountain Juniper, *Sabina scopulorum;* **one-seed Juniper,** S. *monosperma;* and **Utah Juniper,** S. *osteosperma.* Rocky Mountain juniper, also known as western red cedar, can be easily identified by its small, scalelike leaves that overlap one another like shingles, slender and elongate branchlets, and small, bluish purple "berries." Utah juniper has stout branches and dry, rather than resinous, berries. One-seed juniper is distinguished by its Eastern Slope distribution pattern, resinous cones, and large berries. Except in Utah juniper, male and female cones are borne on the same tree. Male cones, small and cylindrical, are located inconspicuously at the ends of the branchlets. The female (seed-producing) cone is round and berrylike, its fleshy scales permanently fused to enclose the seeds. Male cones begin pollen production in late summer or early fall, and the pollen is shed the following spring. Following fertilization, the seeds ripen over one or two seasons; during maturation, the ripening cone changes from green to bluish purple in Rocky Mountain and one-seed juniper, and to reddish brown in Utah juniper. Once the seeds are released from the cone, a prolonged "after-ripening" period is required for the seed coat to break open and release the embryo from dormancy. Seeds that have been through the digestive tract of a fruit-eating bird or mammal tend to germinate faster than seeds that have not. Good cone crops are produced at intervals of two to five years.

Shrubs

Apache Plume, *Fallugia paradoxa.* This attractive member of the rose family is distinguished by its white, apple-

Common shrubs of the piñon-juniper woodlands, from left to right: fendlerbush, Apache plume, shown in fruit (detail of flowers above).

blossom–sized flowers and its small, simple, and deeply lobed leaves. Apache plume tends to grow in clumps, rarely exceeding 6 feet in height. Its slender branches are whitish, the bark becoming shreddy with age. The five-petaled flowers appear in May or early June, followed by clusters of feathery-tailed fruits. When not in flower, the only shrub with which it might be confused is the cliffrose, whose flowers are smaller and cream yellow in color and whose fruits have only five plumes per cluster.

Fendlerbush, *Fendlera rupicola.* Fendlerbush occurs in dry foothill canyons from central Colorado south into New Mexico. The opposite, lanceolate-shaped leaves and four-petaled white flowers readily distinguish fendlerbush from all other woodland shrubs except the mockorange (*Philadelphus microphyllus*); the flowers of fendlerbush have eight stamens per flower, whereas the flowers of mockorange have fifteen. The fruits of both shrubs are narrow, acornlike, and about half an inch long.

Mountain Spray, *Holodiscus dumosus.* This attractive shrub is identified by its serrate, broadly ovate leaves and its pyramidal clusters of white flowers. The inflorescence and seed heads usually remain on the shrub throughout the year. In the Southern Rockies, mountain spray is common along canyon walls and in rocky habitat from central Colorado southward.

Flowers

Claret Cup Cactus, *Echinocereus triglochidiatus.* This exquisite cactus is identified during its blooming season (May to June) by the large, scarlet flowers that appear along the sides of the numerous short stems. When not in bloom, the multistemmed character of the claret cup distinguishes this species from the distinctly solitary-stemmed, magenta-flowered hedgehog cactus (*E. fendleri*).

Showy Four-O'Clock, *Mirabilis multiflora.* This robust and colorful wildflower is widely distributed on open canyonsides in the piñon-juniper zone. Showy four-o'clock is identified by its erect, bushy growth, triangularly chordate and grayish pubescent leaves, and large magenta flowers. The funnel-shaped flowers resemble morning-glory blossoms, and several are clustered together in each involucre.

Common Plants of the Piñon-Juniper Woodlands

Trees and Shrubs

Apache Plume, *Fallugia paradoxa*
Ash, single-leaf, *Fraxinus anomala*
Bitterbrush, *Purshia tridentata*
Cliffrose, *Purshia stansburiana* (formerly *Cowania*)
Fendlerbush, *Fendlera rupicola*
Juniper, one-seed, *Sabina monosperma*
 Rocky Mountain, *Sabina scopulorum*
 Utah, *Sabina osteosperma*
Mahogany, curl-leaf, *Cercocarpus intricatus*
 mountain, *Cercocarpus montanus*
Mockorange, little-leaf, *Philadelphus microphyllus*
Mormon Tea, *Ephedra viridis* and *E. torreyana*
Mountain Spray, *Holodiscus dumosus*

Oak, Gambel, *Quercus gambelii*
Pine, piñon, *Pinus edulis*
Rabbitbrush, *Chrysothamnus* spp.
Sagebrush, big, *Seriphidium tridentatum*
Saltbush, *Atriplex* spp.
Serviceberry, Utah, *Amelanchier utahensis*
  western, *Amelanchier alnifolia*
Skunkbrush, *Rhus aromatica* ssp. *trilobata*

Herbaceous Plants and Cacti

Arabis, false, *Boechera pulchra*
Aster, golden, *Heterotheca villosa*
Bladderpod, *Physaria acutifolia*
Brickellia, *Brickellia* spp.
Cactus, claret cup, *Echinocereus triglochidiatus*
  prickly-pear, *Opuntia* spp.
  hedgehog, *Echinocereus fendleri*
  candelabra, *Cylindropuntia imbricata*
Cheatgrass, *Anisantha tectorum*
Cryptantha, *Cryptantha recurvata, C. gracilis,* and
    C. pterocarya
Feather-grass, New Mexican, *Stipa neomexicana*
Fleabane, *Erigeron* spp.
Four-o'clock, showy, *Mirabilis multiflora*
Galleta grass, *Hilaria jamesii*
Gilia, ballhead, *Ipomopsis congesta*
  prickly, *Leptodactylon pungens*
Grama, blue, *Bouteloua gracilis*
  side-oats, *B. curtipendula*
Junegrass, *Koeleria macrantha*
Mallow, copper, *Sphaeralcea parvifolia*
Milkvetch, *Astragalus* spp.
Mustard, skeleton, *Schoenocrambe linifolia*
Mutton-grass, *Poa fendleriana*
Oreocarya, *Oreocarya* spp.
Paintbrush, Indian, *Castilleja chromosa*
Pincushion, *Chaenactis douglasii*
Ricegrass, Indian, *Stipa hymenoides* (formerly *Oryzopsis*)
Sunflower, little, *Helianthella microcephala*

Environment and Adaptation: Animals of the Piñon-Juniper Woodlands

Many animals are year-round residents of the piñon-juniper woodlands, and the life histories of certain species, such as the piñon jay and the piñon mouse, are intricately tied to these woodlands. The majority of animals, however, visit the woodlands on a seasonal basis, attracted by the diversity and abundance of nesting sites, the rich larder of plant foods, and the shelter these woodlands provide from the harsh winter climate typical of high elevations. The ample supply of seeds and fruits supports large populations of mice and chipmunks—prey species for nocturnal hunters such as the gray fox and the ringtail. Overwintering herds of mule deer, avoiding the deep snows of higher-elevation forests, provide food for larger predators such as the mountain lion and coyote.

The Fine Art of Seed Caching

Seed caching and dispersal by birds and mammals is a critical component of the natural history of piñon-juniper woodlands. Most coniferous trees in the Southern Rockies rely on the wind to disperse their winged seeds to suitable germination sites. Winged seeds are kept tightly sealed in their cones until maturity to protect them from birds and other seed predators. Piñon and limber pine, however, have evolved wingless seeds, which require seed-eating birds to disperse them. Wingless seeds tend to be larger than their winged counterparts, with a greater investment in stored energy and nutrients—attributes that are attractive to the seed eater but also serve to enhance seedling establishment. Clearly, no seedlings can grow from consumed seeds, so how does this mutually beneficial relationship work?

The answer lies in the foraging behavior of the principal harvesters of pine seeds—the jays and the nutcrackers. Though piñon jays, Clark's nutcrackers, and Steller's jays harvest impressive numbers of piñon seeds in the fall, they do not immediately eat the seeds. Instead, they bury much of the harvest in large communal caches—sometimes more than two or three times what the birds could consume. Seed caches serve as supplemental food stores during the winter, when other foods are in short supply. The advantages to the pines in this coevolved system derive from the failure of the birds to recover all the cached seeds. Carefully sequestered in a good seedbed, unconsumed seeds have a favorable chance of germinating when conditions are right.

Clamorous flocks of piñon jays are conspicuous in the piñon-juniper woodlands during the first golden days of autumn. Like the Clark's nutcracker, considered the most proficient harvester of pine seeds, the piñon jay has a long, sharply pointed bill with which to chisel open green cones. Other jays lack this adaptation and must wait for the cones to open naturally before harvesting the seeds. In addition, the length of the piñon jay's bill allows the bird to poke deep between the scales while keeping its facial feathers free of pitch. After extracting a seed, the piñon jay rattles it in its bill—testing its edibility by sound and weight. Inedible (undeveloped) seeds are discarded, while edible (viable) seeds are held for transport in the bird's expandable esophagus. Though lacking the capacious sublingual pouch of the Clark's nutcracker, the piñon jay is capable of transporting nearly sixty seeds at a time—more than double the quantity carried by other jays. This capacity to carry food in quantity minimizes the energy expended in caching or in delivering food to the young.

Piñon jays are a gregarious, highly colonial species. The flock, the critical social unit in piñon jay life, varies in size from small groups of birds to more than one hundred. Social organization is characterized by cooperative feeding of the young, the use of sentinels to watch for predators during foraging bouts, communal food caching, synchronization of reproductive activities, and strong group-cohesion behavior. As long as the seed crop remains good, a flock will occupy a territory of about 8 square miles, which it defends against other flocks. During poor seed years, flocks may band together as they wander over hundreds of miles in search of food.

During August, when the seed crop is ripe, piñon jays forage intensively for a period of two to three weeks. Excess seeds are communally cached — often several miles away — in the flock's traditional nesting area. The flock moves 1 to 2 miles per hour while foraging, with long-distance movements generated by mutual stimulation within the flock. Partly because of the abundance of the food supply, there is virtually no aggression within the foraging flock. Individual jays take turns at sentry duty, remaining at good vantage points along the periphery of the flock. The appearance of potential predators elicits warning calls and mobbing behavior from the sentries, the distraction allowing the flock to seek protective cover.

The reproductive cycle of the piñon jay is entrained in the seasonal rhythm of the woodland. Piñon jays choose their mates during the fall, sealing the bond with a ceremony in which the female is fed piñon seeds by her prospective mate. Breeding activities begin in earnest during February, when courtship behavior intensifies and mated pairs begin leaving the flock to feed. Nest building begins in March, with the eggs of the entire flock being laid within a three- or four-day period. Nestlings and fledglings are cooperatively fed by their parents as well as by other adults. Family groups forage by themselves for much of the spring and summer, the large group flock reforming as the piñon harvest begins anew in late summer.

A Terpenaceous Larder

Juniper seeds, like the seeds of piñon, are wingless and depend on fruit-eating mammals and birds for reliable dispersal. To achieve this end, juniper seeds are presented in an abundant, easily accessible, and nutritious "berry" that attracts avian consumers in large numbers — Bohemian and cedar waxwings, Townsend's solitaires, and robins. These birds digest the calorie-rich pulp that surrounds the seeds, passing the seeds through their digestive tracts intact and ready for germination.

The relationship between the Townsend's solitaire and the juniper provides an elegant example of this mutually beneficial system. During the breeding season, Townsend's solitaires are residents of cool, dense forests at higher elevations and are largely insectivorous. With the coming of fall, these birds migrate to wintering areas in the piñon-juniper woodlands, switching from an insect and fruit diet to one that consists almost exclusively of juniper berries. For the juniper to benefit from avian dispersal, the solitaire must select only ripe berries and must be able to digest the pulp without damaging the seeds. Fruit color provides a simple visual cue to ripeness. Unripe juniper berries are green, whereas ripe berries are blue or copper—colors that are believed to attract fruit-eating birds. Furthermore, to help ensure that its berries escape predation during the two- to three-year ripening period, the juniper imbues the pulp that surrounds the seeds with terpenoid resins whose toxic qualities serve as a deterrent to the would-be seed predator or fruit eater. When a juniper berry is cut open, the translucent sacs in which these volatile, aromatic resins are contained are readily apparent to the naked eye. Terpene levels are consistently higher in immature berries and decline substantially as ripening proceeds—a fact reflected by the Townsend's solitaire's preference for mature fruit.

The Townsend's solitaire avoids the physiological hazards of a terpene-rich food resource by changing the way its digestive system functions. When insects are eaten, they are first routed through an out-pocketing of the main digestive tract, called the gizzard, where they undergo mechanical grinding to release the digestible material from the indigestible chitin. This kind of processing would destroy the thin-shelled juniper seeds and would also break open the resin sacs, releasing harmful terpenoid compounds into the bird's digestive tract. Instead, juniper berries are shunted past the gizzard and into the main part of the digestive tract, where the calorie-rich pulp is digested without the seeds being harmed or the resin sacs breaking down—the bird excretes both seeds and resin sacs undamaged in the feces.

As with the piñon jay, diet has had a profound effect on the social organization of the Townsend's solitaire. In contrast to the piñon jay, however, the solitaire—as its name suggests—is anything but social. On their wintering grounds, male solitaires aggressively defend individual feeding territories. Territory size reflects the quality and abundance of the juniper berry crop, the number of solitaires utilizing the wintering grounds, and individual aggressiveness. Winter territorial defense includes an extensive repertoire of songs and calls, boundary patrols from conspicuous perches, threat postures, pursuit of intruders, and physical combat. Females

THE SOUTHERN ROCKIES

do not establish territories, but move about the wintering grounds as nonterritorial "floaters" tolerated by the males.

Life Histories of Selected Animals

Mammals

Piñon Mouse, *Peromyscus truei.* This buffy brown deer mouse is distinguished by its extremely large ears and conspicuously bicolored tail. The piñon mouse, largely restricted to piñon-juniper habitat, is found from southwestern Wyoming south to Oaxaca, Mexico; on the Eastern Slope, this species is found as far north as the Colorado Springs area. This surprisingly arboreal mouse nests above the ground in a cavity or a hollow branch of a juniper; the nest consists of a ball of shredded bark, with an opening on one side. Piñon mice are especially fond of juniper seeds, selecting mature berries, discarding the resinous pulp surrounding the seed, and chewing a small hole in the seed coat from which to extract the embryonic seedling. Breeding begins in April and continues through September, with two litters of altricial young produced during a single breeding season.

Bushy-tailed Woodrat, *Neotoma cinerea.* This squirrel-size mammal is distinguished from other woodrats by its grayish buff fur, bushy, squirrel-like tail, large ears, and fully furred hind feet. Bushy-tailed woodrats are widespread in the Southern Rockies and are found in rocky areas with vertical fissures or talus and around abandoned, man-made structures from 5,000 feet to timberline. Woodrats are herbivorous, solitary, and largely nocturnal. The collecting instinct is well developed in this species, with an individual commonly accumulating a large pile of sticks, bones, and other debris that serves to restrict predator access at the entrance to its den; denning areas occupied by woodrats for long periods contain urine-cemented accumulations of dark brown fecal pellets. Females bear one or two litters of altricial young yearly.

Gray Fox, *Urocyon cinereoargenteus.* The gray fox is distinguished from the larger red fox by its silvery fur and black middorsal stripe, which extends down the back to the top of the tail; underparts are whitish. In the Southern Rockies, gray foxes prefer shrublands and brushy woodlands where terrain is rocky or broken. This mostly nocturnal carnivore is secretive and inconspicuous over most of its range. Its diet includes small mammals, birds, and fruit (especially juniper berries). Gray foxes are adept at climbing trees to forage for fruit or nesting birds. Mating occurs in February, followed by a gestation period of about nine weeks; newborn foxes are blind but well furred. Male foxes deliver food to the vixen while the young are being reared. Family units break up in autumn, with the young dispersing and the parents separating until the next mating season.

Ringtail, *Bassariscus astutus.* This slender-bodied relative of the raccoon is identified by its white-ringed eyes, its long and ringed tail, and the absence of a black face mask. In the Southern Rockies, ringtails are largely restricted to rocky terrain in the foothill shrublands and piñon-juniper zone. They are carnivorous, nocturnal, and active throughout the year. The species is secretive and rarely observed, though it may hunt in pairs or in extended-family groups. These animals are agile runners and daredevil rock climbers. Dens or daytime resting sites are among rocks or in tree cavities. Territories are marked with urine and accumulations of scat. Vocalizations include chirps, chittering, barks, and hissing. Breeding occurs in spring, with the altricial young born in May or June.

Mountain Lion, *Felis concolor.* This unmistakable cat is distinguished by its large size, short, tawny fur, and long tail. Mountain lions — also called pumas or cougars — are mostly restricted to rugged areas of the mountains, and may be surprisingly common in areas supporting large populations of their favorite diet: mule deer. Other prey includes small to mid-sized mammals and, in rare instances, domestic animals; carrion is seldom utilized. Secretive and solitary, the mountain lion hunts primarily at dawn and dusk. After killing a deer, it covers the leftovers with leaves or brush to be consumed over two or three days. Home range size is variable, depending on the age and sex of the lion, as well as on the season; males average about 48 square miles in winter and spring and nearly 120 square miles in summer and fall. Scrapes — pine needles, leaves, or dirt scraped into a pile with the hind feet — mark home range boundaries. No permanent den is maintained. Lions are promiscuous breeders, mating for the first time at two or three years of age; females give birth to blind but well-furred young, alone, after a gestation period of about ninety-six days; young are weaned at six weeks or so but will stay with the female for up to two years.

Birds

Piñon Jay, *Gymnorhinus cyanocephalus.* The piñon jay is a large blue-to-grayish-blue bird with a short tail and a pale, streaked throat. In the Southern Rockies, the species occurs in piñon-juniper woodlands, and less commonly in ponderosa pine forests. Piñon nuts are the preferred food of this jay, but fruit, insects, and bird eggs and nestlings are taken when available. Piñon jays are gregarious and maintain large, highly organized flocks; social organization includes communal food caching. A bulky nest is built in piñon, juniper, ponderosa pine, or Gambel oak.

Plain Titmouse, *Parus inornatus.* This small, dull gray bird has an erect gray crest. In the Southern Rockies, the species breeds, and occasionally winters, in the piñon-juniper woodlands and oak scrub of the central and southern mountains. The titmouse is insectivorous; when foraging, it mimics

Common birds of the piñon-juniper woodlands, from left to right: bushtit, piñon jay.

the twig-gleaning style of the chickadees and may often be seen hanging upside down from branches. This nonsocial species rarely gathers in large flocks. Titmice roost in tree cavities. Mated pairs remain together for at least two years; males defend territories of several acres during the nesting season. The female selects a nesting site in a tree cavity or old woodpecker hole, but the pair may also dig its own cavity in a rotton portion of a living tree.

Bushtit, *Psaltriparus minimus.* This grayish brown, crest-less bird is identified by its small size, long tail, and rounded wings; the Rocky Mountain race has brown patches on its cheeks, and the wings lack wing bars. Bushtits are locally common in piñon-juniper woodlands or in oak scrub from central Colorado southward. They are insectivorous and highly acrobatic, twittering noisily while foraging. The species is sociable, forming small flocks of twenty or more individuals, except during the breeding season when they remain alone or in pairs. Bushtits build gourd-shaped nests suspended from tree branches or in bushes in late April or early May.

Blue-Gray Gnatcatcher, *Polioptila caerulea.* This slender, bluish gray bird has a narrow bill, white eye ring, and long, thin tail. Blue-gray gnatcatchers are summer residents in piñon-juniper woodlands and scrub oak. The species forages actively for insects in trees and in the brushy understory, often making buzzy, insectlike vocalizations and conspicuously flicking or fanning the tail. Nesting occurs from April through May; the cuplike, lichen-covered nest is built on a horizontal branch or in the crotch of a tree and is often anchored to the branch with spider's silk. Both sexes incubate the eggs.

Reptiles

Collared Lizard, *Crotaphytus collaris.* This large, long-tailed lizard is identified by the twin black collars encircling the neck, the granular scales on the back, and the patterning of light dots on a darker background; the mature male has a blue-green throat, and the sides of breeding females are marked with orange spots or bars. In the Southern Rockies, the species is absent from Wyoming but occurs in Colo-

Collared lizard.

rado and New Mexico, mainly from the Arkansas River south on the Eastern Slope and from the Roan Plateau south on the Western Slope. Collared lizards are insectivorous and will sometimes capture other small lizards. This diurnal species emerges from hibernation in late March and April, remaining active throughout the summer; adults enter hibernation in early September, hatchlings in October. Males are highly territorial, threatening intruders with bobbing displays. Eggs are laid in June or July, with hatchlings first appearing in August.

Common Animals of the Piñon-Juniper Woodlands

Mammals

Long-legged Myotis, *Myotis volans*
Pallid Bat, *Antrozous pallidus*
Mountain (or Nuttall's) Cottontail, *Sylvilagus nuttallii*
Desert Cottontail, *Sylvilagus audubonii*
Black-tailed Jackrabbit, *Lepus californicus*
Colorado Chipmunk, *Tamias quadrivittatus*
Least Chipmunk, *Tamias minimus*
Rock Squirrel, *Spermophilus variegatus*
Deer Mouse, *Peromyscus maniculatus*
Piñon Mouse, *Peromyscus truei*
Rock Mouse, *Peromyscus difficilis*
Bushy-tailed Woodrat, *Neotoma cinerea*
Mexican Woodrat, *Neotoma mexicana*
Porcupine, *Erethizon dorsatum*

Ringtail, *Bassariscus astutus*
Western Spotted Skunk, *Spilogale gracilis*
Long-tailed Weasel, *Mustela frenata*
Coyote, *Canis latrans*
Gray Fox, *Urocyon cinereoargenteus*
Mountain Lion, *Felis concolor*
Mule Deer, *Odocoileus hemionus*

Birds

Red-tailed Hawk, *Buteo jamaicensis*
Golden Eagle, *Aquila chrysaetos*
Mourning Dove, *Zenaida macroura*
Ash-throated Flycatcher, *Myiarchus cinerascens*
Piñon Jay, *Gymnorhinus cyanocephalus*
Scrub Jay, *Aphelocoma coerulescens*
Steller's Jay, *Cyanocitta stelleri*
Clark's Nutcracker, *Nucifraga columbiana*
Common Raven, *Corvus corax*
Mountain Chickadee, *Parus gambeli*
Bushtit, *Psaltriparus minimus*
Plain Titmouse, *Parus inornatus*
Canyon Wren, *Catherpes mexicanus*
Rock Wren, *Salpinctes obsoletus*
Western Bluebird, *Sialia mexicana*
Mountain Bluebird, *Sialia currucoides*
Townsend's Solitaire, *Myadestes townsendi*
Blue-gray Gnatcatcher, *Polioptila caerulea*
Virginia's Warbler, *Vermivora virginiae*
Black-throated Gray Warbler, *Dendroica nigrescens*
Brown Towhee, *Pipilo fuscus*

Reptiles

Collared Lizard, *Crotaphytus collaris*
Sagebrush Lizard, *Sceloporus graciosus*
Eastern Fence Lizard, *Sceloporus undulatus*
Tree Lizard, *Urosaurus ornatus*
Bullsnake, *Pituophis melanoleucus*
Western Rattlesnake, *Crotalus viridis*

Invertebrates

Honey Ant, *Myrmecocystus mexicanus*
Piñon Spindle Gall Midge, *Pinyonia edulicola*
Great Basin Wood Nymph, *Cercyonis sthenele*
Juniper Hairstreak, *Mitoura siva*

CHAPTER FOURTEEN

Ponderosa Pine Forests

WALKING THROUGH A ponderosa pine forest is a sensual delight, the air redolent with the opiate essence of pine and the vanilla-like aroma of sun-warmed bark. John Muir said of ponderosa pine, "Of all the pines, this one gives forth the finest music to the winds." No other conifer in the Southern Rockies has needles as long—or as graceful. Muir also marveled at the "inviting openness" of ponderosa pine forests. Today, few ponderosa forests retain the parklike appearance and large, broad-crowned trees that figured so prominently in historic descriptions. These elegant old-growth forests are the progeny of recurrent and low intensity fires—once a natural component of the ecosystem throughout the West.

Ecological Distribution

The range of ponderosa pine essentially defines the American West. From Nebraska to California, and from southern British Columbia to northern Mexico, ponderosa pine is the dominant forest tree of the montane zone in western North America. Three chemically distinct races of ponderosa pine have evolved as a result of the species' wide geographical distribution. The race present in the Southern Rockies is known as Rocky Mountain ponderosa pine (*Pinus ponderosa* var. *scopulorum* Engelm.), a tree of less generous proportions than the so-called typical variety (*P. ponderosa* var. *ponderosa* Laws) encountered in the Pacific Northwest or the race (*P. ponderosa* var. *arizonica* Engelm.) found in Arizona and other parts of the Southwest.

In the Southern Rockies, ponderosa pine ecosystems occupy warm, dry slopes and gently rolling uplands from 5,600

Ponderosa pine.

to 9,000 feet, on both sides of the Continental Divide. Along the Eastern Slope, forests dominated by ponderosa pine are common on south-facing slopes from the Wyoming border south to the southern end of the Sangre de Cristo Range. Near Colorado Springs, ponderosa pine can be found on scarps extending eastward into the shortgrass prairie; studies of these forest outliers attribute their presence to topography and to the water-holding capacity of soils developed on the Castle Rock conglomerate.

North of the Wyoming border, ponderosa pine forests tend to be restricted to sheltered, low-elevation sites in the foothills. Though this pine occurs sporadically on the Eastern Slope north of the Snowy Range, well-developed stands are largely confined to scarp woodlands, like South Dakota's Pine Ridge, and outlying ranges farther to the east, such as the Bighorn Mountains of northern Wyoming and the Black Hills of South Dakota. The northward attenuation and eventual disappearance of both ponderosa and piñon-juniper woodlands along the Rocky Mountain front is thought to reflect the downward displacement of vegetational zones that occurs with increasing altitude.

On the Western Slope, ponderosa pine forests occupy a narrower elevational range and are not as extensive as those on the Eastern Slope. This pine is largely absent from the western and northwestern mountains of Colorado, where it is replaced by Douglas-fir. South of this area, ponderosa forests are common from the Uncompahgre Plateau south to the Jemez Mountains of New Mexico. At higher elevations within this region, as well as in canyons and on north-facing slopes, ponderosa forests are replaced by mixed coniferous forests. Below 7,500 feet, ponderosa forests are generally replaced by piñon-juniper woodlands throughout much of the southern portion of our range.

Physical Environment

Forests of ponderosa pine are adapted to mid-elevation montane regions characterized by cold winters and warm summers with intense solar radiation and frequent droughts. Summer temperatures rarely exceed 90°F; freezing temperatures can occur from mid-September until late May. The low temperatures typical of higher elevations in the Southern Rockies inhibit the growth of ponderosa pine, thereby determining its upper elevational limit. Average precipitation associated with this forest type varies from about 16 inches in New Mexico and south-central Colorado to more than 25 inches in the Medicine Bow Mountains of Wyoming. Snow seldom exceeds 12 inches in depth and typically melts within a few days.

Community Characteristics

Ponderosa pine forests may be of any size, from single-species stands that cover entire hillsides to small, single- or mixed-species stands. Along their lower altitudinal limits, ponderosa pine forests typically merge with piñon-juniper woodlands, with grasslands, or with various types of shrubland. Along their upper limits, ponderosa forests interfinger with Douglas-fir, spruce-fir forests, or successional forests dominated by aspen or lodgepole pine. On ridges exposed to strong winds, ponderosa pine may occur with limber pine or bristlecone pine.

Ponderosa pine ecosystems reflect differences in elevation, degree of slope, exposure, soil characteristics, stand age, disturbance history, and the relative importance of associated species. South-facing slopes are generally dominated by open, variable-age stands of ponderosa pine or by mixed stands of ponderosa pine and Douglas-fir, with pine predominating on drier sites and Douglas-fir prevalent on the steepest slopes. Under the most moderate conditions, these stands are open and parklike, with numerous grassy clearings. Stands on north-facing slopes are dominated by Douglas-fir and have an almost closed canopy, with a sparse understory of shrubs and herbaceous vegetation. Young stands of ponderosa pine, especially those on more mesic sites, can be very dense.

The amount of shrub and herbaceous understory is highly variable, depending on tree density and moisture availability. In the southern foothills, a well-developed shrub layer dominated by Gambel oak or New Mexican locust may be locally common, especially in areas that have been cut over. Elsewhere, the shrub understory is typically sparse, consisting of species such as wax currant, kinnikinnik, common juniper, big sagebrush, mountain mahogany, and antelope bitterbrush. On gentle slopes, grasses such as mountain muhly or timber oatgrass may form a luxuriant growth, particularly in areas where the soil is deep and fine textured.

Plant Adaptation: Designs for Survival

Competition for available resources — moisture, nutrients, and sunlight — is one of the major factors affecting the growth of ponderosa pine. Successful reproduction depends on an ample seed supply and sufficient moisture to ensure germination and early seedling survival. Ponderosa pine is intolerant of shade, and seedling success is poorest in forests with dense understory vegetation. Seeds germinate best on bare, moist mineral soils with unobstructed sunlight and little competition from other plants. In the Southern Rockies and throughout the Southwest, heavy seed production (an event that occurs at three- to five-year intervals) and higher-than-average moisture in spring and early summer provide optimal conditions for seedling establishment. This fortuitous pairing of events may happen only once every sixty years.

Numerous studies have shown that wide spacing is essential for optimal growth. Mature ponderosa pines have wide-spreading root systems—consisting of deep taproots that can plumb water from depths of up to 6 feet in porous soils or up to 40 feet in fractured bedrock—and networks of lateral roots that fan out through the surface soils for distances of up to 100 feet. Even a young seedling is quick to produce a long taproot. For example, a 3-inch seedling may have a taproot 2 feet long, allowing it to gather moisture from below the rooting level of many herbaceous plants.

Most of the ponderosa pine forests that we see today reflect human intervention—primarily fire suppression and logging. Low-intensity, lightning-initiated ground fires were a natural component of ponderosa pine ecosystems prior to settlement. Under a natural fire cycle, ground fires swept through the forests periodically, clearing away the litter of needles, thinning out dense stands of ponderosa seedlings, and enhancing the fertility of the soil. The degree of thinning produced by fires of this type depends on the quantity of burnable fuel on the forest floor. Thick, fire-resistant bark, functioning much like a suit of asbestos, helps to ensure that a mature ponderosa will be able to withstand all but the most severe fires. Since the early 1900s, however, wildfire prevention and selective logging have resulted in a proliferation of other coniferous species or in increased regeneration of ponderosa pine, both of which greatly increased stocking levels and competition for already limited soil moisture and nutrients.

Overcrowded stands of ponderosa pine tend to be unhealthy and susceptible to diseases and insect infestations. During the past few years, thousands of acres of these unhealthy ponderosa forests in the Southern Rockies have been devastated by infestations of mountain pine beetle. Scientists believe that pine beetle epidemics can occur only when there is an abundance of suitable host trees—weakened, unhealthy trees that cannot fend off the wood-boring beetles with chemical deterrents or by flushing the beetles from their tissues with pitch.

Descriptions of Common Plants

Ponderosa Pine, *Pinus ponderosa.* Ponderosa pine is the largest conifer species in the Southern Rockies, and in favorable locations may grow to be 150 feet in height and more than 3 feet in diameter. The species is readily identified by

THE SOUTHERN ROCKIES

its long needles (up to 7 inches in length), arranged in groups of two or three needles per bundle; a distinct white line, made up of air pores, or *stomata*, runs the length of each needle. The bark of mature trees is thick, orange-brown, and broken into large plates that give off a strong vanilla or butterscotch aroma when warmed by the sun; the bark of immature trees is brownish black, turning to yellow-brown or cinnamon with increasing age. The cones are moderately large and globe shaped, the spine-tipped scales opening at maturity to release dark brown, winged seeds. Ponderosa pine must be at least twenty-five years old before cone production can begin. Mature trees typically have rounded crowns; the more flat-topped crowns of the oldest trees are conspicuous only in old-growth forests. The largest trees in a mature stand may be three hundred to five hundred years old. Younger ponderosas exhibit a more pyramidal crown and may be branched nearly to the ground.

Shrubs

Wax Currant, *Ribes cereum.* Wax currant is a common shrub of dry gulches, canyons, and hillsides, from the plains to the upper montane. The species is identified by its obtusely lobed leaves and pink, funnel-shaped flowers. Sticky hairs coat the surfaces of the translucent, orange-red berries. The fruits are eaten by birds (especially mountain bluebirds) and small mammals, but have a rather insipid taste.

Boulder Raspberry, *Oreobatus deliciosus.* Boulder raspberry (also called Rocky Mountain thimbleberry in some guides) is a handsome shrub found on rocky slopes from the foothills to the montane zone and is especially common on the Eastern Slope. The species is identified by its bright green, round-lobed leaves and its white, roselike flowers. Blooming in late May and June, the five-petaled flowers average about 1.5 inches in diameter and are followed by raspberry-like fruits that are bland and seedy.

Waxflower, *Jamesia americana.* Waxflower grows in rocky crevices or at the base of cliffs and is easily identified by its ovate, opposite leaves, silky leaf undersides, peeling outer bark, and clusters of fragrant, cream white flowers. The species is named for Dr. Edwin James, botanist with the 1820 Long Expedition. Fossils of waxflower have been found in the Oligocene beds of Creede, Colorado.

Common shrubs of the ponderosa pine forest, from top to bottom: waxflower, wax currant, boulder raspberry (with detail of flower), common gooseberry.

Wildflowers

Pasque Flower, *Pulsatilla patens.* One of the earliest flowers of spring, the pasque flower is most abundant on open slopes and mesas, blooming first in the foothills and later in the higher mountains. Flower buds emerge in April and are conspicuous because of the woolly hairs that insulate the sepals, opening on sunny days to reveal crocuslike, lavender

Common wildflowers of the ponderosa pine forest, clockwise from upper left: western wallflower, one-sided penstemon, pasque flower, sulphur flower.

flowers; in early summer the pasque flower is recognized by its ball of feathery-tailed seeds. A whorl of finely dissected leaves appears only after the blossoms fade.

Mountain Ball Cactus, *Pediocactus simpsonii.* Often overlooked, this small, pincushion-like cactus is found in grassy clearings from the foothills to the montane zone. In contrast to the flat pads of the prickly pear (*Opuntia* spp.), this species consists of a flattened ball 2 to 6 inches in diameter, its surface covered with spine-tipped tubercles rather than ribs. Pink, rose-scented flowers appear in spring and are clustered atop the cactus like a crown.

Sulphur Flower, *Eriogonum umbellatum.* This bright yellow flower is abundant on dry hillsides from the foothills to the subalpine. A member of the buckwheat family *(Polygonaceae),* sulphur flower is easily identified by its umbellate (umbrella-like) cluster of small, yellow flowers and by its simple, spatulate leaves.

One-sided Penstemon, *Penstemon secundiflorus.* This showy wildflower is abundant on hillsides in the foothill and montane zones from late spring to early summer. One-sided penstemon is easily distinguished from other blue-flowered penstemons by its large size and by the arrangement of its blue-magenta flowers along one side of the flowering stalk; a sterile stamen, bearded with stiff, yellow hairs, is present and serves to brush the pollen from the abdomens of visiting bees.

Common Plants of the Ponderosa Pine Forest

Trees

Douglas-fir, *Pseudotsuga menziesii*
Juniper, Rocky Mountain, *Sabina scopulorum*
Oak, Gambel, *Quercus gambelii*
Pine, limber, *Pinus flexilus*
  ponderosa, *Pinus ponderosa*

Shrubs

Bitterbrush, *Purshia tridentata*
Buckbrush, *Ceanothus fendleri*
Chokecherry, *Padus virginiana* ssp. *melanocarpa*
Cinquefoil, shrubby, *Pentaphylloides floribunda*
Currant, wax, *Ribes cereum*
Juniper, common, *Juniperus communis*
Kinnikinnik, *Arctostaphylos uva-ursi*
Mahogany, mountain, *Cercocarpus montanus*
Raspberry, boulder, *Oreobatus deliciosus* (formerly
      Rubus)
Sagebrush, big, *Seriphidium tridentatum*
      silver (or fringed), *Artemisia frigida*
Waxflower, *Jamesia americana*

Herbaceous Plants

Blanketflower, *Gaillardia aristata*
Buckwheat, James, *Eriogonum jamesii*
Cactus, mountain ball, *Pediocactus simpsonii*
Candytuft, mountain, *Noccaea montana* (formerly
      Thlaspi)
Daisy, Easter, *Townsendia exscapa*
Dropseed, pine, *Blepharoneuron tricholepis*
Fescue, Arizona, *Festuca arizonica*
      mountain, *Festuca saximontana*
      spike, *Leucopoa kingii*
Fleabane, *Erigeron flagellaris*
Geranium, common wild, *Geranium caespitosum*
Grama, blue, *Bouteloua gracilis*
Grape, Oregon, *Mahonia repens*
Groundsel, *Packera neomexicana* and *P. fendleri*
Gumweed, *Grindelia squarrosa*
Junegrass, *Koeleria macrantha*
Larkspur, *Delphinium nuttallianum*
Lily, sand, *Leucocrinum montanum*
Miner's Candle, *Oreocarya virgata* (formerly
      Cryptantha)
Mistletoe, dwarf, *Arceuthobium vaginatum*
Muhly, mountain, *Muhlenbergia montana*

Oat-grass, poverty, *Danthonia spicata*
Parsley, whiskbroom, *Harbouria trachypleura*
Pasque Flower, *Pulsatilla patens*
Penstemon, one-sided, *Penstemon secundiflorus*
   small-flowered, *Penstemon virens*
Pussy-toes, *Antennaria rosea, A. parvifolia,* and *A.*
   microphylla
Sedge, aridland, *Carex xerantica*
   sun, *Carex pennsylvanica* ssp. *heliophila*
Spring Beauty, *Claytonia rosea*
Sulphur Flower, *Eriogonum umbellatum*
Sunflower, little, *Helianthella uniflora* and *H. parryi*
Wallflower, western, *Erysimum capitatum*

Environment and Adaptation: Animals of the Ponderosa Pine Forest

Ponderosa pine ecosystems provide habitat for a wide diversity of forest animals; at least 57 mammals and 128 bird species occur in these forests. The life histories and distribution patterns of several species—Abert's squirrel, pygmy nuthatch, red crossbill, and flammulated owl—are closely interwoven with that of ponderosa pine. Mature and old-growth forests with well-developed shrub understories are favored by mule deer and elk as winter range. Porcupines can be found in these open woodlands throughout the year, eating herbaceous vegetation on the forest floor during spring and summer and savoring the nutrient-rich inner bark of the ponderosa in other seasons. Grassy clearings and rocky, shrub-covered hillsides provide optimal habitat for chipmunks, golden-mantled ground squirrels, Nuttall's cottontails, and deer mice.

Birds are an important and conspicuous component of ponderosa pine ecosystems. The changing cast of characters includes year-round residents such as pygmy nuthatches, chickadees, juncos, hairy woodpeckers, and Steller's jays, as well as breeding season arrivals—Williamson's sapsucker, mountain bluebird, western tanager, pine siskin, and flam-

From left to right: least chipmunk, golden-mantled ground squirrel.

mulated owl—attracted by the abundance of nesting sites and the diversity of food resources. Strong year-to-year fluctuations in the populations of species that depend on conifer seeds for food, such as the red crossbill, reflect the cyclical nature of the cone crop.

Niche Relationships in Old-Growth Pine Forests

With so many species dependent on the same food resources—conifer seeds and insects—specializations have evolved that limit interspecific competition. Significant differences in size and foraging behavior enable species to use slightly different resources and thus avoid intense competition. For example, the red-breasted nuthatch forages in the top one-third of a tree, effectively segregated from the white-breasted nuthatch, which forages mainly on the trunk and largest branches of the lower two-thirds of the tree, and from the pygmy nuthatch, which forages among the pine needles and smaller branches.

The presence or absence of certain animal species can tell us much about the disturbance history and structural complexity of a ponderosa pine forest. Old-growth forests (forests that are older than two hundred years) exhibit the highest species diversity, largely because these forests tend to be open and have well-developed understories. Stands with trees of various ages are preferred to those in which a single age class predominates. For example, Abert's squirrel and the flammulated owl show a strong preference for old-growth, multiple-aged forests.

Old-growth forests have unique qualities. The complex relationships that bind certain animal species to these old-growth habitats are just beginning to be understood. Unfortunately, the history of ponderosa pine forests throughout the West has been one of heavy use due to their high commercial value and year-round accessibility. In recent years, intensification of harvesting activity has resulted in the continued loss of habitat for species dependent on old–growth — a situation that may eventually cause the disappearance of these species. The most obvious impacts are to cavity nesting birds — nuthatches, flickers, tree swallows, downy woodpeckers, flammulated owls, and mountain bluebirds — because of their vulnerability to forest management practices, such as fuel-wood cutting, that eliminate snags. Outside the breeding season, large cavities provide critical thermal cover and are often used as communal roosts by small birds such as pygmy nuthatches and brown creepers. One Colorado study reported more than fifty pygmy nuthatches sharing a single large cavity in a ponderosa pine.

FLAMMULATED OWLS

Small enough to fit in the palm of your hand, the seldom-seen flammulated owl is often the most abundant raptor in old-growth ponderosa pine and Douglas-fir forests. These mature forests tend to have an abundance of snags and live trees with cavities — a necessity for this obligate cavity nester. In Colorado, radio telemetry studies of this nocturnal, insectivorous owl have shown that it prefers to forage in these forests as opposed to any other forest types. In most cases, the home ranges of nesting flammulated owls include high proportions of old-growth pine forest. In fact, areas of continuous old growth support higher densities of nesting owls than are found in smaller and disjunct stands of old growth. Furthermore, home ranges in continuous old-growth stands are more consistently reoccupied by owls returning in the spring than are ranges located in a mosaic of different forest types.

The flammulated owl's affinity for old-growth pine forests appears to be closely related to the owl's preferred diet, the structure of the forest, and the character of the individual trees where foraging activities occur. There are up to four times as many insect species in old-growth ponderosa pine and Douglas-fir forests as in any other coniferous forest types. In fact, many of these insect species are host-plant specific and are therefore found only in association with ponderosa pine and Douglas-fir. The favored foraging techniques of the flammulated owl require open tree crowns where gleaning can occur while the bird hovers, or spaces between trees where the owl can hawk insects in the air. The research suggests that the future of this owl depends on our ability to preserve sufficient acreages of old-growth ponderosa, as well as the key components of the habitat (such as nest cavities and foraging sites) critical to their survival.

ABERT'S SQUIRRELS

The most distinctive mammal of the ponderosa pine forest is Abert's squirrel, a tassel-eared squirrel confined to the Southern Rockies, the Colorado Plateau, and the Sierra Madre in Mexico. Though this species may be found occasionally in other types of coniferous forest, Abert's squirrels depend mostly on mature forests of ponderosa pine for food and cover. Unlike most other tree squirrels, Abert's squirrel does not cache food. From late spring until early fall, pine seeds constitute nearly the entire diet of this squirrel; a single squirrel may consume the seeds from about seventy-five cones a day. During the winter and spring months, the succulent inner bark of ponderosa pine twigs is consumed; heavily utilized trees are recognized by their denuded branches and the piles of needles and peeled twigs at their bases. Recent studies suggest that the choice of feeding trees may relate to the differential concentration of certain aromatic monoterpenes in the tree's resinous fluids.

MOUNTAIN PINE BEETLE

Abert's squirrel and the mountain pine beetle both rely on the nutrient-rich tissues of ponderosa pine. The infamous mountain pine beetle *(Dendroctonus ponderosae)* has been a major predator of ponderosa pine throughout the West.

Despite the loss of trees to the beetle, it is important to view the pine beetle as an integral part of the ponderosa pine ecosystem — a natural thinning agent in overcrowded stands. Evidence of the importance of the pine beetle as a selective force in the evolution of ponderosa pine can be traced to beetle galleries in petrified wood more than 225 million years old.

The pine beetle completes its entire life cycle, except for a brief flight period, beneath a thick layer of pine bark. The cycle begins in late summer when the eggs are laid (about seventy-five per female) in vertical galleries excavated beneath the bark by the parent beetles. Survival of the beetle brood depends on lower than normal moisture content within the tree. Maintaining this optimal environment for the developing larvae requires an unusual collaboration, or mutualistic relationship, between the adult beetle and some species of *Ceratocysis* and *Trichosporum* known collectively as the "blue-stain fungi." A close look at the head of the adult beetle reveals tiny openings — mycangial pits, or mycangia — that are filled with the spores of these fungi. In the course of tunnel excavation, the spores are spilled into the rays and resin canals of the pine's sapwood. Before long the sapwood will be clogged with tangled strands of fungal hyphae, and the sap will cease to flow. Once hatched, the hungry larvae are nourished by the fungal gardens that prosper within the nursery galleries until cold weather induces inactivity in the fall.

With the coming of spring, the larvae resume feeding on the nutrient-rich tissues of the tree, undergoing a transformation from pupa to adult by early summer. These new adults begin to emerge as early as mid-July, but the majority emerge during the first two weeks of August. Prior to emergence, their own mycangia will be replete with fresh new spores to be introduced into the pines that they will later attack. Following emergence, female beetles pioneer the assault on new host trees, followed by large numbers of males, and the cycle is repeated. Evidence of successful pine beetle infestation includes popcornlike masses of resin on the trunk, boring dust in bark crevices and around the tree's base, blue-stained sapwood, and browning of the tree's needles. Ponderosa pines that have been attacked by large numbers of pine beetles die almost immediately from the combined effects of the beetle's excavations and the physiological drought induced by the blue fungus.

Ponderosa pine is not a passive recipient of the pine beetle's attack. Recent studies have shown that this tree, like
most conifers, has an arsenal of chemical compounds that
serve as natural insecticides; these resins are responsible for
the ponderosa's aromatic bouquet. Tree tissues possessing
high levels of the monoterpene limonene have been shown
to be toxic or inhibitory to the pine beetle, effectively reducing the reproductive success of the beetle as well as the via-
bility of its fungal symbiont. Studies indicate that trees that
survive predation by pine beetles tend to have high concentrations of limonene, suggesting that predation by a specialist
herbivore, such as the mountain pine beetle, would eventually result in directional selection for limonene in a ponderosa pine community.

Mountain pine beetles, on the other hand, have evolved
adaptations that counter the pine's defenses and turn its
chemical arsenal to their own advantage. In the case of ponderosa pine, beetles utilize monoterpenes present to varying degrees in the tree's resinous fluids in both the selection
and the colonization of host trees. For example, the female
beetle requires high concentrations of the monoterpene myr-
cene in order to synthesize the chemical signal, called an
aggregating pheromone, that will encourage male beetles
to follow her to an appropriate host tree. When beetle populations are excessively high, the female beetle may synthesize compounds from the monoterpene alpha-pinene that
mask the attractiveness of her aggregating pheromone and
redirect the male beetles to adjacent host trees — resulting
in the clustering of infested trees in a ponderosa stand.

Life Histories of Selected Animals

Mammals

Abert's (or Tassel-eared) Squirrel, *Sciurus aberti.* This
large, heavy-bodied squirrel is distinguished by its prominent ear tufts and its long, full tail; at least four color phases
are reported for the Southern Rockies — salt-and-pepper,
gray with white belly, pure black, and dark brown. In the
Southern Rockies, Abert's squirrels are found in ponderosa

pine habitat along the Eastern Slope as far north as southern Laramie County, Wyoming, and in the San Juan and Jemez mountains. Strictly diurnal, this squirrel remains active throughout the year. Abert's squirrels do not defend territories but maintain home ranges (often overlapping) averaging about 20 acres in size. Largely solitary, the species forms loose social hierarchies only during the mating season, when males compete for the opportunity to mate with an estrous female. Breeding occurs from late March to May, and one litter of altricial young is born annually. The ball-shaped nest is constructed of pine twigs, with a lining of softer materials, and is built in the crotch of a branch.

Golden-mantled Ground Squirrel, *Spermophilus lateralis.* Commonly mistaken for a large chipmunk, the golden-mantled ground squirrel can be distinguished by its relatively shorter tail, dorsal stripes that run only from hip to shoulder, and absence of stripes on the head. This ground squirrel inhabits a broad elevational range and is most common in open woodlands and forest-edge communities. Though a brazen beggar in tourist areas, the species normally prefers plant material: stems, leaves, flowers, seeds, and fruits; when available, fungi, insects, eggs, nestling birds, and carrion also provide nourishment. Diurnal and asocial, golden-mantles establish and maintain a dominance hierarchy with chases, fights, scent marking, teeth chattering, and other threat displays. These animals enter hibernation in late September or October, their torpidity facilitated by large reserves of body fat; these animals rouse from hibernation every few weeks to feed on cached food. Breeding occurs shortly after emergence in spring, producing a single litter of altricial young.

Least Chipmunk, *Tamias minimus.* This familiar animal is distinguished from the golden-mantled ground squirrel by its smaller size, the presence of head stripes, and its rapid movements. Least chipmunks are found from the foothills and shrubby basins to the alpine tundra on both sides of the Continental Divide, but are largely restricted to higher elevations in the San Juan and Jemez mountains and in the Sangre de Cristo Range, where the species' territory overlaps with that of the Colorado chipmunk *(T. quadrivittatus).* The diet consists largely of seeds from conifers and herbaceous plants (especially those from the sunflower family), as well as fruit, insects, and carrion; food is cached for winter use. Least chipmunks are diurnal, with a peak of activity in the morning, and often forage in trees or shrubs. Least chipmunks appear to be more social than golden-mantled ground squirrels; vocalizations and various tail displays are used to maintain social organization. Home ranges overlap broadly and vary in size from one to several acres. The least chipmunk becomes torpid in October or November, retreating to a nest chamber within its burrow; chipmunks may rouse occasionally to feed on stored food or venture above ground during warm periods. Breeding occurs shortly after emergence, with a litter of altricial young born in early July.

Birds

Flammulated Owl, *Otus flammeolus.* This small, secretive, and strictly nocturnal owl breeds in western mountain forests, especially ponderosa pine, where it may be rare to locally common. The flammulated owl is identified by its dark eyes (it's the only small owl with dark eyes), reddish facial disk, and short tail. The diet consists of night-flying insects, especially moths, which it takes on the wing. Daytime roosts are well hidden by branches and are typically situated close to the trunk. The flammulated owl is most easily located at night, from May until July, when males sing on their territories. This species is an obligate cavity nester, selecting abandoned flicker or woodpecker cavities in pine or aspen adjacent to its foraging areas. The species is migratory in the Southern Rockies, wintering from Mexico southward.

Williamson's Sapsucker, *Sphyrapicus thyroideus.* The male Williamson's sapsucker has a black back, white wing and rump patches, red throat, and yellow belly; the female has a brown head and a brown-and-white barred body. A shy, somewhat secretive bird, the Williamson's drills rows of tiny holes in the bark of pine, fir, aspen, and other trees, from which it drinks sap and also eats the insects that become trapped in the sap; this species also eats ants, spruce budworm moths, and other insects when available. Males arrive on the breeding grounds by early May, establishing their territories by drumming and with threatening displays. Both sexes excavate the nest cavity, and egg laying occurs shortly thereafter. Both sexes incubate the eggs, uttering a harsh "churring" call throughout the nesting period; the male sleeps with the eggs and the young.

Steller's Jay, *Cyanocitta stelleri.* Steller's jay is identified by its dark blue body, black crest, and conspicuous white flecking over the eye. The species is common in coniferous forests throughout western North America. Steller's jay is bold near human habitation but tends to be difficult to approach in forest situations. Somewhat less gregarious than other jays, this species has an amazing repertoire of songs and calls, ranging from soft whisper songs and rolling click calls to more raucous, even hawklike, squawks and calls. These jays are omnivores, foraging on the ground and in trees for insects, seeds, acorns, and other plant foods; they also occasionally take carrion, snakes, and the eggs and young of other birds. Steller's jays build a bulky nest of twigs cemented together with mud, typically situated in a conifer.

Pygmy Nuthatch, *Sitta pygmaea.* The pygmy nuthatch occurs most frequently in open forests of ponderosa pine. This species is easily distinguished from other nuthatches by its gray-brown cap, blue-gray back, and buff underparts. Gregarious except during the nesting season, pygmy nuthatches travel in large, occasionally mixed-species flocks. Their call is a high, rapid "peep-peep." Pygmy nuthatches are insectivorous and forage actively through the tops of pines, searching the needles, cones, and twigs for insects. During the breeding season, pairs of nuthatches excavate their own

From left to right: Steller's jay, pygmy nuthatch.

THE SOUTHERN ROCKIES

cavity nest or utilize an existing one; young are born in June and leave the nest about twenty-two days after hatching. Pygmy nuthatches roost in large, communal cavities during the fall and winter.

Western Tanager, *Piranga ludoviciana.* This brilliantly colored tanager is a common summer inhabitant of coniferous forests throughout western North America. The male has a red head and face, and a yellow-and-black body; the female has grayish upperparts and a yellowish green breast. Upon arriving in the spring, the male perches for a long period in one spot while delivering its robinlike song. Western tanagers are insectivorous, gleaning insects from the branches and foliage and occasionally taking insects on the wing. The nest, built by the female on the outer branches of pines, consists of a loose cup of plant materials.

Evening Grosbeak, *Coccothraustes vespertina.* This conspicuous grosbeak is identified by its conical bill, black tail and wings, and yellow body. Gregarious even during the nesting season, small flocks are often observed foraging for seeds, buds, small fruits, and insects; flocks roost in coniferous trees and are commmon visitors to bird feeders. These birds are fond of salt; flocks can often be seen eating salty soil in areas where salt is spread on roads to melt ice. Evening grosbeaks frequently drink and bathe, eating snow and seeking ice-free stretches of streams during the winter months. During courtship, the male feeds the female and dances before her; both sexes sing during the nesting season. The nest is built by the female in a conifer tree, usually near the end of a branch.

Pine Siskin, *Carduelis pinus.* The breeding range of the pine siskin embraces the coniferous forests of North America. This species is easily identified by its prominent streaking, diagnostic yellow patches at the base of the tail and flight feathers, and forked tail; undulating flight and light, twittery flight notes help in long-distance identification. Unpredictably nomadic, flocks of these birds will appear one day and be gone the next. Pine siskins are gregarious throughout the year; nesting may occur in loose colonies, and breeding siskins may forage in small groups. During the winter months, siskins frequent open fields and may forage with goldfinches and red crossbills in mixed-species flocks. The diet of this species consists largely of seeds, especially conifer seeds, with buds and insects taken when available. Nesting occurs in high evergreens; nestlings are fed in part with regurgitated masses of small seeds.

Common Animals of the Ponderosa Pine Forest

Mammals

Dwarf Shrew, *Sorex nanus*
Merriam's Shrew, *Sorex merriami*
Little Brown Bat, *Myotis lucifugus*
Long-eared Myotis, *Myotis evotis*
Mountain (or Nuttall's) Cottontail, *Sylvilagus nuttallii*
Least Chipmunk, *Tamias minimus*
Colorado Chipmunk, *Tamias quadrivittatus*
Yellow-bellied Marmot, *Marmota flaviventris*
Golden-mantled Ground Squirrel, *Spermophilus lateralis*
Abert's Squirrel, *Sciurus aberti*
Northern Pocket Gopher, *Thomomys talpoides*
Deer Mouse, *Peromyscus maniculatus*
Rock Mouse, *Peromyscus difficilis*
Bushy-tailed Woodrat, *Neotoma cinerea*
Mexican Woodrat, *Neotoma mexicana*
Montane Vole, *Microtus montanus*
Porcupine, *Erethizon dorsatum*
Coyote, *Canis latrans*
Ermine, *Mustela erminea*
Long-tailed Weasel, *Mustela frenata*
Elk, *Cervus elaphus*
Mule Deer, *Odocoileus hemionus*

Birds

Red-tailed Hawk, *Buteo jamaicensis*
Sharp-shinned Hawk, *Accipiter striatus*
Mourning Dove, *Zenaida macroura*
Great Horned Owl, *Bubo virginianus*

Flammulated Owl, *Otus flammeolus*
Northern Pygmy Owl, *Glaucidium gnoma*
Northern Saw-whet Owl, *Aegolius acadicus*
Common Nighthawk, *Chordeiles minor*
Broad-tailed Hummingbird, *Selasphorus platycercus*
Northern Flicker, *Colaptes auratus*
Williamson's Sapsucker, *Sphyrapicus thyroideus*
Hairy Woodpecker, *Picoides villosus*
Downy Woodpecker, *Picoides pubescens*
Western Wood-Pewee, *Contopus sordidulus*
Western Flycatcher, *Empidonax difficilis*
Tree Swallow, *Tachycineta bicolor*
Violet-green Swallow, *Tachycineta thalassina*
Steller's Jay, *Cyanocitta stelleri*
Clark's Nutcracker, *Nucifraga columbiana*
Black-billed Magpie, *Pica pica*
Common Raven, *Corvus corax*
Mountain Chickadee, *Parus gambeli*
Brown Creeper, *Certhia familiaris*
White-breasted Nuthatch, *Sitta carolinensis*
Red-breasted Nuthatch, *Sitta canadensis*
Pygmy Nuthatch, *Sitta pygmaea*
House Wren, *Troglodytes aedon*
Mountain Bluebird, *Sialia currucoides*
Western Bluebird, *Sialia mexicana*
Townsend's Solitaire, *Myadestes townsendi*
American Robin, *Turdus migratorius*
Solitary Vireo, *Vireo solitarius*
Yellow-rumped Warbler, *Dendroica coronata*
Black-headed Grosbeak, *Pheucticus melanocephalus*
Evening Grosbeak, *Coccothraustes vespertina*
Western Tanager, *Piranga ludoviciana*
Pine Siskin, *Carduelis pinus*
Cassin's Finch, *Carpodacus cassinii*
Red Crossbill, *Loxia curvirostra*
Dark-eyed Junco, *Junco hyemalis*
Chipping Sparrow, *Spizella passerina*

Reptiles

Many-lined Skink, *Eumeces multivirgatus*
Milk Snake, *Lampropeltis triangulum*

Butterflies

Pine White, *Neophasia menapia*
Western Pine Elfin, *Incisalia eryphon*
Chryxus Arctic, *Oeneis chryxus*
Red-bordered Brown, *Gyrocheilus patrobas*

CHAPTER FIFTEEN

Douglas-Fir Forests

DOUGLAS-FIR FORESTS provide a striking contrast—both visually and ecologically—to the open pine forests that share their montane habitat. Archibald Menzies, the naturalist who explored Puget Sound with the famous Vancouver Expedition, was the first to collect specimens of Douglas-fir. Unfortunately, Menzies' botanical collections received little attention in the scientific community. The task fell to David Douglas, a Scottish plant collector in the employ of the Horticultural Society of London, to return to the Pacific Northwest in 1825 and essentially rediscover the majestic tree that now bears both their names. In the forests of the Northwest, Douglas-fir is surpassed in size and grandeur only by the giant sequoias. In the Rocky Mountains, however, Douglas-fir forests bear only a fleeting resemblance to those mist-shrouded forests that Menzies marveled at nearly two hundred years ago. Here, tree growth is limited by a short growing season, colder temperatures, and more arid conditions.

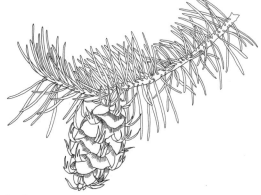

Douglas-fir.

Ecological Distribution

Douglas-fir is one of the most widespread and economically important trees in western North America, and is found from British Columbia south to central Mexico. Botanists recognize two varieties: the Pacific Coast populations of Douglas-fir (*Pseudotsuga menziesii* var. *menziesii*) and the Rocky Mountain Douglas-fir (*P. menziesii* var. *glauca*), distinguished from the Pacific variety by the bluish "bloom" on the needles and by smaller cones.

In the Southern Rockies, Douglas-fir forests can be found from about 6,000 to 9,500 feet on both sides of the Continental Divide. At lower elevations, stands of Douglas-fir are largely confined to sheltered, north-facing slopes and cool ravines, whereas in the upper montane zone, Douglas-fir may be found on all slope aspects, often in association with ponderosa pine. Along the Western Slope, in western and northwestern Colorado, Douglas-fir replaces ponderosa pine as the dominant montane coniferous species.

Physical Environment

Douglas-fir forests are adapted to cool, moist conditions — conditions normally associated, in the foothill and montane zones, with north-facing slopes and narrow ravines. Due to the inclination of the sun, a north-facing slope in northern temperate latitudes will always receive less total insolation than a south-facing slope in the same region. Consequently, air and soil temperatures are cooler, the relative humidity is greater, and more moisture is available for plant life. In addition, the frost-free season is shorter and snow lingers longer than on south-facing slopes.

The upper elevational limit of Douglas-fir, as is true for ponderosa pine, is determined by low summer temperatures; the lower limit depends on soil factors, especially moisture. In general, at their upper elevational limits, species tend to be present primarily on warm slopes or in successional stands; species at their lower limits tend to grow in mesic sites.

Community Characteristics

The correlation of tree species with exposure—Douglas-fir with steep, north-facing slopes and ponderosa pine with south-facing slopes and ridgetops—is most striking at lower elevations in the montane zone. Here, Douglas-fir and ponderosa pine forests interfinger in a complicated way, the relative abundance of the two species varying with the angle of slope and with soil conditions. White fir is a common codominant of Douglas-fir in these forests in the southern half of the Southern Rockies. At higher elevations in the montane zone, expecially in the northern and western mountains, Douglas-fir dominates coniferous forests on all slope aspects. In transitional areas between forest types or on disturbed sites, Douglas-fir may be found in association with aspen, ponderosa pine, lodgepole pine, limber pine, blue spruce, Engelmann spruce, and subalpine fir.

The density of Douglas-fir forests is variable and highly dependent on moisture availability, with the most mesic sites supporting the densest forests. Young stands of Douglas-fir may be exceedingly well stocked, becoming more open with maturity. Mature Douglas-fir forests on steep, north-facing slopes have an almost closed canopy; little sunlight penetrates to the forest floor. In the shadiest forests, a pale green, branching lichen known as Old Man's Beard drapes the lower, light-starved branches. Understory vegetation is sparse and consists mostly of shrubs such as common juniper, kinnikinnik, and waxflower. Where moisture conditions are favorable, a rich moss and lichen flora patterns rock outcrops and rotting stumps.

As a result of lumbering activities and fires, few Douglas-fir forests in the Southern Rockies have retained their primeval character. Consequently, mixed conifer forests generally prevail in areas that were once dominated by Douglas-fir. These disturbed stands tend to be more open and are characterized by shrub and herbaceous species typically associated with drier ponderosa pine or mountain shrub ecosystems.

Plant Adaptation:
Designs for Survival

Rocky Mountain Douglas-fir is relatively resistent to drought — far more so than the coastal variety. To increase its efficiency in absorbing water and nutrients from the soil, the Douglas-fir shares a symbiotic, and possibly obligatory, relationship with certain soil fungi. To understand how this mutually beneficial system functions, it is necessary to know something about the biology of fungi. Unlike higher plants, fungi reproduce by spores. When a spore lands in a suitable environment, it germinates and sends out long filaments, called *hyphae,* that spread through soil or wood. The hyphae grow and divide deep in the soil, producing a mass — called a *mycelium* — which constitutes the main portion or vegetative body of a fungus. When moisture and temperature conditions are right, the mycelium sends up the spore-producing, or reproductive, structure of the fungus — the varicolored mushrooms that we see poking through the forest litter.

Hyphae liberate enzymes that digest dead roots, logs, cones, and other organic matter to provide nutrients for the fungus's growth. Fungi require carbohydrates for growth but, in contrast to green plants, can only obtain them by tapping into the roots of other plants that produce their own food through photosynthesis. To do this, as in the case of Douglas-fir, fungal hyphae envelop the tree's rootlets in a filamentous shroud, with some hyphae penetrating the root's outer tissues. The new structures that are formed are called *mycorrhizae.* Mycorrhizal absorption of water is more efficient than absorption carried on by the unaided root. In the case of Douglas-fir, the increased absorption surface provided by the fungus is believed to be necessary to counterbalance water lost through evaporation. Recent evidence suggests that the presence of mycorrhizae may prolong root life and may also have an antibiotic effect on parasitic fungi that attack tree roots.

Descriptions of Common Plants

Douglas-fir, *Pseudotsuga menziesii.* Douglas-fir is not a true fir, but belongs instead to an entirely different genus found only in western North America and in the mountains of China, Japan, and Taiwan. Douglas-fir is distinguished from other short-needled conifers by its flat, stalked, round-tipped needles, its sharp-pointed winter buds, and its female cones, made conspicuous by the three-pronged bract that protrudes like a snake's tongue from between each cone scale. The male (pollen-producing) cones of the Douglas-fir are small, oblong, and orange-red in color. Unlike the true firs, in which the female (seed-bearing) cones stand straight up on the branches, Douglas-fir cones hang down, falling from the tree intact at maturity. During the single growing season required to reach maturity, female cones change from garnet red to green, and, finally, to a rich brown. The paired seeds are reddish brown and shiny and have a dark brown wing. Seed production may begin when the tree is ten years old, increasing dramatically at twenty-five to thirty years, and reaching maximum production when the tree is between two hundred and three hundred years old.

Shrubs

Mountain-lover, *Paxistima myrsinites.* This small evergreen shrub is a member of the Staff-tree family (*Celastraceae*), of which bittersweet is the best known representative. In contrast to kinnikinnik, which it superficially resembles, the opposite leaves are oval in shape and have finely toothed margins. The reddish, four-petaled flowers are small and inconspicuous. Mountain-lover is especially common in moist, montane forests on the Western Slope but may be found in suitable habitat throughout the Southern Rockies.

Wildflowers

Fairy Slipper Orchid, *Calypso bulbosa.* This small, lovely orchid is found in moist coniferous forests and is locally common on north-facing slopes in certain areas. It is easily identified by its slender, rose-colored petals and whitish, slipper-shaped lip; the interior of the slipper is streaked with purple, and the lip sports a fringe of golden hairs and a spattering of purple dots. Blooming in late May or early June, depending on the elevation, each 4- to 8-inch stalk supports

From left to right: fairy slipper orchid, pipsissewa.

a single, fragrant flower; each flower stalk arises from a tuber and is paired with a solitary, basal leaf that withers after the plant blooms in the spring. Pollination is by insects; germination depends on the presence of symbiotic fungi.

Twinflower, *Linnaea borealis.* This lovely little plant, with its trailing stems and paired evergreen leaves, is named for the Swedish botanist Carl Linnaeus, who discovered it in Lapland. Linnaeus was so fond of this species that many of his portraits show him holding a sprig of it in his hands. Twinflower is a member of the honeysuckle family (*Caprifoliaceae*) and is common in boreal forest situations throughout North America and Europe. It is identified by its prostrate and slightly woody stems, small size (less than 4 inches tall), and paired pink, funnel-shaped flowers. Twinflower is pollinated primarily by small, slender flies.

Heartleaf Arnica, *Arnica cordifolia.* This showy, yellow wildflower can be identified by its solitary, sunflower-like flower head, measuring about 3 inches in diameter, its heart-shaped, opposite leaves, and the white hairs that envelop the stem and involucre. Blooming in late spring and early summer, heartleaf arnica provides a conspicuous floral display in moist coniferous forests of the montane and subalpine zones.

Lichens

Old Man's Beard, *Usnea* spp. This pale green, fruticose lichen is common in Douglas-fir and Engelmann spruce–subalpine fir forests throughout the Southern Rockies. Readily identified by its branching and often pendant growth form, old man's beard is attached to bark or bare wood by a single holdfast. This lichen is especially prolific in dense forests, where it covers stumps and dead branches and sometimes drapes entire trees. Several reports indicate that elk and mule deer may eat old man's beard during the winter months, when other food resources are covered by snow. Because of its sensitivity to pollution, especially acid rain, this lichen is being used by researchers to monitor environmental degradation at several forest sites.

Common Plants of the Douglas-Fir Forest

Trees

Douglas-fir, *Pseudotsuga menziesii*
Fir, white, *Abies concolor*
Juniper, Rocky Mountain, *Sabina scopulorum*
Pine, limber, *Pinus flexilis*
   lodgepole, *Pinus contorta*
   ponderosa, *Pinus ponderosa*

Shrubs

Baneberry, *Actea rubra*
Chokecherry, *Padus virginiana* var. *melanocarpa*
Juniper, common, *Juniperus communis*
Kinnikinnik, *Arctostaphylos uva-ursi*
Maple, Rocky Mountain, *Acer glabrum*
Mountain-ash, *Sorbus scopulina*
Mountain-lover, *Paxistima myrsinites*
Ninebark, *Physocarpus monogynus*

Raspberry, wild, *Rubus idaeus* ssp. *melanolasius*
Rose, wild, *Rosa woodsii*
Thimbleberry, *Rubacer parviflorus*
Waxflower, *Jamesia americana*

Herbaceous Plants and Lichens

Arnica, heartleaf, *Arnica cordifolia*
Aster, smooth, *Aster laevis*
Baby-blue-eyes, *Collinsia parviflora*
Hawkweed, *Chlorocrepis albiflora* and *C. tristis*
Mistletoe, dwarf, *Arceuthobium douglasii*
Old Man's Beard (lichen), *Usnea hirta*
Orchid, fairy slipper, *Calypso bulbosa*
  northern coralroot, *Corallorhiza trifida*
Pipsissewa, *Chimaphila umbellata*
Sedge, elk, *Carex geyeri*
Solomon's Seal, false, *Maianthemum stellatum* (formerly
  Smilacina)
Twinflower, *Linnaea borealis* ssp. *americana*
Twisted-stalk, *Streptopus fassettii*

Environment and Adaptation: Animals of the Douglas-Fir Forest

No mammals or birds are restricted to the Douglas-fir eco-system. Open forests of Douglas-fir, especially those with a well-developed understory, provide food and cover for mule deer and elk. Dense, shady Douglas-fir forests attract mammals normally associated with coniferous forests at higher elevations. For example, boreal forest species such as the chickaree and the snowshoe hare are often encountered in dense stands, whereas the Abert's squirrel and Nuttall's cottontail are more likely to be found in open, mixed forests of Douglas-fir and ponderosa pine.

Birds are perhaps the most conspicuous residents of Douglas-fir forests. Woodpeckers and a variety of smaller birds — Cassin's finches, chickadees, nuthatches, and juncos — are encountered year-round. Townsend's solitaires and king-

THE SOUTHERN ROCKIES

From left to right: hairy woodpecker, dark-eyed junco.

lets are present during the breeding season. The blue grouse, though not common, is found in the densest forests, and on rare occasions you may catch a fleeting glimpse of one of the forest hawks—the small sharp-shinned hawk or the larger Cooper's hawk—as it leaves a hunting perch.

The Western Spruce Budworm

Douglas-fir is susceptible to several insect pests, the most significant being the western spruce budworm. The budworm is the most widely distributed forest defoliator in western North America. Though normally held in check by a combination of predators, parasites, and adverse climatic conditions, major outbreaks of western spruce budworm have occurred in the Southern Rockies during the past few years, some infestations encompassing more than 900,000 acres. Defoliated stands are especially common along the Eastern Slope.

The adult western spruce budworm is a small, mottled orange-brown moth. Following mating, which occurs from late June to early August, the female moths flutter about the crowns of infested trees looking for egg-laying sites on the undersides of the needles; each bright green egg mass includes about twenty-five to forty eggs, which hatch in approximately ten days. Once hatched, the larvae (budworms) do not feed but instead begin building the silken shelters under the bark scales in which they will overwinter.

From late April to May, the budworms emerge and begin to feed, moving from the older needles to the succulent, developing buds. After the buds break open, the budworms loosely web the new foliage and feed until most or all of the new growth is destroyed. If the branch of an infested tree is shaken, wriggling budworms will descend from the foliage on silk strands. The larvae mature thirty to forty days after feeding begins in spring, and pupation occurs within the feeding webs, the adults emerging a week or so later—to begin the cycle anew.

Life Histories of Selected Animals

Birds

Great Horned Owl, *Bubo virginianus.* This large, nocturnal owl is a common resident of the montane forests of the Southern Rockies and is readily identified by its prominent, widely spaced ear tufts and its resonant hoot—"whoo! whoo-whoo-whoo! whoo! whoo!" This species roosts by day, usually in dense foliage; roosting owls are often harassed by noisy flocks of ravens, jays, and other birds. When hunting, great horned owls utilize a perch-wait-and-pounce technique. Their diet is variable and consists of rabbits, hares, rodents, and birds of all sizes. These owls tend to use a feeding post near the nest site, leaving the ground nearby littered with regurgitated pellets of undigestible materials: bones, fur, feathers, and insect chitin. Though solitary outside the breeding season, the male begins territorial hooting in December or January, bonding with a female prior to egg laying—usually by February or March. Both sexes incubate the eggs and deliver food to the nestlings; young owls are able to leave the nest sixty-three to seventy days after hatching.

Hairy Woodpecker, *Picoides villosus.* This robin-sized, black-and-white woodpecker is distinguished from the similar downy woodpecker (*P. pubescens*), which shares most of its range, by its larger size and long bill; both species have a conspicuous white patch on the back, and the males of each have a red patch on the back of the head. Common in both coniferous forests and riparian woodlands, the hairy's presence is often detected by its loud "peek" call note or by its drumming signals. Both sexes use drumming — a series of raps on any resonating surface — as a signaling device. The hairy tends to be noisier and more active than the downy and generally will not tolerate close approach. Resident year-round, adults maintain a large range that includes their nesting territory. Their diet consists mostly of wood-boring insects, which they probe for with their bills and extensible tongues. Both sexes excavate the cavity and incubate the eggs; the young fledge approximately thirty days after hatching.

Mountain Chickadee, *Parus gambeli.* This common chickadee, restricted to the mountain West, is easily distinguished from the similar black-capped chickadee (*P. atricapillus*) by the presence of a white stripe over the eye (missing during late-summer molt). The call is a conspicuous "chicka-dee-dee-dee"; a whistled call of three or four notes, "fee-bee-bay" or "fee-bee, fee-bee" (scaled like the nursery song "Three Blind Mice") is also common. Nesting habitat consists of coniferous forests in the montane and subalpine life zones; the species tends to winter at lower elevations,

From left to right: black-capped chickadee, mountain chickadee.

and may be especially common in riparian or open woodlands, its range overlapping that of the black-capped chickadee. Both species are gregarious and may travel during the winter months in noisy, mixed-species flocks with brown creepers and golden-crowned kinglets. Diet consists mostly of insects "gleaned" from needles, twigs, and bark; seeds of various types are taken when available. Nesting occurs in a natural cavity or in a cavity excavated by both sexes; incubation requires about fourteen days, and young leave the nest at approximately twenty days of age.

Dark-eyed Junco, *Junco hyemalis.* These common birds were once separated into four species — slate-colored, white-winged, Oregon, and gray-headed — but are now considered conspecific; all geographic races have white outer tail feathers that flash conspicuously in flight. Dark-eyed juncos breed in coniferous forests or mixed woodlands; in winter, birds travel in small flocks and may be encountered in a variety of habitats. The song is a musical trill, and a rapid twittering is often delivered in flight. The diet of these ground-foraging birds consists primarily of insects during the breeding season and seeds during the winter months. Winter flocks break up into pairs upon arrival on the nesting grounds. Nests are cup shaped and usually located on the ground; the female incubates the eggs, and young leave the nest eleven to thirteen days after hatching.

Cassin's Finch, *Carpodacus cassinii.* The male Cassin's finch is distinguished by its conspicuous crimson crown, which ends abruptly at the brown-streaked nape; in comparison to the house finch, red plumage areas appear paler in color, and the sides lack brown streaking. Female Cassin's lack red plumage and are identified by the strong brown streaking on the breast and back. The warbled song is more varied than that of other finches and is delivered by the males from a treetop perch or in flight. Outside the breeding season, Cassin's may travel in flocks, often with crossbills and evening grosbeaks, and they are often found at lower elevations during the winter months; family groups are common in summer. This species forages for conifer seeds and buds in the tops of trees or on the ground; summer diet includes insects as well as fruits. Nests are constructed in large conifers, often near the outer end of a limb; females incubate the eggs.

THE SOUTHERN ROCKIES

Common Animals of the Douglas-Fir Forest

Mammals

Masked Shrew, *Sorex cinereus*
Montane Shrew, *Sorex monticola*
Little Brown Bat, *Myotis lucifugus*
Long-eared Myotis, *Myotis volans*
Snowshoe Hare, *Lepus americanus*
Mountain (or Nuttall's) Cottontail, *Sylvilagus nuttallii*
Least Chipmunk, *Tamias minimus*
Colorado Chipmunk, *Tamias quadrivittatus*
Golden-mantled Ground Squirrel, *Spermophilus lateralis*
Abert's Squirrel, *Sciurus aberti*
Red Squirrel (or Chickaree), *Tamiasciurus hudsonicus*
Deer Mouse, *Peromyscus maniculatus*
Bushy-tailed Woodrat, *Neotoma cinerea*
Southern Red-backed Vole, *Clethrionomys gapperi*
Coyote, *Canis latrans*
Long-tailed Weasel, *Mustela frenata*
Mountain Lion, *Felis concolor*
Mule Deer, *Odocoileus hemionus*
Elk, *Cervus elaphus*

Birds

Northern Goshawk, *Accipiter gentilis*
Cooper's Hawk, *Accipiter cooperii*
Sharp-shinned Hawk, *Accipiter striatus*
Blue Grouse, *Dendragapus obscurus*
Great Horned Owl, *Bubo virginianus*
Northern Saw-whet Owl, *Aegolius acadicus*
Northern Flicker, *Colaptes auratus*
Hairy Woodpecker, *Picoides villosus*
Downy Woodpecker, *Picoides pubescens*
Steller's Jay, *Cyanocitta stelleri*
Clark's Nutcracker, *Nucifraga columbiana*

Common Raven, *Corvus corax*
Mountain Chickadee, *Parus gambeli*
Black-capped Chickadee, *Parus atricapillus*
Brown Creeper, *Certhia familiaris*
White-breasted Nuthatch, *Sitta carolinensis*
Red-breasted Nuthatch, *Sitta canadensis*
Pygmy Nuthatch, *Sitta pygmaea*
Townsend's Solitaire, *Myadestes townsendi*
Hermit Thrush, *Catharus guttatus*
Swainson's Thrush, *Catharus ustulatus*
Ruby-crowned Kinglet, *Regulus calendula*
Golden-crowned Kinglet, *Regulus satrapa*
Evening Grosbeak, *Coccothraustes vespertina*
Pine Siskin, *Carduelis pinus*
Yellow-rumped Warbler, *Dendroica coronata*
Cassin's Finch, *Carpodacus cassinii*
Red Crossbill, *Loxia curvirostra*
Dark-eyed Junco, *Junco hyemalis*

CHAPTER SIXTEEN

Open Country: Mountain Grasslands and Meadows

SUMMER'S ARRIVAL IN the mountain grasslands and meadows is a visual poem, rich with shades of green and the jewel-like colors of wildflowers. For most, it is a time of beauty and abundance. The air redolent with their musky scent, a small herd of cow elk and their calves lingers to graze in a secluded meadow. At the meadow's edge, a coyote stands, head cocked, listening to the faint scratching noises of a tunneling pocket gopher. Nearby, the staccato alarm calls of Wyoming ground squirrels protest the coyote's presence, the rodents' heads just visible above the entrances to

Mountain grasslands in North Park, Colorado.
Audrey D. Benedict.

their burrows. Overhead, a mountain bluebird hovers kestrel-like in search of insect prey, an arc of brilliant blue against the billowing clouds.

Ecological Distribution

Herbaceous ecosystems—vegetation communities defined by the dominance of herbs as opposed to shrubs or trees—are classified on the basis of size, moisture regimes, plant associations, and ecosystem history. Natural grasslands and meadows are scattered throughout the foothill, montane, and subalpine forests and are the predominant vegetation type in the intermontane basins and alpine uplands of the Southern Rockies—wherever environmental conditions are unsuitable for tree growth but not so adverse as to preclude the development of a perennial herbaceous layer. These herbaceous ecosystems vary in size from small openings in the forest to more extensive communities covering several thousand acres. The principal ecosystem types described in this chapter include *mountain grasslands* and *dry meadows, moist meadows,* and *successional communities.* Chapter 17 provides a discussion of herbaceous wetlands, and chapter 23 a discussion of alpine tundra ecosystems.

Mountain grasslands occupy large areas characterized by low precipitation, cold temperatures, and relatively fine-textured soils—all factors that discourage tree growth. In the Southern Rockies, mountain grasslands are primarily restricted to the semiarid, intermontane basins: parts of the Shirley and Laramie basins (Wyoming), parts of North, Middle, and South parks, the Wet Mountain Valley, the perimeter of the San Luis Valley, and parts of the upper Rio Grande Basin in Colorado, and the Moreno Valley in New Mexico. Natural meadow ecosystems are generally smaller in areal extent than the mountain grasslands, ranging in size from small patches to communities covering several hundred acres. The distribution of meadows, in contrast to that of the mountain grasslands, reflects localized differences in soil texture, depth, and moisture conditions rather than regional climatic patterns resulting from the rain-shadow effects initiated by the major mountain belts.

Natural meadow ecosystems occur in topographic situations characterized by deep, fine-textured soils: floodplains, valley bottoms, old lake beds, and gently rolling uplands. Many of the larger mountain meadows, such as Moraine Park in Rocky Mountain National Park, are developed on glacier-derived sediments; this distributional pattern is repeated in glaciated valleys throughout the Southern Rockies. Dry meadow ecosystems are typical of well-drained soils; moist meadows predominate in areas with seasonally or permanently high water tables.

Successional herbaceous ecosystems are found on a wide variety of sites. Plant ecologists recognize two types of successional communities — primary and secondary. Primary successional communities occur in areas where physical changes in landscape features, such as the filling in of a pond or changes in the course of a river, have created a new soil surface and initiated the colonization of land that has not been previously vegetated. Secondary successional communities, on the other hand, are found wherever a natural or human disturbance — fire, wind-throw, logging, overgrazing, cultivation, or irrigation — has altered or destroyed the preexisting vegetation.

The Physical Environment

The climatic characteristics of mountain grasslands and meadows are highly variable. Differences in microclimate from one community to another can be correlated with altitude, topographic setting, moisture availability, and the degree of protection afforded by surrounding vegetation types. Lacking an overstory, these ecosystems are exposed repeatedly to the unmoderated influence of solar radiation and the desiccating effects of strong winds, remaining largely snow free during the winter as a result of wind scour. In a general sense, mountain grasslands tend to be associated with climatic conditions that are considered more severe than those typical of most meadow sites. The growing season is short, and frosts may occur at any time. Annual precipitation in the intermontane basins averages less than 15 inches; the driest conditions exist in the San Luis Valley, where the average is less than 10 inches and summer drought is common. Winters tend to be very cold as a result of cold-air drainage from the surrounding mountain slopes. Summers, except in the San Luis Valley, are also quite cool.

Community Characteristics

Images of lush, flower-filled meadows are synonymous with the Southern Rockies. No two meadows ever appear quite the same — the patterns of floral color change constantly as the seasons progress. Mountain grasslands and meadows exhibit great variability from one area to another. Species composition varies conspicuously with altitude, available moisture, geographic position, and in response to the disturbance history of the community. Unfortunately, nearly every herbaceous ecosystem in the Southern Rockies has been altered in some way as a result of grazing, agricultural activities, and/or fire suppression. Because these communities are so variable, only a general discussion of each type is possible within the scope of this book.

Mountain Grasslands and Dry Meadows

Mountain grasslands and dry meadows share several traits. The mineral soils typical of these ecosystems have limited water-storage capacity and are subjected to recurring drought. Bunchgrasses, rather than turf-forming species, predominate; each plant must spread its roots horizontally to tap peripheral moisture reserves, precluding the growth of other plants immediately adjacent. The narrow leaves of grasses and similar plants present a reduced surface area from which evaporative losses can occur, further minimizing these losses with a protective, waxy, cutinous coating. Many broad-leaved species, such as prairie sage, have fine hairs on the leaf surfaces that entrap a layer of moist air, insulating the leaf from excessive heat or dessicating winds.

Though wildflowers may be conspicuous in certain grassland and dry· meadow communities, most fail to approach the luxurious growth associated with moist meadows. Small pockets of moisture-loving species may occur in suitable

THE SOUTHERN ROCKIES

Common grasses of the mountain grasslands, clockwise from left: mountain muhly, junegrass, foxtail barley, cheatgrass.

microsites, but the vegetational zonation typical of many moist or wet meadow ecosystems is largely absent from these drier habitats. Bunchgrasses such as mountain muhly and several species of wheatgrass, as well as weedy species such as yarrow and fringed sage, tend to dominate at lower elevations. Colorful wildflowers such as scarlet paintbrush,

Colorado loco, western wallflower, miner's candle, sulphur flower, blanketflower, and penstemon are common in many montane communities. Shrubs such as shrubby cinquefoil and wax currant may be present in certain areas, reflecting differences in soil characteristics or disturbance history. Subalpine grassland and dry meadow communities are often dominated by bunchgrasses such as Thurber fescue and timber oatgrass. By midsummer, these communites are highlighted by the scattered colors of trumpet gilia, harebell, whiskbroom parsley, orange sneezeweed, and subalpine buckwheat.

Mountain grasslands and dry meadow ecosystems are particularly susceptible to disturbance; differences between ecosystems often reflect the disturbance history of each stand. Prior to settlement, Thurber fescue or Idaho fescue would have made up a large proportion of the bunchgrass communities in the northern and central portions of the Southern Rockies, with Arizona fescue common in the southern portion. Grazing and other land-use practices have had a significant impact. With intense grazing pressure, selective feeding by livestock has encouraged the spread of less palatable species, both native and alien, and has greatly altered the species composition of these ecosystems. Highly competitive species such as Russian-thistle and cheatgrass, as well as big sagebrush and other drought-adapted shrubs, are increasing in abundance at the expense of native bunchgrasses and forbs.

Moist Meadows

Moist meadows in the montane zone are dominated by turf-forming grasses such as red-top, timothy, foxtail barley, and native bluegrass. When moisture conditions are right, spectacular displays of wildflowers such as Rocky Mountain iris, shootingstar, golden banner, black-eyed Susan, aspen-daisy, wild geranium, and fringed gentian are translated into an ever-changing palette of color. Where soils are alkaline, such as in the San Luis Valley, salt-tolerant species such as saltgrass, arrow-grass, alkali grass, and glasswort predominate.

In the high meadows of the subalpine zone, the profu-

Common wildflowers of mountain meadows, clockwise from upper left: trumpet gilia, Colorado locoweed, golden banner, shootingstar.

sion of wildflowers spreads a blaze of color across the land-scape like a firestorm. Species such as rosy paintbrush, groundsel, bistort, wild onion, elephantella, subalpine daisy, and aspen sunflower create clouds of rich color wherever you look. Grasses such as tufted hairgrass, spike trisetum, and Canadian reed-grass are conspicuous in many communities, often sharing dominance with sedges and rushes. Several species of willow and bog birch are also common on certain sites.

Successional Ecosystems

Primary successional herbaceous ecosystems may be difficult to distinguish from climax herbaceous communities without careful observation. Communities that have undergone secondary succession, on the other hand, can often be identified by the presence of charred logs, cut stumps, or other evidence of a previous tree cover. Without further disturbance, secondary successional communities will eventually be invaded by the tree species that were originally present. Aspen is well adapted for invading herb-dominated ecosystems because the young saplings, which are root suckers, do not have to compete with the herbaceous vegetation for water or nutrients. Other tree species, however, may be slow to reinvade because of the competition from herbaceous plants, the absence of shade protection for tree seedlings, or the lack of a nearby seed source.

Successional grasslands and meadows, especially those that have recently been disturbed, are characterized by a decrease in native perennial grasses and an increase in the abundance of annuals and weedy species such as common dandelion, Colorado loco, pussytoes, fringed sage, and prairie sage. In communities where overgrazing is a factor, annuals such as cheatgrass become increasingly important and may share dominance with perennials such as gumweed, coneflower, wild geranium, false hellebore, and sticky cinquefoil. Intense grazing can turn an herb-dominated ecosystem into a shrubland by selectively eliminating the perennial grasses and allowing shrubs and cacti to establish themselves. At higher elevations, northern bedstraw, fireweed, pearly everlasting, and false dandelion predominate on disturbed sites. Fireweed and mullein are common species in areas that have been burned over. On subalpine slopes where avalanches have removed the forest cover, species such as avalanche lily, chimingbells, monkshood, and larkspur are especially common.

Plant Adaptation:
Designs for Survival

Successful reproduction is defined by an individual's passing on its genes to the next generation. Each species has evolved its own repertoire of adaptations to enhance reproductive success. Grasses and sedges employ an efficient, seemingly effortless system of wind pollination. The showy wildflowers of the mountain grasslands and meadows, on the other hand, are insect- or hummingbird-pollinated. The dazzling array of shapes, colors, and fragrances that distinguish these flowers has evolved for the sole function of attracting pollinators and maintaining species' isolation. For services rendered, the pollinator's reward is food—in the form of nectar, pollen, or oil.

The mutualisms that we observe between flowering plants and their pollinators are the result of a long and intimate coevolutionary relationship. Animal pollinators exhibit distinct color, shape, and food-type preferences in the flowers they choose to visit. The pollinator is equipped with one or several anatomical features that maximize collection of pollen or nectar: Beetles have brushlike mouthparts for collecting pollen; hummingbirds have long, narrow bills and tongues for nectar gathering; bees have hollows or pollen baskets on their hind legs for storing pollen during foraging trips; and butterflies, moths, and flies have tubular, bristled proboscises for nectar drinking.

The patches, streaks, and spots of contrasting color—called guide marks or nectar guides—that pattern the inner surfaces of some flowers are believed to direct the pollinator to the location of pollen or to the site of floral nectar glands. These guide marks are generally positioned so that the pollinator must brush against the sex organs of the flower on its way to the nectar or pollen source. Many guide marks are conspicuous, such as the yellow lines on the interior of some penstemon flowers, the brown spots of the wood lily, or the yellow eye typical of forget-me-not flowers. Other guide marks, produced by specialized plant tissues that strongly reflect ultraviolet light (UV), are visible only to the insect eye, which perceives ultraviolet light as a color. When flowers with UV-reflecting tissues, such as marsh-marigold and star gentian, are photographed using a filter that passes only ultraviolet light, a clear pattern of guide marks becomes apparent on what had seemed, to the human eye, to be an unpatterned corolla.

A plant's adaptations for attracting pollinators must be balanced against its need for defending itself against the invertebrate and vertebrate herbivores that abound in mountain grasslands and meadows. The antiherbivore defenses evolved by flowering plants are as diverse as the animals that threaten them. The most obvious defenses are anatomical features, such as spines or thick cuticles, but an array of chemical defenses has also evolved to make certain plants toxic, unpalatable, or simply less nutritious to herbivores. The effects attributed to defensive compounds such as alkaloids, selenium, and phytoestrogens (hormone mimics) include irritation of mucous membranes, acute intoxication, nerve damage, fertility inhibition, congenital malformations, digestive disorders, cancers, and death. A great many poisonous plants are found in mountain grassland and meadow ecosystems. Some of the most common are false hellebore, death camas, lupine, locoweed, golden banner, larkspur, orange sneezeweed, rubberweed, and snakeweed.

In some plants, the levels of chemical defenses fluctuate seasonally, with the highest levels present during periods that are critical for plant reproduction or growth. Those that produce compounds that mimic animal hormones are able to combat insect herbivores by altering their natural pattern of metamorphosis. Variations in the production of phytoestrogens in certain grasses have also been shown to influence the breeding patterns of the montane vole. In late summer and fall, when high phytoestrogen levels coincide with the setting of seed by the grasses, vole reproduction rates are drastically reduced in response to the disruption of ovulation caused by a phytoestrogen-rich grass diet; recent experiments in the laboratory have shown that the higher vole reproduction rates in spring may be associated with plant chemicals that actually stimulate female ovulation and male testicular growth at that time.

Some plants, lacking chemical defenses, enlist the services of an "ant guard" to protect their flowers, seeds, or foliage from herbivorous insects. Although ant-plant mutualisms are generally common in the tropics, a temperate-region example has also been discovered in the Colorado Rockies. The aspen sunflower, a showy species found in subalpine meadows, attracts and rewards its ant guardians (typically of the genus *Formica*) with extrafloral nectar that it produces in bracts encircling the base of its flower head. In return for a steady supply of nectar, which begins several weeks before the flowers open and ends just before the seeds are shed, the ants aggressively deter egg laying by several species of flies whose life cycles are closely tied to these sunflowers and whose larvae would otherwise destroy the flower heads. Research suggests that seed loss to predators may be as high as 90 percent when no guard ants are present.

Descriptions of Common Plants

Mountain Muhly, *Muhlenbergia montana*. This bunchgrass is a common dry-site species encountered on gentle slopes, in open parks, and in ponderosa pine forests. The culm (flowering stem) of this grass ranges in height from 1 to 2 feet. The inflorescence is a narrow, short-branched panicle ranging from 2 to 6 inches long.

Junegrass, *Koeleria macrantha*. This bunchgrass is very common on meadows and slopes, from the foothills to the subalpine. Maturing early in summer, the culm ranges in height from 1 to 2½ feet; the inflorescence is a dense, spikelike panicle and is 1 to 5 inches long.

Parry's Oatgrass, *Danthonia parryi*. This bunchgrass, largely restricted to the Eastern Slope, is a common species of drier meadows, open parks, and open ponderosa pine forests from the upper montane to the subalpine. The culms range in height from 4 to 20 inches; the inflorescence is a spiky, often one-sided panicle that measures from 1 to 2½ inches. Parry's oatgrass is distinguished from timber oatgrass, (*D. intermedia*), a species found in subalpine and alpine environments, by the hairs found on the back of the lemma.

Thurber Fescue, *Festuca thurberi*. This tall, robust bunchgrass is a common species from the montane to the subalpine and may form pure stands on suitable sites. The culms occur in dense tufts and vary in height from 20 to 36 inches. The inflorescence is a loose, slightly drooping, 4- to 6-inch panicle; the lemmas lack awns but have sharp points.

Tufted Hairgrass, *Deschampsia caespitosa.* This luxuriant, medium-to-tall bunchgrass is found in moist meadows from the upper montane through the alpine and is always associated with sites that maintain good winter snow cover. The culms are 2 to 4 feet in height; the leaves are stiff and pointed, pricking the palm of the hand when pressed against it. The inflorescence is an open, purplish panicle with a somewhat feathery appearance.

Prairie Sage and **Fringed Sage,** *Artemisia ludoviciana* and *A. frigida.* These two species, with their silvery green, pubescent, aromatic leaves, are common in dry grasslands and meadows from the foothills to the subalpine. Fringed sage, with its woody base, is actually a small shrub and is distinguished from the herbaceous prairie sage by its finely divided leaves; the leaves of prairie sage are large, lanceolate to deeply lobed, and coated with soft, white hairs. The inflorescence of prairie sage is an elongate cluster of small, pale green flower heads, in contrast to the nodding, yellowish flower heads of fringed sage. Both species are quick to colonize overgrazed meadows and areas where the soil has been disturbed.

Yarrow, *Achillea lanulosa.* This common, widely distributed wildflower is found in dry meadows and grasslands from the foothills to the alpine. Individual plants are approximately 1 foot in height and are easily identified by their finely dissected, fernlike, aromatic leaves and their flat-topped cluster of small white flower heads.

Meadow Pussytoes, *Antennaria rosea.* This small, sunflower family member is typically encountered in dry to moist meadow situations from the foothills to the subalpine, where it may form a matlike ground cover in some areas. It is readily distinguished by its clusters of white flower heads with papery phyllaries (often but not always tinged with pink). The leaves of this species are small, silvery green, and arranged in a basal rosette; stems range in height from 4 to 10 inches.

Orange Sneezeweed, *Dugaldia hoopsii.* This tall, showy member of the sunflower family is found in open meadows and in aspen groves from the montane to the subalpine; it is common on the Western Slope but is found only in the Pikes Peak region of the Eastern Slope. Orange sneezeweed is easily identified by the bright orange-yellow petals of its ray flowers and the darker orange of its disk flowers; in most cases the petals of the ray flowers droop and look slightly wilted. The species is highly poisonous, especially to sheep.

Subalpine Daisy, *Erigeron peregrinus.* This handsome member of the sunflower family is common in moist subalpine and alpine meadows. It is easily identified by its lavender or rose-violet ray flowers, yellow disk flowers, phyllaries in one series rather than shingled, and robust size; the petals of the ray flowers are approximately ⅛ inch wide. A similar species, the aspen-daisy (*E. speciosus*), is encountered in open meadows and aspen groves at lower elevations and is distinguished by its narrower ray-flower petals.

Aspen Sunflower, *Helianthella quinquenervis.* This tall, elegant sunflower is common in moist meadows, aspen groves, and avalanche tracks from the montane to the subalpine. The aspen sunflower is identified by its glossy, leathery leaves (each with five prominent veins) and by its large flower heads (3 to 4 inches in diameter) made up of bright yellow ray flowers and yellowish green disk flowers; the flower heads usually face east.

Golden Banner, *Thermopsis montana.* This showy, lupine-like member of the pea family is common in meadows and open aspen forests from the montane to the subalpine. Golden banner has an erect growth form, large yellow flowers, palmately compound leaves with leaflets in groups of three, and straight, pubescent seedpods. A similar species, *T. divaricarpa*, is more common on the Eastern Slope and produces pods that are curved and mostly hairless. Golden banner is toxic to humans and some other animals.

Colorado Loco, *Oxytropis lambertii.* This widespread member of the pea family is the most common locoweed in open, relatively dry meadows and grasslands from the plains to the subalpine. Colorado loco is readily identified by its showy racemes of magenta flowers; erect growth form; silvery, hairy foliage; and pinnately compound leaves. This species may hybridize with Rocky Mountain loco (*O. sericea*), forming striking variations in color and habit. Because the plants accumulate naturally occurring selenium from the soil, locoweeds are toxic to many animals, especially domestic livestock.

Trumpet Gilia, *Ipomopsis aggregata.* This showy, trumpet-shaped wildflower is common in midsummer meadows from the foothills to the subalpine. The plants are 12 to 15 inches tall, with fernlike leaves and inch-long, trumpet-shaped, scarlet or pink flowers. Pink blooms are especially common on the high mesas of the Western Slope, such as Grand Mesa, the Flattops, and the Uncompahgre Plateau.

Western Shootingstar, *Dodecatheon pulchellum.* This delicate wildflower, a member of the primrose family, is found in moist meadows and along stream courses from the montane to the subalpine. Once called American cyclamen, this species is easily identified by its sharply reflexed, magenta petals and by its five brownish black anthers, which join to form a point. This species may be so abundant, as it is in South Park, that it colors an entire meadow with pink.

False Hellebore, *Veratrum tenuipetalum.* This tall, robust species is found in moist, often overgrazed meadows from the upper montane through the subalpine; it is especially common on the Western Slope and in the southern ranges of the Southern Rockies. It is easily identified by its height (3 feet or more), by its pleated, upright leaves, and by the plumelike inflorescence of greenish white flowers.

Common Plants of the Mountain Grasslands and Meadows

Shrubs

Birch, bog, *Betula glandulosa*
Cinquefoil, shrubby, *Pentaphylloides floribunda*
Currant, prickly, *Ribes lacustre*
Greasewood, *Sarcobatus vermiculatus*
Rabbitbrush, golden, *Chrysothamnus nauseosus*
  sticky-flowered, *Chrysothamnus viscidiflorus*
Sagebrush, big, *Seriphidium tridentatum*
Sage, fringed (or silver), *Artemisia frigida*
Saltbush, four-wing, *Atriplex canescens*
Willow, *Salix* spp.

Grasses, Sedges, and Rushes

Arrow-grass, *Triglochin maritima*
Barley, foxtail, *Critesion jubatum*
Cheatgrass, *Anisantha tectorum,* (formerly *Bromus*)

Fescue, Arizona, *Festuca arizonica*
  Idaho, *Festuca idahoensis*
  Thurber, *Festuca thurberi*
Grama, blue, *Bouteloua gracilis*
Hairgrass, tufted, *Deschampsia caespitosa*
Junegrass, *Koeleria macrantha*
Muhly, mountain, *Muhlenbergia montana*
Needle-and-thread, *Stipa comata*
Needlegrass, *Stipa viridula*
Oatgrass, Parry's, *Danthonia parryi*
  timber, *Danthonia intermedia*
Red-top, *Agrostis gigantea*
Reedgrass, Canadian, *Calamagrostis canadensis*
Ricegrass, Indian, *Stipa hymenoides*
Rush, *Juncus compressus, J. arcticus,* and *J. filiformis*
Saltgrass, *Distichlis spicata* var. *stricta*
Sedge, mountain-loving, *Carex oreocharis*
  Narrow-leaf, *Carex stenophylla* ssp. *eleocharis*
  thick-spiked, *Carex pachystachya*
Squirreltail, *Elymus elymoides* (formerly *Sitanion hystrix*)
Three-awn, *Aristida purpurea*
Timothy, *Phleum pratense*
Trisetum, spike, *Trisetum spicatum*
Wheatgrass, crested, *Agropyron cristatum*
  slender, *Agropyron trachycaulum*
  western, *Agropyron smithii*

Wildflowers

Bedstraw, northern, *Galium septentrionale*
Bergamot, wild (or bee balm), *Monarda fistulosa*
Bistort, American, *Bistorta bistortoides*
Black-eyed Susan, *Rudbeckia hirta*
Blanketflower, *Gaillardia aristata*
Blue-eyed Grass, *Sisyrinchium montanum*
Buckwheat, subalpine, *Eriogonum subalpinum*
Buttercup, *Ranunculus* spp.
Camas, death, *Zigadenus venosus*
Cinquefoil, soft, *Potentilla pulcherrima*
Clover, red, *Trifolium pratense*
Columbine, Colorado, *Aquilegia coerulea*

Coneflower, black, *Rudbeckia occidentalis*
Daisy, aspen, *Erigeron speciosus*
  subalpine, *Erigeron peregrinus*
Dandelion, common, *Taraxacum officinale*
Elephantella, *Pedicularis groenlandica*
Gentian, bottle (or blue), *Pneumonanthe parryi* (formerly
    P. calycosa)
  fragrant, *Gentianopsis barbellata*
  fringed, *Gentianopsis thermalis*
  prairie, *Pneumonanthe affinis*
Geranium, common wild, *Geranium caespitosum*
  sticky, *Geranium viscosissimum*
  white, *Geranium richardsonii*
Gilia, trumpet, *Ipomopsis aggregata*
Golden Banner, *Thermopsis montana*
Gumweed, *Grindelia subalpina*
Harebell, common, *Campanula rotundifolia*
  Parry's, *Campanula parryi*
Hellebore, false, *Veratrum tenuipetalum*
Iris, Rocky Mountain, *Iris missouriensis*
Lily, avalanche, *Erythronium grandiflorum*
  mariposa (or sego), *Calochortus gunnisonii*
Loco, Colorado (or Lambert), *Oxytropis lambertii*
  Rocky Mountain, *Oxytropis sericea*
  showy, *Oxytropis splendens*
  yellow (or field), *Oxytropis campestris* var. *gracilis*
Lupine, *Lupinus* spp.
Miner's Candle, *Oreocarya thyrsiflora* (formerly
    Cryptantha)
Monkshood, *Aconitum columbianum*
Monument Plant (or Green Gentian), *Frasera speciosa*
Mullein, common, *Verbascum thapsus*
Paintbrush, rose, *Castilleja rhexifolia*
  scarlet, *Castilleja miniata* and *C. linariifolia*
Penstemon, *Penstemon* spp.
Prairie Smoke, *Erythrocoma triflora*, (formerly *Geum
    triflorum*)
Pussytoes, *Antennaria* spp.
Sage, prairie, *Artemisia ludoviciana*
Senecio, Fendler's, *Packera fendleri*, (formerly *Senecio*)
Shootingstar, *Dodecatheon pulchellum*
Sneezeweed, orange, *Dugaldia hoopsii*

Sulphur Flower, *Eriogonum umbellatum*
Sunflower, aspen, *Helianthella quinquenervis*
Thistle, Russian, *Salsola australis*
Wallflower, western, *Erysimum capitatum*
Yarrow, *Achillea lanulosa*

Environment and Adaptation: Animals of the Mountain Grasslands and Meadows

The mountain grasslands and meadows of the Southern Rockies provide critical resources for a surprising diversity of animals. The species richness of these ecosystems reflects the influence of the *edge effect*—the increase in species diversity and in biological productivity that characterizes the transition zone, or *ecotone*, between two adjacent ecosystem types. A great many species associated with herbaceous ecosystems—elk, Nuttall's cottontail, least chipmunks, savannah sparrows, and dark-eyed juncos—are edge-loving species that rely on the juxtaposition of the protective cover provided by the forest and the greater productivity associated with herbaceous ecosystems.

In herbaceous ecosystems, the lack of an overstory limits the variety of habitats available for foraging and reproductive activities. Not surprisingly, the resident mammalian fauna is characterized by a preponderance of burrowing animals—northern pocket gophers, Wyoming ground squirrels, prairie dogs, montane voles, and badgers. Most other species utilize these ecosystems on a seasonal or occasional basis. The luxuriant growth of grass and forbs provides prime summer range for elk as well as for domestic grazing animals. Predators such as coyotes and red-tailed hawks are attracted by the abundance of small mammals. Broad-tailed hummingbirds time their nesting to coincide with the flowering of their most important nectar sources—larkspur, trumpet flower, and paintbrush. Other birds—mountain bluebirds, tree swallows, common nighthawks—and several species of bats forage for insects over the meadows, returning to nest or roost within the protection of adjacent forests.

Burrowers Large and Small

The northern pocket gopher is one of the most highly evolved of all burrowing mammals. The body is tubular in shape and equipped with powerful neck and shoulder muscles that enhance its digging prowess. In addition, sensitive whiskers surrounding the mouth and nose assist in tunnel navigation. The forefeet have long, sharply curved claws, and the lips close behind the upper incisors, enabling the pocket gopher to gnaw roots and to use the incisors for tunnel excavation without packing the mouth with soil. Perhaps the most unusual of all adaptations, however, are the capacious, exterior, fur-lined cheek pouches that the pocket gopher uses in food gathering.

During the excavation of extensive tunnel systems, pocket gophers loosen the dirt with their long front claws and, when necessary, their large, chisel-shaped incisors. In some cases, the gopher may also use its upper incisors to anchor its body in place while digging. Excavated dirt is pushed backward under the body and then directed toward the surface or into

From left to right: Wyoming ground squirrel, northern pocket gopher.

a burrow that is no longer being used. Mounds of freshly excavated dirt, each with a small plug of soil blocking the entrance hole, are often conspicuous in mountain meadows and indicate recent pocket-gopher activity. Networks of cylindrical soil casts, called *gopher esker,* or *garlands,* are produced when tunnels in the snow are packed with soil brought up from below ground as a result of winter foraging activities. Abandoned burrow systems, in turn, provide shelter for a variety of other small mammals, tiger salamanders, toads, snakes, and insects.

The ecology of the montane vole, like that of the pocket gopher, corresponds to the grass-dominated ecosystems in which it evolved. Both the montane and the long-tailed vole subsist primarily on grasses and are equipped with evergrowing incisors, allowing them to eat silica-rich, abrasive plant material; as the teeth wear down, they continue to grow from the roots. Additionally, the problem of digesting the complex carbohydrates (cellulose and hemicellulose) found in grasses is solved by microorganism fermentation in a rumen-like foregut—an anatomical adaptation unique to voles and similar to that found in grazing or browsing animals such as elk, deer, and mountain sheep.

Grazers

Historically, the lush herbage of these ecosystems supported enormous herds of bison, pronghorn, and elk—the true aficionados of open country. The last bison in the Southern Rockies was shot in South Park in the late 1800s. Today, pronghorn are relatively rare in the mountains, although small bands are often seen in the San Luis Valley and in North Park. The great herds of elk reported by explorers such as John C. Frémont were largely extirpated by market-hunters prior to the 1900s, but reintroductions and hunting restrictions have reestablished populations in most areas of the Southern Rockies. In Rocky Mountain National Park, where the winter resident elk population has soared to more than 2,000 animals, population control in the absence of natural predation has become a chronic problem. In other areas of the Southern Rockies, however, elk must compete with domestic livestock for grazing space and are further restricted by the appropriation of former elk habitat for use by man.

The ruminant digestive system has played a critical role in the evolutionary success of mountain ungulates. Because of it, these animals are able to rapidly harvest large amounts of forage and then retreat to suitable cover or to the relative safety of the herd—where the real work of digestion can begin. While the animal rests, partially digested food is regurgitated, chewed more thoroughly, shunted to a compartment of the stomach (the omasum) for further mechanical reworking, and then passed to another compartment of the stomach for bacterial processing. Elk, in contrast to mule deer, are primarily grazers rather than browsers. Grasses and forbs dominate the elk's diet during the spring and summer, with shrubs and aspen bark supplementing herbaceous forage during fall and winter. Grass provides substantially more energy, while winter browse plants are a better source of protein. Consequently, by consuming both grass and browse, elk are able to obtain a more nutritionally complete diet than if they were restricted to a single forage type.

During the winter months, the forage available to elk seldom provides sufficient nutrients to meet the metabolic requirements of traveling and foraging in deep snow and withstanding winter temperatures. Fat stores accumulated while the animals were on summer range must be utilized to meet these demands, resulting in substantial weight loss. The ability to survive winter stresses depends to a large degree on the nutritional quality and digestibility of the forage consumed by elk on their summer ranges. Consequently, the maintenance of healthy elk populations depends on the quality and availability of good summer and winter range.

Birds of a Feather

Birds of open country exhibit adaptations in physical appearance and behavior that differ markedly from those of forest species. Cryptic or camouflage coloration is common in many species such as the common snipe, Lincoln's sparrow, vesper sparrow, savannah sparrow, horned lark, and water pipit. These species forage and nest on or near the ground, and their cryptic coloration enables them to blend in with the background vegetation. In much the same way that herd formation benefits grazing animals, flocking behavior provides critical group protection for birds of open country. Additionally, the white, outer tail feathers that distinguish several flocking species—vesper sparrows, horned larks, and juncos—flash conspicuously in flight and serve to maintain visual contact as the birds move from area to area.

Good vision and fine-tuned flight capabilities are critical to the success of many open-country predators. Hawks of the genus *Buteo*, such as the red-tailed hawk, probably have the keenest eyesight known; a red-tailed hawk is believed to be able to detect a mouse from one-third to one-half mile away. The broad, blunt wings typical of *Buteos* and golden eagles provide high lift, allowing them to take off at low speeds, often with heavy prey, and to maintain soaring flight as they hunt; these species often use the natural updrafts (thermals) that develop over open country to stay aloft for long periods. The northern harrier, or marsh hawk, combines keen eyesight, a sound-concentrating, owl-like facial disk, and a somewhat rocking, close-quartering flight style when searching for prey. Marsh hawks have been reported to pluck vole nests from the ground and shake them in midair, catching the tiny mammals as they tumble out.

Insectivorous birds, such as the common nighthawk and the swallows, are equipped with wings that narrow abruptly at the tip, providing high speed and maneuverability for capturing insects in flight; these species also have bristlelike feathers encircling their bills that help to funnel insects toward their mouths. Some species, such as the loggerhead shrike, which feeds on small mammals, birds, and large insects, and the insectivorous mountain bluebird, have perfected a wait-and-watch style of hunting; these birds typically hunt from a suitable perch—a fence post or shrub top—at the meadow's edge, fluttering kestrel-like in the air as they search or swooping down quickly when they spot prey.

Flower-filled meadows are critical to the survival of the broad-tailed hummingbird, the most common hummingbird in the Southern Rockies. Probably evolving in the South American tropics, where flowers bloom throughout the year, hummingbirds are nectar feeders with extremely high metabolic rates but with only limited storage capacities for nec-

Broad-tailed hummingbird (male).

tar in their crops and livers. To cope with the chilling climate and uncertain nectar production associated with more northerly (or higher elevation) habitats, hummingbirds are forced into energy conservation by natural selection. Soon after arriving on their mountain breeding territories in spring, male broad-tails stake out choice feeding territories where nectar-producing flowers are clustered, often restricting females to less productive areas. The situation is further complicated in late July and early August by the arrival of aggressive rufous hummingbirds migrating south, initiating fierce competition for the available nectar. For the female broad-tail, who must meet not only her own energy requirements but also those of her eggs and nestlings, any decline in food supplies—either through competitive exclusion, drought, or inclement weather—necessitates drastic measures to maintain the energy balance. Short-term energy crises occur frequently, but in most cases the female is able to achieve considerable energy conservation through careful insulation of her nest and by lowering her body temperature and entering a brief state of semihibernation, or hypothermia, between foraging bouts. In the most extreme situations, she must abandon her nest and fend for herself.

Life Histories of Selected Animals

Mammals

Masked Shrew, *Sorex cinereus.* This medium-sized shrew is distinguished from voles and mice by its long, pointed snout, its tiny eyes, and the dark, reddish black pigmentation on the tips of its pointed teeth. Masked shrews are common year-round in moist habitats throughout the Southern Rockies. Highly active, shrews forage with rapid, darting movements above ground or burrow through loose litter to locate invertebrates and other prey. Predators apparently find shrews to be unpalatable because of their odiferous glandular secretions. Females bear several litters of four to ten young each year in nests hidden in cavities of old stumps or logs, under rocks, or in the abandoned burrows of other small mammals. Newborn shrews are blind and helpless, but attain self-sufficiency at three to four weeks of age.

Big Brown Bat, *Eptesicus fuscus.* Widely distributed in North America, the big brown bat is distinguished from other brown bats by its large size (only the hoary bat is larger), membranous black ears and wings, and somewhat leisurely flight. The species emerges at dusk to forage on flying insects, and is most common in open country or open woodlands; individuals may chatter audibly during foraging flights. Big brown bats exhibit a predilection for using man-made structures — porches, eaves, bridges, attics, and mine structures — for their diurnal roosts. The species spends the winter alone or in small colonies in a protected hibernaculum near the summer roosting area. Breeding occurs prior to hibernation, but fertilization and implantation of the embryo are delayed until spring. Females generally give birth to one nearly hairless young in mid-June. Development is rapid, and young bats can fly within three to four weeks of birth. This species is long-lived; a record age of nineteen years has been reported.

Nuttall's Cottontail, *Sylvilagus nuttallii.* This medium-sized rabbit is distinguished from the eastern and desert cottontails by its smaller size, shorter ears, dark dorsal color, and habitat preference for forest edge and sagebrush; the desert cottontail prefers open, semiarid grassland and foothill shrub communities and is consistently found at lower elevations than Nuttall's. The diet varies with availability and season, ranging from succulent forbs to woody plants. Cottontails are largely nocturnal, making use of *forms* (unlined depressions) or other sheltered spots for resting during the day. Nuttall's cottontail is typically solitary, but groups may be found foraging close together in grassy clearings bordered by brush. This species breeds throughout the warmer months, giving birth to altricial young in a protected, fur-lined nest.

Wyoming Ground Squirrel, *Spermophilus elegans.* Resembling a diminutive prairie dog in appearance, this ground squirrel is identified by its brownish gray coloring, cinnamon nose, and absence of striping. In the Southern Rockies, the species reaches its southern limits in the Gunnison Basin, but it is believed to be actively expanding its range. Wyoming ground squirrels are common in open grasslands, meadows, and sagebrush stands, at elevations of 6,000 to 12,000 feet. Diet is variable, consisting mostly of grasses, forbs, and some shrubs; carrion is eaten when available. The species is diurnal and highly colonial, with dominance hierarchies, vocalizations, and maintenance of territories circumscribing individual movements and social interactions within the colony. Wyoming ground squirrels begin accumulating fat reserves for hibernation in midsummer, retreating to their burrows in late August or early September. Mating takes place soon after emergence from hibernation in late April, and females bear a single litter of altricial young; young squirrels first appear above ground in early June.

Northern Pocket Gopher, *Thomomys talpoides.* This small rodent is easily identified by its long, curved claws, prominent yellowish orange incisors (always in view because the lips close behind them), and external, fur-lined cheek pouches. In the Southern Rockies, this species occurs from the foothills to the alpine zone and is mostly encountered in sites with well-drained, relatively fine-textured soils. Active year-round, this solitary animal maintains tunnel systems that can be extensive and are distinguished by loose mounds of soil. Mating occurs in April or May, and a single litter of altricial young is born in late spring.

Montane Vole, *Microtus montanus.* This small rodent is distinguished from the more familiar deer mouse by its dark grayish brown fur, small eyes, inconspicuous ears, and pale gray underparts. In the Southern Rockies, the species is common in moist meadows and in open aspen woodlands — wherever a dense cover of grasses and forbs permits these herbivores to construct their elaborate network of runways. Active year-round and typically nocturnal, the montane vole may begin breeding activity beneath the snowpack. Altricial young are born in a ball-shaped, grass nest after a three-week gestation period; the young develop rapidly, and females of the first litter may breed their first summer.

Coyote, *Canis latrans.* This handsome, German-shepherd-sized canid takes its name from the Aztec word *coyotl* and is distinguished from a fox by its larger size, buffy gray fur, and black-tipped tail, which points downward when the animal runs. These highly adaptable animals are encountered in nearly every habitat type, but they prefer open country. The repertoire of coyote vocalizations includes yips, a trailing howl, and a serenade of group yip-howling. Most active at sunrise and sunset, the coyote hunts small prey but will also consume carrion and fruit when available. Coyotes are less social than wolves; the basic social unit consists of an adult male, a female, and their young. Solitary individuals or a mated pair generally follow a habitual hunting trail; cooperative hunting occurs only when food is abundant. Courtship behavior begins two to three months prior to the onset of estrus, which takes place between January and March. Coyotes rarely mate for life, but pairs may remain together for several years. Dens are often located near water. A male provisions the female and their five to seven pups until the pups are about eight weeks old. Longevity is usually less than ten years.

Elk (or Wapiti), *Cervus elaphus.* The American elk is easily identified by its large size, coarse brown fur, dark mane, straw-colored rump patch, and inconspicuous tail. Mature bulls stand 5 feet tall at the shoulder and weigh 750 pounds or more. Grazing occurs mostly just after dawn and at dusk; elk retreat to forest cover during daylight and at night, and the same trails and bedding areas are used repeatedly. Elk are gregarious; wintering herds tend to be quite large, with anywhere from twenty-five to several hundred animals of mixed sexes and ages. Bulls are first to leave the wintering herds, following the retreating snow line to higher elevation meadows. Cows and calves eventually follow the bulls to summer range, and remain there until fall. Breeding begins in mid- to late September with the onset of the rut, which involves the flutelike vocalizations known as bugling, swelling of the chest and neck, antler rubbing and thrashing, wallowing, and ritualized battles with other bulls to assert authority over the harem bands of cows, calves, and yearlings that each has assembled. Once dominance has been asserted, typically by bulls of four or more years in age, cows are bred, each giving birth to a single, precocial calf in late May or June (near the wintering range or during migration to the summer range).

Birds

Red-tailed Hawk, *Buteo jamaicensis.* This common hawk is distinguished from other raptors by its large size, broad wings, brick red tail, brown patagial stripe on the leading edges of its wings, crescent-shaped wrist patches, and diffuse band of brown streaks across its pale breast; plumage can be extremely variable. The call of the red-tail is distinctive — a harsh, descending "kee-e-e-e." These hawks still-hunt from high perches (the tops of trees, utility poles, or rocky outcrops) or while soaring. Consummate soarers, red-tails are often seen making wide, lazy circles in thermals over open country or riding the deflection air currents along ridgelines. When soaring, the wings are held flat and the body does not tilt to and fro. Thought to mate for life, pairs remain faithful to their territories year after year. Red-tail courtship flights can be spectacular and consist of a series of steep dives and climbs. Nests are built of sticks and are typically in the tops of tall trees, on ledges on the sides of canyons, or on rocky outcrops; fresh greenery is brought to the nest throughout the nesting season. Females incubate the eggs, which they lay in late winter or earliest spring; males deliver food to the female while she is on the nest. The young are able to fly after forty-five days.

Northern Harrier, *Circus cyaneus.* Formerly called the marsh hawk, this slender-bodied hawk is distinguished from other medium-sized raptors by its long, narrow wings, owl-like facial disk, and white rump patch; females have brownish upperparts, while males are gray or gray-brown. Conspicuous as it searches for prey because of its acrobatic, close-quartering flight, the northern harrier has a facial disk and large ear openings in the skull that collect the squeaks and scampering noises of its prey; when a harrier detects prey, it may hover briefly and then execute a corkscrew drop to the ground. Courtship flights—consisting of dives, swoops, and wingovers—are spectacular and often occur within a hundred feet or so of the ground. Nests are located on the ground in dense cover. The female incubates the eggs alone, but the male supplies her and the nestlings with food; the male passes the food to the female while both are in flight.

Broad-tailed Hummingbird, *Selasphorus platycercus.* The male broad-tail is easily distinguished by its metallic green crown, rose red gorget, and cricketlike trilling produced by the wings in flight. The only other hummingbird commonly seen in the Southern Rockies during the summer is the rufous (*S. rufus*), an iridescent orange-red species that enters the area only during its migration to and from its breeding range in the Northwest; competitive interactions between these two species can be spectacular. Male broad-tails arrive on the breeding grounds before females. The display flights of the male are conspicuous, with a pendulum-like pattern consisting of a series of U-shaped power dives. The female builds a tiny, lichen-covered nest, typically a few feet above the ground in a tree or shrub, where she alone incubates the eggs and rears the young.

Mountain Bluebird, *Sialia currucoides.* The male mountain bluebird is sky blue, with darkest blue on the upperparts, wings, and tail; the female is a brownish blue overall. Mountain bluebirds are insectivorous, foraging from perches, by fly catching, or by hovering kestrel-like over the ground. The mountain bluebird nests in tree cavities or in nest boxes; the loss of suitable cavity nesting sites has reduced bluebird populations in many areas. Both sexes feed the young until fledging occurs. Family groups flock together in late summer and are common in high-elevation meadows.

Savannah Sparrow, *Passerculus sandwichensis.* This small, common sparrow inhabits open, moist grasslands and meadows with dense cover. It is distinguished from other sparrows of open country by its prominent all-over brown streaking, notched tail, and pink legs and feet; a breast spot is generally present. In the Southern Rockies, this species is a common summer resident and migrant. Savannah sparrows forage on the ground for insects, exhibiting a hopping style and sometimes double-scratching to locate food. When approached, this sparrow runs rapidly through the grass with its head carried low, or it may fly short distances to drop quickly into cover. Males arrive on the breeding grounds before females, establishing territories and giving their buzzy trill from prominent perches.

Common Animals of the Mountain Grasslands and Meadows

Mammals

Masked Shrew, *Sorex cinereus*
Montane Shrew, *Sorex monticolus*
Silver-haired Bat, *Lasionycteris noctivagans*
Big Brown Bat, *Eptesicus fuscus*
Hoary Bat, *Lasiurus cinereus*
Nuttall's Cottontail, *Sylvilagus nuttallii*
White-tailed Jackrabbit, *Lepus townsendii*
Least Chipmunk, *Tamias minimus*
Uinta Chipmunk, *Tamias umbrinus*
Yellow-bellied Marmot, *Marmota flaviventris*
Wyoming Ground Squirrel, *Spermophilus elegans*
Golden-mantled Ground Squirrel, *Spermophilus lateralis*
Northern Pocket Gopher, *Thomomys talpoides*
Valley Pocket Gopher, *Thomomys bottae*
Silky Pocket Mouse, *Perognathus flavus*
Ord's Kangaroo Rat, *Dipodomys ordii*
Western Harvest Mouse, *Reithrodontomys megalotis*
Deer Mouse, *Peromyscus maniculatus*
Northern Grasshopper Mouse, *Onychomys leucogaster*
Montane Vole, *Microtus montanus*
Long-tailed Vole, *Microtus longicaudus*
Western Jumping Mouse, *Zapus princeps*
Coyote, *Canis latrans*
Red Fox, *Vulpes vulpes*
Long-tailed Weasel, *Mustela frenata*
Badger, *Taxidea taxus*
Elk, *Cervus elaphus*

Mule Deer, *Odocoileus hemionus*
Pronghorn, *Antilocapra americana*
Bighorn Sheep, *Ovis canadensis*

Birds

Golden Eagle, *Aquila chrysaetos*
Northern Harrier (or Marsh Hawk), *Circus cyaneus*
Red-tailed Hawk, *Buteo jamaicensis*
Rough-legged Hawk, *Buteo lagopus*
American Kestrel (or Sparrow Hawk), *Falco sparverius*
Prairie Falcon, *Falco mexicanus*
Sharp-tailed Grouse, *Tympanuchus phasianellus*
Great Horned Owl, *Bubo virginianus*
Common Snipe, *Gallinago gallinago*
Common Nighthawk, *Chordeiles minor*
Broad-tailed Hummingbird, *Selasphorus platycercus*
Rufous Hummingbird, *Selasphorus rufus*
Western Kingbird, *Tyrannus verticalis*
Horned Lark, *Eremophila alpestris*
Violet-green Swallow, *Tachycineta thalassina*
Black-billed Magpie, *Pica pica*
Common Raven, *Corvus corax*
Western Bluebird, *Sialia mexicana*
Mountain Bluebird, *Sialia currucoides*
American Robin, *Turdus migratorius*
Loggerhead Shrike, *Lanius ludovicianus*
Water Pipit, *Anthus spinoletta*
Vesper Sparrow, *Pooecetes gramineus*
Savannah Sparrow, *Passerculus sandwichensis*
Lark Sparrow, *Chondestes grammacus*
Chipping Sparrow, *Spizella passerina*
Brewer's Sparrow, *Spizella breweri*
Dark-eyed Junco, *Junco hyemalis*
White-crowned Sparrow, *Zonotrichia leucophrys*
Lincoln's Sparrow, *Melospiza lincolnii*
Western Meadowlark, *Sturnella neglecta*
Red-winged Blackbird, *Agelaius phoeniceus*
Brewer's Blackbird, *Euphagus cyanocephalus*
Brown-headed Cowbird, *Molothrus ater*
American Goldfinch, *Carduelis tristis*

Reptiles and Amphibians

Western Toad, *Bufo boreas*
Striped Chorus Frog, *Pseudacris triseriata*
Short-horned Lizard, *Phrynosoma douglassi*
Western Terrestrial Garter Snake, *Thamnophis elegans*

Butterflies

Queen Alexandra's Sulfur, *Colias alexandra*
Arachne Checkerspot, *Paladryas arachne*
Ruddy Copper, *Chalceria rubida*
Atlantis Fritillary, *Speyeria atlantis*
Pearly Crescentspot, *Phyciodes tharos*
Blue Copper, *Chalceria heteronea*
Phoebus Parnassian, *Parnassius phoebus*
Ochre Ringlet, *Coenonympha ochracea*
Chryxus Arctic, *Oeneis chryxus*
Anicia Checkerspot, *Occidryas anicia*

CHAPTER SEVENTEEN

Streambank and Shoreline: Mountain Wetlands

THE MINGLING OF land and water is a theme repeated with endless variations in the Southern Rockies. In valleys washed with sunshine or in cool, shaded canyons, the lush tangle of vegetation associated with wetland habitats provides a striking contrast to adjacent upland communities. Though seldom extensive, these wetland communities are among the most biologically productive ecosystems in the arid West.

Wetland ecosystems exist in a fragile balance; even subtle changes in the water table can cause irreversible changes. Throughout the Southern Rockies, as in most areas of the West, wetlands are in jeopardy, doomed to increasing fragmentation and dewatering. Much of the destruction is the result of transmountain and other water diversion projects, channelization, development dredge and fill, peat mining, and degradation related to agriculture. Because the region's economic development has been largely concentrated along mountain watercourses and floodplain corridors, riparian ecosystems have been especially hard hit. The future of many mountain wetlands remains uncertain, dependent on our wise stewardship of these important ecosystems.

Ecological Distribution

The term *wetland* is a catchall for lands that are transitional between aquatic and terrestrial ecosystems and where the water table is usually at or near the ground surface during all or part of the year. In the Southern Rockies, ecosystems associated with standing or flowing water are shaped by

Caribou Lake, Indian Peaks Wilderness Area, Colorado.
James B. Benedict.

different ecological processes and form distinctly different communities. For simplicity, however, the mountain wetland ecosystems described in this chapter are broken down into three major types, based on the physiognomy or growth form of the dominant plants: (1) riparian forests; (2) shrub-dominated wetlands; and (3) herbaceous wetlands. Within these broad categories, differences in moisture availability, soil, nutrient characteristics, and plant associations are used to separate wetlands into ecologically distinct communities.

Riparian communities are associated with the banks and borders of bodies of water. Communities bordering flowing waters assume a linear configuration, extending as a somewhat continuous strand of distinctive vegetation through several life zones. Major riparian communities that form continuous strands include those along the Rio Grande, the Arkansas, and the Colorado rivers. Riparian communities

THE SOUTHERN ROCKIES

associated with standing water or with high water tables are found along the shores of ponds and lakes, in ravines and gulches, in association with springs or other areas of groundwater seepage, or in situations where the local geology or topography traps moisture and maintains a high water table.

Most shrub-dominated and herbaceous wetlands persist only in topographic sites where moisture is available in abundance as a result of seasonal or permanent runoff. Such sites include well-watered depressions adjacent to streams, ponds, or lakes, the surfaces of solifluction terraces, and areas where late-lying snow has filled small basins. Successional wetland communities are typical of areas where a pond or lake has filled with sediment. Wetland biologists classify herbaceous and shrub-dominated wetlands on the basis of their soils. Organic soils are those defined as having 20 percent or more organic carbon by weight; these soils, in contrast to the pale color and gravelly or sandy texture typical of most mineral soils, are generally dark colored and somewhat fibrous in texture because they contain partially decomposed plant materials. *Wet meadows* and *marshes* are herbaceous ecosystems developed on sites with mineral soils; *bogs* and *fens*, on the other hand, are herbaceous ecosystems developed on organic soils. The term *carr* is used to refer to a shrub-dominated fen.

Herbaceous wetlands developed on mineral soils occur wherever alluvial sediments accumulate more rapidly than organic materials or where organic material is being lost through microbial activity or oxidation. Wetlands developed on organic soil are largely restricted to valley bottoms and natural depressions—wherever drainage is sluggish and where peat is accumulating in response to the incomplete decomposition of plant and animal remains. The term bog is frequently used—incorrectly—to refer to any soggy, peat-rich wetland. Wetland biologists, however, define a bog as an herbaceous wetland whose principal source of water is surface runoff. Bogs, then, are largely rain fed, or *ombrotrophic,* and tend to be nutrient poor, acidic, and characterized by a depauperate, highly specialized flora. Fens, on the other hand, are nourished by both surface runoff and groundwater sources, resulting in waters with a high nutrient content capable of supporting an extraordinary diversity of plants. Wetland ecologists believe that fens are widespread in the Southern Rockies and that true bogs are exceedingly rare in the Rocky Mountains south of Canada.

The Physical Environment

Water is the primary factor controlling the environment and the associated plant and animal life of mountain wetlands. It is difficult to generalize about the climatic and environmental conditions that characterize these ecosystems because they traverse such a broad elevational range. In placing mountain wetlands within the broad framework of mountain climate, it is important to keep in mind that an increase in elevation is typically associated with a decrease in temperature and an increase in precipitation. Consequently, the linear configuration typical of many riparian communities results in conspicuous changes in the vegetation and associated fauna in relation to the elevation gradient. Though communities tend to intergrade continuously along environmental gradients, each community can be described according to a given range of temperature, humidity, type and amount of precipitation, growing-season length, amount and distribution of wind, and soil condition.

Climatic variables such as precipitation and temperature are strongly influenced by differences in slope and exposure. Precipitation patterns are modified by local conditions, such as whether the ecosystem is located on a west-facing or east-facing slope, and by the geographical position of the ecosystem with regard to regional precipitation regimes. Microclimatic contrasts resulting from variations in the amount of solar radiation received by south-facing slopes as opposed to north-facing slopes can be great. At lower elevations, these differences are often reflected in the character and species composition of the riparian community. Riparian communities located in valleys tend to be colder than communities on slopes or on ridgetops as a result of cold-air drainage and the pooling of cold air that occurs in topographically enclosed basins. During the colder months, visual evidence of the effects of cold-air drainage can be seen at dawn, when a zone of hoar frost often parallels a drainage system or delineates a valley bottom.

Community Characteristics

Mountain wetlands are unique in their combination of high species diversity, high species density, and high productivity. It is not uncommon for a mountain riparian community to contain two to three times the number of species—both plant and animal—as adjacent upland communities. Elevation and factors that affect water chemistry, such as nutrient content, salinity, acidity, and oxygen richness, play a critical role in determining the species composition of a particular wetland community. Most riparian forests, for example, consist of a mosaic of stands that differ in structure, age, and species composition, forming a continuum of change along altitudinal gradients.

Lowland and Foothill Wetlands

The riparian flora of the lowland valleys and foothill canyons is especially rich because of the mixing of lowland and mountain species. Each community type reflects differences in water availability, flooding history, and human disturbance. In the absence of grazing or other types of disturbance, the forest understory consists of a lush growth of shrubs, forbs, grasses, sedges, rushes, and climbing vines. Most lowland riparian communities are dominated by broadleaved species of cottonwood, peachleaf willow, and boxelder; plains cottonwood is most common on the Eastern Slope, while Frémont and Rio Grande cottonwoods dominate the western and southwestern valleys. Some lowland riparian forests contain an abundance of introduced species, such as Russian olive, green ash, and tamarisk. Dense gallery forests, such as New Mexico's beloved *bosques*, prevail on the broadest floodplains and consist of various combinations of the dominant riparian forest species and thickets of coyote willow, sandbar willow, and snowberry.

With increasing elevation, broad-leaved cottonwoods are replaced in most communities by narrowleaf cottonwood; lanceleaf cottonwood, a hybrid of plains and narrowleaf cottonwoods, may also be present. In the moist canyons of

Plains cottonwood, with detail of fruit.

north-central New Mexico, species such as red-osier dogwood, forestiera, and New Mexican locust may be locally
common. In Colorado and northward into southern Wyoming, community associates of narrowleaf cottonwood include shrub willows, mountain alder, and twinberry. Species
such as netleaf hackberry, wild plum, chokecherry, and hawthorn are common in drier canyons and gulches. Cool ravines along the eastern foothills of the Colorado Front Range
harbor Pleistocene relict populations of beaked hazelnut and
wild sarsaparilla, tree species of the eastern United States;
in the foothills near Boulder, North America's southernmost
stand of paper birch occurs with beaked hazelnut.

In the more arid mountain parks and intermontane basins, such as Wyoming's Shirley Basin and Colorado's San
Luis Valley, poor drainage and saline-alkaline soils support
shrub wetlands dominated by greasewood and salt-tolerant
species such as rabbitbrush, fourwing saltbush, cattails, Baltic
rush, and saltgrass. The best watered of these communities
provide critical nesting habitat for waterfowl, both red-
winged and yellow-headed blackbirds, marsh wrens, and sora
rails.

Montane riparian communities are dominated by discontinuous forests of narrowleaf cottonwood, mountain alder, and river birch. Colorado blue spruce and Douglas-fir are

Common trees and shrubs of lowland riparian habitats: netleaf hackberry (top left), sandbar willow (top right), peachleaf willow (center), boxelder (lower left), Russian olive (lower right).

common in the cooler canyons, and may occur with white fir in montane riparian forests from central Colorado south into New Mexico. One or several species of willow as well as shrubs such as red-osier dogwood, Rocky Mountain maple, twinberry, common gooseberry, red elderberry, and shrubby cinquefoil predominate in the understory. In some situations, aspen may form dense stands along the margins of certain wetlands; aspen-dominated communities are often characterized by lush understories of grasses and wildflowers such as cow parsnip and false hellebore.

Herbaceous and shrub-dominated wetlands are common in the montane zone throughout the Southern Rockies. Species diversity tends to be low in these communities, in contrast to most riparian forests or to drier herbaceous communities. Single-species stands are common and are often dominated by sedges, rushes, turf-forming grasses, or, less commonly, water-loving forbs. Where such a community encircles a lake, pond, or moisture-retaining depression, different species associations frequently form discrete bands, each reflecting changes in moisture conditions. In other situations, these communities may form "islands" within drier ecosystem types.

Shrub wetlands dominated by shrubby cinquefoil are common in valley bottoms and may form circular zones around willow-dominated shrub wetlands. The organic soils associated with abandoned stream meanders, floodplain depressions, and the borders of ponds and lakes provide suitable sites for the development of willow carrs and other types of shrub wetlands; the species typically found in these communities include mountain (or yellow-twigged) willow, Geyer willow, river birch, and grasses such as Canadian reedgrass.

Subalpine Wetlands

Subalpine riparian forests are dominated largely by coniferous trees. Blue spruce is the most common species throughout the Southern Rockies and, with few exceptions, is largely confined to floodplains, moist terraces, and shorelines associated with permanent water supplies. White fir is found with blue spruce from the central Southern Rockies south

Common trees and shrubs of mountain riparian habitats, clockwise from upper left: Rocky Mountain maple, narrow-leaf cottonwood, planeleaf willow with detail of male catkins, mountain alder with detail of female catkin, western river birch.

Streambank and Shoreline: Mountain Wetlands

Clockwise from left: white fir, Colorado blue spruce, spruce gall on Colorado blue spruce.

into New Mexico, and hybrids of blue spruce and Engelmann spruce are common throughout this zone. Deciduous species such as narrowleaf cottonwood, aspen, and mountain-ash extend from the montane into the subalpine zone in some areas; small stands of balsam poplar, a possible Pleistocene relict common in the Central and Northern Rockies, are found in scattered locations in the Southern Rockies as far south as Gunnison.

Herbaceous plants form a rank understory in many subalpine riparian forests. Along the rushing streams that grace the higher mountains, tall wildflowers such as cow parsnip, chimingbells, bittercress, twisted stalk, arrowleaf groundsel, larkspur, and monkshood produce a showy, waist-high display. Striking wildflowers such as Parry primrose, yellow monkey-flower, globeflower, northern bog orchid, and marsh-marigold are common in many streamside and shoreline communities. The white rhododendron and the magenta Lewis's monkey-flower, species typical of the flora of the Northern Rockies and the Pacific Northwest, are restricted to moist habitats in the Park Range.

Shrub wetlands and carrs are especially conspicuous in

the broad, glaciated valleys of the subalpine zone. Bog birch and several species of willow dominate these communities. Planeleaf willow is perhaps the most common species and is typical of willow carrs in the San Juans, the Sawatch Range, North Park, the Laramie River Valley, and many areas of the Colorado Front Range. In spots, shrub communities form a dense, almost impenetrable thicket of tough stems and branches. Along narrow streams, willows conspire with mountain alders to keep even the most ardent angler from a promising pool. In late winter and early spring, however, these willow and bog birch communities carry the first luminous hint of spring into the high country, their stems glowing red and golden against the lingering snows. With the arrival of fall, the orange-red leaves of bog birch and the ochre hues of the willows rival the autumn display of aspen.

Herbaceous wetlands in the subalpine zone are dominated by sedges, rushes, grasses, or spikerushes. A moss layer may be well developed in some fens, but in contrast to bogs, it seldom includes *Sphagnum* spp. Fens with an especially high water table may consist of only one or two plant species; rhizomatous species of sedge, such as *Carex utriculata* or *C. aquatilis*, often form dense, continuous mats in these communities. In many communities, wildflowers such as marsh-marigold, queenscrown, kingscrown, white bog-orchid, elephantella, and several species of buttercup may be conspicuous.

From left to right: bog birch, twinberry.

Successional Wetland Communities

Mountain wetlands are diverse, dynamic systems subject to frequent change and, in some situations, to replacement by other ecosystems. Many montane and subalpine wetlands reflect a landscape in transition. For example, the typical successional pattern from subalpine pond or lake to spruce-fir forest involves several distinct stages and begins with a pioneer phase dominated by floating and semiemergent species such as quillwort, pondweed, buttercup, and *Carex aquatilis*. As silt and plant debris build the level of the soil relative to that of the water, an herbaceous wetland, or fen, consisting of sedges, rushes, and grasses such as Canadian reedgrass and tufted hairgrass begins to encroach upon the remaining open water. Eventually, a willow-dominated shrubland colonizes the fen, persisting until sufficient soil develops to a level well above the water table to permit an invasion of the area by Engelmann spruce or subalpine fir. In some cases, cold-air drainage, soil characteristics, or other factors may maintain the shrub wetland and deter tree growth.

Plant Adaptation: Designs for Survival

Floodplain Strategies

Most of the principal tree and shrub species found in mountain wetlands are ecologically restricted to sites that have higher levels of soil moisture than surrounding upland habitats. Willows and cottonwoods are obligate *phreatophytes* (literally, "well plants") and can only survive if their root systems are in reasonably close contact with the water table. Some phreatophytes, such as the introduced tamarisk, are so successful at mining water that they can substantially lower the water table and have become the scourge of watercourses in the arid West. High concentrations of sodium chloride and other salts in the groundwater can reduce a plant's ability to absorb water through its roots. Willows and cottonwoods have a low salt tolerance and will grow only where the salt content of the groundwater is low. Tamarisk, on the other hand, has a high salt tolerance and proliferates wherever heavy use of fertilizers on adjacent agricultural lands is increasing the salinity of the groundwater.

COPING WITH LOW OXYGEN LEVELS

The availability of oxygen is essential to plants, just as it is to animals. Plants require oxygen for root respiration and for the active absorption of minerals by the root cells. Most terrestrial plants take in oxygen through their roots. Because oxygen diffuses many times faster in air than in water, species growing with their roots in water-logged soils are at a distinct disadvantage. Aquatic plants solve the problem of oxygen deficiency by having within their tissues large gas-storage compartments, called *lacunae*, which create a continuous system of air passageways. For riparian trees and shrubs, saturated soils or prolonged intervals of flooding require unusual adaptations for coping with low levels of oxygen. The willow, for example, is stimulated when flooded to produce new, air-filled roots to replace those damaged by flooding. Other species, such as the river birch and the mountain alder, increase the number and effectiveness of the tiny openings in their bark, called *lenticels*, which allow gas exchange with the atmosphere. The wettest sites are successfully occupied by narrowleaf cottonwood, mountain alder, and willows, species able to withstand flooding for portions of two growing seasons and still maintain good root growth. Species such as bog birch, Rocky Mountain maple, river birch, hawthorn, and Colorado blue spruce are able to tolerate flooding for most of a single growing season. No riparian species, however, are able to withstand flooding for periods exceeding two consecutive growing seasons.

NITROGEN FIXATION

Of all the mineral elements required by plants, only nitrogen, critical for plant growth, must be obtained from the atmosphere rather than from the soil in which the plant grows. In areas that have not been previously vegetated, such as on sandbars, colonization by nitrogen-fixing plants plays a critical role in primary succession. *Nitrogen fixation* is the process by which atmospheric nitrogen gas is converted into organic compounds that can be assimilated by the plant and is accomplished primarily by certain free-living bacteria that consume organic matter in the soil, producing ammonia or nitrate as a by-product of their activities. Other types of nitrogen-fixing bacteria live in swellings, or *nodules*, within their host plant's roots and, in a true symbiotic association, supply fixed nitrogen in return for organic molecules secreted by the plant.

If you examine the roots of the mountain alder you will see large numbers of spherical nodules that have formed as a growth response to the presence of the nitrogen-fixing, filamentous bacteria known as *Actinomycetes*. Within these nodules, the bacteria take nitrogen from the air and transform it into nitrate compounds that are water-soluble and transported throughout the tree's tissues. Alder leaves and other nitrogen-rich, decaying tree tissues contribute significant amounts of nitrogen to riparian ecosystems. Trees and shrubs growing in association with mountain alder often exhibit a boost in growth, resulting from the nitrogenous enrichment of their soils. In addition, the alder enhances the nutritive value of the water flowing past it, as well as the lakes, ponds, and rivers into which these waters flow.

REPRODUCTIVE STRATEGIES

Willows are finely tuned to life along the water. The reproductive cycle begins in early spring, and the seeds ripen at about the time that mountain streams and rivers are bankfull. The willow's multitudinous small seeds take to the air in clouds of silken fluff but rarely travel great distances — an advantage since they are short-lived and must land on moist soil and germinate within a few days in order to survive. During the spring, it is common to see whitish mats of new willow seeds along the edges of gravel bars and on mudflats. Willows also frequently resort to vegetative reproduction. Because the persistence of their ecological niche depends to a large degree on the ability to lock riparian soils into place, both shrub and tree willows swiftly develop underground stolons and suckers, and even odd bits of broken stem can take root and sprout. One needs only to follow someone through a dense stand of saplings produced through suckering to appreciate the old-fashioned phrase "willow slaps" used to describe these thickets.

Descriptions of Common Plants

Trees

Plains Cottonwood, *Populus deltoides* ssp. *monilifera.* There is no mistaking the broad, heart-shaped leaves of the plains cottonwood; the leaves of the similar Frémont and Rio Grande cottonwoods have narrow, tapering tips, and their fruiting capsules are distinctly egg-shaped. This massive-trunked tree, with its grayish brown, deeply furrowed bark, is the giant of the lowland riparian forests. Male and female flowers appear on separate plains cottonwood trees in spring before the leaves appear; the ripened, ovoid fruits on the female trees burst open in June to release their abundant, cotton-tufted seeds. The downy seeds, carried far and wide by the wind, collect in soft drifts wherever they come to rest.

Narrowleaf Cottonwood, *Populus angustifolia.* The narrowleaf cottonwood is identified by its narrow, lanceolate leaves and its large, aromatic buds. In contrast to the buds of willows, which are enclosed by a single bud scale, cottonwood buds have overlapping scales. Flowering occurs in spring, before the leaves unfold; male and female catkins grow on separate trees. When the female catkins burst open, they release masses of white cotton and numerous tiny seeds. The seeds remain viable for only a few days and must land on a suitably moist, sandy spot in full sunlight to germinate successfully.

Peachleaf Willow, *Salix amygdaloides.* Named for the resemblance of its narrow, lanceolate leaves to those of the common peach, the peachleaf willow is the only native tree-sized willow in the Southern Rockies. The male and female flowers of this short-lived, fast-growing species appear with the leaves in spring. The cone-shaped fruits mature about a month after flowering and contain numerous tiny seeds.

Boxelder, *Acer negundo.* The boxelder is a member of the maple family and is distinguished from the cottonwoods and willows by its compound, three-part leaves and its two-winged, maplelike fruits (samaras). Male and female flowers appear on separate trees in early spring; the fruits mature by autumn and are a favorite food for fox squirrels, evening grosbeaks, and mice. The boxelder grows quite rapidly for its first fifteen to twenty years, then slows, living a maximum of seventy-five to a hundred years.

Netleaf Hackberry, *Celtis reticulata.* This small, somewhat irregularly shaped tree is typical of drier sites along intermittent streams and rocky riverbanks. Netleaf hackberry is distinguished from other species by its thick, simple leaves with conspicuous netlike veins on the lower surface and orange-red, globe-shaped fruits. The species flowers in early spring, with male and female flowers appearing on the same tree.

Mountain Alder, *Alnus incana* ssp. *tenuifolia.* Mountain alder often forms large, spreading clumps of gray-barked stems and is identified by its double-toothed, obovate leaves and, in winter, by the small, woody cones that decorate its slender, reddish branches. Male and female flowers are produced in separate catkins on the same tree; male catkins are slender and drooping, and female catkins are conelike, clustered, and persistent.

River Birch, *Betula fontinalis.* This small tree, seldom exceeding 30 feet in height, is identified by its oval and sharply pointed leaves, its nonpeeling, coppery red bark, and the nonwoody character of its female catkins. Male and female flowers are borne in separate catkins, but on the same tree. Male catkins develop during the summer, remaining on the tree throughout the winter and into the following spring, when they become limp and pendulous, shedding clouds of pollen. Female catkins emerge in spring and, following pollination, elongate to form conelike structures that consist of numerous three-lobed scales, each scale enclosing a tiny winged seed.

Colorado Blue Spruce, *Picea pungens.* Blue spruce seldom occurs in large stands and is most common in small groves or as scattered trees in moist habitats. It is easily distinguished from other conifers by its narrow, pyramidal growth form, four-sided and sharp-tipped needles, smooth rather than hairy branchlets, and brown, furrowed bark. The degree of "blueness" of Colorado blue spruce is highly variable; some trees may not be blue at all except in the new growth of the season. Male and female cones are produced on the same tree; the female cones are papery when mature, cylindrical, and have wavy-edged scales. Brown, conical galls created by the abnormal growth of shoots infested with spruce gall aphids tip many branchlets. Blue spruce are long-lived, sometimes reaching six hundred to eight hundred years of age.

White fir, *Abies concolor.* White fir is found in the central and southern portions of the Southern Rockies. This elegant conifer is distinguished from subalpine fir *(A. lasiocarpa)* by the broadly pyramidal crown, the frosted appearance of the long, flat needles, and the large, upright greenish yellow cones that adorn its crown. The needles are typically 2 to 3 inches long and have a whitish cast due to the presence of epidermal wax. Female and male cones are produced on the same tree; the female cones are somewhat barrel-shaped and are borne at the top of the tree. Cone production does not begin until a tree is approximately forty years old; on average, heavy seed crops are produced every fifth year.

Shrubs

Shrub Willows, *Salix* spp. A great many species of willow are encountered in wetland habitats, but only a few can be described here. Coyote willow *(S. exigua)* and sandbar willow *(S. interior)* have extremely narrow leaves and are typical of lowland valleys and foothill canyons. Planeleaf willow *(S. planifolia),* a subalpine species, is distinguished by its larger, smooth-surfaced leaves, purplish black or reddish-brown twigs, and hairy capsules. Mountain willow *(S. monticola)* is identified by its erect growth form, yellow-colored branches, and relatively narrow, acute leaves. Blue willow *(S. drummondiana)* occurs from the upper montane to the subalpine and is distinguished by the silky-hairy lower surfaces of its leaves and by the dark blue-green, smooth appearance of the upper leaf surfaces. The male and female flowers, or catkins, of all shrub willows occur on separate plants; the male catkins, because of their silky hairs, tend to be most prominent. Willows reproduce by both sexual and vegetative means.

Bog Birch, *Betula glandulosa.* This low, somewhat robust shrub is widely distributed in the Arctic and in the high mountain areas of North America. Bog birch is identified by its thick, roundish, serrated leaves and by the warty, resinous glands found along its young twigs. Male and female flowers, called catkins, are borne on the same plant; the catkins for the next growing season form during late summer.

Rocky Mountain Maple, *Acer glabrum.* This attractive, large shrub, noted for its rich autumn color, is identified by its three- to five-lobed, maplelike leaves and its two-winged fruits (samaras); the deep green leaves, attached to the twigs by long slender stalks, contrast beautifully with the reddish hue of the twigs, buds, and samaras. Crimson, feltlike blotches on the upper surfaces of the leaves are caused by the galls of eriophyid mites. Clusters of yellowish green flowers appear in early spring, coincident with the leaves; in some cases, male and female flowers are borne on separate plants. At maturity, the two-winged fruit splits in two, each wing enclosing a single seed.

Twinberry, *Distegia involucrata.* This shrub, also known as bush honeysuckle or bearberry, is identified by its dark green oval leaves and paired yellow flowers. Twinberry seldom exceeds 3 feet in height. Individual flowers are somewhat pendant and borne in pairs on a long stalk. Each pair of flowers is enclosed by four fused bracts, which enlarge and turn reddish as the fruits—paired purplish berries—mature. The fruits are considered poisonous.

Wildflowers

Cow parsnip, *Heracleum sphondylium.* This tall, robust member of the parsley family is identified by its three-lobed, coarsely toothed compound leaves, its enormous, flat-topped umbel of white flowers, and the sheathing petiole that envelops its stem leaves. The stems are hollow, and the flowers mature into large, flat seeds. In suitably moist sites, this species may grow to 6 feet in height.

Chimingbells, *Mertensia ciliata.* This graceful wildflower, also known as bluebells or mertensia, is identified by its pendant clusters of bell-shaped blue flowers and by its bluish green, smooth-edged lanceolate leaves. The flowers hang from slender stems that arise from within the leaf axil; pinkish blue hues, especially in the buds, are common. Chimingbells often form large clumps along streams and rivulets, from the upper montane through the subalpine zone.

Monkshood, *Aconitum columbianum.* The purple-blue

Common wildflowers of mountain riparian habitats, clockwise from left: cow parsnip, monkshood, chimingbells.

flowers of monkshood appear along a long stalk and are easily identified by the unusual way in which the uppermost sepal arches over the other floral parts to form a hood. The common name of this species is derived from the resemblance of this hood to that worn by some monks. This species can be extremely toxic to livestock.

Bittercress, *Cardamine cordifolia.* Bittercress, also known as brookcress, is a member of the mustard family and is identified by its white, round-topped racemes of four-petaled flowers and its heart-shaped, toothed leaves.

Yellow Monkey-flower, *Mimulus guttatus.* This lovely wildflower grows around springs and along streambanks and is identified by its bright yellow, snapdragon-like flowers; each flower has a sprinkling of red spots on the lip of the floral tube and a closed throat and is usually less than an inch long. The leaves are broadly ovate in shape and are arranged opposite each other.

Arrowleaf Senecio (or Groundsel), *Senecio triangularis.* Arrowleaf groundsel is identified by the following combination of characters: an unbranched stem, toothed and narrowly triangular leaves, and an open but somewhat round-topped raceme of small, sunflower-like flower heads. Each flower head consists of a ring of yellow ray flowers and a tightly packed cluster of tubular disk flowers, encircled from beneath by a bell-shaped, single series of narrow green bracts.

Northern Bog-Orchid, *Limnorchis hyperborea.* This small-flowered orchid is frequently found along moist streamsides from the foothills to the subalpine zone. All bog-orchids are alike in that their flowers are somewhat crowded together along a stout, erect stalk and their strap-shaped leaves are distributed along the length of the stem. The northern bog-orchid is identified by the green color of its flowering spike and the small spur at the base of the lip of each flower. A similar species, the white bog-orchid (*L. dilatata* ssp. *albiflora*), bears a slender stalk of pure white, fragrant flowers and is found in more open subalpine environments, such as in fens or along the shores of ponds.

Common Plants of the Mountain Wetlands

Trees

Alder, mountain, *Alnus incana* ssp. *tenuifolia*
Ash, mountain, *Sorbus scopulina*

Aspen, quaking, *Populus tremuloides*
Birch, river, *Betula fontinalis*
Boxelder, *Acer negundo*
Cottonwood, Frémont, *Populus deltoides* ssp. *deltoides*
  lanceleaf, *Populus x acuminata* (hybrid)
  narrowleaf, *Populus angustifolia*
  plains, *Populus deltoides* ssp. *monilifera*
  Rio Grande, *Populus deltoides* ssp. *wislizenii*
Douglas-fir, *Pseudotsuga menziesii*
Fir, white, *Abies concolor*
Hackberry, netleaf, *Celtis reticulata*
Hazelnut, beaked, *Corylus cornuta*
Locust, New Mexican, *Robinia neomexicana*
Pine, Mexican white, *Pinus strobiformis*
Poplar, balsam, *Populus balsamifera*
Spruce, Colorado blue, *Picea pungens*
  Engelmann, *Picea engelmannii*
Willow, peachleaf, *Salix amygdaloides*

Shrubs

Birch, bog, *Betula glandulosa*
Chokecherry, *Padus virginiana* var. *melanocarpa*
  (formerly *Prunus*)
Cinquefoil, shrubby, *Pentaphylloides floribunda*
Currant, golden, *Ribes aureum*
Dogwood, red-osier, *Swida sericea* (formerly *Cornus stolonifera*)
Elderberry, red, *Sambucus microbotrys*
Forestiera (or mountain privet), *Forestiera pubescens*
Gooseberry, common, *Ribes inerme*
Greasewood, *Sarcobatus vermiculatus*
Hawthorn, *Crataegus erythropoda*
Maple, Rocky Mountain, *Acer glabrum*
Plum, wild, *Prunus americana*
Serviceberry, Utah, *Amelanchier utahensis*
  western, *Amelanchier alnifolia*
Twinberry (or bush honeysuckle), *Distegia involucrata*
  (formerly *Lonicera*)
Willow, Bebb, *Salix bebbiana*
  blue, *Salix drummondiana*
  bluestem, *Salix irrorata*

coyote, *Salix exigua*
Geyer, *Salix geyeriana*
mountain, *Salix monticola*
planeleaf, *Salix planifolia*
sandbar, *Salix interior*
subalpine, *Salix brachycarpa*
Wolf's, *Salix wolfii*

Vines

Grape, wild, *Vitis riparia*
Virginia Creeper, *Parthenocissus inserta*
Virgins Bower, *Clematis ligusticifolia*

Herbaceous Plants

Angelica, giant, *Angelica ampla*
Arrow-grass, *Triglochin palustris*
Bishops Cap, *Mitella pentandra*
Bittercress, *Cardamine cordifolia*
Bulrush, or Tule, *Schoenoplectus lacustris* ssp. *acutus*
Buttercup, *Ranunculus* spp.
Chimingbells, *Mertensia ciliata*
Cottongrass, *Eriophorum angustifolium*
Cow Parsnip, *Heracleum spondylium*
Elephantella, *Pedicularis groenlandica*
Gentian, star, *Swertia perennis*
Globeflower, *Trollius albiflorus*
Grass-of-Parnassus, *Parnassia parviflora* and *P. fimbriata*
Hairgrass, tufted, *Deschampsia cespitosa*
Hollyhock, mountain, *Iliamna rivularis*
Horsetail (or scouring rush), *Equisetum* spp.
Manna-grass, *Glyceria* spp.
Marsh Marigold, *Psychrophila leptosepala* (formerly
    Caltha)
Mimulus, Lewis', *Mimulus lewisii*
Monkey-flower, yellow, *Mimulus guttatus*
Monkshood, *Aconitum columbianum*
Orchid, northern bog, *Limnorchis hyperborea*
    white bog, *Limnorchis dilatata* ssp. *albiflora*
Pondlily, yellow, *Nuphar luteum*

Pondweed, *Potamogeton* spp.
Primrose, Parry, *Primula parryi*
Reedgrass, Canadian, *Calamagrostis canadensis*
Rush, scouring, *Equisetum* spp.
    subalpine, *Juncus mertensianus*
Saxifrage, brook, *Saxifraga odontoloma*
Senecio, arrowleaf, *Senecio triangularis*
Shootingstar, western, *Dodecatheon pulchellum*
Spikerush, *Eleocharis* spp.
Trefoil, marsh (or water buckbean), *Menyanthes*
    trifoliata
Twisted-stalk, *Streptopus fassettii* (formerly *Streptopus*
    amplexifolius)
Willow-herb, *Epilobium* spp.
Woodrush, common, *Luzula parviflora*

Environment and Adaptation: Animals of Streambank and Shoreline

Framed in moonlight, a beaver swims a steady course across the pond, towing a freshly cut willow sapling. Swooping low over the water, a little brown bat forages on the wing for insects. Nearby, a cow elk grazes in the sedge meadow that encircles the shoreline. With the coming of dawn, the rattling call of a belted kingfisher can be heard as the bird flies upvalley to a morning fishing perch. From a spray-slick boulder, a dipper dives beneath the frothy torrents to poke among the rocks for larval insects. In the tangle of willows and alders lining the streambank, chrome yellow Wilson's warblers flutter from branch to branch gleaning insects. These images exemplify the wilderness spirit inherent in mountain wetlands.

Mountain riparian forests, with their unique mixture of terrestrial and aquatic resources, provide abundant food and protective cover for a diversity of resident and nonresident animal species. Some prefer an aquatic or semiaquatic lifestyle; others concentrate their foraging and breeding activities at different levels in the shrubs and trees; still others forage in the lush understory or seek shelter in the litter of the forest floor. A high rate of net primary productivity — the amount of organic matter created or energy bound by green plants once respiration costs have been subtracted — provides the foundation for the species diversity. Species diversity also depends, however, on a critical factor known as *niche space.* The term niche describes a species' "occupation" within a community; niche space is an abstract term that refers to the total resource space available within a given community. Population ecologists say that diversity creates and sustains diversity. The greater the number of niches available, the greater the variety of species that an ecosystem can support. In the case of most riparian forests, the multistoried structure of the vegetation and the proximity of water provide a multitude of habitat and feeding possibilities. Resource partitioning is necessary, and each species appropriates a space in this highly stratified community by selecting a particular level in which to concentrate its activities, by using different resources, or by using shared resources at different times of the day or year.

Woodcutter, Dam Builder, and Hydrologic Engineer

Adaptations for an aquatic lifestyle are common among many species associated with mountain wetlands. Though the beaver is less than graceful on land, it has achieved a supreme mastery of the water through a variety of adaptations: webbed hind feet, a waterproof coat, a paddlelike tail, nostril and ear valves that close during submersion, small eyes with a transparent inner lid designed for unimpeded underwater vision, and special controls on heart rate and breathing, which permit extended dives. Whereas some animals can modify their immediate environment, the beaver is able to create its own habitat and then manipulate that habitat to suit its needs.

Beavers generally create their own pond by impounding a stream with a dam constructed of logs, sticks, rocks, and mud. Within the pond, the beaver builds a conical lodge of sticks and mud, complete with an underwater entrance. Beavers living along larger streams or rivers do little dam building and make use of bank burrows rather than lodges. The pond not only protects the beaver from most predators, it ensures the proliferation of the beaver's preferred plant foods, provides an all-weather transportation route and a means of floating the harvest home, and, as a side benefit, creates additional stillwater habitat for muskrats, fish, frogs, ducks, and shorebirds.

Long, curved incisor teeth make short work of the beaver's woodcutting tasks, allowing it to cut a willow sapling in seconds and to fell a 6-inch-diameter aspen in a matter of minutes. The problem of a cellulose-rich diet of bark, roots, and other plant materials is efficiently solved by a gland along the digestive tract, which secretes enzymes into the stomach to soften woody tissues. The inner bark of aspen and willow is known to be rich in salicylic acid (the active ingredient in aspirin); interestingly enough, this compound is also the main constituent of castoreum, an oil the beaver secretes from oblong scent glands within its cloaca and uses to waterproof its fur and mark its territory.

Water Sprite and Angler

Bird species associated with mountain wetlands exhibit a variety of adaptations that enable them to exploit their watery habitat. Lured by an abundance of aquatic insects, the American dipper has developed the ability to walk underwater as it forages among the rocks for food. The dipper uses its wings to get to the bottom of a stream and then, using a combination of downward and rearward strokes, is able to overcome its buoyancy and move about on the streambed — often traveling against the current. Dippers are equipped with large preen glands — ten times the size of that of any other passerine bird — which provide the oil needed to waterproof feathers. Additionally, a movable flap over the nostril seals out water during dives, and an extra, transparent eyelid allows the dipper to use its eyes underwater and provides protection from water-borne particles. In keeping with a semiaquatic lifestyle, the dipper's nesting period coincides with the hatching of many aquatic insects, especially the stonefly, which it harvests in large numbers.

Another water-adapted species, the belted kingfisher, prefers to do its hunting from a perch overhanging the water.

A skillful angler, the kingfisher can see fish through the mirrored surface of the water thanks to tiny droplets of red oil that coat the cones of its eyes, reducing glare and distortion. Scanning the water from its perch, the kingfisher may hover briefly before diving headlong into the water, often remaining underwater for several seconds before emerging with a fish or other suitable prey in its beak. Returning to its perch, the kingfisher first kills the fish and then throws it into the air to be swallowed headfirst.

Room to Nest

Mountain riparian communities generally have higher densities of breeding birds than other mountain ecosystems due to the rich variety of available nesting sites and the abundance of food. The dipper chooses its nest site, nearly always near water, with a keen eye toward predator inaccessibility. Streamside ledges, a rock crevice tucked safely behind a cascading waterfall, and the steel girders beneath a bridge are all likely sites. The belted kingfisher excavates its long, tunnel-like burrows near the top of a steep earthen bank adjoining a favorite stream, river, or pond. The lush

Common snipe (top), American dipper (bottom).

riparian tangle provides cover for ground-nesting species such as the Wilson's warbler, Lincoln's and song sparrows, and common snipe. MacGillivray's and yellow warblers build their nests in the shrub layer, taking advantage of dense willow and alder thickets. Waterfowl, such as green-winged teal, mallards, ring-necked ducks, and shorebirds, such as the spotted sandpiper, exploit sedge tussock islands in the more secluded mountain ponds and lakes.

A room with a view is preferred by several species: herons, flycatchers, chickadees, warbling vireos, swallows, robins, and many others. Most great blue and black-crowned night herons nest colonially, in aggregations known as rookeries, generally located in tall cottonwoods. In some areas, black-crowned night heron rookeries may occupy the lower branches of trees already appropriated by great blue herons. Competitive overlap appears to be eliminated by the lifestyles of the two species. The great blue heron is active by day and is often observed standing motionless in shallow water, waiting for prey to come within striking range of its sharp bill. The black-crowned night heron, on the other hand, is largely nocturnal and fishes by alternately stalking and standing motionless.

Amphibians and Reptiles

Mountain riparian communities harbor several species of amphibians and reptiles, including the boreal toad, striped chorus frog, northern leopard frog, western terrestrial garter snake, and smooth green snake. Most amphibians and reptiles cannot live in a cold environment, but three species — the striped chorus frog, the boreal toad, and the tiger salamander — have been found at nearly 12,000 feet in the Southern Rockies. These species are well adapted to cold temperatures, utilizing a combination of behavioral and physiological adaptations that enable them to remain active from spring through fall under a wide range of conditions. Diurnal and nocturnal activity patterns appear to be related to the seasonal progression of temperatures; diurnal activity is common in spring and fall, when cooler temperatures force these animals to be active under optimal opportunities for basking; nocturnal activity dominates the warmer summer weeks. Winter environmental extremes are avoided in underground hibernacula, either in natural cavities or in the abandoned burrows of other animals. During the past decade, a sharp decline in populations of boreal toads and northern leopard frogs has been reported. Long-term studies are currently under way to determine the degree to which acid rain, predation, or disease may be contributing to this decline.

Life Histories of Selected Animals

Mammals

Water Shrew, *Sorex palustris.* This is the largest shrew found in the Southern Rockies and is easily distinguished by its size (total length of adults averages 6 inches), dark gray-black upperparts, silvery gray belly, and fringe of stiff hairs on the hind feet. Water shrews are found along cold mountain streams with overhanging ledges, boulders, and exposed root systems, which provide cover. Masterful swimmers, water shrews are often observed skimming across the surface of the water, propelled by the fringed hind feet, or swimming and foraging underwater. Active year-round and both night and day, water shrews forage energetically for insects, small fish, carrion, and other animal foods. Water shrews are short-lived, seldom surviving their second winter.

Little Brown Bat, *Myotis lucifugus.* This common, medium-sized bat is identified by its dark, glossy coloring and its erratic, zigzagging flight style. Most often observed over water, this bat begins its foraging at dark and continues intermittently until dawn. The diet consists of flying insects, which it locates by sonar. Mating begins in fall and sperm are stored within the uterus of the female throughout hibernation; fertilization is delayed until the females emerge from hibernation in the spring. Upon returning to the summer range, pregnant females establish nursery colonies, which may include several dozen individuals. After a gestation period of less than two months, each female gives birth to a single altricial young. Young bats begin flying and foraging on their own by about three weeks of age.

Beaver, *Castor canadensis.* This large, mostly nocturnal rodent is identified by its paddlelike tail, webbed hind feet, and rich brown fur. Beavers occur wherever permanent streams of moderate grade and a sufficient food supply of aspen, willow, alder, and aquatic plants provide suitable habitat. Active throughout the year, the beaver stores cut saplings and other plant foods underwater for use during the winter. Beaver social life revolves around the mated pair, the yearlings, and the young (called kits). Breeding occurs in January or February; fully furred and open-eyed kits are born in April or May. Beavers are long-lived animals, with many individuals living for fifteen years.

Muskrat, *Ondatra zibethicus.* This medium-sized rodent is identified by its slender and hairless tail, diminutive ears, and partially webbed hind feet. The mink *(Mustela vison)* is more weasel-like in appearance and has a fully furred tail. Muskrats are more common at middle and lower elevations, especially in areas with past or present beaver activity. Muskrats build small, dome-shaped lodges consisting of piles of herbaceous vegetation and equipped with underwater entrances; some individuals utilize bank burrows rather than lodges. The diet is more cosmopolitan than that of the beaver, including virtually any type of aquatic or semiaquatic plant and occasionally animals. Muskrats are promiscuous, and breeding occurs in spring and summer. Females produce two or three litters a year; newborn muskrats are altricial, but the young develop quickly and are largely independent of the female after one month.

Raccoon, *Procyon lotor.* Raccoons are identified by the black facial mask and the alternating rings of yellowish buff and black on the bushy tail. Chiefly nocturnal, the raccoon is an opportunist when it comes to diet, taking amphibians, small mammals, fish, fruit, and other foods as available. Raccoons are promiscuous breeders, the females becoming receptive to males in February or March. Young are born in early spring, and the female cares for the young alone. Adult size is achieved after two years; a life span of ten to twelve years is common.

Striped Skunk, *Mephitis mephitis.* The striped skunk, with its jet black coat, white stripes, and odiferous scent glands, requires little introduction. Chiefly nocturnal, skunks forage for insects, amphibians, ground-nesting birds and their eggs, and fruit. Though active year-round, striped skunks avoid cold, snowy weather by sleeping, relying on stored fat. Mating occurs in March or April and is accompanied by "pacification" courtship behavior. The altricial young are born in May or June and may remain with the mother their first winter.

Red Fox, *Vulpes vulpes.* This small, beautiful canid is distinguished by its normally rust orange upperparts, whitish underparts, and black feet, muzzle, and backs of ears; all color morphs of the red fox have bushy, white-tipped tails. Home range size is variable, averaging between 1 and 3 square miles. Solitary, except during the breeding season, the red fox is largely nocturnal. The diet is omnivorous, consisting of rabbits, small mammals, birds, fish, amphibians, fruits, and insects. The den, usually a renovated burrow or an enlarged natural cavity, is used during inclement weather and becomes the center of activity during the breeding season. Pair-bonds are formed in December or January; a single litter of four to five pups is born blind but furred in early spring. The pups remain within the den until they are about five weeks old; they are weaned at two months and begin joining the parents on hunting trips. The family unit breaks up in autumn.

Birds

Great Blue Heron, *Ardea herodias.* The great blue heron is identified by its large size, bluish gray plumage, serpentine neck, and long legs. The black-crowned night heron *(Nycticorax nycticorax)* is considerably smaller, with a black back and crown, pale gray wings, and white underparts. Male great blue herons conduct ritualized courtship displays as soon as they arrive on the breeding territory in early spring, often returning to the same rookery used in previous years. The male selects the nest site, but the female constructs the nest with materials delivered by the male. Pair-bonds are solidified by passing twigs, by locking bills, and by mutual preening. Both parents rear the young.

Green-winged Teal, *Anas crecca.* This crow-sized, surface-feeding duck is identified by the chestnut head, large green ear patch, and vertical white bar that extends through its gray-streaked breast; the female is a nondescript speckled brown, and both sexes have a green speculum on the wing, visible in flight. While foraging for aquatic insects, teals probe, or "dabble," with their bills in the mud. Arriving shortly after the ice melts, the green-winged teal selects a secluded nest site in a clump of grass or sedges. Eight buff-colored eggs are laid in early summer.

Common Snipe, *Gallinago gallinago.* This secretive, robin-sized bird is identified by its brown-dappled body, short legs, sandpiper-like appearance, and long bill. On breeding grounds, the snipe's circling displays, performed by both sexes, can be spectacular; during the shallow dives associated with this display, air vibrations along the fanned tail produce an eerie, winnowing sound. Most displays occur at twilight or at dawn. The ground call, often delivered in the vicinity of the nest, is a whistled, slow "wheek-a-wheek-a-wheek-a." Largely crepuscular, the snipe forages along the ground, probing with its bill for insects in the mud; the bill is extremely sensitive, with an upper mandible that can be raised and curved to extract worms and clinging larvae. The female selects the nest site, making several scrapes on the ground before choosing one, and incubates the eggs alone. Shortly after hatching, as soon as the young are dry, both parents lead the brood away from the nest.

Belted Kingfisher, *Ceryle torquata.* This pigeon-sized bird is identified by its large, crested head, spear-shaped bill, blue-gray upperparts, and white breast with horizontal breast band. Its call, a reverberating rattle, is delivered from a fishing perch or in flight. The kingfisher is an agile angler, preying on fish, amphibians, and small reptiles. Solitary except during the breeding season, the pair selects a suitable burrow site in a sandy or gravelly stream or river bank within the male's territory. An average of six to seven eggs are laid, and hatching occurs after a period of about three weeks; time to fledging is believed to be at least three weeks.

American Dipper, *Cinclus mexicanus.* Dippers, or water ouzels, are identified by their slate gray coloring, rounded shape, stubby tail, large feet, and underwater foraging style. Common along mountain streams and rivers during the summer, the species abandons these watercourses during the winter in favor of lower-elevation, ice-free waters. When flushed, dippers give a rapid, musical "bzeet" call as they fly low over the water to a new area of the stream. Dippers are often observed bobbing up and down as they perch on a boulder or partially submerged log. Solitary except at nesting time, the female dipper incubates the eggs, but both sexes feed the squawking, demanding young.

Wilson's Warbler, *Wilsonia pusilla.* The male Wilson's warbler is identified by its olive upperparts, yellow face and breast, and small black cap; females are similar in coloring but lack the black cap. A similar species, the common yellowthroat *(Geothlypis trichas),* has a broad black facial mask rather than a cap. Wilson's warblers actively forage for insects in dense shrub thickets, often twitching their tails and flicking their wings in a nervous manner. The song of the male is a hurried, staccato chatter dropping in pitch at the end; the call is a flat "chuff." This species builds a somewhat bulky nest on the ground, often sunken in moss or sedges; Wilson's warblers are subject to nest parasitism by the brown-headed cowbird.

Red-winged Blackbird, *Agelaius phoeniceus.* Male red-winged blackbirds are identified by their black plumage and red shoulder patches (epaulets); the epaulets can be exposed during displays or concealed during times of danger. Female blackbirds are dark brown with mottled breasts. The song of the male is a liquid, gurgling "conk-ka-ree"; the common call is a "chack." The male is strongly territorial during the breeding season, defending an area of marsh within which up to a dozen females may nest. Both sexes become less conspicuous and somewhat secretive in late summer as they undergo molt.

Northern Oriole, *Icterus galbula.* This is the only common oriole in the Southern Rockies. The male is identified by its fiery orange underparts, rump patch, and outer tail feathers; the wings are black with white wing patches, and the orange head is highlighted by a black crown and eye stripe. The female oriole is an inconspicuous grayish yellow. The song is a series of rich, flutelike whistles. Orioles are insectivorous, but will take fruit or nectar at flowers. Males arrive on the breeding territory in late spring. Both sexes participate in nest building, territorial defense, incubating the eggs, and rearing the young.

Lincoln's Sparrow, *Melospiza lincolnii.* Lincoln's sparrow is distinguished from two other species that share its habitat, the fox sparrow *(Passerella iliaca)* and the song sparrow *(M. melodia),* by its slimmer body shape, muted brown streaking, and lighter gray eyebrow stripe and ear coverts. Though relatively common, the Lincoln's sparrow is a shy skulker through brushy habitat, but it can sometimes be attracted by making squeaking noises. When approached or surprised, it may twitch and elevate its crown feathers. Lincoln's sparrows forage on the ground for insects and seeds and may engage in double-scratching to locate food items. The song of the male on the breeding territory is a rapid, bubbling trill; the call note is a low, hard, oft-repeated "tsup." During courtship, the male (like the song sparrow) pounces on its mate in response to the female's behavioral and vocal invitation.

Amphibians and Reptiles

Tiger Salamander, *Ambystoma tigrinum.* This pugnacious-appearing salamander is identified by its stout body and legs, costal grooves, laterally flattened tail, and broad head. The color pattern of tiger salamanders varies considerably; some have yellowish spots or bars on a dark background, while others have dark spots on a light background; larval forms are brownish or greenish and lack spots. Adults may be seen in or out of the water; the larval stage has gills and is aquatic. Metamorphosed tiger salamanders are largely terrestrial and are found in a wide variety of moist habitats at elevations up to 12,000 feet; a body of still water must be present nearby for breeding. Tiger salamanders leave their underground winter chambers and migrate to the breeding ponds

Northern leopard frog (top), tiger salamander (bottom).

Streambank and Shoreline: Mountain Wetlands

anytime from April to July, depending on when the ice melts. Eggs are laid in ponds, and hatching occurs within two to five weeks. The length of the aquatic larval phase is variable; some may metamorphose within two to five months, others after a period of one or two years, whereas some larvae may never metamorphose at all. Metamorphosed salamanders eat snails and aquatic insects, as well as the eggs and larvae of other amphibians; cannibalism occurs frequently among salamander larvae.

Northern Leopard Frog, *Rana pipiens.* This frog is identified by the large dark spots on its back and the prominent dorsolateral folds and midline. This species emerges from its winter retreat in the bottom of a pond in early spring and may remain active through October. Breeding areas are in shallow, still bodies of water. The distinctive call of the male is a prolonged snore, followed by a series of croaks. Females begin laying eggs a few days after the males begin calling; egg masses are attached to vegetation.

Striped Chorus Frog, *Pseudacris triseriata.* This tiny frog is distinguished from other frogs by its size (usually under 2 inches), the stripe that extends through its eye to its groin, and the absence of distinct hind toe webbing. The color patterning of the striped chorus frog is highly variable, with background colors of green, red, or brown. This species occurs to nearly 12,000 feet and is found in or adjacent to any still body of water. Chorus frogs emerge from their underground hibernaculum in late spring, remaining active until September or October. Breeding occurs in both temporary and permanent bodies of water. Males begin their chorus — a slow, staccato trill — soon after emergence in the spring, attracting females to the breeding ponds. During mating, males clasp the females and eggs are released; the tadpoles of this species metamorphose during their first summer, reaching adult size in about seventy-eight days.

Western Terrestrial Garter Snake, *Thamnophis elegans.* This snake is distinguished by its darkish, largely patternless body, the keeled brownish scales on its back, the pale yellowish stripes that run the length of its body and its smooth tail. The western terrestrial garter snake usually is most common below 11,000 feet. Garter snakes emerge from their underground winter chambers in late spring and remain active at moderate elevations through October. When handled, this garter snake may expel a foul-smelling liquid from its anal glands. The diet of the western terrestrial garter snake includes small invertebrates, fish, larval and metamorphosed amphibians, small birds, and small mammals. Like other garter snakes, this species does not lay eggs but gives birth to live young.

Common Animals of Mountain Wetlands

Mammals

Montane Shrew, *Sorex monticolus*
Water Shrew, *Sorex palustris*
Little Brown Bat, *Myotis lucifugus*
Long-legged Myotis, *Myotis volans*
Mountain (or Nuttall's) Cottontail, *Sylvilagus nuttallii*
Least Chipmunk, *Tamias minimus*
Beaver, *Castor canadensis*
Deer Mouse, *Peromyscus maniculatus*
Long-tailed Vole, *Microtus longicaudus*
Montane Vole, *Microtus montanus*
Muskrat, *Ondatra zibethicus*
Western Jumping Mouse, *Zapus princeps*
Coyote, *Canis latrans*
Red Fox, *Vulpes vulpes*
Black Bear, *Ursus americanus*
Raccoon, *Procyon lotor*
Long-tailed Weasel, *Mustela frenata*
Mink, *Mustela vison*
Striped Skunk, *Mephitis mephitis*
Wapiti (or Elk), *Cervus elaphus*
Mule Deer, *Odocoileus hemionus*

Birds

Common Merganser, *Mergus merganser*
Green-winged Teal, *Anas crecca*
Mallard, *Anas platyrhynchos*

Ring-necked Duck, *Aythya collaris*
American Coot, *Fulica americana*
Black-crowned Night Heron, *Nycticorax nycticorax*
Killdeer, *Charadrius vociferus*
Common Snipe, *Gallinago gallinago*
Spotted Sandpiper, *Actitis macularia*
Blue Grouse, *Dendragapus obscurus*
Northern Harrier (or Marsh Hawk), *Circus cyaneus*
Cooper's Hawk, *Accipiter cooperii*
Western Screech Owl, *Otus kennicottii*
Great Horned Owl, *Bubo virginianus*
Saw-whet Owl, *Aegolius acadicus*
Broad-tailed Hummingbird, *Selasphorus platycercus*
Belted Kingfisher, *Ceryle alcyon*
White-throated Swift, *Aeronautes saxatilis*
Hairy Woodpecker, *Picoides villosus*
Dusky Flycatcher, *Empidonax oberholseri*
Willow Flycatcher, *Empidonax traillii*
Western Flycatcher, *Empidonax difficilis*
Tree Swallow, *Tachycineta bicolor*
Bank Swallow, *Riparia riparia*
Cliff Swallow, *Hirundo pyrrhonota*
Black-billed Magpie, *Pica pica*
Mountain Chickadee, *Parus gambelii*
Canyon Wren, *Catherpes mexicanus*
Swainson's Thrush, *Catharus ustulatus*
American Robin, *Turdus migratorius*
American Dipper, *Cinclus mexicanus*
Warbling Vireo, *Vireo gilvus*
Orange-crowned Warbler, *Vermivora celata*
Yellow-rumped Warbler, *Dendroica coronata*
Yellow Warbler, *Dendroica petechia*
MacGillivray's Warbler, *Oporornis tolmiei*
Wilson's Warbler, *Wilsonia pusilla*
Song Sparrow, *Melospiza melodia*
White-crowned Sparrow, *Zonotrichia leucophrys*
Fox Sparrow, *Passerella iliaca*
Lincoln's Sparrow, *Melospiza lincolnii*

Amphibians and Reptiles

Tiger Salamander, *Ambystoma tigrinum*
Boreal Toad, *Bufo boreas*

Striped Chorus Frog, *Pseudacris triseriata*
Northern Leopard Frog, *Rana pipiens*
Smooth Green Snake, *Opheodrys vernalis*
Bullsnake, *Pituophus melanoleucus*
Western Terrestrial Garter Snake, *Thamnophis elegans*

Butterflies

Titiana's Fritillary, *Clossiana titania*
Greenish Blue, *Plebejus saepiolus*
Mourning Cloak, *Nymphalis antiopa*
Common Alpine, *Erebia epipsodea*

CHAPTER EIGHTEEN

Riffle, Pool, and Tarn: Aquatic Communities

FROM THE TINIEST trickle emanating from a melting snowbank to the ink blue depths of a glacial tarn and the sunlit riffles of a mountain stream, the presence of water creates a mosaic of habitats for plants and animals. Aquatic ecosystems are found throughout the Southern Rockies, ranging in elevation from 6,000 to more than 14,000 feet. These ecosystems are divided into two general groups: flowing-water, or *lotic*, habitats; and standing-water, or *lentic*, habitats. Lotic ecosystems range in size from seeps and springs to streams and rivers. Lentic ecosystems include both lakes and ponds as well as a variety of transitional wetland habitats in which the surface of the land is covered, at least seasonally, with shallow water. Both types of ecosystems are described in this chapter. A discussion of the physical and biological features that shape each ecosystem is included to provide an introduction to the complex relationships that govern aquatic communities.

Lotic Ecosystems: Mountain Streams and Rivers

Physical and Biological Features

The physical and biological characteristics of a stream vary markedly as it moves downstream from its source. Changes in the structure and function of the stream's biological communities are closely correlated with changes in physical characteristics—gradient, velocity, width, depth, temperature, substrate, and turbidity. Three broad ecological zones mark the changes in a flowing-water system from its source to its mouth: headwater streams, intermediate-sized streams or small rivers, and large rivers. Each zone is characterized by a different assemblage of organisms specifically adapted to the food resources and living conditions found within that zone.

Stream Animals

Stream animals are classified into the following groups according to the way in which they feed: shredders, collectors, scraper-grazers, and predators. *Shredders* (such as case-building caddisflies, crane fly larvae, and herbivorous mayfly nymphs) are adapted to feed on coarse plant detritus that enters the stream from surrounding terrestrial ecosystems; plant fragments that have been colonized by microscopic decomposers such as bacteria and aquatic fungi are preferred food items. Shredders play an important role in breaking organic material down into finer particles, which are then available to other animals in the food chain.

Collectors (such as net-spinning caddisflies and black fly larvae) capture fine particles of organic matter produced by the feeding activities of the shredders or broken down by mechanical action within the stream. They obtain their food — fragmented, microbe-conditioned organic particles and shredder feces — by filtering or sieving fine particles carried in suspension by the current, or by gathering particles, vacuum-cleaner fashion, from the bottom sediments. Common adaptations for filter feeding include mouth brushes, head fans, and sieve nets fashioned from silk secretions. Most collectors select their food on the basis of particle size rather than food quality, ingesting all manner of fine detritus.

The *scraper-grazer* group includes a diverse array of animals (including snails, caddisfly larvae of the genus *Glossosoma,* and clinging mayflies of the genera *Ephemerella* and *Rhithrogena*) that have mouthparts with rasplike teeth specialized for shearing off diatoms and other microalgae attached to rocks or other surfaces. Other adaptations, such as a streamlined, flattened body and the suckerlike gills of the mayfly *Ephemerella,* enable these organisms to withstand considerable current.

The *predator* group includes all animals (such as stonefly nymphs, water striders, water boatmen, and trout) adapted specifically for the capture of live prey. Though members of other groups may ingest live prey in the course of their feeding, true predators engulf their prey. Some rove from stone to stone, using their large eyes and, in the case of the stonefly nymph, their sensitive antennae to detect prey. Others, such as some dragonfly and damselfly nymphs, ambush their prey, responding to the stimulus of the prey touching an antenna or other receptor. Larger predators, particularly fish, are capable of rapid bursts of speed in pursuit of prey. Terrestrial predators, such as the dipper, kingfisher, and osprey, also exploit the abundant food resources found in streams and rivers.

Lotic Environments: Community Characteristics

Headwater Streams

Headwater streams, with the exception of those flowing through alpine meadows, are narrow and have steep gradients, alternating series of rapids and pools, high levels of dissolved oxygen, cold and relatively constant temperatures, reduced light levels, a paucity of vascular aquatic plants, and substrates that consist of rock rubble of various sizes. Mountain streams typically contain two different habitats: the turbulent riffle and the quiet pool. Riffles are characterized by the periodic growth of attached algae (*periphyton*) during favorable periods and by the algae's subsequent removal, or scouring, during high water. Anyone who has tried to cross from one slippery rock to another in a mountain stream has experienced algal bloom firsthand. Alternating with the riffles are the pools, where the current slows and organic materials settle out. In contrast to riffles, pools serve as sites of decomposition and free carbon dioxide production during summer and fall. This alternation of habitats acts like a conveyor belt, delivering dissolved gases, minerals, sand, silt, and organic materials to downstream reaches.

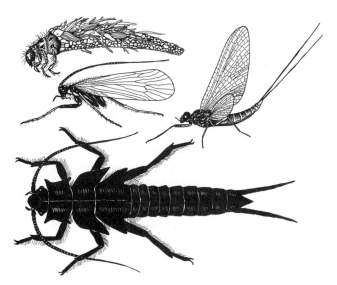

Common stream insects, clockwise from upper left: caddisfly (nymph in case), adult caddisfly, mayfly, stonefly nymph.

The majority of the stream's inhabitants live in the oxygen-rich environment of the riffles, on the undersides of rocks, or in gravel, where they are sheltered from the effects of the current. Characteristic riffle insects include the nymphs of mayflies, caddisflies, true flies, and stoneflies, which depend on flowing water to aid their respiration and to bring them food. Most riffle animals exhibit adaptations that protect them from the current's destructive power: hydrodynamically shaped bodies, suckers or holdfasts, grapple-like appendages, and protective cases constructed of fine gravel or organic debris. In the pools, the dominant insects are the burrowing mayfly nymphs, dragonflies and damselflies, and water striders. Some animals, such as trout, move between riffle and pool at will, selecting the first environment for food, the other for shelter. Researchers suggest that a good trout stream should be about evenly divided between riffles and pools.

Riparian vegetation plays an important role in headwater streams, supplying both shade and organic input. Streams above 10,000 feet are dominated by invertebrate collectors and scraper-grazers, mayflies being the most abundant.

Populations of insects of other orders fluctuate in response to local conditions, with stoneflies often more abundant than caddisflies as elevation increases. Insects belonging to the shredder or predator groups make up only about 20 percent of the fauna of the typical high-altitude stream.

With decreasing elevation, species richness increases dramatically, and shredders and predators assume greater importance. For example, a single riffle may provide habitat for at least six species of the caddisfly genus *Rhyacophila*. Since the major influx of organic matter occurs during autumn leaf drop, shredder life cycles, such as those of the stonefly *Nemoura*, are keyed to this food supply; eggs of most shredders are laid and hatch in the fall, and growth is completed by spring.

The phenomenon known as *invertebrate drift* is an integral part of headwater stream ecosystems and consists of bottom-living invertebrates washed downstream by the current. There are two main types of drift—voluntary and involuntary. In the former, the animal voluntarily lets go of the substrate and allows itself to be transported downstream, where it can colonize new sites. Voluntary drift may be triggered by a decline in flow, changes in current patterns, or high population densities. Invertebrate drift is exploited by predators, such as trout, which time their feeding to coincide with times of maximum drift—dawn and dusk.

Midreaches: Intermediate-sized Streams and Small Rivers

Downstream from the frothy, white cascades that distinguish the headwaters region, a noticeable shift in the character of aquatic communities occurs in response to changes in physical setting and to the coalescing of tributary waters. The most important of these changes include a progressive increase in channel width and depth, a reduction in stream gradient, a decrease in current rate, an increase in flow volume (highest during spring runoff), a reduction in terrestrially derived organic matter, an increase in the amount of in-stream primary production, an increase in solar input, and warmer but more variable water temperatures. Oxygen levels are typically lower than those found in headwater

streams. The streambed consists of boulder- to cobble-sized rubble, gravel, or silt, producing a mosaic of habitats for plant and animal life.

Streams and rivers in this size class, such as the Roaring Fork and Cache la Poudre rivers, exhibit higher species diversity than that found in either headwater or big-river habitats. With the decreasing velocity, warmer waters, and greater accumulation of bottom sediments, animals adapted to life in swift currents are found only in areas with riffles. Shredders are less abundant because of the decline in coarse particulate organic matter entering the stream from terrestrial sources. Collectors, however, are well represented because of the greater concentration of fine sediments produced by the coalescing of headwater streams. Scraper-grazers are also abundant because of the proliferation of attached algae and, to a lesser extent, vascular aquatic plants. Foraging predators such as trout and sculpin and bottom feeders such as minnows and suckers are common in most intermediate-sized streams.

Large Rivers

In their lower reaches, rivers such as the Rio Grande and the Colorado tend to be turbid with sediments gathered from coalescing tributaries. The riverbed is usually covered by mud and silt, except where rocks in the channel create turbulent flow. Primary production is generally low in large rivers, limited largely to planktonic organisms. Flow velocity is highest during spring runoff and declines markedly by fall. Depending on local geology, deep pools may alternate with stretches of rapids.

Biological diversity is significantly lower in large rivers than in upstream waters. Rubble-dwelling insect larvae are replaced by species adapted for burrowing in soft sediments. The prevalence of fine particulate organic matter supports large numbers of collectors specifically adapted to the warmer temperatures and lower dissolved oxygen levels of the river environment, as well as bottom-feeding fish such as the fathead minnow and the bluehead sucker. In the shallows along the banks and in backwater areas, river animals are similar to those found in ponds or lakes; water boatmen and diving beetles are common, and emergent plants provide microhabitats for animals such as snails and water mites. A scoop of mud reveals filter-feeding aquatic earthworms and leeches, and a variety of other organisms that thrive in low-oxygen habitats.

Lentic Ecosystems: Marsh, Pond, and Lake

Marshes, ponds, and lakes are scattered throughout the Southern Rockies. These bodies of water, nourished by streams, groundwater, or runoff, may be either natural or man-made, and most are found in well-defined depressions, in valleys where beavers are active, or behind man-made impoundments. Marshes develop in poorly drained areas and are characterized by a mosaic of emergent, submergent, and floating plant communities, interspersed with areas of open water. Natural lakes and ponds are most common in the glaciated portions of the higher mountains, where water collects in basins at the foot of melting snowfields or behind moraines deposited by retreating glaciers. Lakes and ponds are generally distinguished on the basis of size and depth; ponds tend to be considerably smaller and shallower than lakes and have waters that are relatively uniform in temperature.

Physical Features

LIGHT PENETRATION

The diversity, distribution, and abundance of life in lentic ecosystems is influenced by the penetration of light, seasonal and daily temperature regimes, oxygen levels, and nutrients. Solar radiation provides the primary energy source. In marshes and shallow ponds, light penetrates to the bottom. In deeper waters, light penetrates only to a certain depth, depending on the turbidity of the water. Most lakes can be divided horizontally into two layers on the basis of light penetration—the upper layer, known as the *trophogenic* zone, in which there is sufficient light for photosynthesis; and the lower layer, called the *tropholytic* zone, where light

THE SOUTHERN ROCKIES

penetration is so low that photosynthesis cannot occur and where decomposition is most active.

TEMPERATURE

Patterns of thermal stratification and circulation develop in bodies of water as a result of seasonal changes in temperature and strongly influence community structure. During the summer months, thermal stratification in shallow ponds or lakes is largely diurnal and of short duration, with only slight differences in temperature between the surface and the bottom. Deep-water lakes in the Southern Rockies, on the other hand, experience two thermal overturns, one in spring and one in fall. Thermal overturns are triggered by convection currents set in motion by density differences created by the heating and cooling of the water. These overturns are of critical importance in replenishing the oxygen supply available to organisms in the deepest waters and in mixing nutrients throughout the lake.

OXYGEN

Oxygen enters the aquatic environment by diffusion from the atmosphere and from the photosynthesis of aquatic plants. The oxygen content of pond or lake water is relatively low compared to that of flowing waters because only a small proportion of the water is in direct contact with the air. In general, the amount of oxygen in ponds and lakes is greatest near the surface and decreases sharply with depth, due in part to the respiration of aerobic bacteria and other microbes involved in decomposition. The decomposition of organic matter on the bottom of a pond or lake produces a black, oxygen-poor (anaerobic) mud that smells strongly of hydrogen sulfide. When large quantities of organic matter are decomposing, the oxygen in a pond or shallow lake may decline to such a low level that animals cannot survive.

Sunlight triggers high levels of photosynthetic activity in aquatic plants, especially algae, resulting in the production of significant quantities of oxygen. Oxygen levels are highest in the late afternoon and lowest just before sunrise. In a weed-filled pond on a sunny day, streams of bubbles can be seen rising to the surface when plants release oxygen as a by-product of photosynthesis. In deep water, except in lakes so clear that light penetration permits the growth of phytoplankton even at great depth, oxygen levels are lower than those found in shallow waters. Only during the spring and fall overturns, when oxygen is transferred downward and nutrients brought upward, is life abundant in the tropholytic zone.

Biological Features

Ecological zonation in aquatic ecosystems is correlated with photosynthetic activity. Moving out from the shoreline, the trophogenic zone can be divided into two subzones. The first of these is the *littoral* (shallow-water) zone, where light penetrates to the bottom and aquatic life is richest and most abundant. Beyond the littoral zone, which extends to the limit of rooted plant growth, lies the *limnetic* (open-water) zone. This zone is inhabited by plant and animal plankton, as well as by free-swimming organisms such as fish; the limnetic zone is typically absent from marshes and other shallow-water habitats. Beneath the limnetic zone, below the depth of effective light penetration, lies the *profundal* zone. The abundance and diversity of life in this zone is extremely limited due to reduced oxygen availability and cold temperatures. The bottom of the marsh, pond, or lake, extending from shore to shore, is called the *benthic* zone.

Adaptations for Living in Water

AQUATIC PLANTS

Aquatic plants, in contrast to terrestrial species, lack cuticles and absorb nutrients over their entire surfaces, directly from the surrounding water. Consequently, they have little need for elaborate root systems or for the well-developed conductive tissues found in most land plants. Water provides the supporting medium for the plant, reducing the need for the structural tissues necessary for life on land. Buoyancy is achieved by the presence of large, intercellular air spaces within the plant's tissues; these air spaces may link together to form a continuous passage for the circulation and storage of oxygen produced by photosynthesis. To avoid supersaturation, aquatic plants are often covered with a layer of mucilage.

AQUATIC ANIMALS

Aquatic organisms—whether they live on the water's flexible, tough surface, in the organic muck of the bottom, or in the liquid space in between—are faced with a variety of challenges. Like all animals, they require oxygen, obtaining it in one of two ways. The first method is to collect a supply of air at the surface, stay below until it is exhausted, then quickly resurface to replenish it. Animals that depend on scuba-style procurement include the diving beetles and water scavenger beetles, which carry large bubbles of air beneath their wing cases; the water boatmen, which trap layers of air within the fringes of hairs on their bodies; and the snails, which crawl along upside down beneath the surface film, taking air into the mantle chambers within their shells. The second method of obtaining oxygen involves anatomical adaptations that enable the animal to draw its oxygen directly from the surrounding water, either through the use of gas-exchanging gills, such as those found in many aquatic insect larvae (mayfly and stonefly nymphs, and dragonfly, damselfly, and caddisfly larvae, for example), or by diffusion over the entire, thin-walled body surface (as in aquatic earthworms, planaria, and leeches).

The way in which aquatic animals move about in water is linked to the way in which they obtain oxygen. Those that extract oxygen directly from the water are generally denser than water and move by crawling, either on the bottom or on submerged plants. Animals that collect air from the surface tend to be strong swimmers; most of these species are lighter than water and naturally bob to the surface like corks,

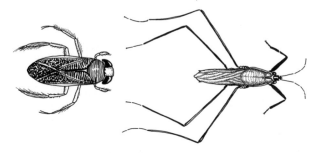

Common pond insects from left to right: water strider, water boatman.

unless they keep swimming or are able to cling to submerged plants. Animals that move about on the surface film of the water, such as the water strider, have water-repellent waxy hairs on their legs and claws that keep them from piercing the surface film.

Community Characteristics

LITTORAL ZONE

The littoral zone is found around the edges of most lakes and usually throughout marshes and ponds. Within this zone, aquatic life varies with water depth, and a distinct ecological zonation can be observed extending from the shoreline to the deeper waters of the limnetic zone. Closest to shore, in the shallowest water, are emergent and floating-leaf vegetation—plants whose roots and lower stems are immersed in water, but whose upper stems and leaves float on or project above the water. Many of these plants produce at least two different types of leaves: the submerged leaf, typically finely dissected; and the emergent leaf, conspicuously broader. Common emergent plants include water crowfoot, water smartweed (or bistort), marestail, pondweed, and yellow pondlily.

Submerged and free-floating aquatic plants are typical of the deeper waters of the littoral zone. Submerged plants are rooted in mud, and most species, such as water moss, water starwort, and water milfoil, have thin, finely dissected or ribbonlike leaves. Free-floating plants occur at or just below the water surface, where they can obtain the light necessary for photosynthesis, and include a great variety of microscopic species (such as green and blue-green algae and diatoms) as well as many higher plants. Some free-floating species, such as duckweed, have thin roots that dangle into the water but do not touch bottom, while others, such as great bladderwort, lack true roots but have evolved bladders on their leaves that serve as insect traps—providing energy through carnivory. Free-floating plants may be found over very deep water and can sometimes form extensive carpets across the surfaces of ponds or shallow lakes.

Many aquatic animals find food and shelter in the diverse microhabitats of the littoral zone. The shimmering surface film is exploited by a specially adapted group of organisms, the *neuston,* that includes the water strider and the marsh treader, as well as spiders and springtails. On the underside of this film, snails and planarian flatworms crawl along in search of algae and other minute plants on which to feed. Here and there, hydras hang upside down from the floating leaves of plants, capturing water fleas and other tiny crustaceans with their stinging tentacles. Beneath the floating-leaf canopy, swarms of single-celled protozoans, rotifers, water fleas, copepods, and fairy shrimp swim freely through the submerged vegetation. Releasing their hold on submerged plants, diving beetles and back swimmers dart swiftly after their tiny prey, rising to the surface occasionally to replenish their supply of air. The littoral bottom receives a constant rain of dead plants and animals from the waters above, supporting a great variety of decomposers and detritus feeders. Because of the abundance of life, the littoral zone serves as the principal hunting ground for both small and large predators — larval insects, fish, larval tiger salamanders, and frogs.

LIMNETIC ZONE

The limnetic zone is populated by minute, suspended plants and animals — phytoplankton and zooplankton. Phytoplankton, including the diatoms, desmids, and filamentous green algae, are the photosynthetic base on which the rest of limnetic life depends. Swimming and drifting with the phytoplankton are the zooplankton — rotifers, copepods, water fleas, and various protozoa. Most limnetic zooplankton are light-colored or translucent, while species found in littoral waters are darker in color, ranging from light yellowish brown to reddish brown, grayish, or almost black. Fish, such as trout, are common visitors to the limnetic zone, their distribution influenced mostly by food supply, oxygen levels, and temperature.

Most zooplankton are filter-feeders, sieving their food — bacteria, algae, detritus, and other smaller zooplankton — from the nutrient-rich soup that surrounds them. Some species, such as the rotifers, have a circlet of moving cilia, which beats to create a current that carries food particles toward the mouth and also serves to propel the animal through the water. When put into motion, the circlet of cilia resembles a turning wheel — thus the species' name, which comes from the Latin *rota,* meaning wheel. Water fleas, typically the most common crustacean found in ponds or lakes, create a constant current with their bristle-edged legs, filtering out food particles that are then directed forward through a ventral groove to the mouthparts. Another group of tiny crustaceans, the copepods, have mouthparts adapted either for seizing food (as in the *Cyclops* spp.), or for filtering; the hairs of the filter are so fine and close together that they can remove an individual bacterium.

The degree to which light is able to penetrate sets the lower limit at which phytoplankton can exist; the depth at which various species live is determined by the optimum conditions for their growth and development. Phytoplankton are more abundant during spring and summer, when nutrient levels, available light, and water temperatures are at maximal levels. Since zooplankton depend on phytoplankton for food, these animals often concentrate in surface waters and tend to be most numerous in productive waters where food is plentiful. In contrast to phytoplankton, which depend largely on the mixing action of currents to move them about, most zooplankton are capable of independent movement, exhibiting both diurnal and seasonal migrations to avoid predation and in response to changing conditions; it is believed that the primary stimulus for vertical migrations is the daily cycle of subsurface illumination.

Planktonic organisms have evolved a number of highly specialized adaptations that allow them to overwinter or to withstand adverse environmental conditions. Many small crustaceans, such as water fleas, produce two kinds of eggs — one type that develops quickly when the habitat is favorable, and another, a thick-shelled resting egg, that is laid in autumn and during times of environmental stress; the resting egg typically remains dormant, sometimes for several years, until favorable conditions return. Other animals, such as certain protozoa and the copepod *Cyclops*, form cysts or cocoons composed of secreted organic membrane and an enveloping mass of detritus. These adaptations tend to be multipurpose — the same device being used to overwinter or as an aestivation mechanism to avoid drying, low oxygen levels, high or low temperatures, or changes in water chemistry.

PROFUNDAL ZONE

The profundal zone lies below the depth of effective light penetration. Consequently, photosynthetic plants, except for

THE SOUTHERN ROCKIES

benthic algae and some bacteria, are absent. The animals found here—particularly fish, water fleas, and opossum shrimp—rely on the rain of organic materials from upper layers for food. Other zooplankton may occupy the profundal zone as part of their daily migrations. Only during the spring and fall overturns, when currents deliver oxygen and organisms from the surface to the deeper waters, is life abundant in this zone. Large, deep-water lakes tend to support more life in the profundal zone because the productivity of the limnetic zone is low in comparison to the volume of water, and decomposition in the benthic zone does not deplete the oxygen supply available for profundal animals.

BENTHIC ZONE

Layers of organic and inorganic sediments at the bottom of the lake or pond constitute the benthic zone. Here, detritus feeders eat the remains of plants and animals that have been decomposed by aquatic fungi and bacteria. In the shallow waters of marshes and most ponds, the littoral bottom extends from shore to shore and is inhabited by a diverse assemblage of aquatic insects—known collectively as *benthos*. In lakes and ponds with deeper waters, the benthic zone includes both the littoral bottom and the biologically impoverished profundal bottom. For the most part, the fauna of the profundal bottom is not unique to that zone but includes only those representatives of the larger littoral bottom fauna that can tolerate severe stagnation.

On the littoral bottom, benthic animals are most abundant in areas with emergent vegetation, which provides surfaces for attachment and cover from predators. Many organisms— species of blue-green algae, diatoms, freshwater sponges, and colonies of bryozoans—attach themselves to the submerged substrate, forming a crustlike growth on stones, logs, and other bottom materials. Burrowing into and living within this living crust are numerous associated animals—rotifers, hydras, copepods, insect larvae, and a wide variety of protozoans. Some benthic animals—scavengers such as water boatmen and predators such as damselfly nymphs, caddisflies, and various beetle larva—roam freely over the surface of the ooze, while others burrow into the organic-rich sediments. The burrowers include tiny clams, segmented worms, roundworms, flatworms, and a host of tiny crustaceans.

Succession

Most ponds, lakes, and marshes are temporary features on the landscape, undergoing changes through time that result in their eventual transformation into terrestrial ecosystems. The continual addition of mineral and organic matter gradually reduces water depth, allowing emergent plants to proliferate from shore to shore. With time, as the bottom rises above the groundwater level, the emergent plants are replaced by sedges, rushes, grasses, and, eventually, shrubs such as willow and bog birch or moisture-loving trees such as aspen.

Life Histories of Selected Animals

Insects

Mayflies, Order Ephemeroptera. The adult mayfly is easily identified by its delicate, gossamer wings and by the two or three long, segmented filaments that project from the end of its slender abdomen. A swarm, or "hatch," of these lovely insects is often observed fluttering over a mountain stream and attracts predators such as trout and fly-catching birds. Mating occurs in the air, and females deposit large numbers of eggs in the water; hatching occurs within a few days. Once hatched, mayflies spend the majority of their lives as dull-colored, aquatic nymphs (naiads) and are distinguished from other aquatic larvae by the paired tracheal gills along the abdomen segments and by the long, fringed caudal filaments at the tip of the abdomen. Nymphs are essentially herbivorous, feeding on plant detritus or algae. When ready to emerge, the nymph floats to the surface or crawls out of the water onto rocks or vegetation. The mayfly is unique among insects in that it has two winged stages in its life cycle. The first of these, called the subimago, sheds its nymphal skin, flies upward, and alights on vegetation. Within minutes or hours, the subimago sheds an exocuticle from its whole body, including the wings, and the adult mayfly is revealed in all its delicate beauty.

Caddisflies, Order Trichoptera. Caddisflies are closely related to butterflies and moths; the wings of the mothlike, terrestrial adult caddisfly are thickly covered with hairs that do not rub off, unlike the scales of a moth's wing. Caddisfly larvae and pupae are aquatic and may be found in both lotic and lentic ecosystems; the larval stage lasts nearly a year, the pupal stage only a few weeks, and the adult form thirty days or less. Caddisfly larvae somewhat resemble caterpillars, with tough, brown heads, soft, pale bodies, and long, thoracic legs. Most larvae are either case-building or net-spinning; a few species are free-living, building a case only when entering pupation. The case-building caddisfly constructs a portable or fixed tubelike case by attaching materials — sand grains, conifer needles, small stones, twigs, and plant fragments — to an inner silken lining spun by the larva; each case is built according to a species-specific pattern and provides excellent camouflage from predators. Net-spinning species, on the other hand, weave delicate, silken nets between stones in a stream, each net having a tunnel leading off to one side and ending in a shelter of stream debris; the larva lives in the shelter, crawling out occasionally to scrape off food particles intercepted by the net. Prior to pupation, larvae seal both ends of their cases, leaving only a small hole to allow entry of water and oxygen. When the pupa-adult is fully formed, it cuts an opening in the case, swims to the surface, and crawls out of the water onto a rock or log; as soon as it is capable of flight, the adult flies off to seek a mate.

Water Boatmen, Order Hemiptera. Water boatmen are distinguished from other aquatic bugs and beetles by their fringed, oarlike hind legs and their diminutive fore legs; they are usually less than half an inch in length and have conspicuously flattened and mottled bodies, large eyes, and mouthparts fused into their rounded heads. A surface breather, the water boatman envelops its body in a layer of air and stores air beneath its wings. Water boatmen swim — head first — in a quick, darting manner, propelled by oarlike movements of the hind legs; most species are also strong fliers and take off easily from the surface of the water. These insects are largely bottom feeders and are the only Hemiptera not wholly predaceous. During courtship, the males of most species produce shrill, chirping noises. Eggs are onion-shaped and attached to the stems of aquatic plants; there are five nymph stages in the life cycle.

Fairy Shrimp, Order Anostraca. Fairy shrimp, sometimes found in shallow ponds and lakes, are most common in temporary pools and in alkaline waters. These delicate, ethereal-looking animals lack the shieldlike, chitinous carapace of their larger relatives and vary in color from translucent whitish to blue, green, orange, or red. The fairy shrimp is remarkably graceful as it alternates between drifting and fast darts, swimming usually on its back, beating its many long, leaflike gill feet. This filter-feeder brings its food—bacteria, rotifers, fine detritus—forward to its mouth by the beating of its legs. Female fairy shrimp are usually more abundant than males; when males are present they are typically paired with females. Eggs, produced by parthenogenesis or by fertilization, are carried in a brood sac; two types of eggs are produced—thin-walled summer eggs and thick-walled winter eggs—and are released in clutches at intervals of two to six days, with 10 to 250 eggs per clutch. The thick-walled, resting eggs are able to withstand desiccation and winter cold.

Trout, Family Salmonidae, Genera *Salmo* and *Salvelinus*. Trout are distinguished from other freshwater fish by their tiny scales (more than one hundred scales in each lateral line), an adipose (fatty) dorsal fin, and well-developed teeth. Color patterns vary, not only with species, but also with habitat, size, and, during the breeding season, sex. All trout, when young, have a series of dark blotches along their sides that disappear with age. Young trout feed largely upon insects and other small invertebrates; as they increase in size, trout may feed on larger organisms and on other fish. Some trout spawn in spring and early summer and others in the fall and winter. All species deposit their eggs in gravel, usually near the head of a riffle; the female prepares the cavity for the eggs while the male defends the territory from other fish until the eggs hatch several weeks later.

Cutthroat Trout, *Salmo clarki*. In general, cutthroat trout (native and nonnative races) are distinguished by the reddish or orange streaks in the folds beneath the lower jaw and by the prominent but sparse pattern of black spots dispersed over the upper body; males in breeding colors may have blood red or orange lower sides. Cutthroats spawn in spring or early summer. Though nonnative cutthroat are common as a result of introductions, pure populations of Colorado cutthroat are largely restricted to northwestern Colorado and southwestern Wyoming; extremely small populations of greenback cutthroat are found in western Boulder and Larimer counties, and transplant populations inhabit certain streams in Rocky Mountain National Park.

Brook Trout, *Salvelinus fontinalis.* This beautiful trout is a native of eastern North America and the only species lacking black spots; back and sides are patterned with light spots (reddish or yellowish) and wavy lines on a dark background. Brook trout are found only in small, cold headwater streams and cold lakes. Spawning occurs in fall.

Brown Trout, *Salmo trutta.* This trout is a native of Europe and is distinguished by the blackish spots (few or none on the tail fin) and small orange or reddish spots that speckle its greenish brown or olive body; the adipose fin is tipped with orange. Spawning occurs in fall.

Rainbow Trout, *Salmo gairdneri.* This trout has been introduced from the West Coast and differs from the cutthroat in that it has a shorter upper jaw; there is usually a diffuse band of rosy scales along the sides and a greater number of black spots. Rainbows spawn in spring.

Common Plants of Aquatic Ecosystems

Bladderwort, great, *Utricularia vulgaris*
　　small, *Utricularia minor*
Bulrush, *Scirpus pallidus* and *S. microcarpus*
Bur-reed, *Sparganium* spp.
Buttercup, birdfoot, *Ranunculus pedatifidus*
　　floating, *Ranunculus hyperboreus* ssp. *intertextus*
　　heart-leaved, *Ranunculus cardiophyllus*
Cattails, *Typha* spp.
Coltsfoot, sweet, *Petasites sagittata*
Crowfoot, small-flowered, *Ranunculus abortivus* ssp.
　　　acrolasius
　　water (white-flowered), *Batrachium trichophyllum*
　　　(formerly *Ranunculus*)
　　yellow-flowered, *Ranunculus gmelinii* var. *hookeri*

Duckweed, *Lemna* spp.
Manna-grass, *Glyceria* spp.
Marestail, *Hippuris vulgaris*
Milfoil, water, *Myriophyllum sibiricum*
Pondlily, yellow, *Nuphar luteum*
Pondweed, *Potamogeton* spp.
Quillwort, *Isoetes bolanderi*
Rushes, *Juncus* spp.
Sedges, *Carex* spp.
Smartweed (or water bistort), *Persicaria amphibia*
  scarlet, *Persicaria coccinea*
Spearwort, *Ranunculus reptans*
Spikerush, *Eleocharis* spp.
Starwort, water, *Callitriche* spp.
Trefoil, marsh, *Menyanthes trifoliata*
Tule, or bulrush, *Schoenoplectus lacustris* ssp. *acutus*
  (formerly *Scirpus acutus*)
Water Moss, *Fontinalis* spp.

Common Animals of Aquatic Ecosystems

Fish

Cutthroat Trout, *Salmo clarki*
Greenback Cutthroat, *Salmo clarki stomias*
Brown Trout, *Salmo trutta*
Rainbow Trout, *Salmo gairdneri*
Brook Trout, *Salvelinus fontinalis*
Brook Stickleback, *Culaea inconstans*
Longnose Dace, *Rhinichthys cataractae*
Speckled Dace, *Rhinichthys osculus*
Colorado Squawfish, *Ptychocheilus lucius*
Roundtail Chub, *Gila robusta*
Rio Grande Chub, *Gila pandora*
Fathead Minnow, *Pimephales promelas*
Red Shiner, *Notropis lutrensis*
Bluehead Sucker, *Catostomus discobolus*
White Sucker, *Catostomus commersoni*

        THE SOUTHERN ROCKIES

Flannelmouth Sucker, *Catostomus latipinnis*
Longnose Sucker, *Catostomus catostomus*
Mottled Sculpin, *Cottus bairdi*

Invertebrates

Caddisfly, (Order Trichoptera)
Mayfly, (Order Ephemeroptera)
Stonefly, (Order Plecoptera)
Dragonfly, (Order Anisoptera)
Damselfly, (Order Zygoptera)
Marsh Treader, (Order Hemiptera, Family
    Hydrometridae)
Water Strider, (Order Hemiptera, Family Gerridae)
Back Swimmer, (Order Hemiptera, Family
    Notonectidae)
Water Boatmen, (Order Hemiptera, Family Corixidae)
Dobson Fly, (Order Megaloptera)
Whirligig Beetle, (Order Coleoptera, Family Gyrinidae)
Water Scavenger Beetle, (Order Coleoptera, Family
    Hydrophilidae)
Riffle Beetle, (Order Coleoptera, Family Psephenidae)
Crane Fly, (Order Diptera, Family Tipulidae)
Mosquitoes, (Order Diptera, Family Culicidae)
Snails, (Gastropoda)
Clams, (Order Pelecypoda, Family Sphaeriidae)
Water Fleas, (Order Cladocera, *Daphnia* spp.)
Copepods, (Order Cyclopoida, *Cyclops* spp.)
Opossum Shrimp, (*Mysis* spp.)
Fairy Shrimp, (Order Anostraca)
Leeches, (Order Hirudinea)
Aquatic Earthworms, (Order Oligochaeta)
Rotifers, (Order Ploima)
Flatworm (or Planaria), (Order Tricladida, Family
    Planariidae)
Fresh Water Sponge, (Family Spongillidae)

CHAPTER NINETEEN

Aspen Forests

FROM THEIR FIRST greening in spring to the golden crescendo that symbolizes autumn in the Rockies, aspen forests occupy a special place in the hearts of most westerners. In a landscape dominated by the somber hues of conifers, the ivory trunks and apple green leaves of the aspen brighten the majestic monotony of the forest palette. In summer, with their hip-high profusion of wildflowers and rich assortment of cavity-nesting birds, aspen forests have an almost tropical quality. With September's arrival, the green of summer dissolves in a blaze of golden light. The soft rustling of the leaves and the sweet, tannin-rich aroma of aspen dust fills the air. Even in winter, the branches swaying in unison to the wind and the black knots that pattern the trunks like

Aspen forest near Kebler Pass, Colorado. *Audrey D. Benedict.*

so many eyes give the forest a curiously animate and welcoming quality.

Ecological Distribution

Aspen is the most widely distributed native tree species in North America, occurring from the Brooks Range of Alaska south to the Mexican state of Querétaro, and from the shores of the Atlantic west to the Pacific. In the Southern Rockies, aspen is found in relatively moist environments from the foothills through the subalpine zone on both sides of the Continental Divide. Though the most extensive aspen forests are found on the Western Slope, the species also occurs in small groves, along riparian corridors, in transitional belts between coniferous forests and open meadows or shrublands, and as scattered individuals in coniferous forests.

Aspen is one of the few plant species that can grow in all mountain vegetation zones except the alpine tundra. It reaches its lower limits in foothill ravines, where cooler temperatures prevail and channelized seepage from higher elevations provides sufficient moisture. From north to south along the mountains, aspen is generally found at progressively higher elevations. In southern Wyoming, the upper limit of aspen occurs at about 10,000 feet. In the mountains of north-central Colorado, krummholz stands of spruce and fir in the timberline ecotone occasionally include dwarfed, gnarled aspen. In the San Juan Mountains of southwestern Colorado, aspen forms extensive forests between 8,500 and 10,500 feet. At the southern end of the Southern Rockies, in the Sangre de Cristos and the Jemez Mountains, aspen forests can be found between 7,500 and 11,500 feet, with aspen taking the place of lodgepole pine as the dominant successional tree species on many middle-elevation slopes.

Physical Environment

The broad altitudinal and ecological range of aspen is evidence of a species that can adapt to wide variations in cli-

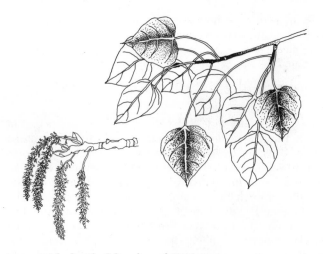

Aspen, with detail of female catkin.

mate. Aspen can tolerate relatively cold temperatures and late-lying snow, but cannot withstand high temperatures or prolonged moisture deprivation. Sites that support major stands of aspen receive more than 25 inches of precipitation annually, experience moderately cold and snowy winters and warm summers, and have reasonably long growing seasons. Large-scale air movements and precipitation patterns in the Southern Rockies tend to maximize precipitation on windward slopes, creating optimal growing conditions for aspen in many areas of the Western Slope. Spring temperatures (from April to June), especially critical because of their influence on the beginning of annual growth and the length of the growing season, increase from north to south along the Southern Rockies. The longer growing season and the additional precipitation associated with the Arizona summer monsoon provide the most likely explanation for the more majestic proportions of aspen in the San Juan and Jemez mountains.

Aspen is a fragile species, especially susceptible to windthrow and damage from snow. Snow damage to aspen saplings is a common phenomenon on mountain slopes with deep snowpacks. As the snowpack builds over the course of the winter, it tends to deform downhill, bending the bases of young aspen in the downslope direction and producing the pistol-butted lower trunks so often exhibited by aspen in deep-snow areas. Avalanching on steep, aspen-covered slopes is common at higher elevations in many ranges, periodically scouring the larger trees from active avalanche chutes and encouraging the development of thickets of even-aged saplings.

Community Characteristics

Aspen forests are highly variable, the composition and character of each community determined by differences in local environmental conditions (such as soil moisture), the age structure of the forest, stand history, tree density within the stand, adjacent vegetation types, and composition of the understory. In many ways, the diversity of these communities results from the occurrence of aspen in successional communities as well as in stable, self-perpetuating stands. Aspen is an aggressive pioneer species, invading sites where the preexisting vegetation has been destroyed by fire or other disturbance. In the Southern Rockies, the majority of aspen-dominated forests are successional (seral) to other types of vegetation. Stable aspen communities, though considerably less common than seral stands, occur in areas where soil conditions are favorable to aspen and where the dense understory discourages invasion by coniferous species.

All aspen forests can be described as multilayered, but the number of layers and the composition of the understory vegetation vary greatly from one stand to another. Under optimal soil and moisture conditions, aspen are often tall and robust, and the understory is a lush tangle of shrubs and herbaceous vegetation. On sites with less than optimal growing conditions—limited moisture, poor soils, or strong winds— aspen stands are characterized by smaller and occasionally stunted trees, and by a less luxuriant understory. In an aspen community with a long history of use as livestock range, the understory is represented by fewer species and by the competitive dominance of the least palatable species.

Seral Communities

Seral communities are best identified by the active replacement of the aspen overstory by coniferous trees. The presence of an uneven-aged coniferous understory is considered a strong indicator of seral status. In a successional aspen community, the tree canopy is usually dominated by aspen for as long as 150 years, or until the slower-growing conifers are able to overtop the aspen. Once the conifers penetrate the aspen canopy, the reduction in light reaching the forest floor limits aspen regeneration because of the species' intolerance to shade and results in a gradual decline in the abundance and vigor of the understory.

In most cases, the aspen overstory in seral communities tends to be single-aged because of the rapidity and uniformity with which aspen regenerates a disturbed stand or expands local populations through vegetative reproduction. Some stands may have domelike appearances, with the oldest trees in the center of the stand and progressively younger and shorter trees occupying the outer, expanding edge. Two-storied stands consisting of trees representing two age classes are often found in areas where grazing, either by wild or domestic animals, has been reduced or eliminated after a long period of overuse.

In most seral communities, conifers such as Engelmann spruce, Colorado blue spruce, subalpine fir, white fir, lodgepole pine, ponderosa pine, and Douglas-fir make up an increasing proportion of the canopy as succession progresses. On certain sites, lodgepole pine, another aggressive colonizer, may share dominance. Where seral communities are being replaced by grass- or shrublands, an absence of young trees indicates a gradual deterioration of aspen clones resulting from suckering suppression or from heavy browsing by wildlife or livestock. Some seral communities occupy an ecotonal position, incorporating understory species that reflect the composition of the adjacent community as well as those more typical of the aspen type.

The understory in most seral communities is luxuriant when compared with the understories of associated coniferous forests. At the dry end of the moisture gradient, the aspen understory is dominated by an herbaceous layer consisting mostly of grasses, with a scattering of wildflowers and medium-sized shrubs. Grasses typical of such communities include purple onion-grass, Thurber fescue, slender wheatgrass, native blue-grass, and blue wild-rye. Dryland sedges such as Geyer's sedge may be common in some communities, and the assortment of wildflowers includes white geranium, northern bedstraw, common harebell, mountain parsley, and yarrow. The shrub layer, where present, consists of widely-spaced, medium-sized shrubs such as common juniper and shrubby cinquefoil. With increasing moisture, wildflowers become more conspicuous and may include meadowrue, golden banner, arnica, mariposa lily, lupine, paintbrush, orange sneezeweed, showy daisy, lovage, and

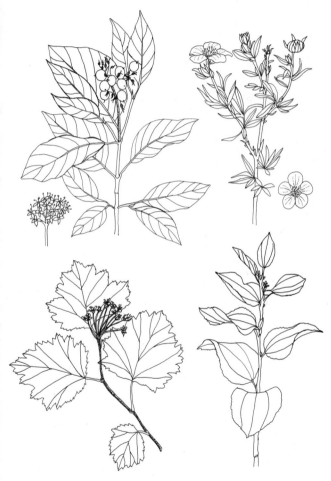

Common shrubs of aspen forests, clockwise from upper left: red-osier dogwood with detail of flowers, shrubby cinquefoil, with flower detail, sticky-laurel, ninebark.

Colorado columbine. Common shrubs in such stands include snowberry and wild rose.

Stable Communities

Forest biologists are only beginning to understand the environmental conditions that encourage the establishment and maintenance of stable or long-lived aspen forests. Stable communities, in contrast to seral stands, may persist for several centuries and exhibit three main characteristics: an uneven-aged structure of the aspen overstory, lack of evidence for successional change in the understory, and an absence of tree species more shade-tolerant than aspen. In the Southern Rockies, stable aspen communities are most common at midelevations and on southerly exposures. Whether or not these communities represent a true climax forest remains uncertain.

Stable forests are generally characterized by a multilayered shrub and herbaceous understory, although in some, the shrub layer may be nonexistent. Scattered conifers may be present, but there is no evidence of conifer reproduction. In certain stands, especially those on south-facing slopes and at lower elevations, tall shrubs form a distinctive layer from 6 to 12 feet in height. Species typical of this layer include serviceberry, ninebark, and chokecherry. A layer consisting of medium-sized shrubs, such as snowberry, red-osier dogwood, thimbleberry, common gooseberry, sticky-laurel, and bush honeysuckle may also be present or may take the place of the tall shrub layer in some stands.

A two-tiered herbaceous layer is common in many stands. The tall herb layer consists of a wide variety of species, including monkshood, cow parsnip, false hellebore, black coneflower, lovage, lousewort, orange sneezeweed, aspen sunflower, and bracken fern. In addition to or instead of the tall herb layer, species such as meadowrue, fleabane daisy, wild geranium, Canada violet, bedstraw, aster, and golden banner may form a continuous carpet of wildflowers across the forest floor. Several vining plants, such as white-flowered peavine and American vetch, use the lush undergrowth as a trellis.

Plant Adaptation: Designs for Survival

Environmental conditions favorable for the germination of aspen seeds and for seedling survival are common in eastern North America, but are exceedingly rare in the West. How, then, has aspen been able to spread into so many habitats? Obviously, at one time, suitable growth conditions must have been more widespread, allowing aspen to increase its distribution. Though reproduction from seed is important in initial establishment, the regeneration or expansion of existing stands is achieved by *clonal growth,* a type of vegetative reproduction to which aspen is superbly adapted. In the case of aspen, the *clone* is defined as a group of genetically related individuals, known as *ramets,* which arise vegetatively from a single "parent" seedling, or *ortet.* During its first year, the ortet produces a multibranching, lateral root system. In subsequent years, especially after a fire or other competition-reducing disturbance, ramets arise from buds along the ortet's root system. Newly formed ramets depend on the parent root for nutrients and water, with the degree of dependency diminishing gradually as the ramet develops its own root system.

The typical aspen forest may consist of a single clone or a mosaic of clones. The boundary between two adjoining clones is often abrupt; distinguishing individual clones within a stand is especially easy in the fall, when the genetically controlled timing of color change and leaf fall within a clone sets it apart from other clones in the stand. The following list of characteristics is useful in distinguishing individual clones within a stand: (1) sex — all trees within a clone are either female or male; (2) timing of flowering and leaf development in spring; (3) leaf color, onset of color change, and leaf drop in fall; (4) shape and size of leaves; (5) leaf serration; and (6) pubescence of dormant buds.

In an undisturbed aspen stand, suckering is somewhat suppressed, but after a stand is burned or cut or when aspen are colonizing an open site, prolific suckering may yield thousands of new trees per acre. Through expansion of the ramet root system and additional suckering, the clone may proliferate over time to cover 100 acres or more. The abundance of light along the leading edge of the expanding clone enhances the survival and proliferation of new ramets, often resulting in the development of a somewhat symmetrical "island" of aspen.

The ability of aspen to regenerate or expand a preexisting stand by clonal growth clearly gives this tree its competitive advantage over many other western tree species. Reliance on the parent rootstock permits rapid initial growth and provides superb insurance against drought during the critical seedling stage. Because of the durability of the rootstocks, the species is able to maintain a suppressed but viable population through long periods of time, even hundreds of years; these persistent rootstocks survive low temperatures, surface fires, and many other types of environmental disturbances, enabling aspen to recolonize a newly disturbed site through the stimulation or reinitiation of vegetative propagation.

The high organic-matter and nutrient content of the soils associated with most aspen communities contrasts markedly with that beneath coniferous forests. Though aspen are capable of growing on a wide variety of soils, their very presence in a community greatly improves the quality of the soil. Because aspen leaves and herbaceous plant material decay more rapidly than conifer needles, the return of nutrients to the soil in an aspen community is relatively quick. More important, however, aspen serves as an efficient nutrient pump, enriching the surface soil layers by withdrawing large quantities of available nutrients from the entire rooting depth and incorporating those nutrients into the upper soil layers.

Avoidance of environmental stress is critical to the survival of aspen. During times of moisture stress, water storage in the aspen's woody tissues — trunks, boles, and branches — provides a reserve supply from which transpiring leaves can draw, an alternative to relying solely on translocation from the roots. Water content of the aspen's trunk and branches is consistently higher during dormancy than when the tree is leafed out; during prolonged drought, aspen trunks shrink in diameter as their water reserves are tapped. The presence of chloroplasts in aspen bark enables the stems, unlike the stems or trunks of most tree species, to carry on photosynthesis. Under conditions of high insolation, the contribution made by bark photosynthesis, while not at net photosynthetic levels, may sufficiently meet the tree's respiratory requirements when leaf photosynthate production is severely reduced as a result of a late spring freeze or insect defoliation.

Descriptions of Common Plants

Trees and Shrubs

Quaking Aspen, *Populus tremuloides.* This medium-sized deciduous tree is distinguished from other members of the willow family by its smooth, pale greenish to ivory-colored bark, ovate and finely serrated leaves, flattened petioles (leaf stalks), and conical buds. Each petiole acts as a pivot for the leaf blade, causing it to flutter in the slightest breeze, giving the entire tree the appearance of trembling — hence the common names "quaking aspen" and "quakies." Male and female flowers appear on separate trees in early spring (April or May), just prior to the leaves. Though seed production may be prolific, successful reproduction is largely by vegetative propagation. The best fall color occurs during autumns characterized by crisp, sunny days, cool nights, and an absence of hard frost.

Red-osier Dogwood, *Swida sericea.* This lovely shrub is common in aspen groves and in mountain riparian communities from the foothills to the subalpine zone. Red-osier dogwood is easily identified by the bright red of its slender branches, and by its opposite, lanceolate leaves, flat-topped clusters of white flowers, and white, berrylike fruits. The flowers consist of four small sepals, four white petals, and four stamens perched atop an ovary (pistil).

Ninebark, *Physocarpus monogynus.* This medium-sized shrub is common in aspen stands and occasionally on dry, rocky hillsides from the foothills to the subalpine zone. A member of the rose family, ninebark is distinguished by its three- to five-lobed, toothed, simple leaves, white to pale rose flowers arranged in an umbrella-like head, and the distinctive peeling and shedding of its outer bark. Each flower has five rounded petals borne on the edge of a small cup. The fruit is an inflated capsule, which splits open at the tip during dry weather to release the seeds but closes during wet weather.

Shrubby Cinquefoil, *Pentaphylloides floribunda.* This common small shrub, a member of the rose family, is found in open aspen and pine forests and mountain meadows, from the montane to the subalpine zone. Shrubby cinquefoil (sometimes called potentilla) is identified by its compound leaves, golden yellow flowers, and shreddy brown bark. The leaves are green on top, their undersides muted by the presence of gray, silky hairs. The roselike flowers have five petals borne on the edge of a shallow cup and are arranged individually along the branches. Flowering begins in June and may continue throughout the summer.

Sticky-laurel, *Ceanothus velutinus.* This medium-sized shrub, a member of the buckthorn family, is found in open forests and in clearings from the foothills to the subalpine zone; the species is especially common on slopes that have been burnt over or otherwise disturbed. Sticky-laurel, also known as snowbrush, is identified by its balsam-scented, oval, evergreen leaves, and by the dense clusters of small white flowers that appear near the ends of its branches in early summer. During dry or cold weather, the edges of the leathery, sticky-surfaced leaves roll under. The roots are dotted with nodules that contain symbiotic, nitrogen-fixing bacteria.

Wildflowers

Mariposa (or Sego) Lily, *Calochortus gunnisonii.* This lovely member of the lily family is found in open aspen woodlands and in mountain meadows from the foothills to the lower alpine tundra. The flower is identified by its tuliplike appearance, white or pale lavender color, yellow petal hairs, and distinctive purple-bearded zone on the inner petals. The leaves are strap-shaped and parallel-veined.

Common Harebell, *Campanula rotundifolia.* This member of the bellflower family is common in open aspen woodlands and mountain meadows, from the foothills to the lower alpine tundra. As its name suggests, the common harebell is distinguished by its blue-violet, bell-shaped flowers, which hang from multiple stems. The stems are extremely slender, with narrow lanceolate leaves.

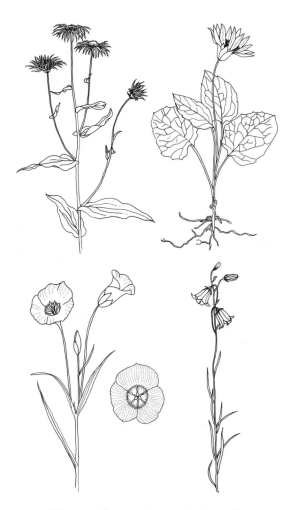

Common wildflowers of aspen forests, clockwise from upper left: showy daisy, heartleaf arnica, common harebell, mariposa lily.

Fendler Meadowrue, *Thalictrum fendleri.* This delicate wildflower, a member of the buttercup family, is abundant in shaded ravines and aspen forests from the montane to the subalpine zone. Meadowrue is identified by its greenish, nodding flowers and by its small, three-lobed leaves, which resemble diminutive columbine leaves. The somewhat inconspicuous flowers of the meadowrue have minute green sepals but no petals. Male and female flowers are borne on separate plants; the male flower is distinguished by the tassel-like appearance of the numerous pointed stamens and the female flower by the several curved ovaries clustered on the receptacle.

Heartleaf Arnica, *Arnica cordifolia.* This showy member of the sunflower family is common in relatively dry aspen and coniferous forests from the foothills to the subalpine zone. Heartleaf arnica is identified by its heart-shaped, opposite leaves, and by its large (2- to 2.5-inch), yellow, sunflower-like flower heads.

Showy Daisy, *Erigeron speciosus.* This member of the sunflower family is conspicuous in moist aspen forests and in meadow-edge habitats, from the foothills to the subalpine zone. Showy daisy, with its lavender ray flowers and yellow disk flowers, is distinguished from other superficially similar species by its mostly hairless, narrowly lanceolate leaves, multiple narrow ray flowers, and two even rows of green bracts that make up the cup that subtends the ray and disk flowers; the flowering stems are little branched, and the flower heads appear singularly at the terminus of each flowering stem.

Black Coneflower, *Rudbeckia occidentalis* var. *montana.* This tall, somewhat unusual member of the sunflower family is found in open aspen forests and moist meadows, from the montane through the subalpine zone. Black coneflower is easily identified by its size (up to 3 feet in height) and by its elongated, conical flower heads. The flower heads of this species are distinctive, consisting solely of disk flowers, and are a dark brownish purple.

Common Wild Geranium, *Geranium caespitosum.* This member of the geranium family is abundant in aspen forests and mountain meadows from the foothills to the subalpine zone. Common wild geranium is identified by its five-petaled, pinkish lavender flowers, multibranched flowering stems, and palmately compound, lobed leaves; a similar species, the white geranium *(G. richardsonii),* has white, somewhat paired flowers and fewer flowering stems. The stems and leaves have a glandular pubescence that makes them sticky to the touch.

Porter Lovage, *Ligusticum porteri.* This moderately tall member of the carrot family is abundant in aspen forests and moist mountain meadows from the foothills to the montane zone. Lovage is easily identified by its fernlike leaves, white flower clusters borne in compound umbels, and carrotlike aroma of its crumbled leaves.

Grays Lousewort, *Pedicularis grayi.* This tall member of the figwort family is common in moist forests from the montane to the subalpine. Grays lousewort is distinguished by its size (up to 3 feet in height), fernlike leaves, and terminal spike of yellow flowers. The flowers are yellowish and streaked with red; the petals of each are fused to form two lips, the upper lip forming an arched, pointed hood (the galea) and the lower lip two-lobed. A similar species, fernleaf lousewort *(P. bracteosa),* has yellow flowers without red streaking.

Common Plants of the Aspen Forests

Trees

Aspen, quaking, *Populus tremuloides*
Fir, subalpine, *Abies lasiocarpa*
Oak, Gambel, *Quercus gambelii*
Pine, lodgepole, *Pinus contorta*
Spruce, Engelmann, *Picea engelmannii*

Shrubs

Blueberry, *Vaccinium* spp.
Chokecherry, *Padus virginiana* ssp. *melanocarpa*
Cinquefoil, shrubby, *Pentaphylloides floribunda*
Dogwood, red-osier, *Swida sericea* (formerly *Cornus stolonifera*)
Gooseberry, common, *Ribes inerme*
Juniper, common, *Juniperus communis*
Kinnikinnik, *Arctostaphylos uva-ursi*
Maple, Rocky Mountain, *Acer glabrum*
Mountain-lover, *Paxistima myrsinites*
Ninebark, *Physocarpus monogynus*

Raspberry, red, *Rubus melanolasius*
Rose, wild, *Rosa woodsii*
Sagebrush, big, *Seriphidium tridentatum*
Serviceberry, western, *Amelanchier alnifolia*
Snowberry, *Symphoricarpos rotundifolius*
Sticky-laurel, *Ceanothus velutinus*
Thimbleberry, *Rubacer parviflorus*
Twinberry (or bush honeysuckle), *Distegia involucrata*

Grasses and Sedges

Bluegrass, *Poa* spp.
Fescue, Thurber, *Festuca thurberi*
Junegrass, *Koeleria macrantha*
Onion-grass, purple, *Bromelica spectabilis*
Sedge, Geyer's (or elk), *Carex geyeri*
Timothy, *Phleum pratense*
Wheatgrass, slender, *Agropyron trachycaulum*
Wild-rye, blue, *Elymus glaucus*

Wildflowers

Arnica, heartleaf, *Arnica cordifolia*
Balsamroot, *Balsamorhiza saggittata*
Bedstraw, *Galium* spp.
Black-eyed Susan, *Rudbeckia hirta*
Chimingbells, *Mertensia brevistyla* and M. *fusiforma*
Cicely, sweet, *Osmorhiza* spp.
Cinquefoil, *Potentilla* spp.
Columbine, Colorado, *Aquilegia coerulea*
Coneflower, black, *Rudbeckia occidentalis*
Cow Parsnip, *Heracleum sphondylium*
Daisy, showy, *Erigeron speciosus*
Dandelion, common, *Taraxacum officinale*
Fireweed, *Chamerion angustifolium*
Fritillary, purple, *Fritillaria atropurpurea*
Golden Banner, *Thermopsis montana*
Harebell, common, *Campanula rotundifolia*
  Parry's, *Campanula parryi*
Hellebore, false, *Veratrum tenuipetalum*

Geranium, wild, *Geranium* spp.
Larkspur, *Delphinium* spp.
Lily, avalanche, *Erythronium grandiflorum*
   mariposa (or sego), *Calochortus gunnisonii*
   wood, *Lilium philadelphicum*
Lousewort, Grays, *Pedicularis grayi* and *P. bracteosa*
Lovage, Porter's, *Ligusticum porteri*
Lupine, *Lupinus* spp.
Meadowrue, Fendler, *Thalictrum fendleri*
Monkshood, *Aconitum columbianum*
Mule's Ears, *Wyethia amplexicaulis*
Paintbrush, *Castilleja* spp.
Parsley, mountain, *Pseudocymopterus montanus*
Peavine, white-flowered, *Lathyrus leucanthus*
Pussytoes, *Antennaria* spp.
Pyrola, green-flowered, *Pyrola chlorantha*
Sage, prairie, *Artemisia ludoviciana*
Sneezeweed, orange, *Dugaldia hoopsii*
Strawberry, wild, *Fragaria* spp.
Sunflower, aspen, *Helianthella quinquenervis*
Valerian, *Valeriana* spp.
Vetch, American, *Vicia* spp.
Violet, Canada, *Viola rydbergii*
Windflower, *Anemone multifida*
Yarrow, *Achillea lanulosa*

Environment and Adaptation: Animals of the Aspen Forests

Aspen forests of the Southern Rockies, because of their broad elevational range and variable composition, provide critical habitat for a rich assortment of resident and nonresident animal species. Similarities between aspen forests and mountain riparian communities are sometimes striking, both in terms of the species found in each and in the range of food resources and habitats available. Not surprisingly, faunal diversity is greater in moist, mature aspen stands than in dry, sparsely stocked forests or in dense, brushy stands of young trees.

Resource Partitioning

Within the aspen community, resource partitioning enables each species to appropriate suitable niche space and to avoid competition with other species. The differential use of space is best illustrated by the high breeding-bird diversity and density associated with many aspen ecosystems. Birds, in contrast to ground-dwelling animals, are able to partition the aspen forest habitat by selecting different vertical strata—ground, shrub understory, tree trunk, or the high canopy—in which to concentrate their foraging and/or nesting activities. Diet and foraging style and location permit the general grouping of aspen forest birds into a series of *feeding guilds:* (1) ground, or low-level, foragers—which eat seeds, fruit, or nectar; (2) ground foragers—which feed on insects; (3) shrub or tree foliage gleaners—which feed on insects; (4) fly catching or on-the-wing foragers—which eat insects; (5) wood borers—which feed on sap and/or insects; and (6) predators—which eat small- to medium-sized mammals and birds.

To the casual observer, the ways in which resources are partitioned may seem somewhat subtle. For example, both Hammond's and western flycatchers breed and forage for insects in aspen forests, avoiding competitive interaction wherever the two species coexist by vertical separation of foraging niches and by taxonomic differences in the composition of their respective diets. The Hammond's consistently forages at higher levels in the forest than does the western flycatcher, exhibiting a distinct dietary preference for beetles rather than for the moths and butterflies preferred by the western flycatcher.

A more obvious example of niche partitioning can be seen in the diurnal-nocturnal hunting patterns and prey preferences of the owls and hawks that use the aspen forests. Six species of owls, ranging in size from the diminutive flammulated owl to the great horned owl, are known to occur in this forest type—in itself a testimony to the ecosystem's biological richness. Among the small, cavity-nesting owls, competition is limited primarily by foraging time and diet. For example, the northern saw-whet owl is a nocturnal predator of small mammals and roosting birds, whereas the flammulated owl is a nocturnal predator of insects, chiefly moths.

The northern pygmy owl, on the other hand, is a diurnal hunter, preying upon small mammals and birds.

Cavity Nesters

Aspen is highly susceptible to fungal diseases that weaken and decay its heartwood, resulting in the development of natural cavities and inviting the excavation of nesting holes by woodpeckers, flickers, and sapsuckers. In fact, cavity-nesting birds make up a large proportion of the breeding-bird species in mature aspen communities. Those species that excavate their own holes, the so-called *primary cavity nesters,* typically abandon their holes after a single season, making them available as nesting habitat for a still larger group of birds, the *secondary cavity nesters,* which includes the flammulated owl, northern saw-whet owl, northern pygmy owl, tree and violet-green swallows, house wren, brown creeper, mountain bluebird, pygmy nuthatch, and mountain chickadee. Cavities are almost always at a premium as a result of natural attrition due to windfall and other causes. Consequently, it is common for a tree with several good cavities to provide "condominium" housing for two or three different species. The sharp decline in cavity-trees that is occurring throughout the West as a result of fuel-wood cutting, residential and resort development, and intensification of logging cannot fail to have a serious impact on cavity-dependent species.

The Herbivore's Larder

Aspen forests provide excellent habitat for a varied group of herbivorous mammals. The smallest of these — mice, voles, and pocket gophers — are most abundant in forests where the lush understory provides protective cover and a diversity of food resources. These small rodents, with the exception of the western jumping mouse, are winter-active but avoid the exigencies of the winter environment by foraging and living beneath the snowpack. During severe winters, patches where bark has been gnawed from lower aspen trunks and from shrubs may be common.

The most important rodent associated with many aspen

ecosystems is the beaver. The winter diet of the beaver consists mostly of aspen and willow, cut and stored the previous autumn. Though beaver can cut aspen of almost any diameter, they prefer young trees in the 2- to 6-inch–diameter range. Diet studies suggest that a mature beaver consumes about 2 to 4 pounds of aspen bark each day and requires an estimated 1,500 pounds of aspen food yearly — roughly equivalent to twenty medium-sized aspen.

The lush shrub and herbaceous understory provides abundant, high-quality forage as well as protective cover for elk and mule deer. During the spring, cow elk and their calves linger in secluded aspen stands and adjacent meadows before resuming their migration to summer range at higher elevations. The elk's consumption of aspen and associated understory vegetation is comparatively light during the summer, when most herds are at higher elevations. Where palatable herbaceous forage is in short supply, or when the snowpack exceeds 20 inches on the winter range, aspen leaves, shoots, and bark may become a major component of the elk diet. In contrast to elk, mule deer are primarily browsers; aspen ranks among the top eight browse plants for this species throughout the year but is especially important during summer and fall. In areas with high concentrations of elk or mule deer, as is common on some wintering grounds or along seasonal migration routes, these animals can have a serious impact on aspen forest ecosystems. Deformed aspen boles are typical of young trees in which the leader, or primary shoot, has been repeatedly nipped by elk and regrowth has occurred from lateral branches.

Black bears are especially common in aspen ecosystems, feeding on aspen buds, catkins, and new leaves in the spring and returning in fall to take advantage of the berry crop produced by the understory shrubbery. Because bears tend to select den sites near their fall feeding areas, dens are often located within or adjacent to aspen and mixed aspen-coniferous communities. Bears are good tree climbers, and their distinctive claw marks, known as "bear registers," are often preserved in the soft bark of the aspen trunk and are easily distinguished from marks made by elk canines; bear claw marks persist in the bark for the life of the tree and often provide a record of repeated climbs of a favorite tree. Black bears are omnivores, occasionally climbing aspen trees to rob bird nests and even ripping open cavity nests to get at the eggs or nestlings within.

Miners and Tent Builders

Insect populations in aspen ecosystems tend to be quite high because of the aspen's palatability to a great many invertebrate species. Few insect infestations are severe enough, however, to affect the aspen host significantly. The silvery-colored, serpentine tracks of a minute moth larva, the aspen leaf miner (*Phyllocnistis* spp.), often form striking patterns on aspen leaves. Leaf miners usually spend the entire larval stage within a single leaf, the proof of their residency revealed by the persistent trails created by their feeding activities as they tunnel through the leaf's spongy tissue. In fact, the larvae of several small moths, flies, beetles, and wasps have coevolved this way of life, each species creating a distinctively shaped mine within the leaf. Despite the obvious constraints, leaf mining offers several adaptive advantages: protection from the elements and some predators and, possibly, a way of avoiding the defensive chemicals that coat the leaves of some plants and are intended to deter externally feeding insect herbivores. When the larvae finish feeding, most either pupate within the mine or cut their way out of the leaf, dropping to the ground to pupate externally.

Another insect, the tent caterpillar (*Malacosoma* spp.), forms large cooperative colonies and is responsible for the periodic defoliation of aspen in many parts of the Southern Rockies. Serious infestations have occurred in the Pikes Peak area, the San Juans, and the Sangre de Cristos of northern New Mexico. The tent caterpillar begins its life cycle and overwinters as a fully formed individual encapsulated within an egg, one of a large mass of eggs deposited by a rather small, nondescript moth. The eggs hatch in early spring, and the emerging caterpillars—often as many as two hundred or three hundred from a single egg mass—venture out en masse to feed on aspen buds and new leaves. Within a few days of hatching, the caterpillars construct a silken tent to protect the colony and to serve as a base from which to launch feeding forays. To maximize feeding efficiency, foraging tent caterpillars create a chemically marked trail system to guide fellow colony members to good foraging areas and away from areas that have been exhausted by feeding. When tent caterpillar populations are high, defoliation drastically reduces the ability of aspen to photosynthesize and reduces stand vigor; infestations attacking the same aspen stand repeatedly over several years may kill entire trees and top-kill others.

Life Histories of Selected Animals

Mammals

Silver-haired Bat, *Lasionycteris noctivagans.* This handsome, medium-sized bat is distinguished by its silver-tipped black pelage, slow flight, and habit of foraging just a few feet above the ground. The silver-haired bat is considered a forest-dwelling species and is rare in extensive open country. Only males are summer residents in the mountain forests of the Southern Rockies; females generally migrate farther north along the Rockies, although both males and females may be present during spring and fall migration. These solitary bats roost mostly in trees, taking advantage of natural cavities in rotting snags, flaps of loose bark, cavity nests, or the dense tree canopy, emerging after dark to begin their slow, low-flying foraging flights for moths and other flying insects. Mating occurs in the fall; the female stores sperm in her reproductive tract during hibernation. The young, usually twins, are born on the female's summer range; young bats generally fly at three to four weeks of age and are sexually mature at the end of their first summer.

Western Jumping Mouse, *Zapus princeps.* The western jumping mouse resides in moist forest and meadow habitat and is identified by its long, nearly naked tail (which is much longer than its body), large hind feet, and bipedal jumping gait. Mostly nocturnal, the western jumping mouse feeds on seeds, some foliage, and occasional insects. In summer, the species constructs a small, ball-shaped nest of fine grasses and other plants in rank vegetation. It accumulates fat in preparation for the eight- to nine-month hibernation period that begins in September and lasts until late spring. Once in the hibernaculum, the jumping mouse securely plugs the burrow entrance with soil. Emergence from hibernation may be triggered by a sustained increase in the temperature of the soil surrounding the nest chamber; individuals with insufficient fat reserves may fail to rouse from hibernation or may rouse when environmental conditions limit survivorship. Males emerge first, from mid-May to mid-June, and mating occurs shortly thereafter. Gestation takes less than three weeks, with the young born in June or July. Following birth, the altricial young are dependent on the mother for at least a month. Western jumping mice are relatively long-lived, surviving four years or longer.

Black Bear, *Ursus americanus.* This unmistakable mammal is identified by its large size, dark brown or blackish fur, stubby tail, and flat-footed gait. The scat of these large omnivores resembles that of humans, and often consists of remains of a single kind of food — beetle wings, undigestible seeds, etc. Black bears are essentially solitary, except during the breeding season and when the females are rearing cubs. Primarily nocturnal and crepuscular, bears wander several miles while foraging but will spend daylight hours in a shallow resting den. Black bears are surprisingly agile runners, able tree climbers, and good swimmers; they will use mud "wallows" to cool off or to rid themselves of insect pests. Mating occurs in early summer, but implantation of the fertilized eggs is delayed until November. Black bears do not hibernate but instead induce a deep sleep during which they rely on body fat accumulated during the previous summer. The sow gives birth to two or three highly altricial young while still within the winter den. The cubs spend their first summer with their mother and disperse their second spring. Maximum longevity ranges between twenty and twenty-five years.

Birds

Northern Goshawk, *Accipiter gentilis.* This large, forest-loving hawk is identified by its conspicuous "eyebrow," fluffy undertail coverts, rounded wings, and relatively long, white-tipped tail. Immature goshawks have brown backs and sides and buff, vertically streaked breasts; adult coloring (appearing during the second year) is bluish gray on the back and sides, and the eye stripe is more prominent. In the Southern Rockies, the northern goshawk prefers mixed aspen and coniferous forest habitat above 7,000 feet. This somewhat secretive species perch-hunts for birds and small- to medium-sized mammals, utilizing a quick, plummeting or gliding flight to surprise and confuse intended prey. The goshawk begins its nesting cycle in mid- to late March, building a bulky nest of branches 30 to 50 feet above the ground in an aspen or conifer; nests are situated quite close to the trunk. Incubation takes approximately thirty days, and after hatching, the young goshawks are able to fly within six to seven weeks.

Red-naped Sapsucker, *Sphyrapicus varius.* Red forecrown, red chin, and black-and-white facial striping distinguish the male red-naped sapsucker from the Williamson's sapsucker *(S. thyroideus)*, which has a black back, red chin patch, and yellow belly. This species returns in late spring to aspen groves or to mixed aspen-coniferous forests. Red-naped sapsuckers drill small holes in aspen and other trees, drinking the sap that collects in these wells with their short, brush-tipped tongues; in addition to sap, the sapsucker feeds on the soft cambial tissue beneath the bark; insects are obtained by gleaning and by fly catching. Red squirrels, warblers,

Red-naped sapsucker feeding nestling at the nest.

hummingbirds, woodpeckers, and several kinds of insects take advantage of sapsucker wells. Upon arrival on the nesting ground, the female sapsucker returns to the nest site of the previous year or, if she does not have a site to return to, selects a temporary territory in which to begin signal drumming (a steady, drumlike roll punctuated at intervals by loud taps). Eventually a male—either her mate from last year or a male returning to a previous nest site—hears her and responds with drumming. During courtship, both sexes engage in bobbing displays as well as in continued drumming. Red-naped sapsuckers are primary cavity nesters, often excavating new cavities in previously used trees. Both sexes excavate the nest hole, incubate the eggs, and feed the young. Young sapsuckers fledge twenty-five to twenty-nine days after hatching.

Tree Swallow, *Tachycineta bicolor.* This swallow is the earliest of the swallows to move north from its wintering grounds, arriving in the Southern Rockies by April in most areas. Tree swallows are identified by their blue-black backs, pure white underparts, and swooping-gliding style of flight. A similar species, the violet-green swallow *(Tachycineta thalassina),* has a white cheek patch that extends over the eye and white flank patches that extend almost over the rump. Tree swallows are insectivorous, coursing back and forth over meadows and bodies of water, catching flying insects on the wing. Though not colonial in their nesting habits, tree swallows often forage together in large groups. During courtship, the male pursues the female with aerial acrobatics. The female, occasionally with the help of her mate, constructs a grassy nest within a preexisting tree cavity or bird box. Both sexes bring food to the young, which are able to fly within sixteen to twenty-four days after hatching.

House Wren, *Troglodytes aedon.* This wee bird is distinguished by its upright tail and brown-checked plumage. The house wren is a migratory species, returning to deciduous woodlands and brushy habitats in early spring. The loud, exuberant, cascading song of this species belies its small size. House wrens are insectivorous, foraging close to or on the ground in dense underbrush. The house wren is aggressive in securing nesting cavities, often harassing or evicting other species from desired sites. Both sexes feed the young; fledging occurs twelve to eighteen days after hatching.

Warbling Vireo, *Vireo gilvus.* The melodious, warbling

From left to right: warbling vireo on nest, tree swallow.

song of this small, gray-green bird provides much of the background music of the summer aspen forest. The warbling vireo is identified by its gray-green back and wings, whitish underparts, absence of wing bars, dusky eyeline, and white eyebrow. A similar species, the solitary vireo *(V. solitarius)*, has prominent wing bars and a white eye ring. The warbling vireo is migratory in the Southern Rockies, arriving on its nesting grounds in May or early June. This species is highly insectivorous, gleaning insects from branches and leaves in the forest canopy. Male warbling vireos are persistent singers, even in the heat of the day or while taking a turn on the nest. The warbling vireo nest is an exquisitely woven cup of fine grasses suspended from a forked branch by spider webs and plant fibers. Both sexes incubate the eggs and then feed the young; the young fledge about twelve to fourteen days after hatching.

Yellow-rumped Warbler, *Dendroica coronata.* This lovely warbler, known as "Audubon's warbler" in the West, is easily identified by its yellow throat, yellow rump patch, yellow crown patch, and bluish gray back and wings. Yellow-rumped warblers are largely migratory in the Southern Rockies, returning to their nesting grounds in aspen groves and mixed aspen-coniferous forests by early May. This species may be abundant and conspicuous during migration, both in spring and fall. The yellow-rumped warbler gleans insects from the canopy foliage as well as from vegetation a few feet from the ground; this species may also fly-catch from a perch and is often observed circling outside the canopy when changing foraging positions. The cup-shaped nest is usually built on a horizontal limb and may be found at various heights above the ground. Both sexes incubate the eggs and feed the young.

Common Animals of the Aspen Forests

Mammals

Montane Shrew, *Sorex monticolus*
Masked Shrew, *Sorex cinereus*
Long-legged Myotis, *Myotis volans*
Silver-haired Bat, *Lasionycteris noctivagans*
Nuttall's Cottontail, *Sylvilagus nuttallii*
Snowshoe Hare, *Lepus americanus*
Least Chipmunk, *Tamias minimus*
Golden-mantled Ground Squirrel, *Spermophilus lateralis*
Pine Squirrel (or Chickaree), *Tamiasciurus hudsonicus*
Deer Mouse, *Peromyscus maniculatus*
Montane Vole, *Microtus montanus*
Long-tailed Vole, *Microtus longicaudus*
Western Jumping Mouse, *Zapus princeps*
Porcupine, *Erithizon dorsatum*
Coyote, *Canis latrans*
Black Bear, *Ursus americanus*
Ermine, *Mustela erminea*
Long-tailed Weasel, *Mustela frenata*
Elk, *Cervus elaphus*
Mule Deer, *Odocoileus hemionus*

Birds

Sharp-shinned Hawk, *Accipiter striatus*
Cooper's Hawk, *Accipiter cooperii*

Northern Goshawk, *Accipiter gentilis*
Red-tailed Hawk, *Buteo jamaicensis*
Blue Grouse, *Dendragapus obscurus*
Flammulated Owl, *Otus flammeolus*
Western Screech Owl, *Otus kennicottii*
Great Horned Owl, *Bubo virginianus*
Northern Pygmy Owl, *Glaucidium gnoma*
Long-eared Owl, *Asio otus*
Saw-whet Owl, *Aegolius acadicus*
Broad-tailed Hummingbird, *Selasphorus platycercus*
Rufous Hummingbird, *Selasphorus rufus*
Red-naped Sapsucker, *Sphyrapicus varius*
Williamson's Sapsucker, *Sphyrapicus thyroideus*
Hairy Woodpecker, *Picoides villosus*
Northern Flicker, *Colaptes auratus*
Western Wood-pewee, *Contopus sordidulus*
Hammond's Flycatcher, *Empidonax hammondii*
Western Flycatcher, *Empidonax difficilis*
Tree Swallow, *Tachycineta bicolor*
Violet-green Swallow, *Tachycineta thalassina*
Steller's Jay, *Cyanocitta stelleri*
Black-billed Magpie, *Pica pica*
Black-capped Chickadee, *Parus atricapillus*
Mountain Chickadee, *Parus gambeli*
Red-breasted Nuthatch, *Sitta canadensis*
White-breasted Nuthatch, *Sitta carolinensis*
Pygmy Nuthatch, *Sitta pygmaea*
House Wren, *Troglodytes aedon*
Mountain Bluebird, *Sialia currucoides*
American Robin, *Turdus migratorius*
Solitary Vireo, *Vireo solitarius*
Warbling Vireo, *Vireo gilvus*
Yellow-rumped (or Audubon's) Warbler, *Dendroica
     coronata*
Dark-eyed Junco, *Junco hyemalis*
Song Sparrow, *Melospiza melodia*

Amphibians and Reptiles

Boreal Toad, *Bufo boreas*
Smooth Green Snake, *Opheodrys vernalis*
Western Terrestrial Garter Snake, *Thamnophis elegans*

Butterflies

Anise Swallowtail, *Papilio zelicaon*
Western Tiger Swallowtail, *Papilio rutulus*
Weidemeyer's Admiral, *Basilarchia weidemeyerii*
Silvery Crescentspot, *Charidryas nycteis*

CHAPTER TWENTY

The Fire Forest: Lodgepole Pine

VIEWED FROM A distance, olive-green forests of lodge-pole pine stand out against the darker green of other conifers. These uniform and seemingly monotonous forests are frequently described as "biological deserts"—a label that belies the beauty inherent in the species' ability to take advantage of environmental adversity. Lodgepole pine is the archetype of the fire forest—the undisputed master of reforestation in the aftermath of fire. The plants and animals that make up the lodgepole pine ecosystem—the pinedrops, coral-root orchids, kinnikinnik, dwarf mistletoe, red squirrels, red-backed voles, martens, nuthatches, woodpeckers, and many others—are among the most fascinating species to be found in the Southern Rockies.

Ecological Distribution

Lodgepole pine is distributed from coastal southeast Alaska and the Yukon Territory south to the mountains of southern California, and east across the Rocky Mountains to the Black Hills of South Dakota. Because of its wide geographic distribution, the species is highly variable and has been separated into four subspecies; the Rocky Mountain subspecies is *Pinus contorta* ssp. *latifolia*. In contrast to the arrow-straight growth form so typical of lodgepoles growing in sheltered forest situations, this species assumes twisted shapes, referred to by the Latin epithet *contorta*, in wind-exposed sites.

In the Southern Rockies, lodgepole pine is found within an elevational range of 7,500 to 11,500 feet. The species

Lodgepole pine.

forms extensive, single-species forests as well as mixed-coniferous stands in the Medicine Bow and Laramie mountains of Wyoming and in the mountains of northern and central Colorado, but occurs only in scattered populations south to the Colorado–New Mexico border. At its southern limit, lodgepole pine occurs along the Eastern Slope of the Sangre de Cristos to the vicinity of the Spanish Peaks, and is absent altogether along the Western Slope of the range. West of the Sangre de Cristos, in the San Juan Mountains and in many of the ranges in the central Southern Rockies, lodgepole pine is exceedingly rare.

In the northern and central ranges of the Southern Rockies, lodgepole pine reaches maximum development in the upper montane and lower subalpine zone, dominating sites between 8,500 and 10,000 feet that have a history of repeated fires. Below 9,000 feet, lodgepole pine forests are most common on northern and eastern exposures; high-elevation lodgepole stands may be found on all slope aspects. At its southern limit, lodgepole pine is largely confined to sheltered, north-facing slopes in a narrow zone between 9,000 and 10,000 feet.

The Physical Environment

The climate generally associated with forests of lodgepole pine is slightly cooler and moister than that of ponderosa pine–Douglas-fir forests but more moderate than that of spruce-fir forests. Summers tend to be warm and subject to intermittent drought. Most precipitation is received as snowfall, and the best growth of lodgepole occurs in areas that average or exceed 20 inches of annual precipitation; the snowpack is consistently deeper and more persistent in lodgepole pine forests of the subalpine zone. Soils supporting stands of lodgepole are highly variable, but most stands occur on coarse-textured soils that are considerably less fertile than those associated with aspen; lodgepole attains maximal growth on soils that are moist but well drained, gravelly-loamy in texture, and only moderately acidic.

Community Characteristics

The character of forests dominated by lodgepole pine varies with their age, stand history, tree density, and degree of species diversity. Lodgepole pine is considered an aggressive pioneer or successional species in the Southern Rockies. Wherever catastrophic fires, insect infestations, or logging have destroyed large areas of the preexisting climax forest, lodgepole pine regenerates vigorously, producing a dense, homogeneous, even-aged forest. On other sites, this pine may be found in uneven-aged, mixed-species stands or as small patches in other forest types. Occasionally, lodgepole pine may invade seral aspen communities or even preempt aspen on sites that have experienced high-temperature crown fires.

At lower elevations, under normal successional processes, lodgepole pine is replaced on cool, somewhat moist sites by Douglas-fir and on warm, dry slopes by ponderosa pine. At higher elevations, lodgepole pine is seral to Engelmann spruce and subalpine fir. The time required for a successional lodgepole forest to be replaced by climax forest species is variable and depends on the type and intensity of the initiating disturbance as well as any changes in the microclimate of the forest floor that might influence the reproductive success of the climax forest species for that site.

Young lodgepole forests colonized as a result of fire or other disturbance are typically even-aged and single-storied, their density and homogeneity giving them the appearance of a tree farm. Limited light penetration beneath the canopy causes the foliage of the lower branches to die, resulting in an interlacing network of dead branches that enhances the impenetrable quality of these forests. A thick layer of acidic pine-needle litter accumulates on the forest floor, resulting in the leaching of nutrients from the soil—in contrast to the direct enhancement of soil nutrients and nutrient cycling that occurs in aspen forest soils. The understory is sparse or absent because the trees use most of the forest's resources. Consequently, very few species other than lodgepole pine occur within these ecosystems. As trees die from lack of sufficient light and nutrition, understory vegetation increases in response to the opening of the forest.

Lodgepole pine forests can form stable, persistent communities where repeated disturbances have disrupted normal successional patterns, where fires or other large-scale disturbances have eliminated the seed source for the normal climax species, or where microclimatic conditions no longer favor regeneration of the climax species. For example, low-elevation stands of lodgepole pine may assume subclimax status on sites where high forest-floor temperatures and intermittent drought in summer are too extreme for Douglas-fir seedlings to gain a foothold. Similar changes in the microclimate in subalpine lodgepole stands can also make it impossible for Engelmann spruce and subalpine fir to reestablish themselves as climax species.

Mature lodgepole forests—those with trees one hundred years old or more—are more open and are characterized by an uneven-aged structure and a better-developed understory. Mixed-species forests occur wherever Douglas-fir, subalpine fir, and Engelmann spruce have been able to establish or reestablish themselves. As was true for younger lodgepole forests, shrubs dominate the understory. The most abundant shrub species in montane lodgepole forests are common juniper, wild rose, and kinnikinnik. At higher elevations, these species are largely replaced by buffaloberry, blueberry, red elderberry, and bush honeysuckle. Herbaceous

From left to right: common juniper, kinnikinnik.

species associated with other montane and subalpine forests may be present in small numbers and include such species as heartleaf arnica, pussytoes, fireweed, wintergreen, spotted coral-root orchid, and pinedrops. The yellow-green, jointed shoots of dwarf mistletoe, a parasitic seed plant that establishes its root system within the bark and outer conducting tissues of the lodgepole, are especially common in open forests.

Plant Adaptation: Designs for Survival

Serotiny

Lodgepole pine is a fire-adapted species. The tree produces its seed crop in cones that do not open at maturity but remain sealed and tightly attached to the branches for many years, until fire or some other agent breaks the resinous bond that prevents the cone from opening. The closed-cone habit, called *serotiny,* is typical of several North American pines. During its lifetime, a lodgepole can accumulate hundreds of the hard, prickly cones along its branches. In the event of a fire, the thin film of resin bonding the cone scales together melts and the scales spread open to release a multitude of tiny, winged seeds. The seeds are readily dispersed by the wind, germinating in large numbers on the fire-readied seedbed. Serotiny benefits the reproductive success of the lodgepole by retaining the seeds in a protected but viable state until a fire or other similar disturbance reduces competition from other species and provides optimal conditions for germination and growth. Lodgepole seedlings are superbly adapted to the intense sunlight, heat, cold, drought, and lack of humus of the fire-scorched seedbed. The price for this fire-initiated fecundity, however, is the almost impenetrable "dog-hair" stand of saplings that characterizes the young lodgepole forest. In a Colorado study, sample plots in a twenty-two-year-old stand established after a fire contained roughly 44,000 trees per acre.

Serotiny is genetically controlled and highly variable in Rocky Mountain populations of lodgepole pine. Individual trees may have either entirely serotinous or nonserotinous cones, or both. In the absence of fire, closed cones open eventually as a result of the mechanical breakdown of the vascular connection between the cone and the parent tree or the deterioration of cone resin with age or with desiccating winds. Studies suggest that Rocky Mountain lodgepoles may even develop a mixed cone serotiny habit with increasing tree age—a distinct evolutionary "advantage" in that the tree can redirect energy from the maintenance of old, perhaps nonviable seed to functions more critical to the tree's survival.

Saprophytes and Parasites

The low surface-light levels and impoverished soils typical of many lodgepole pine forests favor plant species that are opportunistic in their strategies for survival. Two groups of plants, *saprophytes* and *parasites*, fit this requirement precisely. Saprophytes, such as the coral-root orchids and several species of fungi, contain no chlorophyll and are unable to make their own food through photosynthesis, deriving nutrients from dead organic matter in the forest soil. The mycelium from which the fungal fruiting bodies (the "mush-rooms") arise may persist underground for years, fruiting when environmental conditions are conducive to growth, remaining dormant when not. When optimal temperature and moisture conditions prevail, a munificence of mushrooms — chanterelles, morels, pine mushrooms, and scaly urchins — can be found on the forest floor. One interesting species, the honey mushroom, (*Armillaria mellea*), can either grow in dead wood as a saprophyte or become parasitic and attack the roots of living lodgepoles.

Plants such as dwarf mistletoe and pinedrops are true parasites, obtaining nutrients from a living host plant. Pinedrops contains no chlorophyll and is parasitic on the roots of conifers. Dwarf mistletoe, on the other hand, contains some chlorophyll and is able to carry on partial photosynthesis, relying on its lodgepole host for water and minerals. In contrast to pinedrops, which is believed to have little impact on its host, the spread of dwarf mistletoe throughout the crown of a lodgepole pine can seriously impact the tree's normal growth, reduce seed production, and may ultimately kill the tree. Interestingly, dwarf mistletoe development in a lodgepole stand depends directly on the vigor of the host trees: the more vigorous the host, the more vigorous the mistletoe infestation that will result. In fact, sites with optimal lodgepole growth have a higher proportion of mistletoe-infested trees than do poorer sites.

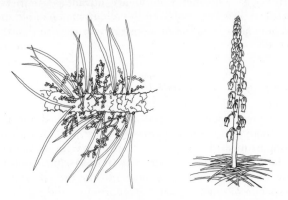

Parasitic plants found in lodgepole pine forests, from left to right (not drawn to scale): dwarf mistletoe, pinedrops.

THE SOUTHERN ROCKIES

Descriptions of Common Plants

Trees and Shrubs

Lodgepole Pine, *Pinus contorta var. latifolia.* This tall, slender-trunked pine is the common pine of the upper montane and subalpine zones of the northern and central Southern Rockies. Lodgepole pine is identified by the persistent cones that dot its branches and by its greenish yellow, somewhat twisted needles, each about 2 inches in length and arranged two needles to a bundle. This slow-growing species can live for several hundred years. Male cones are small and cylindrical and grow in clusters at the branch tips. Female cones take up to two years to develop; immature cones are small, prickly globes. At maturity, female cones are woody and yellowish brown in color (weathering to gray), and each cone scale is armed with a short, curved spine. Seeds are long, reddish brown, and winged; good seed crops are produced every one to three years. The very first railroads to penetrate the Rockies did so on lodgepole ties, most of which were cut in the Medicine Bow Mountains of Wyoming and processed at Tie Siding.

Common Juniper, *Juniperus communis* ssp. *alpina.* This low-growing shrub has a circumpolar distribution and ranges south through the Southern Rockies to New Mexico. It is typically found in dry forests and on open slopes from the foothills to the alpine zone. Common juniper is easily identified by its sharp, needlelike leaves, frost blue female cones, cedary fragrance, and prostrate or spreading growth form. Male and female cones appear on separate plants, although occasionally both sexes can be found on the same plant. Male cones are extremely small and are borne at the tips of branches, disintegrating after pollen release. Female cones resemble berries because of the fusion of the fleshy cone scales. Following fertilization, juniper "berries" require two to three years to reach maturity, changing from pale green to dark blue in color. The female cones are an important food source for small mammals and birds and have a long history of medicinal and culinary use.

Kinnikinnik, *Arctostaphylos uva-ursi.* This creeping, prostrate shrub is circumpolar in its distribution and found in open coniferous woods from the foothills to the subalpine zone. Kinnikinnik, or bearberry, is distinguished by its glossy evergreen leaves, urn-shaped flowers, and deep red berries. The oblanceolate leaves have thick cuticles that protect the plant from drought and desiccating winds. When in bloom, scalloped pink flowers hang from trailing branches, largely hidden by the leaves. Shiny green berries, about a quarter of an inch in diameter and ripening to a cherry red at maturity, may persist on the branches for several seasons.

Wild Rose, *Rosa woodsii.* This upright shrub is found throughout the Southern Rockies but is especially common in dry, open woodlands from the foothills to the subalpine zone. Wild rose is distinguished from other shrubs by its thorny floral stems, compound and serrate leaves, and pink, fragrant, five-petaled flowers. Scarlet, fleshy fruits, called hips, develop in late summer; the hips, which remain on the plant after the leaves have fallen, are an important food for various birds and mammals.

Parasitic Plants

Pinedrops, *Pterospora andromedea.* This unusual plant is most commonly encountered in pine forests from the foothills to the montane zone. Pinedrops is identified by its rich, rusty-rose flowering stalk and its hanging, bell-shaped flowers. This species contains no chlorophyll and is parasitic on the roots of conifers. Clusters of the fleshy, flowering stalks first appear in early summer; stalks average 2 feet in height and become woody as they dry. Seed capsules persist on the stalks after maturity, having opened along suture zones to release abundant, winged seeds.

Dwarf Mistletoe, *Arceuthobium americanum.* The distribution of this parasitic seed plant coincides with the distribution of lodgepole pine in North America. Dwarf mistletoe is identified by the clusters of mustard yellow, jointed shoots that sprout directly from the branches and trunk of the host tree. These leafless shoots are anchored to the tree by modified roots, called haustoria, that are able to tap into the tree's nutrient and water supply; a severe dwarf mistetoe infestation will weaken and even kill the host tree. Mistletoe plants are either male or female; flowering occurs in spring. Female flowers are wind- or insect-pollinated, and the berry-like fruits, each with a single seed, develop by midsummer.

At maturity, typically from late August to early September, the fruit breaks from its base, contracts violently, and shoots the seed several feet into the air; the seed may be expelled at speeds of up to 60 miles per hour and travel distances of up to 30 feet. Each seed is surrounded by a sticky substance that helps it adhere to the surface on which it lands. Seeds that land on or are washed onto a tree branch by the rains will germinate the following spring, establishing their root systems over the next two years; a growth period of three to five years may elapse before the new shoots appear.

Wildflowers

Spotted Coral-root Orchid, *Corallorhiza maculata.* This relatively common orchid is found in dry ponderosa pine and lodgepole pine forests from the foothills to the subalpine zone. The common name refers to the coral-like appearance of its brittle, highly branched root mass. Spotted coral-roots are saprophytes and must obtain their nutrition from dead organic matter in the forest soil; the intertwining of their peculiar root mass with soil-borne fungi and the roots of other plants suggests that this species may be a partial parasite. The asparagus-like flowering stalks appear in early spring, are typically reddish brown in color, and average about 10 inches in height. The small but spectacular flowers appear along a leafless raceme, each flower consisting of a frilly white, purple-spotted lip framed by a fan of reddish brown petals and sepals. Blooming time varies with altitude, extending from late May at lower elevations to mid-July at higher elevations. After flowering, the pendant seed capsules enlarge dramatically, splitting at maturity along longitudinal suture zones to release thousands of dustlike seeds.

One-sided Wintergreen, *Orthilia secunda.* This attractive member of the pyrola family is associated with cool, coniferous forests from the montane to the subalpine. With its rounded, evergreen leaves and its erect, one-sided raceme of pale green flowers, this species is easily distinguished from other members of its family, such as pipsissewa or green pyrola. The leaves, though mostly basal, may extend up the lower third of the flowering stem. The flowers consist of five rounded green petals and hang on short pedicels.

Mountain Pussytoes, *Antennaria parvifolia.* This familiar wildflower, a member of the sunflower or composite family, is found in open coniferous forests and forest clearings from the foothills to the subalpine zone. Pussytoes is identified by its stoloniferous, rosettelike growth form, grayish green leaves, and flowers that resemble a kitten's paw. The leaves of this species are wedge-shaped, thick, and covered with fine hairs. Each 2- to 3-inch flowering stalk arises from a rosette of leaves, the flower head consisting of a tight cluster of white disk flowers.

Fireweed, *Chamerion angustifolium.* This tall, showy member of the evening-primrose family is often found along roadsides and in areas where fires or other disturbances have occurred. In successional lodgepole stands, fireweed is common only in the early stages of reforestation, disappearing as shading intensifies. Fireweed is distinguished by its spire-like racemes of large, rose purple flowers and by its slender, lanceolate leaves. The flowers have four petals, eight stamens, a four-lobed stigma, and an inferior ovary (situated below the petals) that elongates as it ripens. At maturity, elongate seed capsules split open to release a multitude of tufted seeds that are easily dispersed by the wind. The leaves turn a brilliant red in the fall.

Common Plants of the Lodgepole Pine Forest

Trees

Aspen, quaking, *Populus tremuloides*
Fir, subalpine, *Abies lasiocarpa*
Pine, limber, *Pinus flexilis*
  lodgepole, *Pinus contorta*
  ponderosa, *Pinus ponderosa*
Spruce, Engelmann, *Picea engelmannii*

Shrubs

Blueberry, *Vaccinium myrtillus*
  broom, *Vaccinium scoparium*

Buffaloberry, *Shepherdia canadensis*
Elderberry, red, *Sambucus microbotrys*
Juniper, common, *Juniperus communis*
Kinnikinnik, *Arctostaphylos uva-ursi*
Mountain-lover, *Paxistima myrsinites*
Rose, wild, *Rosa woodsii*
Sticky-laurel, *Ceanothus velutinus*
Twinberry (or bush honeysuckle), *Distegia involucrata*
Waxflower, *Jamesia americana*
Willow, Scouler, *Salix scouleriana*

Wildflowers

Arnica, heartleaf, *Arnica cordifolia*
Fireweed, *Chamerion angustifolium*
Locoweed, drop-pod, *Oxytropis deflexa*
Mistletoe, dwarf, *Arceuthobium americanum*
Orchid, fairy slipper, *Calypso bulbosa*
   spotted coral-root, *Corallorhiza maculata*
Pinedrops, *Pterospora andromedea*
Pipsissewa, *Chimaphila umbellata*
Pussytoes, mountain, *Antennaria parvifolia*
Wintergreen, green-flowered, *Pyrola chlorantha*
   one-sided, *Orthilia secunda*

Environment and Adaptation: Animals of the Lodgepole Pine Forest

Lodgepole pine forests offer a limited larder to all but a few species of mammals and birds. The dense growth of trees and the shady character of most successional stands result in a depauperate understory, providing little cover or food. Pine squirrels, or chickarees, take advantage of the beneficent supply of seed-bearing cones, stockpiling them in caches on the forest floor. Red-backed voles excavate tunnels in the piles of cone scales discarded by the squirrels, feasting on leftover lodgepole seeds and on fungi growing in the moist litter. Though the density of breeding birds is low, the brown creeper and several species of woodpeckers, nuthatches, and chickadees are attracted to these forests by the abundance of insects, each species focusing its foraging activities on different parts of the trees or at different vertical levels. These animals, in turn, attract predators such as the marten and the sharp-shinned hawk.

Chickarees

The chickaree is a conifer seed specialist, preferring relatively dense coniferous forests providing ample supplies of cones and suitably moist caching sites. The strident, chattering alarm call of this highly territorial squirrel, as well as the cone-scale middens and freshly cut branch tips that reveal its feeding activities, make it the most conspicuous of all forest animals. Chickarees harvest tightly closed cones, clipping them from the branches in summer and fall and storing them in shallow basins excavated in their middens or at the base of a fallen tree. Not surprisingly, the intensity of territorial behavior varies seasonally and is greatest during the cone-caching period. Though other foods may be consumed when available, cached cones provide the critical food supply during winter and early spring.

To reach the nutritious seeds enclosed within the sealed lodgepole cone, the chickaree must chew through a succession of extremely woody, spine-tipped cone scales — armament intended to frustrate this most skilled seed predator. Studies have shown that chickarees maximize their foraging efficiency in lodgepole forests by discriminative seed predation, selecting trees that have the most easily harvestable cones as well as those that consistently produce a high number of seeds per cone. Coevolution of chickarees and serotinous races of Rocky Mountain lodgepole pine — the overall effect of discriminative seed predation by squirrels — has resulted in the lodgepole's increased reproductive effort toward tissues that protect the seed from predators rather than toward greater seed production. In fact, only an estimated 1 percent of the weight of the typical serotinous lodgepole cone is in its seeds.

Coevolution, however, is a two-way street. Chickarees associated with serotinous races of lodgepole have evolved a larger body and heavier jaw musculature than the Douglas squirrel, a closely related species found in the Pacific Northwest and one that feeds on the more readily obtainable seeds of nonserotinous lodgepoles. A bony ridge atop the skull of the chickaree, nonexistent in most populations of Douglas squirrels, provides additional anchorage for the muscles that work the jaws. For the chickaree and the lodgepole pine, the result is a balanced system in which the chickaree is successful enough to satisfy its appetite for lodgepole seeds — but not so successful that it can decimate the entire lodgepole seed crop.

Of Gleaners and Wood-borers

Many of the bird species associated with lodgepole forests are specialists at extracting bark and wood-boring insects. Nuthatches and brown creepers are equipped with strong feet for clinging to bark and slender pointed bills for picking insects out of bark crevices. Hairy and downy woodpeckers, with their strong grasping feet, picklike bills, long tongues, and stiff-pointed tail feathers that serve to brace the body against the hammering motion of the head, are superbly adapted for digging out wood-boring insects and larvae. The unusually long reach of the woodpecker's barb-tipped tongue is made possible by extensible hyoid bones, which, rearward, divide into two slender bony and muscular horns that curve back around the base of the skull, then up and over the forehead to attach in or near the nostrils. This remarkable adaptation, by which the tongue is protruded, supported, and withdrawn, enables the woodpecker to probe deep into the feeding and nursery galleries created by wood-boring insects.

Life Histories of Selected Animals

Mammals

Pine Squirrel (or Chickaree), *Tamiasciurus hudsonicus.*
This tree squirrel is identified by its small size, chattering call, tuftless ears, white eye ring, dark grayish brown back

and sides (sometimes tinged with red), and grayish white underparts. In the Southern Rockies, chickarees are most common in lodgepole pine and spruce-fir forests. Diurnal and highly territorial, the chickaree defends not only its nesting area but its entire home range. The territorial call is a strident, rolling "cherr" and may be accompanied by vigorous tail-flicking, foot-stamping, and chases. The principal food source is conifer seeds, which the chickaree obtains by cutting and caching cones from late summer through fall. Other foods, including fungi, berries, buds, flowers, inner bark, invertebrates, and the sugar-enriched cambial tissues of mistletoe-infested branches, are eaten when available. A ball-shaped nest of grasses and conifer needles constructed on a branch or in a tree cavity is used throughout the year. Chickarees are solitary except during breeding, when females are receptive to males for a single day during estrus. One or more males may court the female, but only the dominant male succeeds in mating, his approach to the female preceded by a melodious series of "appeasement" vocalizations. The altricial young are usually born in April after a gestation period of approximately forty days. Nursed until early summer, the young undergo a period of training before dispersing from the mother's territory in late summer.

Southern Red-backed Vole, *Clethrionomys gapperi.* This beautiful, forest-dwelling vole is distinguished from the deer mouse by its small eyes and ears, its short tail, and the broad patch of reddish hairs that highlights its buffy gray back. In the Southern Rockies, this boreal species occurs mostly in lodgepole pine and spruce-fir forests at higher elevations. Southern red-backed voles are solitary and active throughout the year, retreating to tunnel systems beneath the snowpack in winter. The principal foods include conifer seeds, fungi, berries, bark, and some invertebrates. In contrast to all other voles except the heather vole, southern red-backed voles have rooted rather than evergrowing molars and are thus poorly adapted to the abrasive diet of grasses favored by most voles. In the Colorado Front Range, red-backed voles are reported to have begun breeding activities beneath the snow in late March. Following a gestation period of about eighteen days, the female gives birth to a litter of two to eight altricial young in a small, globe-shaped nest constructed of grasses and other plants. Female voles reach sexual maturity by about two months of age and may produce several litters per season. Red-backed voles seldom exceed twenty months in age.

Birds

Sharp-shinned Hawk, *Accipiter striatus.* This small accipiter is distinguished from the larger Cooper's hawk (*A. cooperii*) by its pigeonlike size, square tail, rounded wings, slate blue upperparts, reddish streaking on breast and belly, and white undertail coverts. There is no sexual dimorphism; immature birds are brownish above, whitish and streaked with brown below. Sharp-shinned hawks are associated with coniferous forests and mixed woodlands throughout the Southern Rockies, returning to most nesting areas by early spring; some individuals may be present throughout the year, often staking out bird feeders in mountain residential areas that attract large numbers of small birds. These hawks are known for their aerial twists and abrupt changes in direction when pursuing their small avian prey. The style of hunting relies mostly on concealment and ambush. The sharp-shinned hawk typically nests relatively high in an evergreen, constructing a platformlike nest of twigs and branches or renovating the abandoned nest of another raptor. Both sexes incubate the eggs, but the male does most of the hunting during the nesting season. Fledging occurs in as little as twenty-three days.

Downy Woodpecker, *Picoides pubescens.* This bluebird-sized woodpecker is distinguished from the similar hairy woodpecker (*P. villosus*) by its smaller size, small bill, and dark bars on the outer tail feathers. Though less conspicuous than the hairy, the downy is a common resident of coniferous forests and mountain riparian woodlands throughout the Southern Rockies. These woodpeckers forage by clinging to the trunks and branches of trees, digging out subsurface insects and larvae or flaking off the bark to get at insect cocoons or eggs. During the summer, the downy may also forage for surface prey on the foliage and branches. The sexes remain apart during the winter and may defend winter feeding territories as well as the site of their roosting hole. Courtship behavior begins in late winter and is initiated by the onset of drumming by both sexes on trees, utility poles, or other suitable substrates. The territorial call is a slightly softer "pik-pik" than that of the hairy. Once the pair-bond is established or renewed, the pair will seek a nest site and both sexes will work at excavating the nest hole. Following egg laying, both sexes incubate the eggs by day, with the male assuming total responsibility at night. Young downy woodpeckers are fed by both parents and are ready to fly within twenty-one to twenty-four days. Fledglings initially follow the parents but disperse as they become more successful at finding food.

White-breasted Nuthatch, *Sitta carolinensis.* This robust, sparrow-sized nuthatch is distinguished from the diminutive red-breasted nuthatch (*S. canadensis*) by its larger size and all-white face and breast; the red-breasted nuthatch has a rusty-colored breast and dark eye stripe. White-breasted nuthatches are common residents of the coniferous forests of the Southern Rockies. Most birds are observed foraging for bark insects upside down and sideways on trunks and branches, but ground foraging may also occur. The call of this species — a nasal "yank-yank-yank-yank" — is lower pitched than that of the red-breasted. The white-breasted nuthatch is largely insectivorous except in winter, when it eats seeds and is a common visitor to bird feeders. Winter-foraging

From left to right: red-breasted nuthatch, white-breasted nuthatch.

THE SOUTHERN ROCKIES

flocks often include other nuthatches, chickadees, brown creepers, and downy woodpeckers. Pairs may remain close to each other during the winter but will normally roost alone. Nesting occurs in early spring, in a natural tree cavity or in an abandoned woodpecker or sapsucker hole. Both sexes incubate the eggs, which require about twelve days to hatch. Young nuthatches are able to fly within about two weeks of hatching.

Brown Creeper, *Certhia familiaris.* This sparrow-sized bird, with its camouflage coloring of streaky brown, is a fairly common and permanent resident of the dense, coniferous forests of the Southern Rockies. Brown creepers can be difficult to spot and are most often located by their call, a high, lisping, "screep," and then observed spiralling upward along a tree trunk as they forage for bark insects. These birds, equipped with pointed, down-curved beaks, large feet, and stiff tails that serve as braces during foraging, are superbly adapted to their insectivorous niche. Outside the breeding season, brown creepers are solitary but may sometimes be seen foraging in mixed-species flocks. There is some evidence that brown creepers perform altitudinal migrations during cold weather, and communal roosting has been reported. Brown creepers typically nest behind loosened pieces of bark or in abandoned tree cavities, often within 15 feet of the ground, the female constructing a hammock-shaped nest of plant fibers. Incubation takes only two weeks, and the young fledge within two weeks of hatching.

Common Animals of the Lodgepole Pine Forest

Mammals

Masked Shrew, *Sorex cinereus*
Hoary Bat, *Lasiurus cinereus*
Nuttall's Cottontail, *Sylvilagus nuttallii*
Snowshoe Hare, *Lepus americanus*
Least Chipmunk, *Tamias minimus*
Uinta Chipmunk, *Tamias umbrinus*

Red Squirrel, *Tamiasciurus hudsonicus*
Deer Mouse, *Peromyscus maniculatus*
Southern Red-backed Vole, *Clethrionomys gapperi*
Porcupine, *Erethizon dorsatum*
Coyote, *Canis latrans*
Black Bear, *Ursus americanus*
Long-tailed Weasel, *Mustela frenata*
Marten, *Martes americana*
Bobcat, *Felis rufus*
Elk, *Cervus elaphus*
Mule Deer, *Odocoileus hemionus*

Birds

Sharp-shinned Hawk, *Accipiter striatus*
Cooper's Hawk, *Accipiter cooperii*
Northern Goshawk, *Accipiter gentilis*
Blue Grouse, *Dendragapus obscurus*
Great Horned Owl, *Bubo virginianus*
Northern Pygmy Owl, *Glaucidium gnoma*
Saw-whet Owl, *Aegolius acadicus*
Williamson's Sapsucker, *Sphyrapicus thyroideus*
Hairy Woodpecker, *Picoides villosus*
Downy Woodpecker, *Picoides pubescens*
Common Raven, *Corvus corax*
Steller's Jay, *Cyanocitta stelleri*
Gray Jay, *Perisoreus canadensis*
Clark's Nutcracker, *Nucifraga columbiana*
White-breasted Nuthatch, *Sitta carolinensis*
Red-breasted Nuthatch, *Sitta canadensis*
Brown Creeper, *Certhia americana*
Hermit Thrush, *Catharus guttatus*
Yellow-rumped Warbler, *Dendroica coronata*
Pine Siskin, *Carduelis pinus*
Ruby-crowned Kinglet, *Regulus calendula*
Evening Grosbeak, *Coccothraustes vespertina*
Cassin's Finch, *Carpodacus cassinii*
Red Crossbill, *Loxia curvirostra*
Mountain Chickadee, *Parus gambeli*
Dark-eyed Junco, *Junco hyemalis*

CHAPTER TWENTY-ONE

The Wind Forest: Bristlecone Pine and Limber Pine

VENERABLE IN THEIR isolation, the gnarled silhouettes of bristlecone and limber pine grace the mountain skyline. Clinging tenaciously to rocky knob and ridgetop, these trees endure extremes of every sort — strong winds, cold temperatures, drought, and poor soils. Even the sound of the wind whistling through their branches has a distinctly keening sound. Twisted and flayed to the white sinews of their sapwood by the winds, survivors may have only thin ribbons of living tissue encircling their buttressed trunks. Standing like sentinels above the mountain valleys, their silvered trunks glowing rose at sunset, the magnificent snags continue to transfigure the mountain landscape long after their death.

Ecological Distribution

In the Southern Rockies, open woodlands of limber and bristlecone pine dominate dry, rocky ridges and exposed, south-facing slopes. Limber pine occurs in the Rocky Mountains from Canada to northern New Mexico. In the Southern Rockies, it is found on windswept sites from the foothills to timberline, but it is most common above 9,000 feet. Bristlecone pine is represented by two geographically and taxonomically distinct species. Rocky Mountain bristlecone *(Pinus aristata),* the species found in the Southern Rockies, occurs only in Colorado, New Mexico, and the San Francisco Peaks area of Arizona; Great Basin bristlecone *(P. longaeva),*

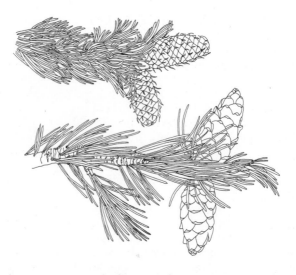

Bristlecone pine (top), limber pine (bottom).

the species that includes the oldest living trees known, is restricted to California, Nevada, and Utah. A distance of 160 miles separates the Rocky Mountain species from the nearest Great Basin bristlecone populations. In the Rocky Mountains, the northern limits of Rocky Mountain bristlecone pine approximate the 40th parallel.

In the Southern Rockies, limber and bristlecone pines may each form pure stands on certain sites or may be found in various combinations with other tree species depending on latitude, elevation, and substrate. Bristlecone and limber pines often occur together where their ranges overlap in the central and southern ranges of the Southern Rockies. At the southern end of the Sangre de Cristo Range, limber pine dominates dry slopes between 7,500 and 10,000 feet and takes the place of lodgepole pine as the successional species on open slopes. Above 10,000 feet, limber pine is occasionally replaced on the driest sites by bristlecone pine, although this species is decidedly rare here. Bristlecone pine increases in importance north along the Sangre de Cristos and is especially common on steep, rocky terrain above 10,000 feet. A nearly pure stand covering about 300 acres is preserved just east of Costilla as part of the Clayton Pass–Bristlecone Pine Research Natural Area in Carson National Forest.

Significant stands of bristlecone have been reported in approximately fifty-four locations in the central and southern ranges of Colorado. In the Spanish Peaks, bristlecone and limber pine form an unusual low-elevation association with woodlands of ponderosa pine and Gambel oak. At higher elevations, bristlecone pine dominates large portions of the dry subalpine forests typical of this region. North and west of the Spanish Peaks, bristlecone pine becomes increasingly uncommon. In the San Juans, bristlecone pine stands occur only on south-facing slopes north of Creede. In the Sawatch Range, mixed stands of bristlecone and limber pine are prominent along Colorado 82 between Twin Lakes and Independence Pass. A timberline stand of bristlecones, believed to include the highest-dwelling erect trees in the Southern Rockies, occurs at 12,300 feet on a southwest-facing slope of the Sawatch Range near the historic town of St. Elmo, Colorado. North of this area, pure stands of bristlecone are relatively common in South Park and in the Mosquito Range; on the flanks of Mount Bross, an especially scenic stand of bristlecones in Pike National Forest is designated as the Windy Ridge–Bristlecone Pine Scenic Area. At the northern limit of the species' range on the Western Slope, stands of bristlecone pine can be seen in upper Gore Canyon (northern Gore Range) and on the rim of Deep Creek Canyon (White River Plateau).

At the southern end of the Colorado Front Range, in the comparatively dry Pikes Peak area, bristlecone is most common on south-facing slopes in the montane and subalpine zones, with limber pine dominating north-facing slopes and filling the role of a successional species in the absence of lodgepole pine. At Mount Evans, bristlecone and limber pine share dominance on high-elevation sites, with bristlecone pine occupying open, south-facing slopes with fine-textured soils and limber pine more prevalent on rocky ridges. A beautiful, easily accessible, 12-acre tract of bristlecone pines, encompassed within the Mount Goliath Natural Area, is located about 3 miles up the Mount Evans road from Echo Lake. Mixed stands of bristlecone and limber pine are also prominent along Interstate 70 near the town of Silver Plume, Colorado.

Bristlecone pine reaches its northern limits along the Colorado Front Range just west of Nederland, near the historic mining town of Caribou. North and west of this area, limber pine takes the place of bristlecone on dry, windswept sites from timberline down to middle elevations. Some scattered populations, such as those at Pawnee Buttes, in northeastern Colorado, occur as low as 6,880 feet. In the Medicine Bow Mountains of Wyoming, limber pine is an important species in lower- and middle-elevation forests, especially because of the rarity of ponderosa pine, but its distribution rarely reaches timberline. In fact, communities of limber pine and aspen often adjoin the sagebrush-grassland transition zone along the mountain valleys of the Medicine Bow Mountains and the Snowy Range.

Physical Environment

Bristlecone and limber pine woodlands occupy areas characterized by strong winds, low temperatures, high solar radiation, a short frost-free season, periodic drought, high surface runoff, and coarse, rocky soils. Average annual precipitation for most sites supporting thriving stands rarely exceeds 30 inches; most sites experience greater effective precipitation in summer than in winter. During the winter months, these ecosystems are largely snow-free as a result of wind scour.

Community Characteristics

Bristlecone and limber pine woodlands are shaped by the harsh conditions of their environment. In contrast to most other forest types, bristlecone and limber pine woodlands are of limited size, ranging from a few trees to stands encompassing a few hundred acres. They can occur as pure stands, as mixtures of the two species, or as minor constituents in other forest types. Climax stands are typical of the windiest, most xeric environments; in the absence of lodgepole pine, bristlecone and limber pine assume a successional role in areas where fire or logging have removed the preexisting tree cover.

Viewed from a distance, these woodlands are easily distinguished from other forest types. In general, the trees tend to be widely spaced, broad-crowned, and comparatively short, rarely exceeding 30 feet in height. On gentle slopes, the woodlands have an open, grovelike appearance and are bright and easy to move through. A high percentage of bare, rocky ground and a sparse understory of shrubs and herbaceous plants are typical of most communities. The most picturesque of these stands usually include several old trees, many ranging in age between a thousand and two thousand years. These gnarled patriarchs, their trunks ice- and sandblasted to a polished platinum, often support only a few living branches. Timberline populations may be erect or somewhat prostrate, often with spectacularly twisted trunks.

The understory composition of bristlecone and limber pine woodlands is highly variable, depending on geographic location, stand elevation, topography, substrate type, and the influence of adjacent vegetation communities. Species diversity tends to be relatively low in most woodlands, except on the most sheltered sites or in successional stands. Dry habitat shrubs such as common juniper, shrubby cinquefoil, kinnikinnik, and sticky-laurel are common in many stands. Herbaceous species typical of lower-elevation woodlands include alumroot, stonecrop, false arabis, wallflower, Fendler sandwort, and alpine penstemon. Species present in high-elevation woodlands include Whipple penstemon and spotted

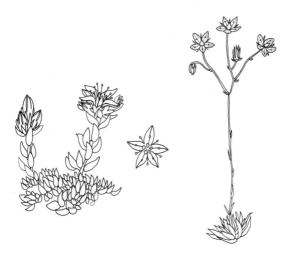

From left to right: stonecrop with detail of flower, spotted saxifrage.

saxifrage. Favorable sites near timberline may support a mixture of alpine species such as whitlow-wort, alpine clover, alpine thistle, purple fringe, and alpine sandwort.

Plant Adaptation: Designs for Survival

To survive under such adverse environmental conditions, bristlecone and limber pine have evolved several strategies. The branches of the limber pine are smooth-barked and flexible, allowing them to bend easily in the wind without breaking. Once established, a limber pine seedling sends down a large taproot, which enables the young tree to anchor itself securely to rocky ridges and bluffs. The ability to retain functional needles for many years, in contrast to the short-lived needles of most conifers, is a characteristic of pines that inhabit high, dry places. The needles of Rocky Mountain bristlecone pine remain functional for ten to fifteen years, requiring the tree to produce only a limited number of new needles each year and providing a stable photosynthetic capacity to sustain the tree during times of environmental stress.

Rocky Mountain bristlecones, the oldest specimens dated between fifteen hundred and two thousand years of age, are the longest-lived trees in the Southern Rockies. Great Basin bristlecones often exceed three thousand years in age, and the world's oldest living tree—a bristlecone known as Methuselah growing in the Schulman Memorial Grove in California's White Mountains—has been dated at more than forty-six hundred years. Many people tend to think that any tree living longer than the norm must be growing under conditions of abundant moisture, moderate temperature, nutrient-rich soils, and protection from severe weather. Not so for the bristlecone pine. The oldest and largest bristlecones typically grow in the harshest, most exposed environments. In these places, soil moisture is scarce, and the tree grows slowly. Slow-growing trees tend to have extremely narrow growth rings, and therefore denser wood, than fast-growing species. The insect, fungal, and bacterial invasions that plague most trees have little impact on bristlecones growing in severe situations because the dense, highly resinous wood produced under harsh circumstances is especially disease resistant. Bristlecones growing under more moderate conditions fail to reach great age because the increased moisture available to these trees encourages the production of less dense, less resinous wood, which is more susceptible to disease and decay.

For long-lived bristlecones, the passage of time is marked by the loss of bark and cambium to porcupines and fire, the gradual death of portions of the pine's root system due to parasitic fungi or desiccation, and the periodic attrition of needled limbs as a result of wind damage, drought, and lightning. What living tissues remain—perhaps only a few needled branches and a strip of living bark and cambium—must strike a balance between the size of the living crown and the amount of bark and active xylem needed to sustain it. Bristlecone is unusual in that its dead wood remains sound throughout the life of the tree. In fact, many bristlecones remain upright or intact for hundreds of years after death.

Descriptions of Common Plants

Trees

Rocky Mountain Bristlecone Pine, *Pinus aristata.* Rocky Mountain bristlecone is identified by its five-needled fascicles, the white dots of resin on individual needles, and its bristle-tipped cone scales. The needles are usually strongly curved, less than 2 inches long, and closely crowded together around all sides of the branches, giving the branch a bottle-brush appearance. The male cones are small, dark orangish, and clustered near the tips of the branchlets. Female cones occur singly or in pairs, near the ends of the branchlets. At maturity, these cones are extremely woody, with purplish brown scales, and difficult to handle because each scale bears a slender, bristlelike prickle. The seeds are brown and oval-shaped, and each has a terminal wing about three times longer than the body of the seed.

Limber Pine, *Pinus flexilis.* Limber pine is distinguished from bristlecone, which it superficially resembles, by its longer and less curved needles, the absence of white resin dots on its needles, and the absence of bristles on its cone scales. Limber pine shares with bristlecone pine the arrangement of its needles in bundles of five and the distinctly tufted appearance produced by the density of needles encircling the branch. The trunk and branches are smooth-barked and silvery gray when young, the trunk becoming scaly and deeply furrowed with age; the branches are extremely flexible, a characteristic that gives limber pine both its common and scientific names. Male cones are small and reddish; young female cones are round and reddish purple. Mature female cones are woody and elongate and have thick, bristleless cone scales. Each square-tipped cone scale bears two large, winged seeds. A year of heavy seed production normally alternates with several years of light production. The large seeds are especially attractive to Clark's nutcrackers, red crossbills, and other seed predators.

Wildflowers

Yellow Stonecrop, *Amerosedum lanceolatum,* formerly *Sedum lanceolatum.* This attractive plant is common on dry, gravelly or rocky ground from the plains to the alpine tundra. It is identified by its fleshy leaves crowded on short shoots and its star-shaped yellow flowers. The leaves have a waxy covering that prevents water loss, enhancing the plant's survival rate in extremely dry environments. When sufficient water is present, this succulent species flourishes; it remains dormant and somewhat shrunken in size during times of moisture stress.

Common Alumroot, *Heuchera parvifolia.* This member of the saxifrage family is typical of rock crevices and cliffsides from the montane to the alpine tundra. Alumroot is identified by its roundish, lobed leaves arranged in a loose rosette at the base of the plant and by the leafless flowering stalks bearing compact clusters of diminutive green flowers.

Spotted Saxifrage, *Ciliaria austromontana,* formerly *Saxifraga bronchialis.* This lovely flower is found in dry forested canyons and rocky cliffs from the foothills to the subalpine zone. This species is easily identified by its matlike growth form, diminutive, awl-shaped leaves, and slender flower stalk bearing several small white flowers. A hand lens reveals the beauty of the flowers, each petal speckled with yellow, orange, and red. The leaves of the spotted saxifrage are evergreen, and mats of this species may form conspicuously green, mosslike cushions on rock ledges during the winter.

Whipple Penstemon, *Penstemon whippleanus.* This tall snapdragon-like flower is common on rocky slopes, along trails, and in open forests from the upper montane through the subalpine zone. Whipple penstemon is easily distinguished from other high-elevation penstemons by its inch-long, purple or wine red flowers and by its robust size. Both dark- and pale-flowered forms are often found in the same population.

Purple Fringe, *Phacelia sericea.* This showy species is common on gravelly, open slopes, around boulders, and in disturbed soils of the subalpine zone. Purple fringe is identified by its silky, fernlike leaves and the dense, spiky cluster of purple flowers from which the stamens and pistils protrude conspicuously.

Common Plants of the Bristlecone Pine and Limber Pine Forests

Trees

Pine, limber, *Pinus flexilis*
  Rocky Mountain bristlecone, *Pinus aristata*

Shrubs

Blueberry (or whortleberry), *Vaccinium scoparium*
Buffaloberry, *Shepherdia canadensis*
Cinquefoil, shrubby, *Pentaphylloides floribunda*
Juniper, common, *Juniperus communis*
Kinnikinnik, *Arctostaphylos uva-ursi*
Raspberry, wild, *Rubus idaeus* ssp. *melanolasius*
Rose, wild, *Rosa woodsii*
Sticky-laurel, *Ceanothus velutinus*

Herbaceous Plants

Alumroot, common, *Heuchera parvifolia*
Arabis, false (or rockcress), *Boechera drummondii*
Buckwheat, alpine, *Eriogonum jamesii* var. *xanthum*
Candytuft, mountain, *Noccaea montanum* (formerly *Thlaspi*)
Clover, alpine, *Trifolium attenuatum*
Draba, or whitlow-wort, *Draba* spp.
Loco, Rocky Mountain, *Oxytropis sericea*
Muhly, mountain, *Muhlenbergia montana*
Mutton-grass, *Poa fendleriana*
Penstemon, alpine, *Penstemon glaber*
  Whipple, *Penstemon whippleanus*
Purple Fringe, *Phacelia sericea*
Pussytoes, *Antennaria parvifolia*
Sandwort, alpine, *Lidia obtusiloba*
  Fendler, *Ergmogone fendleri*
Saxifrage, spotted, *Ciliaria austromontana*
Stonecrop, yellow, *Amerosedum lanceolatum* (formerly *Sedum*)
Thistle, alpine, *Cirsium scopulorum*
Wallflower, *Erysimum capitatum*

Environment and Adaptation: Animals of the Bristlecone and Limber Pine Forests

The harsh conditions and limited resources typical of most bristlecone and limber pine woodlands do not support a diverse fauna. Most animals found here are visitors from adjacent communities, attracted by the seasonal crop of pine seeds, the pine's succulent inner bark, or the availability of nest sites in tree cavities or rocky crevices. For much of the year, however, these woodlands stand alone — with only the wind and the occasional porcupine or Clark's nutcracker for company.

The Solitary Diner

Porcupines are active throughout the year in bristlecone and limber pine woodlands except during the most severe winter weather. Evidence of porcupine activity—patches where bark has been removed and accumulations of inch-long fecal pellets beneath a favorite feeding tree—may be conspicuous in certain stands. Though seemingly clumsy on the ground, the porcupine has long curved claws, a stout tail, powerful thigh muscles, and large foot pads that make it an adept tree climber. Like the woodpecker, the porcupine uses its tail for support when climbing; the underside of the tail is covered with stiff, downward-pointing bristles set in thick connective tissue, which prevent back-sliding.

Getting up the tree is just half the battle. The porcupine must be able to digest and metabolize the cambium, or inner bark, of these trees, its main source of sustenance and one to which it is uniquely adapted. To combat herbivores, trees have evolved a battery of defensive strategies—indigestible, unpalatable, or poisonous substances in their leaves and woody tissues—to reduce the tree's attractiveness to the potential consumer. Seemingly immune to these defenses, the porcupine attacks the bark of a preferred feeding tree with its rootless incisors, first shaving off the dead outer layer of bark and then concentrating its efforts on the cambium, which it processes into a fine puree with its cheek teeth. To gain the maximum benefit from its diet of woody tissues, at least 75 percent of the porcupine's body cavity is taken up by organs devoted to digestion—stomach, caecum, and intestines. Functionally, the caecum resembles the rumen of an elk or deer, housing the symbiotic microflora necessary to convert otherwise indigestible carbohydrates into metabolizable fatty acids, compounds critical in meeting the porcupine's energy requirements.

Despite the efficiency of the porcupine's digestive processes, the low concentration of nitrogen (a building block of proteins) and the excess of indigestible roughage in its fall and winter diet fail to meet the animal's metabolic requirements, causing it to lose a substantial portion of its body weight over the course of the winter. To minimize the effects of this nutritional shortfall, the porcupine limits the breadth of its diet as well as its movements during the winter, concentrating on foraging areas where its preferred trees, typically those with bark most easily digested by a given animal's intestinal microflora, are abundant. In fact, the porcupine's winter foraging area may be less than 15 percent of that used in summer. With the arrival of spring, porcupines may turn their attention to deciduous trees and shrubs, taking advantage of the high protein content of the new buds, catkins, and young leaves. Porcupines generally return to a conifer-based diet by midsummer, the time when the leaves and cambial tissues of deciduous trees begin accumulating tannins and other distasteful compounds that alter proteins and inhibit the intestinal microflora that aid digestion.

Seed Caching

Most coniferous trees rely on the wind to disperse their small, winged seeds. Several mountain pines, however, such as the piñon and limber pines, depend largely on seed-caching birds for dispersal. Limber pine has evolved characteristics similar to those of piñon, making its cones attractive to foraging Clark's nutcrackers and other seed-eating birds. The seed-bearing cones are conspicuously positioned on the branches, and when the cones mature in late summer, the large, high-energy seeds are displayed temptingly on the newly opened cone scales. Superficially, these traits would seem maladaptive for the tree since no seedling can grow from a consumed seed. The advantages to the pine in this coevolved system, however, derive from the failure of the birds to recover all the seeds they have cached. Viable seeds that fail to be retrieved have a better chance of germinating and becoming successfully established than those scattered randomly through wind dispersal.

Clark's nutcracker has evolved both anatomical and behavioral adaptations that make it a proficient harvester of pine seeds. The most striking feature of the nutcracker is its long, sturdy, sharply pointed bill, which it uses as a chisel to pry open green cones or as forceps to extract seeds once the cones have opened. As each seed is extracted, it is subjected to "bill-clicking": the bird rattles the seed in its bill and, assessing its weight or the sound that it makes, determines whether the seed is edible. Inedible seeds are discarded with a toss of the bill, and edible ones, if not eaten

Red crossbill (top), Clark's nutcracker.

at once, are reposited in an expandable pouch located beneath the tongue. This pouch, unique to these birds, can hold as many as 180 limber pine seeds; its use does not interfere with vocalization and permits foraging over wide areas. When the pouch is full, the bird flies off to a favored communal caching area, which may be shared with as many as a dozen other nutcrackers. Most caching sites are located on windswept ridges or south-facing slopes that remain largely snow-free throughout the winter. After selecting a site, the nutcracker uses its bill to excavate a small hole in the soil and deposits one to several seeds in it, carefully covering the cache with soil and marking it with a twig or pebble.

In good cone years, an active nutcracker can store thousands of pine seeds during a fall collecting period—burying many times more seeds than it can possibly consume. Clark's nutcrackers have an extraordinary ability to relocate individual caches. Experiments have shown that seed recovery is dependent not on the nutcracker's sense of smell but on its ability to recognize the arrangement of objects around or marking a cache. During the winter months, cached seeds not only make up the bulk of the diet, but also provide the extra energy required for winter breeding. Particularly surprising, however, is the fact that pine seeds make up almost the entire diet of the nestlings. The nestlings of most other birds are fed insects because most seeds fail to provide sufficient proteins and fat to ensure normal growth. Limber and piñon pine seeds, however, are unusually high in lipids and proteins, and young nutcrackers appear to thrive on them.

Life Histories of Selected Animals

Mammals

Porcupine, *Erethizon dorsatum.* This distinctive rodent is identified by its large size, its thickset appearance, the armament of quills cloaking its back, sides, limbs, and tail, and its waddling gait. Porcupines are relatively common in mountain forests throughout the Southern Rockies but are most abundant in open pine woodlands. Their diet changes seasonally, ranging from the inner bark of trees to forbs. Though timid and rarely known to be aggressive, the porcupine defends itself by turning its back on its attacker, its quills clattering together like so many spears; the animal cannot hurl its quills, but they are so loosely attached that the merest brush against them will result in a painful souvenir of the encounter. Solitary but nonterritorial, porcupines may resort to communal denning in cold weather. Breeding, a complicated affair given the armament, occurs in late autumn or early winter. Den sites are chosen in rocky crevices and hollow logs and under abandoned outbuildings. A single precocial young (rarely twins) is born in April or May after a gestation period of about seven months. Maximum longevity is about ten years.

Birds

Clark's Nutcracker, *Nucifraga columbiana.* This pigeon-sized bird is identified by its gray body, black wings, black central tail feathers, long black bill, and, in flight, white wing patches, rump, and outer tail feathers. Clark's nutcrackers inhabit mountain pine forests throughout the Southern Rockies, especially near timberline. This noisy bird, with its nasal croaking call, is gregarious and often forages for pine seeds in large flocks. Clark's nutcrackers breed in February and March, building their nests in conifers on wind-sheltered slopes near their seed-caching areas. After fledging, the young follow the parents to the caching site, where the parents continue to feed them until July.

Common Raven, *Corvus corax.* This large, all-black bird is distinguished from the crow by its larger size, more massive bill, and long, wedge-shaped tail. This conspicuous, highly intelligent species is widely distributed in the Southern Rockies and can be found from the semidesert shrublands to the alpine tundra. Ravens are omnivorous, functioning both as predator and scavenger. They will take live animals when available and plunder the nests of other birds, but they concentrate largely on the smorgasbord of carrion supplied by high-speed highways. Ravens are gregarious except during the nesting season, and large congregations are often reported at winter roosts. Large numbers of ravens may be seen flying and soaring together, carrying out aerial maneuvers and high-spirited play that resembles the mock dog-fights of fighter jets. Courtship displays are spectacular, replete with pursuit flights, aerial acrobatics, and close-contact, mutual soaring. Pairs mate for life and remain together throughout the year. The nest site is generally situated on a cliffside, atop a utility pole, or, occasionally, in the top of an abandoned outbuilding. Altricial at birth, ravens are slow in developing and do not fledge until about six weeks of age.

Red Crossbill, *Loxia curvirostra.* This sparrow-sized bird is identified by the reddish body of the male or the yellowish olive body of the female, the dark wings, and the bill with crossed tips. The red crossbill is an irregular and uncommon wanderer in the mountain forests. Pine seeds are its dietary staple, but spruce seeds and the buds and catkins of deciduous trees are also utilized when available. The irregular pattern of this bird's occurrence is largely a result of seed crop availability from year to year. The crossbill's beak is uniquely adapted to prying open the scales on conifer cones, allowing the seeds to be easily removed by the tongue. When drinking or collecting highway salt, the bird's bill must be held sideways so that the material can be lapped up with the tongue. Red crossbills use their bills parrot-style when climbing through the branches of a tree while foraging. The call is somewhat chattering, a series of "jip" notes, often a signal of foraging flocks in the vicinity. Red crossbills nest at any time of the year; the frequency of winter nesting suggests that the nestlings need not be fed solely on insects. The nest is built well out on the branch of a conifer.

Common Animals of the Bristlecone Pine and Limber Pine Forests

Mammals

Masked Shrew, *Sorex cinereus*
Nuttall's Cottontail, *Sylvilagus nuttallii*
Snowshoe Hare, *Lepus americanus*
Pine Squirrel (or Chickaree), *Tamiasciurus hudsonicus*
Least Chipmunk, *Tamias minimus*
Golden-mantled Ground Squirrel, *Spermophilus lateralis*
Yellow-bellied Marmot, *Marmota flaviventris*
Deer Mouse, *Peromyscus maniculatus*
Bushy-tailed Woodrat, *Neotoma cinerea*
Porcupine, *Erethizon dorsatum*
Long-tailed Weasel, *Mustela frenata*
Ermine, *Mustela erminea*
Coyote, *Canis latrans*
Bobcat, *Felis rufus*

Birds

Common Raven, *Corvus corax*
Clark's Nutcracker, *Nucifraga columbiana*
Gray Jay, *Perisoreus canadensis*
Steller's Jay, *Cyanocitta stelleri*
Hairy Woodpecker, *Picoides villosus*

White-breasted Nuthatch, *Sitta carolinensis*
Yellow-rumped Warbler, *Dendroica coronata*
Pine Grosbeak, *Pinicola enucleator*
Red Crossbill, *Loxia curvirostra*
Cassin's Finch, *Carpodacus cassinii*
Pine Siskin, *Carduelis pinus*
Dark-eyed Junco, *Junco hyemalis*

CHAPTER TWENTY-TWO

The Snow Forest:
Engelmann Spruce
and Subalpine Fir

CLOSING RANKS AGAINST the open, sun-drenched woodlands typical of lower elevations, forests of Engelmann spruce and subalpine fir share an essential unity with those of the boreal regions of northern Canada. There is always enough of the mysterious in these dark, spired forests to draw one into their midst, enough of the fragrance of melting snow and of spruce needles, the distant fluting of a hermit thrush, the soft clucking of a female blue grouse to her chicks, the fleeting shadow of a marten. Shafts of sunlight pattern the forest floor, spotlighting clumps of curled lousewort amidst a lime green carpet of blueberry and pyrola.

Ecological Distribution

In the Southern Rockies, Engelmann spruce and subalpine fir dominate the subalpine zone and form extensive, largely homogeneous forests between 9,000 feet and timberline. To understand the distributional patterns that characterize these forests we must define several terms used in delimiting the upper forest margin. The term *upper timberline*, hereafter referred to simply as timberline, corresponds to the upper elevational limit of fully erect trees. Above timberline, within a narrow and discontinuous transition zone known as the *forest-tundra ecotone*, trees become increasingly stunted and are finally reduced to prostrate forms in response to the harsh environmental conditions. North American ecologists often use the German word *krummholz* (meaning "crooked

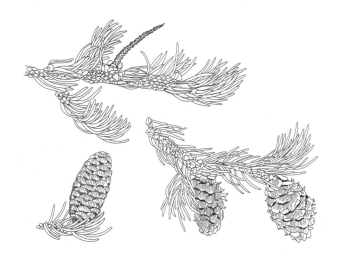

Common trees of the subalpine forest: subalpine fir (lower left), subalpine fir branch showing persistent cone axis after the scales have fallen away at maturity (upper left), and Engelmann spruce.

wood") to describe these stands of wind-deformed trees because of their apparent similarity to those in the European Alps. In many timberline areas of the Southern Rockies, trees tend to grow in clusters, forming discrete stands known as *tree islands*. The term *treelimit* (or treeline) defines the elevational boundary marking the cessation of all tree growth, erect or stunted, and the beginning of alpine tundra. Because the subalpine forest and the forest-tundra ecotone are part of an ecological continuum, both ecosystem types will be described in this chapter.

Within the subalpine forest zone, tree-species dominance shifts in response to elevation and latitude. The most majestic spruce-fir forests are found in the western and central ranges, where a generous winter snowpack and high summer precipitation provide ample moisture for optimal growth. In this region, the subalpine forest extends from about 9,500 feet to 11,000 feet and includes a mixture of Engelmann spruce, subalpine fir, stands of aspen, and lush meadows. On sheltered slopes and in high basins, groves of tall Engelmann spruce are common at timberline. Within the forest-tundra ecotone, both spruce and fir form krummholz islands to about 12,000 feet, but the degree of krummholz development is much less than that found in the windier eastern ranges of the Southern Rockies.

In the central portion of the Southern Rockies, groups of erect Engelmann spruce and lesser amounts of subalpine fir, as well as islands of krummholz vegetation, reach 12,000 feet on sheltered slopes of the Sawatch Range. In the mountains near Crested Butte, spruce-fir forest begins at about 10,500 feet and extends to nearly 11,500 feet, with an Engelmann spruce–dominated krummholz zone to nearly 12,500 feet on south-facing slopes. In the Park and Sierra Madre ranges, the spruce-fir zone begins at about 10,000 feet, with linear, wind-shaped stands, called *ribbon forests,* common along the upper forest margin to nearly 11,000 feet.

At the southern end of the Sangre de Cristo Range, corkbark fir, a variant of subalpine fir identified by its soft, corky bark, shares dominance with Engelmann spruce in the lower subalpine forest. At higher elevations, spruce dominates the forest to treelimit. Treelimit varies from 11,000 feet on northeastern exposures to more than 12,000 feet on southwestern slopes. There is little krummholz development in this area. As one moves north along the Sangre de Cristos, corkbark fir is again restricted to the lower portions of the subalpine forest, and Engelmann spruce dominates the upper forest to treelimit; woodlands of bristlecone pine take the place of spruce-fir forests on the driest subalpine sites. Krummholz communities are rarely encountered here or in the Spanish Peaks to the east. At the northern end of the Sangre de Cristos, corkbark fir continues to be largely absent from the upper subalpine forest, but krummholz becomes increasingly common at timberline.

Farther to the north, in the Colorado Front Range, Engelmann spruce and subalpine fir are codominants throughout most of the subalpine forest zone between 9,500 and 11,000 feet, giving way to limber pine on rocky, windswept slopes. There is usually a dense forest of lodgepole pine at the lower limit of spruce-fir, a result of logging and fire. Engelmann spruce is the dominant species at timberline, which occurs at around 11,000 feet. Extensive krummholz communities occupy the forest-tundra ecotone. Treelimit occurs at around 11,400 feet.

In southern Wyoming, the lower limit of spruce-fir forests also merges with forests dominated by lodgepole pine. Above this zone, dense stands of Engelmann spruce and subalpine fir gradually give way to ribbon forest at about 10,500 feet; well-developed krummholz islands dominated by subalpine fir are common between 11,000 and 11,500 feet. This same pattern is characteristic of the subalpine forest zone in northwestern Colorado.

Physical Environment

Engelmann spruce–subalpine fir forests occupy the highest forested environments in the Southern Rockies. The climate is characterized by long, cold winters, short, cool summers, and high annual precipitation. Mean annual temperature is below 35°F, and frost is possible during any month of the year; winter temperatures are relatively moderate when compared to those in the lower basins or valley bottoms, with few record lows exceeding −15°F. Precipitation, mostly as snowfall, is usually greater than 28 inches and is often as much as 40 inches annually. Snow depths, even with only minimal drifting, are often greater than 5 feet and may be augmented periodically by snow blown down from the alpine tundra. In many areas, the deep snowpack, shaded by the trees, persists well into early summer. Winds can be strong, especially near timberline, and are predominantly from the west; wind-throw of both living and dead trees is a common phenomenon in these forests.

Forest-Tundra Ecotone

The forest-tundra ecotone is characterized by extreme cold and harsh winds, which severely limit growth and reproduction. Throughout most of the ecotone, the average temperature of the warmest month of the year (typically July) is 50°F; sites where this average falls below 50°F generally lie above timberline. In the Southern Rockies, a conspicuous decrease in the elevation of timberline and treelimit occurs with increasing latitude. On average, the growing season is only about forty-five days long, and snow is possible at any time of the year. Mean annual soil temperatures at timberline are close to freezing. Winter winds, often exceeding 80 mph, sweep the snow from exposed tundra ridges and redeposit it in troughs and depressions in the forest-tundra ecotone. Tree islands and ribbon forests act like snow fences, interrupting the free passage of wind-transported snow and encouraging the development of massive drifts to the lee of these communities.

Community Characteristics

Old-growth stands of Engelmann spruce and subalpine fir are among the West's most beautiful forests. The closed canopy, consisting of trees in all stages of life, death, and rebirth, enhances the feeling of a forest primeval. Within these stands, individual spruce trees may exceed 3 feet in diameter, 120 feet in height, and 450 years in age. As the oldest trees die, young ones put on growth spurts to fill the vacated spaces. Silvered snags, pocked with nesting cavities, stand as venerable reminders of forests past. A crisscross maze of fallen trees, their rotting trunks patterned with moss and lichens, impedes passage. Low-growing blueberries and other shade-loving plants form a dense tangle in some areas, while other parts of the forest floor may have only a scattering of plants. Here and there, a rushing mountain stream or a lush, flower-filled meadow provides a visual counterpoint to the forest's shadowy countenance.

Spruce-fir forests are the domain of a distinctive group of shade- and moisture-loving plants. Many species are the same as or similar to those associated with northern boreal forests. Though the understory is often denser than in other

From left to right: buffaloberry, blueberry.

coniferous forests of the Southern Rockies, species diversity is generally low. The shrub understory, where present, is dominated by broom huckleberry and blueberry, with lesser amounts of red elderberry, high-bush cranberry, Colorado currant, buffaloberry, and mountain-lover. With few exceptions, subalpine forest wildflowers tend to be pale in color; they include such species as pipsissewa, wood nymph, broadleaf arnica, curled lousewort, Gray's lousewort, and twinflower. Several orchids, including the rattlesnake plantain, twayblade, and brownie lady's slipper, are found in especially moist, dense forests. The species composition of forest openings and riparian areas within the subalpine zone is strikingly more diverse than that of the forest itself, including colorful wildflowers such as Parry primrose, false hellebore, monkshood, aspen sunflower, and trumpet gilia.

Disturbance and Successional Patterns

The self-perpetuating nature of spruce-fir forests is ensured by the fact that no other tree species can reproduce in the deep shade associated with these stands. In many parts of the Southern Rockies, these forests have remained largely undisturbed because of the rarity of severe fires in such moist environments and because their inaccessibility has proven an impediment to extensive logging or other types of exploitation. Unfortunately, mining activities in the late 1800s and early 1900s were responsible for much cutting and burning. In recent years, damaging infestations of the Engelmann spruce beetle and western spruce budworm have spread through these forests.

When disturbance of climax spruce-fir forests does occur, lodgepole pine or aspen is quick to invade areas below 10,000 feet. These shade-intolerant species eventually produce sufficient shade to limit their own reproduction while creating a suitable microclimate for the establishment of spruce and fir seedlings. Depending on local conditions, this process of conversion may take fifty to one hundred years. On the driest sites, in areas where spruce and fir are unable to regenerate, lodgepole pine or limber pine may form the new climax community. Above 10,000 feet, Engelmann spruce dominates forests disturbed by fires, avalanches, or human activities, largely because its seedlings

Common wildflowers of the subalpine forest, clockwise from upper left: twinflower, wood nymph, Parry primrose, curled lousewort.

have a higher survival rate than those of fir and are more sun-tolerant during initial establishment. However, reforestation in these high-elevation forests is generally slow because of the harsh environmental conditions.

Community Patterns:
The Forest-Tundra Ecotone

Viewed from a distance, the upper limit of the spruce-fir forest may appear as an abrupt boundary, or, as is more often the case, the forest may fragment along its upper margins to form isolated, wind-shaped tree islands and streamlined glades. The dominant tree species within the forest-tundra ecotone is Engelmann spruce, but subalpine fir may be common in some communities. Severely stunted aspen are present in rare situations at timberline, and limber pine or bristlecone pine may be found on the driest and most wind-swept sites. The character of the forest-tundra ecotone is shaped by a rigorous and unforgiving climate. Stunted and wind-battered trees, their crowns often reduced to a one-sided, or "flagged," tuft of foliage on the leeward side of the

Forest-tundra ecotone, Indian Peaks Wilderness Area, Colorado. *James B. Benedict.*

The Snow Forest: Engelmann Spruce and Subalpine Fir   467

stem, become increasingly dwarfed toward treelimit. At tree-limit, the hardiest survivors are forced to hug the ground, assuming cushionlike and even prostrate growth forms on the most exposed sites.

Forest-tundra ecotone communities are characterized by a rich flora consisting of species associated with both subalpine and alpine ecosystems. Shrubs such as Colorado currant, shrubby cinquefoil, bog birch, willow, and several species of blueberry may form a dense growth in certain krummholz communities. Herbaceous plants such as Jacobs ladder and curled lousewort, both shade-loving species, are found within the shelter of the krummholz islands and ribbon forests. Vegetation between the krummholz communities may consist of a well-developed turf formed by grasses, sedges, soil lichens, mosses, and forbs such as alpine avens, globeflower, and American bistort. In the most exposed, gravelly areas, alpine cushion plants such as moss campion and alpine sandwort are common.

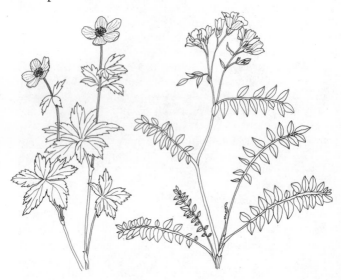

Common wildflowers of the forest-tundra ecotone, from left to right: globeflower, Jacobs ladder.

Plant Adaptation:
Designs for Survival

Conifers and the Winter Environment

Spruce and fir exhibit morphological and physiological adaptations that enable them to withstand the stresses of the winter environment. In contrast to the broader-crowned conifers of lower-elevation forests, the narrow-spired growth form and down-swept branches of spruce and fir minimize snow loading and wind resistance. The spired shape, the result of hormonal suppression of lateral branch growth, becomes especially pronounced along the upper margin of the forest, where many timberline trees resemble upside-down carrots.

Persistent snow loads on the lowest branches of the trees may reduce their resiliency over time, allowing them to remain in contact with the moist litter of the forest floor. It is not unusual for branches affected in this way to produce adventitious roots at the point of soil contact, through a process known as *layering*. Once layering has occurred, the proximal portion of the branch ceases to grow and the rooted branch stem develops its own vertical, central axis. If the layered branch becomes separated from the parent tree, its root system allows it to persist as an independent tree; multiple layered branches sometimes resemble a ring of saplings growing around the parent tree.

PHOTOSYNTHESIS AND GROWTH

Physiological mechanisms are critical to the survival of trees in cold environments. Annual tree growth depends on the maintenance of a favorable balance between the energy gained as a result of photosynthesis and energy expended through respiration. For substantial rates of photosynthesis to occur, minimal leaf temperatures must generally be above 46°F. Studies have shown that spruce and fir are adapted to carry out peak rates of photosynthesis at optimal temperatures lower than are typical for other coniferous species, allowing them to substantially extend their photosynthetic season. In fact, in timberline populations of spruce and fir, the reactivation of photosynthetic processes occurs surprisingly early in the spring, often as long as two months prior to the emergence of new growth.

Experiments have shown that not only does the photosynthetic apparatus of cold-climate conifers shut down during midwinter, but respiratory activity is also reduced. In milder winter climates, coniferous species are able to carry on positive net photosynthesis whenever temperatures are above freezing. In the subalpine forest, however, winter is essentially a time of physiological drought for trees because water reserves in the soil are frozen and unavailable to the roots. Consequently, winter photosynthetic dormancy provides an adaptive advantage in reducing water loss at a time when potential replenishment is greatly limited and when winter transpiration (evaporative water loss) demands must be met by the expenditure of water reserves stored in the trunk and branches.

WINTER DESICCATION AND FREEZING DAMAGE

Orange-brown patches of dead needles are often prominent on the upper portions of krummholz trees in spring and are the result of winter desiccation and frost damage. Whereas a photosynthetic season of sufficient duration is essential for the production of new plant tissue, it is equally important that new shoots have time to mature or "harden off" during their first summer season, maximizing their cold tolerance before the onset of winter conditions. Photosynthesis provides the underlying basis for the completion of this growth process. During maturation, individual plant cells develop lignified cell walls, giving the new foliage greater mechanical strength. Needle succulence, the "soft" appearance typical of new growth, declines markedly as the water content of the tissues is reduced, allowing space for ice crystals to form between cells without causing damage; this adaptation is critical because it reduces the susceptibility of new shoots to frost damage. During the final phase of growth, the needles become encased by a waxy covering known as a *cuticle*, which reduces evaporative water loss. Needle attrition can occur wherever ice-particle abrasion removes the protective cuticle from the foliage or where an inadequate growing season has failed to allow sufficient time for cuticle development and internal frost-proofing of new growth.

Reproduction

In contrast to pines, which require from two to three growing seasons for cone formation, pollination, and seed maturation, Engelmann spruce and subalpine fir have their reproductive stages compressed into less than four months. The male, pollen-producing conelets burst from their buds in late spring. The succulent, female conelets emerge shortly thereafter, their luminous purplish red scales flared slightly to expose the ovules to wind-borne pollen grains. Following pollination, the cones close their scales and begin a gradual transformation in size and texture, the enclosed seeds ripening during the brief summer growing season. The cones of both species reach maturity in autumn, the scales opening to release the winged seeds to the winds.

Engelmann spruce and subalpine fir require shade, relatively cool temperatures, and a moist seedbed to ensure successful germination and establishment. Seed-based regeneration depends on a favorable sequence of events that includes a good seed crop, adequate wind or animal-aided dispersal to suitable germination sites, and amenable weather conditions during the initial seasons of seedling establishment. Though these conditions are admirably met within the cool, shadowy, humid environment of the subalpine forest, cone production and seed-based regeneration are considerably less common in the harsh climate of the forest-tundra ecotone. Seedlings that do become established above timberline generally do so in a sheltered microsite, such as in the lee of a rock or within the protection of existing krummholz trees or shrubs. Once established, the seedling must withstand intense sunlight, summer frosts, prolonged periods of drought, frost heaving, snow molds, and browsing damage by small mammals. Successful seedlings often exhibit some sort of beneficial mycorrhizal-rootlet relationship that maximizes the seedling's ability to draw water and nutrients from the soil.

Forest Parasites

WITCHES' BROOMS

Anyone who has spent much time in spruce-fir forests has noticed the occasional mass of stunted, sickly looking branches high up in a tree. This abnormal proliferation of twigs, which often emits a fetid odor, is called a "witches' broom" and is the tree's response to a parasite-caused infection. In the case of subalpine fir, the culprit is the fir broom rust, a fungus whose life cycle requires alternating generations to parasitize the fir and its alternative host, a small wildflower known as chickweed (*Stellaria* spp.); when inhabiting the fir, the fungus produces spores that infect the chickweed, and when it is inhabiting the chickweed, it produces spores that infect the fir. A witches' broom is an integral part of its host, altering branch structure, causing the virtual elimination of cone production by the infected branch, reducing host vigor, and, in severe cases, initiating the destabilization of the stand in which the host is growing.

SNOW MOLDS

Another unusual parasite, a snow fungus (*Herpotrichia* spp.), is responsible for the black, feltlike weft that often envelops the lower branches of conifers newly emerged from the snow. This remarkable fungus thrives in the icy slush of the melting snowpack, at temperatures at or below 32°F, its fungal hyphae penetrating and subsequently destroying the needles of its host. Though extensive infections of *Herpotrichia* can kill small spruce and fir saplings, most infections of mature trees are localized and apparently do little harm to the host. *Herpotrichia* can be especially damaging when it infects the lee side of krummholz islands, where its proliferation is enhanced by the persistence of wind-drifted snow.

Strategies for Survival Above Timberline

TREE ISLANDS

Each tree responds differently to the harsh environment of the forest-tundra ecotone, and growth is remarkably slow. A spruce or fir with a trunk diameter of just a few inches may be several hundred years old. These trees, majestic spires in the subalpine forest, are dramatically stunted and grow more or less asymmetrically above timberline, assuming a variety of growth forms and distributional patterns that mirror habitat conditions. Limber pine and bristlecone pine are more tolerant of winter desiccation and wind, often developing into erect trees on sites where spruce and fir persist only in prostrate forms.

Tree islands capitalize on the phenomenon of safety in numbers, the clustering of trees providing increased wind protection, mutual mechanical support, ameliorated temperature extremes, higher humidity, and a black-body effect resulting in earlier snowmelt. In fact, some of these tree thickets can be so dense that they are all but impossible to walk through, except during the winter when they are packed so full of wind-drifted snow that one is able to walk right over them. Most tree islands consist of one or two tree species and several shrubs. They may be large or small in areal extent, their shapes—round, oval, linear, etc.—reflecting the degree and character of the local winds. The persistent, largely one-directional winds that blast these dense thickets, pruning away bark, branches, and foliage from the windward sides and giving the crowns of the tallest trees a distinctly one-sided appearance, govern the orientation of tree islands. Where the winter snowpack affords a protective, sheltered environment, krummholz trees may develop a fanlike "skirt" of branches. Cushionlike or prostrate forms are typical of the most severe environments, their wind-pruned surfaces resembling the work of an overzealous bonsai gardener. On gentle slopes, the combination of strong westerly winds and snow distribution patterns often results in the development of ribbon forests. These distinctive formations consist of multiple parallel bands of stunted trees, some bands measuring more than 300 feet in length and each oriented perpendicular to the prevailing wind.

Slow downwind "migration" of tree islands occurs where attrition on the windward side is outpaced by growth and layering regeneration on the leeward. Migrating tree islands can be identified by the trail of dead stems and branches left behind as they move downwind across the forest-tundra ecotone. Research in the Colorado Front Range suggests that some tree islands are moving eastward at the rate of several centimeters each year. The dead stems and branches that remain on the windward sides of the trees provide protection for the viable portions, and their removal for campfires or as curiosities can seriously impact the survival of a tree island.

REPRODUCTION ABOVE TIMBERLINE

The character and development of tree islands in the forest-tundra ecotone reflect both environmental influences and reproductive strategies. Since photosynthetic performance decreases with increasing elevation, most spruce and fir trees above timberline fail to produce cones or, if they do, produce cones with nonviable seeds. Instead, these trees must rely on their ability to spread through layering. Asexual or vegetative regeneration results from the production of adventitious roots wherever the lateral branches of the tree come into prolonged contact with the ground. Though not all rooted branches will develop erect stems, each layered stem has the potential to form a new tree with the same genetic characteristic as its parent. In many cases, these layered branches form circular groups of trees or, where winds are especially strong and one-directional, may be elongated in the downwind direction.

Descriptions of Common Plants

Trees and Shrubs

Engelmann Spruce, *Picea engelmannii.* Engelmann spruce ranges from British Columbia south to New Mexico and Arizona. The species is identified by the thin, scaly bark, dark green, four-sided needles, and fine, soft hairs that envelop its twigs; the needles of the closely related blue spruce are sharper and less flexible and typically have a steely blue color. Immature female cones are purplish red; cones are brown and papery at maturity and hang downward from the branches, sometimes for a year or more after seed dissemination has occurred. Engelmann spruce is relatively long-lived, with many individuals exceeding 450 years of age.

Subalpine fir, *Abies lasiocarpa.* Subalpine fir has the broadest distribution of all North American firs and occurs from the Yukon to southern Arizona and southwestern New Mexico. This tree can be identified at a distance by its narrow, pencil-point crown and by the upright, purple-black cones that decorate the topmost branches. The needles are stalkless, flat, and comparatively blunt, with whitish lines both above and below. On younger trees, the thin, gray bark is patterned with horizontal ridges, conspicuously dotted with resin blisters. On older trees, the bark is broken into narrowly fissured and irregular grayish brown scales. The female cones are borne on the upper side of the topmost branches and remain upright throughout their two-month-long development period. As they reach maturity in early autumn, the cones turn from dark purple to brown and start to fall apart scale by scale, releasing their winged seeds and leaving behind on the tree the black, spiky cone core.

Blueberry (or Huckleberry), *Vaccinium* spp. These diminutive, bright green shrubs are represented by several species in the Southern Rockies, all identified by their small size, alternate arrangement of branches and leaves, narrowly ovate leaves, pinkish urn-shaped flowers, and small red or purple fruits. The most easily identified species is broom blueberry (*V. scoparium*), with its tiny green leaves, densely branching growth habit, and red fruit; the myrtle blueberry (*V. myrtillus*) has larger leaves, a more open and less branching habit, and purple fruit. Blueberry flowers are unusual in that the pollen-producing portion, or anther, of each stamen is drawn out into two narrow tubules with a pore at each end. The viscous pollen is extruded through these tubules as the anthers mature, very much like toothpaste out of a tube, and adheres readily to insect pollinators.

Buffaloberry, *Shepherdia canadensis.* Buffaloberry is a member of the oleaster family (Elaeagnaceae) and is found from Canada and Alaska south along the Rocky Mountains to central New Mexico. It is readily identified by its opposite leaves and branches, elliptical green leaves, rust-colored scales on the undersides of leaves, terminal buds, and orange-red berries. The male and female flowers bloom on separate plants, the diminutive and petalless flowers appearing in early spring, before the leaves emerge.

Red Elderberry, *Sambucus microbotrys.* This lovely shrub, a member of the honeysuckle family (Caprifoliaceae), is distributed from British Columbia south throughout much of the United States. A common species in moist forests, red elderberry is identified by its compound leaves, pyramidal clusters of cream-colored flowers, and terminal bunches of red berries. Each dark green, pinnately compound leaf consists of a main axis with five to nine finely toothed leaflets; two leaves arise at each node, or attachment point, along the stem. The fruit is favored by birds and small mammals but considered to be toxic to humans.

Wildflowers

Wood Nymph, *Moneses uniflora.* This diminutive member of the wintergreen family (Pyrolaceae) occurs in the boreal forests of the Northern Hemisphere and is found in moist, subalpine forests throughout the Rocky Mountains. Though frequently overlooked because of its small size, wood nymph is readily identified by its solitary, nodding, and starlike flower, its basal ovate leaves, and the distinctive lily-of-the-valley fragrance of its flowers.

Curled Lousewort, *Pedicularis racemosa.* Curled lousewort is common in upper montane and subalpine forests from Canada south to New Mexico and California. This species is readily identified by its white, sickle-shaped flowers, finely toothed, lanceolate leaves, and multistemmed growth habit. The flowers are distinctive because the upper two petals of the corolla join to resemble the beak of a parrot and the lower three petals are fused to form a slightly twisted lower lip. The leaves and stems often exhibit a pronounced reddish coloration, which intensifies with the coming of autumn and adds color to the forest floor.

Parry Primrose, *Primula parryi.* Though not a species of dense forests, Parry primrose is found along streambanks within the subalpine forest and in the forest-tundra ecotone. This showy wildflower, a large-flowered member of the primrose family (Primulaceae), is found from southern Montana and Idaho south through the Rocky Mountains to northern New Mexico and Arizona. Parry primrose is robust, with spatulate leaves that arise from a basal rosette and stout stalks that terminate in an umbellate cluster of yellow-centered, rose pink flowers. Each individual flower consists of a five-lobed, funnel-shaped corolla, which opens out to expose its bright yellow center.

Jacobs Ladder, *Polemonium pulcherrium* ssp. *delicatum.* This member of the phlox family (Polemoniaceae) is identified by its delicate blue, bell-shaped flowers and the skunklike odor of its compound leaves. Jacobs ladder derives its name from the ladderlike arrangement of small leaflets that make up each compound leaf.

Globeflower, *Trollius albiflorus.* Globeflower is common in moist forest openings in the subalpine forest, where it often grows in association with marsh-marigold and Parry primrose. This species is identified by its long-petioled,

THE SOUTHERN ROCKIES

palmate leaves and its buttercup-like cream or pale yellow flowers. The flowers are unusual in that there are small, nectar-bearing petals between the multiple golden stamens and the sepals.

Heart-leaved Twayblade, *Listera cordata.* This tiny orchid is common in boreal forest habitats from the sub-Arctic of North America south through the Pacific Northwest and the Rocky Mountains to northern New Mexico. Heart-leaved twayblade is readily identified by its small size (less than 8 inches tall), two heart-shaped leaves arising opposite each other at about the middle of the flowering stalk, and few-flowered inflorescence. Each flower is small and greenish or slightly reddish in color, with a lower lip split into two narrow prongs. Following fertilization of the flowers, the seeds ripen quickly; it is common to find twayblades with both fresh-looking blooms and empty seed capsules.

Brownie Lady's Slipper, *Cypripedium fasciculatum.* Brownie lady's slipper is found in subalpine forests in the Rocky Mountains and Pacific Northwest. This orchid is identified by its robust growth form, multiple ovate leaves, and inflorescence with several nodding, purple-brown flowers. Each flower has a bulbous, pouchlike lip and is topped by three slender purplish green petals.

Common Plants of the Spruce-Fir Forests

Trees

Fir, corkbark, *Abies arizonica*
   subalpine, *Abies lasiocarpa*
   white, *Abies concolor*
Pine, lodgepole, *Pinus contorta*
   Engelmann, *Picea engelmannii*

Shrubs

Birch, bog, *Betula glandulosa*
Blueberry, broom, *Vaccinium scoparium*

    dwarf, *Vaccinium cespitosum*
    myrtle, *Vaccinium myrtillus*
Buffaloberry, *Shepherdia canadensis*
Cinquefoil, shrubby, *Pentaphylloides floribunda*
Cranberry, high-bush, *Viburnum edule*
Currant, Colorado, *Ribes coloradense* and *R. wolfii*
Elderberry, red, *Sambucus microbotrys*
Juniper, common, *Juniperus communis*
Mountain-lover, *Paxistima myrsinites*
Willow, *Salix* spp.

Wildflowers

Arnica, broad-leaf, *Arnica latifolia*
Avens, alpine, *Acomastylis rossii,* (formerly *Geum*)
Bistort, American, *Bistorta bistortoides*
Chickweed, *Stellaria umbellata*
Coneflower, Colorado rayless, *Rudbeckia occidentalis*
Daisy, showy, *Erigeron peregrinus*
Gilia, trumpet, *Ipomopsis aggregata*
Globeflower, *Trollius albiflorus*
Hellebore, false, *Veratrum tenuipetalum*
Jacobs Ladder, *Polemonium pulcherrimum* ssp. *delicatum*
Lady's Slipper, brownie, *Cypripedium fasciculatum*
Lady's Tresses, *Spiranthes romanzoffiana*
Lousewort, curled, *Pedicularis racemosa*
    Grays, *Pedicularis grayi*
Marigold, marsh, *Psychrophila leptosepala,* (formerly
    Caltha)
Monkshood, *Aconitum columbianum*
Orchid, northern bog, *Limnorchis hyperborea*
    heart-leaved twayblade, *Listera cordata*
    rattlesnake plantain, *Goodyera oblongifolia*
Pipsissewa, *Chimaphila umbellata* ssp. *occidentalis*
Primrose, Parry, *Primula parryi*
Pyrola, swamp, *Pyrola rotundifolia* ssp. *asarifolia*
Sunflower, aspen, *Helianthella quinquenervis*
Twinflower, *Linnaea borealis*
Wintergreen, lesser, *Pyrola minor*
    one-sided, *Orthilia secunda*
Wood Nymph, *Moneses uniflora*

Environment and Adaptation: Animals of the Spruce-Fir Forests

To survive in the spruce-fir forests, resident animal species must cope with extreme cold, deep snows (which impede travel and foraging), and a short growing season (which limits both the abundance and diversity of food resources). Not surprisingly, the number of species in these high-elevation forests is considerably less than that found in forest-edge habitats or in lower-elevation forests. Spruce-fir forests provide critical habitat for boreal species such as the three-toed woodpecker, gray jay, pine grosbeak, red crossbill, mountain chickadee, red-breasted nuthatch, chickaree, red-backed vole, marten, and snowshoe hare. Each is uniquely bound to these forests in ways that biologists are only beginning to understand.

The arrival of spring and the beginning of the breeding season mark an increase in both species diversity and abundance. The advertisement songs of hermit thrushes, Townsend's solitaires, mountain chickadees, and ruby-crowned kinglets can be heard above the nasal chatterings of nuthatches and the drumming of woodpeckers. In the tree islands that fringe the forest's upper limits, white-crowned sparrows chirp warnings from the tops of flagged trees. Elk and mule deer follow the retreating line of the snowpack, taking advantage of the lush herbage to be found in forest openings. In the heart of the forest, swift-flying predators such as the northern goshawk and the sharp-shinned hawk dart through the maze of branches in pursuit of their prey. Red foxes move silently along game trails, watchful for the unwary showshoe hare or vole. A marten races along a spruce branch, its unwelcome presence announced by the strident trilling of a chickaree. Unfortunately, the large predators that once roamed these dense forests — the Canada lynx and the wolverine — have largely been extirpated in the Southern Rockies.

Plant-Animal Interactions

After a severe winter or when high populations of snowshoe hares or voles are present, it is common to see shrubs and saplings that have been overbrowsed or debarked. Browsing pressure poses a serious problem to woody plants that are already at a disadvantage as a result of the short growing season. Many such plants combat heavy winter browsing through a process called compensatory growth: vigorous sprouting at the stump or the stimulation of resting buds on surviving branches to produce new shoots with an abundance of larger, chlorophyll-rich leaves.

Another antiherbivore strategy is clearly defensive and involves the production of chemical compounds that make the plant's tissues less palatable and even toxic to herbivores. Some plants concentrate the production of these defensive compounds during the early, or juvenile, stages of growth or when heavy browsing initates the regrowth of juvenile shoots. On the other hand, plants that grow slowly have a limited capacity for compensatory growth and thus maintain their defensive chemical arsenal throughout all stages.

When resin- or phenol-rich plant tissues are consumed in sufficient quantities, they can seriously interfere with the digestive and metabolic processes necessary for survival. Herbivores tend to be very selective in their browsing habits, often choosing less chemically defended genotypes of a preferred browse species. Snowshoe hares appear to be especially sensitive to the resin content of their preferred browse, selecting more mature twigs and leaves rather than the more resin-enriched juvenile growth stages. Feeding experiments with captive hares have shown that they will lose weight rapidly and die if fed a monospecific diet of resinous, juvenile–growth-stage twigs. On the other hand, blue grouse and white-tailed ptarmigan often subsist for several months on a monospecific diet of resin- or phenol-rich leaves and buds. How, then, are some animals able to cope physiologically with plant chemical defenses, while others must avoid these substances? Blue grouse are apparently able to adapt to a moderately toxic diet, largely through the ability to concentrate and detoxify resins in the caecum and to excrete these substances in the form of caecal droppings. Behavioral observations, however, indicate that such an adaptation requires greater expenditure of energy than does the simple avoidance of heavily defended tissues.

Adaptations to Cold and Snow

Animals that overwinter in the spruce-fir forest adapt to seasonal environmental change through a combination of behavioral, morphological, and physiological mechanisms. The chapter on snow includes a discussion of several of these adaptations. The unusually broad and flexible hind feet of the snowshoe hare, the dense mat of winter fur that envelops the feet of the marten, and the stiff tufts of feathers that surround the toes of the white-tailed ptarmigan provide floatation and dramatically improve the ability of these animals to move about on the snow.

Mechanisms for maintaining normal body temperature are of critical importance to the overwintering success of both mammals and birds. The temperature at which it becomes necessary for an animal to increase its metabolic rate in order to balance heat loss to the environment is called the *lower critical temperature,* or LCT. The LCT varies from one species to another and tends to adjust seasonally in most species, generally through changes in insulation thickness. Some animals, such as the chickaree, undergo surprisingly little seasonal LCT adjustment and must rely instead on good nest

From left to right: snowshoe hare, long-tailed weasel.

insulation and high food consumption. The red fox and the porcupine, on the other hand, achieve a substantial drop in their winter LCT's as a result of increased underfur insulation. Gray jays, too, rely on the insulative benefits of their loose, thick feathering, which they can puff out to trap a protective layer of air around the body.

At high elevations, weasels survive at what appears to be the limit of their metabolic capacity. Their unique hunting niche depends on the ability to search through narrow runways and rock piles to find hidden prey unavailable to other predators. Though remarkable for its prowess in tight-squeeze situations, the weasel, with its long, thin body, exposes a relatively large surface area to the air. Weasels are almost constantly expending energy on heat production. Even their resting metabolism is nearly twice that of other mammals of similar mass. Without sufficient food to fuel their metabolic needs, weasels die of starvation after only one or two days. To minimize energy consumption during the winter months, weasels restrict their hunting activities to just a few hours out of each day. Since hunting requires three to five times more energy than resting, time spent in a snug nest prolongs the amount of time the weasel can survive without eating.

In preparation for winter, many animals accumulate reserves of brown fat, a kind of fatty tissue that provides the fuel for metabolic heat production. Birds lack brown fat and, when not generating heat through the muscle activity of flight, must rely on shivering thermogenesis to maintain normal body temperature. Most cold-climate species exhibit an increased capacity for shivering thermogenesis in winter resulting from a seasonal increase in the lipid known as triglyceride and a reduction in the rate of carbohydrate depletion. Chickadees carry this adaptive process one step further, undergoing a torporlike lowering of body temperature triggered by decreasing ambient temperatures. By reducing its body temperature during periods of inactivity, the chickadee effectively minimizes the temperature gradient between body and air, substantially reducing the amount of energy needed to maintain a stable body temperature.

There can be little doubt that a persistent snow cover is the primary selective pressure that led to the evolution of seasonal color change in species such as the snowshoe hare and the long-tailed weasel. The debate over the adaptive benefits of white coloration, however, is represented by two opposing points of view. One suggests that the advantages of cryptic coloration for both predator and prey stimulate the seasonal color change. The other relates the issue to energetics and the fact that white coloration serves to minimize heat exchange with the environment. Unfortunately, the arguments in favor of either point of view are inconclusive. In both cases, changes in temperature and photoperiod appear to play a role in initiating color change to coincide with annual changes in snow cover.

Life Histories of Selected Animals

Mammals

Snowshoe Hare, *Lepus americanus.* This lovely hare is about midway in size between a cottontail and a jackrabbit and is distinguished by its unusually broad hind feet, comparatively short ears, and, in winter, white pelage and black-tipped ears; the transitional pelage typical of early spring and late fall is distinctly dappled, changing to a rusty grayish brown during the summer. Snowshoe hares are boreal mammals and are associated with densely forested habitat from the Arctic Circle southward along the principal mountain ranges to Tennessee, New Mexico, and central California. Snowshoe hares are herbivorous, nocturnal, and relatively solitary, resting by day in shallow depressions excavated beneath dense shrubbery or under fallen trees. Breeding occurs from March through August, and females generally produce two litters of precocial young a year. Young hares reach adult size between three and five months of age but are unable to breed until the following season.

Marten, *Martes americana.* The marten is distinguished by its catlike size, yellowish underside, rich brown upperparts, rounded ears, and bushy, cylindrical tail. These boreal mammals are found in lodgepole pine, spruce-fir, and alpine habitats in the Southern Rockies. Martens are mostly nocturnal and solitary, spending daylight hours and severe weather periods resting in tree holes or abandoned squirrel nests. Active year-round, these carnivores are adept at hunting in trees for red squirrels and birds or on the ground for snowshoe hares and small mammals. Martens are curious and relatively unafraid of humans, often approaching quite closely and emitting a "chuckling" vocalization. Mating occurs in summer, but like most mustelids, implantation is delayed for six to eight months. Though altricial at birth, young martens develop rapidly and leave the nest at two months of age.

Long-tailed Weasel, *Mustela frenata.* This slender-bodied mustelid is easily distinguished by its foot-long size (including the tail), bounding gait, and fur that is chestnut brown above and golden buff below; winter pelage is white except for the black-tipped tail. In the Southern Rockies, the long-tailed weasel is common in a variety of habitats but is especially prevalent near talus and along streams. Weasels prey mostly on small mammals and ground-nesting birds. The entrance to a weasel burrow is often marked with accumulations of scat. Weasels have scent glands that make them unpalatable to most predators. Long-tailed weasels mate in summer, with ovulation induced by copulation. Implantation of the embryo, however, is delayed until the following spring. A litter of altricial young is born in an underground nest-chamber in April. Young weasels develop rapidly, and females are able to begin breeding their first summer.

Birds

Blue Grouse, *Dendragapus obscurus.* This chicken-sized bird is distinguished from other grouse by the sooty gray tail with lighter gray band and mottled gray-brown plumage; males have a yellowish orange comb over each eye. When engaging in sexual displays, males expose an inflatable patch of bare yellow skin ringed by gray-tipped white feathers. In the Southern Rockies, blue grouse occur in a wide variety of conifer, mixed conifer-aspen, and shrubland habitats, retreating to dense forests of lodgepole pine and spruce-fir during fall and winter. During the courtship period in spring, male blue grouse perform displays that include strutting, tail fanning, drumming, inflation of the neck crests, and erection of the neck ruff feathers. Following mating, females construct a well-concealed nest on the ground; females incubate the eggs and rear the young alone. Following fledging, young grouse remain with the mother until early autumn. Blue grouse are solitary during the winter but may occasionally form small unisexual groups.

Northern Saw-whet Owl, *Aegolius acadicus.* This strikingly colored owl is identified by its robinlike size, yellow eyes, prominent reddish streaking on the breast, white-spotted wings, lack of ear tufts, and reddish facial disk. Northern saw-whet owls are found from northeastern Alaska across Canada and southward to northern Mexico; in the Southern Rockies, the species is most common in dense coniferous forests and riparian woodlands. Saw-whet owls are nocturnal hunters of small mammals; birds and insects may be taken when available. The species roosts during the day, selecting a site close to its nesting cavity during the breeding season or in dense evergreens during the winter. Vocalizations consist primarily of a repetitious series of "whoops" said to resemble the sound of a saw blade being sharpened; vocalizations intensify in March and end by June.

Three-toed Woodpecker, *Picoides tridactylus.* The three-toed woodpecker is distinguished from other woodpeckers by its heavily barred sides and variously barred back, and, in the male, by its yellow head patch. Though closely tied to the boreal forests of North America and Eurasia, the species is extending its range south into suitable spruce-dominated habitat along the Rocky Mountains. Three-toed woodpeckers are insectivorous, concentrating on wood-boring beetles and bark insects. Males attract females by drumming and then perform a head-swaying display. Nests are excavated in snags or other suitable trees and are lined with wood chips. Both the male and female incubate the eggs and rear the young; the male roosts nightly in the nest throughout incubation. Following fledging, families remain together throughout much of the summer.

Gray Jay, *Perisoreus canadensis.* Gray jays are identified by their all-over gray coloring and by their darker gray backs and wings. Variously known as the "Canada jay," "whiskey-jack," and "camp-robber," the gray jay is notoriously tame and bold and will often take food—with or without permission—out of the hand. In the Southern Rockies, this boreal species is a year-round resident of high-elevation coniferous forests. Vocalizations are highly variable and may include a whistled "wheeoo" and a lower-pitched "chuck." Gray jays are insectivorous, gleaning insects from the bark and foliage of conifers. This species is often observed caching food, in the form of a saliva-permeated *bolus*, which sustains the jay during winter months and provides food for the young born in early spring. During courtship, the male gray jay employs whisper-singing and ritualized feeding of the female. A bulky but well-woven nest is typically constructed on a horizontal branch; insulative materials cached the previous season enable nest building when snow still covers the ground. Both sexes cooperate in the rearing of the young.

Red-breasted Nuthatch, *Sitta canadensis.* This sparrow-sized bird is distinguished from other nuthatches by its rust-colored underparts, black cap, facial stripes, and slate-blue upperparts; females and juveniles have paler underparts. In the Southern Rockies, this boreal species is most common in high-altitude spruce-fir forests but may be found in both mixed-coniferous forests and deciduous woodlands. The nuthatch's call is a nasal "anck-anck-anck," resembling the sound of a toy horn. Red-breasted nuthatches are insectivorous during much of the year and resemble small woodpeckers in the way that they search in the bark for food; this species concentrates its foraging activities in the top one-third of a tree and commonly descends a tree headfirst, depending on its feet rather than its tail for support. The winter diet consists largely of conifer seeds, with irruptive migrations occurring when the cone crop is poor. Courtship behavior by the male involves a mixture of wing-drooping and swaying displays punctuated by singing; mated pairs remain together through the winter. The red-breasted nuthatch excavates its own nest cavity, surrounding the entrance with a sticky mass of pitch that is maintained throughout nesting.

Ruby-crowned Kinglet, *Regulus calendula.* This diminutive bird is identified by its grayish olive upperparts, dusky breast, two white wing bars, and silvery eye ring; the male's red crown patch is seldom visible except during the breeding season. In the Southern Rockies, this boreal species is a common summer resident of spruce-fir and other types of dense coniferous forests, moving south to lowland sites in winter. Kinglets are insectivorous, gleaning insects mostly from the foliage but occasionally catching them on the wing. These birds are extremely active while foraging, jumping and turning repeatedly as they move about the outer foliage of trees and shrubs. The territorial and courtship song is melodious and ends on a series of descending "tew" notes. The nest consists of a feather-lined cup woven of grasses and moss, suspended from a horizontal branch by spiderwebs. The female incubates the eggs, but both parents feed the brood following hatching.

Hermit Thrush, *Catharus guttatus.* This sparrow-sized bird, renowned for its flutelike song, is identified by its speckled breast, olive brown upperparts, reddish tail, white eye ring, and nervous twitching of the wings. In the Southern Rockies, this boreal species is a common summer resident of high-elevation spruce-fir and mixed-coniferous forests. Hermit thrushes are shy and somewhat inconspicuous, except for their beautiful song resonating throughout the forest at dawn and dusk. Foraging style consists of short, scuffling hops across the forest floor; thrushes supplement their insect diet with berries and other fruit as they become available. Hermit thrushes nest on the ground or, occasionally, a short distance off the ground; the nest is a grass- and fiber-woven cup, often with a middle layer of mud. The female incubates the eggs, but both sexes rear the young.

Pine Grosbeak, *Pinicola enucleator.* This robin-sized bird is identified by its plump appearance, dark tail, two white wing bars, and stubby, strongly down-curved beak; males

Common birds of the subalpine forest: hermit thrush (left), ruby-crowned kinglet (right).

of the species have an all-over wash of rosy red, whereas females and immature males exhibit olive yellow heads. In the Southern Rockies, this boreal species is present year-round and associated with high-elevation spruce-fir and mixed-coniferous forests. Pine grosbeaks forage on conifer and other seeds, ranging widely during times of food shortage. When moving from one foraging area to another, their whistling calls and deeply undulating "roller-coaster" flight styles are reliable field marks. During the breeding season, grosbeaks develop a pair of pouches below the tongue for transporting food to the young. Nesting pairs remain relatively solitary until their broods have fledged, but then form gregarious, loose flocks as they forage through the forest in late summer.

White-crowned Sparrow, *Zonotrichia leucophrys.* This large sparrow is identified by its black-and-white-striped crown (juveniles have buff-and-brown head stripes) and its strongly streaked back and wings. In the Southern Rockies, white-crowned sparrows may be present in a variety of grassland and brushy habitats during migration but are most common during the breeding season in the forest-tundra ecotone. This species is opportunistic, feeding on insects, seeds,

Common birds of the forest-tundra ecotone: gray jay (left), white-crowned sparrow (right).

flower buds, and moss capsules as available; most feeding occurs on the ground. The song consists of one or more whistled notes followed by a resounding, twittering twill; the alarm call is a loud "pink" or "tseep." Nesting occurs on the ground or low in a shrub, in a site chosen by the female. The male feeds the female while she incubates the eggs, but the female normally feeds the young during the first few days after hatching; males may assume the majority of the care and feeding of the young while the female begins a second nest.

Common Animals of the Spruce-Fir Forest and Forest-Tundra Ecotone

Mammals

Montane Shrew, *Sorex monticolus*
Mountain (or Nuttall's) Cottontail, *Sylvilagus nuttallii*
Snowshoe Hare, *Lepus americanus*
Least Chipmunk, *Tamias minimus*
Golden-mantled Ground Squirrel, *Spermophilus lateralis*
Red Squirrel, *Tamiasciurus hudsonicus*
Northern Pocket Gopher, *Thomomys talpoides*
Deer Mouse, *Peromyscus maniculatus*
Southern Red-backed Vole, *Clethrionomys gapperi*
Montane Vole, *Microtus montanus*
Porcupine, *Erethizon dorsatum*
Red Fox, *Vulpes vulpes*
Black Bear, *Ursus americanus*
Marten, *Martes americana*
Long-tailed Weasel, *Mustela frenata*
Ermine, *Mustela erminea*
Lynx, *Felis lynx*
Bobcat, *Felis rufus*
Elk, *Cervus elaphus*
Mule Deer, *Odocoileus hemionus*
Bighorn Sheep, *Ovis canadensis*

Birds

Northern Goshawk, *Accipiter gentilis*
Sharp-shinned Hawk, *Accipiter striatus*
Blue Grouse, *Dendragapus obscurus*
White-tailed Ptarmigan, *Lagopus leucurus*
Northern Saw-whet Owl, *Aegolius acadicus*
Boreal Owl, *Aegolius funereus*
Northern Pygmy Owl, *Glaucidium gnoma*
Hairy Woodpecker, *Picoides villosus*
Three-toed Woodpecker, *Picoides tridactylus*
Olive-sided Flycatcher, *Contopus borealis*
Gray Jay, *Perisoreus canadensis*
Steller's Jay, *Cyanocitta stelleri*
Clark's Nutcracker, *Nucifraga columbiana*
Mountain Chickadee, *Parus gambeli*
Brown Creeper, *Certhia americana*
Red-breasted Nuthatch, *Sitta canadensis*
White-breasted Nuthatch, *Sitta carolinensis*
Ruby-crowned Kinglet, *Regulus calendula*
Golden-crowned Kinglet, *Regulus satrapa*
Townsend's Solitaire, *Myadestes townsendi*
Hermit Thrush, *Catharus guttatus*
Wilson's Warbler, *Wilsonia pusilla*
Red Crossbill, *Loxia curvirostra*
Pine Grosbeak, *Pinicola enucleator*
Cassin's Finch, *Carpodacus cassinii*
Dark-eyed Junco, *Junco hyemalis*
White-crowned Sparrow, *Zonotrichia leucophrys*

CHAPTER TWENTY-THREE

Islands in the Clouds:
Alpine Tundra

ALPINE TUNDRA PROVIDES a surprising counterpoint to the rugged, ice-etched massifs of the Southern Rockies. With the coming of summer, alpine meadows are opulent with the colors of wildflowers — pale blue, magenta, lapis, yellow, and white. Snowbanks linger along lee slopes, their edges marked by chrome yellow snow buttercups. Hidden among the willows at the edge of a meltwater pool, a white-tailed ptarmigan can be heard as she clucks softly to her wandering chicks. A short distance upslope, a marmot basks in sunshine, its body pressed closely to the boulder on which it rests. Nearby, a nasal squawk reveals the presence of a pika in the labyrinthine corridors of the boulder field. High on the ridge above, strong winds send a flock of rosy finches scudding downvalley.

Ecological Distribution

The word *tundra* is Russian and means "land of no trees." It was originally applied to Arctic regions and to the distinctive, cold-adapted vegetation associated with lands north of the Arctic Circle. Because of the physiognomic similarities between Arctic plant communities and those found above treelimit on mountains south of the Arctic Circle, plant ecologists refer to these high-elevation counterparts as *alpine tundra.*

Alpine tundra ecosystems are found on high mountains throughout the Southern Rockies, extending from treelimit at between 11,200 and 12,000 feet to mountain summits exceeding 14,000 feet. The lower limit of the alpine zone corresponds approximately to the 50°F isotherm for the warmest

Alpine tundra in the Colorado Front Range. *Audrey D. Benedict.*

summer month and is variable from one area to another depending on local environmental and microclimatic factors. There is a general decrease in the elevation of treelimit from south to north along the Southern Rockies. In the absence of a clearly defined forest-tundra ecotone, the lower limit of alpine tundra coincides with timberline and may include isolated patches of subalpine vegetation.

Physical Environment

The alpine zone is defined by extremes — high solar radiation, cold temperatures, and strong winds. Due to the heterogeneity of most alpine areas, great environmental contrasts often occur within short distances and within short time spans. In contrast to temperate environments, where the effects of climatic factors on physical, chemical, and biological processes are somewhat muted and difficult to isolate, the role of climate in shaping the alpine environment is readily apparent.

Despite similarities with the Arctic environment in terms of low mean annual temperature and snow-cover duration, several features differentiate midlatitude alpine climates from those of the Arctic. Midlatitude alpine areas experience regular diurnal and seasonal solar radiation regimes, whereas the Arctic receives virtually no solar radiation during the six-month span of the Arctic winter. Because of their high elevations, alpine areas receive intense solar radiation on clear days during the growing season. The twenty-four–hour photoperiod of the Arctic summer, however, tends to equalize the total annual radiation input each area receives.

Alpine Temperatures

Cool summer temperatures are the main reason that trees do not grow in Arctic and alpine tundra environments. In the Southern Rockies, the length of the growing or frost-free season averages less than forty days; daytime temperatures during the summer seldom rise above the low 60s. The alpine temperature regime is subject to highly localized variations resulting from slope and microtopographic differences. For example, while the air temperature a few feet above the ground may be cold, temperatures at or near the ground surface—in the zone where plants grow—may be considerably warmer. Alpine plants themselves may play an important role in modifying the air temperatures of their microenvironments. The temperature inside a lilac-colored flower, for example, may exceed that of the surrounding air by several degrees, and is considerably higher than that within a more reflective white flower.

Precipitation

Annual precipitation in the alpine tundra is highly variable but averages around 40 inches, most falling as snow during the winter months. During the summer, late-lying and permanent snowfields are common in many alpine areas and are especially prominent where strong winds cause substantial redistribution of winter snow. In sites adjacent to persistent snowbanks, meltwater may be present in abundance throughout much of the growing season; plants growing under such conditions must be adapted to cold, saturated soils and to the rill and gully erosion typical of such sites. On the other hand, ridges and other areas blown free of snow are characterized by drought conditions both winter and summer.

Wind

Wind is a critical component of the alpine environment. Wind velocity varies significantly from one area to another as well as on a seasonal basis. In the Southern Rockies, average wind speeds of 25 to 30 miles per hour are common during the winter, with gusts exceeding 100 miles per hour typical of the period from October to February. Summer wind velocity is considerably less, averaging between 18 and 20 miles per hour. The pattern of wind flow is influenced by both small- and large-scale topographic features. Ridges and other upland sites are often subjected to the strongest winds and provide the most severe environments for alpine plants in terms of temperature, drought stress, frost action, and wind abrasion.

The effects of wind on alpine vegetation may be pronounced in certain areas. Wind effectively reduces air and leaf temperatures, increases transpiration rates, and influences the physiognomy of alpine plants as a result of mechanical abrasion caused by wind-transported snow, ice, and soil particles. The pattern of snow accumulation and snowmelt that results from the redistribution of snow by wind is of critical importance in the establishment of alpine vegetation patterns.

Community Characteristics

Alpine landscapes in the Southern Rockies are highly varied, reflecting differences in rock type, geologic structure, and erosional patterns. Geomorphic processes are intensified by the severe climate and steep terrain. The character of a given alpine site is closely linked to its geologic history, which may include glaciation, frost action, patterned ground formation, mass-wasting, or other geomorphic processes. Readers interested in a more detailed discussion of alpine landscape development should refer to chapter 7.

Alpine Plant Communities

Tundra plant communities consist mostly of perennial herbs, graminoids (grasses, sedges, and rushes), cushion plants, low shrubs, lichens, and mosses. Alpine plants tend to be small, low growing, and adapted to a short, cold growing season. Annual species, common at lower elevations, are extremely rare and contribute little to the vegetation cover. Of the three hundred or so plant species that make up the alpine vascular flora, more than 40 percent are restricted to alpine habitats. More than 20 percent of our alpine taxa are circumpolar in their distribution, reaching their southernmost limits of distribution in the Southern Rockies. Only a small number of genera and species are endemic to the alpine of the Southern Rockies or to the Rocky Mountains as a whole. Interestingly, several alpine taxa occur in the Southern Rockies and are also common in the high mountains of central Asia (the Altai-Pamir area).

Visitors to the alpine tundra are often astonished by the diversity of plant communities found within relatively short distances. Alpine ecologists describe tundra vegetation as a mosaic of plant communities arranged into types or continua along environmental gradients that include topography, amount and duration of winter snow cover, temperature, wind exposure, and availability of moisture during the growing season. Superimposed on these environmental gradients are differences in soil chemistry, substrate stability, and disturbance impacts resulting from the activities of pocket gophers and other herbivores. In alpine areas, even a few inches of difference in microtopography, such as might be caused by the presence of rock or shrub, can modify windflow patterns, snow drifting, and other attributes of the microhabitat.

Microhabitat, in combination with the tolerance ranges of individual plant species, plays a critical role in the structure, composition, and distribution of alpine plant communities. To a large degree, the patterns that result can be correlated with available moisture. The harshest environments for tundra plants are found on rocky ridges and other windswept, winter-snow–free sites. Only the hardiest and most drought-resistant species—lichens, mosses, and a few cushion plants—are encountered on such sites. At the opposite end of the moisture spectrum, in areas where snow accumulates to substantial depths during winter and persists late into the growing season, the snow-free period may be too brief to allow for the completion of plant reproductive cycles. The most favorable sites for plants are those where the snow cover provides winter protection but melts early enough for long summer growth.

In the Southern Rockies, alpine plant communities can be grouped into five general types: (1) alpine turfs and meadows; (2) fellfield communities; (3) snowbed communities; (4) alpine wetland communities; and (5) talus, scree, and rock crevice communities. Because of the heterogeneity of the alpine environment, most communities are small, and several distinctly different types may be present in proximity.

Alpine Turfs and Meadows

Alpine turf and meadow communities predominate on level to gently rolling sites that have deep, well-drained, relatively fine-textured soils. Best developed on sites that are geologically stable, the vegetation is generally fairly continuous, consisting of a dense growth of perennial herbs, grasses and grasslike plants, and fruticose lichens. Soil moisture is highly variable from one site to another and reflects winter snow accumulation patterns, ranging from xeric sites where strong winds create snow-free conditions throughout much of the winter to mesic sites where winter snow cover is often substantial and where reserves of soil moisture ensure a lush growth of grasses and forbs. The species associations that characterize specific habitat types form a continuum between xeric-adapted associations and associations that thrive under more mesic conditions.

ALPINE TURFS

Alpine turf, or dry meadow, communities are best developed on geomorphically stable sites that are largely snow free during the winter. Communities may be extensive, covering large areas of boulder-strewn and often frost-patterned uplands, as well as the stabilized fronts of rock glaciers and gently sloping moraines. Distinctive in appearance, turf communities are characterized by dense carpets of sod composed of rhizomatous or tussock-forming perennial sedges, grasses, and forbs. Once established, these durable communities stabilize slopes and reduce erosion, promote continued soil development, and enhance water absorption. Three types of turf are recognized in the tundra of the Southern Rockies: (1) elk sedge, or kobresia, turf (dominated by *Kobresia myosuroides*); (2) false elk sedge turf (dominated by *Carex elynoides*); and (3) rock sedge turf (dominated by *Carex rupestris*). Some alpine ecologists suggest that kobresia turfs represent the climatic climax ecosystem of high tundra regions of the Southern Rockies.

Kobresia turfs are most common on ridgetops, summits, and passes that are relatively snow-free in winter and not excessively windy. The species forms similar turf communities on exposed tundra slopes in the Alps, the Urals, Iceland, Greenland, and the eastern coast of Siberia. Studies of kobresia stands in Rocky Mountain National Park have shown that the restriction of kobresia to sites that are largely snow-free most of the winter results from the fact that kobresia requires approximately six to seven months to complete vegetative and floral development and is therefore intolerant of prolonged snow cover. Compact tussocks of kobresia dominate a typical stand, with a scattering of herbaceous species such as alpine harebell, moss gentian, alpine meadowrue, alpine forget-me-not, alpine primrose, and western yellow paintbrush. As these turfs age, kobresia, with its dense root system, tends to dominate herbaceous species, which are less able to compete for water. In many alpine areas, kobresia turfs are heavily grazed by elk and bighorn sheep.

False elk sedge turfs tolerate shallow snow cover and have a higher incidence of exposed soil and rock. Turfs dominated by this species are less cushiony underfoot than those of kobresia, although the two species are similar in appearance. Differences between the two types of turf are especially conspicuous in the fall, when the straw color of false elk sedge contrasts sharply with the burnished copper swards of kobresia. During early summer, forbs such as alpine parsley, old-man-of-the-mountain, greenleaf chimingbells, and alpine clover provide a colorful display. Rock sedge turfs, in contrast to the more common communities dominated by kobresia or false elk sedge, form small, somewhat open stands in areas with less-well-developed soils. Forbs are less prominent in this community type and include such species as alpine potentilla and draba.

Common plants of alpine meadows, clockwise from upper left: alpine avens, sky pilot, American bistort, old-man-of-the-mountain.

ALPINE MEADOWS

Alpine meadows, in contrast to the compact economy of sedge-dominated turfs, are luxuriant in their profusion of forbs and grasses, providing a summer-long tapestry of wildflower color. Not surprisingly, alpine meadows include more species of wildflowers, grasses, and mosses than are found in any other tundra community in the Southern Rockies. Because of their affinity for moist environments, alpine meadows are found on gentle lee slopes and in shallow basins where they are protected from the harsh winter climate by a blanket of early-melting snow; on some sites the snow cover may persist into late June or early July. Soils tend to be less rocky than turf soils and are relatively deep, rich in organic material, and well drained. Alpine meadows include a variety of vegetation associations whose distribution can be correlated with soil moisture and snow-cover duration.

Meadows dominated by alpine avens and other colorful wildflowers are typical of the most wind-sheltered and moist sites. These meadows are among the most strikingly beautiful tundra communities because of the great diversity of associated tundra plants, including sky pilot, American bistort, alpine wallflower, mountain harebell, alplily, narcissus anemone, and alpine chimingbells. During some years, spectacular displays of American bistort or the endemic old-man-of-the-mountain lend monochromatic splendor. Summer's end is heralded by the elegant white trumpets of Arctic gentian and by a firestorm of autumn color that transforms the foliage of alpine avens to burgundy red and splashes the tundra with gold and ochre.

Though less visually dramatic than the forb-rich communities, subalpine and alpine meadows dominated by tufted hairgrass occur in both the Northern and Southern hemispheres and are common throughout the Southern Rockies. Hairgrass meadows are typical of sites that are covered with snow too long to be tolerated by kobresia but that lack sufficient moisture to support wetland sedges such as Rocky Mountain sedge, *Carex scopulorum*. In early summer, blueleaf potentilla, alpine avens, alpine ragwort, alpine chickweed, and Parry clover bloom brightly among the hairgrass tussocks.

ANIMAL-DISTURBED COMMUNITIES

Alpine turfs and meadows are often heavily used by herbivores. Mounds of loose soil and the sinuous castings or "gopher eskers" left behind by the winter burrowing activities of northern pocket gophers may be conspicuous in many areas. During years when vole populations are high, large patches of vegetation may be severely grazed and meadow areas riddled with small holes and tunnel systems. Animal-disturbed sites, especially those in which pocket gophers or other burrowers have exposed substantial amounts of bare soil, are typically invaded by a distinctive group of species that includes sky pilot, alpine chimingbells, and alpine avens, with lesser amounts of American bistort, yarrow, black-headed sage, and old-man-of-the-mountain. In areas of shallow snow accumulation, Arctic sage, Parry clover, or tufted hairgrass may dominate sites that have experienced repeated digging and grazing by pocket gophers. The occurrence of fellfield species such as moss campion and whiproot clover in patchy turf can often be explained by the ability of these species to invade disturbed sites.

Fellfield Communities

Fell is the Gaelic word for rock. The name *fellfield* is applied to the distinctive plant communities found on rocky, windswept ridgetops and other exposed windward sites. Rocks and bare gravel are conspicuous in most fellfield communities. Fellfield soils, in contrast to soils found in turf or meadow communities, are coarse-textured, with little organic matter and limited profile development; the most severe sites are characterized by periodic deflation of the soil as a result of wind scour. Fellfield communities are characterized by a diversity of plant species whose cushion and matlike growth forms enable them to survive the harsh fellfield environment. Fellfields are remarkably similar to deserts in the severity of their environment. Fellfield plants are subject to severe desiccation both winter and summer as a result of wind exposure, the impoverished and permeable nature of the soil, and the lack of a winter snow cover.

From a distance, the fellfield habitat appears somewhat barren when compared with other tundra communities. In late spring and early summer, however, it resembles a richly colored carpet. More than half of the vegetation is made up of cushion-forming plants such as alpine phlox and moss campion. This growth form, which has evolved independently in diverse plant families, consists of a tightly interwoven cluster of branches and shoots connected to a long, central taproot. Rosette-forming species such as big-rooted spring-

Common plants of fellfield habitats, clockwise from upper left: mountain dryad in fruit, detail of mountain dryad flower, alpine phlox, dwarf clover, moss campion, moss campion showing its growth form and taproot.

beauty and mat-forming species such as dwarf clover and mountain dryad are especially common in certain communities. Based on differences in environmental factors and species composition, three major fellfield types are recognized in the Southern Rockies: (1) fellfields dominated by cushion plants; (2) fellfields dominated by mat-forming species; and (3) fellfields dominated by mountain dryad.

CUSHION PLANT COMMUNITIES

Fellfields dominated by cushion plants are found through-out higher alpine areas of the Southern Rockies. These communities are most common on nonglaciated and relatively stable surfaces that are blown free of snow during the winter. Because of the environmental extremes typical of such sites, they generally have a higher proportion of bare rock and gravel than vegetation cover; cushion plants constitute more than 70 percent of the vegetation cover. The most common species include moss campion, alpine nailwort, alpine phlox, alpine sandwort, and alpine forget-me-not. Dwarf clover and a sprinkling of drought-adapted, erect species such as the little alpine sunflower and spike woodrush may be found in some communities. Soil lichens and mosses are especially prominent, in sharp contrast to the situation in other fellfield habitats.

Cushion and mat-forming species play critical roles in colonizing and stabilizing newly exposed rock and gravel habitats. With their tiny, highly modified leaves, long tap-roots, and compact growth forms, these plants are able to outcompete erect species in invading barren, exposed sites. Though cushion plants may be found in other alpine communities, they tend to be less vigorous here, and are subject to invasion and competition from erect species. In certain situations, cushion plants form the stable vegetation type for a given site, whereas in others, these communities represent a stage of succession in the establishment of a turf or dry meadow. In the successional case, cushions of moss campion and alpine sandwort provide a suitable substrate for the establishment of seedlings of kobresia, alpine avens, western yellow paintbrush, alplily, and many other species.

MAT-FORMING PLANT COMMUNITIES

Fellfield communities dominated by mat-forming species are typical of low alpine sites where the conditions are less severe than those associated with cushion-plant communities and where a shallow snow cover may be present periodi-cally during the winter. Communities dominated by exten-sive mats of alpine clover tend to be most common on level to gently sloping sites with a more favorable moisture re-gime than is associated with most fellfield communities. In late June and early July, a rose-colored carpet of alpine clover gives way to the scattered flowers of alpine wallflower, gold flower, alpine chimingbells, and alpine reedgrass. During certain years, old-man-of-the-mountain may produce a spectacular display on some sites. Soil lichens and mosses are considerably less important than in communities dominated by cushion plants.

MOUNTAIN DRYAD COMMUNITIES

Fellfield communities dominated by mountain dryad are associated with extremely windy sites that are blown free of snow throughout much of the winter. Most communities are found on unstable slopes, with a preference for north-facing slopes, and on soils that tend to be finer-textured and moister than is typical of other fellfield habitats. Most communities are characterized by a large proportion of bare ground and a patchy vegetation cover. With the coming of summer, the dryad's large, white flowers provide a showy display, repeated once again when the mature fruits unfurl their plumes in late summer. Occurring in association with mountain dryad are species such as mat saxifrage, Arctic bluegrass, draba, and goldbloom saxifrage. Soil lichens and mosses are especially prominent in this community.

Mountain dryad is an important pioneer species and soil builder in dry tundra sites because of its wind tolerance, long stout roots, and matlike profusion of branches. In some cases, this diminutive evergreen shrub forms stepped terraces in which the plants occupy the "riser" of each terrace and the "tread" remains largely free of vegetation cover. These miniature terraces generally parallel the contour of the slope and form as a result of the combined influences of surficial frost creep, wind, and the restraining influence of the vegetation cover.

Snowbed Communities

During the long alpine winter, snow accumulates along the walls of cirques and other leeward slopes, in shallow basins, and to the lee of boulders or other obstacles to the wind. In some areas one can find snowbanks that linger well into summer, as well as those that last from one year to the next. Snowbed communities are typical of sites where snowbanks persist well into the alpine summer. Environmental conditions in snowbed communities contrast sharply with those

Common plants of snowbed communities: snow buttercup
(upper left), sibbaldia (upper right), snowlover (center), Parry
clover (lower right), black-headed daisy, with detail showing
dark hairs on the underside of the flowerhead.

of other alpine habitats. Plants covered by winter snow experience warmer and more constant air and soil temperatures, higher humidity, and greater protection from wind
desiccation and abrasion. A late-lying snow cover may also
prevent plants from breaking dormancy too early and pro-

vides a consistent supply of soil moisture once growth begins. On the other hand, a persistent snow cover further shortens the growing season, in some cases to such an extent that certain plants may be unable to complete reproductive activities. Once the snow has melted, saturated soils on slopes are subject to solifluction, while those on level surfaces may experience active frost heaving and needle-ice development. Summer soil temperatures in snowbed sites are also lower than those in nonsaturated areas because of the evaporation of meltwater.

The character and species composition of a given snowbed community corresponds to the duration of the snow cover, which determines the length of the growing season and the amount of moisture present in the soil. Snowbed communities often exhibit concentric bands or zones that mark the progressive stages in the seasonal attrition of a late-lying snowbank. These zoned communities may be conspicuous, with an outer ring of snow buttercups in full bloom while an inner ring of buttercups may just be greening as it emerges from beneath the snow. In more complex situations, there may be a mosaic of vegetation associations that reflect differences in meltwater drainage and localized variations in snow-cover duration. Several distinct snowbed communities in the Southern Rocky Mountains are recognized: (1) microorganism-dominated snowbed communities; (2) sedge-dominated snowbed communities; (3) rush-dominated snowbed communities; and (4) *Sibbaldia-* and *Lepraria*-dominated snowbed communities.

MICROORGANISM-DOMINATED SNOWBED COMMUNITIES

Permanent and late-lying snowbanks contain a diversity of cold-adapted microorganisms, which include bacteria, algae, fungi, and protozoa. These highly specialized organisms form a distinctive microecosystem, complete with producers, consumers, and decomposers. The most conspicuous of these organisms are the snow algae, of which several species occur in the snowbanks of the Southern Rockies. Streaks and patches of red or pinkish snow reveal the presence of the snow alga *Chlamydomonas nivalis,* a species of green algae that smells like watermelon. First appearing in late May or early June, the reddish coloration of the algae is due to the presence of large numbers of resting spores, which become concentrated in depressions on the snow surface as a result of flowing meltwater.

Snow algae persist as spores in the old snow of permanent snowbanks, but they may also appear in snowbanks that melt completely. Though *Chlamydomonas* algae cells are present throughout the year in certain snowbanks, germination is dependent on the presence of meltwater in the snow. The optimal temperature for growth is around 32°F; the species is unable to grow when temperatures exceed 50°F. Any drop in temperature that causes the snowbank to freeze kills the vegetative stages of the algae but has no effect on resting spores. When temperatures are right and sufficient water is present, however, the free-swimming cells are able to reproduce and form spores within only a few days. Studies have shown that these motile algal cells concentrate radionuclides in the snowpack.

SEDGE-DOMINATED SNOWBED COMMUNITIES

Snowbed communities dominated by Pyrenean sedge and black sedge occupy nivation depressions and other sites that remain snow-covered for as long as eleven months of the year. These extremely late-melting sites are characterized by wet to fully saturated soils, a variable proportion of bare soil and rock, and intensive but relatively shallow frost activity. The degree of vegetation cover reflects the duration of the snow cover. Communities dominated by Pyrenean sedge are readily identified by the dull green, droopy tussocks that typify this species. Other snow-tolerant species, such as Drummond's rush, black-headed daisy, and alpine pussytoes may also be common. Few species complete flowering in this community because of the short growing season and the effects of cold meltwater; several species reproduce by vegetative means.

RUSH-DOMINATED SNOWBED COMMUNITIES

Snowbed communities dominated by Drummond's rush are common in late-lying snow areas and are typical of shallow nivation depressions and other sites with a slightly longer snow-free period than those dominated by Pyrenean sedge. In some cases, communities dominated by Drummond's rush may develop around the perimeter of Pyrenean sedge stands. Soils in rush-dominated snowbed sites are normally fast-drying. The dark green color and wiry appearance of Drummond's rush give this community a distinctive appearance. When in bloom, the diminutive rose-colored flowers of the rush are an exquisite surprise with their feathery pink stigmas, yellow stamens, and brown ovaries. Several other flowering species are also common in this community, including saffron ragwort, black-headed daisy, snow buttercup, and alpine willowherb.

SIBBALDIA- AND LEPRARIA-DOMINATED SNOWBED COMMUNITIES

Snowbed communities dominated by Sibbaldia and the pale gray soil lichen *Lepraria arctica* occupy sites that are snow-free for seven to twelve weeks, well drained, and have relatively fine-textured soils. Though this community may appear quite barren from a distance, closer examination reveals a fairly high herb and lichen cover. In many areas, *Lepraria* tends to form polygonal units of a few inches in diameter, each unit separated by narrow dessiccation cracks. The flowering species snow buttercup, alpine avens, and Parry clover are often common. Sites with slightly less persistent snow cover may support such species as Arctic willow, alpine Timothy, tufted hairgrass, and snowlover.

Alpine Wetland Communities

Nourished by melting snowbanks, wetlands of every size and configuration dot the alpine tundra of the Southern Rockies. Alpine wetlands, with their saturated soils, cold temperatures, and active frost processes are strikingly similar to wetlands found in the Arctic. In fact, Arctic wetland species such as koenigia, icegrass, Arctic saxifrage, and golden saxifrage reach their southernmost limits of distribution in the Southern Rockies. Wetland habitats are highly variable, ranging from exposed, gravelly surfaces that are inundated by shallow, meltwater rivulets for most of the growing season to communities characterized by shallow, standing water and a luxuriant growth of water-loving plants. Most communities are situated on relatively flat surfaces below late-lying

Common plants of alpine wetlands, clockwise from upper left: Rocky Mountain sedge, queens crown with detail of individual floret, elephantella, marsh marigold.

snowbanks, in the catchment areas of alpine basins, and adjacent to ponds, lakes, and streams.

BARE GRAVEL SURFACES

Wetland communities developed on saturated gravels are common along streams and in frost-active areas supplied with meltwater from snowbanks or other sources. Gravel habitats with shallow, continuously flowing water should be examined closely for the reddish, seedlinglike leaves of koenigia. This inconspicuous plant, one of the few annual species to be found in the alpine tundra, takes root in the cold, meltwater-washed gravels, in mats of the moss *Calliergon sarmentosum*, or in small bits of sedge peat. Another rare Arctic species, icegrass, is occasionally found growing in association with koenigia. Showy species, such as queens crown, as well as several small rushes (*Juncus castaneus, J. biglumis,* and *J. triglumis*) and Nelson's sedge, are often present in gravelly habitats.

SEDGE-DOMINATED WETLANDS

Wetland sites characterized by shallow, standing water are found downslope from persistent snowbanks, adjacent to ponds and lakes, and on solifluction terraces. These communities often remain saturated throughout the growing season and are dominated by a luxuriant growth of deep green, stiff-leaved tussocks of Rocky Mountain sedge. In lower alpine sites, especially those in somewhat wind-sheltered areas, Nelson willow may share its wetland habitat with marsh-marigold, globeflower, elephantella, queens crown, star gentian, and little gentian. At higher elevations, alpine lousewort, alpine willowherb, and alpine bistort are the most common flowering species in wetland sites. Despite the dense vegetation cover, pocket gopher activity is limited because of the high water table. Voles are common in sedge-dominated wetlands; their nests and runways are concentrated in the better-drained and most hummocky sites.

Talus, Scree, and Rock Crevice Communities

Rocky habitats are found along the bases of cliffs, around the fronts of rock glaciers and moraines, in blockfields, and on slopes mantled with loose rock rubble. During the winter, snow accumulates between the rocks, ensuring a dependable supply of moisture throughout the growing season. The spaces between the rocks provide a remarkably sheltered environment for plants, affording protection from both wind and cold. Plants associated with rocky habitats tend to be present in small numbers, and are restricted to sites with ample soil and moisture. Many species are rugged pioneers, with either long, shallow root systems or with massive taproots that enable them to make the best possible use of their limited space and substrate.

Slope orientation, the degree of protection provided by the rock, and the stability of the substrate largely determine the species composition of a particular habitat. Species typical of lower elevations, such as death camas, prickly currant, and Colorado columbine, grow in lush splendor in the warmest, most stable wind-sheltered sites. Gently sloping talus and scree are dominated by species such as alpine thistle, talus ragwort, and alpine sorrel. Soil-filled rock crevices support big-rooted springbeauty, alumroot, spotted saxifrage, alpine rock-jasmine, and goldbloom saxifrage. Species that are less tolerant of full sun and strong winds, such as alpine kittentails, dwarf columbine, nodding saxifrage, and adoxa are found beneath overhanging ledges and boulders.

Plant Adaptation: Designs for Survival

Alpine plants exhibit a variety of adaptations that enable them to survive and even to flourish in the harsh alpine climate. Morphological adaptations play a critical role in modifying the complex energy environment to which these plants are subjected. To the first-time visitor, the most striking characteristics of alpine plants are their low growth forms and small sizes. By sacrificing height and leaf size, alpine plants take advantage of the more moderate environment near the ground surface, exposing as little plant tissue as possible to cold temperatures and desiccating winds. Additionally, alpine plants typically have two to six times more biomass below ground than above it, investing their energies in an extensive root or rhizome system that provides them with vital life support during times of water or nutrient stress.

The stems, leaves, and flower buds of alpine plants are especially vulnerable. In the most severe environments, delicate tissues, such as those of mountain dryad, are covered with a thick, waxy cuticle. Other species are coated with hairs of various types that provide insulation from the cold,

THE SOUTHERN ROCKIES

reduce water loss due to transpiration, and moderate damage to leaf tissues caused by high levels of ultraviolet radiation. Conspicuous examples are the silky weft of hairs that cloaks the leaves and stem of old-man-of-the-mountain, and the black, heat-absorbing hairs that distinguish the black-headed daisy. Species growing in especially drought-prone habitats often exhibit a rosettelike growth form or have leaves that are greatly reduced in size, or they may have fleshy, succulent leaves that permit substantial water storage.

Discoidal and parabolic flowers dominate cold-climate environments. These flowers, with their deep centers and highly reflective petals, function as solar collectors by focusing heat and light directly on the reproductive organs. By maximizing the limited heat budget of the alpine summer, the adaptively shaped flowers accelerate the development of pollen and seeds and may also provide a beneficial microclimate for pollinating insects. Some species, such as old-man-of-the-mountain, maximize their solar advantage by facing eastward and by providing a wind-sheltered, basking surface for pollinating insects. Heliotropism, the ability of plants to turn so that their flowers remain facing the sun, has been reported for several Arctic species, but its importance has yet to be established for alpine plants.

The Perennial Advantage

Alpine plants must metabolize, grow, and reproduce at consistently cold growing-season air temperatures. Most alpine vascular plants are herbaceous perennials; a few species are biennial, and only 1 to 2 percent of the flora are annuals. Annual species are at a distinct disadvantage because of their need to complete the entire life cycle from germination to seed production within the short span of the alpine summer. Perennial species, on the other hand, can complete their life cycles more rapidly because they do not need to invest valuable time in germination or in the initial stages of growth.

Most tundra perennials, in contrast to lower-elevation species, produce preformed shoots and flower buds that enable them to initiate growth as soon as environmental conditions become favorable. These preformed buds develop in late summer or early fall and overwinter within a protective shroud of dead leaves and other tissue. Once dormancy is broken in the spring, elongation and flowering proceed rapidly, relying on the availability of carbohydrates stored in the root system during the previous growing season. Flowering success, then, depends largely upon environmental conditions of the previous summer or summers rather than on those of the current season.

Photosynthesis and Growth

The abilities to initiate photosynthesis at low temperatures and to draw on stored carbohydrates for rapid initial growth in the spring are essential for species that must cope with the short, cold alpine growing season. Many alpine vascular plants are able to carry on photosynthesis at daytime temperatures as low as 32°F, substantially lower than temperatures reported for plants growing in more moderate climates. The great majority of alpine plants are "summer-green," having leaves that survive for a single summer as well as preformed vegetative buds. The overwintering strategy of summer-green perennials requires massive storage of carbohydrates in roots or rhizomes, which provides the critical food reserves to fuel spring growth. In fact, spring growth is often so rapid that respiration greatly exceeds photosynthetic production and food is consumed at a faster rate than it can be made. Once shoot growth slows and flowering is completed, the respiration rate declines and replenishment of carbohydrate reserves in the roots begins.

Winter photosynthetic activity is reported for alpine species with evergreen leaves, such as mountain dryad, and for a unique group of species classified as having "winter-green" leaves, such as kobresia, tufted hairgrass, and alpine forget-me-not. Winter-green plants have leaves that develop during one summer and survive into the next, contrasting with evergreen species, which last several seasons. The winter-green growth strategy maximizes photosynthetic activity over a longer time span than is possible for summer-green species and concentrates the winter storage of carbohydrates (mostly sugars) in the immature leaves—an advantage that minimizes the time needed for translocation and provides an even quicker "jump-start" for the resumption of growth in the spring.

Anthocyanins and Alpine Plants

Colored pigments are present in all green leaves and are visible to varying degrees depending on the proportion of pigment to chlorophyll present in the leaf at any given time. The bright red color that distinguishes the foliage of many alpine plants just after snowmelt and again at the end of the growing season is due to the presence of *anthocyanin,* a pigment synthesized from sugars stored in the roots. This same pigment is responsible for the scarlet color of maple leaves in the fall and for the red skin of apples. In alpine environments, the intense radiation and cold temperatures that result in low chlorophyll content also encourage the accumulation of anthocyanin in the leaf and young stems; the phenomenon is especially pronounced in species growing in environments with late-lying snow.

The presence of anthocyanin serves several functions. First, it is believed to enhance cold tolerance, acting as a "sink" for excess sugars produced during the cool, bright weather of spring and fall. Second, studies of alpine plants in the Colorado Front Range have shown that anthocyanins absorb ultraviolet radiation, reducing UV transmission and making the leaves of these plants less susceptible to tissue destruction by irradiation. Other studies suggest that the absorption of energy at other wavelengths by anthocyanins may also increase leaf temperature, perhaps moderating the detrimental effects of cold spring temperatures on delicate leaf tissues.

Reproduction in Alpine Environments

The ultimate measure of a species' fitness in the alpine environment is its ability to successfully reproduce. Many alpine plants reproduce sexually, producing flowers and viable seeds during summers when there is adequate sunshine and warmth. Because of the shortness and severity of the alpine summer, however, the seeds of most species mature too late in the season to meet the right combination of temperature and moisture over sufficient time for germination to occur during the same growing season. In fact, in some species, the ripening process may not reach completion until the year following flowering. During some years, weather conditions may not favor flowering, seed production, or germination.

Successful germination in the alpine environment is controlled by suitably warm temperatures and the availability of moisture. In most cases, germination takes place in early summer shortly after snowmelt. Seedlings must have sufficient time to develop root systems and store enough carbohydrates to allow survival through the winter. Late summer germination in species of upland habitats appears to be inhibited by lack of soil moisture, low temperatures, and insufficient time for seedling development. Species typical of wet meadows and other sites that retain soil moisture throughout the growing season normally produce seeds with built-in dormancy mechanisms that protect against premature germination. Seedling growth is very slow in most species; a plant needs several years to grow large enough and store enough carbohydrates to produce flowers.

Many alpine species reproduce by means of runners, stolons, rhizomes, and bulblets. Such methods circumvent the environmental constraints that often interfere with fertilization and seed production and allow rapid colonization of newly exposed ground. Whiplash saxifrage, like the strawberry, sends out threadlike runners across the surface of the ground. At the end of each runner is a tiny plant, which draws nourishment from the parent until it has developed its own set of roots; then the runner withers. One of the most interesting reproductive strategies is that of alpine bistort (*Bistorta vivipara*), which produces bulblets along its flowering stalk. The Latin specific name *vivipara* refers to the plant's ability to bear "young" without going through the seed and seedling process. Viviparous bistort produces both flowers and bulblets; the delicate white flowers are at the top of the flowering stalk and the bulblets toward the bottom. The flowers have never been known to produce viable seed. The bulblets, on the other hand, drop from the parent plant and are able to establish themselves during the same growing season in which they were produced, often showing green sprouts while still attached to the stalk.

Descriptions of Common Plants

Moss Campion, *Silene acaulis* ssp. *subacaulescens.* Races of this cushion-forming species are found in the Arctic and in nearly all tundra areas of the Northern Hemisphere. Moss campion is identified by its bright pink, five-petaled flower, narrow green leaves, growth form, and long taproot. This species generally grows in fellfields and dry meadows and is one of the first colonizers of barren gravel areas. A cushion may live for seventy-five to one hundred years, reaching a diameter of nearly 3 feet.

Black-headed Daisy, *Erigeron melanocephalus.* This species is recognized by its small size, its white ray flowers, and the dark purple hairs that cover the underside of its flower head and upper stem. A similar species, the one-flowered daisy *(E. simplex),* lacks these dark hairs and is found in less moist habitats. Black-headed daisy is found in areas with late-lying snow.

Old-Man-of-the-Mountain, *Rydbergia grandiflora.* This large, conspicuous sunflower derives its common name from the silky hair that covers its stems, foliage, and flowering heads. Old-man-of-the-mountain is distinguished by its east-facing, bright yellow ray and disk flowers and by its feathery leaves. This species stores food for several years before producing flowers, the entire plant dying once the seed matures.

Queens Crown, *Clementsia rhodantha.* This showy alpine wildflower is identified by its ball-shaped cluster of rose-colored flowers and by the prominent midrib that marks the underside of each succulent, lanceolate leaf. Queens crown is endemic to the Southern Rockies and is found in alpine wetlands and other moist habitats.

Parry Clover, *Trifolium parryi.* Of the three species of clover endemic to the alpine of the Rocky Mountains, Parry clover, with its strongly scented, ball-shaped cluster of flowers, is the most "cloverlike." Distinguishing characteristics include the uniformly purple or rose-purple flowers, the papery bracts that subtend the individual flowers, and the three-part leaves; the superficially similar whiproot clover *(T. dasyphyllum)* has bicolored flowers and smaller, more narrow leaves.

Dwarf Clover, *Trifolium nanum.* Dwarf clover is identified by its short-stalked, one- to three-flowered heads, matlike growth form, and tiny leaves. This species is slow-growing and typical of exposed habitats such as fellfields.

Alpine Phlox, *Phlox pulvinata.* Alpine phlox is distinguished by its five-petaled blue flowers and its compact, matlike growth form. Blooming in late June and early July, this fragrant species transforms barren-seeming fellfields with splashes of palest blue. *P. condensata* is the common alpine phlox of the southern half of the Southern Rockies.

Sky Pilot, *Polemonium viscosum.* This showy species is identified by its terminal cluster of blue, funnel-shaped flowers and by its distinctly whorled leaflets. A paler blue race of sky pilot, *P. grayanum,* is common from Mount Evans southwestward. Though white mutants of sky pilot are common, they should not be confused with the sticky-leaved, cream-colored flowers of *P. brandegei,* which occurs in unstable alpine screes and similar rocky habitats.

American Bistort, *Bistorta bistortoides.* Easily identified by its tall, flowering stalk, whitish to pinkish cylindrical flower heads, and lanceolate leaves, American bistort is a conspicuous species in upper montane to alpine meadows in midsummer. Though the flowers of bistort lack petals, the five sepals (called tepals) appear petal-like; at the base of each flower is a tiny brown sheath, called a stipule. Unlike the more diminutive alpine bistort *(B. vivipara),* American bistort reproduces by seeds rather than by bulblets.

Alpine Sorrel, *Oxyria digyna.* The cluster of basal, kidney-shaped leaves and begonia-like flowers identify alpine sorrel, a species typical of alpine rock slides and other rocky habitats. The prefix *oxys* means "sour" in Greek, and the leaves of this species are distinctly sour-sweet.

Big-rooted Springbeauty, *Claytonia megarhiza.* This spectacular species is distinguished by its rosette growth form, broadly spatulate leaves, and encircling ring of white-pink flowers. Big-rooted springbeauty is typical of rocky terrain at high elevations. Pygmy bitterroot *(Oreobroma pygmaea,* formerly *Lewisia),* a diminutive and magenta-flowered relative, is found in gravelly soils of shallow snowbed sites.

White Marsh Marigold, *Psychrophylla leptosepala,* formerly *Caltha.* Marsh-marigold is identified by its white tepals (petals and sepals that are indistinguishable), broadly heart-shaped, basal leaves, and preference for subalpine and alpine snowbed and wetland habitats. Once flowering is completed, the fruits (follicles) become swollen and conspicuous.

Snow Buttercup, *Ranunculus adoneus.* This showy species, with its ruffled, glossy yellow tepals (this flower lacks petals) and finely dissected leaves, is commonly found around melting snowbanks. Snow buttercups are often encountered poking their brilliant yellow flower buds through the melting snow and have been reported to bloom beneath several feet of snow. This species is endemic to the Rocky Mountains.

Alpine Avens, *Acomastylis rossii.* Alpine avens is one of the most common alpine wildflowers, easily recognized by its yellow, roselike flowers and its fernlike leaves. There is no greater generalist in the alpine tundra. It is found in a variety of upland habitats characterized by light winter snow covers and well-drained soils. With the coming of fall, the buildup of anthocyanins in the leaves turns these plants a rich burgundy rust.

Mountain Dryad, *Dryas octopetala* ssp. *hookeriana.* Mountain dryad is identified by its white, eight-petaled flowers, finely toothed, evergreen leaves, and elegantly plumed seed heads. Locally abundant on gravelly, windswept slopes, this species often forms large single-species stands.

Sibbaldia, *Sibbaldia procumbens.* This diminutive member of the rose family is distinguished by its prominent green sepals, tiny yellow petals, and three-part, triple-notched leaves. Sibbaldia is always associated with areas of late-lying snow.

Whiplash Saxifrage, *Hirculus platysepalus* spp. *crandallii.* Whiplash saxifrage is easily identified by its upright, five-petaled yellow flowers, stoloniferous (runner-producing) growth habit, and glandular-pubescent leaves. This small saxifrage is a pioneering species, most often encountered in barren, gravelly sites and rocky crevices.

Snowlover, *Chionophila jamesii.* This lovely little member of the figwort family is distinguished by its one-sided raceme of creamy-white, dorsiventrally flattened flowers. The genus name is Greek and refers to snowlover's preference for snow accumulation sites. The species name honors Edwin James, naturalist on the 1820 Long Expedition, who was first to collect the snowlover.

Elephantella, *Pedicularis groenlandica.* Elephantella, with its fernlike leaves and magenta flowers resembling the heads of elephants, is one of the easiest flowers to identify. This species has a broad elevational range but is most common in moist meadows and wetlands in the subalpine and lower alpine zones.

Rocky Mountain Sedge, *Carex scopulorum.* Rising from a weblike network of rhizomes, the stems of Rocky Mountain sedge form a dense turf in subalpine and alpine wetlands. This is a robust sedge, whose stems well exceed the erect leaves. Each stem is topped with an erect, terminal staminate (male) inflorescence subtended by a cluster of carpellate (female) inflorescences.

Common Plants of the Alpine Tundra

Shrubs

Willow, Arctic, *Salix arctica*
  Nelson (or planeleaf), *Salix planifolia*
  snow, *Salix reticulata* ssp. *nivalis*

Grasses, Sedges, and Rushes

Bentgrass, variable, *Agrostis variablis*
Bluegrass, alpine, *Poa alpina*
  Arctic, *Poa arctica*
  Letterman, *Poa lettermanii*
Fescue, alpine, *Festuca brachyphylla*
  Hall's, *Festuca hallii*
Hairgrass, tufted, *Deschampsia caespitosa*
Kobresia, *Kobresia myosuroides*
Oat, mountain, *Avenula hookeri*
Oatgrass, timber, *Danthonia intermedia*
Rush, Drummond's, *Juncus drummondii*
  chestnut, *Juncus castaneus*
  three-glumed, *Juncus triglumis*
  two-glumed, *Juncus biglumis*
Sedge, black, *Carex nigricans*
  ebony, *Carex ebenea*
  false elk, *Carex elynoides*

fish-scale, *Carex chalciolepis*
Hepburn's, *Carex nardina* ssp. *hepburnii*
Nelson's, *Carex nelsonii*
Pyrenean, *Carex crandallii* (formerly *C. pyrenaica*)
rock, *Carex rupestris*
Rocky Mountain, *Carex scopulorum*
Timothy, alpine, *Phleum commutatum*
Trisetum, spike, *Trisetum spicatum*
Wheatgrass, Scribner's, *Elymus scribneri*
slender, *Elymus trachycaulum*
Wood-rush, spike, *Luzula spicata*

Wildflowers

Adoxa (or Moschatel), *Adoxa moschatellina*
Alplily, *Lloydia serotina*
Alumroot, common (or alpine), *Heuchera parviflora*
Anemone, narcissus (or alpine), *Anemone narcissiflora*
Angelica, Gray's, *Angelica grayi*
Avens, alpine, *Acomastylis rossii*
Bistort, American, *Bistorta bistortoides*
viviparous, *Bistorta vivipara*
Bitteroot, pygmy, *Oreobroma pygmaea*
Braya, dwarf, *Braya humilis*
Butterweed, Fremont's, *Senecio fremontii* var. *blitoides*
Campion, moss, *Silene acaulis*
Candytuft, mountain, *Noccaea montana*
Chimingbells, greenleaf, *Mertensia lanceolata*
Clover, alpine or whiproot, *Trifolium dasyphyllum*
dwarf, *Trifolium nanum*
Parry, *Trifolium parryi*
Columbine, Colorado blue, *Aquilegia coerulea*
dwarf, *Aquilegia saximontana*
Daisy, black-headed, *Erigeron melanocephalus*
one-headed, *Erigeron simplex*
pinnate-leaved, *Erigeron pinniatisectus*
showy, *Erigeron peregrinus*
Draba, Gray's Peak, *Draba grayana*
thick, *Draba crassa*
white, *Draba cana*
Dryad, mountain, *Dryas octopetala* ssp. *hookeriana*

Fern, alpine lady, *Athyrium distentifolium* var.
  americanum
  Christmas, *Polystichum lonchitis*
  grape, *Botrychium* spp.
Fireweed, alpine, *Chamerion latifolium*
Forget-me-not, alpine, *Eritrichum aretioides*
Gentian, Arctic, *Gentianodes algida*
  blue (or bottle), *Pneumonanthe parryi*
  moss (or Siberian), *Chondrophylla prostrata*
  star, *Swertia perennis*
Gilia, snowball, *Ipomopsis globularis*
Goldflower, *Tetraneuris brevifolia*
Harebell, alpine, *Campanula uniflora*
  common or mountain, *Campanula rotundifolia*
Kings Crown, *Rhodiola integrifolia*
Kittentails, alpine, *Besseya alpina*
Koenigia, *Koenigia islandica*
Lousewort, alpine, *Pedicularis scopulorum*
Marigold, white marsh, *Psychrophila leptosepala*
  (formerly *Caltha*)
Mouse-ear, alpine, *Cerastium beeringianum* ssp. *earli*
  field, *Cerastium arvense*
Nailwort, Rocky Mountain or alpine, *Paronychia pulvinata*
Old-Man-of-the-Mountain (or Rydbergia), *Rydbergia*
  grandiflora
Onion, alpine, *Allium* spp.
Paintbrush, western yellow, *Castilleja occidentalis* and
  Castilleja puberula
Parsley, alpine, *Oreoxis alpina*
Phlox, alpine, *Phlox pulvinata*
Poppy, alpine, *Papaver kluanensis*
Primrose, fairy (or alpine), *Primula angustifolia*
  Parry, *Primula parryi*
  rock, *Androsace chamaejasme*
Purple Fringe, *Phacelia sericea*
Queens Crown, *Clementsia rhodantha*
Ragwort, alpine, *Ligularia holmii*
  dandelion, *Ligularia taraxacoides*
  nodding, *Ligularia soldanella*
Sage, Arctic, *Artemisia arctica* ssp. *saxicola*
  black-headed (or alpine), *Artemisia scopulorum*
Sandwort, alpine, *Lidia obtusiloba* (formerly *Minuartia*)
  Fendler, *Eremogone fendleri*

Saxifrage, goldbloom, *Hirculus serpyllifolius* ssp.
   chrysanthus
   nodding, *Saxifraga cernua*
   snowball, *Micranthes rhomboidea*
   spotted, *Ciliaria austromontana*
   whiplash, *Hirculus platysepalus* ssp. *crandallii*
Sibbaldia, *Sibbaldia procumbens*
Sky Pilot, *Polemonium viscosum*
Snow Buttercup, *Ranunculus adoneus*
Snowlover, *Chionophila jamesii*
Sorrel, alpine, *Oxyria digyna*
Springbeauty, big-rooted, *Claytonia megarhiza*
Thistle, alpine, *Cirsium scopulorum*
Violet, twin-flower, *Viola biflora*
Wallflower, alpine, *Erysimum capitatum*
Willowherb, alpine, *Epilobium anagadallidifolium*

Lichens

Antler (or worm) Lichen, *Thamnolia vermicularis*
Yellow Reindeer Lichen, *Cetraria tilesii*
Finger Lichen, *Dactylina* spp.
Iceland Lichen, *Cetraria islandica*
Jewel Lichen, *Xanthoria elegans*
Map Lichen, *Rhizocarpon geographicum*
Snow Lichen, *Cetraria nivalis*
Rock Tripe, *Umbilicaria virginis*

Environment and Adaptation: Animals of the Alpine Tundra

Only a limited number of animal species are year-round residents of the alpine tundra. Of the 19 resident mammalian species, the majority — shrews, pika, voles, pocket gophers, yellow-bellied marmots, and weasels — are small-bodied and can utilize the more moderate microenvironment near the ground surface. In most years, the rigors of the winter environment force large mammals such as bighorn sheep and elk to move to lower elevations in search of more sheltered areas for grazing. Of the half dozen or so birds that breed in the alpine, only the white-tailed ptarmigan remains year-round. No avian or mammalian species are restricted to the alpine zone, although several species are as common here as they are at lower elevations.

The majority of animal species encountered in the alpine zone are present only during the breeding season; others visit on an occasional basis or during migration. Several birds nest in the alpine tundra but winter at lower elevations: brown-capped rosy finches, horned larks, water pipits, rock wrens, spotted sandpipers, ravens, prairie falcons, and black swifts. Elk graze in the tundra during the summer and early autumn, lured by the lush growth of grasses and herbs. Coyotes and red foxes wander up from the mountain valleys, attracted by secluded alpine meadows with an abundance of small mammals and ground-nesting birds. Golden eagles and red-tailed and ferruginous hawks may be seen soaring above timberline as they hunt. Mountain bluebirds, gulls, and kestrels are often conspicuous in late summer and early autumn, when mormon crickets, grasshoppers, and other insects abound in tundra meadows.

Survival Strategies

The fundamental currencies for survival are the abilities to withstand climatic extremes and to secure adequate food. Reproductive success provides the final measure of a species' ability to adapt to the alpine environment. Escaping environmental extremes is largely a function of behavior and of the degree to which an animal is able to move about within its environment to avoid stressful conditions. Birds are the most mobile, of course, with some species moving regularly between the alpine tundra and protective cover or roosting sites in the subalpine or montane zones. Small mammals are able to survive the winter by hibernating, using sheltered microhabitats, storing food, or using adaptive hunting strategies.

Hibernation

The overwintering success of most alpine animals depends on the ability to avoid subfreezing temperatures and excessive heat loss to the environment. For mammals and birds, maintaining a high, constant body temperature is achieved by increasing metabolic heat production several-fold. When food is scarce or unavailable, the higher rate of food intake necessary to fuel metabolic processes is most threatening to small mammals, whose metabolic rates are already at high levels. Hibernation enables these species to conserve energy by allowing their body temperatures to drop to within a few degrees above freezing, greatly reducing the metabolic rate, heart rate, respiration, and other energetically costly functions.

A mammalian hibernator spends the winter in a state of dormancy in an underground burrow or other subterranean shelter where the temperature rarely drops below freezing. Among alpine mammals, hibernation is best-developed in the marmots and the ground squirrels. The annual cycles of these herbivorous animals follow a predictable sequence of events: spring emergence from hibernation, mating, gestation, lactation, emergence of young, prehibernatory fattening, autumnal immergence, and hibernation until the following spring. Spring emergence is cued to environmental factors associated with the onset of vegetative growth, such as increasing air and soil temperatures and a reduction in the snow cover. In the latter stages of hibernation, the increasing frequency of alternating bouts of torpor (dormancy) and arousal enables the animal to monitor and respond to ambient conditions and to emerge at the most opportune time. Arousal from hibernation is energetically costly, however, because the animal must metabolize a considerable amount of its brown-fat reserves in order to rewarm. Premature depletion of these reserves is a common cause of death in hibernating mammals.

YELLOW-BELLIED MARMOTS: HIBERNATION AND THE GROUP ADVANTAGE

Two resources are of critical importance to the overwintering and reproductive success of yellow-bellied marmots: burrows and lush herbage for food. Yellow-bellied marmots are active aboveground for about four months in summer and fall and hibernate during the remainder of the year. Highly social and territorial, marmots form colonies that consist of a single adult male, a "harem" of several adult females,

From top to bottom: yellow-bellied marmot, pika.

several yearlings, and multiple litters of young. Burrows are used as nurseries, resting sites during the day and night, refuges from predators, and communal hibernacula. Marmots spend up to 80 percent of their lives in their burrows, moving between hibernacula and an assortment of summer residence burrows.

Within the marmot social system, competition for the best food and burrows is counteracted by the advantages of group living. The colony provides a measure of social protection, increased alertness to predators, and assurance of a suitable hibernaculum — advantages that ensure colony members a better chance of survival. By sharing home burrows with the colony's juveniles and yearlings, adults enhance their parental investment by providing a safe alternative to premature dispersal. The eventual dispersal of the yearlings after a period of two years reduces competition within the colony and maintains optimal colony size. Larger colonies are at distinct disadvantage because of the greater foraging territory required, the longer distances that must be travelled to obtain food, and the increased risk of predation during foraging trips.

The diet of yellow-bellied marmots consists largely of succulent vegetation. Consumption of other food resources—

insects and animal matter—occurs when vegetation is in short supply or of poor quality. Foraging begins shortly after emergence from hibernation, with individuals fanning out short distances from the home burrow. Most breeding occurs within two weeks of emergence, ensuring that the female and her young have enough time to accumulate sufficient fat to survive hibernation. Foraging intensifies during the months of July and August, the lush vegetation being converted into critical brown-fat reserves. To attain their optimal prehibernation weight, juvenile marmots typically remain active later in the season than adults. The failure of females to produce litters in consecutive years in alpine habitats suggests that the postweaning growth period may not be sufficient to allow postpartum females to accumulate the necessary energy reserves both to survive hibernation and to achieve reproductive success the following spring.

Use of Microhabitats

Small mammals that are unable to migrate or hibernate generally escape climatological extremes by burrowing or by taking advantage of sheltered microenvironments under rocks, snow, and vegetation. These animals are of two types: species that continue foraging throughout the winter, making use of whatever protective cover is available, and those that store food for winter consumption. The first group includes both herbivorous and carnivorous species, such as the northern pocket gopher, shrews, weasels, and most voles. The second group includes the pika, least chipmunk, and deer mouse.

THE BURROWER'S STRATEGY

Northern pocket gophers are common in the alpine tundra of the Southern Rockies. These solitary mammals spend most of their lives underground, leaving behind networks of foraging tunnels and burrow mounds. In fact, these prodigious earth movers may be one of the dominant geomorphic agents in certain alpine areas. It is uncertain whether the pocket gopher's restriction to areas with winter snow cover reflects a need for protective cover to permit winter foraging, or whether the snow is necessary as a buffer against cold temperatures. Evidence of wintertime activity is conspicuous and frequently involves extensive burrowing through the snow to get to new sources of food; such tunnels are then used to dump excavated soil, producing complex patterns of earth tubes, often called "gopher eskers," which are exposed on the surface when meltout occurs.

A NETWORK OF RUNWAYS

Voles, like pocket gophers, prefer habitats with winter snow cover. In contrast to pocket gophers, however, voles forage primarily along the ground surface, their carefully clipped runways typically crisscrossing areas with lush sedge or other herbaceous cover. When montane vole populations are high, surface runways, ball nests, piles of rice-shaped feces, ropelike cords of clipped vegetation, and heavily grazed areas are conspicuous following snowmelt. Another alpine species, the heather vole, does not construct a runway system except in the immediate vicinity of its nest. In contrast to other voles, the heather vole caches food near its nest throughout the year.

PIKAS: LIFE IN THE TALUS

Pikas are superbly adapted to their alpine habitats. This small member of the hare and rabbit family *(Lagomorpha)* inhabits talus slopes and blockfields, which provide refuge from predators, shelter from the sun and from mid-day heat (pikas are heat-sensitive), and protection from the harsh conditions of the alpine winter. The strident, high-pitched calls and nasal squawks of the pika carry well in open country. In contrast to other members of its family, the pika's ears, tail, and feet are small and help to reduce excessive heat loss through the extremities. Additionally, the feet have furred soles, providing a nonskid surface for moving around on rocky surfaces.

Like other lagomorphs, pikas produce two types of feces. The more common type is the dry, fibrous pellets consisting of indigestible waste. The second type is amorphous, soft and somewhat tarry in appearance, and high in protein and other nutrients. The pika reingests the soft feces for an additional round of processing in the digestive system, maximizing the nutritional and caloric contents of the herbaceous diet. Pika urine is highly concentrated and viscous, which allows the excretion of waste products with a minimum consumption of water, an advantage in an environment where free water is often unavailable. Chalk-colored deposits of urine are often conspicuous on rocks within the pika's habitat.

Three main seasonal patterns of activity characterize the typical pika year: breeding from April through June, territorial maintenance and haying from July through October or November, and winter foraging and utilization of stored hay piles. Breeding occurs in late spring, as temperatures increase and the alpine snowpack begins to melt. Male-female territorial overlap is prevalent at this season, and the level of aggression between individuals is fairly low. The first of two litters of young is born within about 30 days of mating and coincides with the melting of the snow cover and the appearance of new vegetation. A second mating occurs shortly after the birth of the first litter, after which time territorial boundaries are redrawn and vigorously defended by both sexes. Vocalizations during the breeding season are varied and consist of "tooth-chattering" (during aggressive encounters), a trill-like call normally delivered by courting males, single-note alarm calls, and long-call exchanges between males and females and between individuals of the same sex.

During the haying season, pikas busily gather vegetation for their winter stores. Vegetation is clipped with the teeth and carried in mouthfuls to a sheltered location among the rocks. Each hay pile amounts to a bushel or so of plant matter. Territorial activity is vigorous during this period, with both male and female pikas defending solitary territories in the vicinity of their hay piles. Territorial behavior includes sharp, single-note calls, often delivered from the top of conspicuous rocks; scent marking, accomplished by rubbing the chin glands on rocks within the territory; chases; and occasional skirmishes.

With the onset of winter, pikas greatly restrict their movements and foraging activities. During good weather, foraging continues via tunnels built beneath the snow. As the snowpack deepens or in times of bad weather, pikas reduce their physical activity and rely on their hay piles for food. Vocalizations are often heard during winter, typically in response to a territorial intrusion or the presence of a predator.

Survival Against All Odds

Rugged terrain with abundant escape cover in the form of cliffs, ledges, and talus slopes provides optimal habitat for the two mountain monarchs of the Southern Rockies — the bighorn sheep and the mountain goat. Mountain goats, an introduced species in the Southern Rockies, are seldom encountered below timberline at any time of the year. Most bighorn, although well adapted to withstand alpine conditions, migrate seasonally to lower elevations where protected winter range remains available to them. In areas where migration routes have been interrupted by human developments, bighorn sheep generally remain in the alpine throughout the year. Indiscriminate hunting, competition with domestic livestock, and introduced sheep diseases decimated bighorn populations throughout the region prior to the 1950s. Today, as a result of both natural recovery and reintroduction efforts, populations are on the increase again in many areas. In Rocky Mountain National Park, the current population is estimated to be about four hundred animals. Biologists

A band of bighorn sheep, Rocky Mountain National Park. *Wendy Shattil/Robert Rozinski*.

THE SOUTHERN ROCKIES

are only beginning to assess the impact and potential problems associated with the introduction and spread of mountain goats into areas historically occupied by bighorn.

Precipitous terrain offers considerable protection from all but the most determined predators. Sheep and goats are remarkably surefooted and adept at moving about their precarious habitats. Bighorn sheep have hooves modified for gripping rocky substrates: the posterior portion of each toe is formed into a round, rubbery pad, and the toes are independently movable and somewhat pincerlike. The mountain goat's hoof, unlike that of other ungulates, has a slightly convex and pliable pad that extends beyond the outer cornified shell. This adaptation permits even greater traction and dexterity. In addition to having remarkable mobility, bighorn rely on keen binocular vision and a well-developed sense of smell to detect danger. If several sheep are together, individuals generally face in different directions so that all approaches are under surveillance.

Bighorn sheep are among the most specialized of all grazers; their ability to survive on a diet of dry, abrasive grasses and herbs of comparatively poor quality gives them a competitive advantage over elk or other grazers. To counteract tooth wear, bighorn sheep, like most grazers, have evolved very long, broad molar teeth that continue to emerge throughout life. Like other ruminants, bighorn harbor microorganisms in a specialized chamber of the digestive tract, the rumen, to break down plant cellulose to volatile fatty acids (acetic, proprionic, and butyric acid) and plant protein to amino acids. In contrast to humans, who primarily use glucose to power metabolic processes, ruminants fuel their metabolic machinery with volatile fatty acids. Bighorn sheep have relatively large rumens compared to other ruminants of equal size, suggesting that the diet on which sheep survive requires a longer processing time than is necessary for soft browse or more succulent forages.

Gregariousness and ritualized social behavior enhance survival of sheep and goats in an extreme environment. The basic unit of sheep society is the band; several bands constitute a herd. Bighorn segregate by sex into male (ram) bands and female-and-juvenile bands. Rams follow the largest-horned male during major movements, whereas females tend to follow the lead of an older lamb-leading ewe. Typically, rams have areas where they concentrate in spring and again before the rut begins in November, and where dominance fights occur. The coexistence of rams is governed by a dominance hierarchy; rams judge the dominance rank of other rams by their horn sizes. Sheep society does not differentiate conduct between individuals based on sex, but only between larger (dominant) and smaller (subordinate) animals. The organization and predictability of sheep society appears designed to maximize familiarity with the habitat, minimize energy wasted, discourage the dispersion of juveniles, and transmit home ranges as a tradition from older to younger generations.

Birds of the Alpine Tundra

Several alpine birds practice behavioral temperature regulation. On days that are windy and cold, if the sun is out, horned larks are often observed basking in the sunshine on the lee sides of rocks or taller clumps of vegetation. On cold nights, these birds may dig shallow roosting holes in the ground with their bills and sleep with their backs approximately level with the ground surface. The use of roosting holes exposes only a minimal amount of the lark's body surface and reduces radiative and convective heat losses. In much the same way, the white-tailed ptarmigan makes use of the insulative value of snow by seeking out soft patches in which to tunnel and roost. During the long alpine winter, ptarmigan spend anywhere from a few hours to a few days in these snow burrows, benefitting by a reduction in heat loss of up to 45 percent.

In alpine tundra, resource petitioning enables species to appropriate suitable niche space and to avoid competition with other species. Water pipits, for example, are entirely insectivorous, and much of their food in spring and early summer consists of cold-numbed or dead insects gleaned from the surfaces of snowbanks or plucked from moist ground as the pipit moves quickly through short vegetation. Pipits nest on the ground, tucking their cup-shaped nests under the edges of rocks or protective grass tussocks; the eggs are chocolate brown, providing both camouflage and additional heat gain. Horned larks also forage on snowbanks for insects, but about a quarter of their food is plant material gathered from drier tundra uplands. Rosy finches are essentially seed

Common birds of the alpine tundra, from top to bottom: water pipit, brown-capped rosy finch, with inset of gray-crowned rosy finch.

eaters, though they feed their nestlings a diet of insects, and are often observed foraging along the edges of receding snowbanks. Rosy finches, in contrast to ground-nesting water pipits and horned larks, are obligate cliff-nesters, placing their nests in rock crevices and under overhangs that provide shelter from the weather.

The courtship and territorial displays of alpine birds resemble those of species associated with grasslands or other open habitats. Male water pipits engage in elaborate song flights, which consist of a steep, vertical ascent accompanied by a simple, somewhat liquid song and followed by a descent to the ground, during which the bird raises and spreads its tail, dangles its legs, flutters its wings, and quickens the tempo of its song. The male horned lark begins its song flight by suddenly rising with rapid wingbeats, climbing in irregular circles (or almost vertically if flying into a strong wind) to a height of several hundred feet. Singing repeatedly, the male continues to flap and soar in circles before folding its wings and plunging Earthward, only to pull out at the last moment and sail across the ground before alighting.

Solar-Powered Insects

Most insects become sluggish and are unable to fly at low temperatures. Flies, with their remarkably low energy requirements and their tolerance of cool temperatures, assume considerable importance as pollinators in alpine environments. Several other flying insects, such as bumblebees and some butterflies, are able to warm up their flight muscles by muscular thermogenesis, a physiological process in which heat is produced internally in a manner analogous to shivering in warm-blooded animals. Bumblebees require a thoracic temperature of nearly 85°F before they are able to fly. To maintain this temperature, these bees must find food at a rate at least equal to the rate at which fuel is consumed in foraging. The bee's ability to move about as a result of muscular thermogenesis when temperatures are low and most other nectar-feeding insects are inactive helps to ensure an adequate food supply.

Butterflies gain the heat they need for metabolic processes and locomotor activity largely from the sun or from their surroundings. Research has shown that butterflies require thoracic temperatures of at least 80°F to initiate flight. Scale color and pubescence, as exemplified by the dark gray scaling of the Phoebus parnassian or the ebony, plushly furred wings of the Magdalena alpine, are important morphological adaptations that increase the solar efficiency of the wings. By changing the orientation of the wings, either through basking to maximize heat gain or by closing the wings dorsally to reduce overheating, butterflies are able to maintain a range of optimal body temperatures similar to those of warm-blooded animals. To further maximize their solar gain, butterflies seek out wind-sheltered microhabitats — such as the flower head of old-man-of-the-mountain — for basking.

Basking positions vary from species to species, and a given subfamily of butterflies often exhibits a characteristic basking style. A great many species simply press the thorax and abdomen closely to a warm rock or other surface. Members of the subfamily Coliadinae (sulfurs) tilt sideways to present the ventral surface of the hind wings perpendicular to the angle of the sun. Several genera of Satyridae (satyrs, wood nymphs, browns, alpines, and arctics), the Lycaenidae (blues, coppers, and hairstreaks), and the Pierinae (whites and orange tips) are body baskers, angling the wings narrowly to maximize solar gain to the body. Most Papilionidae (swallowtails and parnassians) and Nymphalidae (angle-wings, checker-spots, tortoise-shells, admirals, and painted ladies) are open-wing baskers, having the most efficient position for rapidly elevating body temperature.

Insects on Ice

Confronted by the rigors of winter, insects enter a state of hibernation or arrested development known as *diapause*. During diapause, there is no growth or metamorphosis, and the metabolic rate is substantially reduced. In alpine environments, some insects overwinter as eggs, some as larvae, some as pupae, and a few as adults. In most cases, hibernating or diapausal insects seek a sheltered hibernaculum where they are buffered from fluctuating air temperatures, either by shallow burrowing in soil or vegetation or by crawling under rocks or into crevices. Insects that normally complete their life cycles in one season at lower elevations may take two or more seasons at higher elevations. Most butterflies, moths, spiders, and beetles follow this developmental pattern. High-elevation flies and mosquitoes, on the other hand, complete developmental stages in a single season and can reproduce several times in spite of the brevity of the alpine summer.

Alpine insects generally achieve winter-hardiness in one of two ways. Some species, such as beetles, survive the cold by lowering the freezing point of their tissues through the synthesis of compounds such as glycerol or even ethylene glycol, the ingredient in common automobile antifreeze. Other insects actually induce freezing in parts of their bodies. The key to surviving self-induced freezing is to prevent dehydration and ice formation inside cells, while allowing other body cavities (the gut, blood, and spaces between the cells) to gradually fill with ice. These insects, such as the familiar "woolly bear" caterpillar (the overwintering, larval stage of the tiger moth), have the ability to synthesize glycerol and other compounds that reduce the proportion of bodily water locked up in ice.

Life Histories of Selected Animals

Mammals

Pika, *Ochotona princeps.* This small, quick-moving mammal is approximately the size of a juvenile cottontail and has brownish gray fur, rounded ears, and no visible tail. Pikas are restricted to the alpine and subalpine zone and are found almost exclusively in talus or other rock rubble near meadows that provide forage. Vocalizations include a variety of high-pitched, single- and multiple-note calls, and nasal barks. These diurnal herbivores are active year-round, gathering vegetation during the summer months and storing it in small hay piles for use during the winter. Territories are maintained through scent marking, vocalizations, chases, and a variety of aggressive behaviors. One and sometimes two litters of altricial young are born in late June or early July.

Yellow-bellied Marmot, *Marmota flaviventris.* The yellow-bellied marmot, the largest of the ground-dwelling squirrels, is identified by its rusty brown upperparts, grizzled whitish fur about the mouth and chin, and yellowish brown belly. Marmots are encountered in rocky outcrops with adjacent meadows for foraging and are common from the upper foothills to the alpine tundra. These diurnal herbivores are active during the late spring and summer and hibernate during the remainder of the year. Highly social, they form small colonies consisting of a single adult male, a "harem" of adult females, yearlings, and young. Vocalizations include high-pitched whistles, squeals, and tooth-chattering. Breeding occurs in spring, shortly after emergence from hibernation, and each female gives birth to a single litter of altricial young.

Ermine (or Short-tailed Weasel), *Mustela erminea.* The short-tailed weasel, or ermine, is identified by its small size (adults average 8 inches in total length), slender body, and black-tipped tail. In summer, the weasel's upperparts are a rich brown and the belly and chin are pale buff; winter pelage is pure white, except for the black-tipped tail. Like most mustelids, the short-tailed weasel is carnivorous, feeding on small mammals, birds, and insects. Active mostly at dawn and dusk, short-tailed weasels are solitary and maintain winter and summer hunting territories. Mating occurs in late spring, shortly after the female gives birth, but gestation is prolonged for about ten months by delayed implantation.

Bighorn Sheep, *Ovis canadensis.* Bighorn sheep are medium-sized, stocky ungulates with a whitish rump patch and horns. Horns are not shed as antlers are, and the most massive, fully curled horns are characteristic of the oldest rams. The horns of the female are spikelike; the horns of juvenile males resemble those of the female, becoming broader-based and more curled with increasing age. Bighorns prefer remote, rocky terrain with access to escape cover and meadows for grazing. Bighorn sheep are diurnal and active throughout the year, alternating bouts of intense grazing with periods of rest and rumination. Lambing occurs in late May and early June; single lambs are typical, but twin lambs are also reported in some populations.

Birds

White-tailed Ptarmigan, *Lagopus leucurus.* The white-tailed ptarmigan is largely restricted to alpine tundra and is identified by its grouselike appearance, white tail, and reddish eye combs. Winter plumage is white except for the dark bill and red eye comb; summer plumage is mottled brown and black on top and white below. Vocalizations are varied and include soft, henlike clucking and a high-pitched "ku-kriee-kriee" most often heard at dawn or dusk. White-tailed ptarmigan are herbivorous, relying heavily on the buds and woody twigs of alpine willows during the winter. The summer diet consists of a diversity of green leaves and flowers; seeds and the bulblets of alpine bistort may be important. Male territorial establishment consists of "flight screams," "ground challenging," and intimidating postures. Males are typically monogamous, and pair bonds are maintained throughout the breeding season. The timing of breeding and nesting are controlled by climatic events. The female ptarmigan builds a simple scrape nest on the ground, and the male assists the female by acting as sentry at the nest. Juveniles remain with the mother through autumn.

Horned Lark, *Eremophila alpestris.* The horned lark is distinguished by its bold black mustache, black ear tufts, and white outer tail feathers bordering an otherwise black tail.

This species is most often encountered in open country and occurs from the shortgrass prairie to the alpine tundra. Horned larks forage for seeds and insects while walking or running over the ground. Males establish and defend breeding territories; song flights, courtship feeding, and other displays are performed by the male. The female selects a nest site on the ground and excavates a hole for the cup-shaped nest of grass with her bill, often "paving" the nest site on one side with small stones.

Water Pipit, *Anthus spinoletta.* Water pipits are sparrow-sized birds with brownish gray upperparts and pinkish buff underparts with moderate streaking. Pipits prefer low-elevation grasslands and meadows during migration but are largely restricted to alpine tundra during the nesting season. This bird is often observed foraging along the ground or on snowbanks for insects and seeds, the pumping motions of its tail as it moves or perches providing a good field mark. Territorial males engage in elaborate song flights and ground singing. Pipits nest on the ground, constructing cup-shaped nests of grasses tucked beneath rocks or plant tussocks; pipit eggs are brown.

Rosy Finch, *Leucosticte arctoa.* Rosy finches hybridize in areas of overlap and include four subspecies. The brown-capped rosy finch *(L. a. australis)* is identified by its brown cap and brighter rose underparts, wings, and rump; this subspecies is common in the Southern Rockies year-round. The gray-crowned rosy finch *(L. a. tephrocotis),* a winter resident, is distinguished by its silver gray crown and blackish forehead; this subspecies nests largely north and west of the Southern Rockies and is a common breeding bird on the Alaskan tundra. The "Hepburn's," or gray-cheeked rosy finch *(L. a. littoralis),* differs from the gray-crowned by its gray hindcrown and cheeks, and, often, a gray throat. The less common black rosy finch *(L. a. atrata)* has distinctly darker plumage and breeds in the Great Basin and northwestern Rockies. Winter flocks in the Southern Rockies may number several hundred birds and include more than one subspecies. On their breeding grounds, brown-capped rosy finches forage for seeds and occasional insects on the ground and on snowbanks; these birds have gular pouches beneath their tongues for transporting food to the nest site. During the breeding season, aggressive encounters between territorial males are frequent and vigorous. Territorial behavior is unusual in that the area defended by the male changes with the movement of the female. This close defense of the female, with the male in accompaniment wherever she goes, arises out of the strong preponderance of males in both breeding and wintering populations. Rosy finches nest in crevices and holes in cliffs; the female builds the nest and incubates the eggs but is assisted by the male in caring for the nestlings.

Common Animals of the Alpine Tundra

Mammals

Masked Shrew, *Sorex cinereus*
Dwarf Shrew, *Sorex nanus*
Pika, *Ochotona princeps*
White-tailed Jackrabbit, *Lepus townsendii*
Least Chipmunk, *Tamias minimus*
Yellow-bellied Marmot, *Marmota flaviventris*
Golden-mantled Ground Squirrel, *Spermophilus lateralis*
Northern Pocket Gopher, *Thomomys talpoides*
Deer Mouse, *Peromyscus maniculatus*
Bushy-tailed Woodrat, *Neotoma cinerea*
Heather Vole, *Phenacomys intermedius*
Long-tailed Vole, *Microtus longicaudus*
Montane Vole, *Microtis montanus*
Coyote, *Canis latrans*
Marten, *Martes americana*
Short-tailed Weasel, *Mustela erminea*
Long-tailed Weasel, *Mustela frenata*
Badger, *Taxidea taxus*
Bobcat, *Felis rufous*
Elk, *Cervus elaphus*
Mule Deer, *Odocoileus hemionus*
Bighorn Sheep, *Ovis canadensis*
Mountain Goat, *Oreamnos americanus*

Birds

Red-tailed Hawk, *Buteo jamaicensis*
Golden Eagle, *Aquila chrysaetos*
Prairie Falcon, *Falco mexicanus*
American Kestrel, *Falco sparverius*
White-tailed Ptarmigan, *Lagopus leucurus*
Spotted Sandpiper, *Actitis macularia*
Franklin's Gull, *Larus pipixcan*
Black Swift, *Cypseloides niger*
Broad-tailed Hummingbird, *Selasphorus platycercus*
Rufous Hummingbird, *Selasphorus rufus*
Horned Lark, *Eremophila alpestris*
Common Raven, *Corvus corax*
Dipper, *Cinclus mexicanus*
Rock Wren, *Salpinctes obsoletus*
American Robin, *Turdus migratorius*
Mountain Bluebird, *Sialia currucoides*
Water Pipit, *Anthus spinoletta*
Rosy Finch, *Leucosticte arctoa*

Butterflies

Phoebus Parnassian, *Parnassius phoebus*
Western White, *Pontia occidentalis*
Mead's Sulphur, *Colias meadii*
Lustrous Copper, *Chalceria cupreus*
High Mountain Blue, *Agriades franklinii*
Shasta Blue, *Icaricia shasta*
Mormon Fritillary, *Speyeria mormonia*
Bog Fritillary, *Proclossiana eunomia*
Rockslide Checkerspot, *Charidryas damoetas*
Milbert's Tortoiseshell, *Aglais milberti*
Colorado Alpine, *Erebia callias*
Common Alpine, *Erebia epipsodea*
Magdalena Alpine, *Erebia magdalena*
Theano Alpine, *Erebia theano*
Melissa Arctic, *Oeneis melissa*
Polixenes Arctic, *Oeneis polixenes*
Alpine Checkered Skipper, *Pyrgus centaureae*

APPENDIX

Selected References

REGIONAL GUIDES

Chilton, Lance, and others. *New Mexico: A New Guide to the Colorful State*. Albuquerque: University of New Mexico Press, 1984.

Dolson, John. *The Black Canyon of the Gunnison*. Boulder: Pruett Publishing Co., 1982.

Erickson, Kenneth A., and Albert W. Smith. *Atlas of Colorado*. Boulder: Colorado Associated University Press, 1985.

Fenneman, Nevin M. *Physiography of the Western United States*. New York and London: McGraw-Hill Book Co., 1931.

Gregory, Lee. *Colorado Scenic Guide: Northern Region*. Boulder: Johnson Books, 1983.

_____. *Colorado Scenic Guide: Southern Region*. Boulder: Johnson Books, 1984.

Hunt, Charles B. *Natural Regions of the United States*. San Francisco: W. H. Freeman and Co., 1979.

Koch, Don. *An Endless Vista: Colorado's Recreational Lands*. Boulder: Pruett Publishing Co., 1982.

_____. *The Colorado Pass Book: A Guide to Colorado's Backroad Mountain Passes*. Boulder: Pruett Publishing Co., 1980.

Norton, Boyd, and Barbara Norton. *Backroads of Colorado*. Chicago: Rand McNally & Co., 1978.

Rennicke, Jeff. *The Rivers of Colorado*. Colorado Geographic Series, no. 1. Billings and Helena, Mont.: Falcon Press Publishing Co., Inc., 1985.

_____. *Colorado Mountain Ranges*. Colorado Geographic Series, no. 2. Billings and Helena, Mont.: Falcon Press Publishing Co., Inc., 1986.

Scott, Jim. *Pikes Peak Country*. Colorado Geographic Series, no. 3. Billings and Helena, Mont.: Falcon Press Publishing Co., Inc., 1987.

Simmons, Virginia McConnell. *The San Luis Valley.* Boulder: Pruett Publishing Co., 1979.

Smithson, Michael T. *Rocky Mountain: The Story Behind the Scenery.* Las Vegas, Nev.: KC Publications, 1986.

Trimble, Stephen. *Longs Peak: A Rocky Mountain Chronicle.* Estes Park, Colo.: Rocky Mountain Nature Association, 1984.

_____. *Great Sand Dunes: The Shape of the Wind.* Globe, Ariz.: Southwest Parks and Monuments Association, 1978.

Willard, Beatrice Elizabeth, and Susan Quimby Foster. *A Roadside Guide to Rocky Mountain National Park.* Boulder: Johnson Publishing Co. Inc., 1990.

HISTORY

Abbott, Carl, Stephen J. Leonard, and David McComb. *Colorado: A History of the Centennial State.* Boulder: Colorado Associated University Press, 1982.

Arps, Louisa Ward, and Elinor Eppich Kingery. *High Country Names: Rocky Mountain National Park.* Estes Park, Colo.: Rocky Mountain Nature Association, 1977.

Cassells, E. Steve. *The Archaeology of Colorado.* Boulder: Johnson Books, 1983.

Eberhart, Perry. *Guide to the Colorado Ghost Towns and Mining Camps.* Chicago: Swallow Press, 1969.

Hayden, F. V. Annual reports of the United States Geological and Geographical Survey. Washington, D.C.: Government Printing Office, 1873 through 1876.

Lavender, David. *The Rockies.* Lincoln and London: University of Nebraska Press, 1968.

_____. *David Lavender's Colorado.* Garden City, N.Y.: Doubleday, 1976.

_____. *Colorado River Country.* New York: E. P. Dutton, Inc., 1982.

McTighe, James. *Roadside History of Colorado.* Boulder: Johnson Books, 1984.

Noble, David Grant, ed. *Bandelier National Monument: Geology, History, Prehistory.* Santa Fe, N.Mex.: School of American Research, 1980.

Sprague, Marshall. *The Great Gates: The Story of Rocky Mountain Passes.* Lincoln: University of Nebraska Press, 1964.

Stegner, Wallace. *Beyond the Hundredth Meridian: John*

Wesley Powell and the Second Opening of the West. Boston: Houghton Mifflin Co., 1976.

Viola, Herman J. *Exploring the West.* Washington, D.C.: Smithsonian Books, 1987.

HIKING AND CLIMBING GUIDES

Borneman, Walter R., and Lyndon J. Lampert. *A Climbing Guide to Colorado's Fourteeners.* Boulder: Pruett Publishing Co., 1978.

Dannen, Kent, and Donna Dannen. *Rocky Mountain National Park Hiking Trails (Including Indian Peaks).* Charlotte, N.C.: East Woods Press Books, 1978.

Eberhart, Perry, and Philip Schmuck. *The Fourteeners: Colorado's Great Mountains.* Chicago: Swallow Press, 1970.

Hagen, Mary. *Hiking Trails of Northern Colorado.* Boulder: Pruett Publishing Co., 1979.

Martin, Bob. *Hiking Trails of Central Colorado.* Boulder: Pruett Publishing Co., 1983.

Ormes, Robert. *A Guide to the Colorado Mountains.* Colorado Springs: Robert M. Ormes, 1979.

Pixler, Paul. *Hiking Trails of Southwestern Colorado.* Boulder: Pruett Publishing Co., 1981.

Ungnade, Herbert E. *Guide to New Mexico Mountains.* Albuquerque: University of New Mexico Press, 1965.

GEOLOGY TEXTS

Birkeland, Peter W., and Edwin E. Larson. *Putnam's Geology.* 5th ed. New York: Oxford University Press, Inc., 1989.

Bloom, Arthur L. *Geomorphology.* Englewood Cliffs, N.J.: Prentice-Hall, Inc., 1978.

Dott, Robert H., and Roger L. Batten. *Evolution of the Earth.* 3d ed. New York: McGraw-Hill Book Co., 1981.

Embelton, Clifford, and Cuchlaine A. M. King. *Glacial Geology.* New York: John Wiley & Sons, Inc., 1975.

_____. *Periglacial Geomorphology.* New York: John Wiley & Sons, Inc., 1975.

Flint, Richard F. *Glacial and Quaternary Geology.* New York: John Wiley & Sons, Inc., 1971.

Price, Larry W. *Mountains and Man.* Berkeley: University of California Press, 1981.

GEOLOGY OF THE SOUTHERN ROCKIES: BOOKS, PROFESSIONAL VOLUMES, JOURNAL ARTICLES, AND MAPS

Benedict, James B. "Downslope Soil Movement in a Colorado Alpine Region: Rates, Processes, and Climatic Significance." *Arctic and Alpine Research* 2, no. 3 (1970).

————. "Chronology of Cirque Glaciation, Colorado Front Range." *Journal of Quaternary Research* 6, no. 4 (1973).

————. *The Mount Albion Site. A Study of Prehistoric Man and the Altithermal.* Boulder: Center for Mountain Archeology, Research Report no. 1, 1978.

————. *The Fourth of July Valley. Glacial Geology and Archeology of the Timberline Ecotone.* Boulder: Center for Mountain Archeology, Research Report no. 2, 1981.

————. *Arapaho Pass. Glacial Geology and Archeology at the Crest of the Colorado Front Range.* Boulder: Center for Mountain Archeology, Research Report no. 3, 1985.

Beus, Stanley S., ed. *Centennial Field Guide.* Vol. 2, *Rocky Mountain Section of the Geological Society of America.* Boulder: Geological Society of America, 1987.

Bickford, M. E. "The Formation of Continental Crust: A Review of Some Principles; An Application to the Proterozoic Evolution of Southern North America." *Geological Society of America Bulletin* 100 (September 1988): 1375–91.

Curtis, B. F., ed. *Cenozoic History of the Southern Rocky Mountains.* Boulder: Geological Society of America, Memoir 144, 1975.

Dickinson, William R., and others. "Paleogeographic and Paleotectonic Setting of Laramide Sedimentary Basins in the Central Rocky Mountain Region." *Geological Society of America Bulletin* 100 (July 1988): 1023–39.

Duebendorfer, E. M., and R. S. Houston. "Proterozoic Accretionary Tectonics at the Southern Margin of the Archean Craton." *Geological Society of America Bulletin* 98 (May 1987): 554–68.

Epis, R. C., and R. J. Weimer, eds. *Studies in Colorado Field Geology.* Golden, Colo.: Colorado School of Mines, 1976.

Grambling, Jeffrey A., and others. "Proterozoic Tectonic Assembly of New Mexico." *Geology* 16 (August 1988): 724–27.

Kent, Harry C., and Karen W. Porter, eds. *Colorado Geology*. Denver: Rocky Mountain Association of Geologists, 1980.

Kluth, Charles F., and Peter J. Coney. "Plate Tectonics of the Ancestral Rocky Mountains." *Geology* 9 (1980): 10–15.

Lockley, Martin G., and others. "North America's Largest Dinosaur Trackway Site: Implications for Morrison Formation Paleoecology." *Geological Society of America Bulletin* 97 (October 1986): 1163–76.

McPhee, John. *Rising from the Plains*. New York: Farrar/Straus/Giroux, 1986.

Porter, S. C., and others. "Late Wisconsin Mountain Glaciation in the Western United States." In *Late-Quaternary Environments of the United States*, vol. 1, edited by H. E. Wright, Jr. Minneapolis: University of Minnesota Press, 1983.

Tweto, Ogden, comp. *Geologic Map of Colorado*. Denver: U.S. Geological Survey, 1979.

REGIONAL GEOLOGY GUIDEBOOKS

Blackstone, D. L. *Traveler's Guide to the Geology of Wyoming*. Laramie: Wyoming Geological Survey, 1971.

Chronic, Halka. *Roadside Geology of Colorado*. Missoula, Mont.: Mountain Press Publishing Co., 1980.

Chronic, John, and Halka Chronic. *Prairie, Peak, and Plateau*. Denver: Colorado Geological Survey Bulletin 32, 1972.

Hansen, Wallace R. *The Black Canyon of the Gunnison in Depth*. Tucson: Southwest Parks and Monuments Association, 1987.

Hausel, W. Dan, and Richard W. Jones. *Self-Guided Tour of the Geology of Southeastern Wyoming*. Laramie: Geological Survey of Wyoming, 1984.

James, H. L. *Cumbres and Toltec Railroad: Scenic Trips to the Geologic Past No. 11*. Socorro, N.Mex.: New Mexico Bureau of Mines and Mineral Resources, 1974.

Larkin, Robert P., Paul K. Grogger, and Gary L. Peters. *The Southern Rocky Mountains*. K/H Geology Field Guide Series. Dubuque, Iowa: Kendall/Hunt Publishing Company, 1980.

Mears, Brainerd, Jr. and others. *A Geologic Tour of Wyoming from Laramie to Lander, Jackson, and Rock Springs*.

Laramie: Geological Survey of Wyoming Public Information Circular No. 27, 1986.

Muehlberger, William R., Brewster Baldwin, and Roy W. Foster. *High Plains Northeastern New Mexico, Raton, Capulin Mountain, and Clayton: Scenic Trips to the Geologic Past No. 7.* Socorro, N.Mex.: New Mexico Bureau of Mines and Mineral Resources, 1967.

Richmond, Gerald M. *Raising the Roof on the Rockies.* Estes Park, Colo.: Rocky Mountain Nature Association, Inc., 1974.

Sutherland, Patrick K., and Arthur Montgomery. *Trail Guide to the Upper Pecos: Scenic Trips to the Geologic Past No. 6.* Rev. ed. Socorro, N.Mex.: New Mexico Bureau of Mines and Mineral Resources, 1975.

Young, Robert G., and Joann W. Young. *Colorado West: Land of Geology and Wildflowers.* Grand Junction, Colo.: Wheelwright Press, 1977.

CLIMATE

Barry, Roger G. *Mountain Weather and Climate.* London: Methuen, 1981.

Brinkmann, Waltraud A. R. *A Climatological Study of Strong Downslope Winds in the Boulder Area.* The University of Colorado (INSTAAR Occasional Paper No. 7) and N.C.A.R. (Cooperative Thesis No. 27), 1973.

Bryson, Reid A. "Ancient Climes on the Great Plains." *Natural History* 89, no. 6 (1980).

Caldwell, M. M. "Solar Ultraviolet Radiation as an Ecological Factor for Alpine Plants." *Ecological Monographs,* 38 (1969): 243–68.

Hansen, Wallace R., John Chronic, and John Matelock. *Climatography of the Front Range Urban Corridor and Vicinity, Colorado.* Geological Survey Professional Paper 1019, U.S. Government Printing Office, Washington, D.C., 1978.

Ives, J. D., and R. G. Barry, eds. *Arctic and Alpine Environments.* London: Methuen, 1974.

Ives, Ronald L. "Weather Phenomena of the Colorado Rockies." *Journal of the Franklin Institute* 226 (Dec., 1938): 691–755.

Keen, Richard A. *Skywatch: The Western Weather Guide.* Golden, Colo.: Fulcrum, Incorporated, 1987.

Lutgens, Frederick K., and Edward J. Tarbuck. *The At-*

mosphere: An Introduction to Meteorology. Englewood Cliffs, N.J.: Prentice-Hall, Inc., 1979.

Price, Larry W. *Mountains and Man.* Berkeley: University of California Press, 1981.

Reifsnyder, William F. *Weathering the Wilderness.* San Francisco: Sierra Club Books, 1980.

Reiter, E. R., and J. L. Rasmussen. *Proceedings of the Symposium on Mountain Meteorology,* Atmospheric Science paper No. 122, Fort Collins, Colo., 1967.

Schaefer, Victor J., and John A. Day. *A Field Guide to the Atmosphere.* The Peterson Field Guide Series No. 26. Boston: Houghton Mifflin Company, 1981.

Strahler, Arthur N., and Alan H. Strahler. *Modern Physical Geography.* 3d ed. New York: John Wiley & Sons, 1987.

SNOW AND WINTER ENVIRONMENTS

Alford, Donald. "Snow" in *Arctic and Alpine Environments.* London: Methuen, p. 85–110, 1974.

Armstrong, Richard L., and Jack D. Ives, eds. "Avalanche Release and Snow Characteristics, San Juan Mountains, Colorado." University of Colorado, Institute of Arctic and Alpine Research, Occasional Paper 19, 1976.

Gray, D. M., and D. H. Male, eds. *Handbook of Snow: Principles, Processes, Management and Use.* New York: Pergamon Press, 1981.

Halfpenny, James C., and Roy Douglas Ozanne. *Winter: An Ecological Handbook.* Boulder: Johnson Publishing Company, 1989.

LaChapelle, Edward R. *Field Guide to Snow Crystals.* Seattle: University of Washington Press, 1969.

Marchand, Peter J. *Life in the Cold: An Introduction to Winter Ecology.* Hanover, N.H.: University Press of New England, 1987.

Martinelli, M. Jr., *Snow Avalanche Sites: Their Identification and Evaluation.* U.S. Dept. of Agriculture, Forest Service, Agriculture Information Bulletin 360, 1974.

Merritt, J. F., ed. *Winter Ecology of Small Mammals.* Carnegie Museum Natural History Special Publication no. 10, Pittsburgh, 1984.

Perla, Ronald I., and M. Martinelli, Jr. *Avalanche Handbook.* U.S. Dept. of Agriculture, Forest Service, Agriculture Handbook 489, 1976.

Schmidt-Nielson, K. *Animal Physiology: Adaptation and Environment.* 3d ed. New York: Cambridge University Press, 1983.

GENERAL NATURAL HISTORY AND ECOLOGY

Arno, Stephen F., and Ramona P. Hammerly. *Timberline: Mountain and Arctic Forest Frontiers.* Seattle: The Mountaineers, 1984.

Chabot, B. F., and H. A. Mooney, eds. *Physiological Ecology of North American Plant Communities.* New York: Chapman and Hall, 1985.

Cushman, Ruth Carol, and Stephen R. Jones. *The Shortgrass Prairie.* Boulder: Pruett Publishing Co., 1988.

DeByle, Norbert V., and Robert P. Winokur, eds. *Aspen: Ecology and Management in the Western United States.* U.S.D.A. Forest Service General Technical Report RM-119, Rocky Mountain Forest and Range Experiment Station, Fort Collins, Colorado, 1985.

Grant, Susan. *Beauty and the Beast: The Coevolution of Animals and Plants.* New York: Charles Scribner's Sons, 1984.

Lanner, Ronald M. *The Piñon Pine: A Natural and Cultural History.* Reno: University of Nevada Press, 1981.

Marr, John W. *Ecosystems of the East Slope of the Colorado Front Range.* Boulder: Colorado Associated University Press, 1967.

Mutel, Cornelia Fleisher, and John C. Emerick. *From Grassland to Glacier: The Natural History of Colorado.* Boulder: Johnson Books, 1984.

Ricklefs, Robert E. *Ecology,* 2d ed. New York: Chiron Press, Inc., 1979.

Tranquellini, W. *Physiological Ecology of the Alpine Timberline.* Berlin: Springer-Verlag, 1979.

Whittaker, Robert H. *Communities and Ecosystems.* 2d ed. New York: MacMillan Publishing Co., Inc., 1975.

Windell, J. T., B. E. Williard, D. J. Cooper, S. Q. Foster, C. F. Knud-Hansen, L. P. Rink, and G. N. Kiladis. *An ecological characterization of Rocky Mountain montane and subalpine wetlands.* U.S. Fish and Wildlife Serv. Biol. Rep 86(11), 1986.

Zwinger, Ann H., and Beatrice E. Willard. *Land Above the Trees: A Guide to American Alpine Tundra.* New York: Harper & Row, 1972.

Barnard, Carolyn M., and Loren D. Potter. *New Mexico Grasses: A Vegetative Key*. Albuquerque: University of New Mexico Press, 1984.

Duft, Joseph E., and Robert K. Mosely. *Alpine Wildflowers of the Rocky Mountains*. Missoula, Mont.: Mountain Press Publishing Company, 1989.

Elias, Thomas S. *The Complete Trees of North America*. New York: Van Nostrand Rheingold Company, 1980.

Elmore, Francis H. *Shrubs and Trees of the Southwest Uplands*. Globe, Ariz.: Southwest Parks and Monuments Association, 1976.

Foxx, Teralene S., and Dorothy Hoard. *Flowers of the Southwestern Forests and Woodlands*. Los Alamos: Los Alamos Historical Society, 1984.

Harrington, H. D. *Edible Native Plants of the Rocky Mountains*. Albuquerque: University of New Mexico Press, 1967.

Hermann, Frederick J., *Manual of the Carices of the Rocky Mountains and Colorado Basin*. Agriculture Handbook No. 374. Washington, D.C.: U.S. Government Printing Office, 1970.

Martin, William C., and Charles H. Hutchins. *Spring Wildflowers of New Mexico*. Albuquerque: University of New Mexico Press, 1984.

_____. *Summer Wildflowers of New Mexico*. Albuquerque: University of New Mexico Press, 1986.

Nelson, Ruth Ashton. *Handbook of Rocky Mountain Plants*, 3d ed. Estes Park, Colo.: Skyland Publishers, 1969.

_____. *Plants of Rocky Mountain National Park*. Estes Park, Colo.: Rocky Mountain Nature Association, 1982.

Smith, Alexander H. *A Field Guide to Western Mushrooms*. Ann Arbor: The University of Michigan Press, 1975.

Stubbendiek, J., Stephan L. Hatch, and Kathie J. Kjar. *North American Range Plants*. Lincoln: University of Nebraska Press, 1982.

Weber, William A. *Colorado Flora: Eastern Slope*. Boulder: University Press of Colorado, 1990.

_____. *Colorado Flora: Western Slope*. Boulder: Colorado Associated University Press, 1987.

_____. *Rocky Mountain Flora*, 5th ed. Boulder: Colorado Associated University Press, 1976.

_____. Guide to the Mosses of Colorado. Occasional Paper no. 6, Institute of Arctic and Alpine Research, University of Colorado, July 1973.

Willard, Bettie E., and Michael T. Smithson. *Alpine Wildflowers of the Rocky Mountains.* Estes Park, Colo.: Rocky Mountain Nature Association, no date given.

MAMMALS

Armstrong, David M. *Distribution of Mammals in Colorado.* Monograph no. 3. Lawrence: University of Kansas Natural History Museum, 1972.

_____. *Mammals of the Canyon Country.* Moab, Utah: Canyonlands Natural History Association, 1982.

_____. *Rocky Mountain Mammals.* Boulder: Colorado Associated University Press, 1987.

Boyce, Mark S., and Larry D. Hayden-Wing, eds. *North American Elk: Ecology, Behavior and Management.* Laramie: The University of Wyoming, 1979.

Chapman, Joseph A., and George A. Feldhamer. *Wild Mammals of North America: Biology, Management, and Economics.* Baltimore: Johns Hopkins University Press, 1982.

Clark, Tim W., and Mark R. Stromberg. *Mammals in Wyoming.* Lawrence, Kan.: University of Kansas Museum of Natural History, Publication Series No. 10, 1987.

Connor, Douglas A. "Life in a Rock Pile." *Natural History,* June 1983, 51–57.

Findley, James S., and others. *Mammals of New Mexico.* Albuquerque: University of New Mexico Press, 1975.

Fox, M. W., ed. *The Wild Canids: Their Systematics, Behavioral Ecology and Evolution.* New York: Van Nostrand Reinhold Company, 1975.

Geist, Valerius. *Mountain Sheep, a Study in Behavior and Evolution.* Chicago: University of Chicago Press, 1971.

Gittleman, John L. *Carnivore Behavior, Ecology, and Evolution.* Ithaca: Cornell University Press, 1989.

Gurnell, John. *The Natural History of Squirrels.* London: Christopher Helm, 1987.

Halfpenny, James. *A Field Guide to Mammal Tracking in Western North America.* Boulder: Johnson Books, 1986.

Hall, E. R. *The Mammals of North America,* 2 vols. New York: John Wiley & Sons, 1981.

Johns, Dennis W., and Kenneth B. Armitage. 1979. "Behavioral Ecology of Alpine Yellow-bellied Marmots." *Behavioral Ecology and Social Biology* 5: 133–157.

Jones, J. K., Jr., D. M. Armstrong, R. S. Hoffman, and C. Jones. *Mammals of the Northern Great Plains.* Lincoln: University of Nebraska Press, 1983.

Meaney, Carron A. "Olfactory Communication in Pikas *(Ochotona princeps).*" Ph.D. thesis, University of Colorado, 1983.

Murie, Jan O., and Gail D. Michener, eds. *The Biology of Ground-dwelling Squirrels.* Lincoln: University of Nebraska Press, 1984.

Murie, Olaus J. *The Elk of North America.* Harrisburg, Pa.: The Stackpole Co., 1951.

_____. *A Field Guide to Animal Tracks.* The Peterson Field Guide Series No. 9. Boston: Houghton Mifflin Company, 1954.

Scott, J., D. M. Armstrong, S. J. Bissell, and J. Freeman. *The Bats of Colorado: Shadows in the Night.* Denver: Colorado Division of Wildlife, 1984.

Van Soest, Peter J. *Nutritional Ecology of the Ruminant.* Ithaca: Comstock Publishing Associates, Cornell University Press, 1982.

Wallmo, O. C., ed. *Mule and Black-tailed Deer of North America.* Lincoln: University of Nebraska Press, 1981.

BIRDS

Angell, Tony. *Ravens, Crows, Magpies and Jays.* Seattle: University of Washington Press, 1978.

Calder, William A. *Size, Function, and Life History.* Cambridge: Harvard University Press, 1984.

Erlich, Paul R., David R. Dobkin, and Darryl Wheye. *The Birder's Handbook: A Field Guide to the Natural History of North American Birds.* New York: Simon & Schuster Inc., 1988.

Harrison, Hal H. *A Field Guide to Western Bird's Nests,* The Peterson Field Guide Series No. 25. Boston: Houghton Mifflin Company, 1979.

Johnsgard, Paul A. *The Grouse of North America.* Lincoln: University of Nebraska Press, 1983.

_____. *The Hummingbirds of North America.* Washington, D.C.: Smithsonian Institution Press, 1983.

National Geographic Society. *Field Guide to the Birds of*

North America, 2d ed. Washington, D.C.: National Geographic Society, 1983.

Peterson, Roger Tory. *Western Birds,* 3d ed. Peterson Field Guide No. 2. Boston: Houghton Mifflin Company, 1990.

Price, Frank E., and Carl E. Bock. 1983. *Population Ecology of the Dipper (Cinclus mexicanus) in the Front Range of Colorado.* Studies in Avian Biology No. 7. Lawrence, Kansas: Allen Press.

Reynolds, Richard T., and Brian D. Linkhart. "The Nesting Biology of Flammulated Owls in Colorado." Symposium on the Biology and Conservation of Northern Forest Owls, Winnipeg, Manitoba, Canada, February 3–7, 1987.

Robbins, Chandler S., Bertel Bruun, and Herbert S. Zim. *Birds of North America,* rev. ed. New York: Golden Press, 1983.

Tomback, D. F. "Nutcrackers and Pines: Coevolution or Coadaptation?" In Nitecki, N.H., ed. *Coevolution.* Chicago: University of Chicago Press, 1983.

Vander Wall, Stephen, and Russell P. Balda. "Remembrance of Seeds Stashed." *Natural History,* September 1983, 60–64.

AMPHIBIANS AND REPTILES

Baxter, George T., and Michael D. Stone. *Amphibians and Reptiles of Wyoming,* Bulletin No. 16. Cheyenne: Wyoming Fish and Game Department, 1980.

Hammerson, Geoffrey A. *Amphibians and Reptiles in Colorado.* Denver: Colorado Division of Wildlife, 1982.

Smith, Hobart M., and Edmund D. Brodie, Jr. *Reptiles of North America: A Guide to Field Identification.* New York: Golden Press, 1982.

FISH

Koster, William J. *Guide to the Fishes of New Mexico.* Albuquerque: University of New Mexico Press, 1957.

Woodling, John D. *Game Fish of Colorado.* Pub. Code DOW-M-1-25-84. Colorado Division of Wildlife, Denver, 1980.

_____. *Colorado's Little Fish: A Guide to the Minnows and Other Lesser Known Fishes in the State of Colorado.* Denver: Colorado Division of Wildlife, 1985.

INVERTEBRATES

Brewer, Jo, and Dave Winter. *Butterflies and Moths: A Companion to Your Field Guide*. Englewood Cliffs, N.J.: Phalarope Books, Prentice Hall, 1986.

Borror, Donald J., and Richard E. White. *A Field Guide to the Insects*. The Peterson Field Guide Series No. 19. Boston: Houghton Mifflin Company, 1970.

Gregg, Robert E. *The Ants of Colorado*. Boulder: University of Colorado Press, 1963.

Ferris, Clifford D., and F. Martin Brown, eds. *Butterflies of the Rocky Mountain States*. Norman: University of Oklahoma Press, 1980.

Inouye, David W. "The Ant and the Sunflower." *Natural History*, June 1984, 48–53.

McCafferty, W. Patrick. *Aquatic Entomology: The Fisherman's and Ecologist's Illustrated Guide to Insects and Their Relatives*. Boston: Jones and Bartlett Publishers, Inc., 1981.

Merritt, R. W., and K. W. Cummins. *An Introduction to the Aquatic Insects of North America*. Dubuque, Iowa: Kendall/Hunt Publishing Co., 1978.

Milne, Lorus, and Margery Milne. *The Audubon Society Field Guide to North American Insects & Spiders*. New York: Alfred A. Knopf, 1980.

Pennak, Robert W. *Freshwater Invertebrates of the United States*. 2d ed. New York: John Wiley & Sons, Inc., 1978.

Pyle, Robert Michael. *The Audubon Society Field Guide to North American Butterflies*. New York: Alfred A. Knopf, 1981.

INDEX

NOTE: Page numbers in *italics* refer to illustrations. Page numbers in **boldface** refer to major discussions.

Casper, Wyoming, 148
Cassidy, Butch, 21
Cassin's finch, **306**
Castle Peak, 24, 98
Castle Rock Conglomerate, 94
Caterpillars
    tent, 415–416
    "woolly bear," 533
Cathedral Peak, 98
Cattle ranching, 34, 35, 36, 178
Caves
    Cave of the Winds, 61, 65
    Deep Creek Canyon, 26
    Groaning, 68
    Tererro, 69
Cavity nesters, 413
Cedar, western red. *See* Juniper,
    Rocky Mountain
Cenozoic era, 39, 90–124
    Quaternary epoch, 106–124
    Tertiary epoch, 90–105
Centennial Valley, 77, 148
Central City Mining District,
    93
Central Colorado Trough, 71–72,
    88
Cuerno Verde, Chief, 14
Chaffee Group, 67
Chalk Cliffs, 27
Cheatgrass, *313*, 314, 316
Chemical defenses, 206, 255–256,
    318
Chert, 46
Cheyenne, Wyoming, 148
Cheyenne Belt, 57, 60
Chickadees, *305*, **305–306**, 482
Chickarees, 435, 436–437, **437–
    438**, 481–482
Chickweed, witches' broom and,
    472
Chimayosos Peak, 57
Chimingbells, *356*, 357
Chinle Formation, 77, 79, *80*

Chinook winds, *136*, 138–139
Chipmunks
    Colorado, **244–245**
    least, *283*, **288–289**
Chokecherry, 202, **239–240**, *239*
Chugwater Formation, 77
Cimarron, New Mexico, 148
Cimarron Range, 16, 102
Cinquefoil, shrubby, *401*, **406**
Cirque, 108–109
Clark's nutcrackers, 261, 262, 454–
    456, *455*, **456–457**
Clayton's Pass-Bristlecone Pine Re-
    search Natural Area, 444
Climate, 125–148
    alpine tundra, 492–494
    aquatic community and, 383–
        384
    aspen forest, 397–399
    atmospheric circulation and,
        129–131
    bristlecone-limber pine forest,
        446
    Douglas-fir forest, 296
    geology and, 104, 118–124
    Holocene glaciation, 116
    lodgepole pine forest, 426
    microclimates, 132–133
    mountains and, 126–129, 132–
        141
    mountain wetland, 342
    open grassland and meadow,
        311–312
    paleoclimatic history and, 106–
        107
    piñon-juniper woodland, 253
    Pleistocene (Ice Age), 106, 111
    ponderosa pine forest, 274
    precipitation, 135–137
    regional controls, 125–129
    regional patterns, 147–148
    seasonal patterns, 141–147
    shortgrass prairie, 172–173

THE SOUTHERN ROCKIES

THE SOUTHERN ROCKIES

Woodlands. *See* Piñon-juniper
  woodlands
Wood nymph, *466*, **476**
Woodpeckers
  downy, **439–440**
  hairy, *303*, **305**
  three-toed, **485**
Woodrats
  bushy-tailed, **265**
  Mexican, **245**
Woody plants. *See* Shrubs; Trees
Wren
  house, **419**
  rock, **247**

Wyoming Basin, 142
Wyoming mountain ranges, 9–10

Yale, Mount, 27
Yampa River, 31, 32
Yampa Williams Fork Mountains,
  25
Yarrow, **320**
Ypsilon Peak, 11

Zerkel, Mount, 31
Zinc, 93
Zooplankton, 387–388, 389